Early Christianity

Roman Roads Reader

Early Christianity

Roman Roads Reader

Patristic Selections

Companion Book for *Romans: Early Christianity*,
a curriculum by Roman Roads Media.

ROMAN
ROADS
MEDIA

Early Christianity : Roman Roads Reader

Published by Roman Roads Media, LLC
121 E 3rd St., Moscow ID 83843
509-906-8635 | www.romanroadsmedia.com
copyright@romanroadsmedia.com

Layout and editing: George Callihan
Cover Design: Daniel Foucachon
Front Cover Photo: St. Jean, Lyon, France. Arches of 1st Church of Gaul.

Printed in the United States of America.

Early Christianity: Roman Roads Reader: / Roman Roads Media, LLC.
ISBN: 978-0-9897028-9-8

14 15 16 17 18 19 20 21 10 9 8 7 6 5 4 3 2 1

This book has been designed to accompany the *Old Western Culture* curriculum by Roman Roads Media. To find out more about this course, visit www.romanroadsmedia.com

Other titles in the *Old Western Culture* Series by Roman Roads Media:

The Greeks:
-- **The Epics** (*The Iliad & The Odyssey*)
-- **Drama and Lyric** (*The Tragedies, Comedies, and Minor Poets*)
-- **The Histories** *(Herodotus, Thucydides, and Xenophon)*
-- **The Philosophers** (*Plato and Aristotle*)

The Romans:
-- **The Aeneid** *(The Aeneid, Ovid, and Lucretius)*
-- **The Historians** *(Livy, Tacitus, Salust, Julius Caesar, Plutarch, and Cicero)*
-- **Early Christianity** *(Clementine, Ignatius, Irenaeus, Justin Martyr, and Eusebius)*
-- **Nicene Christianity** *(Athanasius, Augustine, and Boethius)*

Christendom:
-- **Early Medievals** *(St. Benedict, Bede, Charlemagne, and Alfred the Great)*
-- **The Defense of the Faith** *(Anselm, Geffrey of Monmoth, The Golden Legend)*
-- **The Medieval Mind** *(Dante and Aquinas)*
-- **The Reformation** *(Erasmus, Calvin, Cranmer, Spencer, and Chaucer)*

Early Moderns:
-- **Early British Poetry** *(Metaphysical Poets, Milton, Shakespeare, and Bunyan)*
-- **The Rise of Enlightenment** *(Bacon, Descartes, Locke, Rousseau, Jefferson, Burke, and Alexis de Toqueville)*
-- **Later British Poetry** *(Neo-Classical Poetry, Victorian Poetry, and Romantic Poetry)* -- **The Novels** *(Austen, Dickens, Dostoevsky, Hugo)*

Other curriculum by Roman Roads Media:

Grammar of Poetry (Matt Whitling)
Fitting Words: Classical Rhetoric for the Christian Student (James Nance)
Introductory Logic (James Nance)
Intermediate Logic (James Nance)

Roman Roads Media
121 E 3rd St
Moscow, Idaho
83843
www.romanroadsmedia.com

Roman Roads combines its technical expertise with the experience of established authorities in the field of classical education to create quality video courses and resources tailored to the homeschooler. Just as the first century roads of the Roman Empire were the physical means by which the early church spread the gospel far and wide, so Roman Roads Media uses today's technology to bring timeless truth, goodness, and beauty into your home. By combining excellent instruction augmented with visual aids and examples, we help inspire in your children a lifelong love of learning.

Printed in the United States of America

ISBN: 978-0-9897028-9-8

Contents

THE DIDACHE

Unknown

TRANSLATED BY TIM SAUDER

1

There are two ways: one of life and one of death; and the difference between the two ways is great.

The way of life is this: first, you should love God, who made you; secondly, love your neighbor as yourself; and whatever things you do not desire to be done to you, do not do them to someone else. Now the words of this teaching are this: Bless those who curse you and pray for your enemies, and fast for those who are persecuting you. For what credit is it if you love those who love you? Do not the Gentiles do the same thing? But love those hating you, and you will not have an enemy.

Keep yourself from fleshly and bodily cravings. If anyone hits you on the right cheek, turn the other one to him also. And you will be acting maturely. If someone should force you to go one mile, go with him two. If someone takes your coat, give him your shirt also. If anyone should take from you what is yours, do not demand that he give it back, for you cannot.

Give to everyone asking you and do not refuse, for the Father desires to give to everyone from His own gifts. Blessed is the one who gives according to the commandment, for he is innocent. But the one who receives without need shall account for his receiving. Furthermore, being held, he shall be examined concerning what he has done, and he shall not be released until he has given back the last cent. It has been said concerning this, "Let your money sweat in your hands until you know whom you should give it to."

2

And this is the second commandment of the teaching: you shall not kill; you shall not commit adultery; you shall not corrupt children, nor practice sexual deviation; you shall not steal; nor practice calling on spiritual guides; nor use sorcery; you shall not procure an abortion, nor practice infanticide; you shall not covet your neighbor's goods. You shall not commit perjury, nor accuse someone falsely; you shall not speak evil nor hold a grudge. You shall not be double minded nor double tongued, for the double tongue is the snare of death. Your word shall not be false or empty, but do what you say. You shall not be covetous or extortionate, or hypocritical, or malicious or proud. You shall not plan evil against your neighbor. You should not hate anyone; but you should reprove some, and you should pray for some, and you should love some more then your own life.

3

My child, flee from evil and from every appearance of evil. Do not be ruled by your passions, for this leads to murder. Neither be jealous, quarrelsome, or quick- tempered. For murders are born out of such things. Do not let yourself develop lust, for this leads to sexual immorality. Do not be foul-mouthed, nor raise your eyes, for this leads to adultery. My child, do not regard omens, for this leads to idolatry. Do not be a sorcerer, nor be involved in astrology or magic purifications. Do not desire to see these things, for that is how idolatry comes. My child, do not be a liar, for lying leads to thievery. Do not be fond of money and do not try to build your own image, for that also leads to thievery. My child, do not be a grumbler, for it leads to blasphemy. Do not be self-willed nor entertain evil thoughts, for that is how blasphemy starts. Be meek, for the meek shall inherit the earth. Be patient and long suffering, devoid of evil, gentle and good, and trembling continually at the words that you have heard. Do not exalt yourself nor act presumptuously. Do not join yourself with the proud, but walk with the righteous and humble men. Accept everything that happens to you as good, knowing that nothing happens apart from God.

4

My child, you should remember night and day the one who speaks to you the Word of God, and honor him as you would the Lord; for where the delegated authority speaks, there is the Lord. And you should seek every day the presence of the saints, in order that you may be supported by their words. You should not desire division, but make peace between those quarreling. Judge righteously; do not favor anyone in reproving transgressions. Do not be double-minded as to whether anything should or should not be. Do not be one who stretches out his hand to receive but withdraws it in giving. Give a ransom for your sins if you have it to give. Do not hesitate to give, nor give in a grumbling manner, for you know who is the good Paymaster who rewards? You should not turn away the needy, but share all things with your brother, not saying that anything is your own. For if we are sharers in the eternal things, much more should we be in the physical things. Do not withhold your hand from your son or your daughter, but from their youth teach them the fear of God. Do not give orders to your slave or your handmaiden--those who hope in the same God--when you are bitter, lest they stop fearing God who is over you both. For He does not come to call men according to their social status, but He calls those whom the Spirit has prepared. And you slaves submit in fear and reverence to your masters as God's delegated authority over you. You should hate all hypocrisy and all that is not pleasing to the Lord. Do not forsake the commandments of the Lord, and keep (the teachings) you have received, not adding and not taking away. In church, you should confess your faults; and do not go to prayer with an evil conscience. This is the Way of Life.

5

But the Way of Death is this: first of all, it is evil and full of curses, lusts, adulteries, murders, thefts, idolatries, witchcrafts, sorceries, robberies, false witnesses, hypocrisies, double-mindedness, fraud, arrogance, boastfulness, jealousies, foul speech, pride, persecutors of the good, haters of truth, lovers of a lie, not regarding the reward of the righteous, not holding to the good or to the righteous judgment, spending sleepless nights not for good, but for wickedness; far from whom is gentleness and patience; loving useless things, seeking rewards, unmerciful to the poor, not helping the hardworking person, not regarding the one who made them, child murderers, destroyers of God's creation, turning away the needy, oppressing the distressed, wrongfully assisting the rich, unjust judges of the poor, altogether sinful. May you be delivered, my children, from all of these things?

6

See that no one misleads you from the pathway of this teaching, since it would be contrary to God. For if you are able to bear the whole yoke of the Lord, you should be mature. If you are not able, do what you can.

Concerning meat, do what you can; but keep from that which is offered to idols, for it is the worship of dead gods.

7

And concerning baptism, in this manner baptize: when you have gone over these things, baptize in the name of the Father, and the Son, and the Holy Spirit, in running water. If you do not have running water, baptize in other water. If you are not able to use cold water, use warm. And if you have neither, pour water on the head three times, in the name of the Father, the Son, and the Holy Spirit. And before baptism, the one baptizing and the one to be baptized should fast, as well as any others who are able. And you should instruct the one being baptized to fast one or two days before.

8

And let not your fasts be with those of the hypocrites, for they fast on Mondays and Thursdays, but you fast Wednesdays and Fridays. Do not pray as the hypocrites but as the Lord commanded in His gospel. Pray like this: Our Father in heaven, hallowed is Your name, Your kingdom come and Your will be done on earth as it is in heaven. Give us our daily bread for today and forgive our debts as we forgive those who owe us. Please do not lead us into a test, but deliver us from the evil one. For You have the power and the glory forever. Pray like this three times a day.

9

Concerning the Eucharist give thanks like this: First for the cup:

We give thanks to You, our Father, for Your holy vine of David, Your servant, which You made known to us through Jesus, Your Servant. Glory to You forever.

Concerning the broken bread:

We give thanks to You, our Father, for the life and knowledge that You made known to us through Jesus, Your Servant. Glory to You forever. As this broken bread was scattered over the hills and was brought together becoming one, so gather Your Church from the ends of the earth into Your kingdom, for You have all power and glory forever through Jesus Christ.

Do not let anyone eat or drink of your Eucharist meal except the ones who have been baptized into the name of the Lord. For the Lord said concerning this: "do not give that which is holy to the dogs."

10

After you are filled, give thanks like this: We thank you, Holy Father, for Your Holy name which you made to dwell in our hearts, and for knowledge and faith and immortality as You made known to us through Jesus, Your Servant. Glory to You forever. You, Lord Almighty, created all things to show forth Your name. You give both food and drink to man to enjoy, and everlasting life through Your Servant. Above all, we thank You because You are mighty. Glory to You forever. Remember Lord, Your Church, to deliver her from all evil and mature her in Your love. And gather her from the four winds, separated into Your kingdom which You have made for her, because You have the power and glory forever. Let grace come and this world pass away. Hosanna to the Son of David! If anyone is holy, let him come. If anyone is not, let him repent. Maranatha (Lord come). Amen. Allow the prophets now to give thanks as they desire.

11

Whoever, therefore, who comes and teaches you all these things mentioned, receive him. But if the one teaching changes what has been taught to another teaching in order to destroy these things, do not listen to him. However, if his motive is to add righteousness and knowledge of the Lord, receive him as you would the Lord. Now concerning the apostles and prophets, act according to the requirements of the Gospel. Every apostle coming to you, welcome as you would the Lord. And he should not remain more than one day, and if he has a need also another. But if he remains three days, he is a false prophet. And when the apostle goes forth, he should take nothing except a loaf of bread, until he arrives at his night's lodging. If he asks for money he is a false prophet. Also, you should not test or judge and prophet speaking in the Spirit, for every sin will be forgiven, but this sin shall not be forgiven. But not everyone speaking in the Spirit is a prophet, but only if he should have a lifestyle of the Lord'scharacter. Therefore, by his lifestyle you will know a false prophet from a true prophet. And any prophet ordering a meal in the Spirit should not eat of it; otherwise he is a false prophet. And every prophet who teaches the truth but does not do what he teaches is a false prophet. But every prophet who stands the test and is genuine, even if he uses symbolic imagery in the church, so long as he does not teach others to do the same, should not be judged. His judgment comes from God, for so did the prophets of old. But whoever should say in the Spirit, "Give me money or something else," do not listen to them. But if, concerning others in need, he says, "give", let no one judge him.

12

Receive everyone coming in the name of the Lord. Later, by testing him, you will find out about him, where he deviates from the standard. If the one coming is just traveling through, help him as much as you can. He should not remain with you more than three days if that is necessary. But if he desires to settle among you and has a trade, let him work for his bread. But if he has no trade, you should provide for him according to your own discretion. In no way should anyone live among you unemployed as a Christian. And if he is not willing to do this, he is making a trade of Christ. Beware of this kind of person.

13

But every genuine prophet who desires to settle among you is worthy of his food. Likewise, every genuine teacher is worthy; like a workman, he is worthy of his food. Therefore, of all the first produce of the wine press and the threshing floor, and of the oxen and the sheep, take the first fruits and give it to the prophets. For they are your high priests. And if you do not have a prophet, give such first fruits to the poor. If you should make bread, take it and give according to the commandment. Likewise, if you have opened a jar of wine or oil, take the first fruits and give to the prophets. And also take the first fruits of your money and clothes and all your possessions. As it seems best, give according to the commandment.

14

And when coming together on the Lord's own day, break bread and give thanks after confessing your transgressions. In that manner, your sacrifice will be pure. And do not let anyone coming with a quarrel against a brother join you until they get reconciled, in order that your sacrifice is not impure. For this has been spoken of by the Lord, "in every place and time offer me a pure sacrifice, for I am a great King," says the Lord, "and My name is wonderful among the nations."

15

Appoint for yourselves, therefore bishops and deacons worthy of the Lord: gentlemen, not lovers of money, true and approved. For they minister also to you the ministry of prophets and teachers. Therefore, do not despise them, for they are to be honored among you along with the prophets and teachers. Do not reprove one another in anger, but in peace, as we have been shown in the Gospel. And do not let anyone speak to a person who is unloving to his neighbor, nor let him hear a word from you, until he repents. Pray and give and live as you have found in the Gospel of our Lord.

16

Watch over your life. Do not let your lamps be extinguished or your body unclothed, but be ready; for you do not know the hour in which our Lord comes. Assemble yourselves together frequently to seek the things that benefit your souls, for all the time of your faith will not profit you unless you are perfect at the last. For in the last days, false prophets and seducers will increase, turning the sheep into wolves; and love will be turned into hate. For lawlessness will increase and they will hate and persecute and betray one another. And then the deceiver of the world will appear as though he were the Son of God, and he shall do signs and wonders and the earth shall be delivered into his hands; and he will commit immoralities which have never been done since the age began. Then shall the race of men come into the fire of proving trial and many shall be made to stumble and perish. But those who remain established in their faith shall be saved under the very curse. And then the signs of truth shall be revealed. First, a sign spread out in heaven; then a sign of the sound of a trumpet; and third, the resurrection of the dead, but not all of the dead. But as it was said, "the Lord shall come and all His Holy Ones with Him."Then the world shall see the Lord coming in the clouds of heaven."

THE FIRST EPISTLE OF CLEMENT OF ROME

Clement of Rome

TRANSLATED BY J.B. LIGHTFOOT

1 Clement prologue:1

The Church of God which sojourneth in Rome to the Church of God which sojourneth in Corinth, to them which are called and sanctified by the will of God through our Lord Jesus Christ. Grace to you and peace from Almighty God through Jesus Christ be multiplied.

1:1 By reason of the sudden and repeated calamities and reverses which are befalling us, brethren, we consider that we have been somewhat tardy in giving heed to the matters of dispute that have arisen among you, dearly beloved, and to the detestable and unholy sedition, so alien and strange to the elect of God, which a few headstrong and self-willed persons have kindled to such a pitch of madness that your name, once revered and renowned and lovely in the sight of all men, hath been greatly reviled.

1:2 For who that had sojourned among you did not approve your most virtuous and steadfast faith? Who did not admire your sober and forbearing piety in Christ? Who did not publish abroad your magnificent disposition of hospitality? Who did not congratulate you on your perfect and sound knowledge?

1:3 For ye did all things without respect of persons, and ye walked after the ordinances of God, submitting yourselves to your rulers and rendering to the older men among you the honor which is their due. On the young too ye enjoined modest and seemly thoughts: and the women ye charged to perform all their duties in a blameless and seemly and pure conscience, cherishing their own husbands, as is meet; and ye taught them to keep in the rule of obedience, and to manage the affairs of their household in seemliness, with all discretion.

2:1 And ye were all lowly in mind and free from arrogance, yielding rather than claiming submission, *more glad to give than to receive*, and content with the provisions which God supplieth. And giving heed unto His words, ye laid them up diligently in your hearts, and His sufferings were before your eyes.

2:2 Thus a profound and rich peace was given to all, and an insatiable desire of doing good. An abundant outpouring also of the Holy Spirit fell upon all;

2:3 and, being full of holy counsel, in excellent zeal and with a pious confidence ye stretched out your hands to Almighty God, supplicating Him to be propitious, if unwillingly ye had committed any sin.

2:4 Ye had conflict day and night for all the brotherhood, that the number of His elect might be saved with fearfulness and intentness of mind.

2:5 Ye were sincere and simple and free from malice one towards another.

2:6 Every sedition and every schism was abominable to you. Ye mourned over the transgressions of your neighbors: ye judged their shortcomings to be your own.

2:7 Ye repented not of any well-doing, but were *ready unto every good work.*

2:8 Being adorned with a most virtuous and honorable life, ye performed all your duties in the fear of Him. The commandments and the ordinances of the Lord were *written on the tablets of your hearts.*

3:1 All glory and enlargement was given unto you, and that was fulfilled which is written *My beloved ate and drank and was enlarged and waxed fat and kicked.*

3:2 Hence come jealousy and envy, strife and sedition, persecution and tumult, war and captivity.

3:3 So men were stirred up, *the mean against the honorable*, the ill reputed against the highly reputed, the foolish against the wise, the *young against the elder.*

3:4 For this cause *righteousness* and peace *stand aloof*, while each man hath forsaken the fear of the Lord and become purblind in the faith of Him, neither walketh in the ordinances of His commandments nor liveth according to that which becometh Christ, but each goeth after the lusts of his evil heart, seeing that they have conceived an unrighteous and ungodly jealousy, through which also *death entered into the world.*

4:1 For so it is written, *And it came to pass after certain days that Cain brought of the fruits of the earth a sacrifice unto God, and Abel he also brought of the firstlings of the sheep and of their* fatness.

4:2 *And God looked upon Abel and upon his gifts, but unto Cain and unto his sacrifices He gave no heed.*

4:3 *And Cain sorrowed exceedingly, and his countenance fell.*

4:4 *And God said unto Cain, Wherefore art thou very sorrowful and wherefore did thy countenance fall? If thou hast offered aright and hast not divided aright, didst thou not sin? Hold thy peace.*

4:5 *Unto thee shall he turn, and thou shalt rule over him.* {This last phrase has also been translated: *Be at peace: thine offering returns to thyself, and thou shalt again possess it.*}

4:6 *And Cain said unto Abel his brother, Let us go over unto the plain. And it came to pass, while they were in the plain, that Cain rose up against Abel his brother and slew him.*

4:7 Ye see, brethren, jealousy and envy wrought a brother's murder.

4:8 By reason of jealousy our father Jacob ran away from the face of Esau his brother.

4:9 Jealousy caused Joseph to be persecuted even unto death, and to come even unto bondage.

4:10 Jealousy compelled Moses to flee from the face of Pharaoh king of Egypt while it was said to him by his own countryman, *Who made thee a judge or a decider over us, Wouldest thou slay me, even as yesterday thou slewest the Egyptian?*

4:11 By reason of jealousy Aaron and Miriam were lodged outside the camp.

4:12 Jealousy brought Dathan and Abiram down alive to hades, because they made sedition against Moses the servant of God.

4:13 By reason of jealousy David was envied not only by the Philistines, but was persecuted also by Saul [king of Israel].

5:1 But, to pass from the examples of ancient days, let us come to those champions who lived nearest to our time. Let us set before us the noble examples which belong to our generation.

5:2 By reason of jealousy and envy the greatest and most righteous pillars of the Church were persecuted, and contended even unto death.

5:3 Let us set before our eyes the good Apostles.

5:4 There was Peter who by reason of unrighteous jealousy endured not one not one but many labors, and thus having borne his testimony went to his appointed place of glory.

5:5 By reason of jealousy and strife Paul by his example pointed out the prize of patient endurance. After that he had been seven times in bonds, had been driven into exile, had been stoned, had preached in the East and in the West, he won the noble renown which was the reward of his faith,

5:6 having taught righteousness unto the whole world and having reached the farthest bounds of the West; and when he had borne his testimony before the rulers, so he departed from the world and went unto the holy place, having been found a notable pattern of patient endurance.

6:1 Unto these men of holy lives was gathered a vast multitude of the elect, who through many indignities and tortures, being the victims of jealousy, set a brave example among ourselves.

6:2 By reason of jealousy women being persecuted, after that they had suffered cruel and unholy insults as Danaids and Dircae, safely reached the goal in the race of faith, and received a noble reward, feeble though they were in body.

6:3 Jealousy hath estranged wives from their husbands and changed the saying of our father Adam, *This now is bone of my bones and flesh of my flesh.*

6:4 Jealousy and strife have overthrown great cities and uprooted great nations.

7:1 These things, dearly beloved, we write, not only as admonishing you, but also as putting ourselves in remembrance. For we are in the same lists, and the same contest awaiteth us.

7:2 Wherefore let us forsake idle and vain thoughts; and let us conform to the glorious and venerable rule which hath been handed down to us;

7:3 and let us see what is good and what is pleasant and what is acceptable in the sight of Him that made us.

7:4 Let us fix our eyes on the blood of Christ and understand how precious it is unto His Father, because being shed for our salvation it won for the whole world the grace of repentance.

7:5 Let us review all the generations in turn, and learn how from generation to generation the Master hath given a place for repentance unto them that desire to turn to Him.

7:6 Noah preached repentance, and they that obeyed were saved.

7:7 Jonah preached destruction unto the men of Nineveh; but they, repenting of their sins, obtained pardon of God by their supplications and received salvation, albeit they were aliens from God.

8:1 The ministers of the grace of God through the Holy Spirit spake concerning repentance.

8:2 Yea and the Master of the universe Himself spake concerning repentance with an oath:

8:3 *for, as I live saith the Lord, I desire not the death of the sinner, so much as his repentance,*

8:4 and He added also a merciful judgment: *Repent ye, O house of Israel, of your iniquity; say unto the sons of My people, Though your sins reach from the earth even unto the heaven, and though they be redder than scarlet and blacker than sackcloth, and ye turn unto Me with your whole heart and say Father, I will give ear unto you as unto a holy people.*

8:5 And in another place He saith on this wise, *Wash, be ye clean. Put away your iniquities from your souls out of My sight. Cease from your iniquities; learn to do good; seek out judgmcl; defend him that is wronged: give judgment for the orphan, and execute righteousness for the widow; and come and let us reason together, saith He; and though your sins be as crimson, I will make them white as snow; and though they be as scarlet, I will make them white as wool. And if ye be willing and will hearken unto Me, ye shall eat the good things of the earth; but if ye be not willing, neither hearken unto Me, a sword shall devour you; for the mouth of the Lord hath spoken these things.*

8:6 Seeing then that He desireth all His beloved to be partakers of repentance, He confirmed it by an act of His almighty will.

9:1 Wherefore let us be obedient unto His excellent and glorious will; and presenting ourselves as suppliants of His mercy and goodness, let us fall down before Him and betake ourselves unto His compassions, forsaking the vain toil and the strife and the jealousy which leadeth unto death.

9:2 Let us fix our eyes on them that ministered perfectly unto His excellent glory.

9:3 Let us set before us Enoch, who being found righteous in obedience was translated, and his death was not found.

9:4 Noah, being found faithful, by his ministration preached regeneration unto the world, and through him the Master saved the living creatures that entered into the ark in concord.

10:1 Abraham, who was called the 'friend,' was found faithful in that he rendered obedience unto the words of God.

10:2 He through obedience went forth from his land and from his kindred and from his father's house, that leaving a scanty land and a feeble kindred and a mean house he might inherit the promises of God.

10:3 For He saith unto him *Go forth from thy land and from thy kindred and from thy father's house unto the land which I shall show thee, and I will make thee into a great nation, and I will bless thee and will magnify thy name, and thou shalt be blessed. And I will bless them that bless thee, and I will curse them that curse thee; and in thee shall all the tribes of the earth be blessed.*

10:4 And again, when he was parted from Lot, God said unto him *Look up with thine eyes, and behold from the place where thou now art, unto the north and the south and the sunrise and the sea; for all the land which thou seest, I will give it unto thee and to thy seed for ever;*

10:5 *and I will make thy seed as the dust of the earth. If any man can count the dust of the earth, then shall thy seed also be counted.*

10:6 And again He saith; *God led Abraham forth and said unto him, Look up unto the heaven and count the stars, and see whether thou canst number them. So shall thy seed be. And Abraham believed God, and it was reckoned unto him for righteousness.*

10:7 For his faith and hospitality a son was given unto him in old age, and by obedience he offered him a sacrifice unto God on one of the mountains which He showed him.

11:1 For his hospitality and godliness Lot was saved from Sodom, when all the country round about was judged by fire and brimstone; the Master having thus fore shown that He forsaketh not them which set their hope on Him, but appointeth unto punishment and torment them which swerve aside.

11:2 For when his wife had gone forth with him, being otherwise minded and not in accord, she was appointed for a sign hereunto, so that she became a pillar of salt unto this day, that it might be known unto all men that they which are double-minded and they which doubt concerning the power of God are set for a judgment and for a token unto all the generations.

12:1 For her faith and hospitality Rahab the harlot was saved.

12:2 For when the spies were sent forth unto Jericho by Joshua the son of Nun, the king of the land perceived that they were come to spy out his country, and sent forth men to seize them, that being seized they might be put to death.

12:3 So the hospitable Rahab received them and hid them in the upper chamber under the flax stalks.

12:4 And when the messengers of the king came near and said, *The spies of our land entered in unto thee: bring them forth, for the king so ordereth:* then she answered, *The men truly, whom ye seek, entered in unto me, but they departed forthwith and are sojourning on the way;* and she pointed out to them the opposite road.

12:5 And she said unto the men, *Of a surety I perceive that the Lord your God delivereth this city unto you; for the fear and the dread of you is fallen upon the inhabitants thereof. When therefore it shall come to pass that ye take it, save me and the house of my father.*

12:6 And they said unto her, *It shall be even so as thou hast spoken unto us. Whensoever therefore thou perceivest that we are coming, thou shalt gather all thy folk beneath thy roof and they shall be saved; for as many as shall be found without the house shall perish.*

12:7 And moreover they gave her a sign, that she should hang out from her house a scarlet thread, thereby showing beforehand that through the blood of the Lord there shall be redemption unto all them that believe and hope on God.

12:8 Ye see, dearly beloved, not only faith, but prophecy, is found in the woman.

13:1 Let us therefore be lowly minded, brethren, laying aside all arrogance and conceit and folly and anger, and let us do that which is written. For the Holy Ghost saith, *Let not the wise man boast in his wisdom, nor the strong in his strength, neither the rich in his riches; but he that boasteth let him boast in the Lord, that he may seek Him out, and do judgment and righteousness* most of all remembering the words of the Lord Jesus which He spake, teaching forbearance and long-suffering:

13:2 for thus He spake *Have mercy, that ye may receive mercy: forgive, that it may be forgiven to you. As ye do, so shall it be done to you. As ye give, so shall it be given unto you. As ye judge, so shall ye be judged. As ye show kindness, so shall kindness be showed unto you. With what measure ye mete, it shall be measured withal to you.*

13:3 With this commandment and these precepts let us confirm ourselves, that we may walk in obedience to His hallowed words, with lowliness of mind.

13:4 For the holy Word saith, *Upon whom shall I look, save upon him that is gentle and quiet and feareth Mine oracles?*

14:1 Therefore it is right and proper, brethren, that we should be obedient unto God, rather than follow those who in arrogance and unruliness have set themselves up as leaders in abominable jealousy.

14:2 For we shall bring upon us no common harm, but rather great peril, if we surrender ourselves recklessly to the purposes of men who launch out into strife and seditions, so as to estrange us from that which is right.

14:3 Let us be good one towards another according to the compassion and sweetness of Him that made us. For it is written:

14:4 *The good shall be dwellers in the land, and the innocent shall be left on it but they that transgress shall be destroyed utterly from it.*

14:5 And again He saith *I saw the ungodly lifted up on high and exalted as the cedars of Lebanon. And I passed by, and behold he was not; and sought out his place, and I found it not. Keep innocence and behold uprightness; for there is a remnant for the peaceful man.*

15:1 Therefore let us cleave unto them that practice peace with godliness, and not unto them that desire peace with dissimulation.

15:2 For He saith in a certain place *This people honoreth Me with their lips, but their heart is far from Me,*

15:3 and again, *they blessed with their mouth, but they cursed with their heart.*

15:4 And again He saith, *They loved Him with their mouth, and with their tongue they lied unto Him; and their heart was not upright with Him, neither were they steadfast in His covenant.*

15:5 *For this cause let the deceitful lips be made dumb which speak iniquity against the righteous.* And again *May the Lord utterly destroy all the deceitful lips, the tongue that speaketh proud things, even them that say, Let us magnify our tongue; our lips are our own; who is lord over us?*

15:6 *For the misery of the needy and for the groaning of the poor I will now arise, saith the Lord. I will set him in safety; I will deal boldly by him.*

16:1 For Christ is with them that are lowly of mind, not with them that exalt themselves over the flock.

16:2 The scepter of the majesty of God, even our Lord Jesus Christ, came not in the pomp of arrogance or of pride, though He might have done so, but in lowliness of mind, according as the Holy Spirit spake concerning Him.

16:3 For He saith *Lord, who believed our report? and to whom was the arm of the Lord revealed? We announced Him in His presence. As a child was He, as a root in a thirsty ground. There is no form in Him, neither glory. And we beheld Him, and He had no form nor comeliness, but His form was mean, lacking more than the form of men. He was a man of stripes and of toil, and knowing how to bear infirmity: for His face is turned away. He was dishonored and held of no account.*

16:4 *He beareth our sins and suffereth pain for our sakes: and we accounted Him to be in toil and in stripes and in affliction.*

16:5 *And He was wounded for our sins and hath been afflicted for our iniquities. The chastisement of our peace is upon Him. With His bruises we were healed.*

16:6 *We all went astray like sheep, each man went astray in his own path:*

16:7 *and the Lord delivered Him over for our sins. And He openeth not His mouth, because He is afflicted. As a sheep He was led to slaughter; and as a lamb before his shearer is dumb, so openeth He not His mouth. In His humiliation His judgment was taken away.*

16:8 *His generation who shall declare? For His life is taken away from the earth.*

16:9 *For the iniquities of my people He is come to death.*

16:10 *And I will give the wicked for His burial, and the rich for His death; for He wrought no iniquity, neither was guile found in His mouth. And the Lord desireth to cleanse Him from His stripes.*

16:11 *If ye offer for sin, your soul shall see along lived seed.*

16:12 *And the Lord desireth to take away from the toil of His soul, to show Him light and to mould Him with understanding, to justify a Just One that is a good servant unto many. And He shall bear their sins.*

16:13 *Therefore He shall inherit many, and shall divide the spoils of the strong; because His soul was delivered unto death, and He was reckoned unto the transgressors;*

16:14 *and He bare the sins of many, and for their sins was He delivered up.*

16:15 And again He Himself saith; *But I am a worm and no man, a reproach of men and an outcast of the people.*

16:16 *All they that beheld me mocked at me; they spake with their lips; they wagged their heads, saying, He hoped on the Lord; let Him deliver him, or let Him save him, for He desireth him.*

16:17 Ye see, dearly beloved, what is the pattern that hath been given unto us; for, if the Lord was thus lowly of mind, what should we do, who through Him have been brought under the yoke of His grace?

17:1 Let us be imitators also of them which went about in goatskins and sheepskins, preaching the coming of Christ. We mean Elijah and Elisha and likewise Ezekiel, the prophets, and besides them those men also that obtained a good report.

17:2 Abraham obtained an exceeding good report and was called the friend of God; and looking steadfastly on the glory of God, he saith in lowliness of mind, But I am dust and ashes.

17:3 Moreover concerning Job also it is thus written; *And Job was righteous and unblamable, one that was true and honored God and abstained from all evil.*

17:4 Yet he himself accuseth himself saying, *No man from filth; no, not though his life be but for a day.*

17:5 Moses was called *faithful in all His house*, and through his ministration God judged Egypt with the plagues and the torments which befell them. Howbeit he also, though greatly glorified, yet spake no proud words, but said, when an oracle was given to him at the bush, *Who am I, that Thou sendest me?*

17:6 *Nay, I am feeble of speech and slow of tongue.* And again he saith, *But I am smoke from the pot.*

18:1 But what must we say of David that obtained a good report? of whom God said, *I have found a man after My heart, David the son of Jesse: with eternal mercy have I anointed him.*

18:2 Yet he too saith unto God *Have mercy upon me, O God, according to Thy great mercy; and according to the multitude of Thy compassions, blot out mine iniquity.*

18:3 *Wash me yet more from mine iniquity, and cleanse me from my sin. For I acknowledge mine iniquity, and my sin is ever before me. Against Thee only did I sin, and I wrought evil in Thy sight; that Thou mayest be justified in Thy words, and mayest conquer in Thy pleading.*

18:4 *For behold, in iniquities was I conceived, and in sins did my mother bear me. For behold Thou hast loved truth: the dark and hidden things of Thy wisdom hast Thou showed unto me.*

18:5 *Thou shalt sprinkle me with hyssop, and I shall be made clean. Thou shalt wash me, and I shall become whiter than snow.*

18:6 *Thou shalt make me to hear of joy and gladness. The bones which have been humbled shall rejoice.*

18:7 *Turn away Thy face from my sins, and blot out all mine iniquities.*

18:8 *Make a clean heart within me, O God, and renew a right spirit in mine inmost parts. Cast me not away from Thy presence, and take not Thy Holy Spirit from me.*

18:9 *Restore unto me the joy of Thy salvation, and strengthen me with a princely spirit.*

18:10 *I will teach sinners Thy ways, and godless men shall be converted unto Thee.*

18:11 *Deliver me from bloodguiltiness, O God, the God of my salvation. My tongue shall rejoice in Thy righteousness.*

18:12 *Lord, Thou shalt open my mouth, and my lips shall declare Thy praise.*

18:13 *For, if Thou hadst desired sacrifice, I would have given it: in whole burnt offerings Thou wilt have no pleasure.*

18:14 *A sacrifice unto God is a contrite spirit; a contrite and humbled heart God will not despise.*

19:1 The humility therefore and the submissiveness of so many and so great men, who have thus obtained a good report, hath through obedience made better not only us but also the generations which were before us, even them that received His oracles in fear and truth.

19:2 Seeing then that we have been partakers of many great and glorious doings, let us hasten to return unto the goal of peace which hath been handed down to us from the beginning, and let us look steadfastly unto the Father and Maker of the whole world, and cleave unto His splendid and excellent gifts of peace and benefits.

19:3 Let us behold Him in our mind, and let us look with the eyes of our soul unto His long-suffering will. Let us note how free from anger He is towards all His creatures.

20:1 The heavens are moved by His direction and obey Him in peace.

20:2 Day and night accomplish the course assigned to them by Him, without hindrance one to another.

20:3 The sun and the moon and the dancing stars according to His appointment circle in harmony within the bounds assigned to them, without any swerving aside.

20:4 The earth, bearing fruit in fulfillment of His will at her proper seasons, putteth forth the food that supplieth abundantly both men and beasts and all living things which are thereupon, making no dissension, neither altering anything which He hath decreed.

20:5 Moreover, the inscrutable depths of the abysses and the unutterable statutes of the nether regions are constrained by the same ordinances.

20:6 The basin of the boundless sea, gathered together by His workmanship *into it's reservoirs*, passeth not the barriers wherewith it is surrounded; but even as He ordered it, so it doeth.

20:7 For He said, *So far shalt thou come, and thy waves shall be broken within thee.*

20:8 The ocean which is impassable for men, and the worlds beyond it, are directed by the same ordinances of the Master.

20:9 The seasons of spring and summer and autumn and winter give way in succession one to another in peace.

20:10 The winds in their several quarters at their proper season fulfill their ministry without disturbance; and the ever flowing fountains, created for enjoyment and health, without fail give their breasts which sustain the life for men. Yea, the smallest of living things come together in concord and peace.

20:11 All these things the great Creator and Master of the universe ordered to be in peace and concord, doing good unto all things, but far beyond the rest unto us who have taken refuge in His compassionate mercies through our Lord Jesus Christ,

20:12 to whom be the glory and the majesty for ever and ever. Amen.

21:1 Look ye, brethren, lest His benefits, which are many, turn unto judgment to all of us, if we walk not worthily of Him, and do those things which are good and well pleasing in His sight with concord.

21:2 For He saith in a certain place, *The Spirit of the Lord is a lamp searching the closets of the belly.*

21:3 Let us see how near He is, and how that nothing escapeth Him of our thoughts or our devices which we make.

21:4 It is right therefore that we should not be deserters from His will.

21:5 Let us rather give offense to foolish and senseless men who exalt themselves and boast in the arrogance of their words, than to God.

21:6 Let us fear the Lord Jesus [Christ], whose blood was given for us. Let us reverence our rulers; let us honor our elders; let us instruct our young men in the lesson of the fear of God. Let us guide our women toward that which is good:

21:7 let them show forth their lovely disposition of purity; let them prove their sincere affection of gentleness; let them make manifest the moderation of their tongue through their silence; let them show their love, not in factious preferences but without partiality towards all them that fear God, in holiness. Let our children be partakers of the instruction which is in Christ:

21:8 let them learn how lowliness of mind prevaileth with God, what power chaste love hath with God, how the fear of Him is good and great and saveth all them that walk therein in a pure mind with holiness.

21:9 For He is the searcher out of the intents and desires; whose breath is in us, and when He listeth, He shall take it away.

22:1 Now all these things the faith which is in Christ confirmeth: for He Himself through the Holy Spirit thus invite thus: *Come, my children, hearken unto Me, I will teach you the fear of the Lord.*

22:2 *What man is he that desireth life and loveth to see good days?*

22:3 *Make thy tongue to cease from evil, and thy lips that they speak no guile.*

22:4 *Turn aside from evil and do good.*

22:5 *Seek peace and ensue it.*

22:6 *The eyes of the Lord are over the righteous, and His ears are turned to their prayers. But the face of the Lord is upon them that do evil, to destroy their memorial from the earth.*

22:7 *The righteous cried out, and the Lord heard him, and delivered him from all his troubles. Many are the troubles of the righteous, and the Lord shall deliver him from them all.*

22:8 *And again Many are the stripes of the sinner, but them that set their hope on the Lord mercy shall compass about.*

23:1 The Father, who is pitiful in all things, and ready to do good, hath compassion on them that fear Him, and kindly and lovingly bestoweth His favors on them that draw nigh unto Him with a single mind.

23:2 Therefore let us not be double-minded, neither let our soul indulge in idle humors respecting His exceeding and glorious gifts.

23:3 Let this scripture be far from us where He saith *Wretched are the double-minded, Which doubt in their soul and say, These things we did hear in the days of our fathers also, and behold we have grown old, and none of these things hath befallen us.*

23:4 *Ye fools, compare yourselves unto a tree; take a vine. First it sheddeth its leaves, then a shoot cometh, then a leaf, then a flower, and after these a sour berry, then a full ripe grape.* Ye see that in a little time the fruit of the tree attaineth unto mellowness.

23:5 Of a truth quickly and suddenly shall His will be accomplished, the scripture also bearing witness to it, saying *He shall come quickly and shall not tarry; and the Lord shall come suddenly into His temple, even the Holy One, whom ye expect.*

24:1 Let us understand, dearly beloved, how the Master continually showeth unto us the resurrection that shall be hereafter; whereof He made the Lord Jesus Christ the firstfruit, when He raised Him from the dead.

24:2 Let us behold, dearly beloved, the resurrection which happeneth at its proper season.

24:3 Day and night show unto us the resurrection. The night falleth asleep, and day ariseth; the day departeth, and night cometh on.

24:4 Let us mark the fruits, how and in what manner the sowing taketh place.

24:5 *The sower goeth forth* and casteth into the earth each of the seeds; and these falling into the earth dry and bare decay: then out of their decay the mightiness of the Master's providence raiseth them up, and from being one they increase manifold and bear fruit.

25:1 Let us consider the marvelous sign which is seen in the regions of the east, that is, in the parts about Arabia.

25:2 There is a bird, which is named the phoenix. This, being the only one of its kind, liveth for five hundred years; and when it hath now reached the time of its dissolution that it should die, it maketh for itself a coffin of frankincense and myrrh and the other spices, into the which in the fullness of time it entereth, and so it dieth.

25:3 But, as the flesh rotteth, a certain worm is engendered, which is nurtured from the moisture of the dead creature and putteth forth wings. Then, when it is grown lusty, it taketh up that coffin where are the bones of its parent, and carrying them journeyeth from the country of Arabia even unto Egypt, to the place called the City of the Sun;

25:4 and in the daytime in the sight of all, flying to the altar of the Sun, it layeth them thereupon; and this done, it setteth forth to return.

25:5 So the priests examine the registers of the times, and they find that it hath come when the five hundredth year is completed.

26:1 Do we then think it to be a great and marvelous thing, if the Creator of the universe shall bring about the resurrection of them that have served Him with holiness in the assurance of a good faith, seeing that He showeth to us even by a bird the magnificence of His promise?

26:2 For He saith in a certain place *And Thou shalt raise me up, and I will praise Thee; and; I went to rest and slept, I was awaked, for Thou art with me.*

26:3 And again Job saith *And Thou shall raise this my flesh which hath endured all these things.*

27:1 With this hope therefore let our souls be bound unto Him that is faithful in His promises and that is righteous in His judgments.

27:2 He that commanded not to lie, much more shall He Himself not lie: for nothing is impossible with God save to lie.

27:3 Therefore let our faith in Him be kindled within us, and let us understand that all things are nigh unto Him.

27:4 By a word of His majesty He compacted the universe; and by a word He can destroy it.

27:5 *Who shall say unto Him, What hast thou done? or who shall resist the might of His strength?* When He listeth, and as He listeth, He will do all things; and nothing shall pass away of those things that He hath decreed.

27:6 All things are in His sight, and nothing escapeth His counsel,

27:7 seeing that *The heavens declare the glory of God, and the firmament proclaimeth His handiwork. Day uttereth word unto day, and night proclaimeth knowledge unto night; and there are neither words nor speeches, whose voices are not heard.*

28:1 Since therefore all things are seen and heard, let us fear Him and forsake the abominable lusts of evil works, that we maybe shielded by His mercy from the coming judgments.

28:2 For where can any of us escape from His strong hand? And what world will receive any of them that desert from His service?

28:3 For the holy writing saith in a certain place *Where shall I go, and where shall I be hidden from Thy face? If I ascend into the heaven, Thou art there; if I depart into the farthest parts of the earth, there is Thy right hand; if I make my bed in the depths, there is Thy Spirit.*

28:4 Whither then shall one depart, or where shall one flee, from Him that embraceth the universe?

29:1 Let us therefore approach Him in holiness of soul, lifting up pure and undefiled hands unto Him, with love towards our gentle and compassionate Father who made us an elect portion unto Himself.

29:2 For thus it is written: *When the Most High divided the nations, when He dispersed the sons of Adam, He fixed the boundaries of the nations according to the number of the angels of God. His people Jacob became the portion of the Lord, and Israel the measurement of His inheritance.*

29:3 And in another place He saith, *Behold, the Lord taketh for Himself a nation out of the midst of the nations, as a man taketh the first fruits of his threshing floor; and the holy of holies shall come forth from that nation.*

30:1 Seeing then that we are the special portion of a Holy God, let us do all things that pertain unto holiness, forsaking evil speakings, abominable and impure embraces, drunkennesses and tumults and hateful lusts, abominable adultery, hateful pride.

30:2 *For God,* He saith, *resisteth the proud, but giveth grace to the lowly.*

30:3 Let us therefore cleave unto those to whom grace is given from God. Let us clothe ourselves in concord, being lowlyminded and temperate, holding ourselves aloof from all back biting and evil speaking, being justified by works and not by words.

30:4 For He saith, *He that saith much shall hear also again. Doth the ready talker think to be righteous?*

30:5 *Blessed is the offspring of a woman that liveth but a short time. Be not thou abundant in words.*

30:6 Let our praise be with God, and not of ourselves: for God hateth them that praise themselves.

30:7 Let the testimony to our well doing be given by others, as it was given unto our fathers who were righteous.

30:8 Boldness and arrogance and daring are for them that are accursed of God; but forbearance and humility and gentleness are with them that are blessed of God.

31:1 Let us therefore cleave unto His blessing, and let us see what are the ways of blessing. Let us study the records of the things that have happened from the beginning.

31:2 Wherefore was our father Abraham blessed? Was it not because he wrought righteousness and truth through faith?

31:3 Isaac with confidence, as knowing the future, was led a willing sacrifice.

31:4 Jacob with humility departed from his land because of his brother, and went unto Laban and served; and the twelve tribes of Israel were given unto him.

32:1 If any man will consider them one by one in sincerity, he shall understand the magnificence of the gifts that are given by Him.

32:2 For of Jacob are all the priests and levites who minister unto the altar of God; of him is the Lord Jesus as concerning the flesh; of him are kings and rulers and governors in the line of Judah; yea and the rest of his tribes are held in no small honor, seeing that God promised saying, *Thy seed shall be as the stars of heaven.*

32:3 They all therefore were glorified and magnified, not through themselves or their own works or the righteous doing which they wrought, but through His will.

32:4 And so we, having been called through His will in Christ Jesus, are not justified through ourselves or through our own wisdom or understanding or piety or works which we wrought in holiness of heart, but through faith, whereby the Almighty God justified all men that have been from the beginning; to whom be the glory for ever and ever. Amen.

33:1 What then must we do, brethren? Must we idly abstain from doing good, and forsake love? May the Master never allow this to befall us at least; but let us hasten with instancy and zeal to accomplish every good work.

33:2 For the Creator and Master of the universe Himself rejoiceth in His works.

33:3 For by His exceeding great might He established the heavens, and in His incomprehensible wisdom He set them in order. And the earth He separated from the water that surroundeth it, and He set it firm on the sure foundation of His own will; and the living creatures which walk upon it He commanded to exist by His ordinance. Having before created the sea and the living creatures therein, He enclosed it by His own power.

33:4 Above all, as the most excellent and exceeding great work of His intelligence, with His sacred and faultless hands He formed man in the impress of His own image.

33:5 For thus saith God *Let us make man after our image and after our likeness. And God made man; male and female made He them.*

33:6 So having finished all these things, He praised them and blessed them and said, *Increase and multiply.*

33:7 We have seen that all the righteous were adorned in good works. Yea, and the Lord Himself having adorned Himself with worlds rejoiced.

33:8 Seeing then that we have this pattern, let us conform ourselves with all diligence to His will; let us with all our strength work the work of righteousness.

34:1 The good workman receiveth the bread of his work with boldness, but the slothful and careless dareth not look his employer in the face.

34:2 It is therefore needful that we should be zealous unto well doing, for of Him are all things:

34:3 since He forewarneth us saying, *Behold, the Lord, and His reward is before His face, to recompense each man according to his work.*

34:4 He exhorteth us therefore to believe on Him with our whole heart, and to be not idle nor careless unto every good work.

34:5 Let our boast and our confidence be in Him: let us submit ourselves to His will; let us mark the whole host of His angels, how they stand by and minister unto His will.

34:6 For the scripture saith, *Ten thousands of ten thousands stood by Him, and thousands of thousands ministered unto Him: and they cried aloud, Holy, holy, holy is the Lord of Sabaoth; all creation is full of His glory.*

34:7 Yea, and let us ourselves then, being gathered together in concord with intentness of heart, cry unto Him as from one mouth earnestly that we may be made partakers of His great and glorious promises.

34:8 For He saith, *Eye hath not seen and ear hath not heard, and it hath not entered into the heart of man what great things He hath prepared for them that patiently await Him.*

35:1 How blessed and marvelous are the gifts of God, dearly beloved!

35:2 Life in immortality, splendor in righteousness, truth in boldness, faith in confidence, temperance in sanctification! And all these things fall under our apprehension.

35:3 What then, think ye, are the things preparing for them that patiently await Him? The Creator and Father of the ages, the All holy One Himself knoweth their number and their beauty.

35:4 Let us therefore contend, that we may be found in the number of those that patiently await Him, to the end that we may be partakers of His promised gifts.

35:5 But how shall this be, dearly beloved? If our mind be fixed through faith towards God; if we seek out those things which are well pleasing and acceptable unto Him; if we accomplish such things as beseem His faultless will, and follow the way of truth, casting off from ourselves all unrighteousness and iniquity, covetousness, strifes, malignities and deceits, whisperings and backbitings, hatred of God, pride and arrogance, vainglory and inhospitality.

35:6 For they that do these things are hateful to God; and not only they that do them, but they also that consent unto them.

35:7 For the scripture saith, *But unto the sinner said God, Wherefore dost thou declare Mine ordinances, and takest My covenant upon thy lips?*

35:8 *Yet Thou didst hate instruction and didst cast away My words behind thee. If thou sawest a thief thou didst keep company with him, and with the adulterers thou didst set thy portion. Thy mouth multiplied wickedness and thy tongue wove deceit. Thou sattest and spakest against thy brother, and against the son of thy mother thou didst lay a stumbling block.*

35:9 *These things Thou hast done, and I kept silence. Thou thoughtest, unrighteous man, that I should be like unto thee.*

35:10 *I will convict thee and will set thee face to face with thyself.*

35:11 *Now understand ye these things, ye that forget God, lest at any time He seize you as a lion, and there be none to deliver.*

35:12 *The sacrifice of praise shall glorify Me, and there is the way wherein I will show him the salvation of God.*

36:1 This is the way, dearly beloved, wherein we found our salvation, even Jesus Christ the High priest of our offerings, the Guardian and Helper of our weakness.

36:2 Through Him let us look steadfastly unto the heights of the heavens; through Him we behold as in a mirror His faultless and most excellent visage; through Him the eyes of our hearts were opened; through Him our foolish and darkened mind springeth up unto the light; through Him the Master willed that we should taste of the immortal knowledge *Who being the brightness of His majesty is so much greater than angels, as He hath inherited a more excellent name.*

36:3 For so it is written *Who maketh His angels spirits and His ministers aflame of fire*

36:4 but of His Son the Master said thus, *Thou art My Son, I this day have begotten thee. Ask of Me, and I will give Thee the Gentiles for Thine inheritance, and the ends of the earth for Thy possession.*

36:5 And again He saith unto Him *Sit Thou on My right hand, until I make Thine enemies a footstool for Thy feet.*

36:6 Who then are these enemies? They that are wicked and resist His will.

37:1 Let us therefore enlist ourselves, brethren, with all earnestness in His faultless ordinances.

37:2 Let us mark the soldiers that are enlisted under our rulers, how exactly, how readily, how submissively, they execute the orders given them.

37:3 All are not prefects, nor rulers of thousands, nor rulers of hundreds, nor rulers of fifties, and so forth; but each man in his own rank executeth the orders given by the king and the governors.

37:4 The great without the small cannot exist, neither the small without the great. There is a certain mixture in all things, and therein is utility.

37:5 Let us take our body as an example. The head without the feet is nothing; so likewise the feet without the head are nothing: even the smallest limbs of our body are necessary and useful for the whole body: but all the members conspire and unite in subjection, that the whole body maybe saved.

38:1 So in our case let the whole body be saved in Christ Jesus, and let each man be subject unto his neighbor, according as also he was appointed with his special grace.

38:2 Let not the strong neglect the weak; and let the weak respect the strong. Let the rich minister aid to the poor; and let the poor give thanks to God, because He hath given him one through whom his wants may be supplied. Let the wise display his wisdom, not in words, but in good works. He that is lowly in mind, let him not bear testimony to himself, but leave testimony to be borne to him by his neighbor. He that is pure in the flesh, let him be so, and not boast, knowing that it is Another who bestoweth his continence upon him.

38:3 Let us consider, brethren, of what matter we were made; who and what manner of beings we were, when we came into the world; from what a sepulchre and what darkness He that molded and created us brought us into His world, having prepared His benefits aforehand ere ever we were born.

38:4 Seeing therefore that we have all these things from Him, we ought in all things to give thanks to Him, to whom be the glory for ever and ever. Amen.

39:1 Senseless and stupid and foolish and ignorant men jeer and mock at us, desiring that they themselves should be exalted in their imaginations.

39:2 For what power hath a mortal? or what strength hath a child of earth?

39:3 For it is written; *There was no form before mine eyes; only I heard a breath and a voice.*

39:4 *What then? Shall a mortal be clean in the sight of the Lord; or shall a man be unblamable for his works? seeing that He is distrustful against His servants and noteth some perversity against His angels.*

39:5 *Nay, the heaven is not clean in His sight. Away then, ye that dwell in houses of clay, whereof, even of the same clay, we ourselves are made. He smote them like a moth, and from morn to even they are no more. Because they could not succor themselves, they perished.*

39:6 *He breathed on them and they died, because they had no wisdom.*

39:7 *But call thou, if perchance one shall obey thee, or if thou shalt see one of the holy angels. For wrath killeth the foolish man, and envy slayeth him that has gone astray.*

39:8 *And I have seen fools throwing out roots, but forthwith their habitation was eaten up.*

39:9 *Far be their sons from safety. May they be mocked at the gates of inferiors, and there shall be none to deliver them. For the things which are prepared for them, the righteous shall eat; but they themselves shall not be delivered from evils.*

40:1 Forasmuch then as these things are manifest beforehand, and we have searched into the depths of the Divine knowledge, we ought to do all things in order, as many as the Master hath commanded us to perform at their appointed seasons.

40:2 Now the offerings and ministrations He commanded to be performed with care, and not to be done rashly or in disorder, but at fixed times and seasons.

40:3 And where and by whom He would have them performed, He Himself fixed by His supreme will: that all things being done with piety according to His good pleasure might be acceptable to His will.

40:4 They therefore that make their offerings at the appointed seasons are acceptable and blessed: for while they follow the institutions of the Master they cannot go wrong.

40:5 For unto the high priest his proper services have been assigned, and to the priests their proper office is appointed, and upon the levites their proper ministrations are laid. The layman is bound by the layman's ordinances.

41:1 Let each of you, brethren, in his own order give thanks unto God, maintaining a good conscience and not transgressing the appointed rule of his service, but acting with all seemliness.

41:2 Not in every place, brethren, are the continual daily sacrifices offered, or the freewill offerings, or the sin offerings and the trespass offerings, but in Jerusalem alone. And even there the offering is not made in every place, but before the sanctuary in the court of the altar; and this too through the high priest and the afore said ministers, after that the victim to be offered hath been inspected for blemishes.

41:3 They therefore who do any thing contrary to the seemly ordinance of His will receive death as the penalty.

41:4 Ye see, brethren, in proportion as greater knowledge hath been vouchsafed unto us, so much the more are we exposed to danger.

42:1 The Apostles received the Gospel for us from the Lord Jesus Christ; Jesus Christ was sent forth from God.

42:2 So then Christ is from God, and the Apostles are from Christ. Both therefore came of the will of God in the appointed order.

42:3 Having therefore received a charge, and having been fully assured through the resurrection of our Lord Jesus Christ and confirmed in the word of God with full assurance of the Holy Ghost, they went forth with the glad tidings that the kingdom of God should come.

42:4 So preaching everywhere in country and town, they appointed their firstfruits, when they had proved them by the Spirit, to be bishops and deacons unto them that should believe.

42:5 And this they did in no new fashion; for indeed it had been written concerning bishops and deacons from very ancient times; for thus saith the scripture in a certain place, *I will appoint their bishops in righteousness and their deacons in faith.*

43:1 And what marvel, if they which were entrusted in Christ with such a work by God appointed the aforesaid persons? seeing that even the blessed Moses who was *a faithful servant in all His house* recorded for a sign in the sacred books all things that were enjoined upon him. And him also the rest of the prophets followed, bearing witness with him unto the laws that were ordained by him.

43:2 For he, when jealousy arose concerning the priesthood, and there was dissension among the tribes which of them was adorned with the glorious name, commanded the twelve chiefs of the tribes to bring to him rods inscribed with the name of each tribe. And he took them and tied them and sealed them with the signet rings of the chiefs of the tribes, and put them away in the tabernacle of the testimony on the table of God.

43:3 And having shut the tabernacle he sealed the keys and likewise also the doors.

43:4 And he said unto them, Brethren, the tribe whose rod shall bud, this hath God chosen to be priests and ministers unto Him.

43:5 Now when morning came, he called together all Israel, even the six hundred thousand men, and showed the seals to the chiefs of the tribes and opened the tabernacle of the testimony and drew forth the rods. And the rod of Aaron was found not only with buds, but also bearing fruit.

43:6 What think ye, dearly beloved? Did not Moses know beforehand that this would come to pass? Assuredly he knew it. But that disorder might not arise in Israel, he did thus, to the end that the Name of the true and only God might be glorified: to whom he the glory for ever and ever. Amen...

44:1 And our Apostles knew through our Lord Jesus Christ that there would be strife over the name of the bishop's office.

44:2 For this cause therefore, having received complete foreknowledge, they appointed the aforesaid persons, and afterwards they provided a continuance, that if these should fall asleep, other approved men should succeed to their ministration. Those therefore who were appointed by them, or afterward by other men of repute with the consent of the whole Church, and have ministered unblamably to the flock of Christ in lowliness of mind, peacefully and with all modesty, and for long time have borne a good report with all these men we consider to be unjustly thrust out from their ministration.

44:3 For it will be no light sin for us, if we thrust out those who have offered the gifts of the bishop's office unblamably and holily.

44:4 Blessed are those presbyters who have gone before, seeing that their departure was fruitful and ripe: for they have no fear lest any one should remove them from their appointed place.

44:5 For we see that ye have displaced certain persons, though they were living honorably, from the ministration which had been respected by them blamelessly.

45:1 Be ye contentious, brethren, and jealous about the things that pertain unto salvation.

45:2 Ye have searched the scriptures, which are true, which were given through the Holy Ghost;

45:3 and ye know that nothing unrighteous or counterfeit is written in them. Ye will not find that righteous persons have been thrust out by holy men.

45:4 Righteous men were persecuted, but it was by the lawless; they were imprisoned, but it was by the unholy. They were stoned by transgressors: they were slain by those who had conceived a detestable and unrighteous jealousy.

45:5 Suffering these things, they endured nobly.

45:6 For what must we say, brethren? Was Daniel cast into the lions' den by them that feared God?

45:7 Or were Ananias and Azarias and Misael shut up in the furnace of fire by them that professed the excellent and glorious worship of the Most High? Far be this from our thoughts. Who then were they that did these things? Abominable men and full of all wickedness were stirred up to such a pitch of wrath, as to bring cruel suffering upon them that served God in a holy and blameless purpose, not knowing that the Most High is the champion and protector of them that in a pure conscience serve His excellent Name: unto whom be the glory for ever and ever. Amen.

45:8 But they that endured patiently in confidence inherited glory and honor; they were exalted, and had their names recorded by God in their memorial for ever and ever. Amen.

46:1 To such examples as these therefore, brethren, we also ought to cleave.

46:2 For it is written; *Cleave unto the saints, for they that cleave unto them shall be sanctified.*

46:3 And again He saith in another place; *With the guiltless man thou shalt be guiltless, and with the elect thou shalt be elect, and with the crooked thou shalt deal crookedly.*

46:4 Let us therefore cleave to the guiltless and righteous: and these are the elect of God.

46:5 Wherefore are there strifes and wraths and factions and divisions and war among you?

46:6 Have we not one God and one Christ and one Spirit of grace that was shed upon us? And is there not one calling in Christ?

46:7 Wherefore do we tear and rend asunder the members of Christ, and stir up factions against our own body, and reach such a pitch of folly, as to forget that we are members one of another?

46:8 Remember the words of Jesus our Lord: for He said, *Woe unto that man; it were good for him if he had not been born, rather than that at he should offend one of Mine elect. It were better for him that a millstone were hanged about him, and be cast into the sea, than that he should pervert one of Mine elect.*

46:9 Your division hath perverted many; it hath brought many to despair, many to doubting, and all of us to sorrow. And your sedition still continueth.

47:1 Take up the epistle of the blessed Paul the Apostle.

47:2 What wrote he first unto you in the beginning of the Gospel?

47:3 Of a truth he charged you in the Spirit concerning himself and Cephas and Apollos, because that even then ye had made parties.

47:4 Yet that making of parties brought less sin upon you; for ye were partisans of Apostles that were highly reputed, and of a man approved in their sight.

47:5 But now mark ye, who they are that have perverted you and diminished the glory of your renowned love for the brotherhood.

47:6 It is shameful, dearly beloved, yes, utterly shameful and unworthy of your conduct in Christ, that it should be reported that the very steadfast and ancient Church of the Corinthians, for the sake of one or two persons, maketh sedition against its presbyters.

47:7 And this report hath reached not only us, but them also which differ from us, so that ye even heap blasphemies on the Name of the Lord by reason of your folly, and moreover create peril for yourselves.

48:1 Let us therefore root this out quickly, and let us fall down before the Master and entreat Him with tears, that He may show Himself propitious and be reconciled unto us, and may restore us to the seemly and pure conduct which belongeth to our love of the brethren.

48:2 For this is a gate of righteousness opened unto life, as it is written; *Open me the gates of righteousness, that I may enter in thereby and preach the Lord.*

48:3 *This is the gate of the Lord; the righteous shall enter in thereby.*

48:4 Seeing then that many gates are opened, this is that gate which is in righteousness, even that which is in Christ, whereby all are blessed that have entered in and direct their path in holiness and righteousness, performing all things without confusion.

48:5 Let a man be faithful, let him be able to expound a deep saying, let him be wise in the discernment of words, let him be strenuous in deeds, let him be pure;

48:6 for so much the more ought he to be lowly in mind, in proportion as he seemeth to be the greater; and he ought to seek the common advantage of all, and not his own.

49:1 Let him that hath love in Christ fulfill the commandments of Christ.

49:2 Who can declare the bond of the love of God?

49:3 Who is sufficient to tell the majesty of its beauty?

49:4 The height, where unto love exalteth, is unspeakable.

49:5 Love joineth us unto God; *love covereth a multitude of sins*; love endureth all things, is long-suffering in all things. There is nothing coarse, nothing arrogant in love. Love hath no divisions, love maketh no seditions, love doeth all things in concord. In love were all the elect of God made perfect; without love nothing is well pleasing to God:

49:6 in love the Master took us unto Himself; for the love which He had toward us, Jesus Christ our Lord hath given His blood for us by the will of God, and His flesh for our flesh and His life for our lives.

50:1 Ye see, dearly beloved, how great and marvelous a thing is love, and there is no declaring its perfection.

50:2 Who is sufficient to be found therein, save those to whom God shall vouchsafe it? Let us therefore entreat and ask of His mercy, that we may be found blameless in love, standing apart from the factiousness of men. All the generations from Adam unto this day have passed away: but they that by God's grace were perfected in love dwell in the abode of the pious; and they shall be made manifest in the visitation of the Kingdom of God.

50:3 For it is written; *Enter into the closet for a very little while until Mine anger and Mine wrath shall pass away, and I will remember a good day and will raise you from your tombs.*

50:4 Blessed were we, dearly beloved, if we should be doing the commandments of God in concord of love, to the end that our sins may through love be forgiven us.

50:5 For it is written; *Blessed are they whose iniquities are forgiven, and whose sins are covered. Blessed is the man to whom the Lord shall impute no sin, neither is guile in his mouth.*

50:6 This declaration of blessedness was pronounced upon them that have been elected by God through Jesus Christ our Lord, to whom be the glory for ever and ever. Amen.

51:1 For all our transgressions which we have committed through any of the wiles of the adversary, let us entreat that we may obtain forgiveness. Yea and they also, who set themselves up as leaders of faction and division, ought to look to the common ground of hope.

51:2 For such as walk in fear and love desire that they themselves should fall into suffering rather than their neighbors; and they pronounce condemnation against themselves rather than against the harmony which hath been handed down to us nobly and righteously.

51:3 For it is good for a man to make confession of his trespasses rather than to harden his heart, as the heart of those was hardened who made sedition against Moses the servant of God; whose condemnation was clearly manifest,

51:4 for they went down to hades alive, and *Death shall be their shepherd.*

51:5 Pharaoh and his host and all the rulers of Egypt, *their chariots and their horsemen*, were overwhelmed in the depths of the Red Sea, and perished for none other reason but because their foolish hearts were hardened after that the signs and the wonders had been wrought in the land of Egypt by the hand of Moses the servant of God.

52:1 The Master, brethren, hath need of nothing at all. He desireth not anything of any man, save to confess unto Him.

52:2 For the elect David saith; *I will confess unto the Lord, and it shall please Him more than a young calf that groweth horns and hoofs. Let the poor see it, and rejoice.*

52:3 And again He saith; *Sacrifice to God a sacrifice of praise, and pay thy vows to the Most High: and call upon Me in the day of thine affliction, and I will deliver thee, and thou shalt glorify Me.*

52:4 *For a sacrifice unto God is a broken spirit.*

53:1 For ye know, and know well, the sacred scriptures, dearly beloved, and ye have searched into the oracles of God. We write these things therefore to put you in remembrance.

53:2 When Moses went up into the mountain and had spent forty days and forty nights in fasting and humiliation, God said unto him; *Moses, Moses, come down , quickly hence, for My people whom thou leadest forth from the land of Egypt have wrought iniquity: they have transgressed quickly out of the way which thou didst command unto them: they have made for themselves molten images.*

53:3 *And the Lord said unto him; I have spoken unto thee once and twice, saying, I have seen this people, and behold it is stiff-necked. Let Me destroy them utterly, and I will blot out their name from under heaven, and I will make of thee a nation great and wonderful and numerous more than this.*

53:4 And Moses said; *Nay, not so, Lord Forgive this people their sin, or blot me also out of the book of the living.*

53:5 O mighty love! O unsurpassable perfection! The servant is bold with his Master; he asketh forgiveness for the multitude, or he demandeth that himself also be blotted out with them.

54:1 Who therefore is noble among you? Who is compassionate? Who is fulfilled with love?

54:2 Let him say; If by reason of me there be faction and strife and divisions, I retire, I depart, whither ye will, and I do that which is ordered by the people: only let the flock of Christ be at peace with its duly appointed presbyters.

54:3 He that shall have done this, shall win for himself great renown in Christ, and every place will receive him: for *the earth is the Lord's and the fullness thereof.*

54:4 Thus have they done and will do, that live as citizens of that kingdom of God which bringeth no regrets.

55:1 But, to bring forward examples of Gentiles also; many kings and rulers, when some season of pestilence pressed upon them, being taught by oracles have delivered themselves over to death, that they might rescue their fellow citizens through their own blood. Many have retired from their own cities, that they might have no more seditions.

55:2 We know that many among ourselves have delivered themselves to bondage, that they might ransom others. Many have sold themselves to slavery, and receiving the price paid for themselves have fed others.

55:3 Many women being strengthened through the grace of God have performed many manly deeds.

55:4 The blessed Judith, when the city was beleaguered, asked of the elders that she might be suffered to go forth into the camp of the aliens.

55:5 So she exposed herself to peril and went forth for love of her country and of her people which were beleaguered; and the Lord delivered Holophernes into the hand of a woman.

55:6 To no less peril did Esther also, who was perfect in faith, expose herself, that she might deliver the twelve tribes of Israel, when they were on the point to perish. For through her fasting and her humiliation she entreated the all seeing Master, the God of the ages; and He, seeing the humility of her soul, delivered the people for whose sake she encountered the peril.

56:1 Therefore let us also make intercession for them that are in any transgression, that forbearance and humility may be given them, to the end that they may yield not unto us, but unto the will of God. For so shall the compassionate remembrance of them with God and the saints be fruitful unto them, and perfect.

56:2 Let us accept chastisement, whereat no man ought to be vexed, dearly beloved. The admonition which we give one to another is good and exceeding useful; for it joineth us unto the will of God.

56:3 For thus saith the holy word; *The Lord hath indeed chastened me, and hath not delivered me over unto death.*

56:4 *For whom the Lord loveth He chasteneth, and scourgeth every son whom He receiveth.*

56:5 *For the righteous*, it is said, *shall chasten me in mercy and shall reprove me, but let not the mercy of sinners anoint my head.*

56:6 And again He saith; *Blessed is the man whom the Lord hath reproved, and refuse not thou the admonition of the Almighty. For He causeth pain, and he restoreth again:*

56:7 *He hath smitten, and His hands have healed.*

56:8 *Six times shall He rescue thee from afflictions and at the seventh no evil shall touch thee.*

56:9 *In famine he shall deliver thee from death, and in war He shall release thee from the arm of the sword.*

56:10 *And from the scourge of the tongue He shall hide thee and thou shalt not be afraid when evils approach.*

56:11 *Thou shalt laugh at the unrighteous and wicked, and of the wild beasts thou shalt not be afraid.*

56:12 *For wild beasts shall be at peace with thee.*

56:13 *Then shalt thou know that thy house shall be at peace: and the abode of thy tabernacle shall not go wrong,*

56:14 *and thou shalt know that thy seed is many, and thy children as the plenteous herbage of the field.*

56:15 *And thou shalt come to the grave as ripe corn reaped in due season, or as the heap of the threshing floor gathered together at the right time.*

56:16 Ye see, dearly beloved, how great protection there is for them that are chastened by the Master: for being a kind father He chasteneth us to the end that we may obtain mercy through His holy chastisement.

57:1 Ye therefore that laid the foundation of the sedition, submit yourselves unto the presbyters and receive chastisement unto repentance, bending the knees of your heart.

57:2 Learn to submit yourselves, laying aside the arrogant and proud stubbornness of your tongue. For it is better for you to be found little in the flock of Christ and to have your name on God's roll, than to be had in exceeding honor and yet be cast out from the hope of Him.

57:3 For thus saith the All virtuous Wisdom; *Behold I will pour out for you a saying of My breath, and I will teach you My word.*

57:4 *Because I called and ye obeyed not, and I held out words and ye heeded not, but made My councils of none effect, and were disobedient unto My reproofs; therefore I also will laugh at your destruction, and will rejoice over you when ruin cometh upon you, and when confusion overtaketh you suddenly, and your overthrow is at hand like a whirlwind,*

57:5 *or when ye call upon Me, yet will I not here you. Evil men shall seek me and not find me: for they hated wisdom, and chose not the fear of the Lord, neither would they give head unto My councils, but mocked at My reproofs.*

57:6 *Therefore they shall eat the fruits of their own way, and shall be filled with their own ungodliness.*

57:7 *For because they wronged babes, they shall be slain, and inquisition shall destroy the ungodly. But he that heareth Me shall dwell safely trusting in hope, and shall be quiet from all fear of all evil.*

58:1 Let us therefore be obedient unto His most holy and glorious Name, thereby escaping the threatenings which were spoken of old by the mouth of Wisdom against them which disobey, that we may dwell safely, trusting in the most holy Name of His majesty.

58:2 Receive our counsel, and ye shall have no occasion of regret. For as God liveth, and the Lord Jesus Christ liveth, and the Holy Spirit, who are the faith and the hope of the elect, so surely shall he, who with lowliness of mind and instant in gentleness hath without regretfulness performed the ordinances and commandments that are given by God, be enrolled and have a name among the number of them that are saved through Jesus Christ, through whom is the glory unto Him for ever and ever. Amen.

59:1 But if certain persons should be disobedient unto the words spoken by Him through us, let them understand that they will entangle themselves in no slight transgression and danger;

59:2 but we shall be guiltless of this sin. And we will ask, with instancy of prayer and supplication, that the Creator of the universe may guard intact unto the end the number that hath been numbered of His elect throughout the whole world, through His beloved Son Jesus Christ, through whom He called us from darkness to light, from ignorance to the full knowledge of the glory of His Name.

59:3 [Grant unto us, Lord,] that we may set our hope on Thy Name which is the primal source of all creation, and open the eyes of our hearts, that we may know Thee, who alone abidest *Highest in the lofty, Holy in the holy;* who *layest low in the insolence of the proud*, who *settest the lowly on high*, and *bringest the lofty low*; who *makest rich and makest poor*; who *killest and makest alive*; who alone art the Benefactor of spirits and the God of all flesh; who *lookest into the abysses*, who scanest the works of man; the Succor of them that are in peril, the *Savior of them that are in despair*; The Creator and Overseer of every spirit; who multipliest the nations upon earth, and hast chosen out from all men those that love Thee through Jesus Christ, Thy beloved Son, through whom Thou didst instruct us, didst sanctify us, didst honor us.

59:4 We beseech Thee, Lord and Master, to be *our help and succor*. Save those among us who are in tribulation; have mercy on the lowly; lift up the fallen; show Thyself unto the needy; heal the ungodly; convert the wanderers of Thy people; feed the hungry; release our prisoners; raise up the weak; comfort the fainthearted. *Let all the Gentiles know that Thou art the God alone*, and Jesus Christ is Thy Son, and *we are Thy people and the sheep of Thy pasture.*

60:1 Thou through Thine operations didst make manifest the everlasting fabric of the world. Thou, Lord, didst create the earth. Thou that art faithful throughout all generations, righteous in Thy judgments, marvelous in strength and excellence, Thou that art wise in creating and prudent in establishing that which Thou hast made, that art good in the things which are seen and faithful with them that trust on Thee, *pitiful and compassionate,* forgive us our iniquities and our unrighteousnesses and our transgressions and shortcomings.

60:2 Lay not to our account every sin of Thy servants and Thine handmaids, but cleanse us with the cleansing of Thy truth, and *guide our steps to walk in holiness* and righteousness and singleness *of heart* and *to do such things as are good and well pleasing in Thy sight* and in the sight of our rulers.

60:3 Yea, Lord, *make Thy face to shine upon us* in peace for our good, that we may be sheltered *by Thy mighty hand and* delivered from every sin *by Thine uplifted arm.* And deliver us from them that hate us wrongfully.

60:4 Give concord and peace to us and to all that dwell on the earth, as Thou gavest to our fathers, *when they called on* Thee *in faith and truth* with holiness, [that we may be saved,] while we render obedience to Thine almighty and most excellent Name, and to our rulers and governors upon the earth.

61:1 Thou, Lord and Master, hast given them the power of sovereignty through Thine excellent and unspeakable might, that we knowing the glory and honor which Thou hast given them may submit ourselves unto them, in nothing resisting Thy will. Grant unto them therefore, O Lord, health peace, concord, stability, that they may administer the government which Thou hast given them without failure.

61:2 For Thou, O heavenly Master, King of the ages, givest to the sons of men glory and honor and power over all things that are upon the earth. Do Thou, Lord, direct their counsel according to that which is good and well pleasing in Thy sight, that, administering in peace and gentleness with Godliness the power which Thou hast given them, they may obtain Thy favor.

61:3 O Thou, who alone art able to do these things and things far more exceeding good than these for us, we praise Thee through the High priest and Guardian of our souls, Jesus Christ, through whom be the glory and the majesty unto Thee both now and for all generations and for ever and ever. Amen.

62:1 As touching those things which befit our religion and are most useful for a virtuous life to such as would guide [their steps] in holiness and righteousness, we have written fully unto you, brethren.

62:2 For concerning faith and repentance and genuine love and temperance and sobriety and patience we have handled every argument, putting you in remembrance, that ye ought to please Almighty God in righteousness and truth and long suffering with holiness, laying aside malice and pursuing concord in love and peace, being instant in gentleness; even as our fathers, of whom we spake before, pleased Him, being lowly minded toward their Father and God and Creator and towards all men.

62:3 And we have put you in mind of these things the more gladly, since we knew well that we were writing to men who are faithful and highly accounted and have diligently searched into the oracles of the teaching of God.

63:1 Therefore it is right for us to give heed to so great and so many examples and to submit the neck and occupying the place of obedience to take our side with them that are the leaders of our souls, that ceasing from this foolish dissension we may attain unto the goal which lieth before us in truthfulness, keeping aloof from every fault.

63:2 For ye will give us great joy and gladness, if ye render obedience unto the things written by us through the Holy Spirit, and root out the unrighteous anger of your jealousy, according to the entreaty which we have made for peace and concord in this letter.

63:3 And we have also sent faithful and prudent men that have walked among us from youth unto old age unblamably, who shall also be witnesses between you and us.

63:4 And this we have done that ye might know that we have had, and still have, every solicitude that ye should be speedily at peace.

64:1 Finally may the All seeing God and Master of spirits and Lord of all flesh, who chose the Lord Jesus Christ, and us through Him for a peculiar people, grant unto every soul that is called after His excellent and holy Name faith, fear, peace, patience, long-suffering, temperance, chastity and soberness, that they may be well pleasing unto His Name through our High priest and Guardian Jesus Christ, through whom unto Him be glory and majesty, might and honor, both now and for ever and ever. Amen.

65:1 Now send ye back speedily unto us our messengers Claudius Ephebus and Valerius Bito, together with Fortunatus also, in peace and with joy, to the end that they may the more quickly report the peace and concord which is prayed for and earnestly desired by us, that we also may the more speedily rejoice over your good order.

65:2 The grace of our Lord Jesus Christ be with you and with all men in all places who have been called by God and through Him, through whom be glory and honor, power and greatness and eternal dominion, unto Him, from the ages past and forever and ever. Amen.

THE LETTERS OF IGNATIUS

Ignatius

TRANSLATED BY ALEXANDER ROBERTS AND JAMES DONALDSON

The Epistle of Ignatius to the Ephesians

Ignatius, who is also called Theopharus, to the Church which is at Ephesus, in Asia, deservedly most happy, being blessed in the greatness and fulness of God the Father, and predestinated before the beginning of time, that it should be always for an enduring and unchangeable glory, being united and elected through the true passion by the will of the Father, and Jesus Christ, our God: Abundant happiness through Jesus Christ, and His undefiled grace.

Chapter I.—Praise of the Ephesians.

I have become acquainted with your name, much-beloved in God, which ye have acquired by the habit of righteousness, according to the faith and love in Jesus Christ our Saviour. Being the followers of God, and stirring up yourselves by the blood of God, ye have perfectly accomplished the work which was beseeming to you. For, on hearing that I came bound from Syria for the common name and hope, trusting through your prayers to be permitted to fight with beasts at Rome, that so by martyrdom I may indeed become the disciple of Him "who gave Himself for us, an offering and sacrifice to God,"[ye hastened to see me]. I received, therefore, your whole multitude in the name of God, through Onesimus, a man of inexpressible love, and your bishop in the flesh, whom I pray you by Jesus Christ to love, and that you would all seek to be like him. And blessed be He who has granted unto you, being worthy, to obtain such an excellent bishop.

Chapter II.—Congratulations and entreaties.

As to my fellow-servant Burrhus, your deacon in regard to God and blessed in all things, I beg that he may continue longer, both for your honour and that of your bishop. And Crocus also, worthy both of God and you, whom I have received as the manifestation of your love, hath in all things refreshed me, as the Father of our Lord Jesus Christ shall also refresh him; together with Onesimus, and Burrhus, and Euplus, and Fronto, by means of whom, I have, as to love, beheld all of you. May I always have joy of you, if indeed I be worthy of it. It is therefore befitting that you should in every way glorify Jesus Christ, who hath glorified you, that by a unanimous obedience "ye may be perfectly joined together in the same mind, and in the same judgment, and may all speak the same thing concerning the same thing," and that, being subject to the bishop and the presbytery, ye may in all respects be sanctified.

Chapter III.—Exhortations to unity.

I do not issue orders to you, as if I were some great person. For though I am bound for the name [of Christ], I am not yet perfect in Jesus Christ. For now I begin to be a disciple, and I speak to you as fellow-disciples with me. For it was needful for me to have been stirred up by you in faith, exhortation, patience, and long-suffering. But inasmuch as love suffers me not to be silent in regard to you, I have therefore taken upon me first to exhort you that ye would all run together in accordance with the will of God. For even Jesus Christ, our inseparable life, is the[manifested] will of the Father; as also bishops, settled everywhere to the utmost bounds[of the earth], are so by the will of Jesus Christ.

Chapter IV.—The same continued.

Wherefore it is fitting that ye should run together in accordance with the will of your bishop, which thing also ye do. For your justly renowned presbytery, worthy of God, is fitted as exactly to the bishop as the strings are to the harp. Therefore in your concord and harmonious love, Jesus Christ is sung. And do ye, man by man, become a choir, that being harmonious in love, and taking up the song of God in unison, ye may with one voice sing to the Father through Jesus Christ, so that He may both hear you, and perceive by your works that ye are indeed the members of His Son. It is profitable, therefore, that you should live in an unblameable unity, that thus ye may always enjoy communion with God.

Chapter V.—The praise of unity.

For if I in this brief space of time, have enjoyed such fellowship with your bishop--I mean not of a mere human, but of a spiritual nature-

-how much more do I reckon you happy who are so joined to him as the Church is to Jesus Christ, and as Jesus Christ is to the Father, that so all things may agree in unity! Let no man deceive himself: if any one be not within the altar, he is deprived of the bread of God. For if the prayer of one or two possesses such power, how much more that of the bishop and the whole Church ! He, therefore, that does not assemble with the Church, has even by this manifested his pride, and condemned himself. For it is written, "God resisteth the proud." Let us be careful, then, not to set ourselves in opposition to the bishop, in order that we may be subject to God.

Chapter VI.—Have respect to the Bishop as to Christ Himself.

Now the more any one sees the bishop keeping silence, the more ought he to revere him. For we ought to receive every one whom the Master of the house sends to be over His household, as we would do Him that sent him. It is manifest, therefore, that we should look upon the bishop even as we would upon the Lord Himself. And indeed Onesimus himself greatly commends your good order in God, that ye all live according to the truth, and that no sect has any dwelling- place among you. Nor, indeed, do ye hearken to any one rather than to Jesus Christ speaking in truth.

Chapter VII.—Beware of false teachers.

For some are in the habit of carrying about the name[of Jesus Christ] in wicked guile, while yet they practise things unworthy of God, whom ye must flee as ye would wild beasts. For they are ravening dogs, who bite secretly, against whom ye must be on your guard, inasmuch as they are men who can scarcely be cured. There is one Physician who is possessed both of flesh and spirit; both made and not made; God existing in flesh; true life in death; both of Mary and of God; first possible and then impossible, even Jesus Christ our Lord.

Chapter VIII.—Renewed praise of the Ephesians.

Let not then any one deceive you, as indeed ye are not deceived, inasmuch as ye are wholly devoted to God. For since there is no strife raging among you which might distress you, ye are certainly living in accordance with God's will. I am far inferior to you, and require to be sanctified by your Church of Ephesus, so renowned throughout the world. They that are carnal cannot do those things which are spiritual, nor they that are spiritual the things which are carnal; even as faith cannot do the works of unbelief, nor unbelief the works of faith. But even those things which ye do according to the flesh are spiritual; for ye do all things in Jesus Christ.

Chapter IX.—Ye have given no heed to false teachers.

Nevertheless, I have heard of some who have passed on from this to you, having false doctrine, whom ye did not suffer to sow among you, but stopped your ears, that ye might not receive those things which were sown by them, as being stones of the temple of the Father, prepared for the building of God the Father, and drawn up on high by the instrument of Jesus Christ, which is the cross, making use of the Holy Spirit as a rope, while your faith was the means by which you ascended, and your love the way which led up to God. Ye, therefore, as well as all your fellow-travellers, are God-bearers, temple-bearers, Christ-bearers, bearers of holiness, adorned in all respects with the commandments of Jesus Christ, in whom also I exult that I have been thought worthy, by means of this Epistle, to converse and rejoice with you, because with respect to your Christian life ye love nothing but God only.

Chapter X.—Exhortations to prayer, humility, etc.

And pray ye without ceasing in behalf of other men. For there is in them hope of repentance that they may attain to God. See, then, that they be instructed by your works, if in no other way. Be ye meek in response to their wrath, humble in opposition to their boasting: to their blasphemies return your prayers; in contrast to their error, be ye stedfast in the faith; and for their cruelty, manifest your gentleness. While we take care not to imitate their conduct, let us be found their brethren in all true kindness; and let us seek to be followers of the Lord(who ever more unjustly treated, more destitute, more condemned?), that so no plant of the devil may be found in you, but ye may remain in all holiness and sobriety in Jesus Christ, both with respect to the flesh and spirit.

Chapter XI.—An exhortation to fear God, etc.

The last times are come upon us. Let us therefore be of a reverent spirit, and fear the long-suffering of God, that it tend not to our condemnation. For let us either stand in awe of the wrath to come, or show regard for the grace which is at present displayed--one of two things. Only[in one way or another] let us be found in Christ Jesus unto the true life. Apart from Him, let nothing attract you, for whom I bear about these bonds, these spiritual jewels, by which may I arise through your prayers, of which I entreat I may always be a partaker, that I may be found in the lot of the Christians of Ephesus, who have always been of the same mind with the apostles through the power of Jesus Christ.

Chapter XII.—Praise of the Ephesians.

I know both who I am, and to whom I write. I am a condemned man, ye have been the objects of mercy; I am subject to danger, ye are established in safety. Ye are the persons through whom those pass that are cut off for the sake of God. Ye are initiated into the mysteries of the Gospel with Paul, the holy, the martyred, the deservedly most happy, at whose feet may I be found, when I shall attain to God; who in all his Epistles makes mention of you in Christ Jesus.

Chapter XIII.—Exhortation to meet together frequently for the worship of God.

Take heed, then, often to come together to give thanks to God, and show forth His praise. For when ye assemble frequently in the same place, the powers of Satan are destroyed, and the destruction at which he aims is prevented by the unity of your faith. Nothing is more precious than peace, by which all war, both in heaven and earth, is brought to an end.

Chapter XIV.—Exhortations to faith and love.

None of these things is hid from you, if ye perfectly possess that faith and love towards Christ Jesus which are the beginning and the end of life. For the beginning is faith, and the end is love. Now these two. being inseparably connected together, are of God, while all other things which are requisite for a holy life follow after them. No man [truly] making a profession of faith sinneth; nor does he that possesses love hate any one. The tree is made manifest by its fruit; so those that profess themselves to be Christians shall be recognised by their conduct. For there is not now a demand for mere profession, but that a man be found continuing in the power of faith to the end.

Chapter XV.—Exhortation to confess Christ by silence as well as speech.

It is better for a man to be silent and be [a Christian], than to talk and not to be one. It is good to teach, if he who speaks also acts. There is then one Teacher, who spake and it was done; while even those things which He did in silence are worthy of the Father. He who possesses the word of Jesus, is truly able to hear even His very silence, that he may be perfect, and may both act as he speaks, and be recognised by his silence. There is nothing which is hid from God, but our very secrets are near to Him. Let us therefore do all things as those who have Him dwelling in us, that we may be His temples, and He may be in us as our God, which indeed He is, and will manifest Himself before our faces. Wherefore we justly love Him.

Chapter XVI.—The fate of false teachers.

Do not err, my brethren. Those that corrupt families shall not inherit the kingdom of God. If, then, those who do this as respects the flesh have suffered death, how much more shall this be the case with any one who corrupts by wicked doctrine the faith of God, for which Jesus Christ was crucified! Such an one becoming defiled [in this way], shall go away into everlasting fire, and so shall every one that hearkens unto him.

Chapter XVII.—Beware of false doctrines.

For this end did the Lord suffer the ointment to be poured upon His head, that He might breathe immortality into His Church. Be not ye anointed with the bad odour of the doctrine of the prince of this world; let him not lead you away captive from the life which is set before you.

And why are we not all prudent, since we have received the knowledge of God, which is Jesus Christ? Why do we foolishly perish, not recognising the gift which the Lord has of a truth sent to us?

Chapter XVIII.—The Glory of the Cross.

Let my spirit be counted as nothing for the sake of the cross, which is a stumbling-block to those that do not believe, but to us salvation and life eternal. "Where is the wise man? where the disputer?" Where is the boasting of those who are styled prudent? For our God, Jesus Christ, was, according to the appointment of God, conceived in the womb by Mary, of the seed of David, but by the Holy Ghost. He was born and baptized, that by His passion He might purify the water.

Chapter XIX.—Three celebrated mysteries.

Now the virginity of Mary was hidden from the prince of this world, as was also her offspring, and the death of the Lord; three mysteries of renown, which were wrought in silence by God. How, then, was He manifested to the world? A star shone forth in heaven above all the other stars, the light of Which was inexpressible, while its novelty struck men with astonishment. And all the rest of the stars, with the sun and moon, formed a chorus to this star, and its light was exceedingly great above them all. And there was agitation felt as to whence this new spectacle came, so unlike to everything else [in the heavens]. Hence every kind of magic was destroyed, and every bond of wickedness disappeared; ignorance was removed, and the old kingdom abolished, God Himself being manifested in human form for the renewal of eternal life. And now that took a beginning which had been prepared by God. Henceforth all things were in a state of tumult, because He meditated the abolition of death.

Chapter XX.—Promise of another letter.

If Jesus Christ shall graciously permit me through your prayers, and if it be His will, I shall, in a second little work which I will write to you, make further manifest to you [the nature of] the dispensation of which I have begun [to treat], with respect to the new man, Jesus Christ, in His faith and in His love, in His suffering and in His resurrection. Especially [will I do this if the Lord make known to me that ye come together man by man in common through grace, individually, in one faith, and in Jesus Christ, who was of the seed of David according to the flesh, being both the Son of man and the Son of God, so that ye obey the bishop and the presbytery with an undivided mind, breaking one and the same bread, which is the medicine of immortality, and the antidote to prevent us from dying, but [which causes] that we should live for ever in Jesus Christ.

Chapter XXI.—Conclusion.

My soul be for yours and theirs whom, for the honour of God, ye have sent to Smyrna; whence also I write to you, giving thanks unto the Lord, and loving Polycarp even as I do you. Remember me, as Jesus Christ also remembered you. Pray ye for the Church which is in Syria, whence I am led bound to Rome, being the last of the faithful who are there, even as I have been thought worthy to be chosen to show forth the honour of God. Farewell in God the Father, and in Jesus Christ, our common hope.

The Epistle of Ignatius to the Magnesians

Ignatius, who is also called Theophorus, to the [Church] blessed in the grace of God the Father, in Jesus Christ our Saviour, in whom I salute the Church which is at Magnesia, near the Moeander, and wish it abundance of happiness in God the father, and in Jesus Christ.

Chapter I.—Reason of writing the epistle.

Having been informed of your godly love, so well-ordered, I rejoiced greatly, and determined to commune with you in the faith of Jesus Christ. For as one who has been thought worthy of the most honourable of all names, in those bonds which I bear about, I commend the Churches, in which I pray for a union both of the flesh and spirit of Jesus Christ, the constant source of our life, and of faith and love, to which nothing is to be preferred, but especially of Jesus and the Father, in whom, if we endure all the assaults of the prince of this world, and escape them, we shall enjoy God.

Chapter II.--I rejoice in your messengers.

Since, then, I have had the privilege of seeing you, through Damas your most worthy bishop, and through your worthy presbyters Bassus and Apollonius, and through my fellow-servant the deacon Sotio, whose friendship may I ever enjoy, inasmuch as he is subject to the bishop as to the grace of God, and to the presbytery as to the law of Jesus Christ, [I now write to you].

Chapter III.—Honour your youthful Bishop

Now it becomes you also not to treat your bishop too familiarly on account of his youth, but to yield him all reverence, having respect to the power of God the Father, as I have known even holy presbyters do, not judging rashly, from the manifest youthful appearance [of their bishop], but as being themselves prudent in God, submitting to him, or rather not to him, but to the Father of Jesus Christ, the bishop of us all. It is therefore fitting that you should, after no hypocritical fashion, obey [your bishop], in honour of Him who has wired us [so to do], since he that does not so deceives not [by such conduct] the bishop that is visible, but seeks to mock Him that is invisible. And all such conduct has reference not to man, but to God, who knows all secrets.

Chapter IV.—Some wickedly act independently of the Bishop.

It is fitting, then, not only to be called Christians, but to be so in reality: as some indeed give one the title of bishop, but do all things without him. Now such persons seem to me to be not possessed of a good conscience, seeing they are not stedfastly gathered together according to the commandment.

Chapter V.—Death is the fate of all such.

Seeing, then, all things have an end, these two things are simultaneously set before us--death and life; and every one shall go unto his own place. For as there are two kinds of coins, the one of God, the other of the world, and each of these has its special character stamped upon it,[so is it also here.] The unbelieving are of this world; but the believing have, in love, the character of God the Father by Jesus Christ, by whom, if we are not in readiness to die into His passion, His life is not in us.

Chapter VI.—Preserve harmony.

Since therefore I have, in the persons before mentioned, beheld the whole multitude of you in faith and love, I exhort you to study to do all things with a divine harmony, while your bishop presides in the place of God, and your presbyters in the place of the assembly of the apostles, along with your deacons, who are most dear to me, and are entrusted with the ministry of Jesus Christ, who was with the Father before the beginning of time, and in the end was revealed. Do ye all then, imitating the same divine conduct, pay respect to one another, and let no one look upon his neighbour after the flesh, but do ye continually love each other in Jesus Christ. Let nothing exist among you that may divide you ; but be ye united with your bishop, and those that preside over you, as a type and evidence of your immortality.

Chapter VII.—Do nothing without the Bishop and Presbyters.

As therefore the Lord did nothing without the Father, being united to Him, neither by Himself nor by the apostles, so neither do ye anything without the bishop and presbyters. Neither endeavour that anything appear reasonable and proper to yourselves apart; but being come together into the same place, let there be one prayer, one supplication, one mind, one hope, in love and in joy undefiled. There is one Jesus Christ, than whom nothing is more excellent. Do ye therefore all run together as into one temple of God, as to one altar, as to one Jesus Christ, who came forth from one Father, and is with and has gone to one.

Chapter VIII.—Caution against false doctrines.

Be not deceived with strange doctrines, nor with old fables, which are unprofitable. For if we still live according to the Jewish law, we acknowledge that we have not received grace. For the divinest prophets lived according to Christ Jesus. On this account also they were persecuted, being inspired by His grace to fully convince the unbelieving that there is one God, who has manifested Himself by Jesus Christ His Son, who is His eternal Word, not proceeding forth from silence, and who in all things pleased Him that sent Him.

Chapter IX.—Let us live with Christ.

If, therefore, those who were brought up in the ancient order of things have come to the possession of a new hope, no longer observing the Sabbath, but living in the observance of the Lord's Day, on which also our life has sprung up again by Him and by His death--whom some deny, by which mystery we have obtained faith, and therefore endure, that we may be found the disciples of Jesus Christ, our only Master--how shall we be able to live apart from Him, whose disciples the prophets themselves in the Spirit did wait for Him as their Teacher? And therefore He whom they rightly waited for, being come, raised them from the dead.

Chapter X.—Beware of Judaizing.

Let us not, therefore, be insensible to His kindness. For were He to reward us according to our works, we should cease to be. Therefore, having become His disciples, let us learn to live according to the principles of Christianity. For whosoever is called by any other name besides this, is not of God. Lay aside, therefore, the evil, the old, the sour leaven, and be ye changed into the new leaven, which is Jesus Christ. Be ye salted in Him, lest any one among you should be corrupted, since by your savour ye shall be convicted. It is absurd to profess Christ Jesus, and to Judaize. For Christianity did not embrace Judaism, but Judaism Christianity, that so every tongue which believeth might be gathered together to God.

Chapter XI.—I write these things to warn you.

These things [I address to you], my beloved, not that I know any of you to be in such a state; but, as less than any of you, I desire to guard you beforehand, that ye fall not upon the hooks of vain doctrine, but that ye attain to full assurance in regard to the birth, and passion, and resurrection which took place in the time of the government of Pontius Pilate, being truly and certainly accomplished by Jesus Christ, who is our hope, from which may no one of you ever be turned aside.

Chapter XII.—Ye are superior to me.

May I enjoy you in all respects, if indeed I be worthy! For though I am bound, I am not worthy to be compared to any of you that are at liberty. I know that ye are not puffed up, for ye have Jesus Christ in yourselves. And all the more when I commend you, I know that ye cherish modesty of spirit; as it is written, "The righteous man is his own accuser."

Chapter XIII.—Be established in faith and unity.

Study, therefore, to be established in the doctrines of the Lord and the apostles, that so all things, whatsoever ye do, may prosper both in the flesh and spirit; in faith and love; in the Son, and in the Father, and in the Spirit; in the beginning and in the end; with your most admirable bishop, and the well-compacted spiritual crown of your presbytery, and the deacons who are according to God. Be ye subject to the bishop, and to one another, as Jesus Christ to the Father, according to the flesh, and the apostles to Christ, and to the Father, and to the Spirit; that so there may be a union beth fleshly and spiritual.

Chapter XIV.—Your prayers requested.

Knowing as I do that ye are full of God, I have but briefly exhorted you. Be mindful of me in your prayers, that I may attain to God; and of the Church which is in Syria, whence I am not worthy to derive my name: for I stand in need of your united prayer in God, and your love, that the Church which is in Syria may be "deemed worthy of being refreshed by your Church.

Chapter XV.—Salutations.

The Ephesians from Smyrna (whence I also write to you), who are here for the glory of God, as ye also are, who have in all things refreshed me, salute you, along with Polycarp, the bishop of the Smyrnaeans. The rest of the Churches, in honour of Jesus Christ, also salute you. Fare ye well in the harmony of God, ye who have obtained the inseparable Spirit, who is Jesus Christ.

The Epistle of Ignatius to the Trallians

Ignatius, who is also called Theophorus, to the holy Church which is at Tralles, in Asia, beloved of God, the Father of Jesus Christ, elect, and worthy of God, possessing peace through the flesh, and blood, and passion of Jesus Christ, who is our hope, through our rising again to Him, which also I salute in its fulness, and in the apostalical character, and wish abundance of happiness.

Chapter I.—Acknowledgement of their excellence.

I know that ye possess an unblameable and sincere mind in patience, and that not only in present practice, but according to inherent nature, as Polybius your bishop has shown me, who has come to Smyrna by the will of God and Jesus Christ, and so sympathized in the joy which I, who am bound in Christ Jesus, possess, that I beheld your whole multitude in him. Having therefore received through him the testimony of your good-will, according to God, I gloried to find you, as I knew you were, the followers of God.

Chapter II.—Be subject to the Bishop, etc.

For, since ye are subject to the bishop as to Jesus Christ, ye appear to me to live not after the manner of men, but according to Jesus Christ, who died for us, in order, by believing in His death, ye may escape from death. It is therefore necessary that, as ye indeed do, so without the bishop ye should do nothing, but should also be subject to the presbytery, as to the apostle of Jesus Christ, who is our hope, in whom, if we live, we shall [at last] be found. It is fitting also that the deacons, as being [the ministers] of the mysteries of Jesus Christ, should in every respect be pleasing to all. For they are not ministers of meat and drink, but servants of the Church of God. They are bound, therefore, to avoid all grounds of accusation [against them], as they would do fire.

Chapter III.—Honour the Deacons, etc.

In like manner, let all reverence the deacons as an appointment of Jesus Christ, and the bishop as Jesus Christ, who is the Son of the Father, and the presbyters as the sanhedrin of God, and assembly of the apostles.

Apart from these, there is no Church. Concerning all this, I am persuaded that ye are of the same opinion. For I have received the manifestations of your love, and still have it with me, in your bishop, whose very appearance is highly instructive, and his meekness of itself a power; whom I imagine even the ungodly must reverence, seeing they are also pleased that I do not spare myself. But shall I, when permitted to write on this point, reach such a height of self-esteem, that though being a condemned man, I should issue commands to you as if I were an apostle?

Chapter IV.--I have need of humility.

I have great knowledge in God, but I restrain myself, lest, I should perish through boasting. For now it is needful for me to be the more fearful; and not give heed to those that puff me up. For they that speak to me [in the way of commendation] scourge me. For I do indeed desire to suffer, but I know not if I be worthy to do so. For this longing, though it is not manifest to many, all the more vehemently assails me. I therefore have need of meekness, by which the prince of this world is brought to nought.

Chapter V.--I will not teach you profound doctrines.

Am I not able to write to you of heavenly things? But I fear to do so, lest I should inflict injury on you who are but babes [in Christ]. Pardon me in this respect, lest, as not being able to receive [such doctrines], ye should be strangled by them. For even I, though I am bound [for Christ], yet am not on that account able to understand heavenly things, and the places of the angels, and their gatherings under their respective princes, things visible and invisible. Without reference to such abstruse subjects, I am still but a learner [in other respects]; for many things are wanting to us, that we come not short of God.

Chapter VI.—Abstain from the poison of heretics.

I therefore, yet not I, but the love of Jesus Christ, entreat you that ye use Christian nourishment only, and abstain from herbage of a different kind; I mean heresy. For those [that are given to this] mix up Jesus Christ with their own poison, speaking things which are unworthy of credit, like those who administer a deadly drug in sweet wine, which he who is ignorant of does greedily take, with a fatal pleasure leading to his own death.

Chapter VII.—The same continued.

Be on your guard, therefore, against such persons. And this will be the case with you if you are not puffed up, and continue in intimate union with Jesus Christ our God, and the bishop, and the enactments of the apostles. He that is within the altar is pure, but he that is without is not pure; that is, he who does anything apart from the bishop, and presbytery, and deacons, such a man is not pure in his conscience.

Chapter VIII.—Be on your guard against the snares of the Devil.

Not that I know there is anything of this kind among you; but I put you on your guard, inasmuch as I love you greatly, and foresee the snares of the devil. Wherefore, clothing yourselves with meekness, be ye renewed in faith, that is the flesh of the Lord, and in love, that is the blood of Jesus Christ. Let no one of you cherish any grudge against his neighbour. Give no occasion to the Gentiles, lest by means of a few foolish men the whole multitude [of those that believe] in God be evil spoken of. For, "Woe to him by whose vanity my name is blasphemed among any."

Chapter IX.—Reference to the history of Christ.

Stop your ears, therefore, when any one speaks to you at variance with Jesus Christ, who was descended from David, and was also of Mary; who was truly born, and did eat and drink. He was truly persecuted under Pontius Pilate; He was truly crucified, and [truly] died, in the sight of beings in heaven, and on earth, and under the earth. He was also truly raised from the dead, His Father quickening Him, even as after the same manner His Father will so raise up us who believe in Him by Christ Jesus, apart from whom we do not possess the true life.

Chapter X.—The reality of Christ's passion.

But if, as some that are without God, that is, the unbelieving, say, that He only seemed to suffer (they themselves only seeming to exist), then why am I in bonds? Why do I long to be exposed to s the wild beasts?

Do I therefore die in vain? Am I not then guilty of falsehood against [the cross of] the Lord?

Chapter XI.—Avoid the deadly errors of the Docetae.

Flee, therefore, those evil offshoots [of Satan], which produce death-bearing fruit, whereof if any one tastes, he instantly dies. For these men are not the planting of the Father. For if they were, they would appear as branches of the cross, and their fruit would be incorruptible. By it He calls you through His passion, as being His members. The head, therefore, cannot be born by itself, without its members; God, who is [the Saviour] Himself, having promised their union.

Chapter XII.—Continue in unity and love.

I salute you from Smyrna, together with the Churches of God which are with me, who have refreshed me in all things, both in the flesh and in the spirit. My bonds, which I carry about with me for the sake of Jesus Christ (praying that I may attain to God), exhort you. Continue in harmony among yourselves, and in prayer with one another; for it becomes every one of you, and especially the presbyters, to refresh the bishop, to the hon-our of the Father, of Jesus Christ, and of the apostles. I entreat you in love to hear me, that I may not, by having written, be a testimony against you. And do ye also pray for me, who have need of your love, along with the mercy of God, that I may be worthy of the lot for which I am destined, and that I may not be found reprobate.

Chapter XIII.—Conclusion.

The love of the Smyrnaeans and Ephesians salutes you. Remember in your prayers the Church which is in Syria, from which also I am not worthy to receive my appellation, being the last of them. Fare ye well in Jesus Christ, while ye continue subject to the bishop, as to the command [of God], and in like manner to the presbytery. And do ye, every man, love one another with an undivided heart. Let my spirit be sanctified by yours, not only now, but also when I shall attain to God. For I am as yet exposed to danger. But the Father is faithful in Jesus Christ to fulfil both mine and your petitions: in whom may ye be found unblameable.

The Epistle of Ignatius to the Romans

Ignatius, who is also called Theophorus, to the Church which has obtained mercy, through the majesty of the Mast High Father, and Jesus Christ, His only-begotten Son; the Church which is beloved and enlightened by the will of Him that willeth all things which are according to the love of Jesus Christ our God, which also presides in the place of the report of the Romans, worthy of God, worthy of honour, worthy of the highest happiness, worthy of praise, worthy of obtaining her every desire, worthy of being deemed holy, and which presides over love, is named from Christ, and from the Father, which I also salute in the name of Jesus Christ, the San of the Father: to those who are united, both according ta the flesh and spirit, to every one of His commandments; who are filled inseparably with the grace of God, and are purified from every strange taint, [I wish] abundance of happiness unblameably, in Jesus Christ our God.

Chapter I.—As a prisoner, I hope to see you.

Through prayer to God I have obtained the privilege of seeing your most worthy faces, and have even been granted more than I requested; for I hope as a prisoner in Christ Jesus to salute you, if indeed it be the will of God that I be thought worthy of attaining unto the end. For the beginning has been well ordered, if I may obtain grace to cling to my lot without hindrance unto the end. For I am afraid of your love, lest it should do me an injury. For it is easy for you to accomplish what you please; but it is difficult for me to attain to God, if ye spare me. But it is difficult for me to attain to God, if ye do not spare me, under the pretence of carnal affection.

Chapter II.—Do not save me from martyrdom.

For it is not my desire to act towards you as a man-pleaser, but as pleasing God, even as also ye please Him. For neither shall I ever have such [another] opportunity of attaining to God; nor will ye, if ye shall now be silent, ever be entitled to the honour of a better work. For if ye are silent concerning me, I shall become God's; but if you show your love to my flesh, I shall again have to run my race. Pray, then, do not seek to confer any greater favour upon me than that I be sacrificed to God while the altar is still prepared; that, being gathered together in love, ye may sing praise to the Father, through Christ Jesus, that God has deemed me, the bishop of Syria, worthy to be sent for from the east unto the west. It is good to set from the world unto God, that I may rise again to Him.

Chapter III.—Pray rather that I may attain to martyrdom.

Ye have never envied anyone; ye have taught others. Now I desire that those things may be confirmed [by your conduct], which in your instructions ye enjoin [on others]. Only request in my behalf both inward and outward strength, that I may not only speak, but [truly] will, so that I may not merely be called a Christian, but really found to be one. For if I be truly found [a Christian], I may also be called one, and be then deemed faithful, when I shall no longer appear to the world. Nothing visible is eternal. "For the things which are seen are temporal, but the things which are not seen are eternal. The Christian is not the result of persuasion, but of power. When he is hated by the world, he is beloved of God. For says [the Scripture], "If ye were of this world, the world would love its own; but now ye are not of the world, but I have chosen you out of it: continue in fellowship with me."

Chapter IV.—Allow me to fall a prey to the wild beasts.

I write to all the Churches, and impress on them all, that I shall willingly die for God, unless ye hinder me. I beseech of you not to show an unseasonable goodwill towards me. Suffer me to become food for the wild beasts, through whose instrumentality it will be granted me to attain to God. I am the wheat of God, and am ground by the teeth of the wild beasts, that I may be found the pure bread of God. Rather entice the wild beasts, that they may become my tomb, and may leave nothing of my body; so that when I have fallen asleep [in death], I may not be found troublesome to any one. Then shall I be a true disciple of Jesus Christ, when the world shall not see so much as my body. Entreat the Lord for me, that by these instruments I may be found a sacrifice to God. I do not, as Peter and Paul, issue commandments unto you. They were apostles of Jesus Christ, but I am the very least [of believers]: they were free, as the servants of God; while I am, even until now, a servant. But when I suffer, I shall be the freedman of Jesus Christ, and shall rise again emancipated in Him. And now, being in bonds for Him, I learn not to desire anything worldly or vain.

Chapter V.—I desire to die.

From Syria even unto Rome I fight with beasts, both by land and sea, both by night and day, being bound to ten leopards, I mean a band of soldiers, who, even when they receive benefits, show themselves all the worse. But I am the more instructed by their injuries [to act as a disciple of Christ]; "yet am I not thereby justified." May I enjoy the wild beasts that are prepared for me; and I pray that they may be found eager to rush upon me, which also I will entice to devour me speedily, and not deal with me as with some, whom, out of fear, they have not touched. But if they be unwilling to assail me, I will compel them to do so. Pardon me [in this] I know what is for my benefit. Now I begin to be a disciple. And let no one, of things visible or invisible, envy me that I should attain to Jesus Christ. Let fire and the cross; let the crowds of wild beasts; let tearings, breakings, and dislocations of bones; let cutting off of members; let shatterings of the whole body; and let all the dreadful torments of the devil come upon me: only let me attain to Jesus Christ.

Chapter VI.—By death I shall attain true life.

All the pleasures of the world, and all the kingdoms of this earth, shall profit me nothing. It is better for me to die in behalf of Jesus Christ, than to reign over all the ends of the earth. "For what shall a man be profited, if he gain the whole world, but lose his own soul?" Him I seek, who died for us: Him I desire, who rose again for our sake. This is the gain which is laid up for me. Pardon me, brethren: do not hinder me from living, do not wish to keep me in a state of death; and while I desire to belong to God, do not ye give me over to the world. Suffer me to obtain pure light: when I have gone thither, I shall indeed be a man of God. Permit me to be an imitator of the passion of my God. If any one has Him within himself, let him consider what I desire, and let him have sympathy with me, as knowing how I am straitened.

Chapter VII.—Reason of desiring to die.

The prince of this world would fain carry me away, and corrupt my disposition towards God. Let none of you, therefore, who are [in Rome] help him; rather be ye on my side, that is, on the side of God. Do not speak of Jesus Christ, and yet set your desires on the world. Let not envy find a dwelling-place among you; nor even should I, when present with you, exhort you to it, be ye persuaded to listen to me, but rather give credit to those things which I now write to you. For though I am alive while I write to you, yet I am eager to die. My love has been crucified, and there is no fire in me desiring to be fed; but there is within me a water that liveth and speaketh, saying to me inwardly, Come to the Father. I have no delight in corruptible food, nor in the pleasures of this life. I desire the bread of God, the heavenly bread, the bread of life, which is the flesh of Jesus Christ, the Son of God, who became afterwards of the seed of David and Abraham; and I desire the drink of God, namely His blood, which is incorruptible love and eternal life.

Chapter VIII.—Be ye favourable to me.

I no longer wish to live after the manner of men, and my desire shall be fulfilled if ye consent. Be ye willing, then, that ye also may have your desires fulfilled. I entreat you in this brief letter; do ye give credit to me. Jesus Christ will reveal these things to you, [so that ye shall know] that I speak truly. He is the mouth altogether free from falsehood, by which the Father has truly spoken. Pray ye for me, that I may attain [the object of my desire]. I have not written to you according to the flesh, but according to the will of God. If I shall suffer, ye have wished [well] to me; but if I am rejected, ye have hated me.

Chapter IX.—Pray for the Church in Syria.

Remember in your prayers the Church in Syria, which now has God for its shepherd, instead of me. Jesus Christ alone will oversee it, and your love [will also regard it]. But as for me, I am ashamed to be counted one of them; for indeed I am not worthy, as being the very last of them, and one born out of due time. But I have obtained mercy to be somebody, if I shall attain to God. My spirit salutes you, and the love of the Churches that have received me in the name of Jesus Christ, and not as a mere passer-by. For even those Churches which were not near to me in the way, I mean according to the flesh, have gone before me, city by city, [to meet me.]

Chapter X.—Conclusion.

Now I write these things to you from Smyrna by the Ephesians, who are deservedly most happy. There is also with me, along with many others, Crocus, one dearly beloved by me. As to those who have gone before me from Syria to Rome for the glory of God, I believe that you are acquainted with them; to whom, [then,] do ye make known that I am at hand. For they are all worthy, both of God and of you; and it is becoming that you should refresh them in all things. I have written these things unto you, on the day before the ninth of the Kalends of September (that is, on the twenty-third day of August). Fare ye well to the end, in the patience of Jesus Christ. Amen.

The Epistle of Ignatius to the Philadelphians

Ignatius, who is also called Theophorus, to the Church of God the Father, and our Lord Jesus Christ, which is at Philadelphia, in Asia, which has obtained mercy, and is established in the harmony of God, and rejoiceth unceasingly in the passion of our Lord, and is filled with all mercy through his resurrection; which I salute in the blood of Jesus Christ, who is our eternal and enduring joy, especially if [men] are in unity with the bishop, the presbyters, and the deacons, who have been appointed according to the mind of Jesus Christ, whom He has established in security, after His own will, and by His Holy Spirit.

Chapter I.—Praise of the Bishop.

Which bishop, I know, obtained the ministry which pertains to the common [weal], not of himself, neither by men, nor through vainglory, but by the love of God the Father, and the Lord Jesus Christ; at whose meekness I am struck with admiration, and who by his silence is able to accomplish more than those who vainly talk. For he is in harmony with the commandments [of God], even as the harp is with its strings. Wherefore my soul declares his mind towards God a happy one, knowing it to be virtuous and perfect, and that his stability as well as freedom from all anger is after the example of the infinite meekness of the living God.

Chapter II.—Maintain union with the Bishop.

Wherefore, as children of light and truth, flee from division and wicked doctrines; but where the shepherd is, there do ye as sheep follow. For there are many wolves that appear worthy of credit, who, by means of a pernicious pleasure, carry captives those that are running towards God; but in your unity they shall have no place.

Chapter III.—Avoid schismatics.

Keep yourselves from those evil plants which Jesus Christ does not tend, because they are not the planting of the Father. Not that I have found any division among you, but exceeding purity. For as many as are of God and of Jesus Christ are also with the bishop. And as many as shall, in the exercise of repentance, return into the unity of the Church, these, too, shall belong to God, that they may live according to Jesus Christ. Do not err, my brethren. If any man follows him that makes a schism in the Church, he shall not inherit the kingdom of God. If any one walks according to a strange opinion, he agrees not with the passion [of Christ.].

Chapter IV.—Have but one Eucharist, etc.

Take ye heed, then, to have but one Eucharist. For there is one flesh of our Lord Jesus Christ, and one cup to [show forth] the unity of His blood; one altar; as there is one bishop, along with the presbytery and deacons, my fellow-servants: that so, whatsoever ye do, ye may do it according to [the will of] God.

Chapter V.—Pray for me.

My brethren, I am greatly enlarged in loving you; and rejoicing exceedingly [over you], I seek to secure your safety. Yet it is not I, but Jesus Christ, for whose sake being bound I fear the more, inasmuch as I am not yet perfect. But your prayer to God shall make me perfect, that I may attain to that portion which through mercy has been allotted me, while I flee to the Gospel as to the flesh of Jesus, and to the apostles as to the presbytery of the Church. And let us also love the prophets, because they too have proclaimed the Gospel, and placed their hope in Him, and waited for Him; in whom also believing, they were saved, through union to Jesus Christ, being holy men, worthy of love and admiration, having had witness borne to them by Jesus Christ, and being reckoned along with in the Gospel of the common hope.

Chapter VI.—Do not accept Judaism.

But if any one preach the Jewish law unto you, listen not to him. For it is better to hearken to Christian doctrine from a man who has been circumcised, than to Judaism from one uncircumcised. But if either of such persons do not speak concerning Jesus Christ, they are in my judgment but as monuments and sepulchres of the dead, upon which are written only the names of men. Flee therefore the wicked devices and snares of the prince of this world, lest at any time being conquered by his artifices, ye grow weak in your love. But be ye all joined together with an undivided heart. And I thank my God that I have a good conscience in respect to you, and that no one has it in his power to boast, either privately or publicly, that I have burdened any one either in much or in little. And I wish for all among whom I have spoken, that they may not possess that for a testimony against them.

Chapter VII.--I have exhorted you to unity.

For though some would nave deceived me according to the flesh, yet the Spirit, as being from God, is not deceived. For it knows both whence it comes and whither it goes, and detects the secrets [of the heart]. For, when I was among you, I cried, I spoke with a loud voice: Give heed to the bishop, and to the presbytery and deacons. Now, some suspected me of having spoken thus, as knowing beforehand the division caused by some among you. But He is my witness, for whose sake I am in bonds, that I got no intelligence from any man. But the Spirit proclaimed these words: Do nothing without the bishop; keep your bodies as the temples of God; love unity; avoid divisions; be the followers of Jesus Christ, even as He is of His Father.

Chapter VIII.—The same continued.

I therefore did what belonged to me, as a man devoted to unity. For where there is division and wrath, God doth not dwell. To all them that repent, the Lord grants forgiveness, if they turn in penitence to the unity of God, and to communion with the bishop. I trust [as to you] in the grace of Jesus Christ, who shall free you from every bond. And I exhort you to do nothing out of strife, but according to the doctrine of Christ. When I heard some saying, If I do not find it in the ancient Scriptures, I will not believe the Gospel; on my saying to them, It is written, they answered me, That remains to be proved. But to me Jesus Christ is in the place of all that is ancient: His cross, and death, and resurrection, and the faith which is by Him, are undefiled monuments of antiquity; by which I desire, through your prayers, to be justified.

Chapter IX.—The Old Testament is good: the New Testament is better.

The priests indeed are good, but the High Priest is better; to whom the holy of holies has been committed, and who alone has been trusted with the secrets of God. He is the door of the Father, by which enter in

Abraham, and Isaac, and Jacob, and the prophets, and the apostles, and the Church. All these have for their object the attaining to the unity of God. But the Gospel possesses something transcendent [above the former dispensation], viz., the appearance of our Lord Jesus Christ, His passion and resurrection. For the beloved prophets announced Him, but the Gospel is the perfection of immortality. All these things are good together, if ye believe in love.

Chapter X.—Congratulate the inhabitants of Antioch on the close of the persecution.

Since, according to your prayers, and the compassion which ye feel in Christ Jesus, it is reported to me that the Church which is at Antioch in Syria possesses peace, it will become you, as a Church of God, to elect a deacon to act as the ambassador of God[for you] to[the brethren there], that he may rejoice along with them when they are met together, and glorify the name[of God], Blessed is he in Jesus Christ, who shall be deemed worthy of such a ministry; and ye too shall be glorified. And if ye are willing, it is not beyond your power to do this, for the sake of God; as also the nearest Churches have sent, in some cases bishops, and in others presbyters and deacons.

Chapter XI.—Thanks and salutation.

Now, as to Philo the deacon, of Cilicia, a man of reputation, who still ministers to me in the word of God, along with Rheus Agathopus, an elect man, who has followed me from Syria, not regarding his life,-

-these bear witness in your behalf; and I myself give thanks to God for you, that ye have received them, even as the Lord you. But may those that dishonoured them be forgiven through the grace of Jesus Christ! The love of the brethren at Troas salutes you; whence also I write to you by Burrhus, who was sent along with me by the Ephesians and Smyrnaeans, to show their respect. May the Lord Jesus Christ honour them, in whom they hope, in flesh, and soul, and faith, and love, and concord! Fare ye well in Christ Jesus, our common hope.

The Epistle of Ignatius to the Smyrnaeans

Ignatius, who is also called Theophorus, to the Church of God the Father, and of the beloved Jesus Christ, which has through mercy obtained every kind of gift, which is filled with faith and love, and is deficient in no gift, most worthy of God, and adorned with holiness: the Church which is at Smyrna, in Asia, wishes abundance of happiness, through the immaculate Spirit and word of God.

Chapter I.—Thanks to God for your faith.

I glorify God, even Jesus Christ, who has given you such wisdom. For I have observed that ye are perfected in an immoveable faith, as if ye were nailed to the cross of our Lord Jesus Christ, both in the flesh and in the spirit, and are established in love through the blood of Christ, being fully persuaded with respect to our Lord, that He was truly of the seed of David according to the flesh, and the Son of God according to the will and power of God; that He was truly born of a virgin, was baptized by John, in order that all righteousness might be fulfilled by Him; and was truly, under Pontius Pilate and Herod the tetrarch, nailed[to the cross] for us in His flesh. Of this fruit we are by His divinely-blessed passion, that He might set up a standard s for all ages, through His resurrection, to all His holy and faithful[followers], whether among Jews or Gentiles, in the one body of His Church.

Chapter II.—Christ's true passion.

Now, He suffered all these things for our sakes, that we might be saved. And He suffered truly, even as also He truly raised up Himself, not, as certain unbelievers maintain, that He only seemed to suffer, as they themselves only seem to be[Christians]. And as they believe, so shall it happen unto them, when they shall be divested of their bodies, and be mere evil spirits.

Chapter III.—Christ was possessed of a body after his resurrection.

For I know that after His resurrection also He was still possessed of flesh, and I believe that He is so now. When, for instance, He came to those who were with Peter, He said to them, "Lay hold, handle Me, and see that I am not an incorporeal spirit." And immediately they touched Him, and believed, being convinced both by His flesh and spirit. For this cause also they despised death, and were found its conquerors. And after his resurrection He did eat and drink with them, as being possessed of flesh, although spiritually He was united to the Father.

Chapter IV.—Beware of these heretics.

I give you these instructions, beloved, assured that ye also hold the same opinions[as I do]. But I guard you beforehand from those beasts in the shape of men, whom you must not only not receive, but, if it be possible, not even meet with; only you must pray to God for them, if by any means they may be brought to repentance, which, however, will be very difficult. Yet Jesus Christ, who is our true life; has the power of[effecting] this. But if these things were done by our Lord only in appearance, then am I also only in appearance bound. And why have I also surrendered myself to death, to fire, to the sword, to the wild beasts? But,[in fact,] he who is near to the sword is near to God; he that is among the wild beasts is in company with God; provided only he be so m the name of Jesus Christ. I undergo all these things that I may suffer together with Him, He who became a perfect man inwardly strengthening me.

Chapter V.—Their dangerous errors.

Some ignorantly deny Him, or rather have been denied by Him, being the advocates of death rather than of the truth. These persons neither have the prophets persuaded, nor the law of Moses, nor the Gospel even to this day, nor the sufferings we have individually endured. For they think also the same thing regarding us. For what does any one profit me, if he commends me, but blasphemes my Lord, not confessing that He was[truly] possessed of a body? But he who does not acknowledge this, has in fact altogether denied Him, being enveloped in death. I have not, however, thought good to write the names of such persons, inasmuch as they are unbelievers. Yea, far be it from me to make any mention of them, until they repent and return to[a true belief in] Christ's passion, which is our resurrection.

Chapter VI—Unbelievers in the blood of Christ shall be condemned.

Let no man deceive himself. Both the things which are in heaven, and the glorious angels, and rulers, both visible and invisible, if they believe not in the blood of Christ, shall, in consequence, incur condemnation. "He that is able to receive it, let him receive it." Let not[high] place puff any one up: for that which is worth all is a faith and love, to which nothing is to be preferred. But consider those who are of a different opinion with respect to the grace of Christ which has come unto us, how opposed they are to the will of God. They have no regard for love; no care for the widow, or the orphan, or the oppressed; of the bond, or of the free; of the hungry, or of the thirsty.

Chapter VII.—Let us stand aloof from such heretics.

They abstain from the Eucharist and from prayer, because they confess not the Eucharist to be the flesh of our Saviour Jesus Christ, which suffered for our sins, and which the Father, of His goodness, raised up again. Those, therefore, who speak against this gift of God, incur death in the midst of their disputes. But it were better for them to treat it with respect, that they also might rise again. It is fitting, therefore, that ye should keep aloof from such persons, and not to speak of them either in private or in public, but to give heed to the prophets, and above all, to the Gospel, in which the passion[of Christ] has been revealed to us, and the resurrection has been fully proved. But avoid all divisions, as the beginning of evils.

Chapter VIII.—Let nothing be done without the Bishop.

See that ye all follow the bishop, even as Jesus Christ does the Father, and the presbytery as ye would the apostles; and reverence the deacons, as being the institution of God. Let no man do anything connected with the Church without the bishop. Let that be deemed a proper Eucharist, which is[administered] either by the bishop, or by one to whom he has entrusted it. Wherever the bishop shall appear, there let the multitude[of the people] also be; even as, wherever Jesus Christ is, there is the Catholic Church. It is not lawful without the bishop either to baptize or to celebrate a love-feast; but whatsoever he shall approve of, that is also pleasing to God, so that everything that is done may be secure and valid.

Chapter IX.—Honour the Bishop.

Moreover, it is in accordance with reason that we should return to soberness[of conduct], and, while yet we have opportunity, exercise repentance towards God. It is well to reverence both God and the bishop. He who honours the bishop has been honoured by God; he who does anything without the knowledge of the bishop, does[in reality] serve the devil. Let all things, then, abound to you through grace, for ye are worthy. Ye have refreshed me in all things, and Jesus Christ[shall refresh] you. Ye have loved me when absent as well as when present. May God recompense you, for whose sake, while ye endure all things, ye shall attain unto Him.

Chapter X.—Acknowledgement of their kindness.

Ye have done well in receiving Philo and Rheus Agathopus as servants of Christ our God, who have followed me for the sake of God, and who give thanks to the Lord in your behalf, because ye have in every way refreshed them. None of these things shall be lost to you. May my spirit be for you, and my bonds, which ye have not despised or been ashamed of; nor shall Jesus Christ, our perfect hope, be ashamed of you.

Chapter XI.—Request to them to send a messenger to Antioch.

Your prayer has reached to the Church which is at Antioch in Syria. Coming from that place bound with chains, most acceptable to God, I salute all; I who am not worthy to be styled from thence, inasmuch as I am the least of them. Nevertheless, according to the will of God, I have been thought worthy[of this honour], not that I have any sense[of having deserved it], but by the grace of God, which I wish may be perfectly given to me, that through your prayers I may attain to God. In order, therefore, that your work may be complete both on earth and in heaven, it is fitting that, for the honour of God, your Church should elect some worthy delegate; so that he, journeying into Syria, may congratulate them that they are[now] at peace, and are restored to their proper greatness, and that their proper constitution has been re-established among them. It seems then to me a becoming thing, that you should send some one of your number with an epistle, so that, in company with them, he may rejoice over the tranquility which, according to the will of God, they have obtained, and because that, through your prayers, they have now reached the harbour. As persons who are perfect, ye should also aim at those things which are perfect. For when ye are desirous to do well, God is also ready to assist you.

Chapter XII.—Salutations.

The love of the brethren at Troas salutes you; whence also I write to The love of your brethren at Troas salutes you; whence also I write to you by Burrhus, whom ye sent with me, together with the Ephesians, your brethren, and who has in all things refreshed me. And I would that all may imitate him, as being a pattern of a minister of God. Grace will reward him in all things. I salute your most worthy bishop, and your very venerable presbytery, and your deacons, my fellow-servants, and all of you individually, as well as generally, in the name of Jesus Christ, and in His flesh and blood, in His passion and resurrection, both corporeal and spiritual, in union with God and you. Grace, mercy, peace, and patience, be with you for evermore!

Conclusion.

I salute the families of my brethren, with their wives and children, and and the virgins who are called widows. Be ye strong, I pray, in the power of the Holy Ghost. Philo, who is with me, greets you. I salute the house of Tavias, and pray that it may be confirmed in faith and love, both corporeal and spiritual. I salute Alce; my well-beloved, and the incomparable Daphnus, and Eutecnus, and all by name. Fare ye well in the grace of God.

The Epistle of Ignatius to Polycarp

Ignatius, who is also called Theophorus, to Polycarp, Bishop of the Church of the Smyrnaeans, or rather, who has, as his own bishop, God the Father, and the Lord Jesus Christ: [wishes] abundance of happiness.

Chapter I.—Commendation and exhortation.

Having obtained good proof that thy mind is fixed in God as upon an immoveable rock, I loudly glorify [His name] that I have been thought worthy [to behold] thy blameless face, which may I ever enjoy in God! I entreat thee, by the grace with which thou art clothed, to press forward in thy course, and to exhort all that they may be saved. Maintain thy position with all care, both in the flesh and spirit. Have a regard to preserve unity, than which nothing is better. Bear with all, even as the Lord does with thee. Support all in love, as also thou doest. Give thyself to prayer without ceasing. Implore additional understanding to what thou already hast. Be watchful, possessing a sleepless spirit. Speak to every man separately, as God enables thee. Bear the infirmities of all, as being a perfect athlete [in the Christian life]: where the labour is great, the gain is all the more.

Chapter II.—Exhortations.

If thou lovest the good disciples, no thanks are due to thee on that account; but rather seek by meekness to subdue the more troublesome. Every kind of wound is not healed with the same plaster. Mitigate violent attacks [of disease] by gentle applications. Be in all things "wise as a serpent, and harmless as a dove." For this purpose thou art composed of both flesh and spirit, that thou mayest deal tenderly with those [evils] that present themselves visibly before thee. And as respects those that are not seen, pray that [God] would reveal them unto thee, in order that thou mayest be wanting in nothing, but mayest abound in every gift. The times call for thee, as pilots do for the winds, and as on tossed with tempest seeks for the haven, so that both thou [and those under thy care] may attain to God. Be sober as an athlete of God: the prize set before thee is immortality and eternal life, of which thou art also persuaded. In all things may my soul be for thing, and my bonds also, which thou hast loved.

Chapter III.—Exhortations.

Let not those who seem worthy of credit, but teach strange doctrines, fill thee with apprehension. Stand firm, as does an anvil which is beaten. It is the part of a noble athlete to be wounded, and yet to conquer. And especially, we ought to bear all things for the sake of God, that He also may bear with us. Be ever becoming more zealous than what thou art. Weigh carefully the times. Look for Him who is above all time, eternal and invisible, yet who became visible for our sakes; impalpable and impassible, yet who became passible on our account; and who in every kind of way suffered for our sakes.

Chapter IV.—Exhortations.

Let not widows be neglected. Be thou, after the Lord, their protector s and friend. Let nothing be done without thy consent; neither do thou anything without the approval of God, which indeed thou dost not, inasmuch as thou art stedfast. Let your assembling together be of of frequent occurrence: seek after all by name. Do not despise either male or female slaves, yet neither let them be puffed up with conceit, but rather let them submit themselves the more, for the glory of God, that they my obtain from God a better liberty. Let them not long to be set free [from slavery] at the public expense, that they be not found slaves to their own desires.

Chapter V.—The duties of husbands and wives.

Flee evil arts; but all the more discourse in public regarding them. Speak to my sisters, that they love the Lord, and be satisfied with their husbands both in the flesh and spirit. In like manner also, exhort my brethren, in the name of Jesus Christ, that they love their wives, even as the Lord the Church. If any one can continue in a state of purity, to the honour of Him who is Lord of the flesh, let him so remain without boasting. If he begins to boast, he is undone; and if he reckon himself greater than the bishop, he is ruined. But it becomes both men and women who marry, to form their union with the approval of the bishop, that their marriage may be according to God, and not after their own lust. Let all things be done to the honour of God.

Chapter VI.—The duties of the Christian flock.

Give ye heed to the bishop, that God also may give heed to you. My soul be for theirs that are submissive to the bishop, to the presbyters, and to the deacons, and may my portion be along with them in God! Labour together with one another; strive in company together; run together; suffer together; sleep together; and awake together, as the stewards, and associates, and servants of God. Please ye Him under whom ye fight, and from whom ye receive your wages. Let none of you be found a deserter. Let your baptism endure as your arms; your faith as your helmet; your love as your spear; your patience as a complete panoply. Let your works be the charge assigned to you, that ye may receive a worthy recompense. Be long-suffering, therefore, with one another, in meekness, as God is towards you.May I have joy of you for ever!

Chapter VII.—Request that Polycarp would send a messenger to Antioch.

Seeing that the Church which is at Antioch in Syria is, as report has informed me, at peace, through your prayers, I also am the more encouraged, resting without anxiety in God, if indeed by means of suffering I may attain to God, so that, through your prayers, I may be found a disciple [of Christ]. It is fitting, O Polycarp, most blessed in God, to assemble a very solemn council, and to elect one whom you greatly love, and know to be a man of activity, who may be designated the messenger of God; and to bestow on him this honour that he may go into Syria, and glorify your ever active love to the praise of Christ. A Christian has not power over himself, but must always be ready for s the service of God. Now, this work is both God's and yours, when ye shall have completed it to His glory. For I trust that, through grace, ye are prepared for every good work pertaining to God. Knowing, therefore, your energetic love of the truth, I have exhorted you by this brief Epistle.

Chapter VIII.—Let other Churches also send to Antioch.

Inasmuch as I have not been able to write to all the Churches, because I must suddenly sail from Troas to Neapolis, as the will [of the emperor] enjoins, [I beg that] thou, as being acquainted with the purpose of God, wilt write to the adjacent Churches, that they also may act in like manner, such as are able to do so sending messengers, and the others transmitting letters through those persons who are sent by thee, that thou mayest be glorified by a work which shall be remembered for ever, as indeed thou art worthy to be. I salute all by name, and in particutar the wife of Epitropus, with all her house and children. I salute Attalus, my beloved. I salute him who shall be deemed worthy to go [from you] into Syria. Grace shall be with him for ever, and with Polycarp that sends him. I pray for your happiness for ever in our God, Jesus Christ, by whom continue ye in the unity and under the protection of God, I salute Alce, my dearly beloved. Fare ye well in the Lord.

LETTER TO THE PHILIPPIANS

Polycarp

TRANSLATED BY J. B. LIGHTFOOT

Polycarp and the presbyters that are with him unto the Church of God which sojourneth at Philippi; mercy unto you and peace from God Almighty and Jesus Christ our Savior be multiplied.

1

I rejoiced with you greatly in our Lord Jesus Christ, for that ye received the followers of the true Love and escorted them on their way, as befitted you—those men encircled in saintly bonds which are the diadems of them that be truly chosen of God and our Lord; and that the steadfast root of your faith which was famed from primitive times abideth until now and beareth fruit unto our Lord Jesus Christ, who endured to face even death for our sins, *whom God raised, having loosed the pangs of Hades; on whom, though ye saw Him not, ye believe with joy unutterable and full of glory;* unto which joy many desire to enter in; forasmuch as ye know that it is *by grace ye are saved, not of works,* but by the will of God through Jesus Christ.

2

Wherefore gird up your loins and serve God in fear and truth, forsaking the vain and empty talking and the error of the many, *for that ye have believed on Him that raised our Lord Jesus Christ from the dead and gave unto him glory* and a throne on His right hand; unto whom all things were made subject that are in heaven and that are on the earth; to whom every creature that hath breath doeth service; who cometh as *judge of quick and dead*; whose blood God will require of them that are disobedient unto Him. Now *He that raised Him from the dead will raise us also*; if we do His will and walk in His commandments and love the things which He loved, abstaining from all unrighteousness, covetousness, love of money, evil speaking, false witness; *not rendering evil for evil or railing for railing* or blow for blow or cursing for cursing; but remembering the words which the Lord spake, as He taught; *Judge not that ye be not judged. Forgive, and it shall be forgiven to you. Have mercy that ye may receive mercy. With what measure ye mete, it shall be measured to you again*; and again *Blessed are the poor and they that are persecuted for righteousness' sake, for theirs is the kingdom of God.*

3

These things, brethren, I write unto you concerning righteousness, not because I laid this charge upon myself, but because ye invited me. For neither am I, nor is any other like unto me, able to follow the wisdom of the blessed and glorious Paul, who when he came among you taught face to face with the men of that day the word which concerneth truth carefully and surely; who also, when he was absent, wrote a letter unto you, into the which if ye look diligently, ye shall be able to be builded up unto the faith given to you, *which is the mother of us all,* while hope followeth after and love goeth before— love toward God and Christ and toward our neighbor. For if any man be occupied with these, he hath fulfilled the commandment of righteousness; for he that hath love is far from all sin.

4

But the love of money is the beginning of all troubles. Knowing therefore that *we brought nothing into the world neither can we carry anything out*, let us arm ourselves with the armor of righteousness, and let us teach ourselves first to walk in the commandment of the Lord; and then our wives also, to walk in the faith that hath been given unto them and in love and purity, cherishing their own husbands in all truth and loving all men equally in all chastity, and to train their children in the training of the fear of God. Our widows must be sober-minded as touching the faith of the Lord, making intercession without ceasing for all men, abstaining from all calumny, evil speaking, false witness, love of money, and every evil thing, knowing that they are God's altar, and that all sacrifices are carefully inspected, and nothing escapeth Him either of their thoughts or intents or any of the secret things of the heart.

5

Knowing then that *God is not mocked*, we ought to walk worthily of His commandment and His glory. In like manner deacons should be blameless in the presence of His righteousness, as deacons of God and Christ and not of men; not calumniators, not double-tongued, not lovers of money, temperate in all things, compassionate, diligent, walking according to the truth of the Lord who became a *minister (deacon) of all.* For if we be well pleasing unto Him in this present world, we shall receive the future world also, according as He promised us to raise us from the dead, and that if we conduct ourselves worthily of Him *we shall also reign with Him*, if indeed we have faith. In like manner also the younger men must be blameless in all things, caring for purity before everything and curbing themselves from every evil. For it is a good thing to refrain from lusts in the world, for every *lust warreth against the Spirit, and neither whoremongers nor effeminate persons nor defilers of themselves with men shall inherit the kingdom of God*, neither they that do untoward things. Wherefore it is right to abstain from all these things, submitting yourselves to the presbyters and deacons as to God and Christ. The virgins must walk in a blameless and pure conscience.

6

And the presbyters also must be compassionate, merciful towards all men, *turning back the sheep that are gone astray*, visiting all the infirm, not neglecting a widow or an orphan or a poor man: but *providing always for that which is honorable in the sight of God and of men*, abstaining from all anger, respect of persons, unrighteous judgment, being far from all love of money, not quick to believe anything against any man, not hasty in judgment, knowing that we all are debtors of sin. If then we entreat the Lord that He would forgive us, we also ought to forgive: for we are before the eyes of our Lord and God, and we must *all stand at the judgment-seat of Christ*, and *each man must give an account of himself*. Let us therefore so serve Him with fear and all reverence, as He himself gave commandment and the Apostles who preached the Gospel to us and the prophets who proclaimed beforehand the coming of our Lord; being zealous as touching that which is good, abstaining from offenses and from the false brethren and from them that bear the name of the Lord in hypocrisy, who lead foolish men astray.

7

For every one *who shall not confess that Jesus Christ is come in the flesh, is antichrist*: and whosoever shall not confess the testimony of the Cross, is of the devil; and whosoever shall pervert the oracles of the Lord to his own lusts and say that there is neither resurrection nor judgment, that man is the first-born of Satan. Wherefore let us forsake the vain doing of the many and their false teachings, and turn unto the word which was delivered unto us from the beginning, *being sober unto prayer* and constant in fastings, entreating the all-seeing God with supplications that He *bring us not into temptation*, according as the Lord said, *The Spirit is indeed willing, but the flesh is weak*.

8

Let us therefore without ceasing hold fast by our hope and by the earnest of our righteousness, which is Jesus Christ *who took up our sins in His own body upon the tree, who did no sin, neither was guile found in His mouth,* but for our sakes He endured all things, that we might live in Him. Let us therefore become imitators of His endurance; and if we should suffer for His name's sake, let us glorify Him. For He gave this example to us in His own person, and we believed this.

9

I exhort you all therefore to be obedient unto the word of righteousness and to practice all endurance, which also ye saw with your own eyes in the blessed Ignatius and Zosimus and Rufus, yea and in others also who came from among yourselves, as well as in Paul himself and the rest of the Apostles; being persuaded that all these *ran not in vain* but in faith and righteousness, and that they are in their due place in the presence of the Lord, with whom also they suffered. For they *loved not the present world*, but Him that died for our sakes and was raised by God for us.

10

Stand fast therefore in these things and follow the example of the Lord, *being firm in the faith* and *immovable, in love of the brotherhood kindly affectioned one to another*, partners with the truth, *forestalling one another* in the gentleness of the Lord, despising no man. *When ye are able to do good,* defer it not, for *Pitifulness delivereth from death. Be ye all subject one to another, having your conversation unblamable among the gentiles, that your good works* both ye may receive praise and the Lord may not be blasphemed in you. But *woe to him through whom the name of the Lord be blasphemed.* Therefore teach all men soberness, in which ye yourselves also walk.

11

I was exceedingly grieved for Valens, who aforetime was a presbyter among you, because he is so ignorant of the office which was given unto him. I warn you therefore that ye refrain from covetousness, and that ye be pure and truthful. Refrain from all evil. But he who cannot govern himself in these things, how doth he enjoin this upon another? If a man refrain not from covetousness, he shall be defiled by idolatry, and shall be judged as one of the Gentiles who *know not the judgment of the Lord. Nay, know we not, that the saints shall judge the world*, as Paul teacheth? But I have not found any such thing in you, neither have heard thereof, among whom the blessed Paul labored, who were his *letters* in the beginning.

For *he boasteth of you in* all those *churches* which alone at that time knew God; for we knew Him not as yet. Therefore I am exceedingly grieved for him and for his wife, unto whom may the Lord grant true repentance. Be ye therefore yourselves also sober herein, and *hold not such as enemies*, but restore them as frail and erring members, that ye may save the whole body of you. For so doing, ye do edify one another.

12

For I am persuaded that ye are well trained in the sacred writings, and nothing is hidden from you. But to myself this is not granted. Only, as it is said in these scriptures, *Be ye angry and sin not*, and *Let not the sun set on your wrath.* Blessed is he that remembereth this; and I trust that this is in you. Now may the God and Father of our Lord Jesus Christ, and the eternal High-priest Himself the [Son of] God Jesus Christ, build you up in faith and truth, and in all gentleness and in all avoidance of wrath and in forbearance and long suffering and in patient endurance and in purity; and may He grant unto you a lot and portion among His saints, and to us with you, and to all that are under heaven, who shall believe on our Lord and God Jesus Christ and on His Father *that raised him from the dead. Pray for all the saints.* Pray also *for kings* and powers and princes and *for them that persecute* and hate *you* and for *the enemies of the cross*, that your fruit may be *manifest among all men*, that ye may be perfect in Him.

13

Ye wrote to me, both ye yourselves and Ignatius, asking that if any one should go to Syria he might carry thither the letters from you. And this I will do, if I get a fit opportunity, either I myself, or he whom I shall send to be ambassador on your behalf also. The letters of Ignatius which were sent to us by him, and others as many as we had by us, we send unto you, according as ye gave charge; the which are subjoined to this letter; from which ye will be able to gain great advantage. For they comprise faith and endurance and every kind of edification, which pertaineth unto our Lord. Moreover concerning Ignatius himself and those that were with him, if ye have any sure tidings, certify us.

14

I write these things to you by Crescens, whom I commended to you recently and now commend unto you: for he hath walked blamelessly with us; and I believe also with you in like manner. But ye shall have his sister commended, when she shall come to you. Fare ye well in the Lord Jesus Christ in grace, ye and all yours. Amen.

A PLEA FOR THE CHRISTIANS

Athenagoras

TRANSLATED BY REVEREND B. P. PRATTEN

A PLEA FOR THE CHRISTIANS BY ATHENAGORAS THE ATHENIAN: PHILOSOPHER AND CHRISTIAN

To the Emperors Marcus Aurelius Anoninus and Lucius Aurelius Commodus, conquerors of Armenia and Sarmatia, and more than all, philosophers.

Chapter I: Injustice shown towards the Christians.

In your empire, greatest of sovereigns, different nations have different customs and laws; and no one is hindered by law or fear of punishment from following his ancestral usages, however ridiculous these may be. A citizen of Ilium calls Hector a god, and pays divine honours to Helen, taking her for Adrasteia. The Lacedaemonian venerates Agamemnon as Zeus, and Phylonoe the daughter of Tyndarus; and the man of Tenedos worships Tennes. The Athenian sacrifices to Erechtheus as Poseidon. The Athenians also perform religious rites and celebrate mysteries in honour of Agraulus and Pandrosus, women who were deemed guilty of impiety for opening the box. In short, among every nation and people, men offer whatever sacrifices and celebrate whatever mysteries they please. The Egyptians reckon among their gods even cats, and crocodiles, and serpents, and asps, and dogs. And to all these both you and the laws give permission so to act, deeming, on the one hand, that to believe in no god at all is impious and wicked, and on the other, that it is necessary for each man to worship the gods he prefers, in order that through fear of the deity, men may be kept from wrong-doing. But why--for do not, like the multitude, be led astray by hearsay--why is a mere name odious to you?

Names are not deserving of hatred: it is the unjust act that calls for penalty and punishment. And accordingly, with admiration of your mildness and gentleness, and your peaceful and benevolent disposition towards every man, individuals live in the possession of equal rights; and the cities, according to their rank, share in equal honour; and the whole empire, under your intelligent sway, enjoys profound peace. But for us who are called Christians you have not in like manner cared; but although we commit no wrong--nay, as will appear in the sequel of this discourse, are of all men most piously and righteously disposed towards the Deity and towards your government--you allow us to be harassed, plundered, and persecuted, the multitude making war upon us for our name alone. We venture, therefore, to lay a statement of our case before you--and you will team from this discourse that we suffer unjustly, and contrary to all law and reason--and we beseech you to bestow some consideration upon us also, that we may cease at length to be slaughtered at the instigation of false accusers. For the fine imposed by our persecutors does not aim merely at our property, nor their insults at our reputation, nor the damage they do us at any other of our greater interests.

These we hold in contempt, though to the generality they appear matters of great importance; for we have learned, not only not to return blow for blow, nor to go to law with those who plunder and rob us, but to those who smite us on one side of the face to offer the other side also, and to those who take away our coat to give likewise our cloak. But, when we have surrendered our property, they plot against our very bodies and souls, pouring upon us wholesale charges of crimes of which we are guiltless even in thought, but which belong to these idle praters themselves, and to the whole tribe of those who are like them.

Chapter II: Claim to be treated as others when accused.

If, indeed, any one can convict us of a crime, be it small or great, we do not ask to be excused from punishment, but are prepared to undergo the sharpest and most merciless inflictions. But if the accusation relates merely to our name--and it is undeniable, that up to the present time the stories told about us rest on nothing better than the common undiscriminating popular talk, nor has any Christian been convicted of crime--it will devolve on you, illustrious and benevolent and most learned sovereigns, to remove by law this despiteful treatment, so that, as throughout the world both individuals and cities partake of your beneficence, we also may feel grateful to you, exulting that we are no longer the victims of false accusation. For it does not comport with your justice, that others when charged with crimes should not be punished till they are convicted, but that in our case the name we bear should have more force than the evidence adduced on the trial, when the judges, instead of inquiring whether the person arraigned have committed any crime, vent their insults on the name, as if that were itself a crime. But no name in and by itself is reckoned either good or bad; names appear bad or good according as the actions underlying them are bad or good. You, however, have yourselves a dear knowledge of this, since you are well instructed in philosophy and all learning. For this reason, too, those who are brought before you for trial, though they may be arraigned on the gravest charges, have no fear, because they know that you will inquire respecting their previous life, and not be influenced by names if they mean nothing, nor by the charges contained in the indictments if they should be false: they accept with equal satisfaction, as regards its fairness, the sentence whether of condemnation or acquittal. What, therefore, is conceded as the common right of all, we claim for ourselves, that we shall not be hated and punished because we are called Christians (for what has the name to do with our being bad men?), but be tried on any charges which may be brought against us, and either be released on our disproving them, or punished if convicted of crime--not for the name (for no Christian is a bad man unless he falsely profess our doctrines), but for the wrong which has been done. It is thus that we see the philosophers judged. None of them before trial is deemed by the judge either good or bad on account of his science or art, but if found guilty of wickedness he is punished, without thereby affixing any stigma on philosophy (for he is a bad man for not cultivating philosophy in a lawful manner, but science is blameless), while if he refutes the false charges he is acquitted. Let this equal justice, then, be done to us. Let the life of the accused persons be investigated, but let the name stand free from all imputation. I must at the outset of my defence entreat you, illustrious emperors, to listen to me impartially: not to be carried away by the common irrational talk and prejudge the case, but to apply your desire of knowledge and love of truth to the examination of our doctrine also. Thus, while you on your part will not err through ignorance, we also, by disproving the charges arising out of the undiscerning rumour of the multitude, shall cease to be assailed.

Chapter III: Charges brought against the Christians.

Three things are alleged against us: atheism, Thyestean feasts, OEdipodean intercourse. But if these charges are true, spare no class:

proceed at once against our crimes; destroy us root and branch, with our wives and children, if any Christian is found to live like the brutes. And yet even the brutes do not touch the flesh of their own kind; and they pair by a law of nature, and only at the regular season, not from simple wantonness; they also recognise those from whom they receive benefits. If any one, therefore, is more savage than the brutes, what punishment that he can endure shall be deemed adequate to such offences? But, if these things are only idle tales and empty slanders, originating in the fact that virtue is opposed by its very nature to vice, and that contraries war against one another by a divine law (and you are yourselves witnesses that no such iniquities are committed by us, for you forbid informations to be laid against us), it remains for you to make inquiry concerning our life, our opinions, our loyalty and obedience to you and your house and government, and thus at length to grant to us the same rights (we ask nothing more) as to those who persecute us. For we shall then conquer them, unhesitatingly surrendering, as we now do, our very lives for the truth's sake.

Chapter IV: The Christians are not Atheists, but acknowledge only one God.

As regards, first of all, the allegation that we are atheists--for I will meet the charges one by one, that we may not be ridiculed for having no answer to give to those who make them--with reason did the Athenians adjudge Diagoras guilty of atheism, in that he not only divulged the Orphic doctrine, and published the mysteries of Eleusis and of the Cabiri, and chopped up the wooden statue of Hercules to boil his turnips, but openly declared that there was no God at all. But to us, who distinguish God from matter, and teach that matter is one thing and God another, and that they are separated by a wide interval (for that the Deity is uncreated and eternal, to be beheld by the understanding and reason alone, while matter is created and perishable), is it not absurd to apply the name of atheism? If our sentiments were like those of Diagoras, while we have such incentives to piety--in the established order, the universal harmony, the magnitude, the colour, the form, the arrangement of the world-- with reason might our reputation for impiety, as well as the cause of our being thus harassed, be charged on ourselves. But, since our doctrine acknowledges one God, the Maker of this universe, who is Himself uncreated (for that which is does not come to be, but that which is not) but has made all things by the Logos which is from Him, we are treated unreasonably in both respects, in that we are both defamed and persecuted.

Chapter V: Testimony of the poets to the unity of God.

Poets and philosophers have not been voted atheists for inquiring concerning God. Euripides, speaking of those who, according to popular preconception, are ignorantly called gods, says doubtingly:- "If Zeus indeed does reign in heaven above, He ought not on the righteous ills to send." But speaking of Him who is apprehended by the understanding as matter of certain knowledge, he gives his opinion decidedly, and with intelligence, thus:- "Seest thou on high him who, with humid arms, Clasps both the boundless ether and the earth? Him reckon Zeus, and him regard as God." For, as to these so-called gods, he neither saw any real existences, to which a name is usually assigned, underlying them ("Zeus," for instance: "who Zeus is I know not, but by report"), nor that any names were given to realities which actually do exist (for of what use are names to those who have no real existences underlying them?); but Him he did see by means of His works, considering with an eye to things unseen the things which are manifest in air, in ether, on earth. Him therefore, from whom proceed all created things, and by whose Spirit they are governed, he concluded to be God; and Sophocles agrees with him, when he says:- "There is one God, in truth there is but one, Who made the heavens, and the broad earth beneath." [Euripides is speaking] of the nature of God, which fills His works with beauty, and teaching both where God must be, and that He must be One.

Chapter VI: Opinions of the Philosophers as to the one God.

Philolaus, too, when he says that all things are included in God as in a stronghold, teaches that He is one, and that He is superior to matter. Lysis and Opsimus thus define God: the one says that He is an ineffable number, the other that He is the excess of the greatest number beyond that which comes nearest to it. So that since ten is the greatest number according to the Pythagoreans, being the Tetractys, and containing all the arithmetic and harmonic principles, and the Nine stands next to it, God is a unit--that is, one. For the greatest number exceeds the next least by one. Then there are Plato and Aristotle--not that I am about to go through all that the philosophers have said about God, as if I wished to exhibit a complete summary of their opinions; for I know that, as you excel all men in intelligence and in the power of your rule, in the same proportion do you surpass them all in an accurate acquaintance with all learning, cultivating as you do each several branch with more success than even those who have devoted themselves exclusively to any one. But, inasmuch as it is impossible to demonstrate without the citation of names that we are not alone in confining the notion of God to unity, I have ventured on an enumeration of opinions. Plato, then, says, "To find out the Maker and Father of this universe is difficult; and, when found, it is impossible to declare Him to all," conceiving of one uncreated and eternal God. And if he recognises others as well, such as the sun, moon, and stars, yet he recognises them as created: "gods, offspring of gods, of whom I am the Maker, and the Father of works which are indissoluble apart from my will; but whatever is compounded can be dissolved." If, therefore, Plato is not an atheist for conceiving of one uncreated God, the Framer of the universe, neither are we atheists who acknowledge and firmly hold that He is God who has framed all things by the Logos, and holds them in being by His Spirit. Aristotle, again, and his followers, recognising the existence of one whom they regard as a sort of compound living creature (zwon), speak of God as consisting of soul and body, thinking His body to be the etherial space and the planetary stars and the sphere of the fixed stars, moving in circles; but His soul, the reason which presides over the motion of the body, itself not subject to motion, but becoming the cause of motion to the other. The Stoics also, although by the appellations they employ to suit the changes of matter, which they say is permeated by the Spirit of God, they multiply the Deity in name, yet in reality they consider God to be one.

For, if God is an artistic fire advancing methodically to the production of the several things in the world, embracing in Himself all the seminal principles by which each thing is produced in accordance with fate, and if His Spirit pervades the whole world, then God is one according to them, being named Zeus in respect of the fervid part (to zeon) of matter, and Hera in respect of the air (o ahr), and called by other names in respect of that particular part of matter which He pervades.

Chapter VII: Superiority of the Christian doctrine respecting God.

Since, therefore, the unity of the Deity is confessed by almost all, even against their will, when they come to treat of the first principles of the universe, and we in our turn likewise assert that He who arranged this universe is God,--why is it that they can say and write with impunity what they please concerning the Deity, but that against us a law lies in force, though we are able to demonstrate what we apprehend and justly believe, namely that there is one God, with proofs and reason accordant with truth? For poets and philosophers, as to other subjects so also to this, have applied themselves in the way of conjecture, moved, by reason of their affinity with the afflatus from God, each one by his own soul, to try whether he could find out and apprehend the truth; but they have not been found competent fully to apprehend it, because they thought fit to learn, not from God concerning God, but each one from himself; hence they came each to his own conclusion respecting God, and matter, and forms, and the world. But we have for witnesses of the things we apprehend and believe, prophets, men who have pronounced concerning God and the things of God, guided by the Spirit of God. And you too will admit, excelling all others as you do in intelligence and in piety towards the true God (to ontws qeion), that it would be irrational for us to cease to believe in the Spirit from God, who moved the mouths of the prophets like musical instruments, and to give heed to mere human opinions.

Chapter VIII: Absurdities of Polytheism.

As regards, then, the doctrine that there was from the beginning one God, the Maker of this universe, consider it in this wise, that you may be acquainted with the argumentative grounds also of our faith. If there were from the beginning two or more gods, they were either in one and the same place, or each of them separately in his own. In one and the same place they could not be. For, if they are gods, they are not alike; but because they are uncreated they are unlike:-- for created things are like their patterns; but the uncreated are unlike, being neither produced from any one, nor formed after the pattern of any one. Hand and eye and foot are parts of one body, making up together one man: is God in this sense one? And indeed Socrates was compounded and divided into parts, just because he was created and perishable; but God is uncreated, and, impassible, and indivisible-- does not, therefore, consist of parts. But if, on the contrary, each of them exists separately, since He that made the world is above the things created, and about the things He has made and set in order, where can the other or the rest be? For if the world, being made spherical, is confined within the circles of heaven, and the Creator of the world is above the things created, managing that by His providential care of these, what place is there for the second god, or for the other gods? For he is not in the world, because it belongs to the other; nor about the world, for God the Maker of the world is above it. But if he is neither in the world nor about the world (for all that surrounds it is occupied by this one), where is he? Is he above the world and [the first] God? In another world, or about another? But if he is in another or about another, then he is not about us, for he does not govern the world; nor is his power great, for he exists in a circumscribed space. But if he is neither in another world (for all things are filled by the other), nor about another (for all things are occupied by the other), he clearly does not exist at all, for there is no place in which he can be. Or what does he do, Seeing there is another to whom the world belongs, and he is above the Maker of the world, and yet is neither in the world nor about the world? Is there, then, some other place where he can stand? But God, and what belongs to God, are above him. And what, too, shall be the place, seeing that the other fills the regions which are above the world? Perhaps he exerts a providential care? [By no means.] And yet, unless he does so, he has done nothing. If, then, he neither does anything nor exercises providential care, and if there is not another place in which he is, then this Being of whom we speak is the one God from the beginning, and the sole Maker of the world.

Chapter IX: The testimony of the Prophets.

If we satisfied ourselves with advancing such considerations as these, our doctrines might by some be looked upon as human. But, since the voices of the prophets confirm our arguments--for I think that you also, with your great zeal for knowledge, and your great attainments in learning, cannot be ignorant of the writings either of Moses or of Isaiah and Jeremiah, and the other prophets, who, lifted in ecstasy above the natural operations of their minds by the impulses of the Divine Spirit, uttered the things with which they were inspired, the Spirit making use of them as a flute-player breathes into a flute;-

-what, then, do these men say? The LORD is our God; no other can be compared with Him." And again: "I am God, the first and the last, and besides Me there is no God." In like manner: "Before Me there was no other God, and after Me there shall be none; I am God, and there is none besides Me." And as to His greatness: "Heaven is My throne, and the earth is the footstool of My feet: what house win ye build for Me, or what is the place of My rest?" But I leave it to you, when you meet with the books themselves, to examine carefully the prophecies contained in them, that you may on fitting grounds defend us from the abuse cast upon us.

Chapter X: The Christians worship the Father, Son, and Holy Ghost.

That we are not atheists, therefore, seeing that we acknowledge one God, uncreated, eternal, invisible, impassible, incomprehensible, illimitable, who is apprehended by the understanding only and the reason, who is encompassed by light, and beauty, and spirit, and power ineffable, by whom the universe has been created through His Logos, and set in order, and is kept in being--I have sufficiently demonstrated. [I say "His Logos"], for we acknowledge also a Son of God. Nor let any one think it ridiculous that God should have a Son. For though the poets, in their fictions, represent the gods as no better than men, our mode of thinking is not the same as theirs, concerning either God the Father or the Son. But the Son of God is the Logos of the Father, in idea and in operation; for after the pattern of Him and by Him were all things made, the Father and the Son being one. And, the Son being in the Father and the Father in the Son, in oneness and power of spirit, the understanding and reason (nous kai logos) of the Father is the Son of God. But if, in your surpassing intelligence, it occurs to you to inquire what is meant by the Son, I will state briefly that He is the first product of the Father, not as having been brought into existence (for from the beginning, God, who is the eternal mind [nous], had the Logos in Himself, being from eternity instinct with Logos [logikos]; but inasmuch as He came forth to be the idea and energizing power of all material things, which lay like a nature without attributes, and an inactive earth, the grosser particles being mixed up with the lighter. The prophetic Spirit also agrees with our statements. "The Lord," it says, "made me, the beginning of His ways to His works." The Holy Spirit Himself also, which operates in the prophets, we assert to be an effluence of God, flowing from Him, and returning back again like a beam of the sun. Who, then, would not be astonished to hear men who speak of God the Father, and of God the Son, and of the Holy Spirit, and who declare both their power in union and their distinction in order, called atheists? Nor is our teaching in what relates to the divine nature confined to these points; but we recognise also a multitude of angels and ministers, whom God the Maker and Framer of the world distributed and ap pointed to their several posts by His Logos, to occupy themselves about the elements, and the heavens, and the world, and the things in it, and the goodly ordering of them all.

Chapter XI: The moral teaching of the Christians repels the charge brought against them.

If I go minutely into the particulars of our doctrine, let it not surprise you. It is that you may not be carried away by the popular and irrational opinion, but may have the truth clearly before you. For presenting the opinions themselves to which we adhere, as being not human but uttered and taught by God, we shall be able to persuade you not to think of us as atheists. What, then, are those teachings in which we are brought up? "I say unto you, Love your enemies; bless them that curse you; pray for them that persecute you; that ye may be the sons of your Father who is in heaven, who causes His sun to rise on the evil and the good, and sends rain on the just and the unjust." Allow me here to lift up my voice boldly in loud and audible outcry, pleading as I do before philosophic princes. For who of those that reduce syllogisms, and clear up ambiguities, and explain etymologies, or of those who teach homonyms and synonyms, and predicaments and axioms, and what is the subject and what the predicate, and who promise their disciples by these and such like instructions to make them happy: who of them have so purged their souls as, instead of hating their enemies, to love them; and, instead of speaking ill of those who have reviled them (to abstain from which is of itself an evidence of no mean forbearance), to bless them; and to pray for those who plot against their lives? On the contrary, they never cease with evil intent to search out skilfully the secrets of their art, and are ever bent on working some ill, making the art of words and not the exhibition of deeds their business and profession. But among us you will find uneducated persons, and artisans, and old women, who, if they are unable in words to prove the benefit of our doctrine, yet by their deeds exhibit the benefit arising from their persuasion of its truth: they do not rehearse speeches, but exhibit good works; when struck, they do not strike again; when robbed, they do not go to law; they give to those that ask of them, and love their neighbours as themselves.

Chapter XII: Consequent absurdity of the charge of Atheism.

Should we, then, unless we believed that a God presides over the human race, thus purge ourselves from evil? Most certainly not. But, because we are persuaded that we shall give an account of everything in the present life to God, who made us and the world, we adopt a temperate and benovolent and generally despised method of life, believing that we shall suffer no such great evil here, even should our lives be taken from us, compared with what we shall there receive for our meek and benevolent and moderate life from the great Judge. Plato indeed has said that Minos and Rhadamanthus will judge and punish the wicked; but we say that, even if a man be Minos or Rhadamanthus himself, or their father, even he will not escape the judgment of God. Are, then, those who consider life. to be comprised in this, "Let us eat and drink, for to-morrow we die," and who regard death as a deep sleep and forgetfulness ("sleep and death, twin-brothers"), to be accounted pious; while men who reckon the present life of very small worth indeed, and who are conducted to the future life by this one thing alone, that they know God and His Logos, what is the oneness of the Son with the Father, what the communion of the Father with the Son, what is the Spirit, what is the unity of these three, the Spirit, the Son, the Father, and their distinction in unity; and who know that the life for which we look is far better than can be described in words, provided we arrive at it pure from all wrong-doing; who, moreover, carry our benevolence to such an extent, that we not only love our friends ("for if ye love them," He says, "that love you, and lend to them that lend to you, what reward will ye have?"),--shall we, I say, when such is our character, and when we live such a life as this, that we may escape condemnation at last, not be accounted pious? These, however, are only small matters taken from great, and a few things from many, that we may not further trespass on your patience; for those who test honey and whey, judge by a small quantity whether the whole is good.

Chapter XIII: Why the Christians do not offer sacrifices.

But, as most of those who charge us with atheism, and that because they have not even the dreamiest conception of what God is, and are doltish and utterly unacquainted with natural and divine things, and such as measure piety by the rule of sacrifices, charges us with not acknowledging the same gods as the cities, be pleased to attend to the following considerations, O emperors, on both points. And first, as to our not sacrificing: the Framer and Father of this universe does not need blood, nor the odour of burnt-offerings, nor the fragrance of flowers and incense, forasmuch as He is Himself perfect fragrance, needing nothing either within or without; but the noblest sacrifice to Him is for us to know who stretched out and vaulted the heavens, and fixed the earth in its place like a centre, who gathered the water into seas and divided the light from the darkness, who adorned the sky with stars and made the earth to bring forth seed of every kind, who made animals and fashioned man. When, holding God to be this Framer of all things, who preserves them in being and superintends them all by knowledge and administrative skill, we "lift up holy hands" to Him, what need has He further of a hecatomb? "For they, when mortals have transgress'd or fail'd To do aright, by sacrifice and pray'r, Libations and burnt-offerings, may be soothed." And what have I to do with holocausts, which God does not stand in need of?--though indeed it does behove us to offer a bloodless sacrifice and "the service of our reason."

Chapter XIV: Inconsistency of those who accuse the Christians.

Then, as to the other complaint, that we do not pray to and believe in the same gods as the cities, it is an exceedingly silly one. Why, the very men who charge us with atheism for not admitting the same gods as they acknowledge, are not agreed among themselves concerning the gods. The Athenians have set up as gods Celeus and Metanira: the Lacedaemonians Menelaus; and they offer sacrifices and hold festivals to him, while the men of Ilium cannot endure the very sound of his name, and pay their adoration to Hector. The Ceans worship Aristaeus, considering him to be the same as Zeus and Apollo; the Thasians Theagenes, a man who committed murder at the Olympic games; the Samians Lysander, notwithstanding all the slaughters and all the crimes perpetrated by him; Alcman and Hesiod Medea, and the Cilicians Niobe; the Sicilians Philip the son of Butacides; the Amathusians Onesilus; the Carthaginians Hamilcar. Time would fail me to enumerate the whole. When, therefore, they differ among themselves concerning their gods, why do they bring the charge against us of not agreeing with them? Then look at the practices prevailing among the Egyptians: are they not perfectly ridiculous? For in the temples at their solemn festivals they beat their breasts as for the dead, and sacrifice to the same beings as gods; and no wonder, when they look upon the brutes as gods, and shave themselves when they die, and bury them in temples, and make public lamentation. If, then, we are guilty of impiety because we do not practise a piety corresponding with theirs, then all cities and all nations are guilty of impiety, for they do not all acknowledge the same gods.

Chapter XV: The Christians distinguish God from Matter.

But grant that they acknowledge the same. What then? Because the multitude, who cannot distinguish between matter and God, or see how great is the interval which lies between them, pray to idols made of matter, are we therefore, who do distinguish and separate the uncreated and the created, that which is and that which is not, that which is apprehended by the understanding and that which is perceived by the senses, and who give the fitting name to each of them,--are we to come and worship images? If, indeed, matter and God are the same, two names for one thing, then certainly, in not regarding stocks and stones, gold and silver, as gods, we are guilty of impiety. But if they are at the greatest possible remove from one another--as far asunder as the artist and the materials of his art--why are we called to account? For as is the potter and the clay (matter being the clay, and the artist the potter), so is God, the Framer of the world, and matter, which is subservient to Him for the purposes of His art. But as the clay cannot become vessels of itself without art, so neither did matter, which is capable of taking all forms, receive, apart from God the Framer, distinction and shape and order. And as we do not hold the pottery of more worth than him who made it, nor the vessels or glass and gold than him who wrought them; but if there is anything about them elegant in art we praise the artificer, and it is he who reaps the glory of the vessels: even so with matter and God

--the glory and honour of the orderly arrangement of the world belongs of right not to matter, but to God, the Framer of matter. So that, if we were to regard the various forms of matter as gods, we should seem to be without any sense of the true God, because we should be putting the things which are dissoluble and perishable on a level with that which is eternal.

Chapter XVI: The Christians do not worship the universe.

Beautiful without doubt is the world, excelling, as well in its magnitude as in the arrangement of its parts, both those in the oblique circle and those about the north, and also in its spherical form. Yet it is not this, but its Artificer, that we must worship. For when any of your subjects come to you, they do not neglect to pay their homage to you, their rulers and lords, from whom they will obtain whatever they need, and address themselves to the magnificence of your palace; but, if they chance to come upon the royal residence, they bestow a passing glance of admiration on its beautiful structure: but it is to you yourselves that they show honour, as being "all in all." You sovereigns, indeed, rear and adorn your palaces for yourselves; but the world was not created because God needed it; for God is Himself everything to Himself,--light unapproachable, a perfect world, spirit, power, reason. If, therefore, the world is an instrument in tune, and moving in well-measured time, I adore the Being who gave its harmony, and strikes its notes, and sings the accordant strain, and not the instrument. For at the musical contests the adjudicators do not pass by the lute-players and crown the lutes. Whether, then, as Plato says, the world be a product of divine art, I admire its beauty, and adore the Artificer; or whether it be His essence and body, as the Peripatetics affirm, we do not neglect to adore God, who is the cause of the motion of the body, and descend "to the poor and weak elements," adoring in the impassible air (as they term it), passible matter; or, if any one apprehends the several parts of the world to be powers of God, we do not approach and do homage to the powers, but their Maker and Lord. I do not ask of matter what it has not to give, nor passing God by do I pay homage to the elements, which can do nothing more than what they were bidden; for, although they are beautiful to look upon, by reason of the art of their Framer, yet they still have the nature of matter. And to this view Plato also bears testimony; "for," says he, "that which is called heaven and earth has received many blessings from the Father, but yet partakes of body; hence it cannot possibly be free from' change." If, therefore, while I admire the heavens and the elements in respect of their art, I do not worship them as gods, knowing that the law of dissolution is upon them, how can I call those objects gods of which I know the makers to be men? Attend, I beg, to a few words on this subject.

Chapter XVII: The names of the gods and their images are but of recent date.

An apologist must adduce more precise arguments than I have yet given, both concering the names of the gods, to show that they are of recent origin, and concerning their images, to show that they are, so to say, but of yesterday. You yourselves, however, are thoroughly acquainted with these matters, since you are versed in all departments of knowledge, and are beyond all other men familiar with the ancients. I assert, then, that it was Orpheus, and Homer, and Hesiod who s gave both genealogies and names to those whom they call gods. Such, too, is the testimony of Herodotus. "My opinion," he says, "is that Hesiod and Homer preceded me by four hundred years, and no more; and it was they who framed a theogony for the Greeks, and gave the gods their names, and assigned them their several honours and functions, and described their forms." Representations of the gods, again, were not in use at all, so long as statuary, and painting, and sculpture were unknown; nor did they become common until Saurias the Samian, and Crato the Sicyonian, and Cleanthes the Corinthian, and the Corinthian damsel appeared, when drawing in outline was invented by Saurias, who sketched a horse in the sun, and painting by Crato, who painted in oil on a whitened tablet the outlines of a man and woman; and the art of making figures in relief (koroplaqikh) was invented by the damsel, who, being in love with a person, traced his shadow on a wall as he lay asleep, and her father, being delighted with the exactness of the resemblance (he was a potter), carved out the sketch and filled it up with clay: this figure is still preserved at Corinth. After these, Daedalus and Theodorus the Milesian further invented sculpture and statuary. You perceive, then, that the time since representations of form and the making of images began is so short, that we can name the artist of each particular god. The image of Artemis at Ephesus, for example, and that of Athena (or rather of Athela, for so is she named by those who speak more in the style of the mysteries; for thus was the ancient image made of the olive-tree called), and the sitting figure of the same goddess, were made by Endoeus, a pupil of Daedalus; the Pythian god was the work of Theodorus and Telecles; and the Delian god and Artemis are due to the art of Tectaeus and Angelio; Hera in Samos and in Argos came from the hands of Smilis, and the other statues were by Phidias; Aphrodite the courtezan in Cnidus is the production of Praxiteles; Asclepius in Epidaurus is the work of Phidias. In a word, of not one of these statues can it be said that it was not made by man. If, then, these are gods, why did they not exist from the beginning? Why, in sooth, are they younger than those who made them? Why, in sooth, in order to their coming into existence, did they need the aid of men and art? They are nothing but earth, and stones, and matter, and curious art.

Chapter XVIII: The gods themselves have been created, as the poets confess.

But, since it is affirmed by some that, although these are only images, yet there exist gods in honour of whom they are made; and that the supplications and sacrifices presented to the images are to be referred to the gods, and are in fact made to the gods; and that there is not any other way of coming to them, for "'Tis hard for man To meet in presence visible a God;" and whereas, in proof that such is the fact, they adduce the eneregies possessed by certain images, let us examine into the power attached to their names. And I would beseech you, greatest of emperors, before I enter on this discussion, to be indulgent to me while I bring forward true considerations; for it is not my design to show the fallacy of idols, but, by disproving the calumnies vented against us, to offer a reason for the course of life we follow. May you, by considering yourselves, be able to discover the heavenly kingdom also! For as all things are subservient to you, father and son, who have received the kingdom from above (for "the king's soul is in the hand of God," saith the prophetic Spirit), so to the one God and the Logos proceeding from. Him, the Son, apprehended by us as inseparable from Him, all things are in like manner subjected. This then especially I beg you carefully to consider. The gods, as they affirm, were not from the beginning, but every one of them has come into existence just like ourselves. And in this opinion they all agree. Homer speaks of "Old Oceanus, The sire of gods, and Tethys;" and Orpheus (who, moreover, was the first to invent their names, and recounted their births, and narrated the exploits of each, and is believed by them to treat with greater truth than others of divine things, whom Homer himself follows in most matters, especially in reference to the gods)--he, too, has fixed their first origin to be from water:- "Oceanus, the origin of all." For, according to him, water was the beginning of all things, and from water mud was formed, and from both was produced an animal, a dragon with the head of a lion growing to it, and between the two heads there was the face of a god, named Heracles and Kronos. This Heracles generated an egg of enormous size, which, on becoming full, was, by the powerful friction of its generator, burst into two, the part at the top receiving the form of heaven (ouranos), and the lower part that of earth (gh). The goddess Ge, moreover, came forth with a body; and Ouranos, by his union with Ge, begat females, Clotho, Lachesis, and Atropos; and males, the hundred-handed Cottys, Gyges, Briareus, and the Cyclopes Brontes, and Steropes, and Argos, whom also he bound and hurled down to Tartarus, having learnt that he was to be ejected from his government by his children; whereupon Ge, being enraged, brought forth the Titans. "The godlike Gala bore to Ouranos Sons who are by the name of Titans known, Because they vengeance took on Ouranos, Majestic, glitt'ring with his starry crown."

Chapter XIX: The Philosophers agree with the poets respecting the gods.

Such was the beginning of the existence both of their gods and of the universe. Now what are we to make of this? For each of those things to which divinity is ascribed is conceived of as having existed from the first. For, if they have come into being, having previously had no existence, as those say who treat of the gods, they do not exist. For, a thing is either uncreated and eternal, or created and perishable. Nor do I think one thing and the philosophers another. "What is that which always is, and has no origin; or what is that which has been originated, yet never is?" Discoursing of the intelligible and the sensible, Plato teaches that that which always is, the intelligible, is unoriginated, but that which is not, the sensible, is originated, beginning to be and ceasing to exist. In like manner, the Stoics also say that all things will be burnt up and will again exist, the world receiving another beginning. But if, although there is, according to them, a twofold cause, one active and governing, namely providence, the other passive and changeable, namely matter, it is nevertheless impossible for the world, even though under the care of Providence, to remain in the same state, because it is created--how can the constitution of these gods remain, who are not self-existent, but have been originated? And in what are the gods superior to matter, since they derive their constitution from water? But not even water, according to them, is the beginning of all things. From simple and homogeneous elements what could be constituted? Moreover, matter requires an artificer, and the artificer requires matter. For how could figures be made without matter or an artificer? Neither, again, is it reasonable that matter should be older than God; for the efficient cause must of necessity exist before the things that are made.

Chapter XX: Absurd representations of the gods.

If the absurdity of their theology were confined to saying that the gods were created, and owed their constitution to water, since I have demonstrated that nothing is made which is not also liable to dissolution, I might proceed to the remaining charges. But, on the one hand, they have described their bodily forms: speaking of Hercules, for instance, as a god in the shape of a dragon coiled up; of others as hundred-handed; of the daughter of Zeus, whom he begat of his mother Rhea; or of Demeter, as having two eyes in the natural order, and two in her forehead, and the face of an animal on the back part of her neck, and as having also horns, so that Rhea, frightened at her monster of a child, fled from her, and did not give her the breast (qhlh), whence mystically she is called Athela, but commonly Phersephone and Kore, though she is not the same as Athena, who is called Kore from the pupil of the eye;--and, on the other hand, they have described their admirable achievements, as they deem them: how Kronos, for instance, mutilated his father, and hurled him down from his chariot, and how he murdered his children, and swallowed the males of them; and how Zeus bound his father, and cast him down to Tartarus, as did Ouranos also to his sons, and fought with the Titans for the government; and how he persecuted his mother Rhea when she refused to wed him, and, she becoming a she-dragon, and he himself being changed into a dragon, bound her with what is called the Herculean knot, and accomplished his purpose, of which fact the rod of Hermes is a symbol; and again, how he violated his daughter Phersephone, in this case also assuming the form of a dragon, and became the father of Dionysus. In face of narrations like these, I must say at least this much, What that is becoming or useful is there in such a history, that we must believe Kronos, Zeus, Kore, and the rest, to be gods? Is it the descriptions of their bodies? Why, what man of judgment and reflection will believe that a viper was begotten by a god (thus Orpheus:- "But from the sacred womb Phanes begat Another offspring, horrible and fierce, In sight a frightful viper, on whose head Were hairs: its face was comely; but the rest, From the neck downwards, bore the aspect dire Of a dread dragon"); or who will admit that Phanes himself, being a first-born god (for he it was that was produced from the egg), has the body or shape of a dragon, or was swallowed by Zeus, that Zeus might be too large to be contained? For if they differ in no respect from the lowest brutes (since it is evident that the Deity must differ from the things of earth and those that are derived from matter), they are not gods. How, then, I ask, can we approach them as suppliants, when their origin resembles that of cattle, and they themselves have the form of brutes, and are ugly to behold?

Chapter XXI: Impure loves ascribed to the gods.

But should it be said that they only had fleshly forms, and possess blood and seed, and the affections of anger and sexual desire, even then we must regard such assertions as nonsensical and ridiculous; for there is neither anger, nor desire and appetite, nor procreative seed, in gods. Let them, then, have fleshly forms, but let them be superior to wrath and anger, that Athena may not be seen "Burning with rage and inly wroth with Jove;" nor Hera appear thus:- "Juno's breast Could not contain her rage." And let them be superior to grief:- "A woful sight mine eyes behold: a man I love in flight around the walls! My heart For Hector grieves." For I call even men rude and stupid who give way to anger and grief. But when the "father of men and gods" mourns for his son,- "Woe, woe! that fate decrees my best belov'd Sarpedon, by Patroclus' hand to fall;" and is not able while he mourns to rescue him from his peril:- "The son of Jove, yet Jove preserv'd him not;" who would not blame the folly of those who, with tales like these, are lovers of the gods, or rather, live without any god? Let them have fleshly forms, but let not Aphrodite be wounded by Diomedes in her body: - "The haughty son of Tydeus, Diomed, Hath wounded me;" or by Ares in her soul:- "Me, awkward me, she scorns; and yields her charms To that fair lecher, the strong god of arms."

"The weapon pierced the flesh."

He who was terrible in battle, the ally of Zeus against the Titans, is shown to be weaker than Diomedes:- "He raged, as Mars, when brandishing his spear." Hush! Homer, a god never rages. But you describe the god to me as blood-stained, and the bane of mortals:- "Mars, Mars, the bane of mortals, stained with blood;" and you tell of his adultery and his bonds:- "Then, nothing loth, th' enamour'd fair he led, And sunk transported on the conscious bed. Down rushed the toils." Do they not pour forth impious stuff of this sort in abundance concerning the gods? Ouranos is mutilated; Kronos is bound, and thrust down to Tartarus; the Titans revolt; Styx dies in battle: yea, they even represent them as mortal; they are in love with one another; they are in love with human beings:- "AEneas, amid Ida's jutting peaks, Immortal Venus to Anchises bore." Are they not in love? Do they not suffer? Nay, verily, they are gods, and desire cannot touch them! Even though a god assume flesh in pursuance of a divine purpose," he is therefore the slave of desire.

"For never yet did such a flood of love, For goddess or for mortal, fill my soul; Not for Ixion's beauteous wife, who bore Pirithous, sage in council as the gods; Nor the neat-footed maiden Danae, A crisius' daughter, her who Perseus bore, Th' observ'd of all; nor noble Phoenix child; . . . . . . nor for Semele; Nor for Alcmena fair; . . . No, nor for Ceres, golden-tressed queen; Nor for Latona bright; nor for thyself."

He is created, he is perishable, with no trace of a god in him. Nay, they are even the hired servants of men:- "Admetus' halls, in which I have endured To praise the menial table, though a god."

And they tend cattle:- "And coming to this laud, I cattle fed, For him that was my host, and kept this house."

Admetus, therefore, was superior to the god. 0 prophet and wise one, and who canst foresee for others the things that shall be, thou didst not divine the slaughter of thy beloved, but didst even kill him with thine own hand, dear as he was:- "And I believed Apollo's mouth divine Was full of truth, as well as prophet's art.

(AEschylus is reproaching Apollo for being a false prophet:)- "The very one who slugs while at the feast, The one who said these things, alas! is he Who slew my son."

Chapter XXII: Pretended symbolical explanations.

But perhaps these things are poetic vagary, and there is some natural explanation of them, such as this by Empedocles:- "Let Jove be fire, and Juno source of life, With Pluto and Nestis, who bathes with tears The human founts." If, then, Zeus is fire, and Hera the earth, and Aidoneus the air, and Nestis water, and these are elements--fire, water, air--none of them is a god, neither Zeus, nor Hera, nor Aidoneus; for from matter separated into parts by God is their constitution and origin:- "Fire, water, earth, and the air's gentle height, And harmony with these."

Here are things which without harmony cannot abide; which would be brought to ruin by strife: how then can any one say that they are gods? Friendship, according to Empedocles, has an aptitude to govern, things that are compounded are governed, and that which is apt to govern has the dominion; so that if we make the power of the governed and the governing one and the same, we shall be, unawares to ourselves putting perishable and fluctuating and changeable matter on an equality with the uncreated, and eternal, and ever self- accordant God. Zeus is, according to the Stoics, the fervid part of nature; Hera is the air (ahr)--the very name, if it be joined to itself, signifying this; Poseidon is what is drunk (water, posis). But these things are by different persons explained of natural objects in different ways. Some call Zeus twofold masculine-feminine air; others the season which brings about mild weather, on which account it was that he alone escaped from Kronos. But to the Stoics it may be said, If you acknowledge one God, the supreme and uncreated and eternal One, and as many compound bodies as there are changes of matter, and say that the Spirit of God, which pervades matter, obtains according to its variations a diversity of names the forms of matter will become the body of God; but when the elements are destroyed in the conflagration, the names will necessarily perish along with the forms, the Spirit of God alone remaining. Who, then, can believe that those bodies, of which the variation according to matter is allied to corruption, are gods? But to those who say that Kronos is time, and Rhea the earth, and that she becomes pregnant by Kronos, and brings forth, whence she is regarded as the mother of all; and that he begets and devours his offspring; and that the mutilation is the intercourse of the male with the female, which cuts off the seed and casts it into the womb, and generates a human being, who has in himself the sexual desire, which is Aphrodite; and that the madness of Kronos is the turn of season, which destroys animate and inanimate things; and that the bonds and Tartarus are time, which is changed by seasons and disappears;--to such persons we say, If Kronos is time, he changes; if a season, he turns about; if darkness, or frost, or the moist part of nature, none of these is abiding; but the Deity is immortal, and immoveable, and unalterable: so that neither is Kronos nor his image God. As regards Zeus again: If he is air, born of Kronos, of which the male part is called Zeus and the female Hera (whence both sister and wife), he is subject to change; if a season, he turns about: but the Deity neither changes nor shifts about. But why should I trespass on your patience by saying more, when you know so well what has been said by each of those who have resolved these things into nature, or what various writers have thought concerning nature, or what they say concerning Athena, whom they affirm to be the wisdom (fronhsis) pervading all things; and concerning Isis, whom they call the birth of all time (fusis aiwnos), from whom all have sprung, and by whom all exist; or concerning Osiris, on whose murder by Typhon his brother Isis with her son Orus sought after his limbs, and finding them honoured them with a sepulchre, which sepulchre is to this day called the tomb of Osiris? For whilst they wander up and down about the forms of matter, they miss to find the God who can only be beheld by the reason, while they deify the elements and their several parts, applying different names to them at different times: calling the sowing of the corn, for instance, Osiris (hence they say, that in the mysteries, on the finding of the members of his body, or the fruits, Isis is thus addressed: We have found, we wish thee joy), the fruit of the vine Dionysus, the vine itself Semele, the heat of the sun the thunderbolt. And yet, in fact, they who refer the fables to actual gods, do anything rather than add to their divine character; for they do not perceive, that by the very defence they make for the gods, they confirm the things which are alleged concerning them. What have Europa, and the bull, and the swan, and Leda, to do with the earth and air, that the abominable intercourse of Zeus with them should be taken for the intercourse of the earth and air? But missing to discover the greatness of God, and not being able to rise on high with their reason (for they have no affinity for the heavenly place), they pine away among the forms of matter, and rooted to the earth, deify the changes of the elements: just as if any one should put the ship he sailed in the place of the steersman. But as the ship, although equipped with everything, is of no use if it have not a steersman, so neither are the elements, though arranged in perfect order, of any service apart from the providence of God. For the ship will not sail of itself; and the elements without their Framer will not move.

Chapter XXIII: Opinions of Thales and Plato.

You may say, however, since you excel all men in understanding, How comes it to pass, then, that some of the idols manifest power, if those to whom we erect the statues are not gods? For it is not likely that images destitute of life and motion can of themselves do anything without a mover. That in various places, cities, and nations, certain effects are brought about in the name of idols, we are far from denying. None the more, however, if some have received benefit, and others, on the contrary, suffered harm, shall we deem those to be gods who have produced the effects in either case. But I have made careful inquiry, both why it is that you think the idols to have this power, and who they are that, usurping their names, produce the effects. It is necessary for me, however, in attempting to show who they are that produce the effects ascribed to the idols, and that they are not gods, to have recourse to some witnesses from among the philosophers. First Thales, as those Who have accurately examined his opinions report, divides [superior beings] into God, demons, and heroes. God he recognises as the Intelligence (nous) of the world; by demons he understands beings possessed of Soul (yukikai); and by heroes the separated souls of men, the good being the good souls, and the bad the worthless. Plato again, while withholding his assent on other points, also divides [superior beings] into the uncreated God and those produced by' the uncreated One for the adornment of heaven, the planets, and the fixed stars, and into demons; concerning which demons, while he does not think fit to speak himself, he thinks that those ought to be listened to who have spoken about them. "To speak concerning the other demons, and to know their origin, is beyond our powers; but we ought to believe those who have before spoken, the descendants of gods, as they say--and surely they must be well acquainted with their own ancestors: it is impossible, therefore, to disbelieve the sons of gods, even though they speak without probable or convincing proofs; but as they profess to tell of their own family affairs, we are bound, in pursuance of custom, to believe them. In this way, then, let us hold and speak as they do concerning the origin of the gods themselves. Of Ge and Ouranos were born Oceanus and Tethys; and of these Phorcus, Kronos, and Rhea, and the rest; and of Kronos and Rhea, Zeus, Hera, and all the others, who, we know, are all called their brothers; besides other descendants again of these." Did, then, he who had contemplated the eternal Intelligence and God who is apprehended by reason, and declared His attributes--His real existence, the simplicity of His nature, the good that flows forth from Him that is truth, and discoursed of primal power, and how "all things are about the King of all, and all things exist for His sake, and He is the cause of all;" and about two and three, that He is "the second moving about the seconds, and the third about the thirds;" --did this man think, that to learn the truth concerning those who are said to have been produced from sensible things, namely earth and heaven, was a task transcending his powers? It is not to be believed for a moment. But because he thought it impossible to believe that gods beget and are brought forth, since everything that begins to be is followed by an end, and (for this is much more difficult) to change the views of the multitude, who receive the fables without examination, on this account it was that he declared it to be beyond his powers to know and to speak concerning the origin of the other demons, since he was unable either to admit or teach that gods were begotten. And as regards that saying of his, "The great sovereign in heaven, Zeus, driving a winged car, advances first, ordering and managing all things, and there follow him a host of gods and demons," this does not refer to the Zeus who is said to have sprung from Kronos; for here the name is given to the Maker of the universe. This is shown by Plato himself: not being able to designate Him by another title that should be suitable, he availed himself of the popular name, not as peculiar to God, but for distinctness, because it is not possible to discourse of God to all men as fully as one might; and he adds at the same time the epithet "Great," so as to distinguish the heavenly from the earthly, the uncreated from the created, who is younger than heaven and earth, and younger than the Cretans, who stole him away, that he might not be killed by his father.

Chapter XXIV: Concering the angels and giants.

What need is there, in speaking to you who have searched into every department of knowledge, to mention the poets, or to examine opinions of another kind? Let it suffice to say thus much. If the poets and philosophers did not acknowledge that there is one God, and concerning these gods were not of opinion, some that they are demons, others that they are matter, and others that they once were men, there might be some show of reason for our being harassed as we are, since we employ language which makes a distinction between God and matter, and the natures of the two. For, as we acknowledge a God, and a Son his Logos, and a Holy Spirit, united in essence,the Father, the Son, the Spirit, because the Son is the Intelligence, Reason, Wisdom of the Father, and the Spirit an effluence, as light from fire; so also do we apprehend the existence of other powers, which exercise dominion about matter, and by means of it, and one in particular, which is hostile to God: not that anything is really opposed to God, like strife to friendship, according to Empedocles, and night to day, according to the appearing and disappearing of the stars (for even if anything had placed itself in opposition to God, it would have ceased to exist, its structure being destroyed by-the power and might of God), but that to the good that is in God, which belongs of necessity to Him, and co-exists with Him, as colour with body, without which it has no existence (not as being part of it, but as an attendant property co-existing with it, united and blended, just as it is natural for fire to be yellow and the ether dark blue),--to the good that is in God, I say, the spirit which is about matter, who was created by God; just as the other angels were created by Him, and entrusted with the control of matter and the forms of matter, is opposed. For this is the office of the angels,--to exercise providence for God over the things created and ordered by Him; so that God may have the universal and general providence of the whole, while the particular parts are provided for by the angels appointed over them. Just as with men, who have freedom of choice as to both virtue and vice (for you would not either honour the good or punish the bad, unless vice and virtue were in their own power; and some are diligent in the matters entrusted to them by you, and others faithless), so is it among the angels. Some, free agents, you will observe, such as they were created by God, continued in those things for which God had made and over which He had ordained them; but some outraged both the constitution of their nature and the government entrusted to them: namely, this ruler of matter and its various forms, and others of those who were placed about this first firmament (you know that we say nothing without witnesses, but state the things which have been declared by the prophets); these fell into impure love of virgins, and were subjugated by the flesh, and he became negligent and wicked in the management of the things entrusted to him. Of these lovers of virgins, therefore, were begotten those who are called giants. And if something has been said by the poets, too, about the giants, be not surprised at this: worldly Wisdom and divine differ as much from each other as truth and plausibility: the one is of heaven and the other of earth; and indeed, according to the prince of matter,- "We know we oft speak lies that look like troths."

Chapter XXV: The poets and Philosophers have denied a divine providence.

These angels, then, who have fallen from heaven, and haunt the air and the earth, and are no longer able to rise to heavenly things, and the souls of the giants, which are the demons who wander about the world, perform actions similar, the one (that is, the demons) to the natures they have received, the other (that is, the angels) to the appetites they have indulged. But the prince of matter, as may be seen merely from what transpires, exercises a control and management contrary to the good that is in God:- "Ofttimes this anxious thought has crossed my mind, Whether 'tis chance or deity that rules The small affairs of men; and, spite of hope As well as justice, drives to exile some Stripped of all means of life, while others still Continue to enjoy prosperity."

Prosperity and adversity, contrary to hope and justice, made it impossible for Euripides to say to whom belongs the administration of earthly affairs, which is of such a kind that one might say of it:- "How then, while seeing these things, can we say There is a race of gods, or yield to laws?"

The same thing led Aristotle to say that the things below the heaven are not under the care of Providence, although the eternal providence of God concerns itself equally with us below, "The earth, let willingness move her or not, Must herbs produce, and thus sustain my flocks," - and addresses itself to the deserving individually, according to truth and not according to opinion; and all other things, according to the general constitution of nature, are provided for by the law of reason. But because the demoniac movements and operations proceeding from the adverse spirit produce these disorderly sallies, and moreover move men, some in one way and some in another, as individuals and as nations, separately and in common, in accordance with the tendency of matter on the one hand, and of the affinity for divine things on the other, from within and from without,--some who are of no mean reputation have therefore thought that this universe is constituted without any definite order, and is driven hither and thither by an irrational chance. But they do not understand, that of those things which belong to the constitution of the whole world there is nothing out of order or neglected, but that each one of them has been produced by reason, and that, therefore, they do not transgress the order prescribed to them; and that man himself, too, so far as He that made him is concerned, is well ordered, both by his original nature, which has one common character for all, and by the constitution of his body, which does not transgress the law imposed upon it, and by the termination of his life, which remains equal and common to all alike; but that, according to the character peculiar to himself and the operation of the ruling prince and of the demons his followers, he is impelled and moved in this direction or in that, notwithstanding that all possess in common the same original constitution of mind.

Chapter XXVI: The demons allure men to the worship of images.

They who draw men to idols, then, are the aforesaid demons, who are eager for the blood of the sacrifices, and lick them; but the gods that please the multitude, and whose names are given to the images, were men, as may be learned from their history. And that it is the demons who act under their names, is proved by the nature of their operations. For some castrate, as Rhea; others wound and slaughter, as Artemis; the Tauric goddess puts all strangers to death. I pass over those who lacerate with knives and scourges of bones, and shall not attempt to describe all the kinds of demons; for it is not the part of a god to incite to things against nature.

"But when the demon plots against a man, He first inflicts some hurt upon his mind."

But God, being perfectly good, is eternally doing good. That, moreover, those who exert the power are not the same as those to whom the statues are erected, very strong evidence is afforded by Troas and

Parium. The one has statues of Neryllinus, a man of our own times; and Parium of Alexander and Proteus: both the sepulchre and the statue of Alexander are still in the forum. The other statues of Neryllinus, then, are a public ornament, if indeed a city can be adorned by such objects as these; but one of them is supposed to utter oracles and to heal the sick, and on this account the people of the Troad offer sacrifices to this statue, and overlay it with gold, and hang chaplets upon it. But of the statues of Alexander and Proteus (the latter, you are aware, threw himself into the fire near Olympia), that of Proteus is likewise said to utter oracles; and to that of Alexander- "Wretched Paris, though in form so fair, Thou slave of woman" - sacrifices are offered and festivals are held at the public cost, as to a god who can hear. Is it, then, Neryllinus, and Proteus, and Alexander who exert these energies in connection with the statues, or is it the nature of the matter itself? But the matter is brass. And what can brass do of itself, which may be made again into a different form, as Amasis treated the footpan, as told by Herodotus? And Neryllinus, and Proteus, and Alexander, what good are they to the sick? For what the image is said now to effect, it effected when Neryllinus was alive and sick.

Chapter XXVII: Artifices of the demons.

What then? In the first place, the irrational and fantastic movements of the soul about opinions produce a diversity of images (eidwla) from time to time: some they derive from matter, and some they fashion and bring forth for themselves; and this happens to a soul especially when it par takes of the material spirit and becomes mingled with it, looking not at heavenly things and their Maker, but downwards to earthly things, wholly at the earth, as being now mere flesh and blood, and no longer pure spirit. These irrational and fantastic movements of the soul, then, give birth to empty visions in the mind, by which it becomes madly set on idols. When, too, a tender and susceptible soul, which has no knowledge or experience of sounder doctrines, and is unaccustomed to contemplate truth, and to consider thoughtfully the Father and Maker of all things, gets impressed with false opinions respecting itself, then the demons who hover about matter, greedy of sacrificial odours and the blood of victims, and ever ready to lead men into error, avail themselves of these delusive movements of the souls of the multitude; and, taking possession of their thoughts, cause to flow into the mind empty visions as if coming from the idols and the statues; and when, too, a soul of itself, as being immortal, moves comformably to reason, either predicting the future or healing the present, the demons claim the glory for themselves.

Chapter XXVIII: The heathen gods were simply men.

But it is perhaps necessary, in accordance with what has already been adduced, to say a little about their names. Herodotus, then, and Alexander the son of Philip, in his letter to his mother (and each of them is said to have conversed with the priests at Heliopolis, and Memphis, and Thebes), affirm that they learnt from them that the gods had been men. Herodotus speaks thus: "Of such a nature were, they said, the beings represented by these images, they were very far indeed from being gods. However, in the times anterior to them it was otherwise; then Egypt had gods for its rulers, who dwelt upon the earth with men, one being always supreme above the rest. The last of these was Horus the son of Osiris, called by the Greeks Apollo. He deposed Typhon, and ruled over Egypt as its last god-king. Osiris is named Dionysus (Bacchus) by the Greeks." "Almost all the names of the gods came into Greece from Egypt." Apollo was the son of Dionysus and Isis, as He rodotus likewise affirms: "According to the Egyptians, Apollo and Diana are the children of Bacchus and Isis; while Latona is their nurse and their preserver." These beings of heavenly origin they had for their first kings: partly from ignorance of the true worship of the Deity, partly from gratitude for their government, they esteemed them as gods together with their wives. "The male kine, if clean, and the male calves are used for sacrifice by the Egyptians universally; but the females, they are not allowed to sacrifice, since they are sacred to Isis. The statue of this goddess has the form of a woman but with horns like a cow, resembling those of the Greek representations of Io." And who can be more deserving of credit in making these statements, than those who in family succession son from father, received not only the priesthood, but also the history? For it is not likely that the priests, who make if their business to commend the idols to men's reverence, would assert falsely that they were men. If Herodotus alone had said that the Egyptians spoke in their histories of the gods as of men, when he says, "What they told me concerning their religion it is not my intention to repeat, except only the names of their deities, things of very trifling importance," it would behove us not to credit even Herodotus as being a fabulist. But as Alexander and Hermes surnamed Trismegistus, who shares with them in the attribute of eternity, and innumerable others, not to name them individually, [declare the same], no room is left even for doubt that they, being kings, were esteemed gods. That they were men, the most learned of the Egyptians also testify, who, while saying that ether, earth, sun, moon, are gods, regard the rest as mortal men, and the temples as their sepulchres. Apollodorus, too, asserts the same thing in his treatise concerning the gods.

But Herodotus calls even their sufferings mysteries. "The ceremonies at the feast of Isis in the city of Busiris have been already spoken of. It is there that the whole multitude, both of men and women, many thousands in number, beat them selves at the close of the sacrifice in honour of a god whose name a religious scruple forbids me to mention." If they are gods, they are also immortal; but if people are beaten for them, and their sufferings are mysteries, they are men, as Herodotus himself says: "Here, too, in this same precinct of Minerva at Sais, is the burial-place of one whom I think it not right to mention in such a connection. It stands behind the temple against the back wall, which it entirely covers. There are also some large stone obelisks in the enclosure, and there is a lake near them, adorned with an edging of stone. In form it is circular, and in size, as it seemed to me, about equal to the lake at Delos called the Hoop. On this lake it is that the Egyptians represent by night his sufferings whose name I refrain from mentioning, and this representation they call their mysteries." And not only is the sepulchre of Osiris shown, but also his embalming: "When a body is brought to them, they show the bearer various models of corpses made in wood, and painted so as to resemble nature. The most perfect is said to be after the manner of him whom I do not think it religious to name in connection with such a matter."

Chapter XXIX: Proof of the same from the poets.

But among the Greeks, also, those who are eminent in poetry and history say the same thing. Thus of Heracles:- "That lawless wretch, that man of brutal strength, Deaf to Heaven's voice, the social rite transgressed."

Such being his nature, deservedly did he go mad, and deservedly did he light the funeral pile and burn himself to death. Of Asklepius, Hesiod says:- "The mighty father both of gods and men Was filled with wrath, and from Olympus' top With flaming thunderbolt cast down and slew Latona's well-lov'd son--such was his ire."

And Pindar:- "But even wisdom is ensnared by gain.

The brilliant bribe of gold seen in the hand Ev'n him perverted: therefore Kronos' son With both hands quickly stopp'd his vital breath, And by a bolt of fire ensured his doom.'

Either, therefore, they were gods and did not hanker after gold- "O gold, the fairest prize to mortal men, Which neither mother equals in delight, Nor children dear" - for the Deity is in want of nought, and is superior to carnal desire, nor did they die; or, having been born men, they were wicked by reason of ignorance, and overcome by love of money. What more need I say, or refer to Castor, or Pollux, or Amphiaraus, who, having been born, so to speak, only the other day, men of men, are looked upon as gods, when they imagine even Ino after her madness and its consequent sufferings to have become a goddess?

"Sea-rovers will her name Leucothea."

And her son:- "August Palaemon, sailors will invoke."

Chapter XXX: Reasons why Divinity has been ascribed to men.

For if detestable and god-hated men had the reputation of being gods, and the daughter of Derceto, Semiramis, a lascivious and blood-stained woman, was esteemed a Syria goddess; and if, on account of Derceto, the Syrians worship doves and Semiramis (for, a thing impossible, a woman was changed into a dove: the story is in Ctesias), what wonder if some should be called gods by their people on the ground of their rule and sovereignty (the Sibyl, of whom Plato also makes mention, says:- "It was the generation then the tenth, Of men endow'd with speech, since forth the flood Had burst upon the men of former times, And Kronos, Japetus, and Titan reigned, Whom men, of Ouranos and Gaia Proclaimed the noblest sons, and named them so, Because of men endowed with gift of speech They were the first"); and others for their strength, as Heracles and Perseus; and others for their art, as Asclepius? Those, therefore, to whom either the subjects gave honour or the rulers themselves [assumed it], obtained the name, some from fear, others from revenge. Thus Antinous, through the benevolence of your ancestors towards their subjects, came to be regarded as a god. But those who came after adopted the worship without examination.

"The Cretans always lie; for they, O king, Have built a tomb to thee who art not dead."

Though you believe, O Callimachus, in the nativity of Zeus, you do not believe in his sepulchre; and whilst you think to obscure the truth, you in fact proclaim him dead, even to those who are ignorant; and if you see the cave, you call to mind the childbirth of Rhea; but when you see the coffin, you throw a shadow over his death, not considering that the unbegotten God alone is eternal. For either the tales told by the multitude and the poets about the gods are unworthy of credit, and the reverence shown them is superfluous (for those do not exist, the tales concerning whom are untrue); or if the births, the amours, the murders, the thefts, the castrations, the thunderbolts, are true, they no longer exist, having ceased to be since they were born, having previously had no being. And on what principle must we believe some things and disbelieve others, when the poets have written their stories in order to gain greater veneration for them? For surely those through whom they have got to be considered gods, and who have striven to represent their deeds as worthy of reverence, cannot have invented their sufferings. That, therefore, we are not atheists, acknowledging as we do God the Maker of this universe and His Logos, has been proved according to my ability, if not according to the importance of the subject.

Chapter XXXI: Confutation of the other charges brought against the Christians.

But they have further also made up stories against us of impious feasts and forbidden intercourse between the sexes, both that they may appear to themselves to have rational grounds of hatred, and because they think either by fear to lead us away from our way of life, or to render the rulers harsh and inexorable by the magnitude of the charges they bring. But they lose their labour with those who know that from of old it has been the custom, and not in our time only, for vice to make war on virtue. Thus Pythagoras, with three hundred others, was burnt to death; Heraclitus and Democritus were banished, the one from the city of the Ephesians, the other from Abdera, because he was charged with being mad; and the Athenians condemned Socrates to death. But as they were none the worse in respect of virtue because of the opinion of the multitude, so neither does the undiscriminating calumny of some persons cast any shade upon us as regards rectitude of life, for with God we stand in good repute. Nevertheless, I will meet these charges also, although I am well assured that by what has been already said I have cleared myself to you. For as you excel all men in intelligence, you know that those whose life is directed towards God as its rule, so that each one among us may be blameless and irreproachable before Him, will not entertain even the thought of the slightest sin. For if we believed that we should live only the present life, then we might be suspected of sinning, through being enslaved to flesh and blood, or overmastered by gain or carnal desire; but since we know that God is witness to what we think and what we say both by night and by day, and that He, being Himself light, sees all things in our heart, we are persuaded that when we are removed from the present life we shall live another life, better than the present one, and heavenly, not earthly (since we shall abide near God, and with God, free from all change or suffering in the soul, not as flesh, even though we shall have flesh, but as heavenly spirit), or, falling with the rest, a worse one and in fire; for God has not made us as sheep or beasts of burden, a mere by-work, and that we should perish and be annihilated. On these grounds it is not likely that we should wish to do evil, or deliver ourselves over to the great Judge to be punished.

Chapter XXXII: Elevated morality of the Christians.

It is, however, nothing wonderful that they should get up tales about us such as they tell of their own gods, of the incidents of whose lives they make mysteries. But it behoved them, if they meant to condemn shameless and promiscuous intercourse, to hate either Zeus, who begat children of his mother Rhea and his daughter Kore, and took his own sister to wife, or Orpheus, the inventor of these tales, which made Zeus more unholy and detestable than Thyestes himself; for the latter defiled his daughter in pursuance of an oracle, and when he wanted to obtain the kingdom and avenge himself. But we are so far from practising promiscuous intercourse, that it is not lawful among us to indulge even a lustful look. "For," saith He, "he that looketh on a woman to lust after her, hath committed adultery already in his heart." Those, then, who are forbidden to look at anything more than that for which God formed the eyes, which were intended to be a light to us, and to whom a wanton look is adultery, the eyes being made for other purposes, and who are to be called to account for their very thoughts, how can any one doubt that such persons practise self-control? For our account lies not with human laws, which a bad man can evade (at the outset I proved to you, sovereign lords, that our doctrine is from the teaching of God), but we have a law which makes the measure of rectitude to consist in dealing with our neighbour as ourselves. On this account, too, according to age, we recognise some as sons and daughters, others we regard as brothers and sisters, and to the more advanced in life we give the honour due to fathers and mothers. On behalf of those, then, to whom we apply the names of brothers and sisters, and other designations of relationship, we exercise the greatest care that their bodies should remain undefiled and uncorrupted; for the Logos again says to us, "If any one kiss a second time because it has given him pleasure, [he sins];" adding, "Therefore the kiss, or rather the salutation, should be given with the greatest care, since, if there be mixed with it the least defilement of thought, it excludes us from eternal life."

Chapter XXXIII: Chastity of the Christians with respect to marriage.

Therefore, having the hope of eternal life, we despise the things of this life, even to the pleasures of the soul, each of us reckoning her his wife whom he has married according to the laws laid down by us, and that only for the purpose of having children. For as the husbandman throwing the seed into the ground awaits the harvest, not sowing more upon it, so to us the procreation of children is the measure of our indulgence in appetite. Nay, you would find many among us, both men and women, growing old unmarried, in hope of living in closer communion with God. But if the remaining in virginity and in the state of an eunuch brings nearer to God, while the indulgence of carnal thought and desire leads away from Him, in those cases in which we shun the thoughts, much more do we reject the deeds. For we bestow our attention; not on the study of words, but on the exhibition and teaching of actions,--that a person should either remain as he was born, or be content with one marriage; for a second marriage is only a specious adultery. "For whosoever puts away his wife," says He, "and marries another, commits adultery;" not permitting a man to send her away whose virginity he has brought to an end, nor to marry again. For he who deprives himself of his first wife, even though she be dead, is a cloaked adulterer, resisting the hand of God, because in the beginning God made one man and one woman, and dissolving the strictest union of flesh with flesh, formed for the intercourse of the race.

Chapter XXXIV: The vast difference in morals between the Christians and their accusers.

But though such is our character (Oh! why should I speak of things unfit to be uttered?), the things said of us are an example of the proverb, "The harlot reproves the chaste." For those who have set up a market for fornication and established infamous resorts for the young for every kind of vile pleasure,--who do not abstain even from males, males with males committing shocking abominations, outraging all the noblest and comeliest bodies in all sorts of ways, so dishonouring the fair workmanship of God (for beauty on earth is not self-made, but sent hither by the hand and will of God),--these men, I say, revile us for the very things which they are conscious of themselves, and ascribe to their own gods, boasting of them as noble deeds, and worthy of the gods. These adulterers and paederasts defame the eunuchs and the once-married (while they themselves live like fishes; for these gulp down whatever fails in their way, and the stronger chases the weaker: and, in fact, this is to feed upon human flesh, to do violence in contravention of the very laws which you and your ancestors, with due care for all that is fair and right, have enacted), so that not even the governors of the provinces sent by you suffice for the hearing of the complaints against those, to whom it even is not lawful, when they are struck, not to offer themselves for more blows, nor when defamed not to bless: for it is not enough to be just (and justice is to return like for like), but it is incumbent on us to be good and patient of evil.

Chapter XXXV: The Christians condemn and detest all cruelty.

What man of sound mind, therefore, will affirm, while such is our character, that we are murderers? For we cannot eat human flesh till we have killed some one. The former charge, therefore, being false, if any one should ask them in regard to the second, whether they have seen what they assert, not one of them would be so barefaced as to say that he had. And yet we have slaves, some more and some fewer, by whom we could not help being seen; but even of these, not one has been found to invent even such things against us. For when they know that we cannot endure even to see a man put to death, though justly; who of them can accuse us of murder or cannibalism? Who does not reckon among the things of greatest interest the contests of gladiators and wild beasts, especially those which are given by you? But we, deeming that to see a man put to death is much the same as killing him, have abjured such spectacles. How, then, when we do not even look on, lest we should contract guilt and pollution, can we put people to death? And when we say that those women who use drugs to bring on abortion commit murder, and will have to give an account to God s for the abortion, on what principle should we commit murder? For it does not belong to the same person to regard the very foetus in the womb as a created being, and therefore an object of God's care, and when it has passed into life, to kill it; and not to expose an infant, because those who expose them are chargeable with child-murder, and on the other hand, when it has been reared to destroy it. But we are in all things always alike and the same, submitting ourselves to reason, and not ruling over it.

Chapter XXXVI: Bearing of the doctrine of the resurrection on the practices of the Christians.

Who, then, that believes in a resurrection, would make himself into a tomb for bodies that will rise again? For it is not the part of the same persons to believe that our bodies will rise again, and to eat them as if they would not; and to think that the earth will give back the bodies held by it, but that those which a man has entombed in himself will not be demanded back. On the contrary, it is reasonable to suppose, that those who think they shall have no account to give of the present life, ill or well spent, and that there is no resurrection, but calculate on the soul perishing with the body, and being as it were quenched in it, will refrain from no deed of daring; but as for those who are persuaded that nothing will escape the scrutiny of God, but that even the body which has ministered to the irrational impulses of the soul, and to its desires, will be punished along with it, it is not likely that they will commit even the smallest sin. But if to any one it appears sheer nonsense that the body which has mouldered away, and been dissolved, and reduced to nothing, should be reconstructed, we certainly cannot with any reason be accused of wickedness with reference to those that believe not, but only of folly; for with the opinions by which we deceive ourselves we injure no one else. But that it is not our belief alone that bodies will rise again, but that many philosophers also hold the same view, it is out of place to show just now, lest we should be thought to introduce topics irrelevant to the matter in hand, either by speaking of the intelligible and the sensible, and the nature of these respectively, or by contending that the incorporeal is older than the corporeal, and that the intelligible precedes the sensible, although we become acquainted with the latter earliest, since the corporeal is formed from the incorporeal, by the combination with it of the intelligible, and that the sensible is formed from the intelligible; for nothing hinders, according to Pythagoras and Plato, that when the dissolution of bodies takes place, they should, from the very same elements of which they were constructed at first, be constructed again. But let us defer the discourse concerning the resurrection.

Chapter XXXVII: Entreaty to be fairly judged.

And now do you, who are entirely in everything, by nature and by education, upright, and moderate, and benevolent, and worthy of your rule, now that I have disposed of the several accusations, and proved that we are pious, and gentle, and temperate in spirit, bend your royal head in approval. For who are more deserving to obtain the things they ask, than those who, like us, pray for your government, that you may, as is most equitable, receive the kingdom, son from father, and that your empire may receive increase and addition, all men becoming subject to your sway? And this is also for our advantage, that we may lead a peaceable and quiet life, and may ourselves readily perform all that is commanded us.

EPISTLE TO DIOGNETUS

Unknown

TRANSLATED BY ALEXANDER ROBERTS AND JAMES DONALDSON

Chapter 1. Occasion of the epistle

Since I see you, most excellent Diognetus, exceedingly desirous to learn the mode of worshipping God prevalent among the Christians, and inquiring very carefully and earnestly concerning them, what God they trust in, and what form of religion they observe, so as all to look down upon the world itself, and despise death, while they neither esteem those to be gods that are reckoned such by the Greeks, nor hold to the superstition of the Jews; and what is the affection which they cherish among themselves; and finally, why this new kind or practice [of piety] has only now entered into the world, and not long ago; I cordially welcome this your desire, and I implore God, who enables us both to speak and to hear, to grant to me so to speak, that, above all, I may hear you have been edified, and to you so to hear, that I who speak may have no cause of regret for having done so.

Chapter 2. The vanity of idols

Come, then, after you have freed yourself from all prejudices possessing your mind, and laid aside what you have been accustomed to, as something apt to deceive you, and being made, as if from the beginning, a new man, inasmuch as, according to your own confession, you are to be the hearer of a new [system of] doctrine; come and contemplate, not with your eyes only, but with your understanding, the substance and the form of those whom you declare and deem to be gods.

Is not one of them a stone similar to that on which we tread? Is not a second brass, in no way superior to those vessels which are constructed for our ordinary use? Is not a third wood, and that already rotten? Is not a fourth silver, which needs a man to watch it, lest it be stolen? Is not a fifth iron, consumed by rust? Is not a sixth earthenware, in no degree more valuable than that which is formed for the humblest purposes?

Are not all these of corruptible matter? Are they not fabricated by means of iron and fire? Did not the sculptor fashion one of them, the brazier a second, the silversmith a third, and the potter a fourth? Was not every one of them, before they were formed by the arts of these [workmen] into the shape of these [gods], each in its own way subject to change? Would not those things which are now vessels, formed of the same materials, become like to such, if they met with the same artificers? Might not these, which are now worshipped by you, again be made by men vessels similar to others? Are they not all deaf? Are they not blind? Are they not without life? Are they not destitute of feeling? Are they not incapable of motion? Are they not all liable to rot? Are they not all corruptible?

These things you call gods; these you serve; these you worship; and you become altogether like them. For this reason you hate the Christians, because they do not deem these to be gods. But do not you yourselves, who now think and suppose [such to be gods], much more cast contempt upon them than they [the Christians do]? Do you not much more mock and insult them, when you worship those that are made of stone and earthenware, without appointing any persons to guard them; but those made of silver and gold you shut up by night, and appoint watchers to look after them by day, lest they be stolen? And by those gifts which you mean to present to them, do you not, if they are possessed of sense, rather punish [than honour] them? But if, on the other hand, they are destitute of sense, you convict them of this fact, while you worship them with blood and the smoke of sacrifices. Let any one of you suffer such indignities! Let any one of you endure to have such things done to himself! But not a single human being will, unless compelled to it, endure such treatment, since he is endowed with sense and reason. A stone, however, readily bears it, seeing it is insensible. Certainly you do not show [by your conduct] that he [your God] is possessed of sense. And as to the fact that Christians are not accustomed to serve such gods, I might easily find many other things to say; but if even what has been said does not seem to any one sufficient, I deem it idle to say anything further.

Chapter 3. Superstitions of the Jews

And next, I imagine that you are most desirous of hearing something on this point, that the Christians do not observe the same forms of divine worship as do the Jews. The Jews, then, if they abstain from the kind of service above described, and deem it proper to worship one God as being Lord of all, [are right]; but if they offer Him worship in the way which we have described, they greatly err. For while the Gentiles, by offering such things to those that are destitute of sense and hearing, furnish an example of madness; they, on the other hand by thinking to offer these things to God as if He needed them, might justly reckon it rather an act of folly than of divine worship. For He that made heaven and earth, and all that is therein, and gives to us all the things of which we stand in need, certainly requires none of those things which He Himself bestows on such as think of furnishing them to Him. But those who imagine that, by means of blood, and the smoke of sacrifices and burnt-offerings, they offer sacrifices [acceptable] to Him, and that by such honours they show Him respect, — these, by supposing that they can give anything to Him who stands in need of nothing, appear to me in no respect to differ from those who studiously confer the same honour on things destitute of sense, and which therefore are unable to enjoy such honours.

Chapter 4. The other observances of the Jews

But as to their scrupulosity concerning meats, and their superstition as respects the Sabbaths, and their boasting about circumcision, and their fancies about fasting and the new moons, which are utterly ridiculous and unworthy of notice—I do not think that you require to learn anything from me. For, to accept some of those things which have been formed by God for the use of men as properly formed, and to reject others as useless and redundant—how can this be lawful? And to speak falsely of God, as if He forbade us to do what is good on the Sabbath-days—how is not this impious? And to glory in the circumcision of the flesh as a proof of election, and as if, on account of it, they were specially beloved by God—how is it not a subject of ridicule? And as to their observing months and days, Galatians 4:10 as if waiting upon the stars and the moon, and their distributing, according to their own tendencies, the appointments of God, and the vicissitudes of the seasons, some for festivities, and others for mourning—who would deem this a part of divine worship, and not much rather a manifestation of folly? I suppose, then, you are sufficiently convinced that the Christians properly abstain from the vanity and error common [to both Jews and Gentiles], and from the busybody spirit and vain boasting of the Jews; but you must not hope to learn the mystery of their peculiar mode of worshipping God from any mortal.

Chapter 5. The manners of the Christians

For the Christians are distinguished from other men neither by country, nor language, nor the customs which they observe. For they neither inhabit cities of their own, nor employ a peculiar form of speech, nor lead a life which is marked out by any singularity. The course of conduct which they follow has not been devised by any speculation or deliberation of inquisitive men; nor do they, like some, proclaim themselves the advocates of any merely human doctrines. But, inhabiting Greek as well as barbarian cities, according as the lot of each of them has determined, and following the customs of the natives in respect to clothing, food, and the rest of their ordinary conduct, they display to us their wonderful and confessedly striking method of life. They dwell in their own countries, but simply as sojourners. As citizens, they share in all things with others, and yet endure all things as if foreigners. Every foreign land is to them as their native country, and every land of their birth as a land of strangers. They marry, as do all [others]; they beget children; but they do not destroy their offspring. They have a common table, but not a common bed. They are in the flesh, but they do not live after the flesh. 2 Corinthians 10:3 They pass their days on earth, but they are citizens of heaven. Philippians 3:20 They obey the prescribed laws, and at the same time surpass the laws by their lives. They love all men, and are persecuted by all. They are unknown and condemned; they are put to death, and restored to life. 2 Corinthians 6:9 They are poor, yet make many rich; 2 Corinthians 6:10 they are in lack of all things, and yet abound in all; they are dishonoured, and yet in their very dishonour are glorified. They are evil spoken of, and yet are justified; they are reviled, and bless; 2 Corinthians 4:12 they are insulted, and repay the insult with honour; they do good, yet are punished as evil-doers. When punished, they rejoice as if quickened into life; they are assailed by the Jews as foreigners, and are persecuted by the Greeks; yet those who hate them are unable to assign any reason for their hatred.

Chapter 6. The relation of Christians to the world

To sum up all in one word— what the soul is in the body, Christians are in the world. The soul is dispersed through all the members of the body, and Christians are scattered through all the cities of the world. The soul dwells in the body, yet is not of the body; and Christians dwell in the world, yet are not of the world. The invisible soul is guarded by the visible body, and Christians are known indeed to be in the world, but their godliness remains invisible. The flesh hates the soul, and wars against it, 1 Peter 2:11 though itself suffering no injury, because it is prevented from enjoying pleasures; the world also hates the Christians, though in nowise injured, because they abjure pleasures. The soul loves the flesh that hates it, and [loves also] the members; Christians likewise love those that hate them. The soul is imprisoned in the body, yet preserves that very body; and Christians are confined in the world as in a prison, and yet they are the preservers of the world. The immortal soul dwells in a mortal tabernacle; and Christians dwell as sojourners in corruptible [bodies], looking for an incorruptible dwelling in the heavens. The soul, when but ill-provided with food and drink, becomes better; in like manner, the Christians, though subjected day by day to punishment, increase the more in number. God has assigned them this illustrious position, which it were unlawful for them to forsake.

Chapter 7. The manifestation of Christ

For, as I said, this was no mere earthly invention which was delivered to them, nor is it a mere human system of opinion, which they judge it right to preserve so carefully, nor has a dispensation of mere human mysteries been committed to them, but truly God Himself, who is almighty, the Creator of all things, and invisible, has sent from heaven, and placed among men, [Him who is] the truth, and the holy and incomprehensible Word, and has firmly established Him in their hearts. He did not, as one might have imagined, send to men any servant, or angel, or ruler, or any one of those who bear sway over earthly things, or one of those to whom the government of things in the heavens has been entrusted, but the very Creator and Fashioner of all things— by whom He made the heavens— by whom he enclosed the sea within its proper bounds— whose ordinances all the stars faithfully observe— from whom the sun has received the measure of his daily course to be observed — whom the moon obeys, being commanded to shine in the night, and whom the stars also obey, following the moon in her course; by whom all things have been arranged, and placed within their proper limits, and to whom all are subject— the heavens and the things that are therein, the earth and the things that are therein, the sea and the things that are therein— fire, air, and the abyss— the things which are in the heights, the things which are in the depths, and the things which lie between. This [messenger] He sent to them. Was it then, as one might conceive, for the purpose of exercising tyranny, or of inspiring fear and terror? By no means, but under the influence of clemency and meekness.

As a king sends his son, who is also a king, so sent He Him; as God He sent Him; as to men He sent Him; as a Saviour He sent Him, and as seeking to persuade, not to compel us; for violence has no place in the character of God. As calling us He sent Him, not as vengefully pursuing us; as loving us He sent Him, not as judging us. For He will yet send Him to judge us, and who shall endure His appearing? ... Do you not see them exposed to wild beasts, that they may be persuaded to deny the Lord, and yet not overcome? Do you not see that the more of them are punished, the greater becomes the number of the rest? This does not seem to be the work of man: this is the power of God; these are the evidences of His manifestation.

Chapter 8. The miserable state of men before the coming of the Word

For, who of men at all understood before His coming what God is? Do you accept of the vain and silly doctrines of those who are deemed trustworthy philosophers? Of whom some said that fire was God, calling that God to which they themselves were by and by to come; and some water; and others some other of the elements formed by God. But if any one of these theories be worthy of approbation, every one of the rest of created things might also be declared to be God. But such declarations are simply the startling and erroneous utterances of deceivers; and no man has either seen Him, or made Him known, but He has revealed Himself. And He has manifested Himself through faith, to which alone it is given to behold God. For God, the Lord and Fashioner of all things, who made all things, and assigned them their several positions, proved Himself not merely a friend of mankind, but also long-suffering [in His dealings with them]. Yea, He was always of such a character, and still is, and will ever be, kind and good, and free from wrath, and true, and the only one who is [absolutely] good; Matthew 19:17 and He formed in His mind a great and unspeakable conception, which He communicated to His Son alone. As long, then, as He held and preserved His own wise counsel in concealment, He appeared to neglect us, and to have no care over us. But after He revealed and laid open, through His beloved Son, the things which had been prepared from the beginning, He conferred every blessing all at once upon us, so that we should both share in His benefits, and see and be active [in His service]. Who of us would ever have expected these things? He was aware, then, of all things in His own mind, along with His Son, according to the relation subsisting between them.

Chapter 9. Why the Son was sent so late

As long then as the former time endured, He permitted us to be borne along by unruly impulses, being drawn away by the desire of pleasure and various lusts. This was not that He at all delighted in our sins, but that He simply endured them; nor that He approved the time of working iniquity which then was, but that He sought to form a mind conscious of righteousness, so that being convinced in that time of our unworthiness of attaining life through our own works, it should now, through the kindness of God, be vouchsafed to us; and having made it manifest that in ourselves we were unable to enter into the kingdom of God, we might through the power of God be made able. But when our wickedness had reached its height, and it had been clearly shown that its reward, punishment and death, was impending over us; and when the time had come which God had before appointed for manifesting His own kindness and power, how the one love of God, through exceeding regard for men, did not regard us with hatred, nor thrust us away, nor remember our iniquity against us, but showed great long-suffering, and bore with us, He Himself took on Him the burden of our iniquities, He gave His own Son as a ransom for us, the holy One for transgressors, the blameless One for the wicked, the righteous One for the unrighteous, the incorruptible One for the corruptible, the immortal One for those who are mortal. For what other thing was capable of covering our sins than His righteousness? By what other one was it possible that we, the wicked and ungodly, could be justified, than by the only Son of God? O sweet exchange! O unsearchable operation! O benefits surpassing all expectation! That the wickedness of many should be hid in a single righteous One, and that the righteousness of One should justify many transgressors! Having therefore convinced us in the former time that our nature was unable to attain to life, and having now revealed the Saviour who is able to save even those things which it was [formerly] impossible to save, by both these facts He desired to lead us to trust in His kindness, to esteem Him our Nourisher, Father, Teacher, Counsellor, Healer, our Wisdom, Light, Honour, Glory, Power, and Life, so that we should not be anxious concerning clothing and food.

Chapter 10. The blessings that will flow from faith

If you also desire [to possess] this faith, you likewise shall receive first of all the knowledge of the Father. For God has loved mankind, on whose account He made the world, to whom He rendered subject all the things that are in it, to whom He gave reason and understanding, to whom alone He imparted the privilege of looking upwards to Himself, whom He formed after His own image, to whom He sent His only-begotten Son, to whom He has promised a kingdom in heaven, and will give it to those who have loved Him. And when you have attained this knowledge, with what joy do you think you will be filled? Or, how will you love Him who has first so loved you? And if you love Him, you will be an imitator of His kindness. And do not wonder that a man may become an imitator of God. He can, if he is willing. For it is not by ruling over his neighbours, or by seeking to hold the supremacy over those that are weaker, or by being rich, and showing violence towards those that are inferior, that happiness is found; nor can any one by these things become an imitator of God. But these things do not at all constitute His majesty. On the contrary he who takes upon himself the burden of his neighbour; he who, in whatsoever respect he may be superior, is ready to benefit another who is deficient; he who, whatsoever things he has received from God, by distributing these to the needy, becomes a god to those who receive [his benefits]: he is an imitator of God. Then you shall see, while still on earth, that God in the heavens rules over [the universe]; then you shall begin to speak the mysteries of God; then shall you both love and admire those that suffer punishment because they will not deny God; then shall you condemn the deceit and error of the world when you shall know what it is to live truly in heaven, when you shall despise that which is here esteemed to be death, when you shall fear what is truly death, which is reserved for those who shall be condemned to the eternal fire, which shall afflict those even to the end that are committed to it. Then shall you admire those who for righteousness' sake endure the fire that is but for a moment, and shall count them happy when you shall know [the nature of] that fire.

Chapter 11. These things are worthy to be known and believed

I do not speak of things strange to me, nor do I aim at anything inconsistent with right reason; but having been a disciple of the Apostles, I have become a teacher of the Gentiles. I minister the things delivered to me to those that are disciples worthy of the truth. For who that is rightly taught and begotten by the loving Word, would not seek to learn accurately the things which have been clearly shown by the Word to His disciples, to whom the Word being manifested has revealed them, speaking plainly [to them], not understood indeed by the unbelieving, but conversing with the disciples, who, being esteemed faithful by Him, acquired a knowledge of the mysteries of the Father? For which reason He sent the Word, that He might be manifested to the world; and He, being despised by the people [of the Jews], was, when preached by the Apostles, believed on by the Gentiles. This is He who was from the beginning, who appeared as if new, and was found old, and yet who is ever born afresh in the hearts of the saints. This is He who, being from everlasting, is today called the Son; through whom the Church is enriched, and grace, widely spread, increases in the saints, furnishing understanding, revealing mysteries, announcing times, rejoicing over the faithful, giving to those that seek, by whom the limits of faith are not broken through, nor the boundaries set by the fathers passed over. Then the fear of the law is chanted, and the grace of the prophets is known, and the faith of the gospels is established, and the tradition of the Apostles is preserved, and the grace of the Church exults; which grace if you grieve not, you shall know those things which the Word teaches, by whom He wills, and when He pleases. For whatever things we are moved to utter by the will of the Word commanding us, we communicate to you with pains, and from a love of the things that have been revealed to us.

Chapter 12. The importance of knowledge to true spiritual life

When you have read and carefully listened to these things, you shall know what God bestows on such as rightly love Him, being made [as you are] a paradise of delight, presenting in yourselves a tree bearing all kinds of produce and flourishing well, being adorned with various fruits. For in this place the tree of knowledge and the tree of life have been planted; but it is not the tree of knowledge that destroys— it is disobedience that proves destructive. Nor truly are those words without significance which are written, how God from the beginning planted the tree of life in the midst of paradise, revealing through knowledge the way to life, and when those who were first formed did not use this [knowledge] properly, they were, through the fraud of the Serpent, stripped naked. For neither can life exist without knowledge, nor is knowledge secure without life. Wherefore both were planted close together. The Apostle, perceiving the force [of this conjunction], and blaming that knowledge which, without true doctrine, is admitted to influence life, declares, Knowledge puffs up, but love edifies. For he who thinks he knows anything without true knowledge, and such as is witnessed to by life, knows nothing, but is deceived by the Serpent, as not loving life. But he who combines knowledge with fear, and seeks after life, plants in hope, looking for fruit. Let your heart be your wisdom; and let your life be true knowledge inwardly received. Bearing this tree and displaying its fruit, you shall always gather in those things which are desired by God, which the Serpent cannot reach, and to which deception does not approach; nor is Eve then corrupted, but is trusted as a virgin; and salvation is manifested, and the Apostles are filled with understanding, and the Passover of the Lord advances, and the choirs are gathered together, and are arranged in proper order, and the Word rejoices in teaching the saints—by whom the Father is glorified: to whom be glory for ever. Amen.

FIRST APOLOGY

Justin Martyr

TRANSLATED BY MARCUS DODS AND GEORGE REITH

Chapter 1. Address

To the Emperor Titus Ælius Adrianus Antoninus Pius Augustus Cæsar, and to his son Verissimus the Philosopher, and to Lucius the Philosopher, the natural son of Cæsar, and the adopted son of Pius, a lover of learning, and to the sacred Senate, with the whole People of the Romans, I, Justin, the son of Priscus and grandson of Bacchius, natives of Flavia Neapolis in Palestine, present this address and petition in behalf of those of all nations who are unjustly hated and wantonly abused, myself being one of them.

Chapter 2. Justice demanded

Reason directs those who are truly pious and philosophical to honour and love only what is true, declining to follow traditional opinions, if these be worthless. For not only does sound reason direct us to refuse the guidance of those who did or taught anything wrong, but it is incumbent on the lover of truth, by all means, and if death be threatened, even before his own life, to choose to do and say what is right. Do you, then, since you are called pious and philosophers, guardians of justice and lovers of learning, give good heed, and hearken to my address; and if you are indeed such, it will be manifested. For we have come, not to flatter you by this writing, nor please you by our address, but to beg that you pass judgment, after an accurate and searching investigation, not flattered by prejudice or by a desire of pleasing superstitious men, nor induced by irrational impulse or evil rumours which have long been prevalent, to give a decision which will prove to be against yourselves. For as for us, we reckon that no evil can be done us, unless we be convicted as evil- doers or be proved to be wicked men; and you, you can kill, but not hurt us.

Chapter 3. Claim of judicial investigation

But lest any one think that this is an unreasonable and reckless utterance, we demand that the charges against the Christians be investigated, and that, if these be substantiated, they be punished as they deserve; [or rather, indeed, we ourselves will punish them.] But if no one can convict us of anything, true reason forbids you, for the sake of a wicked rumour, to wrong blameless men, and indeed rather yourselves, who think fit to direct affairs, not by judgment, but by passion. And every sober-minded person will declare this to be the only fair and equitable adjustment, namely, that the subjects render an unexceptional account of their own life and doctrine; and that, on the other hand, the rulers should give their decision in obedience, not to violence and tyranny, but to piety and philosophy. For thus would both rulers and ruled reap benefit. For even one of the ancients somewhere said, "Unless both rulers and ruled philosophize, it is impossible to make states blessed." It is our task, therefore, to afford to all an opportunity of inspecting our life and teachings, lest, on account of those who are accustomed to be ignorant of our affairs, we should incur the penalty due to them for mental blindness; and it is your business, when you hear us, to be found, as reason demands, good judges. For if, when you have learned the truth, you do not what is just, you will be before God without excuse.

Chapter 4. Christians unjustly condemned for their mere name

By the mere application of a name, nothing is decided, either good or evil, apart from the actions implied in the name; and indeed, so far at least as one may judge from the name we are accused of, we are most excellent people. But as we do not think it just to beg to be acquitted on account of the name, if we be convicted as evil-doers, so, on the other hand, if we be found to have committed no offense, either in the matter of thus naming ourselves, or of our conduct as citizens, it is your part very earnestly to guard against incurring just punishment, by unjustly punishing those who are not convicted. For from a name neither praise nor punishment could reasonably spring, unless something excellent or base in action be proved. And those among yourselves who are accused you do not punish before they are convicted; but in our case you receive the name as proof against us, and this although, so far as the name goes, you ought rather to punish our accusers. For we are accused of being Christians, and to hate what is excellent (Chrestian) is unjust. Again, if any of the accused deny the name, and say that he is not a Christian, you acquit him, as having no evidence against him as a wrong-doer; but if any one acknowledge that he is a Christian, you punish him on account of this acknowledgment. Justice requires that you inquire into the life both of him who confesses and of him who denies, that by his deeds it may be apparent what kind of man each is. For as some who have been taught by the Master, Christ, not to deny Him, give encouragement to others when they are put to the question, so in all probability do those who lead wicked lives give occasion to those who, without consideration, take upon them to accuse all the Christians of impiety and wickedness. And this also is not right. For of philosophy, too, some assume the name and the garb who do nothing worthy of their profession; and you are well aware, that those of the ancients whose opinions and teachings were quite diverse, are yet all called by the one name of philosophers. And of these some taught atheism; and the poets who have flourished among you raise a laugh out of the uncleanness of Jupiter with his own children. And those who now adopt such instruction are not restrained by you; but, on the contrary, you bestow prizes and honours upon those who euphoniously insult the gods.

Chapter 5. Christians charged with atheism

Why, then, should this be? In our case, who pledge ourselves to do no wickedness, nor to hold these atheistic opinions, you do not examine the charges made against us; but, yielding to unreasoning passion, and to the instigation of evil demons, you punish us without consideration or judgment. For the truth shall be spoken; since of old these evil demons, effecting apparitions of themselves, both defiled women and corrupted boys, and showed such fearful sights to men, that those who did not use their reason in judging of the actions that were done, were struck with terror; and being carried away by fear, and not knowing that these were demons, they called them gods, and gave to each the name which each of the demons chose for himself. And when Socrates endeavoured, by true reason and examination, to bring these things to light, and deliver men from the demons, then the demons themselves, by means of men who rejoiced in iniquity, compassed his death, as an atheist and a profane person, on the charge that "he was introducing new divinities;" and in our case they display a similar activity. For not only among the Greeks did reason (Logos) prevail to condemn these things through Socrates, but also among the Barbarians were they condemned by Reason (or the Word, the Logos) Himself, who took shape, and became man, and was called Jesus Christ; and in obedience to Him, we not only deny that they who did such things as these are gods, but assert that they are wicked and impious demons, whose actions will not bear comparison with those even of men desirous of virtue.

Chapter 6. Charge of atheism refuted

Hence are we called atheists. And we confess that we are atheists, so far as gods of this sort are concerned, but not with respect to the most true God, the Father of righteousness and temperance and the other virtues, who is free from all impurity. But both Him, and the Son (who came forth from Him and taught us these things, and the host of the other good angels who follow and are made like to Him), and the prophetic Spirit, we worship and adore, knowing them in reason and truth, and declaring without grudging to every one who wishes to learn, as we have been taught.

Chapter 7. Each Christian must be tried by his own life

But some one will say, Some have ere now been arrested and convicted as evil-doers. For you condemn many, many a time, after inquiring into the life of each of the accused severally, but not on account of those of whom we have been speaking. And this we acknowledge, that as among the Greeks those who teach such theories as please themselves are all called by the one name "Philosopher", though their doctrines be diverse, so also among the Barbarians this name on which accusations are accumulated is the common property of those who are and those who seem wise. For all are called Christians. Wherefore we demand that the deeds of all those who are accused to you be judged, in order that each one who is convicted may be punished as an evil-doer, and not as a Christian; and if it is clear that any one is blameless, that he may be acquitted, since by the mere fact of his being a Christian he does no wrong. For we will not require that you punish our accusers; they being sufficiently punished by their present wickedness and ignorance of what is right.

Chapter 8. Christians confess their faith in God

And reckon that it is for your sakes we have been saying these things; for it is in our power, when we are examined, to deny that we are Christians; but we would not live by telling a lie. For, impelled by the desire of the eternal and pure life, we seek the abode that is with God, the Father and Creator of all, and hasten to confess our faith, persuaded and convinced as we are that they who have proved to God by their works that they followed Him, and loved to abide with Him where there is no sin to cause disturbance, can obtain these things. This, then, to speak shortly, is what we expect and have learned from Christ, and teach. And Plato, in like manner, used to say that Rhadamanthus and Minos would punish the wicked who came before them; and we say that the same thing will be done, but at the hand of Christ, and upon the wicked in the same bodies united again to their spirits which are now to undergo everlasting punishment; and not only, as Plato said, for a period of a thousand years. And if any one say that this is incredible or impossible, this error of ours is one which concerns ourselves only, and no other person, so long as you cannot convict us of doing any harm.

[margin handwriting: What about the thief on the Cross?]

Chapter 9. Folly of idol worship

And neither do we honour with many sacrifices and garlands of flowers such deities as men have formed and set in shrines and called gods; since we see that these are soulless and dead, and have not the form of God (for we do not consider that God has such a form as some say that they imitate to His honour), but have the names and forms of those wicked demons which have appeared. For why need we tell you who already know, into what forms the craftsmen, (Isaiah 44:9-20; Jeremiah 10:3.) carving and cutting, casting and hammering, fashion the materials? And often out of vessels of dishonour, by merely changing the form, and making an image of the requisite shape, they make what they call a god; which we consider not only senseless, but to be even insulting to God, who, having ineffable glory and form, thus gets His name attached to things that are corruptible, and require constant service. And that the artificers of these are both intemperate, and, not to enter into particulars, are practised in every vice, you very well know; even their own girls who work along with them they corrupt. What infatuation! That dissolute men should be said to fashion and make gods for your worship, and that you should appoint such men the guardians of the temples where they are enshrined; not recognising that it is unlawful even to think or say that men are the guardians of gods.

Chapter 10. How God is to be served

But we have received by tradition that God does not need the material offerings which men can give, seeing, indeed, that He Himself is the provider of all things. And we have been taught, and are convinced, and do believe, that He accepts those only who imitate the excellences which reside in Him, temperance, and justice, and philanthropy, and as many virtues as are peculiar to a God who is called by no proper name. And we have been taught that He in the beginning did of His goodness, for man's sake, create all things out of unformed matter; and if men by their works show themselves worthy of this His design, they are deemed worthy, and so we have received— of reigning in company with Him, being delivered from corruption and suffering. For as in the beginning He created us when we were not, so do we consider that, in like manner, those who choose what is pleasing to Him are, on account of their choice, deemed worthy of incorruption and of fellowship with Him. For the coming into being at first was not in our own power; and in order that we may follow those things which please Him, choosing them by means of the rational faculties He has Himself endowed us with, He both persuades us and leads us to faith. And we think it for the advantage of all men that they are not restrained from learning these things, but are even urged thereto. For the restraint which human laws could not effect, the Word, inasmuch as He is divine, would have effected, had not the wicked demons, taking as their ally the lust of wickedness which is in every man, and which draws variously to all manner of vice, scattered many false and profane accusations, none of which attach to us.

Chapter 11. What kingdom Christians look for

And when you hear that we look for a kingdom, you suppose, without making any inquiry, that we speak of a human kingdom; whereas we speak of that which is with God, as appears also from the confession of their faith made by those who are charged with being Christians, though they know that death is the punishment awarded to him who so confesses. For if we looked for a human kingdom, we should also deny our Christ, that we might not be slain; and we should strive to escape detection, that we might obtain what we expect. But since our thoughts are not fixed on the present, we are not concerned when men cut us off; since also death is a debt which must at all events be paid.

Chapter 12. Christians live as under God's eye

And more than all other men are we your helpers and allies in promoting peace, seeing that we hold this view, that it is alike impossible for the wicked, the covetous, the conspirator, and for the virtuous, to escape the notice of God, and that each man goes to everlasting punishment or salvation according to the value of his actions. For if all men knew this, no one would choose wickedness even for a little, knowing that he goes to the everlasting punishment of fire; but would by all means restrain himself, and adorn himself with virtue, that he might obtain the good gifts of God, and escape the punishments. For those who, on account of the laws and punishments you impose, endeavour to escape detection when they offend (and they offend, too, under the impression that it is quite possible to escape your detection, since you are but men), those persons, if they learned and were convinced that nothing, whether actually done or only intended, can escape the knowledge of God, would by all means live decently on account of the penalties threatened, as even you yourselves will admit. But you seem to fear lest all men become righteous, and you no longer have any to punish. Such would be the concern of public executioners, but not of good princes. But, as we before said, we are persuaded that these things are prompted by evil spirits, who demand sacrifices and service even from those who live unreasonably; but as for you, we presume that you who aim at [a reputation for] piety and philosophy will do nothing unreasonable. But if you also, like the foolish, prefer custom to truth, do what you have power to do. But just so much power have rulers who esteem opinion more than truth, as robbers have in a desert. And that you will not succeed is declared by the Word, than whom, after God who begot Him, we know there is no ruler more kingly and just. For as all shrink from succeeding to the poverty or sufferings or obscurity of their fathers, so whatever the Word forbids us to choose, the sensible man will not choose. That all these things should come to pass, I say, our Teacher foretold, He who is both Son and Apostle of God the Father of all and the Ruler, Jesus Christ; from whom also we have the name of Christians. Whence we become more assured of all the things He taught us, since whatever He beforehand foretold should come to pass, is seen in fact coming to pass; and this is the work of God, to tell of a thing before it happens, and as it was foretold so to show it happening. It were possible to pause here and add no more, reckoning that we demand what is just and true; but because we are well aware that it is not easy suddenly to change a mind possessed by ignorance, we intend to add a few things, for the sake of persuading those who love the truth, knowing that it is not impossible to put ignorance to flight by presenting the truth.

Chapter 13. Christians serve God rationally

What sober-minded man, then, will not acknowledge that we are not atheists, worshipping as we do the Maker of this universe, and declaring, as we have been taught, that He has no need of streams of blood and libations and incense; whom we praise to the utmost of our power by the exercise of prayer and thanksgiving for all things wherewith we are supplied, as we have been taught that the only honour that is worthy of Him is not to consume by fire what He has brought into being for our sustenance, but to use it for ourselves and those who need, and with gratitude to Him to offer thanks by invocations and hymns for our creation, and for all the means of health, and for the various qualities of the different kinds of things, and for the changes of the seasons; and to present before Him petitions for our existing again in incorruption through faith in Him. Our teacher of these things is Jesus Christ, who also was born for this purpose, and was crucified under Pontius Pilate, procurator of Judæa, in the times of Tiberius Cæsar; and that we reasonably worship Him, having learned that He is the Son of the true God Himself, and holding Him in the second place, and the prophetic Spirit in the third, we will prove. For they proclaim our madness to consist in this, that we give to a crucified man a place second to the unchangeable and eternal God, the Creator of all; for they do not discern the mystery that is herein, to which, as we make it plain to you, we pray you to give heed.

Chapter 14. The demons misrepresent Christian doctrine

For we forewarn you to be on your guard, lest those demons whom we have been accusing should deceive you, and quite divert you from reading and understanding what we say. For they strive to hold you their slaves and servants; and sometimes by appearances in dreams, and sometimes by magical impositions, they subdue all who make no strong opposing effort for their own salvation. And thus do we also, since our persuasion by the Word, stand aloof from them (i.e., the demons), and follow the only unbegotten God through His Son — we who formerly delighted in fornication, but now embrace chastity alone; we who formerly used magical arts, dedicate ourselves to the good and unbegotten God; we who valued above all things the acquisition of wealth and possessions, now bring what we have into a common stock, and communicate to every one in need; we who hated and destroyed one another, and on account of their different manners would not live with men of a different tribe, now, since the coming of Christ, live familiarly with them, and pray for our enemies, and endeavour to persuade those who hate us unjustly to live conformably to the good precepts of Christ, to the end that they may become partakers with us of the same joyful hope of a reward from God the ruler of all. But lest we should seem to be reasoning sophistically, we consider it right, before giving you the promised explanation, to cite a few precepts given by Christ Himself. And be it yours, as powerful rulers, to inquire whether we have been taught and do teach these things truly. Brief and concise utterances fell from Him, for He was no sophist, but His word was the power of God.

Chapter 15. What Christ himself taught

Concerning chastity, He uttered such sentiments as these: "Whosoever looks upon a woman to lust after her, has committed adultery with her already in his heart before God." And, "If your right eye offend you, cut it out; for it is better for you to enter into the kingdom of heaven with one eye, than, having two eyes, to be cast into everlasting fire." And, "Whosoever shall marry her that is divorced from another husband, commits adultery." And, "There are some who have been made eunuchs of men, and some who were born eunuchs, and some who have made themselves eunuchs for the kingdom of heaven's sake; but all cannot receive this saying." (Matthew 19:12) So that all who, by human law, are twice married, are in the eye of our Master sinners, and those who look upon a woman to lust after her. For not only he who in act commits adultery is rejected by Him, but also he who desires to commit adultery: since not only our works, but also our thoughts, are open before God. And many, both men and women, who have been Christ's disciples from childhood, remain pure at the age of sixty or seventy years; and I boast that I could produce such from every race of men. For what shall I say, too, of the countless multitude of those who have reformed intemperate habits, and learned these things? For Christ called not the just nor the chaste to repentance, but the ungodly, and the licentious, and the unjust; His words being, "I came not to call the righteous, but sinners to repentance." (Matthew 9:13) For the heavenly Father desires rather the repentance than the punishment of the sinner. And of our love to all, He taught thus: "If you love them that love you, what new thing are you doing? For even fornicators do this. But I say unto you, Pray for your enemies, and love them that hate you, and bless them that curse you, and pray for them that despitefully use you." (Matthew 5:46, 44; Luke 6:28) And that we should communicate to the needy, and do nothing for glory, He said, "Give to him that asks, and from him that would borrow turn not away; for if you lend to them of whom you hope to receive, what new thing are you doing? Even the publicans do this. Lay not up for yourselves treasure upon earth, where moth and rust does corrupt, and where robbers break through; but lay up for yourselves treasure in heaven, where neither moth nor rust does corrupt. For what is a man profited, if he shall gain the whole world, and lose his own soul? Or what shall a man give in exchange for it? Lay up treasure, therefore, in heaven, where neither moth nor rust does corrupt." And, "Be kind and merciful, as your Father also is kind and merciful, and makes His sun to rise on sinners, and the righteous, and the wicked. Take no thought what you shall eat, or what you shall put on: are you not better than the birds and the beasts? And God feeds them. Take no thought, therefore, what you shall eat, or what you shall put on; for your heavenly Father knows that you have need of these things. But seek the kingdom of heaven, and all these things shall be added unto you. For where his treasure is, there also is the mind of a man." And, "Do not these things to be seen of men; otherwise you have no reward from your Father which is in heaven." (Matthew 6:1)

Chapter 16. Concerning patience and swearing

And concerning our being patient of injuries, and ready to serve all, and free from anger, this is what He said: "To him that smites you on the one cheek, offer also the other; and him that takes away your cloak or coat, forbid not. And whosoever shall be angry, is in danger of the fire. And every one that compels you to go with him a mile, follow him two. And let your good works shine before men, that they, seeing them, may glorify your Father which is in heaven." For we ought not to strive; neither has He desired us to be imitators of wicked men, but He has exhorted us to lead all men, by patience and gentleness, from shame and the love of evil. And this indeed is proved in the case of many who once were of your way of thinking, but have changed their violent and tyrannical disposition, being overcome either by the constancy which they have witnessed in their neighbours' lives, or by the extraordinary forbearance they have observed in their fellow-travellers when defrauded, or by the honesty of those with whom they have transacted business.

And with regard to our not swearing at all, and always speaking the truth, He enjoined as follows: "Swear not at all; but let your yea be yea, and your nay, nay; for whatsoever is more than these comes of evil." (Matthew 5:34,

27) And that we ought to worship God alone, He thus persuaded us: "The greatest commandment is, You shall worship the Lord your God, and Him only shall you serve, with all your heart, and with all your strength, the Lord God that made you." (Mark 12:30) And when a certain man came to Him and said, "Good Master," He answered and said, "There is none good but God only, who made all things." (Matthew 19:6, 17) And let those who are not found living as He taught, be understood to be no Christians, even though they profess with the lip the precepts of Christ; for not those who make profession, but those who do the works, shall be saved, according to His word: "Not every one who says to Me, Lord, Lord, shall enter into the kingdom of heaven, but he that does the will of My Father which is in heaven. For whosoever hears Me, and does My sayings, hears Him that sent Me. And many will say unto Me, Lord, Lord, have we not eaten and drunk in Your name, and done wonders? And then will I say unto them, Depart from Me, you workers of iniquity. Then shall there be wailing and gnashing of teeth, when the righteous shall shine as the sun, and the wicked are sent into everlasting fire. For many shall come in My name, clothed outwardly in sheep's clothing, but inwardly being ravening wolves. By their works you shall know them. And every tree that brings not forth good fruit, is hewn down and cast into the fire." And as to those who are not living pursuant to these His teachings, and are Christians only in name, we demand that all such be punished by you.

Chapter 17. Christ taught civil obedience

And everywhere we, more readily than all men, endeavour to pay to those appointed by you the taxes both ordinary and extraordinary, as we have been taught by Him; for at that time some came to Him and asked Him, if one ought to pay tribute to Cæsar; and He answered, "Tell Me, whose image does the coin bear?) And they said, "Cæsar's." And again He answered them, "Render therefore to Cæsar the things that are Cæsar's, and to God the things that are God's." Whence to God alone we render worship, but in other things we gladly serve you, acknowledging you as kings and rulers of men, and praying that with your kingly power you be found to possess also sound judgment. But if you pay no regard to our prayers and frank explanations, we shall suffer no loss, since we believe (or rather, indeed, are persuaded) that every man will suffer punishment in eternal fire according to the merit of his deed, and will render account according to the power he has received from God, as Christ intimated when He said, "To whom God has given more, of him shall more be required." (Luke 12:48)

Chapter 18. Proof of immortality and the resurrection

For reflect upon the end of each of the preceding kings, how they died the death common to all, which, if it issued in insensibility, would be a godsend to all the wicked. But since sensation remains to all who have ever lived, and eternal punishment is laid up (i.e., for the wicked), see that you neglect not to be convinced, and to hold as your belief, that these things are true. For let even necromancy, and the divinations you practise by immaculate children, and the evoking of departed human souls, and those who are called among the magi, Dream-senders and Assistant-spirits (Familiars), and all that is done by those who are skilled in such matters — let these persuade you that even after death souls are in a state of sensation; and those who are seized and cast about by the spirits of the dead, whom all call dæmoniacs or madmen; and what you repute as oracles, both of Amphilochus, Dodana, Pytho, and as many other such as exist; and the opinions of your authors, Empedocles and Pythagoras, Plato and Socrates, and the pit of Homer, and the descent of Ulysses to inspect these things, and all that has been uttered of a like kind. Such favour as you grant to these, grant also to us, who not less but more firmly than they believe in God; since we expect to receive again our own bodies, though they be dead and cast into the earth, for we maintain that with God nothing is impossible.

Chapter 19. The resurrection possible

And to any thoughtful person would anything appear more incredible, than, if we were not in the body, and some one were to say that it was possible that from a small drop of human seed bones and sinews and flesh be formed into a shape such as we see? For let this now be said hypothetically: if you yourselves were not such as you now are, and born

No man has ever seen a dead man not rise so you can't disprove it

of such parents [and causes], and one were to show you human seed and a picture of a man, and were to say with confidence that from such a substance such a being could be produced, would you believe before you saw the actual production? No one will dare to deny [that such a statement would surpass belief]. In the same way, then, you are now incredulous because you have never seen a dead man rise again. But as at first you would not have believed it possible that such persons could be produced from the small drop, and yet now you see them thus produced, so also judge that it is not impossible that the bodies of men, after they have been dissolved, and like seeds resolved into earth, should in God's appointed time rise again and put on incorruption. For what power worthy of God those imagine who say, that each thing returns to that from which it was produced, and that beyond this not even God Himself can do anything, we are unable to conceive; but this we see clearly, that they would not have believed it possible that they could have become such and produced from such materials, as they now see both themselves and the whole world to be. And that it is better to believe even what is impossible to our own nature and to men, than to be unbelieving like the rest of the world, we have learned; for we know that our Master Jesus Christ said, that "what is impossible with men is possible with God," (Matthew 19:26) and, "Fear not them that kill you, and after that can do no more; but fear Him who after death is able to cast both soul and body into hell." (Matthew 10:28) And hell is a place where those are to be punished who have lived wickedly, and who do not believe that those things which God has taught us by Christ will come to pass.

Chapter 20. Heathen analogies to Christian doctrine

And the Sibyl and Hystaspes said that there should be a dissolution by God of things corruptible. And the philosophers called Stoics teach that even God Himself shall be resolved into fire, and they say that the world is to be formed anew by this revolution; but we understand that God, the Creator of all things, is superior to the things that are to be changed. If, therefore, on some points we teach the same things as the poets and philosophers whom you honour, and on other points are fuller and more divine in our teaching, and if we alone afford proof of what we assert, why are we unjustly hated more than all others? For while we say that all things have been produced and arranged into a world by God, we shall seem to utter the doctrine of Plato; and while we say that there will be a burning up of all, we shall seem to utter the doctrine of the

Plato

Stoics: and while we affirm that the souls of the wicked, being endowed with sensation even after death, are punished, and that those of the good being delivered from punishment spend a blessed existence, we shall seem to say the same things as the poets and philosophers; and while we maintain that men ought not to worship the works of their hands, we say the very things which have been said by the comic poet Menander, and other similar writers, for they have declared that the workman is greater than the work.

Chapter 21. Analogies to the history of Christ

And when we say also that the Word, who is the first-birth of God, was produced without sexual union, and that He, Jesus Christ, our Teacher, was crucified and died, and rose again, and ascended into heaven, we propound nothing different from what you believe regarding those whom you esteem sons of Jupiter. For you know how many sons your esteemed writers ascribed to Jupiter: Mercury, the interpreting word and teacher of all; Æsculapius, who, though he was a great physician, was struck by a thunderbolt, and so ascended to heaven; and Bacchus too, after he had been torn limb from limb; and Hercules, when he had committed himself to the flames to escape his toils; and the sons of Leda, and Dioscuri; and Perseus, son of Danae; and Bellerophon, who, though sprung from mortals, rose to heaven on the horse Pegasus. For what shall I say of Ariadne, and those who, like her, have been declared to be set among the stars? And what of the emperors who die among yourselves, whom you deem worthy of deification, and in whose behalf you produce some one who swears he has seen the burning Cæsar rise to heaven from the funeral pyre? And what kind of deeds are recorded of each of these reputed sons of Jupiter, it is needless to tell to those who already know. This only shall be said, that they are written for the advantage and encouragement of youthful scholars; for all reckon it an honourable thing to imitate the gods. But far be such a thought concerning the gods from every well-conditioned soul, as to believe that Jupiter himself, the governor and creator of all things, was both a parricide and the son of a parricide, and that being overcome by the love of base and shameful pleasures, he came in to Ganymede and those many women whom he had violated and that his sons did like actions. But, as we said above, wicked devils perpetrated these things. And we have learned that those only are deified who have lived near to God in holiness and virtue; and we believe that those who live wickedly and do not repent are punished in everlasting fire.

Justin argues that the Roman beliefs are fulfilled in Christ

Chapter 22. Analogies to the sonship of Christ

Moreover, the Son of God called Jesus, even if only a man by ordinary generation, yet, on account of His wisdom, is worthy to be called the Son of God; for all writers call God the Father of men and gods. And if we assert that the Word of God was born of God in a peculiar manner, different from ordinary generation, let this, as said above, be no extraordinary thing to you, who say that Mercury is the angelic word of God. But if any one objects that He was crucified, in this also He is on a par with those reputed sons of Jupiter of yours, who suffered as we have now enumerated. For their sufferings at death are recorded to have been not all alike, but diverse; so that not even by the peculiarity of His sufferings does He seem to be inferior to them; but, on the contrary, as we promised in the preceding part of this discourse, we will now prove Him superior— or rather have already proved Him to be so— for the superior is revealed by His actions. And if we even affirm that He was born of a virgin, accept this in common with what you accept of Perseus. And in that we say that He made whole the lame, the paralytic, and those born blind, we seem to say what is very similar to the deeds said to have been done by Æsculapius.

Chapter 23. The argument

And that this may now become evident to you— (firstly) that whatever we assert in conformity with what has been taught us by Christ, and by the prophets who preceded Him, are alone true, and are older than all the writers who have existed; that we claim to be acknowledged, not because we say the same things as these writers said, but because we say true things: and (secondly) that Jesus Christ is the only proper Son who has been begotten by God, being His Word and first-begotten, and power; and, becoming man according to His will, He taught us these things for the conversion and restoration of the human race: and (thirdly) that before He became a man among men, some, influenced by the demons before mentioned, related beforehand, through the instrumentality of the poets, those circumstances as having really happened, which, having fictitiously devised, they narrated, in the same manner as they have caused to be fabricated the scandalous reports against us of infamous and impious actions, of which there is neither witness nor proof— we shall bring forward the following proof.

Chapter 24. Varieties of heathen worship

In the first place [we furnish proof], because, though we say things similar to what the Greeks say, we only are hated on account of the name of Christ, and though we do no wrong, are put to death as sinners; other men in other places worshipping trees and rivers, and mice and cats and crocodiles, and many irrational animals. Nor are the same animals esteemed by all; but in one place one is worshipped, and another in another, so that all are profane in the judgment of one another, on account of their not worshipping the same objects. And this is the sole accusation you bring against us, that we do not reverence the same gods as you do, nor offer to the dead libations and the savour of fat, and crowns for their statues, and sacrifices. For you very well know that the same animals are with some esteemed gods, with others wild beasts, and with others sacrificial victims.

Chapter 25. False Gods abandoned by Christians

And, secondly, because we— who, out of every race of men, used to worship Bacchus the son of Semele, and Apollo the son of Latona (who in their loves with men did such things as it is shameful even to mention), and Proserpine and Venus (who were maddened with love of Adonis, and whose mysteries also you celebrate), or Æsculapius, or some one or other of those who are called gods— have now, through Jesus Christ, learned to despise these, though we be threatened with death for it, and have dedicated ourselves to the unbegotten and impossible God; of whom we are persuaded that never was he goaded by lust of Antiope, or such other women, or of Ganymede, nor was rescued by that hundred-handed giant whose aid was obtained through Thetis, nor was anxious on this account that her son Achilles should destroy many of the Greeks because of his concubine Briseis. Those who believe these things we pity, and those who invented them we know to be devils.

He claims that those who made the stories are devils.

Chapter 26. Magicians not trusted by Christians

And, thirdly, because after Christ's ascension into heaven the devils put forward certain men who said that they themselves were gods; and they were not only not persecuted by you, but even deemed worthy of honours. There was a Samaritan, Simon, a native of the village called

Gitto, who in the reign of Claudius Cæsar, and in your royal city of Rome, did mighty acts of magic, by virtue of the art of the devils operating in him. He was considered a god, and as a god was honoured by you with a statue, which statue was erected on the river Tiber, between the two bridges, and bore this inscription, in the language of Rome:— Simoni Deo Sancto, To Simon the holy God. And almost all the Samaritans, and a few even of other nations, worship him, and acknowledge him as the first god; and a woman, Helena, who went about with him at that time, and had formerly been a prostitute, they say is the first idea generated by him. And a man, Menander, also a Samaritan, of the town Capparetæa, a disciple of Simon, and inspired by devils, we know to have deceived many while he was in Antioch by his magical art. He persuaded those who adhered to him that they should never die, and even now there are some living who hold this opinion of his. And there is Marcion, a man of Pontus, who is even at this day alive, and teaching his disciples to believe in some other god greater than the Creator. And he, by the aid of the devils, has caused many of every nation to speak blasphemies, and to deny that God is the maker of this universe, and to assert that some other being, greater than He, has done greater works. All who take their opinions from these men, are, as we before said, called Christians; just as also those who do not agree with the philosophers in their doctrines, have yet in common with them the name of philosophers given to them. And whether they perpetrate those fabulous and shameful deeds — the upsetting of the lamp, and promiscuous intercourse, and eating human flesh— we know not; but we do know that they are neither persecuted nor put to death by you, at least on account of their opinions. But I have a treatise against all the heresies that have existed already composed, which, if you wish to read it, I will give you.

Chapter 27. Guilt of exposing children

But as for us, we have been taught that to expose newly-born children is the part of wicked men; and this we have been taught lest we should do any one an injury, and lest we should sin against God, first, because we see that almost all so exposed (not only the girls, but also the males) are brought up to prostitution. And as the ancients are said to have reared herds of oxen, or goats, or sheep, or grazing horses, so now we see you rear children only for this shameful use; and for this pollution a multitude of females and hermaphrodites, and those who commit unmentionable iniquities, are found in every nation. And you receive the hire of these, and duty and taxes from them, whom you ought to exterminate from your realm. And any one who uses such persons, besides the godless and infamous and impure intercourse, may possibly be having intercourse with his own child, or relative, or brother. And there are some who prostitute even their own children and wives, and some are openly mutilated for the purpose of sodomy; and they refer these mysteries to the mother of the gods, and along with each of those whom you esteem gods there is painted a serpent, a great symbol and mystery. Indeed, the things which you do openly and with applause, as if the divine light were overturned and extinguished, these you lay to our charge; which, in truth, does no harm to us who shrink from doing any such things, but only to those who do them and bear false witness against us.

Chapter 28. God's care for men

God put the will to chose good or evil in mens hearts

For among us the prince of the wicked spirits is called the serpent, and Satan, and the devil, as you can learn by looking into our writings. And that he would be sent into the fire with his host, and the men who follow him, and would be punished for an endless duration, Christ foretold. For the reason why God has delayed to do this, is His regard for the human race. For He foreknows that some are to be saved by repentance, some even that are perhaps not yet born. In the beginning He made the human race with the power of thought and of choosing the truth and doing right, so that all men are without excuse before God; for they have been born rational and contemplative. And if any one disbelieves that God cares for these things, he will thereby either insinuate that God does not exist, or he will assert that though He exists He delights in vice, or exists like a stone, and that neither virtue nor vice are anything, but only in the opinion of men these things are reckoned good or evil. And this is the greatest profanity and wickedness.

Chapter 29. Continence of Christians

And again [we fear to expose children], lest some of them be not picked up, but die, and we become murderers. But whether we marry, it is only that we may bring up children; or whether we decline marriage, we live continently. And that you may understand that promiscuous intercourse is not one of our mysteries, one of our number a short time ago presented to Felix the governor in Alexandria a petition, craving that permission might be given to a surgeon to make him an eunuch. For the surgeons there said that they were forbidden to do this without the permission of the governor. And when Felix absolutely refused to sign such a permission, the youth remained single, and was satisfied with his own approving conscience, and the approval of those who thought as he did. And it is not out of place, we think, to mention here Antinous, who was alive but lately, and whom all were prompt, through fear, to worship as a god, though they knew both who he was and what was his origin.

Chapter 30. Was Christ not a magician?

But lest any one should meet us with the question, What should prevent that He whom we call Christ, being a man born of men, performed what we call His mighty works by magical art, and by this appeared to be the Son of God? We will now offer proof, not trusting mere assertions, but being of necessity persuaded by those who prophesied [of Him] before these things came to pass, for with our own eyes we behold things that have happened and are happening just as they were predicted; and this will, we think appear even to you the strongest and truest evidence.

Chapter 31. Of the Hebrew prophets

There were, then, among the Jews certain men who were prophets of God, through whom the prophetic Spirit published beforehand things that were to come to pass, ere ever they happened. And their prophecies, as they were spoken and when they were uttered, the kings who happened to be reigning among the Jews at the several times carefully preserved in their possession, when they had been arranged in books by the prophets themselves in their own Hebrew language. And when Ptolemy king of Egypt formed a library, and endeavoured to collect the writings of all men, he heard also of these prophets, and sent to Herod, who was at that time king of the Jews, requesting that the books of the prophets be sent to him. And Herod the king did indeed send them, written, as they were, in the foresaid Hebrew language. And when their contents were found to be unintelligible to the Egyptians, he again sent and requested that men be commissioned to translate them into the Greek language. And when this was done, the books remained with the Egyptians, where they are until now. They are also in the possession of all Jews throughout the world; but they, though they read, do not understand what is said, but count us foes and enemies; and, like yourselves, they kill and punish us whenever they have the power, as you can well believe. For in the Jewish war which lately raged, Barchochebas, the leader of the revolt of the Jews, gave orders that Christians alone should be led to cruel punishments, unless they would deny Jesus Christ and utter blasphemy. In these books, then, of the prophets we found Jesus our Christ foretold as coming, born of a virgin, growing up to man's estate, and healing every disease and every sickness, and raising the dead, and being hated, and unrecognised, and crucified, and dying, and rising again, and ascending into heaven, and being, and being called, the Son of God. We find it also predicted that certain persons should be sent by Him into every nation to publish these things, and that rather among the Gentiles [than among the Jews] men should believe in Him. And He was predicted before He appeared, first 5000 years before, and again 3000, then 2000, then 1000, and yet again 800; for in the succession of generations prophets after prophets arose.

Chapter 32. Christ predicted by Moses

Moses then, who was the first of the prophets, spoke in these very words: "The sceptre shall not depart from Judah, nor a lawgiver from between his feet, until He come for whom it is reserved; and He shall be the desire of the nations, binding His foal to the vine, washing His robe in the blood of the grape." (Genesis 49:10) It is yours to make accurate inquiry, and ascertain up to whose time the Jews had a lawgiver and king of their own. Up to the time of Jesus Christ, who taught us, and interpreted the prophecies which were not yet understood, [they had a lawgiver] as was foretold by the holy and divine Spirit of prophecy through Moses, "that a ruler would not fail the Jews until He should come for whom the kingdom was reserved" (for Judah was the forefather of the Jews, from whom also they have their name of Jews); and after He (i.e., Christ) appeared, you began to rule the Jews, and gained possession of all their territory. And the prophecy, "He shall be the expectation of the nations," signified that there would be some of all nations who should look for Him to come again. And this indeed you can see for yourselves, and be convinced of by fact. For of all races of men there are some who look for Him who was crucified in Judæa, and after whose crucifixion the land was straightway surrendered to you as spoil of war. And the prophecy, "binding His foal to the vine, and washing His robe in the blood of the grape," was a significant symbol of the things that were to happen to Christ, and of what He was to do.

For the foal of an ass stood bound to a vine at the entrance of a village, and He ordered His acquaintances to bring it to Him then; and when it was brought, He mounted and sat upon it, and entered Jerusalem, where was the vast temple of the Jews which was afterwards destroyed by you. And after this He was crucified, that the rest of the prophecy might be fulfilled. For this "washing His robe in the blood of the grape" was predictive of the passion He was to endure, cleansing by His blood those who believe in Him. For what is called by the Divine Spirit through the prophet "His robe," are those men who believe in Him in whom abides the seed of God, the Word. And what is spoken of as "the blood of the grape," signifies that He who should appear would have blood, though not of the seed of man, but of the power of God. And the first power after God the Father and Lord of all is the Word, who is also the Son; and of Him we will, in what follows, relate how He took flesh and became man. For as man did not make the blood of the vine, but God, so it was hereby intimated that the blood should not be of human seed, but of divine power, as we have said above. And Isaiah, another prophet, foretelling the same things in other words, spoke thus: A star shall rise out of Jacob, and a flower shall spring from the root of Jesse; and His arm shall the nations trust. (Isaiah 11:1) And a star of light has arisen, and a flower has sprung from the root of Jesse— this Christ. For by the power of God He was conceived by a virgin of the seed of Jacob, who was the father of Judah, who, as we have shown, was the father of the Jews; and Jesse was His forefather according to the oracle, and He was the son of Jacob and Judah according to lineal descent.

Chapter 33. Manner of Christ's birth predicted

And hear again how Isaiah in express words foretold that He should be born of a virgin; for he spoke thus: "Behold, a virgin shall conceive, and bring forth a son, and they shall say for His name, 'God with us.'" (Isaiah 7:14) For things which were incredible and seemed impossible with men, these God predicted by the Spirit of prophecy as about to come to pass, in order that, when they came to pass, there might be no unbelief, but faith, because of their prediction. But lest some, not understanding the prophecy now cited, should charge us with the very things we have been laying to the charge of the poets who say that Jupiter went in to women through lust, let us try to explain the words. This, then, "Behold, a virgin shall conceive," signifies that a virgin should conceive without intercourse. For if she had had intercourse with any one whatever, she was no longer a virgin; but the power of God having come upon the virgin, overshadowed her, and caused her while yet a virgin to conceive. And the angel of God who was sent to the same virgin at that time brought her good news, saying, "Behold, you shall conceive of the Holy Ghost, and shall bear a Son, and He shall be called the Son of the Highest, and you shall call His name Jesus; for He shall save His people from their sins," (Luke 1:32; Matthew 1:21) — as they who have recorded all that concerns our Saviour Jesus Christ have taught, whom we believed, since by Isaiah also, whom we have now adduced, the Spirit of prophecy declared that He should be born as we intimated before. It is wrong, therefore, to understand the Spirit and the power of God as anything else than the Word, who is also the first-born of God, as the foresaid prophet Moses declared; and it was this which, when it came upon the virgin and overshadowed her, caused her to conceive, not by intercourse, but by power. And the name Jesus in the Hebrew language means Σωτήϱ (Saviour) in the Greek tongue. Wherefore, too, the angel said to the virgin, "You shall call His name Jesus, for He shall save His people from their sins." And that the prophets are inspired by no other than the Divine Word, even you, as I fancy, will grant.

Chapter 34. Place of Christ's birth foretold

And hear what part of earth He was to be born in, as another prophet, Micah, foretold. He spoke thus: "And you, Bethlehem, the land of Judah, are not the least among the princes of Judah; for out of you shall come forth a Governor, who shall feed My people." (Micah 5:2) Now there is a village in the land of the Jews, thirty-five stadia from Jerusalem, in which Jesus Christ was born, as you can ascertain also from the registers of the taxing made under Cyrenius, your first procurator in Judæa.

Chapter 35. Other fulfilled prophecies

And how Christ after He was born was to escape the notice of other men until He grew to man's estate, which also came to pass, hear what was foretold regarding this. There are the following predictions:

— "Unto us a child is born, and unto us a young man is given, and the government shall be upon His shoulders;" (Isaiah 9:6) which is significant of the power of the cross, for to it, when He was crucified, He applied His shoulders, as shall be more clearly made out in the ensuing discourse. And again the same prophet Isaiah, being inspired by the prophetic Spirit, said, "I have spread out my hands to a disobedient and gainsaying people, to those who walk in a way that is not good. They now ask of me judgment, and dare to draw near to God." (Isaiah 65:2, Isaiah 58:2) And again in other words, through another prophet, He says, "They pierced My hands and My feet, and for My vesture they cast lots." And indeed David, the king and prophet, who uttered these things, suffered none of them; but Jesus Christ stretched forth His hands, being crucified by the Jews speaking against Him, and denying that He was the Christ. And as the prophet spoke, they tormented Him, and set Him on the judgment-seat, and said, Judge us. And the expression, "They pierced my hands and my feet," was used in reference to the nails of the cross which were fixed in His hands and feet. And after He was crucified they cast lots upon His vesture, and they that crucified Him parted it among them. And that these things did happen, you can ascertain from the Acts of Pontius Pilate. And we will cite the prophetic utterances of another prophet, Zephaniah, to the effect that He was foretold expressly as to sit upon the foal of an ass and to enter Jerusalem. The words are these: "Rejoice greatly, O daughter of Zion; shout, O daughter of Jerusalem: behold, your King comes unto you; lowly, and riding upon an ass, and upon a colt the foal of an ass." (Zechariah 9:9)

Chapter 36. Different modes of prophecy

But when you hear the utterances of the prophets spoken as it were personally, you must not suppose that they are spoken by the inspired themselves, but by the Divine Word who moves them. For sometimes He declares things that are to come to pass, in the manner of one who foretells the future; sometimes He speaks as from the person of God the Lord and Father of all; sometimes as from the person of Christ; sometimes as from the person of the people answering the Lord or His Father, just as you can see even in your own writers, one man being the writer of the whole, but introducing the persons who converse. And this the Jews who possessed the books of the prophets did not understand, and therefore did not recognise Christ even when He came, but even hate us who say that He has come, and who prove that, as was predicted, He was crucified by them.

Chapter 37. Utterances of the Father

And that this too may be clear to you, there were spoken from the person of the Father through Isaiah the prophet, the following words: "The ox knows his owner, and the ass his master's crib; but Israel does not know, and My people has not understood. Woe, sinful nation, a people full of sins, a wicked seed, children that are transgressors, you have forsaken the Lord." And again elsewhere, when the same prophet speaks in like manner from the person of the Father, "What is the house that you will build for Me? Says the Lord. The heaven is My throne, and the earth is My footstool." (Isaiah 66:1) And again, in another place, "Your new moons and your sabbaths My soul hates; and the great day of the fast and of ceasing from labour I cannot away with; nor, if you come to be seen of Me, will I hear you: your hands are full of blood; and if you bring fine flour, incense, it is abomination unto Me: the fat of lambs and the blood of bulls I do not desire. For who has required this at your hands? But loose every bond of wickedness, tear asunder the tight knots of violent contracts, cover the houseless and naked, deal your bread to the hungry." (Isaiah 1:14, Isaiah 58:6) What kind of things are taught through the prophets from [the person of] God, you can now perceive.

Chapter 38. Utterances of the Son

And when the Spirit of prophecy speaks from the person of Christ, the utterances are of this sort: "I have spread out My hands to a disobedient and gainsaying people, to those who walk in a way that is not good." (Isaiah 65:2) And again: "I gave My back to the scourges, and My cheeks to the buffetings; I turned not away My face from the shame of spittings; and the Lord was My helper: therefore was I not confounded: but I set My face as a firm rock; and I knew that I should not be ashamed, for He is near that justifies Me." (Isaiah 50:6) And again, when He says, "They cast lots upon My vesture, and pierced My hands and My feet. And I lay down and slept, and rose again, because the Lord sustained Me." And again, when He says, "They spoke with their lips, they wagged the head, saying, Let Him deliver Himself." And that all these things happened to Christ at the hands of the Jews, you can ascertain. For when He was crucified, they did shoot out the lip, and wagged their heads, saying, "Let Him who raised the dead save Himself." (Matthew 27:39)

Chapter 39. Direct predictions by the Spirit

And when the Spirit of prophecy speaks as predicting things that are to come to pass, He speaks in this way: "For out of Zion shall go forth the law, and the word of the Lord from Jerusalem. And He shall judge among the nations, and shall rebuke many people; and they shall beat their swords into ploughshares, and their spears into pruning-hooks: nation shall not lift up sword against nation, neither shall they learn war any more." (Isaiah 2:3) And that it did so come to pass, we can convince you. For from Jerusalem there went out into the world, men, twelve in number, and these illiterate, of no ability in speaking: but by the power of God they proclaimed to every race of men that they were sent by Christ to teach to all the word of God; and we who formerly used to murder one another do not only now refrain from making war upon our enemies, but also, that we may not lie nor deceive our examiners, willingly die confessing Christ. For that saying, "The tongue has sworn but the mind is unsworn," might be imitated by us in this matter. But if the soldiers enrolled by you, and who have taken the military oath, prefer their allegiance to their own life, and parents, and country, and

25

all kindred, though you can offer them nothing incorruptible, it were verily ridiculous if we, who earnestly long for incorruption, should not endure all things, in order to obtain what we desire from Him who is able to grant it.

Chapter 40. Christ's advent foretold

And hear how it was foretold concerning those who published His doctrine and proclaimed His appearance, the above-mentioned prophet and king speaking thus by the Spirit of prophecy "Day unto day utters speech, and night unto night shows knowledge. There is no speech nor language where their voice is not heard. Their voice has gone out into all the earth, and their words to the ends of the world. In the sun has He set His tabernacle, and he as a bridegroom going out of his chamber shall rejoice as a giant to run his course." And we have thought it right and relevant to mention some other prophetic utterances of David besides these; from which you may learn how the Spirit of prophecy exhorts men to live, and how He foretold the conspiracy which was formed against Christ by Herod the king of the Jews, and the Jews themselves, and Pilate, who was your governor among them, with his soldiers; and how He should be believed on by men of every race; and how God calls Him His Son, and has declared that He will subdue all His enemies under Him; and how the devils, as much as they can, strive to escape the power of God the Father and Lord of all, and the power of Christ Himself; and how God calls all to repentance before the day of judgment comes. These things were uttered thus: "Blessed is the man who has not walked in the counsel of the ungodly, nor stood in the way of sinners, nor sat in the seat of the scornful: but his delight is in the law of the Lord; and in His law will he meditate day and night. And he shall be like a tree planted by the rivers of waters, which shall give his fruit in his season; and his leaf shall not wither, and whatsoever he does shall prosper. The ungodly are not so, but are like the chaff which the wind drives away from the face of the earth. Therefore the ungodly shall not stand in the judgment, nor sinners in the council of the righteous. For the Lord knows the way of the righteous; but the way of the ungodly shall perish. Why do the heathen rage, and the people imagine new things? The kings of the earth set themselves, and the rulers take counsel together, against the Lord, and against His Anointed, saying, Let us break their bands asunder, and cast their yoke from us. He that dwells in the heavens shall laugh at them, and the Lord shall have them in derision. Then shall He speak to them in His wrath, and vex them in His sore displeasure. Yet have I been set by Him a King on Zion His holy hill, declaring the decree of the Lord. The Lord said to Me, You are My Son; this day have I begotten You. Ask of Me, and I shall give You the heathen for Your inheritance, and the uttermost parts of the earth as Your possession. You shall herd them with a rod of iron; as the vessels of a potter shall You dash them in pieces. Be wise now, therefore, O you kings; be instructed, all you judges of the earth. Serve the Lord with fear, and rejoice with trembling. Embrace instruction, lest at any time the Lord be angry, and you perish from the right way, when His wrath has been suddenly kindled. Blessed are all they that put their trust in Him."

Chapter 41. The crucifixion predicted

And again, in another prophecy, the Spirit of prophecy, through the same David, intimated that Christ, after He had been crucified, should reign, and spoke as follows: "Sing to the Lord, all the earth, and day by day declare His salvation. For great is the Lord, and greatly to be praised, to be feared above all the gods. For all the gods of the nations are idols of devils; but God made the heavens. Glory and praise are before His face, strength and glorying are in the habitation of His holiness. Give Glory to the Lord, the Father everlasting. Receive grace, and enter His presence, and worship in His holy courts. Let all the earth fear before His face; let it be established, and not shaken. Let them rejoice among the nations. The Lord has reigned from the tree."

Chapter 42. Prophecy using the past tense

But when the Spirit of prophecy speaks of things that are about to come to pass as if they had already taken place, — as may be observed even in the passages already cited by me, — that this circumstance may afford no excuse to readers [for misinterpreting them], we will make even this also quite plain. The things which He absolutely knows will take place, He predicts as if already they had taken place. And that the utterances must be thus received, you will perceive, if you give your attention to them. The words cited above, David uttered 1500 years before Christ became a man and was crucified; and no one of those who lived before Him, nor yet of His contemporaries, afforded joy to the Gentiles by being crucified. But our Jesus Christ, being crucified and dead, rose again, and having ascended to heaven, reigned; and by those things which were published in His name among all nations by the apostles, there is joy afforded to those who expect the immortality promised by Him.

Chapter 43. Responsibility asserted

But lest some suppose, from what has been said by us, that we say that whatever happens, happens by a fatal necessity, because it is foretold as known beforehand, this too we explain. We have learned from the prophets, and we hold it to be true, that punishments, and chastisements, and good rewards, are rendered according to the merit of each man's actions. Since if it be not so, but all things happen by fate, neither is anything at all in our own power. For if it be fated that this man, e.g., be good, and this other evil, neither is the former meritorious nor the latter to be blamed. And again, unless the human race have the power of avoiding evil and choosing good by free choice, they are not accountable for their actions, of whatever kind they be. But that it is by free choice they both walk uprightly and stumble, we thus demonstrate. We see the same man making a transition to opposite things. Now, if it had been fated that he were to be either good or bad, he could never have been capable of both the opposites, nor of so many transitions. But not even would some be good and others bad, since we thus make fate the cause of evil, and exhibit her as acting in opposition to herself; or that which has been already stated would seem to be true, that neither virtue nor vice is anything, but that things are only reckoned good or evil by opinion; which, as the true word shows, is the greatest impiety and wickedness. But this we assert is inevitable fate, that they who choose the good have worthy rewards, and they who choose the opposite have their merited awards. For not like other things, as trees and quadrupeds, which cannot act by choice, did God make man: for neither would he be worthy of reward or praise did he not of himself choose the good, but were created for this end; nor, if he were evil, would he be worthy of punishment, not being evil of himself, but being able to be nothing else than what he was made.

Chapter 44. Not nullified by prophecy

And the holy Spirit of prophecy taught us this, telling us by Moses that God spoke thus to the man first created: "Behold, before your face are good and evil: choose the good." And again, by the other prophet Isaiah, that the following utterance was made as if from God the Father and Lord of all: "Wash you, make you clean; put away evils from your souls; learn to do well; judge the orphan, and plead for the widow: and come and let us reason together, says the Lord: And if your sins be as scarlet, I will make them white as wool; and if they be red like as crimson, I will make them white as snow. And if you be willing and obey Me, you shall eat the good of the land; but if you do not obey Me, the sword shall devour you: for the mouth of the Lord has spoken it." (Isaiah 1:16, etc.) And that expression, "The sword shall devour you," does not mean that the disobedient shall be slain by the sword, but the sword of God is fire, of which they who choose to do wickedly become the fuel. Wherefore He says, "The sword shall devour you: for the mouth of the Lord has spoken it." And if He had spoken concerning a sword that cuts and at once dispatches, He would not have said, shall devour. And so, too, Plato, when he says, "The blame is his who chooses, and God is blameless," took this from the prophet Moses and uttered it. For Moses is more ancient than all the Greek writers. And whatever both philosophers and poets have said concerning the immortality of the soul, or punishments after death, or contemplation of things heavenly, or doctrines of the like kind, they have received such suggestions from the

The greek writers gain their knowledge from the prophets!

prophets as have enabled them to understand and interpret these things. And hence there seem to be seeds of truth among all men; but they are charged with not accurately understanding [the truth] when they assert contradictories. So that what we say about future events being foretold, we do not say it as if they came about by a fatal necessity; but God foreknowing all that shall be done by all men, and it being His decree that the future actions of men shall all be recompensed according to their several value, He foretells by the Spirit of prophecy that He will bestow meet rewards according to the merit of the actions done, always urging the human race to effort and recollection, showing that He cares and provides for men. But by the agency of the devils death has been decreed against those who read the books of Hystaspes, or of the Sibyl, or of the prophets, that through fear they may prevent men who read them from receiving the knowledge of the good, and may retain them in slavery to themselves; which, however, they could not always effect. For not only do we fearlessly read them, but, as you see, bring them for your inspection, knowing that their contents will be pleasing to all. And if we persuade even a few, our gain will be very great; for, as good husbandmen, we shall receive the reward from the Master.

So true! humanity knows truth Romans 1:20

humans are led astray by false doctrine

Chapter 45. Christ's session in heaven foretold

And that God the Father of all would bring Christ to heaven after He had raised Him from the dead, and would keep Him there until He has subdued His enemies the devils, and until the number of those who are foreknown by Him as good and virtuous is complete, on whose account He has still delayed the consummation— hear what was said by the prophet David. These are his words: "The Lord said unto My Lord, Sit at My right hand, until I make Your enemies Your footstool. The Lord shall send to You the rod of power out of Jerusalem; and rule You in the midst of Your enemies. With You is the government in the day of Your power, in the beauties of Your saints: from the womb of morning have I begotten You." That which he says, "He shall send to You the rod of power out of Jerusalem," is predictive of the mighty word, which His apostles, going forth from Jerusalem, preached everywhere; and though death is decreed against those who teach or at all confess the name of Christ, we everywhere both embrace and teach it. And if you also read these words in a hostile spirit, you can do no more, as I said before, than kill us; which indeed does no harm to us, but to you and all who unjustly hate us, and do not repent, brings eternal punishment by fire.

Chapter 46. The Word in the world before Christ

But lest some should, without reason, and for the perversion of what we teach, maintain that we say that Christ was born one hundred and fifty years ago under Cyrenius, and subsequently, in the time of Pontius Pilate, taught what we say He taught; and should cry out against us as though all men who were born before Him were irresponsible — let us anticipate and solve the difficulty. We have been taught that Christ is the first-born of God, and we have declared above that He is the Word of whom every race of men were partakers; and those who lived reasonably are Christians, even though they have been thought atheists; as, among the Greeks, Socrates and Heraclitus, and men like them; and among the barbarians, Abraham, and Ananias, and Azarias, and Misael, and Elias, and many others whose actions and names we now decline to recount, because we know it would be tedious. So that even they who lived before Christ, and lived without reason, were wicked and hostile to Christ, and slew those who lived reasonably. But who, through the power of the Word, according to the will of God the Father and Lord of all, He was born of a virgin as a man, and was named Jesus, and was crucified, and died, and rose again, and ascended into heaven, an intelligent man will be able to comprehend from what has been already so largely said. And we, since the proof of this subject is less needful now, will pass for the present to the proof of those things which are urgent.

Chapter 47. Desolation of Judæa foretold

That the land of the Jews, then, was to be laid waste, hear what was said by the Spirit of prophecy. And the words were spoken as if from the person of the people wondering at what had happened. They are these: "Sion is a wilderness, Jerusalem a desolation. The house of our sanctuary has become a curse, and the glory which our fathers blessed is burned up with fire, and all its glorious things are laid waste: and You refrain Yourself at these things, and have held Your peace, and have humbled us very sore." (Isaiah 64:10-12) And you are convinced that Jerusalem has been laid waste, as was predicted. And concerning its desolation, and that no one should be permitted to inhabit it, there was the following prophecy by Isaiah: "Their land is desolate, their enemies consume it before them, and none of them shall dwell therein." (Isaiah 1:7) And that it is guarded by you lest any one dwell in it, and that death is decreed against a Jew apprehended entering it, you know very well.

Chapter 48. Christ's work and death foretold

And that it was predicted that our Christ should heal all diseases and raise the dead, hear what was said. There are these words: "At His coming the lame shall leap as an hart, and the tongue of the stammerer shall be clear speaking: the blind shall see, and the lepers shall be cleansed; and the dead shall rise, and walk about." (Isaiah 35:6) And that He did those things, you can learn from the Acts of Pontius Pilate. And how it was predicted by the Spirit of prophecy that He and those who hoped in Him should be slain, hear what was said by Isaiah. These are the words: "Behold now the righteous perishes, and no man lays it to heart; and just men are taken away, and no man considers. From the presence of wickedness is the righteous man taken, and his burial shall be in peace: he is taken from our midst." Isaiah 57:1

Chapter 49. His rejection by the Jews foretold

And again, how it was said by the same Isaiah, that the Gentile nations who were not looking for Him should worship Him, but the Jews who always expected Him should not recognise Him when He came. And the words are spoken as from the person of Christ; and they are these: "I was manifest to them that asked not for Me; I was found of them that sought Me not: I said, Behold Me, to a nation that called not on My name. I spread out My hands to a disobedient and gainsaying people, to those who walked in a way that is not good, but follow after their own sins; a people that provokes Me to anger to My face." (Isaiah 65:1-3) For the Jews having the prophecies, and being always in expectation of the Christ to come, did not recognise Him; and not only so, but even treated Him shamefully. But the Gentiles, who had never heard anything about Christ, until the apostles set out from Jerusalem and preached concerning Him, and gave them the prophecies, were filled with joy and faith, and cast away their idols, and dedicated themselves to the Unbegotten God through Christ. And that it was foreknown that these infamous things should be uttered against those who confessed Christ, and that those who slandered Him, and said that it was well to preserve the ancient customs, should be miserable, hear what was briefly said by

Isaiah; it is this: "Woe unto them that call sweet bitter, and bitter sweet." (Isaiah 5:20)

Chapter 50. His humiliation predicted

But that, having become man for our sakes, He endured to suffer and to be dishonoured, and that He shall come again with glory, hear the prophecies which relate to this; they are these: "Because they delivered His soul unto death, and He was numbered with the transgressors, He has borne the sin of many, and shall make intercession for the transgressors. For, behold, My Servant shall deal prudently, and shall be exalted, and shall be greatly extolled. As many were astonished at You, so marred shall Your form be before men, and so hidden from them Your glory; so shall many nations wonder, and the kings shall shut their mouths at Him. For they to whom it was not told concerning Him, and they who have not heard, shall understand. O Lord, who has believed our report? And to whom is the arm of the Lord revealed? We have declared before Him as a child, as a root in a dry ground. He had no form, nor glory; and we saw Him, and there was no form nor comeliness: but His form was dishonoured and marred more than the sons of men. A man under the stroke, and knowing how to bear infirmity, because His face was turned away: He was despised, and of no reputation. It is He who bears our sins, and is afflicted for us; yet we did esteem Him smitten, stricken, and afflicted. But He was wounded for our transgressions, He was bruised for our iniquities, the chastisement of peace was upon Him, by His stripes we are healed. All we, like sheep, have gone astray; every man has wandered in his own way. And He delivered Him for our sins; and He opened not His mouth for all His affliction. He was brought as a sheep to the slaughter, and as a lamb before his shearer is dumb, so He opens not His mouth. In His humiliation, His judgment was taken away." (Isaiah 52:13-15, Isaiah 53:1-8) Accordingly, after He was crucified, even all His acquaintances forsook Him, having denied Him; and afterwards, when He had risen from the dead and appeared to them, and had taught them to read the prophecies in which all these things were foretold as coming to pass, and when they had seen Him ascending into heaven, and had believed, and had received power sent thence by Him upon them, and went to every race of men, they taught these things, and were called apostles.

Chapter 51. The majesty of Christ

And that the Spirit of prophecy might signify to us that He who suffers these things has an ineffable origin, and rules His enemies, He spoke thus: "His generation who shall declare? Because His life is cut off from the earth: for their transgressions He comes to death. And I will give the wicked for His burial, and the rich for His death; because He did no violence, neither was any deceit in His mouth. And the Lord is pleased to cleanse Him from the stripe. If He be given for sin, your soul shall see His seed prolonged in days. And the Lord is pleased to deliver His soul from grief, to show Him light, and to form Him with knowledge, to justify the righteous who richly serves many. And He shall bear our iniquities. Therefore He shall inherit many, and He shall divide the spoil of the strong; because His soul was delivered to death: and He was numbered with the transgressors; and He bore the sins of many, and He was delivered up for their transgressions." (Isaiah 53:8-12) Hear, too, how He was to ascend into heaven according to prophecy. It was thus spoken: "Lift up the gates of heaven; be opened, that the King of glory may come in. Who is this King of glory? The Lord, strong and mighty." And how also He should come again out of heaven with glory, hear what was spoken in reference to this by the prophet Jeremiah. His words are: "Behold, as the Son of man He comes in the clouds of heaven, and His angels with Him." Daniel 7:13

Chapter 52. Certain fulfilment of prophecy

Since, then, we prove that all things which have already happened had been predicted by the prophets before they came to pass, we must necessarily believe also that those things which are in like manner predicted, but are yet to come to pass, shall certainly happen. For as the things which have already taken place came to pass when foretold, and even though unknown, so shall the things that remain, even though they be unknown and disbelieved, yet come to pass. For the prophets have proclaimed two advents of His: the one, that which is already past, when He came as a dishonoured and suffering Man; but the second, when, according to prophecy, He shall come from heaven with glory, accompanied by His angelic host, when also He shall raise the bodies of all men who have lived, and shall clothe those of the worthy with immortality, and shall send those of the wicked, endued with eternal sensibility, into everlasting fire with the wicked devils. And that these things also have been foretold as yet to be, we will prove. By Ezekiel the prophet it was said: "Joint shall be joined to joint, and bone to bone, and flesh shall grow again; and every knee shall bow to the Lord, and every tongue shall confess Him." (Ezekiel 37:7-8; Isaiah 45:24) And in what kind of sensation and punishment the wicked are to be, hear from what was said in like manner with reference to this; it is as follows: "Their worm shall not rest, and their fire shall not be quenched;" (Isaiah 66:24) and then shall they repent, when it profits them not. And what the people of the Jews shall say and do, when they see Him coming in glory, has been thus predicted by Zechariah the prophet: "I will command the four winds to gather the scattered children; I will command the north wind to bring them, and the south wind, that it keep not back. And then in Jerusalem there shall be great lamentation, not the lamentation of mouths or of lips, but the lamentation of the heart; and they shall rend not their garments, but their hearts. Tribe by tribe they shall mourn, and then they shall look on Him whom they have pierced; and they shall say, Why, O Lord, have You made us to err from Your way? The glory which our fathers blessed, has for us been turned into shame."

Chapter 53. Summary of the prophecies

Though we could bring forward many other prophecies, we forbear, judging these sufficient for the persuasion of those who have ears to hear and understand; and considering also that those persons are able to see that we do not make mere assertions without being able to produce proof, like those fables that are told of the so-called sons of Jupiter. For with what reason should we believe of a crucified man that He is the first-born of the unbegotten God, and Himself will pass judgment on the whole human race, unless we had found testimonies concerning Him published before He came and was born as man, and unless we saw that things had happened accordingly— the devastation of the land of the Jews, and men of every race persuaded by His teaching through the apostles, and rejecting their old habits, in which, being deceived, they had their conversation; yea, seeing ourselves too, and knowing that the Christians from among the Gentiles are both more numerous and more true than those from among the Jews and Samaritans? For all the other human races are called Gentiles by the Spirit of prophecy; but the Jewish and Samaritan races are called the tribe of Israel, and the house of Jacob. And the prophecy in which it was predicted that there should be more believers from the Gentiles than from the Jews and Samaritans, we will produce: it ran thus: "Rejoice, O barren, you that do not bear; break forth and shout, you that do not travail, because many more are the children of the desolate than of her that has an husband." (Isaiah 54:1)

For all the Gentiles were "desolate" of the true God, serving the works of their hands; but the Jews and Samaritans, having the word of God delivered to them by the prophets, and always expecting the Christ, did not recognise Him when He came, except some few, of whom the Spirit of prophecy by Isaiah had predicted that they should be saved. He spoke as from their person: "Unless the Lord had left us a seed, we should have been as Sodom and Gomorrha." (Isaiah 1:9) For Sodom and Gomorrha are related by Moses to have been cities of ungodly men, which God burned with fire and brimstone, and overthrew, no one of their inhabitants being saved except a certain stranger, a Chaldæan by birth, whose name was Lot; with whom also his daughters were rescued. And those who care may yet see their whole country desolate and burned, and remaining barren. And to show how those from among the Gentiles were foretold as more true and more believing, we will cite what was said by Isaiah the prophet; for he spoke as follows "Israel is uncircumcised in heart, but the Gentiles are uncircumcised in the flesh." So many things therefore, as these, when they are seen with the eye, are enough to produce conviction and belief in those who embrace the truth, and are not bigoted in their opinions, nor are governed by their passions.

Chapter 54. Origin of heathen mythology

But those who hand down the myths which the poets have made, adduce no proof to the youths who learn them; and we proceed to demonstrate that they have been uttered by the influence of the wicked demons, to deceive and lead astray the human race. For having heard it proclaimed through the prophets that the Christ was to come, and that the ungodly among men were to be punished by fire, they put forward many to be called sons of Jupiter, under the impression that they would be able to produce in men the idea that the things which were said with regard to Christ were mere marvellous tales, like the things which were said by the poets. And these things were said both among the Greeks and among all nations where they [the demons] heard the prophets foretelling that Christ would specially be believed in; but that in hearing what was said by the prophets they did not accurately understand it, but imitated what was said of our Christ, like men who are in error, we will make plain. The prophet Moses, then, was, as we have already said, older than all writers; and by him, as we have also said before, it was thus predicted: "There shall not fail a prince from Judah, nor a lawgiver from between his feet, until He come for whom it is reserved; and He shall be the desire of the Gentiles, binding His foal to the vine, washing His robe in the blood of the grape." (Genesis 49:10) The devils, accordingly, when they heard these prophetic words, said that Bacchus was the son of Jupiter, and gave out that he was the discoverer of the vine, and they number wine [or, the ass] among his mysteries; and they taught that, having been torn in pieces, he ascended into heaven. And because in the prophecy of Moses it had not been expressly intimated whether He who was to come was the Son of God, and whether He would, riding on the foal, remain on earth or ascend into heaven, and because the name of "foal" could mean either the foal of an ass or the foal of a horse, they, not knowing whether He who was foretold would bring the foal of an ass or of a horse as the sign of His coming, nor whether He was the Son of God, as we said above, or of man, gave out that Bellerophon, a man born of man, himself ascended to heaven on his horse Pegasus. And when they heard it said by the other prophet Isaiah, that He should be born of a virgin, and by His own means ascend into heaven, they pretended that Perseus was spoken of. And when they knew what was said, as has been cited above, in the prophecies written aforetime, "Strong as a giant to run his course," they said that Hercules was strong, and had journeyed over the whole earth. And when, again, they learned that it had been foretold that He should heal every sickness, and raise the dead, they produced Æsculapius.

Chapter 55. Symbols of the cross

But in no instance, not even in any of those called sons of Jupiter, did they imitate the being crucified; for it was not understood by them, all the things said of it having been put symbolically. And this, as the prophet foretold, is the greatest symbol of His power and role; as is also proved by the things which fall under our observation. For consider all the things in the world, whether without this form they could be administered or have any community. For the sea is not traversed except that trophy which is called a sail abide safe in the ship; and the earth is not ploughed without it: diggers and mechanics do not their work, except with tools which have this shape. And the human form differs from that of the irrational animals in nothing else than in its being erect and having the hands extended, and having on the face extending from the forehead what is called the nose, through which there is respiration for the living creature; and this shows no other form than that of the cross. And so it was said by the prophet, "The breath before our face is the Lord Christ." And the power of this form is shown by your own symbols on what are called "vexilla" [banners] and trophies, with which all your state possessions are made, using these as the insignia of your power and government, even though you do so unwittingly. And with this form you consecrate the images of your emperors when they die, and you name them gods by inscriptions. Since, therefore, we have urged you both by reason and by an evident form, and to the utmost of our ability, we know that now we are blameless even though you disbelieve; for our part is done and finished.

Chapter 56. The demons still mislead men

But the evil spirits were not satisfied with saying, before Christ's appearance, that those who were said to be sons of Jupiter were born of him; but after He had appeared, and been born among men, and when they learned how He had been foretold by the prophets, and knew that He should be believed on and looked for by every nation, they again, as was said above, put forward other men, the Samaritans Simon and Menander, who did many mighty works by magic, and deceived many, and still keep them deceived. For even among yourselves, as we said before, Simon was in the royal city Rome in the reign of Claudius Cæsar, and so greatly astonished the sacred senate and people of the Romans, that he was considered a god, and honoured, like the others whom you honour as gods, with a statue. Wherefore we pray that the sacred senate and your people may, along with yourselves, be arbiters of this our memorial, in order that if any one be entangled by that man's doctrines, he may learn the truth, and so be able to escape error; and as for the statue, if you please, destroy it.

Chapter 57. And cause persecution

The devils have no power over Christ's Judgement and his Grace.

Destruction fire

Nor can the devils persuade men that there will be no conflagration for the punishment of the wicked; as they were unable to effect that Christ should be hidden after He came. But this only can they effect, that they who live irrationally, and were brought up licentiously in wicked customs, and are prejudiced in their own opinions, should kill and hate us; whom we not only do not hate, but, as is proved, pity and endeavour to lead to repentance. For we do not fear death, since it is acknowledged we must surely die; and there is nothing new, but all things continue the same in this administration of things; and if satiety overtakes those who enjoy even one year of these things, they ought to give heed to our

bigoted: An obstinate belief in ones own opinions

doctrines, that they may live eternally free both from suffering and from want. But if they believe that there is nothing after death, but declare that those who die pass into insensibility, then they become our benefactors when they set us free from sufferings and necessities of this life, and prove themselves to be wicked, and inhuman, and bigoted. For they kill us with no intention of delivering us, but cut us off that we may be deprived of life and pleasure.

Chapter 58. And raise up heretics

And, as we said before, the devils put forward Marcion of Pontus, who is even now teaching men to deny that God is the maker of all things in heaven and on earth, and that the Christ predicted by the prophets is His Son, and preaches another god besides the Creator of all, and likewise another son. And this man many have believed, as if he alone knew the truth, and laugh at us, though they have no proof of what they say, but are carried away irrationally as lambs by a wolf, and become the prey of atheistical doctrines, and of devils. For they who are called devils attempt nothing else than to seduce men from God who made them, and from Christ His first-begotten; and those who are unable to raise themselves above the earth they have riveted, and do now rivet, to things earthly, and to the works of their own hands; but those who devote themselves to the contemplation of things divine, they secretly beat back; and if they have not a wise sober-mindedness, and a pure and passionless life, they drive them into godlessness.

Chapter 59. Plato's obligation to Moses

And that you may learn that it was from our teachers— we mean the account given through the prophets— that Plato borrowed his statement that God, having altered matter which was shapeless, made the world, hear the very words spoken through Moses, who, as above shown, was the first prophet, and of greater antiquity than the Greek writers; and through whom the Spirit of prophecy, signifying how and from what materials God at first formed the world, spoke thus: "In the beginning God created the heaven and the earth. And the earth was invisible and unfurnished, and darkness was upon the face of the deep; and the Spirit of God moved over the waters. And God said, Let there be light; and it was so." So that both Plato and they who agree with him, and we ourselves, have learned, and you also can be convinced, that by the word of God the whole world was made out of the substance spoken of before by Moses. And that which the poets call Erebus, we know was spoken of formerly by Moses. (Deuteronomy 32:22)

Chapter 60. Plato's doctrine of the cross

And the physiological discussion concerning the Son of God in the Timæus of Plato, where he says, "He placed him crosswise in the universe, he borrowed in like manner from Moses;" for in the writings of Moses it is related how at that time, when the Israelites went out of Egypt and were in the wilderness, they fell in with poisonous beasts, both vipers and asps, and every kind of serpent, which slew the people; and that Moses, by the inspiration and influence of God, took brass, and made it into the figure of a cross, and set it in the holy tabernacle, and said to the people, "If you look to this figure, and believe, you shall be saved thereby." (Numbers 21:8) And when this was done, it is recorded that the serpents died, and it is handed down that the people thus escaped death. Which things Plato reading, and not accurately understanding, and not apprehending that it was the figure of the cross, but taking it to be a placing crosswise, he said that the power next to the first God was placed crosswise in the universe. And as to his speaking of a third, he did this because he read, as we said above, that which was spoken by Moses, "that the Spirit of God moved over the waters." For he gives the second place to the Logos which is with God, who he said was placed crosswise in the universe; and the third place to the Spirit who was said to be borne upon the water, saying, "And the third around the third." And hear how the Spirit of prophecy signified through Moses that there should be a conflagration. He spoke thus: "Everlasting fire shall descend, and shall devour to the pit beneath." Deuteronomy 32:22 It is not, then, that we hold the same opinions as others, but that all speak in imitation of ours. Among us these things can be heard and learned from persons who do not even know the forms of the letters, who are uneducated and barbarous in speech, though wise and believing in mind; some, indeed, even maimed and deprived of eyesight; so that you may understand that these things are not the effect of human wisdom, but are uttered by the power of God.

Chapter 61. Christian baptism

I will also relate the manner in which we dedicated ourselves to God when we had been made new through Christ; lest, if we omit this, we seem to be unfair in the explanation we are making. As many as are persuaded and believe that what we teach and say is true, and undertake to be able to live accordingly, are instructed to pray and to entreat God with fasting, for the remission of their sins that are past, we praying and fasting with them. Then they are brought by us where there is water, and are regenerated in the same manner in which we were ourselves regenerated. For, in the name of God, the Father and Lord of the universe, and of our Saviour Jesus Christ, and of the Holy Spirit, they then receive the washing with water. For Christ also said, "Unless you be born again, you shall not enter into the kingdom of heaven." (John 3:5) Now, that it is impossible for those who have once been born to enter into their mothers' wombs, is manifest to all. And how those who have sinned and repent shall escape their sins, is declared by Esaias the prophet, as I wrote above; he thus speaks: "Wash you, make you clean; put away the evil of your doings from your souls; learn to do well; judge the fatherless, and plead for the widow: and come and let us reason together, says the Lord. And though your sins be as scarlet, I will make them white like wool; and though they be as crimson, I will make them white as snow. But if you refuse and rebel, the sword shall devour you: for the mouth of the Lord has spoken it." Isaiah 1:16-20 And for this [rite] we have learned from the apostles this reason. Since at our birth we were born without our own knowledge or choice, by our parents coming together, and were brought up in bad habits and wicked training; in order that we may not remain the children of necessity and of ignorance, but may become the children of choice and knowledge, and may obtain in the water the remission of sins formerly committed, there is pronounced over him who chooses to be born again, and has repented of his sins, the name of God the Father and Lord of the universe; he who leads to the laver the person that is to be washed calling him by this name alone. For no one can utter the name of the ineffable God; and if any one dare to say that there is a name, he raves with a hopeless madness. And this washing is called illumination, because they who learn these things are illuminated in their understandings. And in the name of Jesus Christ, who was crucified under Pontius Pilate, and in the name of the Holy Ghost, who through the prophets foretold all things about Jesus, he who is illuminated is washed.

Chapter 62. Its imitation by demons

And the devils, indeed, having heard this washing published by the prophet, instigated those who enter their temples, and are about to approach them with libations and burnt-offerings, also to sprinkle themselves; and they cause them also to wash themselves entirely, as they depart [from the sacrifice], before they enter into the shrines in which their images are set. And the command, too, given by the priests to those who enter and worship in the temples, that they take off their shoes, the devils, learning what happened to the above- mentioned prophet Moses, have given in imitation of these things. For at that juncture, when Moses was ordered to go down into Egypt and lead out the people of the Israelites who were there, and while he was tending the flocks of his maternal uncle in the land of Arabia, our Christ conversed with him under the appearance of fire from a bush, and said, "Put off your shoes, and draw near and hear." And he, when he had put off his shoes and drawn near, heard that he was to go down into Egypt and lead out the people of the Israelites there; and he received mighty power from Christ, who spoke to him in the appearance of fire, and went down and led out the people, having done great and marvellous things; which, if you desire to know, you will learn them accurately from his writings.

Chapter 63. How God appeared to Moses

And all the Jews even now teach that the nameless God spoke to Moses; whence the Spirit of prophecy, accusing them by Isaiah the prophet mentioned above, said "The ox knows his owner, and the ass his master's crib; but Israel does not know Me, and My people do not understand." (Isaiah 1:3) And Jesus the Christ, because the Jews knew not what the Father was, and what the Son, in like manner accused them; and Himself said, "No one knows the Father, but the Son; nor the Son, but the Father, and they to whom the Son reveals Him." (Matthew 11:27) Now the Word of God is His Son, as we have before said. And He is called Angel and Apostle; for He declares whatever we ought to know, and is sent forth to declare whatever is revealed; as our Lord Himself says, "He that hears Me, hears Him that sent Me." (Luke 10:16) From the writings of Moses also this will be manifest; for thus it is written in them, "And the Angel of God spoke to Moses, in a flame of fire out of the bush, and said, I am that I am, the God of Abraham, the God of Isaac, the God of Jacob, the God of your fathers; go down into Egypt, and bring forth My people." (Exodus 3:6) And if you wish to learn what follows, you can do so from the same writings; for it is impossible to relate the whole here. But so much is written for the sake of proving that Jesus the Christ is the Son of God and His Apostle, being of old the Word, and appearing sometimes in the form of fire, and sometimes in the likeness of angels; but now, by the will of God, having become man for the human race, He endured all the sufferings which the devils instigated the senseless Jews to inflict upon Him; who, though they have it expressly affirmed in the writings of Moses, "And the angel of God spoke to Moses in a flame of fire in a bush, and said, I am that I am, the God of Abraham, and the God of Isaac, and the God of Jacob," yet maintain that He who said this was the Father and Creator of the universe. Whence also the Spirit of prophecy rebukes them, and says, "Israel does not know Me, my people have not understood Me." (Isaiah 1:3) And again, Jesus, as we have already shown, while He was with them, said, "No one knows the Father, but the Son; nor the Son but the Father, and those to whom the Son will reveal Him." (Matthew 11:27) The Jews, accordingly, being throughout of opinion that it was the Father of the universe who spoke to Moses, though He who spoke to him was indeed the Son of God, who is called both Angel and Apostle, are justly charged, both by the Spirit of prophecy and by Christ Himself, with knowing neither the Father nor the Son. For they who affirm that the Son is the Father, are proved neither to have become acquainted with the Father, nor to know that the Father of the universe has a Son; who also, being the first-begotten Word of God, is even God. And of old He appeared in the shape of fire and in the likeness of an angel to Moses and to the other prophets; but now in the times of your reign, having, as we before said, become Man by a virgin, according to the counsel of the Father, for the salvation of those who believe in Him, He endured both to be set at nought and to suffer, that by dying and rising again He might conquer death. And that which was said out of the bush to Moses, "I am that I am, the God of Abraham, and the God of Isaac, and the God of Jacob, and the God of your fathers," (Exodus 3:6) this signified that they, even though dead, are yet in existence, and are men belonging to Christ Himself. For they were the first of all men to busy themselves in the search after God; Abraham being the father of Isaac, and Isaac of Jacob, as Moses wrote.

Chapter 64. Further misrepresentations of the truth

From what has been already said, you can understand how the devils, in imitation of what was said by Moses, asserted that Proserpine was the daughter of Jupiter, and instigated the people to set up an image of her under the name of Kore [Cora, i.e., the maiden or daughter] at the spring-heads. For, as we wrote above, Moses said, "In the beginning God made the heaven and the earth. And the earth was without form and unfurnished: and the Spirit of God moved upon the face of the waters." In imitation, therefore, of what is here said of the Spirit of God moving on the waters, they said that Proserpine [or Cora] was the daughter of Jupiter. And in like manner also they craftily feigned that Minerva was the daughter of Jupiter, not by sexual union, but, knowing that God conceived and made the world by the Word, they say that Minerva is the first conception [ἔννοια]; which we consider to be very absurd, bringing forward the form of the conception in a female shape. And in like manner the actions of those others who are called sons of Jupiter sufficiently condemn them.

Chapter 65. Administration of the sacraments

But we, after we have thus washed him who has been convinced and has assented to our teaching, bring him to the place where those who are called brethren are assembled, in order that we may offer hearty prayers in common for ourselves and for the baptized [illuminated] person, and for all others in every place, that we may be counted worthy, now that we have learned the truth, by our works also to be found good citizens and keepers of the commandments, so that we may be saved with an everlasting salvation. Having ended the prayers, we salute one another with a kiss. There is then brought to the president of the brethren bread and a cup of wine mixed with water; and he taking them, gives praise and glory to the Father of the universe, through the name of the Son and of the Holy Ghost, and offers thanks at considerable length for our being counted worthy to receive these things at His hands. And when he has concluded the prayers and thanksgivings, all the people present express their assent by saying Amen. This word Amen answers in the Hebrew language to γένοιτο [so be it]. And when the president has given thanks, and all the people have expressed their assent, those who are called by us deacons give to each of those present to partake of the bread and wine mixed with water over which the thanksgiving was pronounced, and to those who are absent they carry away a portion.

Chapter 66. Of the Eucharist

And this food is called among us Εὐχαριστία [the Eucharist], of which no one is allowed to partake but the man who believes that the things which we teach are true, and who has been washed with the washing that is for the remission of sins, and unto regeneration, and who is so living as Christ has enjoined. For not as common bread and common drink do we receive these; but in like manner as Jesus Christ our Saviour, having been made flesh by the Word of God, had both flesh and blood for our salvation, so likewise have we been taught that the food which is blessed by the prayer of His word, and from which our blood and flesh by transmutation are nourished, is the flesh and blood of that Jesus who was made flesh. For the apostles, in the memoirs composed by them, which are called Gospels, have thus delivered unto us what was enjoined upon them; that Jesus took bread, and when He had given thanks, said, "This do in remembrance of Me, (Luke 22:19) this is My body;" and that, after the same manner, having taken the cup and given thanks, He said, "This is My blood;" and gave it to them alone. Which the wicked devils have imitated in the mysteries of Mithras, commanding the same thing to be done. For, that bread and a cup of water are placed with certain incantations in the mystic rites of one who is being initiated, you either know or can learn.

Chapter 67. Weekly worship of the Christians

And we afterwards continually remind each other of these things. And the wealthy among us help the needy; and we always keep together; and for all things wherewith we are supplied, we bless the Maker of all through His Son Jesus Christ, and through the Holy Ghost. And on the day called Sunday, all who live in cities or in the country gather together to one place, and the memoirs of the apostles or the writings of the prophets are read, as long as time permits; then, when the reader has ceased, the president verbally instructs, and exhorts to the imitation of these good things. Then we all rise together and pray, and, as we before said, when our prayer is ended, bread and wine and water are brought, and the president in like manner offers prayers and thanksgivings, according to his ability, and the people assent, saying Amen; and there is a distribution to each, and a participation of that over which thanks have been given, and to those who are absent a portion is sent by the deacons. And they who are well to do, and willing, give what each thinks fit; and what is collected is deposited with the president, who succours the orphans and widows and those who, through sickness or any other cause, are in want, and those who are in bonds and the strangers sojourning among us, and in a word takes care of all who are in need. But Sunday is the day on which we all hold our common assembly, because it is the first day on which God, having wrought a change in the darkness and matter, made the world; and Jesus Christ our Saviour on the same day rose from the dead. For He was crucified on the day before that of Saturn (Saturday); and on the day after that of Saturn, which is the day of the Sun, having appeared to His apostles and disciples, He taught them these things, which we have submitted to you also for your consideration.

Chapter 68. Conclusion

And if these things seem to you to be reasonable and true, honour them; but if they seem nonsensical, despise them as nonsense, and do not decree death against those who have done no wrong, as you would against enemies. For we forewarn you, that you shall not escape the coming judgment of God, if you continue in your injustice; and we ourselves will invite you to do that which is pleasing to God. And though from the letter of the greatest and most illustrious Emperor Adrian, your father, we could demand that you order judgment to be given as we have desired, yet we have made this appeal and explanation, not on the ground of Adrian's decision, but because we know that what we ask is just. And we have subjoined the copy of Adrian's epistle, that you may know that we are speaking truly about this. And the following is the copy:—

APPENDIX

Epistle of Adrian in behalf of the Christians

I have received the letter addressed to me by your predecessor Serenius Granianus, a most illustrious man; and this communication I am unwilling to pass over in silence, lest innocent persons be disturbed, and occasion be given to the informers for practising villany. Accordingly, if the inhabitants of your province will so far sustain this petition of theirs as to accuse the Christians in some court of law, I do not prohibit them from doing so. But I will not suffer them to make use of mere entreaties and outcries. For it is far more just, if any one desires to make an accusation, that you give judgment upon it. If, therefore, any one makes the accusation, and furnishes proof that the said men do anything contrary to the laws, you shall adjudge punishments in proportion to the offenses. And this, by Hercules, you shall give special heed to, that if any man shall, through mere calumny, bring an accusation against any of these persons, you shall award to him more severe punishments in proportion to his wickedness.

Epistle of Antoninus to the common assembly of Asia

The Emperor Cæsar Titus Ælius Adrianus Antoninus Augustus Pius, Supreme Pontiff, in the fifteenth year of his tribuneship, Consul for the third time, Father of the fatherland, to the Common Assembly of Asia, greeting: I should have thought that the gods themselves would see to it that such offenders should not escape. For if they had the power, they themselves would much rather punish those who refuse to worship them; but it is you who bring trouble on these persons, and accuse as the opinion of atheists that which they hold, and lay to their charge certain other things which we are unable to prove. But it would be advantageous to them that they should be thought to die for that of which they are accused, and they conquer you by being lavish of their lives rather than yield that obedience which you require of them. And regarding the earthquakes which have already happened and are now occurring, it is not seemly that you remind us of them, losing heart whenever they occur, and thus set your conduct in contrast with that of these men; for they have much greater confidence towards God than you yourselves have. And you, indeed, seem at such times to ignore the gods, and you neglect the temples, and make no recognition of the worship of God. And hence you are jealous of those who do serve Him, and persecute them to the death. Concerning such persons, some others also of the governors of provinces wrote to my most divine father; to whom he replied that they should not at all disturb such persons, unless they were found to be attempting anything against the Roman government. And to myself many have sent intimations regarding such persons, to whom I also replied in pursuance of my father's judgment. But if any one has a matter to bring against any person of this class, merely as such a person, let the accused be acquitted of the charge, even though he should be found to be such an one; but let the accuser be amenable to justice.

Epistle of Marcus Aurelius to the senate, in which he testifies that the Christians were the cause of his victory

The Emperor Cæsar Marcus Aurelius Antoninus, Germanicus, Parthicus, Sarmaticus, to the People of Rome, and to the sacred Senate greeting: I explained to you my grand design, and what advantages I gained on the confines of Germany, with much labour and suffering, in consequence of the circumstance that I was surrounded by the enemy; I myself being shut up in Carnuntum by seventy-four cohorts, nine miles off. And the enemy being at hand, the scouts pointed out to us, and our general Pompeianus showed us that there was close on us a mass of a mixed multitude of 977,000 men, which indeed we saw; and I was shut up by this vast host, having with me only a battalion composed of the first, tenth, double and marine legions. Having then examined my own position, and my host, with respect to the vast mass of barbarians and of the enemy, I quickly betook myself to prayer to the gods of my country. But being disregarded by them, I summoned those who among us go by the name of Christians. And having made inquiry, I discovered a great number and vast host of them, and raged against them, which was by no means becoming; for afterwards I learned their power. Wherefore they began the battle, not by preparing weapons, nor arms, nor bugles; for such preparation is hateful to them, on account of the God they bear about in their conscience. Therefore it is probable that those whom we suppose to be atheists, have God as their ruling power entrenched in their conscience. For having cast themselves on the ground, they prayed not only for me, but also for the whole army as it stood, that they might be delivered from the present thirst and famine. For during five days we had got no water, because there was none; for we were in the heart of Germany, and in the enemy's territory. And simultaneously with their casting themselves on the ground, and praying to God (a God of whom I am ignorant), water poured from heaven, upon us most refreshingly cool, but upon the enemies of Rome a withering hail. And immediately we recognised the presence of God following on the prayer — a God unconquerable and indestructible. Founding upon this, then, let us pardon such as are Christians, lest they pray for and obtain such a weapon against ourselves. And I counsel that no such person be accused on the ground of his being a Christian. But if any one be found laying to the charge of a Christian that he is a Christian, I desire that it be made manifest that he who is accused as a Christian, and acknowledges that he is one, is accused of nothing else than only this, that he is a Christian; but that he who arraigns him be burned alive. And I further desire, that he who is entrusted with the government of the province shall not compel the Christian, who confesses and certifies such a matter, to retract; neither shall he commit him. And I desire that these things be confirmed by a decree of the Senate. And I command this my edict to be published in the Forum of Trajan, in order that it may be read. The prefect Vitrasius Pollio will see that it be transmitted to all the provinces round about, and that no one who wishes to make use of or to possess it be hindered from obtaining a copy from the document I now publish.

AGAINST HERESIES

Irenaeus

TRANSLATED BY PHILIP SCHAFF ET AL

BOOK III

Preface.

Thou hast indeed enjoined upon me, my very dear friend, that I should bring to light the Valentinian doctrines, concealed, as their votaries imagine; that I should exhibit their diversity, and compose a treatise in refutation of them. I therefore have undertaken—showing that they spring from Simon, the father of all heretics—to exhibit both their doctrines and successions, and to set forth arguments against them all. Wherefore, since the conviction of these men and their exposure is in many points but one work, I have sent unto thee [certain] books, of which the first comprises the opinions of all these men, and exhibits their customs, and the character of their behaviour. In the second, again, their perverse teachings are cast down and overthrown, and, such as they really are, laid bare and open to view. But in this, the third book I shall adduce proofs from the Scriptures, so that I may come behind in nothing of what thou hast enjoined; yea, that over and above what thou didst reckon upon, thou mayest receive from me the means of combating and vanquishing those who, in whatever manner, are propagating falsehood. For the love of God, being rich and ungrudging, confers upon the suppliant more than he can ask from it. Call to mind then, the things which I have stated in the two preceding books, and, taking these in connection with them, thou shalt have from me a very copious refutation of all the heretics; and faithfully and strenuously shalt thou resist them in defence of the only true and life-giving faith, which the Church has received from the apostles and imparted to her sons. For the Lord of all gave to His apostles the power of the Gospel, through whom also we have known the truth, that is, the doctrine of the Son of God; to whom also did the Lord declare: "He that heareth you, heareth Me; and he that despiseth you, despiseth Me, and Him that sent Me."

Chapter I.—The apostles did not commence to preach the Gospel, or to place anything on record until they were endowed with the gifts and power of the Holy Spirit. They preached one God alone, Maker of heaven and earth.

1. We have learned from none others the plan of our salvation, than from those through whom the Gospel has come down to us, which they did at one time proclaim in public, and, at a later period, by the will of God, handed down to us in the Scriptures, to be the ground and pillar of our faith. For it is unlawful to assert that they preached before they possessed "perfect knowledge," as some do even venture to say, boasting themselves as improvers of the apostles. For, after our Lord rose from the dead, [the apostles] were invested with power from on high when the Holy Spirit came down [upon them], were filled from all [His gifts], and had perfect knowledge: they departed to the ends of the earth, preaching the glad tidings of the good things [sent] from God to us, and proclaiming the peace of heaven to men, who indeed do all equally and individually possess the Gospel of God. Matthew also issued a written Gospel among the Hebrews in their own dialect, while Peter and Paul were preaching at Rome, and laying the foundations of the Church. After their departure, Mark, the disciple and interpreter of Peter, did also hand down to us in writing what had been preached by Peter. Luke also, the companion of Paul, recorded in a book the Gospel preached by him. Afterwards, John, the disciple of the Lord, who also had leaned upon His breast, did himself publish a Gospel during his residence at Ephesus in Asia.

2. These have all declared to us that there is one God, Creator of heaven and earth, announced by the law and the prophets; and one Christ the Son of God. If any one do not agree to these truths, he despises the companions of the Lord; nay more, he despises Christ Himself the Lord; yea, he despises the Father also, and stands self- condemned, resisting and opposing his own salvation, as is the case with all heretics.

Chapter II.—The heretics follow neither Scripture nor tradition.

1. When, however, they are confuted from the Scriptures, they turn round and accuse these same Scriptures, as if they were not correct, nor of authority, and [assert] that they are ambiguous, and that the truth

cannot be extracted from them by those who are ignorant of tradition. For [they allege] that the truth was not delivered by means of written documents, but vivâ voce: wherefore also Paul declared, "But we speak wisdom among those that are perfect, but not the wisdom of this world." And this wisdom each one of them alleges to be the fiction of his own inventing, forsooth; so that, according to their idea, the truth properly resides at one time in Valentinus, at another in Marcion, at another in Cerinthus, then afterwards in Basilides, or has even been indifferently in any other opponent, who could speak nothing pertaining to salvation. For every one of these men, being altogether of a perverse disposition, depraving the system of truth, is not ashamed to preach himself.

2. But, again, when we refer them to that tradition which originates from the apostles, [and] which is preserved by means of the succession of presbyters in the Churches, they object to tradition, saying that they themselves are wiser not merely than the presbyters, but even than the apostles, because they have discovered the unadulterated truth. For [they maintain] that the apostles intermingled the things of the law with the words of the Saviour; and that not the apostles alone, but even the Lord Himself, spoke as at one time from the Demiurge, at another from the intermediate place, and yet again from the Pleroma, but that they themselves, indubitably, unsulliedly, and purely, have knowledge of the hidden mystery: this is, indeed, to blaspheme their Creator after a most impudent manner! It comes to this, therefore, that these men do now consent neither to Scripture nor to tradition.

3. Such are the adversaries with whom we have to deal, my very dear friend, endeavouring like slippery serpents to escape at all points. Where-fore they must be opposed at all points, if per-chance, by cutting off their retreat, we may succeed in turning them back to the truth. For, though it is not an easy thing for a soul under the influence of error to repent, yet, on the other hand, it is not altogether impossible to escape from error when the truth is brought alongside it.

Chapter III.—A refutation of the heretics, from the fact that, in the various Churches, a perpetual succession of bishops was kept up.

1. It is within the power of all, therefore, in every Church, who may wish to see the truth, to contemplate clearly the tradition of the apostles manifested throughout the whole world; and we are in a position to reckon up those who were by the apostles instituted bishops in the Churches, and [to demonstrate] the succession of these men to our own times; those who neither taught nor knew of anything like what these [heretics] rave about. For if the apostles had known hidden mysteries, which they were in the habit of imparting to "the perfect" apart and privily from the rest, they would have delivered them especially to those to whom they were also committing the Churches themselves. For they were desirous that these men should be very perfect and blameless in all things, whom also they were leaving behind as their successors, delivering up their own place of government to these men; which men, if they discharged their functions honestly, would be a great boon [to the Church], but if they should fall away, the direst calamity.

2. Since, however, it would be very tedious, in such a volume as this, to reckon up the successions of all the Churches, we do put to confusion all those who, in whatever manner, whether by an evil self- pleasing, by vainglory, or by blindness and perverse opinion, assemble in unauthorized meetings; [we do this, I say,] by indicating that tradition derived from the apostles, of the very great, the very ancient, and universally known Church founded and organized at Rome by the two most glorious apostles, Peter and Paul; as also [by pointing out] the faith preached to men, which comes down to our time by means of the successions of the bishops. For it is a matter of necessity that every Church should agree with this Church, on account of its pre-eminent authority, that is, the faithful everywhere, inasmuch as the apostolical tradition has been preserved continuously by those [faithful men] who exist everywhere.

3. The blessed apostles, then, having founded and built up the Church, committed into the hands of Linus the office of the episcopate. Of this Linus, Paul makes mention in the Epistles to Timothy. To him succeeded Anacletus; and after him, in the third place from the apostles, Clement was allotted the bishopric. This man, as he had seen the blessed apostles, and had been conversant with them, might be said to have the preaching of the apostles still echoing [in his ears], and their traditions before his eyes. Nor was he alone [in this], for there were many still

remaining who had received instructions from the apostles. In the time of this Clement, no small dissension having occurred among the brethren at Corinth, the Church in Rome despatched a most powerful letter to the Corinthians, exhorting them to peace, renewing their faith, and declaring the tradition which it had lately received from the apostles, proclaiming the one God, omnipotent, the Maker of heaven and earth, the Creator of man, who brought on the deluge, and called Abraham, who led the people from the land of Egypt, spake with Moses, set forth the law, sent the prophets, and who has prepared fire for the devil and his angels. From this document, whosoever chooses to do so, may learn that He, the Father of our Lord Jesus Christ, was preached by the Churches, and may also understand the apostolical tradition of the Church, since this Epistle is of older date than these men who are now propagating falsehood, and who conjure into existence another god beyond the Creator and the Maker of all existing things. To this Clement there succeeded Evaristus. Alexander followed Evaristus; then, sixth from the apostles, Sixtus was appointed; after him, Telephorus, who was gloriously martyred; then Hyginus; after him, Pius; then after him, Anicetus. Sorer having succeeded Anicetus, Eleutherius does now, in the twelfth place from the apostles, hold the inheritance of the episcopate. In this order, and by this succession, the ecclesiastical tradition from the apostles, and the preaching of the truth, have come down to us. And this is most abundant proof that there is one and the same vivifying faith, which has been preserved in the Church from the apostles until now, and handed down in truth.

Polycarp was instructed by the apostles.

4. But Polycarp also was not only instructed by apostles, and conversed with many who had seen Christ, but was also, by apostles in Asia, appointed bishop of the Church in Smyrna, whom I also saw in my early youth, for he tarried [on earth] a very long time, and, when a very old man, gloriously and most nobly suffering martyrdom, departed this life, having always taught the things which he had learned from the apostles, and which the Church has handed down, and which alone are true. To these things all the Asiatic Churches testify, as do also those men who have succeeded Polycarp down to the present time,—a man who was of much greater weight, and a more stedfast witness of truth, than Valentinus, and Marcion, and the rest of the heretics. He it was who, coming to Rome in the time of Anicetus caused many to turn away from the aforesaid heretics to the Church of God, proclaiming that he had received this one and sole truth from the apostles,—that, namely, which

is handed down by the Church. There are also those who heard from him that John, the disciple of the Lord, going to bathe at Ephesus, and perceiving Cerinthus within, rushed out of the bath-house without bathing, exclaiming, "Let us fly, lest even the bath-house fall down, because Cerinthus, the enemy of the truth, is within." And Polycarp himself replied to Marcion, who met him on one occasion, and said, "Dost thou know me?" "I do know thee, the first-born of Satan." Such was the horror which the apostles and their disciples had against holding even verbal communication with any corrupters of the truth; as Paul also says, "A man that is an heretic, after the first and second admonition, reject; knowing that he that is such is subverted, and sinneth, being condemned of himself." There is also a very powerful Epistle of Polycarp written to the Philippians, from which those who choose to do so, and are anxious about their salvation, can learn the character of his faith, and the preaching of the truth. Then, again, the Church in Ephesus, founded by Paul, and having John remaining among them permanently until the times of Trajan, is a true witness of the tradition of the apostles.

Chapter IV.—The truth is to be found nowhere else but in the Catholic Church, the sole depository of apostolical doctrine. Heresies are of recent formation, and cannot trace their origin up to the apostles.

1. Since therefore we have such proofs, it is not necessary to seek the truth among others which it is easy to obtain from the Church; since the apostles, like a rich man [depositing his money] in a bank, lodged in her hands most copiously all things pertaining to the truth: so that every man, whosoever will, can draw from her the water of life. For she is the entrance to life; all others are thieves and robbers. On this account are we bound to avoid them, but to make choice of the thing pertaining to the Church with the utmost diligence, and to lay hold of the tradition of the truth. For how stands the case? Suppose there arise a dispute relative to some important question among us, should we not have recourse to the most ancient Churches with which the apostles held constant intercourse, and learn from them what is certain and clear in regard to the present question? For how should it be if the apostles themselves had not left us writings? Would it not be necessary, [in that case,] to follow the course of the tradition which they handed down to those to whom they did commit the Churches?

2. To which course many nations of those barbarians who believe in Christ do assent, having salvation written in their hearts by the Spirit, without paper or ink, and, carefully preserving the ancient tradition, believing in one God, the Creator of heaven and earth, and all things therein, by means of Christ Jesus, the Son of God; who, because of His surpassing love towards His creation, condescended to be born of the virgin, He Himself uniting man through Himself to God, and having suffered under Pontius Pilate, and rising again, and having been received up in splendour, shall come in glory, the Saviour of those who are saved, and the Judge of those who are judged, and sending into eternal fire those who transform the truth, and despise His Father and His advent. Those who, in the absence of written documents, have believed this faith, are barbarians, so far as regards our language; but as regards doctrine, manner, and tenor of life, they are, because of faith, very wise indeed; and they do please God, ordering their conversation in all righteousness, chastity, and wisdom. If any one were to preach to these men the inventions of the heretics, speaking to them in their own language, they would at once stop their ears, and flee as far off as possible, not enduring even to listen to the blasphemous address. Thus, by means of that ancient tradition of the apostles, they do not suffer their mind to conceive anything of the [doctrines suggested by the] portentous language of these teachers, among whom neither Church nor doctrine has ever been established.

3. For, prior to Valentinus, those who follow Valentinus had no existence; nor did those from Marcion exist before Marcion; nor, in short, had any of those malignant-minded people, whom I have above enumerated, any being previous to the initiators and inventors of their perversity. For Valentinus came to Rome in the time of Hyginus, flourished under Pius, and remained until Anicetus. Cerdon, too, Marcion's predecessor, himself arrived in the time of Hyginus, who was the ninth bishop. Coming frequently into the Church, and making public confession, he thus remained, one time teaching in secret, and then again making public confession; but at last, having been denounced for corrupt teaching, he was excommunicated from the assembly of the brethren. Marcion, then, succeeding him, flourished under Anicetus, who held the tenth place of the episcopate. But the rest, who are called Gnostics, take rise from Menander, Simon's disciple, as I have shown; and each one of them appeared to be both the father and the high priest of that doctrine into which he has been initiated. But all these (the

Marcosians) broke out into their apostasy much later, even during the intermediate period of the Church.

Chapter V.—Christ and His apostles, without any fraud, deception, or hypocrisy, preached that one God, the Father, was the founder of all things. They did not accommodate their doctrine to the prepossessions of their hearers.

1. Since, therefore, the tradition from the apostles does thus exist in the Church, and is permanent among us, let us revert to the Scriptural proof furnished by those apostles who did also write the Gospel, in which they recorded the doctrine regarding God, pointing out that our Lord Jesus Christ is the truth, and that no lie is in Him. As also David says, prophesying His birth from a virgin, and the resurrection from the dead, "Truth has sprung out of the earth." The apostles, likewise, being disciples of the truth, are above all falsehood; for a lie has no fellowship with the truth, just as darkness has none with light, but the presence of the one shuts out that of the other. Our Lord, therefore, being the truth, did not speak lies; and whom He knew to have taken origin from a defect, He never would have acknowledged as God, even the God of all, the Supreme King, too, and His own Father, an imperfect being as a perfect one, an animal one as a spiritual, Him who was without the Pleroma as Him who was within it. Neither did His disciples make mention of any other God, or term any other Lord, except Him, who was truly the God and Lord of all, as these most vain sophists affirm that the apostles did with hypocrisy frame their doctrine according to the capacity of their hearers, and gave answers after the opinions of their questioners,—fabling blind things for the blind, according to their blindness; for the dull according to their dulness; for those in error according to their error. And to those who imagined that the Demiurge alone was God, they preached him; but to those who are capable of comprehending the unnameable Father, they did declare the unspeakable mystery through parables and enigmas: so that the Lord and the apostles exercised the office of teacher not to further the cause of truth, but even in hypocrisy, and as each individual was able to receive it!

2. Such [a line of conduct] belongs not to those who heal, or who give life: it is rather that of those bringing on diseases, and increasing ignorance; and much more true than these men shall the law be found,

which pronounces every one accursed who sends the blind man astray in the way. For the apostles, who were commissioned to find out the wanderers, and to be for sight to those who saw not, and medicine to the weak, certainly did not address them in accordance with their opinion at the time, but according to revealed truth. For no persons of any kind would act properly, if they should advise blind men, just about to fall over a precipice, to continue their most dangerous path, as if it were the right one, and as if they might go on in safety. Or what medical man, anxious to heal a sick person, would prescribe in accordance with the patient's whims, and not according to the requisite medicine? But that the Lord came as the physician of the sick, He does Himself declare saying, "They that are whole need not a physician, but they that are sick; I came not to call the righteous, but sinners to repentance." How then shall the sick be strengthened, or how shall sinners come to repentance? Is it by persevering in the very same courses? or, on the contrary, is it by undergoing a great change and reversal of their former mode of living, by which they have brought upon themselves no slight amount of sickness, and many sins? But ignorance, the mother of all these, is driven out by knowledge. Wherefore the Lord used to impart knowledge to His disciples, by which also it was His practice to heal those who were suffering, and to keep back sinners from sin. He therefore did not address them in accordance with their pristine notions, nor did He reply to them in harmony with the opinion of His questioners, but according to the doctrine leading to salvation, without hypocrisy or respect of person.

3. This is also made clear from the words of the Lord, who did truly reveal the Son of God to those of the circumcision— Him who had been foretold as Christ by the prophets; that is, He set Himself forth, who had restored liberty to men, and bestowed on them the inheritance of incorruption. And again, the apostles taught the Gentiles that they should leave vain stocks and stones, which they imagined to be gods, and worship the true God, who had created and made all the human family, and, by means of His creation, did nourish, increase, strengthen, and preserve them in being; and that they might look for His Son Jesus Christ, who redeemed us from apostasy with His own blood, so that we should also be a sanctified people,—who shall also descend from heaven in His Father's power, and pass judgment upon all, and who shall freely give the good things of God to those who shall have kept His commandments. He, appearing in these last times, the chief

cornerstone, has gathered into one, and united those that were far off and those that were near; that is, the circumcision and the uncircumcision, enlarging Japhet, and placing him in the dwelling of Shem.

Chapter VI—The Holy Ghost, throughout the Old Testament Scriptures, made mention of no other God or Lord, save him who is the true God.

1. Therefore neither would the Lord, nor the Holy Spirit, nor the apostles, have ever named as God, definitely and absolutely, him who was not God, unless he were truly God; nor would they have named any one in his own person Lord, except God the Father ruling over all, and His Son who has received dominion from His Father over all creation, as this passage has it: "The Lord said unto my Lord, Sit Thou at my right hand, until I make Thine enemies Thy footstool." Here the [Scripture] represents to us the Father addressing the Son; He who gave Him the inheritance of the heathen, and subjected to Him all His enemies. Since, therefore, the Father is truly Lord, and the Son truly Lord, the Holy Spirit has fitly designated them by the title of Lord. And again, referring to the destruction of the Sodomites, the Scripture says, "Then the Lord rained upon Sodom and upon Gomorrah fire and brimstone from the Lord out of heaven." For it here points out that the Son, who had also been talking with Abraham, had received power to judge the Sodomites for their wickedness. And this [text following] does declare the same truth: "Thy throne, O God, is for ever and ever; the sceptre of Thy kingdom is a right sceptre. Thou hast loved righteousness, and hated iniquity: therefore God, Thy God, hath anointed Thee." For the Spirit designates both [of them] by the name, of God—both Him who is anointed as Son, and Him who does anoint, that is, the Father. And again: "God stood in the congregation of the gods, He judges among the gods." He [here] refers to the Father and the Son, and those who have received the adoption; but these are the Church. For she is the synagogue of God, which God—that is, the Son Himself— has gathered by Himself. Of whom He again speaks: "The God of gods, the Lord hath spoken, and hath called the earth." Who is meant by God? He of whom He has said, "God shall come openly, our God, and shall not keep silence;" that is, the Son, who came manifested to men who said, "I have openly appeared to those who seek Me not." But of what gods [does he speak]? [Of those] to whom He says, "I have said, Ye are

we are adopted into the family

gods, and all sons of the Most High." To those, no doubt, who have received the grace of the "adoption, by which we cry, Abba Father."

2. Wherefore, as I have already stated, no other is named as God, or is called Lord, except Him who is God and Lord of all, who also said to Moses, "I am that I am. And thus shalt thou say to the children of Israel: He who is, hath sent me unto you;" and His Son Jesus Christ our Lord, who makes those that believe in His name the sons of God. And again, when the Son speaks to Moses, He says, "I am come down to deliver this people." For it is He who descended and ascended for the salvation of men. Therefore God has been declared through the Son, who is in the Father, and has the Father in Himself

—He who is, the Father bearing witness to the Son, and the Son announcing the Father.—As also Esaias says, "I too am witness," he declares, "saith the Lord God, and the Son whom I have chosen, that ye may know, and believe, and understand that I am."

3. When, however, the Scripture terms them [gods] which are no gods, it does not, as I have already remarked, declare them as gods in every sense, but with a certain addition and signification, by which they are shown to be no gods at all. As with David: "The gods of the heathen are idols of demons;" and, "Ye shall not follow other gods." For in that he says "the gods of the heathen"—but the heathen are ignorant of the true God—and calls them "other gods," he bars their claim [to be looked upon] as gods at all. But as to what they are in their own person, he speaks concerning them; "for they are," he says, "the idols of demons." And Esaias: "Let them be confounded, all who blaspheme God, and carve useless things; even I am witness, saith God." He removes them from [the category of] gods, but he makes use of the word alone, for this [purpose], that we may know of whom he speaks. Jeremiah also says the same: "The gods that have not made the heavens and earth, let them perish from the earth which is under the heaven." For, from the fact of his having subjoined their destruction, he shows them to be no gods at all. Elias, too, when all Israel was assembled at Mount Carmel, wishing to turn them from idolatry, says to them, "How long halt ye between two opinions? If the Lord be God, follow Him." And again, at the burnt-offering, he thus addresses the idolatrous priests: "Ye shall call upon the name of your gods, and I will call on the name of the Lord my God; and the Lord that will hearken by fire, He is God."

Now, from the fact of the prophet having said these words, he proves that these gods which were reputed so among those men, are no gods at all. He directed them to that God upon whom he believed, and who was truly God; whom invoking, he exclaimed, "Lord God of Abraham, God of Isaac, and God of Jacob, hear me to-day, and let all this people know that Thou art the God of Israel."

Irenæus's prayer

4. Wherefore I do also call upon thee, Lord God of Abraham, and God of Isaac, and God of Jacob and Israel, who art the Father of our Lord Jesus Christ, the God who, through the abundance of Thy mercy, hast had a favour towards us, that we should know Thee, who hast made heaven and earth, who rulest over all, who art the only and the true God, above whom there is none other God; grant, by our Lord Jesus Christ, the governing power of the Holy Spirit; give to every reader of this book to know Thee, that Thou art God alone, to be strengthened in Thee, and to avoid every heretical, and godless, and impious doctrine.

False gods and the term God and how it's used

5. And the Apostle Paul also, saying, "For though ye have served them which are no gods; ye now know God, or rather, are known of God," has made a separation between those that were not [gods] and Him who is God. And again, speaking of Antichrist, he says, "who opposeth and exalteth himself above all that is called God, or that is worshipped." He points out here those who are called gods, by such as know not God, that is, idols. For the Father of all is called God, and is so; and Antichrist shall be lifted up, not above Him, but above those which are indeed called gods, but are not. And Paul himself says that this is true: "We know that an idol is nothing, and that there is none other God but one. For though there be that are called gods, whether in heaven or in earth; yet to us there is but one God, the Father, of whom are all things, and we through Him; and one Lord Jesus Christ, by whom are all things, and we by Him." For he has made a distinction, and separated those which are indeed called gods, but which are none, from the one God the Father, from whom are all things, and, he has confessed in the most decided manner in his own person, one Lord Jesus Christ. But in this [clause], "whether in heaven or in earth," he does not speak of the formers of the world, as these [teachers] expound it; but his meaning is similar to that of Moses, when it is said, "Thou shalt not make to thyself any image for God, of whatsoever things are in heaven above, whatsoever in the earth beneath, and whatsoever in the waters under the

earth." And he does thus explain what are meant by the things in heaven: "Lest when," he says, "looking towards heaven, and observing the sun, and the moon, and the stars, and all the ornament of heaven, falling into error, thou shouldest adore and serve them." And Moses himself, being a man of God, was indeed given as a god before Pharaoh; but he is not properly termed Lord, nor is called God by the prophets, but is spoken of by the Spirit as "Moses, the faithful minister and servant of God," which also he was.

Chapter VII.—Reply to an objection founded on the words of St. Paul (2 Cor. iv. 4). St. Paul occasionally uses words not in their grammatical sequence.

1. As to their affirming that Paul said plainly in the Second [Epistle] to the Corinthians, "In whom the god of this world hath blinded the minds of them that believe not," and maintaining that there is indeed one god of this world, but another who is beyond all principality, and beginning, and power, we are not to blame if they, who give out that they do themselves know mysteries beyond God, know not how to read Paul. For if any one read the passage thus—according to Paul's custom, as I show elsewhere, and by many examples, that he uses transposition of words—"In whom God," then pointing it off, and making a slight interval, and at the same time read also the rest [of the sentence] in one [clause], "hath blinded the minds of them of this world that believe not," he shall find out the true [sense]; that it is contained in the expression, "God hath blinded the minds of the unbelievers of this world." And this is shown by means of the little interval [between the clause]. For Paul does not say, "the God of this world," as if recognising any other beyond Him; but he confessed God as indeed God. And he says, "the unbelievers of this world," because they shall not inherit the future age of incorruption. I shall show from Paul himself, how it is that God has blinded the minds of them that believe not, in the course of this work, that we may not just at present distract our mind from the matter in hand, [by wandering] at large.

2. From many other instances also, we may discover that the apostle frequently uses a transposed order in his sentences, due to the rapidity of his discourses, and the impetus of the Spirit which is in him. An example occurs in the [Epistle] to the Galatians, where he expresses himself as follows: "Wherefore then the law of works? It was added,

hyperbaton: A figure of speech
Where a phrase is made discontinuous by the insertion of other words.

until the seed should come to whom the promise was made; [and it was] ordained by angels in the hand of a Mediator." For the order of the words runs thus: "Wherefore then the law of works? Ordained by angels in the hand of a Mediator, it was added until the seed should come to whom the promise was made,"— man thus asking the question, and the Spirit making answer. And again, in the Second to the Thessalonians, speaking of Antichrist, he says, "And then shall that wicked be revealed, whom the Lord Jesus Christ shall slay with the Spirit of His mouth, and shall destroy him with the presence of his coming; [even him] whose coming is after the working of Satan, with all power, and signs, and lying wonders." Now in these [sentences] the order of the words is this: "And then shall be revealed that wicked, whose coming is after the working of Satan, with all power, and signs, and lying wonders, whom the Lord Jesus shall slay with the Spirit of His mouth, and shall destroy with the presence of His coming." For he does not mean that the coming of the Lord is after the working of Satan; but the coming of the wicked one, whom we also call Antichrist. If, then, one does not attend to the [proper] reading [of the passage], and if he do not exhibit the intervals of breathing as they occur, there shall be not only incongruities, but also, when reading, he will utter blasphemy, as if the advent of the Lord could take place according to the working of Satan. *why?* So therefore, in such passages, the hyperbaton must be exhibited by the reading, and the apostle's meaning following on, preserved; and thus we do not read in that passage, "the god of this world," but, "God," whom we do truly call God; and we hear [it declared of] the unbelieving and the blinded of *interesting* this world, that they shall not inherit the world of life which is to come.

Chapter VIII.—Answer to an objection, arising from the words of Christ (Matt. vi. 24). God alone is to be really called God and Lord, for He is without beginning and end.

1. This calumny, then, of these men, having been squashed, it is clearly proved that neither the prophets nor the apostles did ever name another God, or call [him] Lord, except the true and only God. Much more [would this be the case with regard to] the Lord Himself, who did also direct us to "render unto Cæsar the things that are Cæsar's, and to God the things that are God's;" naming indeed Cæsar as Cæsar, but confessing God as God. In like manner also, that [text] which says, "Ye cannot serve two masters," He does Himself interpret, saying, "Ye cannot serve God and mammon;" acknowledging God indeed as God, but mentioning mammon, a thing having also an existence. He does not

call mammon Lord when He says, "Ye cannot serve two masters;" but He teaches His disciples who serve God, not to be subject to mammon, nor to be ruled by it. For He says, "He that committeth sin is the slave of sin." Inasmuch, then, as He terms those "the slaves of sin" who serve sin, but does not certainly call sin itself God, thus also He terms those who serve mammon "the slaves of mammon," not calling mammon God. For mammon is, according to the Jewish language, which the Samaritans do also use, a covetous man, and one who wishes to have more than he ought to have. But according to the Hebrew, it is by the addition of a syllable (adjunctive) called Mamuel, and signifies gulosum, that is, one whose gullet is insatiable. Therefore, according to both these things which are indicated, we cannot serve God and mammon.

hmm

2. But also, when He spoke of the devil as strong, not absolutely so, but as in comparison with us, the Lord showed Himself under every aspect and truly to be the strong man, saying that one can in no other way "spoil the goods of a strong man, if he do not first bind the strong man himself, and then he will spoil his house." Now we were the vessels and the house of this [strong man] when we were in a state of apostasy; for he put us to whatever use he pleased, and the unclean spirit dwelt within us. For he was not strong, as opposed to Him who bound him, and spoiled his house; but as against those persons who were his tools, inasmuch as he caused their thought to wander away from God: these did the Lord snatch from his grasp. As also Jeremiah declares, "The Lord hath redeemed Jacob, and has snatched him from the hand of him that was stronger than he." If, then, he had not pointed out Him who binds and spoils his goods, but had merely spoken of him as being strong, the strong man should have been unconquered. But he also subjoined Him who obtains and retains possession; for he holds who binds, but he is held who is bound. And this he did without any comparison, so that, apostate slave as he was, he might not be compared to the Lord: for not he alone, but not one of created and subject things, shall ever be compared to the Word of God, by whom all things were made, who is our Lord Jesus Christ.

The enemy is not strong. God has broken his grip on us.

3. For that all things, whether Angels, or Archangels, or Thrones, or Dominions, were both established and created by Him who is God over all, through His Word, John has thus pointed out. For when he had spoken of the Word of God as having been in the Father, he added, "All

things were made by Him, and without Him was not anything made." David also, when he had enumerated [His] praises, subjoins by name all things whatsoever I have mentioned, both the heavens and all the powers therein: "For He commanded, and they were created; He spake, and they were made." Whom, therefore, did He command? The Word, no doubt, "by whom," he says, "the heavens were established, and all their power by the breath of His mouth." But that He did Himself make all things freely, and as He pleased, again David says, "But our God is in the heavens above, and in the earth; He hath made all things whatsoever He pleased." But the things established are distinct from Him who has established them, and what have been made from Him who has made them. For He is Himself uncreated, both without beginning and end, and lacking nothing. He is Himself sufficient for Himself; and still further, He grants to all others this very thing, existence; but the things which have been made by Him have received a beginning. But whatever things had a beginning, and are liable to dissolution, and are subject to and stand in need of Him who made them, must necessarily in all respects have a different term [applied to them], even by those who have but a moderate capacity for discerning such things; so that He indeed who made all things can alone, together with His Word, properly be termed God and Lord: but the things which have been made cannot have this term applied to them, neither should they justly assume that appellation which belongs to the Creator.

Chapter IX.—One and the same God, the Creator of heaven and earth, is He whom the prophets foretold, and who was declared by the Gospel. Proof of this, at the outset, from St. Matthew's Gospel.

1. This, therefore, having been clearly demonstrated here (and it shall yet be so still more clearly), that neither the prophets, nor the apostles, nor the Lord Christ in His own person, did acknowledge any other Lord or God, but the God and Lord supreme: the prophets and the apostles confessing the Father and the Son; but naming no other as God, and confessing no other as Lord: and the Lord Himself handing down to His disciples, that He, the Father, is the only God and Lord, who alone is God and ruler of all; —it is incumbent on us to follow, if we are their disciples indeed, their testimonies to this effect. For Matthew the apostle— knowing, as one and the same God, Him who had given promise to Abraham, that He would make his seed as the stars of

heaven, and Him who, by His Son Christ Jesus, has called us to the knowledge of Himself, from the worship of stones, so that those who were not a people were made a people, and she beloved who was not beloved—declares that John, when preparing the way for Christ, said to those who were boasting of their relationship [to Abraham] according to the flesh, but who had their mind tinged and stuffed with all manner of evil, preaching that repentance which should call them back from their evil doings, said, "O generation of vipers, who hath shown you to flee from the wrath to come? Bring forth therefore fruit meet for repentance. And think not to say within yourselves, We have Abraham [to our] father: for I say unto you, that God is able of these stones to raise up children unto Abraham." He preached to them, therefore, the repentance from wickedness, but he did not declare to them another God, besides Him who made the promise to Abraham; he, the forerunner of Christ, of whom Matthew again says, and Luke likewise, "For this is he that was spoken of from the Lord by the prophet, The voice of one crying in the wilderness, Prepare ye the way of the Lord, make straight the paths of our God. Every valley shall be filled, and every mountain and hill brought low; and the crooked shall be made straight, and the rough into smooth ways; and all flesh shall see the salvation of God." There is therefore one and the same God, the Father of our Lord, who also promised, through the prophets, that He would send His forerunner; and His salvation—that is, His Word

—He caused to be made visible to all flesh, [the Word] Himself being made incarnate, that in all things their King might become manifest. For it is necessary that those [beings] which are judged do see the judge, and know Him from whom they receive judgment; and it is also proper, that those which follow on to glory should know Him who bestows upon them the gift of glory.

2. Then again Matthew, when speaking of the angel, says, "The angel of the Lord appeared to Joseph in sleep." Of what Lord he does himself interpret: "That it may be fulfilled which was spoken of the Lord by the prophet, Out of Egypt have I called my son." "Behold, a virgin shall conceive, and shall bring forth a son, and they shall call his name Emmanuel; which is, being interpreted, God with us." David likewise speaks of Him who, from the virgin, is Emmanuel: "Turn not away the face of Thine anointed. The Lord hath sworn a truth to David, and will not turn from him. Of the fruit of thy body will I set upon thy seat." And again: "In Judea is God known; His place has been made in peace,

Prophecy

and His dwelling in Zion." Therefore there is one and the same God, who was proclaimed by the prophets and announced by the Gospel; and His Son, who was of the fruit of David's body, that is, of the virgin of [the house of] David, and Emmanuel; whose star also Balaam thus prophesied: "There shall come a star out of Jacob, and a leader shall rise in Israel." But Matthew says that the Magi, coming from the east, exclaimed "For we have seen His star in the east, and are come to worship Him;" and that, having been led by the star into the house of Jacob to Emmanuel, they showed, by these gifts which they offered, who it was that was worshipped; myrrh, because it was He who should die and be buried for the mortal human race; gold, because He was a King, "of whose kingdom is no end;" and frankincense, because He was God, who also "was made known in Judea," and was "declared to those who sought Him not."

3. And then, [speaking of His] baptism, Matthew says, "The heavens were opened, and He saw the Spirit of God, as a dove, coming upon Him: and lo a voice from heaven, saying, This is my beloved Son, in whom I am well pleased." For Christ did not at that time descend upon Jesus, neither was Christ one and Jesus another: but the Word of God—who is the Saviour of all, and the ruler of heaven and earth, who is Jesus, as I have already pointed out, who did also take upon Him flesh, and was anointed by the Spirit from the Father—was made Jesus Christ, as Esaias also says, "There shall come forth a rod from the root of Jesse, and a flower shall rise from his root; and the Spirit of God shall rest upon Him: the spirit of wisdom and understanding, the spirit of counsel and might, the spirit of knowledge and piety, and the spirit of the fear of God, shall fill Him. He shall not judge according to glory, nor reprove after the manner of speech; but He shall dispense judgment to the humble man, and reprove the haughty ones of the earth." And again Esaias, pointing out beforehand His unction, and the reason why he was anointed, does himself say, "The Spirit of God is upon Me, because He hath anointed Me: He hath sent Me to preach the Gospel to the lowly, to heal the broken up in heart, to proclaim liberty to the captives, and sight to the blind; to announce the acceptable year of the Lord, and the day of vengeance; to comfort all that mourn." For inasmuch as the Word of God was man from the root of Jesse, and son of Abraham, in this respect did the Spirit of God rest upon Him, and anoint Him to preach the Gospel to the lowly. But inasmuch as He was God, He did not judge according to glory, nor reprove after the manner of speech.

For "He needed not that any should testify to Him of man, for He Himself knew what was in man." For He called all men that mourn; and granting forgiveness to those who had been led into captivity by their sins, He loosed them from their chains, of whom Solomon says, "Every one shall be holden with the cords of his own sins." Therefore did the Spirit of God descend upon Him, [the Spirit] of Him who had promised by the prophets that He would anoint Him, so that we, receiving from the abundance of His unction, might be saved. Such, then, [is the witness] of Matthew.

Chapter X.—Proofs of the foregoing, drawn from the Gospels of Mark and Luke.

1. Luke also, the follower and disciple of the apostles, referring to Zacharias and Elisabeth, from whom, according to promise, John was born, says: "And they were both righteous before God, walking in all the commandments and ordinances of the Lord blameless." And again, speaking of Zacharias: "And it came to pass, that while he executed the priest's office before God in the order of his course, according to the custom of the priest's office, his lot was to burn incense;" and he came to sacrifice, "entering into the temple of the Lord." Whose angel Gabriel, also, who stands prominently in the presence of the Lord, simply, absolutely, and decidedly confessed in his own person as God and Lord, Him who had chosen Jerusalem, and had instituted the sacerdotal office. For he knew of none other above Him; since, if he had been in possession of the knowledge of any other more perfect God and Lord besides Him, he surely would never—as I have already shown —have confessed Him, whom he knew to be the fruit of a defect, as absolutely and altogether God and Lord. And then, speaking of John, he thus says: "For he shall be great in the sight of the Lord, and many of the children of Israel shall he turn to the Lord their God. And he shall go before Him in the spirit and power of Elias, to make ready a people prepared for the Lord." For whom, then, did he prepare the people, and in the sight of what Lord was he made great? Truly of Him who said that John had something even "more than a prophet," and that "among those born of women none is greater than John the Baptist;" who did also make the people ready for the Lord's advent, warning his fellow-servants, and preaching to them repentance, that they might receive remission from the Lord when He should be present, having been converted to Him, from whom they had been alienated because of sins and transgressions. As also David says, "The alienated are sinners

from the womb: they go astray as soon as they are born." And it was on account of this that he, turning them to their Lord, prepared, in the spirit and power of Elias, a perfect people for the Lord.

2. And again, speaking in reference to the angel, he says: "But at that time the angel Gabriel was sent from God, who did also say to the virgin, Fear not, Mary; for thou hast found favour with God." And he says concerning the Lord: "He shall be great, and shall be called the Son of the Highest: and the Lord God shall give unto Him the throne of His father David: and He shall reign over the house of Jacob for ever; and of His kingdom there shall be no end." For who else is there who can reign uninterruptedly over the house of Jacob for ever, except Jesus Christ our Lord, the Son of the Most High God, who promised by the law and the prophets that He would make His salvation visible to all flesh; so that He would become the Son of man for this purpose, that man also might become the son of God. And Mary, exulting because of this, cried out, prophesying on behalf of the Church, "My soul doth magnify the Lord, and my spirit hath rejoiced in God my Saviour. For He hath taken up His child Israel, in remembrance of His mercy, as He spake to our fathers, Abraham, and his seed for ever." By these and such like [passages] the Gospel points out that it was God who spake to the fathers; that it was He who, by Moses, instituted the legal dispensation, by which giving of the law we know that He spake to the fathers. This same God, after His great goodness, poured His compassion upon us, through which compassion "the Day-spring from on high hath looked upon us, and appeared to those who sat in darkness and the shadow of death, and has guided our feet into the way of peace;" as Zacharias also, recovering from the state of dumbness which he had suffered on account of unbelief, having been filled with a new spirit, did bless God in a new manner. For all things had entered upon a new phase, the Word arranging after a new manner the advent in the flesh, that He might win back to God that human nature (hominem) which had departed from God; and therefore men were taught to worship God after a new fashion, but not another god, because in truth there is but "one God, who justifieth the circumcision by faith, and the uncircumcision through faith." But Zacharias prophesying, exclaimed, "Blessed be the Lord God of Israel; for He hath visited and redeemed His people, and hath raised up an horn of salvation for us in the house of His servant David; as He spake by the mouth of His holy prophets, which have been since the world begun; salvation from our enemies, and from the hand of all that

hate us; to perform the mercy [promised] to our fathers, and to remember His holy covenant, the oath which He swore to our father Abraham, that He would grant unto us, that we, being delivered out of the hand of our enemies, might serve Him without fear, in holiness and righteousness before Him, all our days." Then he says to John: "And thou, child, shalt be called the prophet of the Highest: for thou shalt go before the face of the Lord to prepare His ways; to give knowledge of salvation to His people, for the remission of their sins." For this is the knowledge of salvation which was wanting to them, that of the Son of God, which John made known, saying, "Behold the Lamb of God, who taketh away the sin of the world. This is He of whom I said, After me cometh a man who was made before me; because He was prior to me: and of His fulness have all we received." This, therefore, was the knowledge of salvation; but [it did not consist in] another God, nor another Father, nor Bythus, nor the Pleroma of thirty Æons, nor the Mother of the (lower) Ogdoad: but the knowledge of salvation was the knowledge of the Son of God, who is both called and actually is, salvation, and Saviour, and salutary. Salvation, indeed, as follows: "I have waited for Thy salvation, O Lord." And then again, Saviour: "Behold my God, my Saviour, I will put my trust in Him." But as bringing salvation, thus: "God hath made known His salvation (salutare) in the sight of the heathen." For He is indeed Saviour, as being the Son and Word of God; but salutary, since [He is] Spirit; for he says: "The Spirit of our countenance, Christ the Lord." But salvation, as being flesh: for "the Word was made flesh, and dwelt among us." This knowledge of salvation, therefore, John did impart to those repenting, and believing in the Lamb of God, who taketh away the sin of the world.

3. And the angel of the Lord, he says, appeared to the shepherds, proclaiming joy to them: "For there is born in the house of David, a Saviour, which is Christ the Lord. Then [appeared] a multitude of the heavenly host, praising God, and saying, Glory in the highest to God, and on earth peace, to men of good will." The falsely-called Gnostics say that these angels came from the Ogdoad, and made manifest the descent of the superior Christ. But they are again in error, when saying that the Christ and Saviour from above was not born, but that also, after the baptism of the dispensational Jesus, he, [the Christ of the Pleroma,] descended upon him as a dove. Therefore, according to these men, the angels of the Ogdoad lied, when they said, "For unto you is born this day a Saviour, who is Christ the Lord, in the city of David." For neither

was Christ nor the Saviour born at that time, by their account; but it was he, the dispensational Jesus, who is of the framer of the world, the [Demiurge], and upon whom, after his baptism, that is, after [the lapse of] thirty years, they maintain the Saviour from above descended. But why did [the angels] add, "in the city of David," if they did not proclaim the glad tidings of the fulfilment of God's promise made to David, that from the fruit of his body there should be an eternal King? For the Framer [Demiurge] of the entire universe made promise to David, as David himself declares: "My help is from God, who made heaven and earth;" and again: "In His hand are the ends of the earth, and the heights of the mountains are His. For the sea is His, and He did Himself make it; and His hands founded the dry land. Come ye, let us worship and fall down before Him, and weep in the presence of the Lord who made us; for He is the Lord our God." The Holy Spirit evidently thus declares by David to those hearing him, that there shall be those who despise Him who formed us, and who is God alone. Wherefore he also uttered the foregoing words, meaning to say: See that ye do not err; besides or above Him there is no other God, to whom ye should rather stretch out [your hands], thus rendering us pious and grateful towards Him who made, established, and [still] nourishes us. What, then, shall happen to those who have been the authors of so much blasphemy against their Creator? This identical truth was also what the angels [proclaimed]. For when they exclaim, "Glory to God in the highest, and in earth peace," they have glorified with these words Him who is the Creator of the highest, that is, of super-celestial things, and the Founder of everything on earth: who has sent to His own handiwork, that is, to men, the blessing of His salvation from heaven. Wherefore he adds: "The shepherds returned, glorifying God for all which they had heard and seen, as it was told unto them." For the Israelitish shepherds did not glorify another god, but Him who had been announced by the law and the prophets, the Maker of all things, whom also the angels glorified. But if the angels who were from the Ogdoad were accustomed to glorify any other, different from Him whom the shepherds [adored], these angels from the Ogdoad brought to them error and not truth.

4. And still further does Luke say in reference to the Lord: "When the days of purification were accomplished, they brought Him up to Jerusalem, to present Him before the Lord, as it is written in the law of the Lord, That every male opening the womb shall be called holy to the Lord; and that they should offer a sacrifice, as it is said in the law of the

Lord, a pair of turtle-doves, or two young pigeons:" in his own person most clearly calling Him Lord, who appointed the legal dispensation. But "Simeon," he also says, "blessed God, and said, Lord, now lettest Thou Thy servant depart in peace; for mine eyes have seen Thy salvation, which Thou hast prepared before the face of all people; a light for the revelation of the Gentiles, and the glory of Thy people Israel." And "Anna" also, "the prophetess," he says, in like manner glorified God when she saw Christ, "and spake of Him to all them who were looking for the redemption of Jerusalem." Now by all these one God is shown forth, revealing to men the new dispensation of liberty, the covenant, through the new advent of His Son.

5. Wherefore also Mark, the interpreter and follower of Peter, does thus commence his Gospel narrative: "The beginning of the Gospel of Jesus Christ, the Son of God; as it is written in the prophets, Behold, I send My messenger before Thy face, which shall prepare Thy way. The voice of one crying in the wilderness, Prepare ye the way of the Lord, make the paths straight before our God." Plainly does the commencement of the Gospel quote the words of the holy prophets, and point out Him at once, whom they confessed as God and Lord; Him, the Father of our Lord Jesus Christ, who had also made promise to Him, that He would send His messenger before His face, who was John, crying in the wilderness, in "the spirit and power of Elias," "Prepare ye the way of the Lord, make straight paths before our God." For the prophets did not announce one and another God, but one and the same; under various aspects, however, and many titles. For varied and rich in attribute is the Father, as I have already shown in the book preceding this; and I shall show [the same truth] from the prophets themselves in the further course of this work. Also, towards the conclusion of his Gospel, Mark says: "So then, after the Lord Jesus had spoken to them, He was received up into heaven, and sitteth on the right hand of God;" confirming what had been spoken by the prophet: "The Lord said to my Lord, Sit Thou on My right hand, until I make Thy foes Thy footstool." Thus God and the Father are truly one and the same; He who was announced by the prophets, and handed down by the true Gospel; whom we Christians worship and love with the whole heart, as the Maker of heaven and earth, and of all things therein.

Chapter XI—Proofs in continuation, extracted from St. John's Gospel. The Gospels are four in number, neither more nor less. Mystic reasons for this.

1. John, the disciple of the Lord, preaches this faith, and seeks, by the proclamation of the Gospel, to remove that error which by Cerinthus had been disseminated among men, and a long time previously by those termed Nicolaitans, who are an offset of that "knowledge" falsely so called, that he might confound them, and persuade them that there is but one God, who made all things by His Word; and not, as they allege, that the Creator was one, but the Father of the Lord another; and that the Son of the Creator was, forsooth, one, but the Christ from above another, who also continued impassible, descending upon Jesus, the Son of the Creator, and flew back again into His Pleroma; and that Monogenes was the beginning, but Logos was the true son of Monogenes; and that this creation to which we belong was not made by the primary God, but by some power lying far below Him, and shut off from communion with the things invisible and ineffable. The disciple of the Lord therefore desiring to put an end to all such doctrines, and to establish the rule of truth in the Church, that there is one Almighty God, who made all things by His Word, both visible and invisible; showing at the same time, that by the Word, through whom God made the creation, He also bestowed salvation on the men included in the creation; thus commenced His teaching in the Gospel: "In the beginning was the Word, and the Word was with God, and the Word was God. The same was in the beginning with God. All things were made by Him, and without Him was nothing made. What was made was life in Him, and the life was the light of men. And the light shineth in darkness, and the darkness comprehended it not." "All things," he says, "were made by Him;" therefore in "all things" this creation of ours is [included], for we cannot concede to these men that [the words] "all things" are spoken in reference to those within their Pleroma. For if their Pleroma do indeed contain these, this creation, as being such, is not outside, as I have demonstrated in the preceding book; but if they are outside the Pleroma, which indeed appeared impossible, it follows, in that case, that their Pleroma cannot be "all things:" therefore this vast creation is not outside [the Pleroma].

2. John, however, does himself put this matter beyond all controversy on our part, when he says, "He was in this world, and the world was made by Him, and the world knew Him not. He came unto His own

[things], and His own [people] received Him not." But according to Marcion, and those like him, neither was the world made by Him; nor did He come to His own things, but to those of another. And, according to certain of the Gnostics, this world was made by angels, and not by the Word of God. But according to the followers of Valentinus, the world was not made by Him, but by the Demiurge. For he (Soter) caused such similitudes to be made, after the pattern of things above, as they allege; but the Demiurge accomplished the work of creation. For they say that he, the Lord and Creator of the plan of creation, by whom they hold that this world was made, was produced from the Mother; while the Gospel affirms plainly, that by the Word, which was in the beginning with God, all things were made, which Word, he says, "was made flesh, and dwelt among us."

3. But, according to these men, neither was the Word made flesh, nor Christ, nor the Saviour (Soter), who was produced from [the joint contributions of] all [the Æons]. For they will have it, that the Word and Christ never came into this world; that the Saviour, too, never became incarnate, nor suffered, but that He descended like a dove upon the dispensational Jesus; and that, as soon as He had declared the unknown Father, He did again ascend into the Pleroma. Some, however, make the assertion, that this dispensational Jesus did become incarnate, and suffered, whom they represent as having passed through Mary just as water through a tube; but others allege him to be the Son of the Demiurge, upon whom the dispensational Jesus descended; while others, again, say that Jesus was born from Joseph and Mary, and that the Christ from above descended upon him, being without flesh, and impassible. But according to the opinion of no one of the heretics was the Word of God made flesh. For if anyone carefully examines the systems of them all, he will find that the Word of God is brought in by all of them as not having become incarnate (sine carne) and impassible, as is also the Christ from above. Others consider Him to have been manifested as a transfigured man; but they maintain Him to have been neither born nor to have become incarnate; whilst others [hold] that He did not assume a human form at all, but that, as a dove, He did descend upon that Jesus who was born from Mary. Therefore the Lord's disciple, pointing them all out as false witnesses, says, "And the Word was made flesh, and dwelt among us."

4. And that we may not have to ask, Of what God was the Word made flesh? he does himself previously teach us, saying, "There was a man sent from God, whose name was John. The same came as a witness, that he might bear witness of that Light. He was not that Light, but [came] that he might testify of the Light." By what God, then, was John, the forerunner, who testifies of the Light, sent [into the world]? Truly it was by Him, of whom Gabriel is the angel, who also announced the glad tidings of his birth: [that God] who also had promised by the prophets that He would send His messenger before the face of His Son, who should prepare His way, that is, that he should bear witness of that Light in the spirit and power of Elias. But, again, of what God was Elias the servant and the prophet? Of Him who made heaven and earth, as he does himself confess. John, therefore, having been sent by the founder and maker of this world, how could he testify of that Light, which came down from things unspeakable and invisible? For all the heretics have decided that the Demiurge was ignorant of that Power above him, whose witness and herald John is found to be. Wherefore the Lord said that He deemed him "more than a prophet." For all the other prophets preached the advent of the paternal Light, and desired to be worthy of seeing Him whom they preached; but John did both announce [the advent] beforehand, in a like manner as did the others, and actually saw Him when He came, and pointed Him out, and persuaded many to believe on Him, so that he did himself hold the place of both prophet and apostle. For this is to be more than a prophet, because, "first apostles, secondarily prophets;" but all things from one and the same God Himself.

5. That wine, which was produced by God in a vineyard, and which was first consumed, was good. None of those who drank of it found fault with it; and the Lord partook of it also. But that wine was better which the Word made from water, on the moment, and simply for the use of those who had been called to the marriage. For although the Lord had the power to supply wine to those feasting, independently of any created substance, and to fill with food those who were hungry, He did not adopt this course; but, taking the loaves which the earth had produced, and giving thanks, and on the other occasion making water wine, He satisfied those who were reclining [at table], and gave drink to those who had been invited to the marriage; showing that the God who made the earth, and commanded it to bring forth fruit, who established the waters, and brought forth the fountains, was He who in these last times

bestowed upon mankind, by His Son, the blessing of food and the favour of drink: the Incomprehensible [acting thus] by means of the comprehensible, and the Invisible by the visible; since there is none beyond Him, but He exists in the bosom of the Father.

6. For "no man," he says, "hath seen God at any time," unless "the only-begotten Son of God, which is in the bosom of the Father, He hath declared [Him]." For He, the Son who is in His bosom, declares to all the Father who is invisible. Wherefore they know Him to whom the Son reveals Him; and again, the Father, by means of the Son, gives knowledge of His Son to those who love Him. By whom also Nathanael, being taught, recognised [Him], he to whom also the Lord bare witness, that he was "an Israelite indeed, in whom was no guile." The Israelite recognised his King, therefore did he cry out to Him, "Rabbi, Thou art the Son of God, Thou art the King of Israel." By whom also Peter, having been taught, recognised Christ as the Son of the living God, when [God] said, "Behold My dearly beloved Son, in whom I am well pleased: I will put my Spirit upon Him, and He shall show judgment to the Gentiles. He shall not strive, nor cry; neither shall any man hear His voice in the streets. A bruised reed shall He not break, and smoking flax shall He not quench, until He send forth judgment into contention; and in His name shall the Gentiles trust."

7. Such, then, are the first principles of the Gospel: that there is one God, the Maker of this universe; He who was also announced by the prophets, and who by Moses set forth the dispensation of the law,—[principles] which proclaim the Father of our Lord Jesus Christ, and ignore any other God or Father except Him. So firm is the ground upon which these Gospels rest, that the very heretics themselves bear witness to them, and, starting from these [documents], each one of them endeavours to establish his own peculiar doctrine. For the Ebionites, who use Matthew's Gospel only, are confuted out of this very same, making false suppositions with regard to the Lord. But Marcion, mutilating that according to Luke, is proved to be a blasphemer of the only existing God, from those [passages] which he still retains. Those, again, who separate Jesus from Christ, alleging that Christ remained impassible, but that it was Jesus who suffered, preferring the Gospel by Mark, if they read it with a love of truth, may have their errors rectified. Those, moreover, who follow Valentinus, making copious use of that

according to John, to illustrate their conjunctions, shall be proved to be totally in error by means of this very Gospel, as I have shown in the first book. Since, then, our opponents do bear testimony to us, and make use of these [documents], our proof derived from them is firm and true.

8. It is not possible that the Gospels can be either more or fewer in number than they are. For, since there are four zones of the world in which we live, and four principal winds, while the Church is scattered throughout all the world, and the "pillar and ground" of the Church is the Gospel and the spirit of life; it is fitting that she should have four pillars, breathing out immortality on every side, and vivifying men afresh. From which fact, it is evident that the Word, the Artificer of all, He that sitteth upon the cherubim, and contains all things, He who was manifested to men, has given us the Gospel under four aspects, but bound together by one Spirit. As also David says, when entreating His manifestation, "Thou that sittest between the cherubim, shine forth." For the cherubim, too, were four-faced, and their faces were images of the dispensation of the Son of God. For, [as the Scripture] says, "The first living creature was like a lion," symbolizing His effectual working, His leadership, and royal power; the second [living creature] was like a calf, signifying [His] sacrificial and sacerdotal order; but "the third had, as it were, the face as of a man,"—an evident description of His advent as a human being; "the fourth was like a flying eagle," pointing out the gift of the Spirit hovering with His wings over the Church. And therefore the Gospels are in accord with these things, among which Christ Jesus is seated. For that according to John relates His original, effectual, and glorious generation from the Father, thus declaring, "In the beginning was the Word, and the Word was with God, and the Word was God." Also, "all things were made by Him, and without Him was nothing made." For this reason, too, is that Gospel full of all confidence, for such is His person. But that according to Luke, taking up [His] priestly character, commenced with Zacharias the priest offering sacrifice to God. For now was made ready the fatted calf, about to be immolated for the finding again of the younger son. Matthew, again, relates His generation as a man, saying, "The book of the generation of Jesus Christ, the son of David, the son of Abraham;" and also, "The birth of Jesus Christ was on this wise." This, then, is the Gospel of His humanity; for which reason it is, too, that [the character of] a humble and meek man is kept up through the whole Gospel. Mark, on the other hand, commences with [a reference to] the prophetical spirit coming

down from on high to men, saying, "The beginning of the Gospel of Jesus Christ, as it is written in Esaias the prophet,"— pointing to the winged aspect of the Gospel; and on this account he made a compendious and cursory narrative, for such is the prophetical character. And the Word of God Himself used to converse with the ante-Mosaic patriarchs, in accordance with His divinity and glory; but for those under the law he instituted a sacerdotal and liturgical service. Afterwards, being made man for us, He sent the gift of the celestial Spirit over all the earth, protecting us with His wings. Such, then, as was the course followed by the Son of God, so was also the form of the living creatures; and such as was the form of the living creatures, so was also the character of the Gospel. For the living creatures are quadriform, and the Gospel is quadriform, as is also the course followed by the Lord. For this reason were four principal (καθολικαί) covenants given to the human race: one, prior to the deluge, under Adam; the second, that after the deluge, under Noah; the third, the giving of the law, under Moses; the fourth, that which renovates man, and sums up all things in itself by means of the Gospel, raising and bearing men upon its wings into the heavenly kingdom.

9. These things being so, all who destroy the form of the Gospel are vain, unlearned, and also audacious; those, [I mean,] who represent the aspects of the Gospel as being either more in number than as aforesaid, or, on the other hand, fewer. The former class [do so], that they may seem to have discovered more than is of the truth; the latter, that they may set the dispensations of God aside. For Marcion, rejecting the entire Gospel, yea rather, cutting himself off from the Gospel, boasts that he has part in the [blessings of] the Gospel. Others, again (the Montanists), that they may set at nought the gift of the Spirit, which in the latter times has been, by the good pleasure of the Father, poured out upon the human race, do not admit that aspect [of the evangelical dispensation] presented by John's Gospel, in which the Lord promised that He would send the Paraclete; but set aside at once both the Gospel and the prophetic Spirit. Wretched men indeed! who wish to be pseudo-prophets, forsooth, but who set aside the gift of prophecy from the Church; acting like those (the Encratitæ) who, on account of such as come in hypocrisy, hold themselves aloof from the communion of the brethren. We must conclude, moreover, that these men (the Montanists) can not admit the Apostle Paul either. For, in his Epistle to the Corinthians, he speaks expressly of prophetical gifts, and recognises

men and women prophesying in the Church. Sinning, therefore, in all these particulars, against the Spirit of God, they fall into the irremissible sin. But those who are from Valentinus, being, on the other hand, altogether reckless, while they put forth their own compositions, boast that they possess more Gospels than there really are. Indeed, they have arrived at such a pitch of audacity, as to entitle their comparatively recent writing "the Gospel of Truth," though it agrees in nothing with the Gospels of the Apostles, so that they have really no Gospel which is not full of blasphemy. For if what they have published is the Gospel of truth, and yet is totally unlike those which have been handed down to us from the apostles, any who please may learn, as is shown from the Scriptures themselves, that that which has been handed down from the apostles can no longer be reckoned the Gospel of truth. But that these Gospels alone are true and reliable, and admit neither an increase nor diminution of the aforesaid number, I have proved by so many and such [arguments]. For, since God made all things in due proportion and adaptation, it was fit also that the outward aspect of the Gospel should be well arranged and harmonized. The opinion of those men, therefore, who handed the Gospel down to us, having been investigated, from their very fountainheads, let us proceed also to the remaining apostles, and inquire into their doctrine with regard to God; then, in due course we shall listen to the very words of the Lord.

Chapter XII.—Doctrine of the rest of the apostles.

1. The Apostle Peter, therefore, after the resurrection of the Lord, and His assumption into the heavens, being desirous of filling up the number of the twelve apostles, and in electing into the place of Judas any substitute who should be chosen by God, thus addressed those who were present: "Men [and] brethren, this Scripture must needs have been fulfilled, which the Holy Ghost, by the mouth of David, spake before concerning Judas, which was made guide to them that took Jesus. For he was numbered with us: ... Let his habitation be desolate, and let no man dwell therein; and, His bishoprick let another take;"— thus leading to the completion of the apostles, according to the words spoken by David. Again, when the Holy Ghost had descended upon the disciples, that they all might prophesy and speak with tongues, and some mocked them, as if drunken with new wine, Peter said that they were not drunken, for it was the third hour of the day; but that this was what had been spoken by the prophet: "It shall come to pass in the last days, saith God, I will pour out of my Spirit upon all flesh, and they shall prophesy."

The God, therefore, who did promise by the prophet, that He would send His Spirit upon the whole human race, was He who did send; and God Himself is announced by Peter as having fulfilled His own promise.

2. For Peter said, "Ye men of Israel, hear my words; Jesus of Nazareth, a man approved by God among you by powers, and wonders, and signs, which God did by Him in the midst of you, as ye yourselves also know: Him, being delivered by the determined counsel and foreknowledge of God, by the hands of wicked men ye have slain, affixing [to the cross]: whom God hath raised up, having loosed the pains of death; because it was not possible that he should be holden of them. For David speaketh concerning Him, I foresaw the Lord always before my face; for He is on my right hand, lest I should be moved: therefore did my heart rejoice, and my tongue was glad; moreover also, my flesh shall rest in hope: because Thou wilt not leave my soul in hell, neither wilt Thou give Thy Holy One to see corruption." Then he proceeds to speak confidently to them concerning the patriarch David, that he was dead and buried, and that his sepulchre is with them to this day. He said, "But since he was a prophet, and knew that God had sworn with an oath to him, that of the fruit of his body one should sit in his throne; foreseeing this, he spake of the resurrection of Christ, that He was not left in hell, neither did His flesh see corruption. This Jesus," he said, "hath God raised up, of which we all are witnesses: who, being exalted by the right hand of God, receiving from the Father the promise of the Holy Ghost, hath shed forth this gift which ye now see and hear. For David has not ascended into the heavens; but he saith himself, The Lord said unto my Lord, Sit Thou on My right hand, until I make Thy foes Thy footstool. Therefore let all the house of Israel know assuredly, that God hath made that same Jesus, whom ye have crucified, both Lord and Christ." And when the multitudes exclaimed, "What shall we do then?" Peter says to them, "Repent, and be baptized everyone of you in the name of Jesus for the remission of sins, and ye shall receive the gift of the Holy Ghost." Thus the apostles did not preach another God, or another Fulness; nor, that the Christ who suffered and rose again was one, while he who flew off on high was another, and remained impassible; but that there was one and the same God the Father, and Christ Jesus who rose from the dead; and they preached faith in Him, to those who did not believe on the Son of God, and exhorted them out of the prophets, that the Christ whom God promised to send, He sent in Jesus, whom they crucified and God raised up.

3. Again, when Peter, accompanied by John, had looked upon the man lame from his birth, before that gate of the temple which is called Beautiful, sitting and seeking alms, he said to him, "Silver and gold I have none; but such as I have give I thee: In the name of Jesus Christ of Nazareth, rise up and walk. And immediately his legs and his feet received strength; and he walked, and entered with them into the temple, walking, and leaping, and praising God." Then, when a multitude had gathered around them from all quarters because of this unexpected deed, Peter addressed them: "Ye men of Israel, why marvel ye at this; or why look ye so earnestly on us, as though by our own power we had made this man to walk? The God of Abraham, the God of Isaac, and the God of Jacob, the God of our fathers, hath glorified His Son, whom ye delivered up for judgment, and denied in the presence of Pilate, when he wished to let Him go. But ye were bitterly set against the Holy One and the Just, and desired a murderer to be granted unto you; but ye killed the Prince of life, whom God hath raised from the dead, whereof we are witnesses. And in the faith of His name, him, whom ye see and know, hath His name made strong; yea, the faith which is by Him, hath given him this perfect soundness in the presence of you all. And now, brethren, I wot that through ignorance ye did this wickedness. … But those things which God before had showed by the mouth of all the prophets, that His Christ should suffer, He hath so fulfilled. Repent ye therefore, and be converted, that your sins may be blotted out, and that the times of refreshing may come to you from the presence of the Lord; and He shall send Jesus Christ, prepared for you beforehand, whom the heaven must indeed receive until the times of the arrangement of all things, of which God hath spoken by His holy prophets. For Moses truly said unto our fathers, Your Lord God shall raise up to you a Prophet from your brethren, like unto me; Him shall ye hear in all things whatsoever He shall say unto you. And it shall come to pass, that every soul, whosoever will not hear that Prophet, shall be destroyed from among the people. And all [the prophets] from Samuel, and henceforth, as many as have spoken, have likewise foretold of these days. Ye are the children of the prophets, and of the covenant which God made with our fathers, saying unto Abraham, And in thy seed shall all the kindreds of the earth be blessed. Unto you first, God, having raised up His Son, sent Him blessing you, that each may turn himself from his iniquities." Peter, together with John, preached to them this plain message of glad tidings, that the promise which God made to the fathers had been fulfilled by Jesus; not certainly proclaiming another god, but the Son of God, who

also was made man, and suffered; thus leading Israel into knowledge, and through Jesus preaching the resurrection of the dead, and showing, that whatever the prophets had proclaimed as to the suffering of Christ, these had God fulfilled.

4. For this reason, too, when the chief priests were assembled, Peter, full of boldness, said to them, "Ye rulers of the people, and elders of Israel, if we this day be examined by you of the good deed done to the impotent man, by what means he has been made whole; be it known to you all, and to all the people of Israel, that by the name of Jesus Christ of Nazareth, whom ye crucified, whom God raised from the dead, even by Him doth this man stand here before you whole. This is the stone which was set at nought of you builders, which is become the head-stone of the corner. [Neither is there salvation in any other: for] there is none other name under heaven, which is given to men, whereby we must be saved:" Thus the apostles did not change God, but preached to the people that Christ was Jesus the crucified One, whom the same God that had sent the prophets, being God Himself, raised up, and gave in Him salvation to men.

5. They were confounded, therefore, both by this instance of healing ("for the man was above forty years old on whom this miracle of healing took place"), and by the doctrine of the apostles, and by the exposition of the prophets, when the chief priests had sent away Peter and John. [These latter] returned to the rest of their fellow- apostles and disciples of the Lord, that is, to the Church, and related what had occurred, and how courageously they had acted in the name of Jesus. The whole Church, it is then said, "when they had heard that, lifted up the voice to God with one accord, and said, Lord, Thou art God, which hast made heaven, and earth, and the sea, and all that in them is; who, through the Holy Ghost, by the mouth of our father David, Thy servant, hast said, Why did the heathen rage, and the people imagine vain things? The kings of the earth stood up, and the rulers were gathered together against the Lord, and against His Christ. For of a truth, in this city, against Thy holy Son Jesus, whom Thou hast anointed, both Herod and Pontius Pilate, with the Gentiles, and the people of Israel, were gathered together, to do whatsoever Thy hand and Thy counsel determined before to be done." These [are the] voices of the Church from which every Church had its origin; these are the voices of the metropolis of the citizens of

the new covenant; these are the voices of the apostles; these are voices of the disciples of the Lord, the truly perfect, who, after the assumption of the Lord, were perfected by the Spirit, and called upon the God who made heaven, and earth, and the sea,— who was announced by the prophets,— and Jesus Christ His Son, whom God anointed, and who knew no other [God]. For at that time and place there was neither Valentinus, nor Marcion, nor the rest of these subverters [of the truth], and their adherents. Wherefore God, the Maker of all things, heard them. For it is said, "The place was shaken where they were assembled together; and they were all filled with the Holy Ghost, and they spake the word of God with boldness" to every one that was willing to believe. "And with great power," it is added, "gave the apostles witness of the resurrection of the Lord Jesus," saying to them, "The God of our fathers raised up Jesus, whom ye seized and slew, hanging [Him] upon a beam of wood: Him hath God raised up by His right hand to be a Prince and Saviour, to give repentance to Israel, and forgiveness of sins. And we are in this witnesses of these words; as also is the Holy Ghost, whom God hath given to them that believe in Him." "And daily," it is said, "in the temple, and from house to house, they ceased not to teach and preach Christ Jesus," the Son of God. For this was the knowledge of salvation, which renders those who acknowledge His Son's advent perfect towards God.

6. But as some of these men impudently assert that the apostles, when preaching among the Jews, could not declare to them another god besides Him in whom they (their hearers) believed, we say to them, that if the apostles used to speak to people in accordance with the opinion instilled into them of old, no one learned the truth from them, nor, at a much earlier date, from the Lord; for they say that He did Himself speak after the same fashion. Wherefore neither do these men themselves know the truth; but since such was their opinion regarding God, they had just received doctrine as they were able to hear it. According to this manner of speaking, therefore, the rule of truth can be with nobody; but all learners will ascribe this practice to all [teachers], that just as every person thought, and as far as his capability extended, so was also the language addressed to him. But the advent of the Lord will appear superfluous and useless, if He did indeed come intending to tolerate and to preserve each man's idea regarding God rooted in him from of old. Besides this, also, it was a much heavier task, that He whom the Jews had seen as a man, and had fastened to the cross, should be preached as

Christ the Son of God, their eternal King. Since this, however, was so, they certainly did not speak to them in accordance with their old belief. For they, who told them to their face that they were the slayers of the Lord, would themselves also much more boldly preach that Father who is above the Demiurge, and not what each individual bid himself believe [respecting God]; and the sin was much less, if indeed they had not fastened to the cross the superior Saviour (to whom it behoved them to ascend), since He was impassible. For, as they did not speak to the Gentiles in compliance with their notions, but told them with boldness that their gods were no gods, but the idols of demons; so would they in like manner have preached to the Jews, if they had known another greater or more perfect Father, not nourishing nor strengthening the untrue opinion of these men regarding God. Moreover, while destroying the error of the Gentiles, and bearing them away from their gods, they did not certainly induce another error upon them; but, removing those which were no gods, they pointed out Him who alone was God and the true Father.

7. From the words of Peter, therefore, which he addressed in Cæsarea to Cornelius the centurion, and those Gentiles with him, to whom the word of God was first preached, we can understand what the apostles used to preach, the nature of their preaching, and their idea with regard to God. For this Cornelius was, it is said, "a devout man, and one who feared God with all his house, giving much alms to the people, and praying to God always. He saw therefore, about the ninth hour of the day, an angel of God coming in to him, and saying, Thine alms are come up for a memorial before God. Wherefore send to Simon, who is called Peter." But when Peter saw the vision, in which the voice from heaven said to him, "What God hath cleansed, that call not thou common," this happened [to teach him] that the God who had, through the law, distinguished between clean and unclean, was He who had purified the Gentiles through the blood of His Son—He whom also Cornelius worshipped; to whom Peter, coming in, said, "Of a truth I perceive that God is no respecter of persons: but in every nation, he that feareth Him, and worketh righteousness, is acceptable to Him." He thus clearly indicates, that He whom Cornelius had previously feared as God, of whom he had heard through the law and the prophets, for whose sake also he used to give alms, is, in truth, God. The knowledge of the Son was, however, wanting to him; therefore did [Peter] add, "The word, ye know, which was published throughout all Judea, beginning from

Galilee, after the baptism which John preached, Jesus of Nazareth, how God anointed Him with the Holy Ghost, and with power; who went about doing good, and healing all that were oppressed of the devil; for God was with Him. And we are witnesses of all those things which He did both in the land of the Jews and in Jerusalem; whom they slew, hanging Him on a beam of wood: Him God raised up the third day, and showed Him openly; not to all the people, but unto us, witnesses chosen before of God, who did eat and drink with Him after the resurrection from the dead. And He commanded us to preach unto the people, and to testify that it is He which was ordained of God to be the Judge of quick and dead. To Him give all the prophets witness, that, through His name, every one that believeth in Him does receive remission of sins." The apostles, therefore, did preach the Son of God, of whom men were ignorant; and His advent, to those who had been already instructed as to God; but they did not bring in another god. For if Peter had known any such thing, he would have preached freely to the Gentiles, that the God of the Jews was indeed one, but the God of the Christians another; and all of them, doubtless, being awe-struck because of the vision of the angel, would have believed whatever he told them. But it is evident from Peter's words that he did indeed still retain the God who was already known to them; but he also bare witness to them that Jesus Christ was the Son of God, the Judge of quick and dead, into whom he did also command them to be baptized for the remission of sins; and not this alone, but he witnessed that Jesus was Himself the Son of God, who also, having been anointed with the Holy Spirit, is called Jesus Christ. And He is the same being that was born of Mary, as the testimony of Peter implies. Can it really be, that Peter was not at that time as yet in possession of the perfect knowledge which these men discovered afterwards? According to them, therefore, Peter was imperfect, and the rest of the apostles were imperfect; and so it would be fitting that they, coming to life again, should become disciples of these men, in order that they too might be made perfect. But this is truly ridiculous. These men, in fact, are proved to be not disciples of the apostles, but of their own wicked notions. To this cause also are due the various opinions which exist among them, inasmuch as each one adopted error just as he was capable [of embracing it]. But the Church throughout all the world, having its origin firm from the apostles, perseveres in one and the same opinion with regard to God and His Son.

8. But again: Whom did Philip preach to the eunuch of the queen of the Ethiopians, returning from Jerusalem, and reading Esaias the prophet, when he and this man were alone together? Was it not He of whom the prophet spoke: "He was led as a sheep to the slaughter, and as a lamb dumb before the shearer, so He opened not the mouth?" "But who shall declare His nativity? for His life shall be taken away from the earth." [Philip declared] that this was Jesus, and that the Scripture was fulfilled in Him; as did also the believing eunuch himself: and, immediately requesting to be baptized, he said, "I believe Jesus Christ to be the Son of God." This man was also sent into the regions of Ethiopia, to preach what he had himself believed, that there was one God preached by the prophets, but that the Son of this [God] had already made [His] appearance in human nature (secundum hominem), and had been led as a sheep to the slaughter; and all the other statements which the prophets made regarding Him.

9. Paul himself also—after that the Lord spoke to him out of heaven, and showed him that, in persecuting His disciples, he persecuted his own Lord, and sent Ananias to him that he might recover his sight, and be baptized—"preached," it is said, "Jesus in the synagogues at Damascus, with all freedom of speech, that this is the Son of God, the Christ." This is the mystery which he says was made known to him by revelation, that He who suffered under Pontius Pilate, the same is Lord of all, and King, and God, and Judge, receiving power from Him who is the God of all, because He became "obedient unto death, even the death of the cross." And inasmuch as this is true, when preaching to the Athenians on the Areopagus—where, no Jews being present, he had it in his power to preach God with freedom of speech—he said to them: "God, who made the world, and all things therein, He, being Lord of heaven and earth, dwelleth not in temples made with hands; neither is He touched by men's hands, as though He needed anything, seeing He giveth to all life, and breath, and all things; who hath made from one blood the whole race of men to dwell upon the face of the whole earth, predetermining the times according to the boundary of their habitation, to seek the Deity, if by any means they might be able to track Him out, or find Him, although He be not far from each of us. For in Him we live, and move, and have our being, as certain men of your own have said, For we are also His offspring. Inasmuch, then, as we are the offspring of God, we ought not to think that the Deity is like unto gold or silver, or stone graven by art or man's device. Therefore God, winking at the times of

ignorance, does now command all men everywhere to turn to Him with repentance; because He hath appointed a day, on which the world shall be judged in righteousness by the man Jesus; whereof He hath given assurance by raising Him from the dead." Now in this passage he does not only declare to them God as the Creator of the world, no Jews being present, but that He did also make one race of men to dwell upon all the earth; as also Moses declared: "When the Most High divided the nations, as He scattered the sons of Adam, He set the bounds of the nations after the number of the angels of God;" but that people which believes in God is not now under the power of angels, but under the Lord's [rule]. "For His people Jacob was made the portion of the Lord, Israel the cord of His inheritance." And again, at Lystra of Lycia (Lycaonia), when Paul was with Barnabas, and in the name of our Lord Jesus Christ had made a man to walk who had been lame from his birth, and when the crowd wished to honour them as gods because of the astonishing deed, he said to them: "We are men like unto you, preaching to you God, that ye may be turned away from these vain idols to [serve] the living God, who made heaven, and earth, and the sea, and all things that are therein; who in times past suffered all nations to walk in their own ways, although He left not Himself without witness, performing acts of goodness, giving you rain from heaven, and fruitful seasons, filling your hearts with food and gladness." But that all his Epistles are consonant to these declarations, I shall, when expounding the apostle, show from the Epistles themselves, in the right place. But while I bring out by these proofs the truths of Scripture, and set forth briefly and compendiously things which are stated in various ways, do thou also attend to them with patience, and not deem them prolix; taking this into account, that proofs [of the things which are] contained in the Scriptures cannot be shown except from the Scriptures themselves.

10. And still further, Stephen, who was chosen the first deacon by the apostles, and who, of all men, was the first to follow the footsteps of the martyrdom of the Lord, being the first that was slain for confessing Christ, speaking boldly among the people, and teaching them, says: "The God of glory appeared to our father Abraham, … and said to him, Get thee out of thy country, and from thy kindred, and come into the land which I shall show thee; … and He removed him into this land, wherein ye now dwell. And He gave him none inheritance in it, no, not so much as to set his foot on; yet He promised that He would give it to him for a possession, and to his seed after him. … And God spake on this wise,

That his seed should sojourn in a strange land, and should be brought into bondage, and should be evil-entreated four hundred years; and the nation whom they shall serve will I judge, says the Lord. And after that shall they come forth, and serve me in this place. And He gave him the covenant of circumcision: and so [Abraham] begat Isaac." And the rest of his words announce the same God, who was with Joseph and with the patriarchs, and who spake with Moses.

11. And that the whole range of the doctrine of the apostles proclaimed one and the same God, who removed Abraham, who made to him the promise of inheritance, who in due season gave to him the covenant of circumcision, who called his descendants out of Egypt, preserved outwardly by circumcision—for he gave it as a sign, that they might not be like the Egyptians—that He was the Maker of all things, that He was the Father of our Lord Jesus Christ, that He was the God of glory,—they who wish may learn from the very words and acts of the apostles, and may contemplate the fact that this God is one, above whom is no other. But even if there were another god above Him, we should say, upon [instituting] a comparison of the quantity [of the work done by each], that the latter is superior to the former. For by deeds the better man appears, as I have already remarked; and, inasmuch as these men have no works of their father to adduce, the latter is shown to be God alone. But if any one, "doting about questions," do imagine that what the apostles have declared about God should be allegorized, let him consider my previous statements, in which I set forth one God as the Founder and Maker of all things, and destroyed and laid bare their allegations; and he shall find them agreeable to the doctrine of the apostles, and so to maintain what they used to teach, and were persuaded of, that there is one God, the Maker of all things. And when he shall have divested his mind of such error, and of that blasphemy against God which it implies, he will of himself find reason to acknowledge that both the Mosaic law and the grace of the new covenant, as both fitted for the times [at which they were given], were bestowed by one and the same God for the benefit of the human race.

12. For all those who are of a perverse mind, having been set against the Mosaic legislation, judging it to be dissimilar and contrary to the doctrine of the Gospel, have not applied themselves to investigate the causes of the difference of each covenant. Since, therefore, they have been

deserted by the paternal love, and puffed up by Satan, being brought over to the doctrine of Simon Magus, they have apostatized in their opinions from Him who is God, and imagined that they have themselves discovered more than the apostles, by finding out another god; and [maintained] that the apostles preached the Gospel still somewhat under the influence of Jewish opinions, but that they themselves are purer [in doctrine], and more intelligent, than the apostles. Wherefore also Marcion and his followers have betaken themselves to mutilating the Scriptures, not acknowledging some books at all; and, curtailing the Gospel according to Luke and the Epistles of Paul, they assert that these are alone authentic, which they have themselves thus shortened. In another work, however, I shall, God granting [me strength], refute them out of these which they still retain. But all the rest, inflated with the false name of "knowledge," do certainly recognise the Scriptures; but they pervert the interpretations, as I have shown in the first book. And, indeed, the followers of Marcion do directly blaspheme the Creator, alleging him to be the creator of evils, [but] holding a more tolerable theory as to his origin, [and] maintaining that there are two beings, gods by nature, differing from each other,—the one being good, but the other evil. Those from Valentinus, however, while they employ names of a more honourable kind, and set forth that He who is Creator is both Father, and Lord, and God, do [nevertheless] render their theory or sect more blasphemous, by maintaining that He was not produced from any one of those Æons within the Pleroma, but from that defect which had been expelled beyond the Pleroma. Ignorance of the Scriptures and of the dispensation of God has brought all these things upon them. And in the course of this work I shall touch upon the cause of the difference of the covenants on the one hand, and, on the other hand, of their unity and harmony.

13. But that both the apostles and their disciples thus taught as the Church preaches, and thus teaching were perfected, wherefore also they were called away to that which is perfect— Stephen, teaching these truths, when he was yet on earth, saw the glory of God, and Jesus on His right hand, and exclaimed, "Behold, I see the heavens opened, and the Son of man standing on the right hand of God." These words he said, and was stoned; and thus did he fulfil the perfect doctrine, copying in every respect the Leader of martyrdom, and praying for those who were slaying him, in these words: "Lord, lay not this sin to their charge." Thus were they perfected who knew one and the same God, who from

beginning to end was present with mankind in the various dispensations; as the prophet Hosea declares: "I have filled up visions, and used similitudes by the hands of the prophets." Those, therefore, who delivered up their souls to death for Christ's Gospel—how could they have spoken to men in accordance with old-established opinion? If this had been the course adopted by them, they should not have suffered; but inasmuch as they did preach things contrary to those persons who did not assent to the truth, for that reason they suffered. It is evident, therefore, that they did not relinquish the truth, but with all boldness preached to the Jews and Greeks. To the Jews, indeed, [they proclaimed] that the Jesus who was crucified by them was the Son of God, the Judge of quick and dead, and that He has received from His Father an eternal kingdom in Israel, as I have pointed out; but to the Greeks they preached one God, who made all things, and Jesus Christ His Son.

14. This is shown in a still clearer light from the letter of the apostles, which they forwarded neither to the Jews nor to the Greeks, but to those who from the Gentiles believed in Christ, confirming their faith. For when certain men had come down from Judea to Antioch—where also, first of all, the Lord's disciples were called Christians, because of their faith in Christ—and sought to persuade those who had believed on the Lord to be circumcised, and to perform other things after the observance of the law; and when Paul and Barnabas had gone up to Jerusalem to the apostles on account of this question, and the whole Church had convened together, Peter thus addressed them: "Men, brethren, ye know how that from the days of old God made choice among you, that the Gentiles by my mouth should hear the word of the Gospel, and believe. And God, the Searcher of the heart, bare them witness, giving them the Holy Ghost, even as to us; and put no difference between us and them, purifying their hearts by faith. Now therefore why tempt ye God, to impose a yoke upon the neck of the disciples, which neither our fathers nor we were able to bear? But we believe that, through the grace of our Lord Jesus Christ, we are to be saved, even as they." After him James spoke as follows: "Men, brethren, Simon hath declared how God did purpose to take from among the Gentiles a people for His name. And thus do the words of the prophets agree, as it is written, After this I will return, and will build again the tabernacle of David, which is fallen down; and I will build the ruins thereof, and I will set it up: that the residue of men may seek after the Lord, and all the Gentiles, among whom my name has been invoked,

saith the Lord, doing these things. Known from eternity is His work to God. Wherefore I for my part give judgment, that we trouble not them who from among the Gentiles are turned to God: but that it be enjoined them, that they do abstain from the vanities of idols, and from fornication, and from blood; and whatsoever they wish not to be done to themselves, let them not do to others." And when these things had been said, and all had given their consent, they wrote to them after this manner: "The apostles, and the presbyters, [and] the brethren, unto those brethren from among the Gentiles who are in Antioch, and Syria, and Cilicia, greeting: Forasmuch as we have heard that certain persons going out from us have troubled you with words, subverting your souls, saying, Ye must be circumcised, and keep the law; to whom we gave no such commandment: it seemed good unto us, being assembled with one accord, to send chosen men unto you with our beloved Barnabas and Paul; men who have delivered up their soul for the name of our Lord Jesus Christ. We have sent therefore Judas and Silas, that they may declare our opinion by word of mouth. For it seemed good to the Holy Ghost, and to us, to lay upon you no greater burden than these necessary things; that ye abstain from meats offered to idols, and from blood, and from fornication; and whatsoever ye do not wish to be done to you, do not ye to others: from which preserving yourselves, ye shall do well, walking in the Holy Spirit." From all these passages, then, it is evident that they did not teach the existence of another Father, but gave the new covenant of liberty to those who had lately believed in God by the Holy Spirit. But they clearly indicated, from the nature of the point debated by them, as to whether or not it were still necessary to circumcise the disciples, that they had no idea of another god.

15. Neither [in that case] would they have had such a tenor with regard to the first covenant, as not even to have been willing to eat with the Gentiles. For even Peter, although he had been sent to instruct them, and had been constrained by a vision to that effect, spake nevertheless with not a little hesitation, saying to them: "Ye know how it is an unlawful thing for a man that is a Jew to keep company with, or to come unto, one of another nation; but God hath shown me that I should not call any man common or unclean. Therefore came I without gainsaying;" indicating by these words, that he would not have come to them unless he had been commanded. Neither, for a like reason, would he have given them baptism so readily, had he not heard them prophesying when the Holy Ghost rested upon them. And therefore did

he exclaim, "Can any man forbid water, that these should not be baptized, who have received the Holy Ghost as well as we?" He persuaded, at the same time, those that were with him, and pointed out that, unless the Holy Ghost had rested upon them, there might have been some one who would have raised objections to their baptism. And the apostles who were with James allowed the Gentiles to act freely, yielding us up to the Spirit of God. But they themselves, while knowing the same God, continued in the ancient observances; so that even Peter, fearing also lest he might incur their reproof, although formerly eating with the Gentiles, because of the vision, and of the Spirit who had rested upon them, yet, when certain persons came from James, withdrew himself, and did not eat with them. And Paul said that Barnabas likewise did the same thing. Thus did the apostles, whom the Lord made witnesses of every action and of every doctrine—for upon all occasions do we find Peter, and James, and John present with Him— scrupulously act according to the dispensation of the Mosaic law, showing that it was from one and the same God; which they certainly never would have done, as I have already said, if they had learned from the Lord [that there existed] another Father besides Him who appointed the dispensation of the law.

Chapter XIII—Refutation of the opinion, that Paul was the only apostle who had knowledge of the truth.

1. With regard to those (the Marcionites) who allege that Paul alone knew the truth, and that to him the mystery was manifested by revelation, let Paul himself convict them, when he says, that one and the same God wrought in Peter for the apostolate of the circumcision, and in himself for the Gentiles. Peter, therefore, was an apostle of that very God whose was also Paul; and Him whom Peter preached as God among those of the circumcision, and likewise the Son of God, did Paul [declare] also among the Gentiles. For our Lord never came to save Paul alone, nor is God so limited in means, that He should have but one apostle who knew the dispensation of His Son. And again, when Paul says, "How beautiful are the feet of those bringing glad tidings of good things, and preaching the Gospel of peace," he shows clearly that it was not merely one, but there were many who used to preach the truth. And again, in the Epistle to the Corinthians, when he had recounted all those who had seen God after the resurrection, he says in continuation, "But whether it were I or they, so we preach, and so ye believed,"

acknowledging as one and the same, the preaching of all those who saw God after the resurrection from the dead.

2. And again, the Lord replied to Philip, who wished to behold the Father, "Have I been so long a time with you, and yet thou hast not known Me, Philip? He that sees Me, sees also the Father; and how sayest thou then, Show us the Father? For I am in the Father, and the Father in Me; and henceforth ye know Him, and have seen Him." To these men, therefore, did the Lord bear witness, that in Himself they had both known and seen the Father (and the Father is truth). To allege, then, that these men did not know the truth, is to act the part of false witnesses, and of those who have been alienated from the doctrine of Christ. For why did the Lord send the twelve apostles to the lost sheep of the house of Israel, if these men did not know the truth? How also did the seventy preach, unless they had themselves previously known the truth of what was preached? Or how could Peter have been in ignorance, to whom the Lord gave testimony, that flesh and blood had not revealed to him, but the Father, who is in heaven? Just, then, as "Paul [was] an apostle, not of men, neither by man, but by Jesus Christ, and God the Father," [so with the rest;] the Son indeed leading them to the Father, but the Father revealing to them the Son.

3. But that Paul acceded to [the request of] those who summoned him to the apostles, on account of the question [which had been raised], and went up to them, with Barnabas, to Jerusalem, not without reason, but that the liberty of the Gentiles might be confirmed by them, he does himself say, in the Epistle to the Galatians: "Then, fourteen years after, I went up again to Jerusalem with Barnabas, taking also Titus. But I went up by revelation, and communicated to them that Gospel which I preached among the Gentiles." And again he says, "For an hour we did give place to subjection, that the truth of the gospel might continue with you." If, then, any one shall, from the Acts of the Apostles, carefully scrutinize the time concerning which it is written that he went up to Jerusalem on account of the forementioned question, he will find those years mentioned by Paul coinciding with it. Thus the statement of Paul harmonizes with, and is, as it were, identical with, the testimony of Luke regarding the apostles.

Chapter XIV.—If Paul had known any mysteries unrevealed to the other apostles, Luke, his constant companion and fellow-traveller, could not have been ignorant of them; neither could the truth have possibly lain hid from him, through whom alone we learn many and most important particulars of the Gospel history.

1. But that this Luke was inseparable from Paul, and his fellow- labourer in the Gospel, he himself clearly evinces, not as a matter of boasting, but as bound to do so by the truth itself. For he says that when Barnabas, and John who was called Mark, had parted company from Paul, and sailed to Cyprus, "we came to Troas;" and when Paul had beheld in a dream a man of Macedonia, saying, "Come into Macedonia, Paul, and help us," "immediately," he says, "we endeavoured to go into Macedonia, understanding that the Lord had called us to preach the Gospel unto them. Therefore, sailing from Troas, we directed our ship's course towards Samothracia." And then he carefully indicates all the rest of their journey as far as Philippi, and how they delivered their first address: "for, sitting down," he says, "we spake unto the women who had assembled;" and certain believed, even a great many. And again does he say, "But we sailed from Philippi after the days of unleavened bread, and came to Troas, where we abode seven days." And all the remaining [details] of his course with Paul he recounts, indicating with all diligence both places, and cities, and number of days, until they went up to Jerusalem; and what befell Paul there, how he was sent to Rome in bonds; the name of the centurion who took him in charge; and the signs of the ships, and how they made shipwreck; and the island upon which they escaped, and how they received kindness there, Paul healing the chief man of that island; and how they sailed from thence to Puteoli, and from that arrived at Rome; and for what period they sojourned at Rome. As Luke was present at all these occurrences, he carefully noted them down in writing, so that he cannot be convicted of falsehood or boastfulness, because all these [particulars] proved both that he was senior to all those who now teach otherwise, and that he was not ignorant of the truth. That he was not merely a follower, but also a fellow-labourer of the apostles, but especially of Paul, Paul has himself declared also in the Epistles, saying: "Demas hath forsaken me, … and is departed unto Thessalonica; Crescens to Galatia, Titus to Dalmatia. Only Luke is with me." From this he shows that he was always attached to and inseparable from him. And again he says, in the Epistle to the Colossians: "Luke, the beloved physician, greets you." But surely if

Luke, who always preached in company with Paul, and is called by him "the beloved," and with him performed the work of an evangelist, and was entrusted to hand down to us a Gospel, learned nothing different from him (Paul), as has been pointed out from his words, how can these men, who were never attached to Paul, boast that they have learned hidden and unspeakable mysteries?

2. But that Paul taught with simplicity what he knew, not only to those who were [employed] with him, but to those that heard him, he does himself make manifest. For when the bishops and presbyters who came from Ephesus and the other cities adjoining had assembled in Miletus, since he was himself hastening to Jerusalem to observe Pentecost, after testifying many things to them, and declaring what must happen to him at Jerusalem, he added: "I know that ye shall see my face no more. Therefore I take you to record this day, that I am pure from the blood of all. For I have not shunned to declare unto you all the counsel of God. Take heed, therefore, both to yourselves, and to all the flock over which the Holy Ghost has placed you as bishops, to rule the Church of the Lord, which He has acquired for Himself through His own blood." Then, referring to the evil teachers who should arise, he said: "I know that after my departure shall grievous wolves come to you, not sparing the flock. Also of your own selves shall men arise, speaking perverse things, to draw away disciples after them." "I have not shunned," he says, "to declare unto you all the counsel of God." Thus did the apostles simply, and without respect of persons, deliver to all what they had themselves learned from the Lord. Thus also does Luke, without respect of persons, deliver to us what he had learned from them, as he has himself testified, saying, "Even as they delivered them unto us, who from the beginning were eye-witnesses and ministers of the Word."

3. Now if any man set Luke aside, as one who did not know the truth, he will, [by so acting,] manifestly reject that Gospel of which he claims to be a disciple. For through him we have become acquainted with very many and important parts of the Gospel; for instance, the generation of John, the history of Zacharias, the coming of the angel to Mary, the exclamation of Elisabeth, the descent of the angels to the shepherds, the words spoken by them, the testimony of Anna and of Simeon with regard to Christ, and that twelve years of age He was left behind at Jerusalem; also the baptism of John, the number of the Lord's years

when He was baptized, and that this occurred in the fifteenth year of Tiberius Cæsar. And in His office of teacher this is what He has said to the rich: "Woe unto you that are rich, for ye have received your consolation;" and "Woe unto you that are full, for ye shall hunger; and ye who laugh now, for ye shall weep;" and, "Woe unto you when all men shall speak well of you: for so did your fathers to the false prophets." All things of the following kind we have known through Luke alone (and numerous actions of the Lord we have learned through him, which also all [the Evangelists] notice): the multitude of fishes which Peter's companions enclosed, when at the Lord's command they cast the nets; the woman who had suffered for eighteen years, and was healed on the Sabbath-day; the man who had the dropsy, whom the Lord made whole on the Sabbath, and how He did defend Himself for having performed an act of healing on that day; how He taught His disciples not to aspire to the uppermost rooms; how we should invite the poor and feeble, who cannot recompense us; the man who knocked during the night to obtain loaves, and did obtain them, because of the urgency of his importunity; how, when [our Lord] was sitting at meat with a Pharisee, a woman that was a sinner kissed His feet, and anointed them with ointment, with what the Lord said to Simon on her behalf concerning the two debtors; also about the parable of that rich man who stored up the goods which had accrued to him, to whom it was also said, "In this night they shall demand thy soul from thee; whose then shall those things be which thou hast prepared?" and similar to this, that of the rich man, who was clothed in purple and who fared sumptuously, and the indigent Lazarus; also the answer which He gave to His disciples when they said, "Increase our faith;" also His conversation with Zaccheus the publican; also about the Pharisee and the publican, who were praying in the temple at the same time; also the ten lepers, whom He cleansed in the way simultaneously; also how He ordered the lame and the blind to be gathered to the wedding from the lanes and streets; also the parable of the judge who feared not God, whom the widow's importunity led to avenge her cause; and about the fig-tree in the vineyard which produced no fruit. There are also many other particulars to be found mentioned by Luke alone, which are made use of by both Marcion and Valentinus. And besides all these, [he records] what [Christ] said to His disciples in the way, after the resurrection, and how they recognised Him in the breaking of bread.

4. It follows then, as of course, that these men must either receive the rest of his narrative, or else reject these parts also. For no persons of common sense can permit them to receive some things recounted by Luke as being true, and to set others aside, as if he had not known the truth. And if indeed Marcion's followers reject these, they will then possess no Gospel; for, curtailing that according to Luke, as I have said already, they boast in having the Gospel [in what remains]. But the followers of Valentinus must give up their utterly vain talk; for they have taken from that [Gospel] many occasions for their own speculations, to put an evil interpretation upon what he has well said. If, on the other hand, they feel compelled to receive the remaining portions also, then, by studying the perfect Gospel, and the doctrine of the apostles, they will find it necessary to repent, that they may be saved from the danger [to which they are exposed].

Chapter XV.—Refutation of the Ebionites, who disparaged the authority of St. Paul, from the writings of St. Luke, which must be received as a whole. Exposure of the hypocrisy, deceit, and pride of the Gnostics. The apostles and their disciples knew and preached one God, the Creator of the world.

1. But again, we allege the same against those who do not recognise Paul as an apostle: that they should either reject the other words of the Gospel which we have come to know through Luke alone, and not make use of them; or else, if they do receive all these, they must necessarily admit also that testimony concerning Paul, when he (Luke) tells us that the Lord spoke at first to him from heaven: "Saul, Saul, why persecutest thou Me? I am Jesus Christ, whom thou persecutest;" and then to Ananias, saying regarding him: "Go thy way; for he is a chosen vessel unto Me, to bear My name among the Gentiles, and kings, and the children of Israel. For I will show him, from this time, how great things he must suffer for My name's sake." Those, therefore, who do not accept of him [as a teacher], who was chosen by God for this purpose, that he might boldly bear His name, as being sent to the forementioned nations, do despise the election of God, and separate themselves from the company of the apostles. For neither can they contend that Paul was no apostle, when he was chosen for this purpose; nor can they prove Luke guilty of falsehood, when he proclaims the truth to us with all diligence. It may be, indeed, that it was with this view that God set forth

very many Gospel truths, through Luke's instrumentality, which all should esteem it necessary to use, in order that all persons, following his subsequent testimony, which treats upon the acts and the doctrine of the apostles, and holding the unadulterated rule of truth, may be saved. His testimony, therefore, is true, and the doctrine of the apostles is open and stedfast, holding nothing in reserve; nor did they teach one set of doctrines in private, and another in public.

2. For this is the subterfuge of false persons, evil seducers, and hypocrites, as they act who are from Valentinus. These men discourse to the multitude about those who belong to the Church, whom they do themselves term "vulgar," and "ecclesiastic." By these words they entrap the more simple, and entice them, imitating our phraseology, that these [dupes] may listen to them the oftener; and then these are asked regarding us, how it is, that when they hold doctrines similar to ours, we, without cause, keep ourselves aloof from their company; and [how it is, that] when they say the same things, and hold the same doctrine, we call them heretics? When they have thus, by means of questions, overthrown the faith of any, and rendered them uncontradicting hearers of their own, they describe to them in private the unspeakable mystery of their Pleroma. But they are altogether deceived, who imagine that they may learn from the Scriptural texts adduced by heretics, that [doctrine] which their words plausibly teach. For error is plausible, and bears a resemblance to the truth, but requires to be disguised; while truth is without disguise, and therefore has been entrusted to children. And if any one of their auditors do indeed demand explanations, or start objections to them, they affirm that he is one not capable of receiving the truth, and not having from above the seed [derived] from their Mother; and thus really give him no reply, but simply declare that he is of the intermediate regions, that is, belongs to animal natures. But if any one do yield himself up to them like a little sheep, and follows out their practice, and their "redemption," such an one is puffed up to such an extent, that he thinks he is neither in heaven nor on earth, but that he has passed within the Pleroma; and having already embraced his angel, he walks with a strutting gait and a supercilious countenance, possessing all the pompous air of a cock. There are those among them who assert that that man who comes from above ought to follow a good course of conduct; wherefore they do also pretend a gravity [of demeanour] with a certain superciliousness. The majority, however, having become scoffers also, as if already perfect, and living without regard [to

appearances], yea, in contempt [of that which is good], call themselves "the spiritual," and allege that they have already become acquainted with that place of refreshing which is within their Pleroma.

3. But let us revert to the same line of argument [hitherto pursued]. For when it has been manifestly declared, that they who were the preachers of the truth and the apostles of liberty termed no one else God, or named him Lord, except the only true God the Father, and His Word, who has the pre-eminence in all things; it shall then be clearly proved, that they (the apostles) confessed as the Lord God Him who was the Creator of heaven and earth, who also spoke with Moses, gave to him the dispensation of the law, and who called the fathers; and that they knew no other. The opinion of the apostles, therefore, and of those (Mark and Luke) who learned from their words, concerning God, has been made manifest.

Chapter XVI.—Proofs from the apostolic writings, that Jesus Christ was one and the same, the only begotten Son of God, perfect God and perfect man.

1. But there are some who say that Jesus was merely a receptacle of Christ, upon whom the Christ, as a dove, descended from above, and that when He had declared the unnameable Father He entered into the Pleroma in an incomprehensible and invisible manner: for that He was not comprehended, not only by men, but not even by those powers and virtues which are in heaven, and that Jesus was the Son, but that Christ was the Father, and the Father of Christ, God; while others say that He merely suffered in outward appearance, being naturally impassible. The Valentinians, again, maintain that the dispensational Jesus was the same who passed through Mary, upon whom that Saviour from the more exalted [region] descended, who was also termed Pan, because He possessed the names (vocabula) of all those who had produced Him; but that [this latter] shared with Him, the dispensational one, His power and His name; so that by His means death was abolished, but the Father was made known by that Saviour who had descended from above, whom they do also allege to be Himself the receptacle of Christ and of the entire Pleroma; confessing, indeed, in tongue one Christ Jesus, but being divided in [actual] opinion: for, as I have already observed, it is the practice of these men to say that there was one Christ, who was produced by Monogenes, for the confirmation of the Pleroma; but that

another, the Saviour, was sent [forth] for the glorification of the Father; and yet another, the dispensational one, and whom they represent as having suffered, who also bore [in himself] Christ, that Saviour who returned into the Pleroma. I judge it necessary therefore to take into account the entire mind of the apostles regarding our Lord Jesus Christ, and to show that not only did they never hold any such opinions regarding Him; but, still further, that they announced through the Holy Spirit, that those who should teach such doctrines were agents of Satan, sent forth for the purpose of overturning the faith of some, and drawing them away from life.

2. That John knew the one and the same Word of God, and that He was the only begotten, and that He became incarnate for our salvation, Jesus Christ our Lord, I have sufficiently proved from the word of John himself. And Matthew, too, recognising one and the same Jesus Christ, exhibiting his generation as a man from the Virgin, even as God did promise David that He would raise up from the fruit of his body an eternal King, having made the same promise to Abraham a long time previously, says: "The book of the generation of Jesus Christ, the son of David, the son of Abraham." Then, that he might free our mind from suspicion regarding Joseph, he says: "But the birth of Christ was on this wise. When His mother was espoused to Joseph, before they came together, she was found with child of the Holy Ghost." Then, when Joseph had it in contemplation to put Mary away, since she proved with child, [Matthew tells us of] the angel of God standing by him, and saying: "Fear not to take unto thee Mary thy wife: for that which is conceived in her is of the Holy Ghost. And she shall bring forth a son, and thou shalt call His name Jesus; for He shall save His people from their sins. Now this was done, that it might be fulfilled which was spoken of the Lord by the prophet: Behold, a virgin shall conceive, and bring forth a son, and they shall call His name Emmanuel, which is, God with us;" clearly signifying that both the promise made to the fathers had been accomplished, that the Son of God was born of a virgin, and that He Himself was Christ the Saviour whom the prophets had foretold; not, as these men assert, that Jesus was He who was born of Mary, but that Christ was He who descended from above. Matthew might certainly have said, "Now the birth of Jesus was on this wise;" but the Holy Ghost, foreseeing the corrupters [of the truth], and guarding by anticipation against their deceit, says by Matthew, "But the birth of Christ was on this wise;" and that He is Emmanuel, lest perchance we

might consider Him as a mere man: for "not by the will of the flesh nor by the will of man, but by the will of God was the Word made flesh;" and that we should not imagine that Jesus was one, and Christ another, but should know them to be one and the same.

3. Paul, when writing to the Romans, has explained this very point: "Paul, an apostle of Jesus Christ, predestinated unto the Gospel of God, which He had promised by His prophets in the holy Scriptures, concerning His Son, who was made to Him of the seed of David according to the flesh, who was predestinated the Son of God with power through the Spirit of holiness, by the resurrection from the dead of our Lord Jesus Christ." And again, writing to the Romans about Israel, he says: "Whose are the fathers, and from whom is Christ according to the flesh, who is God over all, blessed for ever." And again, in his Epistle to the Galatians, he says: "But when the fulness of time had come, God sent forth His Son, made of a woman, made under the law, to redeem them that were under the law, that we might receive the adoption;" plainly indicating one God, who did by the prophets make promise of the Son, and one Jesus Christ our Lord, who was of the seed of David according to His birth from Mary; and that Jesus Christ was appointed the Son of God with power, according to the Spirit of holiness, by the resurrection from the dead, as being the first begotten in all the creation; the Son of God being made the Son of man, that through Him we may receive the adoption,—humanity sustaining, and receiving, and embracing the Son of God. Wherefore Mark also says: "The beginning of the Gospel of Jesus Christ, the Son of God; as it is written in the prophets." Knowing one and the same Son of God, Jesus Christ, who was announced by the prophets, who from the fruit of David's body was Emmanuel, "the messenger of great counsel of the Father;" through whom God caused the day-spring and the Just One to arise to the house of David, and raised up for him an horn of salvation, "and established a testimony in Jacob;" as David says when discoursing on the causes of His birth: "And He appointed a law in Israel, that another generation might know [Him,] the children which should he born from these, and they arising shall themselves declare to their children, so that they might set their hope in God, and seek after His commandments." And again, the angel said, when bringing good tidings to Mary: "He shall he great, and shall be called the Son of the Highest; and the Lord shall give unto Him the throne of His father David;" acknowledging that He who is the Son of the Highest, the same is

Himself also the Son of David. And David, knowing by the Spirit the dispensation of the advent of this Person, by which He is supreme over all the living and dead, confessed Him as Lord, sitting on the right hand of the Most High Father.

4. But Simeon also —he who had received an intimation from the Holy Ghost that he should not see death, until first he had beheld Christ Jesus— taking Him, the first-begotten of the Virgin, into his hands, blessed God, and said, "Lord, now lettest Thou Thy servant depart in peace, according to Thy word: because mine eyes have seen Thy salvation, which Thou hast prepared before the face of all people; a light to lighten the Gentiles, and the glory of Thy people Israel;" confessing thus, that the infant whom he was holding in his hands, Jesus, born of Mary, was Christ Himself, the Son of God, the light of all, the glory of Israel itself, and the peace and refreshing of those who had fallen asleep. For He was already despoiling men, by removing their ignorance, conferring upon them His own knowledge, and scattering abroad those who recognised Him, as Esaias says: "Call His name, Quickly spoil, Rapidly divide." Now these are the works of Christ. He therefore was Himself Christ, whom Simeon carrying [in his arms] blessed the Most High; on beholding whom the shepherds glorified God; whom John, while yet in his mother's womb, and He (Christ) in that of Mary, recognising as the Lord, saluted with leaping; whom the Magi, when they had seen, adored, and offered their gifts [to Him], as I have already stated, and prostrated themselves to the eternal King, departed by another way, not now returning by the way of the Assyrians. "For before the child shall have knowledge to cry, Father or mother, He shall receive the power of Damascus, and the spoils of Samaria, against the king of the Assyrians;" declaring, in a mysterious manner indeed, but emphatically, that the Lord did fight with a hidden hand against Amalek. For this cause, too, He suddenly removed those children belonging to the house of David, whose happy lot it was to have been born at that time, that He might send them on before into His kingdom; He, since He was Himself an infant, so arranging it that human infants should be martyrs, slain, according to the Scriptures, for the sake of Christ, who was born in Bethlehem of Judah, in the city of David.

5. Therefore did the Lord also say to His disciples after the resurrection, "O thoughtless ones, and slow of heart to believe all that the prophets

have spoken! Ought not Christ to have suffered these things, and to enter into His glory?" And again does He say to them: "These are the words which I spoke unto you while I was yet with you, that all things must be fulfilled which were written in the law of Moses, and in the prophets, and in the Psalms, concerning Me. Then opened He their understanding, that they should understand the Scriptures, and said unto them, Thus it is written, and thus it behoved Christ to suffer, and to rise again from the dead, and that repentance for the remission of sins be preached in His name among all nations." Now this is He who was born of Mary; for He says: "The Son of man must suffer many things, and be rejected, and crucified, and on the third day rise again." The Gospel, therefore, knew no other son of man but Him who was of Mary, who also suffered; and no Christ who flew away from Jesus before the passion; but Him who was born it knew as Jesus Christ the Son of God, and that this same suffered and rose again, as John, the disciple of the Lord, verifies, saying: "But these are written, that ye might believe that Jesus is the Christ, the Son of God, and that believing ye might have eternal life in His name,"—foreseeing these blasphemous systems which divide the Lord, as far as lies in their power, saying that He was formed of two different substances. For this reason also he has thus testified to us in his Epistle: "Little children, it is the last time; and as ye have heard that Antichrist doth come, now have many antichrists appeared; whereby we know that it is the last time. They went out from us, but they were not of us; for if they had been of us, they would have continued with us: but [they departed], that they might be made manifest that they are not of us. Know ye therefore, that every lie is from without, and is not of the truth. Who is a liar, but he that denieth that Jesus is the Christ? This is Antichrist."

6. But inasmuch as all those before mentioned, although they certainly do with their tongue confess one Jesus Christ, make fools of themselves, thinking one thing and saying another; for their hypotheses vary, as I have already shown, alleging, [as they do,] that one Being suffered and was born, and that this was Jesus; but that there was another who descended upon Him, and that this was Christ, who also ascended again; and they argue, that he who proceeded from the Demiurge, or he who was dispensational, or he who sprang from Joseph, was the Being subject to suffering; but upon the latter there descended from the invisible and ineffable [places] the former, whom they assert to be incomprehensible, invisible, and impassible: they thus wander from the

truth, because their doctrine departs from Him who is truly God, being ignorant that His only-begotten Word, who is always present with the human race, united to and mingled with His own creation, according to the Father's pleasure, and who became flesh, is Himself Jesus Christ our Lord, who did also suffer for us, and rose again on our behalf, and who will come again in the glory of His Father, to raise up all flesh, and for the manifestation of salvation, and to apply the rule of just judgment to all who were made by Him. There is therefore, as I have pointed out, one God the Father, and one Christ Jesus, who came by means of the whole dispensational arrangements [connected with Him], and gathered together all things in Himself. But in every respect, too, He is man, the formation of God; and thus He took up man into Himself, the invisible becoming visible, the incomprehensible being made comprehensible, the impassible becoming capable of suffering, and the Word being made man, thus summing up all things in Himself: so that as in super-celestial, spiritual, and invisible things, the Word of God is supreme, so also in things visible and corporeal He might possess the supremacy, and, taking to Himself the pre-eminence, as well as constituting Himself Head of the Church, He might draw all things to Himself at the proper time.

7. With Him is nothing incomplete or out of due season, just as with the Father there is nothing incongruous. For all these things were foreknown by the Father; but the Son works them out at the proper time in perfect order and sequence. This was the reason why, when Mary was urging [Him] on to [perform] the wonderful miracle of the wine, and was desirous before the time to partake of the cup of emblematic significance, the Lord, checking her untimely haste, said, "Woman, what have I to do with thee? mine hour is not yet come"— waiting for that hour which was foreknown by the Father. This is also the reason why, when men were often desirous to take Him, it is said, "No man laid hands upon Him, for the hour of His being taken was not yet come;" nor the time of His passion, which had been foreknown by the Father; as also says the prophet Habakkuk, "By this Thou shalt be known when the years have drawn nigh; Thou shalt be set forth when the time comes; because my soul is disturbed by anger, Thou shalt remember Thy mercy." Paul also says: "But when the fulness of time came, God sent forth His Son." By which is made manifest, that all things which had been foreknown of the Father, our Lord did accomplish in their order, season, and hour, foreknown and fitting, being indeed one and the same,

but rich and great. For He fulfils the bountiful and comprehensive will of His Father, inasmuch as He is Himself the Saviour of those who are saved, and the Lord of those who are under authority, and the God of all those things which have been formed, the only-begotten of the Father, Christ who was announced, and the Word of God, who became incarnate when the fulness of time had come, at which the Son of God had to become the Son of man.

8. All, therefore, are outside of the [Christian] dispensation, who, under pretext of knowledge, understand that Jesus was one, and Christ another, and the Only-begotten another, from whom again is the Word, and that the Saviour is another, whom these disciples of error allege to be a production of those who were made Æons in a state of degeneracy. Such men are to outward appearance sheep; for they appear to be like us, by what they say in public, repeating the same words as we do; but inwardly they are wolves. Their doctrine is homicidal, conjuring up, as it does, a number of gods, and simulating many Fathers, but lowering and dividing the Son of God in many ways. These are they against whom the Lord has cautioned us beforehand; and His disciple, in his Epistle already mentioned, commands us to avoid them, when he says: "For many deceivers are entered into the world, who confess not that Jesus Christ is come in the flesh. This is a deceiver and an antichrist. Take heed to them, that ye lose not what ye have wrought." And again does he say in the Epistle: "Many false prophets are gone out into the world. Hereby know ye the Spirit of God: Every spirit that confesseth that Jesus Christ is come in the flesh is of God; and every spirit which separates Jesus Christ is not of God, but is of antichrist." These words agree with what was said in the Gospel, that "the Word was made flesh, and dwelt among us." Wherefore he again exclaims in his Epistle, "Every one that believeth that Jesus is the Christ, has been born of God;" knowing Jesus Christ to be one and the same, to whom the gates of heaven were opened, because of His taking upon Him flesh: who shall also come in the same flesh in which He suffered, revealing the glory of the Father.

9. Concurring with these statements, Paul, speaking to the Romans, declares: "Much more they who receive abundance of grace and righteousness for [eternal] life, shall reign by one, Christ Jesus." It follows from this, that he knew nothing of that Christ who flew away

from Jesus; nor did he of the Saviour above, whom they hold to be impassible. For if, in truth, the one suffered, and the other remained incapable of suffering, and the one was born, but the other descended upon him who was born, and left him again, it is not one, but two, that are shown forth. But that the apostle did know Him as one, both who was born and who suffered, namely Christ Jesus, he again says in the same Epistle: "Know ye not, that so many of us as were baptized in Christ Jesus were baptized in His death? that like as Christ rose from the dead, so should we also walk in newness of life." But again, showing that Christ did suffer, and was Himself the Son of God, who died for us, and redeemed us with His blood at the time appointed beforehand, he says: "For how is it, that Christ, when we were yet without strength, in due time died for the ungodly? But God commendeth His love towards us, in that, while we were yet sinners, Christ died for us. Much more, then, being now justified by His blood, we shall be saved from wrath through Him. For if, when we were enemies, we were reconciled to God by the death of His Son; much more, being reconciled, we shall be saved by His life." He declares in the plainest manner, that the same Being who was laid hold of, and underwent suffering, and shed His blood for us, was both Christ and the Son of God, who did also rise again, and was taken up into heaven, as he himself [Paul] says: "But at the same time, [it, is] Christ [that] died, yea rather, that is risen again, who is even at the right hand of God." And again, "Knowing that Christ, rising from the dead, dieth no more:" for, as himself foreseeing, through the Spirit, the subdivisions of evil teachers [with regard to the Lord's person], and being desirous of cutting away from them all occasion of cavil, he says what has been already stated, [and also declares:] "But if the Spirit of Him that raised up Jesus from the dead dwell in you, He that raised up Christ from the dead shall also quicken your mortal bodies." This he does not utter to those alone who wish to hear: Do not err, [he says to all:] Jesus Christ, the Son of God, is one and the same, who did by suffering reconcile us to God, and rose from the dead; who is at the right hand of the Father, and perfect in all things; "who, when He was buffeted, struck not in return; who, when He suffered, threatened not;" and when He underwent tyranny, He prayed His Father that He would forgive those who had crucified Him. For He did Himself truly bring in salvation: since He is Himself the Word of God, Himself the Only-begotten of the Father, Christ Jesus our Lord.

Chapter XVII.—The apostles teach that it was neither Christ nor the Saviour, but the Holy Spirit, who did descend upon Jesus. The reason for this descent.

1. It certainly was in the power of the apostles to declare that Christ descended upon Jesus, or that the so-called superior Saviour [came down] upon the dispensational one, or he who is from the invisible places upon him from the Demiurge; but they neither knew nor said anything of the kind: for, had they known it, they would have also certainly stated it. But what really was the case, that did they record, [namely,] that the Spirit of God as a dove descended upon Him; this Spirit, of whom it was declared by Isaiah, "And the Spirit of God shall rest upon Him," as I have already said. And again: "The Spirit of the Lord is upon Me, because He hath anointed Me." That is the Spirit of whom the Lord declares, "For it is not ye that speak, but the Spirit of your Father which speaketh in you." And again, giving to the disciples the power of regeneration into God, He said to them, "Go and teach all nations, baptizing them in the name of the Father, and of the Son, and of the Holy Ghost." For [God] promised, that in the last times He would pour Him [the Spirit] upon [His] servants and handmaids, that they might prophesy; wherefore He did also descend upon the Son of God, made the Son of man, becoming accustomed in fellowship with Him to dwell in the human race, to rest with human beings, and to dwell in the workmanship of God, working the will of the Father in them, and renewing them from their old habits into the newness of Christ.

2. This Spirit did David ask for the human race, saying, "And stablish me with Thine all-governing Spirit;" who also, as Luke says, descended at the day of Pentecost upon the disciples after the Lord's ascension, having power to admit all nations to the entrance of life, and to the opening of the new covenant; from whence also, with one accord in all languages, they uttered praise to God, the Spirit bringing distant tribes to unity, and offering to the Father the first-fruits of all nations. Wherefore also the Lord promised to send the Comforter, who should join us to God. For as a compacted lump of dough cannot be formed of dry wheat without fluid matter, nor can a loaf possess unity, so, in like manner, neither could we, being many, be made one in Christ Jesus without the water from heaven. And as dry earth does not bring forth unless it receive moisture, in like manner we also, being originally a dry tree, could never have brought forth fruit unto life without the voluntary rain from above. For our bodies have received unity among themselves

by means of that laver which leads to incorruption; but our souls, by means of the Spirit. Wherefore both are necessary, since both contribute towards the life of God, our Lord compassionating that erring Samaritan woman—who did not remain with one husband, but committed fornication by [contracting] many marriages—by pointing out, and promising to her living water, so that she should thirst no more, nor occupy herself in acquiring the refreshing water obtained by labour, having in herself water springing up to eternal life. The Lord, receiving this as a gift from His Father, does Himself also confer it upon those who are partakers of Himself, sending the Holy Spirit upon all the earth.

3. Gideon, that Israelite whom God chose, that he might save the people of Israel from the power of foreigners, foreseeing this gracious gift, changed his request, and prophesied that there would be dryness upon the fleece of wool (a type of the people), on which alone at first there had been dew; thus indicating that they should no longer have the Holy Spirit from God, as saith Esaias, "I will also command the clouds, that they rain no rain upon it," but that the dew, which is the Spirit of God, who descended upon the Lord, should be diffused throughout all the earth, "the spirit of wisdom and understanding, the spirit of counsel and might, the spirit of knowledge and piety, the spirit of the fear of God." This Spirit, again, He did confer upon the Church, sending throughout all the world the Comforter from heaven, from whence also the Lord tells us that the devil, like lightning, was cast down. Wherefore we have need of the dew of God, that we be not consumed by fire, nor be rendered unfruitful, and that where we have an accuser there we may have also an Advocate, the Lord commending to the Holy Spirit His own man, who had fallen among thieves, whom He Himself compassionated, and bound up his wounds, giving two royal denaria; so that we, receiving by the Spirit the image and superscription of the Father and the Son, might cause the denarium entrusted to us to be fruitful, counting out the increase [thereof] to the Lord.

4. The Spirit, therefore, descending under the predestined dispensation, and the Son of God, the Only-begotten, who is also the Word of the Father, coming in the fulness of time, having become incarnate in man for the sake of man, and fulfilling all the conditions of human nature, our Lord Jesus Christ being one and the same, as He Himself the Lord doth testify, as the apostles confess, and as the prophets announce,—all

the doctrines of these men who have invented putative Ogdoads and Tetrads, and imagined subdivisions [of the Lord's person], have been proved falsehoods. These men do, in fact, set the Spirit aside altogether; they understand that Christ was one and Jesus another; and they teach that there was not one Christ, but many. And if they speak of them as united, they do again separate them: for they show that one did indeed undergo sufferings, but that the other remained impassible; that the one truly did ascend to the Pleroma, but the other remained in the intermediate place; that the one does truly feast and revel in places invisible and above all name, but that the other is seated with the Demiurge, emptying him of power. It will therefore be incumbent upon thee, and all others who give their attention to this writing, and are anxious about their own salvation, not readily to express acquiescence when they hear abroad the speeches of these men: for, speaking things resembling the [doctrine of the] faithful, as I have already observed, not only do they hold opinions which are different, but absolutely contrary, and in all points full of blasphemies, by which they destroy those persons who, by reason of the resemblance of the words, imbibe a poison which disagrees with their constitution, just as if one, giving lime mixed with water for milk, should mislead by the similitude of the colour; as a man superior to me has said, concerning all that in any way corrupt the things of God and adulterate the truth, "Lime is wickedly mixed with the milk of God."

Chapter XVIII.—Continuation of the foregoing argument. Proofs from the writings of St. Paul, and from the words of Our Lord, that Christ and Jesus cannot be considered as distinct beings; neither can it be alleged that the Son of God became man merely in appearance, but that He did so truly and actually.

1. As it has been clearly demonstrated that the Word, who existed in the beginning with God, by whom all things were made, who was also always present with mankind, was in these last days, according to the time appointed by the Father, united to His own workmanship, inasmuch as He became a man liable to suffering, [it follows] that every objection is set aside of those who say, "If our Lord was born at that time, Christ had therefore no previous existence." For I have shown that the Son of God did not then begin to exist, being with the Father from the beginning; but when He became incarnate, and was made man, He

commenced afresh the long line of human beings, and furnished us, in a brief, comprehensive manner, with salvation; so that what we had lost in Adam—namely, to be according to the image and likeness of God—that we might recover in Christ Jesus.

2. For as it was not possible that the man who had once for all been conquered, and who had been destroyed through disobedience, could reform himself, and obtain the prize of victory; and as it was also impossible that he could attain to salvation who had fallen under the power of sin,—the Son effected both these things, being the Word of God, descending from the Father, becoming incarnate, stooping low, even to death, and consummating the arranged plan of our salvation, upon whom [Paul], exhorting us unhesitatingly to believe, again says, "Who shall ascend into heaven? that is, to bring down Christ; or who shall descend into the deep? that is, to liberate Christ again from the dead." Then he continues, "If thou shall confess with thy mouth the Lord Jesus, and shalt believe in thine heart that God hath raised Him from the dead, thou shall be saved." And he renders the reason why the Son of God did these things, saying, "For to this end Christ both lived, and died, and revived, that He might rule over the living and the dead." And again, writing to the Corinthians, he declares, "But we preach Christ Jesus crucified;" and adds, "The cup of blessing which we bless, is it not the communion of the blood of Christ?"

3. But who is it that has had fellowship with us in the matter of food? Whether is it he who is conceived of by them as the Christ above, who extended himself through Horos, and imparted a form to their mother; or is it He who is from the Virgin, Emmanuel, who did eat butter and honey, of whom the prophet declared, "He is also a man, and who shall know him?" He was likewise preached by Paul: "For I delivered," he says, "unto you first of all, that Christ died for our sins, according to the Scriptures; and that He was buried, and rose again the third day, according to the Scriptures." It is plain, then, that Paul knew no other Christ besides Him alone, who both suffered, and was buried, and rose gain, who was also born, and whom he speaks of as man. For after remarking, "But if Christ be preached, that He rose from the dead," he continues, rendering the reason of His incarnation, "For since by man came death, by man [came] also the resurrection of the dead." And everywhere, when [referring to] the passion of our Lord, and to His

human nature, and His subjection to death, he employs the name of Christ, as in that passage: "Destroy not him with thy meat for whom Christ died." And again: "But now, in Christ, ye who sometimes were far off are made nigh by the blood of Christ." And again: "Christ has redeemed us from the curse of the law, being made a curse for us: for it is written, Cursed is every one that hangeth upon a tree." And again: "And through thy knowledge shall the weak brother perish, for whom Christ died;" indicating that the impassible Christ did not descend upon Jesus, but that He Himself, because He was Jesus Christ, suffered for us; He, who lay in the tomb, and rose again, who descended and ascended,—the Son of God having been made the Son of man, as the very name itself doth declare. For in the name of Christ is implied, He that anoints, He that is anointed, and the unction itself with which He is anointed. And it is the Father who anoints, but the Son who is anointed by the Spirit, who is the unction, as the Word declares by Isaiah, "The Spirit of the Lord is upon me, because He hath anointed me,"—pointing out both the anointing Father, the anointed Son, and the unction, which is the Spirit.

4. The Lord Himself, too, makes it evident who it was that suffered; for when He asked the disciples, "Who do men say that I, the Son of man, am?" and when Peter had replied, "Thou art the Christ, the Son of the living God;" and when he had been commended by Him [in these words], "That flesh and blood had not revealed it to him, but the Father who is in heaven," He made it clear that He, the Son of man, is Christ the Son of the living God. "For from that time forth," it is said, "He began to show to His disciples, how that He must go unto Jerusalem, and suffer many things of the priests, and be rejected, and crucified, and rise again the third day." He who was acknowledged by Peter as Christ, who pronounced him blessed because the Father had revealed the Son of the living God to him, said that He must Himself suffer many things, and be crucified; and then He rebuked Peter, who imagined that He was the Christ as the generality of men supposed [that the Christ should be], and was averse to the idea of His suffering, [and] said to the disciples, "If any man will come after Me, let him deny himself, and take up his cross, and follow Me. For whosoever will save his life, shall lose it; and whosoever will lose it for My sake shall save it." For these things Christ spoke openly, He being Himself the Saviour of those who should be delivered over to death for their confession of Him, and lose their lives.

5. If, however, He was Himself not to suffer, but should fly away from Jesus, why did He exhort His disciples to take up the cross and follow Him,—that cross which these men represent Him as not having taken up, but [speak of Him] as having relinquished the dispensation of suffering? For that He did not say this with reference to the acknowledging of the Stauros (cross) above, as some among them venture to expound, but with respect to the suffering which He should Himself undergo, and that His disciples should endure, He implies when He says, "For whosoever will save his life, shall lose it; and whosoever will lose, shall find it." And that His disciples must suffer for His sake, He [implied when He] said to the Jews, "Behold, I send you prophets, and wise men, and scribes: and some of them ye shall kill and crucify." And to the disciples He was wont to say, "And ye shall stand before governors and kings for My sake; and they shall scourge some of you, and slay you, and persecute you from city to city." He knew, therefore, both those who should suffer persecution, and He knew those who should have to be scourged and slain because of Him; and He did not speak of any other cross, but of the suffering which He should Himself undergo first, and His disciples afterwards. For this purpose did He give them this exhortation: "Fear not them which kill the body, but are not able to kill the soul; but rather fear Him who is able to send both soul and body into hell;" [thus exhorting them] to hold fast those professions of faith which they had made in reference to Him. For He promised to confess before His Father those who should confess His name before men; but declared that He would deny those who should deny Him, and would be ashamed of those who should be ashamed to confess Him. And although these things are so, some of these men have proceeded to such a degree of temerity, that they even pour contempt upon the martyrs, and vituperate those who are slain on account of the confession of the Lord, and who suffer all things predicted by the Lord, and who in this respect strive to follow the footprints of the Lord's passion, having become martyrs of the suffering One; these we do also enrol with the martyrs themselves. For, when inquisition shall be made for their blood, and they shall attain to glory, then all shall be confounded by Christ, who have cast a slur upon their martyrdom. And from this fact, that He exclaimed upon the cross, "Father, forgive them, for they know not what they do," the long-suffering, patience, compassion, and goodness of Christ are exhibited, since He both suffered, and did Himself exculpate those who had maltreated Him. For the Word of God, who said to us, "Love your enemies, and pray for those that hate you," Himself did this very thing upon the cross; loving the human race

to such a degree, that He even prayed for those putting Him to death. If, however, any one, going upon the supposition that there are two [Christs], forms a judgment in regard to them, that [Christ] shall be found much the better one, and more patient, and the truly good one, who, in the midst of His own wounds and stripes, and the other [cruelties] inflicted upon Him, was beneficent, and unmindful of the wrongs perpetrated upon Him, than he who flew away, and sustained neither injury nor insult.

6. This also does likewise meet [the case] of those who maintain that He suffered only in appearance. For if He did not truly suffer, no thanks to Him, since there was no suffering at all; and when we shall actually begin to suffer, He will seem as leading us astray, exhorting us to endure buffering, and to turn the other cheek, if He did not Himself before us in reality suffer the same; and as He misled them by seeming to them what He was not, so does He also mislead us, by exhorting us to endure what He did not endure Himself. [In that case] we shall be even above the Master, because we suffer and sustain what our Master never bore or endured. But as our Lord is alone truly Master, so the Son of God is truly good and patient, the Word of God the Father having been made the Son of man. For He fought and conquered; for He was man contending for the fathers, and through obedience doing away with disobedience completely: for He bound the strong man, and set free the weak, and endowed His own handiwork with salvation, by destroying sin. For He is a most holy and merciful Lord, and loves the human race.

7. Therefore, as I have already said, He caused man (human nature) to cleave to and to become, one with God. For unless man had overcome the enemy of man, the enemy would not have been legitimately vanquished. And again: unless it had been God who had freely given salvation, we could never have possessed it securely. And unless man had been joined to God, he could never have become a partaker of incorruptibility. For it was incumbent upon the Mediator between God and men, by His relationship to both, to bring both to friendship and concord, and present man to God, while He revealed God to man. For, in what way could we be partaken of the adoption of sons, unless we had received from Him through the Son that fellowship which refers to Himself, unless His Word, having been made flesh, had entered into communion with us? Wherefore also He passed through every stage of

life, restoring to all communion with God. Those, therefore, who assert that He appeared putatively, and was neither born in the flesh nor truly made man, are as yet under the old condemnation, holding out patronage to sin; for, by their showing, death has not been vanquished, which "reigned from Adam to Moses, even over them that had not sinned after the similitude of Adam's transgression." But the law coming, which was given by Moses, and testifying of sin that it is a sinner, did truly take away his (death's) kingdom, showing that he was no king, but a robber; and it revealed him as a murderer. It laid, however, a weighty burden upon man, who had sin in himself, showing that he was liable to death. For as the law was spiritual, it merely made sin to stand out in relief, but did not destroy it. For sin had no dominion over the spirit, but over man. For it behoved Him who was to destroy sin, and redeem man under the power of death, that He should Himself be made that very same thing which he was, that is, man; who had been drawn by sin into bondage, but was held by death, so that sin should be destroyed by man, and man should go forth from death. For as by the disobedience of the one man who was originally moulded from virgin soil, the many were made sinners, and forfeited life; so was it necessary that, by the obedience of one man, who was originally born from a virgin, many should be justified and receive salvation. Thus, then, was the Word of God made man, as also Moses says: "God, true are His works." But if, not having been made flesh, He did appear as if flesh, His work was not a true one. But what He did appear, that He also was: God recapitulated in Himself the ancient formation of man, that He might kill sin, deprive death of its power, and vivify man; and therefore His works are true.

Chapter XIX.—Jesus Christ was not a mere man, begotten from Joseph in the ordinary course of nature, but was very God, begotten of the Father most high, and very man, born of the Virgin.

1. But again, those who assert that He was simply a mere man, begotten by Joseph, remaining in the bondage of the old disobedience, are in a state of death having been not as yet joined to the Word of God the Father, nor receiving liberty through the Son, as He does Himself declare: "If the Son shall make you free, ye shall be free indeed." But, being ignorant of Him who from the Virgin is Emmanuel, they are deprived of His gift, which is eternal life; and not receiving the incorruptible Word, they remain in mortal flesh, and are debtors to death, not obtaining the antidote of life. To whom the Word says,

mentioning His own gift of grace: "I said, Ye are all the sons of the Highest, and gods; but ye shall die like men." He speaks undoubtedly these words to those who have not received the gift of adoption, but who despise the incarnation of the pure generation of the Word of God, defraud human nature of promotion into God, and prove themselves ungrateful to the Word of God, who became flesh for them. For it was for this end that the Word of God was made man, and He who was the Son of God became the Son of man, that man, having been taken into the Word, and receiving the adoption, might become the son of God. For by no other means could we have attained to incorruptibility and immortality, unless we had been united to incorruptibility and immortality. But how could we be joined to incorruptibility and immortality, unless, first, incorruptibility and immortality had become that which we also are, so that the corruptible might be swallowed up by incorruptibility, and the mortal by immortality, that we might receive the adoption of sons?

2. For this reason [it is, said], "Who shall declare His generation?" since "He is a man, and who shall recognise Him?" But he to whom the Father which is in heaven has revealed Him, knows Him, so that he understands that He who "was not born either by the will of the flesh, or by the will of man," is the Son of man, this is Christ, the Son of the living God. For I have shown from the Scriptures, that no one of the sons of Adam is as to everything, and absolutely, called God, or named Lord. But that He is Himself in His own right, beyond all men who ever lived, God, and Lord, and King Eternal, and the Incarnate Word, proclaimed by all the prophets, the apostles, and by the Spirit Himself, may be seen by all who have attained to even a small portion of the truth. Now, the Scriptures would not have testified these things of Him, if, like others, He had been a mere man. But that He had, beyond all others, in Himself that pre-eminent birth which is from the Most High Father, and also experienced that pre- eminent generation which is from the Virgin, the divine Scriptures do in both respects testify of Him: also, that He was a man without comeliness, and liable to suffering; that He sat upon the foal of an ass; that He received for drink, vinegar and gall; that He was despised among the people, and humbled Himself even to death and that He is the holy Lord, the Wonderful, the Counsellor, the Beautiful in appearance, and the Mighty God, coming on the clouds as the Judge of all men;—all these things did the Scriptures prophesy of Him.

3. For as He became man in order to undergo temptation, so also was He the Word that He might be glorified; the Word remaining quiescent, that He might be capable of being tempted, dishonoured, crucified, and of suffering death, but the human nature being swallowed up in it (the divine), when it conquered, and endured [without yielding], and performed acts of kindness, and rose again, and was received up [into heaven]. He therefore, the Son of God, our Lord, being the Word of the Father, and the Son of man, since He had a generation as to His human nature from Mary—who was descended from mankind, and who was herself a human being—was made the Son of man. Wherefore also the Lord Himself gave us a sign, in the depth below, and in the height above, which man did not ask for, because he never expected that a virgin could conceive, or that it was possible that one remaining a virgin could bring forth a son, and that what was thus born should be "God with us," and descend to those things which are of the earth beneath, seeking the sheep which had perished, which was indeed His own peculiar handiwork, and ascend to the height above, offering and commending to His Father that human nature (hominem) which had been found, making in His own person the first-fruits of the resurrection of man; that, as the Head rose from the dead, so also the remaining part of the body—[namely, the body] of everyman who is found in life—when the time is fulfilled of that condemnation which existed by reason of disobedience, may arise, blended together and strengthened through means of joints and bands by the increase of God, each of the members having its own proper and fit position in the body. For there are many mansions in the Father's house, inasmuch as there are also many members in the body.

Chapter XX.—God showed himself, by the fall of man, as patient, benign, merciful, mighty to save. Man is therefore most ungrateful, if, unmindful of his own lot, and of the benefits held out to him, he do not acknowledge divine grace.

1. Long-suffering therefore was God, when man became a defaulter, as foreseeing that victory which should be granted to him through the Word. For, when strength was made perfect in weakness, it showed the kindness and transcendent power of God. For as He patiently suffered Jonah to be swallowed by the whale, not that he should be swallowed up and perish altogether, but that, having been cast out again, he might

be the more subject to God, and might glorify Him the more who had conferred upon him such an unhoped-for deliverance, and might bring the Ninevites to a lasting repentance, so that they should be converted to the Lord, who would deliver them from death, having been struck with awe by that portent which had been wrought in Jonah's case, as the Scripture says of them, "And they returned each from his evil way, and the unrighteousness which was in their hands, saying, Who knoweth if God will repent, and turn away His anger from us, and we shall not perish?"—so also, from the beginning, did God permit man to be swallowed up by the great whale, who was the author of transgression, not that he should perish altogether when so engulphed; but, arranging and preparing the plan of salvation, which was accomplished by the Word, through the sign of Jonah, for those who held the same opinion as Jonah regarding the Lord, and who confessed, and said, "I am a servant of the Lord, and I worship the Lord God of heaven, who hath made the sea and the dry land." [This was done] that man, receiving an unhoped-for salvation from God, might rise from the dead, and glorify God, and repeat that word which was uttered in prophecy by Jonah: "I cried by reason of mine affliction to the Lord my God, and He heard me out of the belly of hell;" and that he might always continue glorifying God, and giving thanks without ceasing, for that salvation which he has derived from Him, "that no flesh should glory in the Lord's presence;" and that man should never adopt an opposite opinion with regard to God, supposing that the incorruptibility which belongs to him is his own naturally, and by thus not holding the truth, should boast with empty superciliousness, as if he were naturally like to God. For he (Satan) thus rendered him (man) more ungrateful towards his Creator, obscured the love which God had towards man, and blinded his mind not to perceive what is worthy of God, comparing himself with, and judging himself equal to, God.

2. This, therefore, was the [object of the] long-suffering of God, that man, passing through all things, and acquiring the knowledge of moral discipline, then attaining to the resurrection from the dead, and learning by experience what is the source of his deliverance, may always live in a state of gratitude to the Lord, having obtained from Him the gift of incorruptibility, that he might love Him the more; for "he to whom more is forgiven, loveth more:" and that he may know himself, how mortal and weak he is; while he also understands respecting God, that He is immortal and powerful to such a degree as to confer immortality

upon what is mortal, and eternity upon what is temporal; and may understand also the other attributes of God displayed towards himself, by means of which being instructed he may think of God in accordance with the divine greatness. For the glory of man [is] God, but [His] works [are the glory] of God; and the receptacle of all His wisdom and power [is] man. Just as the physician is proved by his patients, so is God also revealed through men. And therefore Paul declares, "For God hath concluded all in unbelief, that He may have mercy upon all;" not saying this in reference to spiritual Æons, but to man, who had been disobedient to God, and being cast off from immortality, then obtained mercy, receiving through the Son of God that adoption which is [accomplished] by Himself. For he who holds, without pride and boasting, the true glory (opinion) regarding created things and the Creator, who is the Almighty God of all, and who has granted existence to all; [such an one,] continuing in His love and subjection, and giving of thanks, shall also receive from Him the greater glory of promotion, looking forward to the time when he shall become like Him who died for him, for He, too, "was made in the likeness of sinful flesh," to condemn sin, and to cast it, as now a condemned thing, away beyond the flesh, but that He might call man forth into His own likeness, assigning him as [His own] imitator to God, and imposing on him His Father's law, in order that he may see God, and granting him power to receive the Father; [being] the Word of God who dwelt in man, and became the Son of man, that He might accustom man to receive God, and God to dwell in man, according to the good pleasure of the Father.

3. On this account, therefore, the Lord Himself, who is Emmanuel from the Virgin, is the sign of our salvation, since it was the Lord Himself who saved them, because they could not be saved by their own instrumentality; and, therefore, when Paul sets forth human infirmity, he says: "For I know that there dwelleth in my flesh no good thing," showing that the "good thing" of our salvation is not from us, but from God. And again: "Wretched man that I am, who shall deliver me from the body of this death?" Then he introduces the Deliverer, [saying,] "The grace of Jesus Christ our Lord." And Isaiah declares this also, [when he says:] "Be ye strengthened, ye hands that hang down, and ye feeble knees; be ye encouraged, ye feeble-minded; be comforted, fear not: behold, our God has given judgment with retribution, and shall recompense: He will come Himself, and will save us." Here we see, that not by ourselves, but by the help of God, we must be saved.

4. Again, that it should not be a mere man who should save us, nor [one] without flesh—for the angels are without flesh—[the same prophet] announced, saying: "Neither an elder, nor angel, but the Lord Himself will save them because He loves them, and will spare them: He will Himself set them free." And that He should Himself become very man, visible, when He should be the Word giving salvation, Isaiah again says: "Behold, city of Zion: thine eyes shall see our salvation." And that it was not a mere man who died for us, Isaiah says: "And the holy Lord remembered His dead Israel, who had slept in the land of sepulture; and He came down to preach His salvation to them, that He might save them." And Amos (Micah) the prophet declares the same: "He will turn again, and will have compassion upon us: He will destroy our iniquities, and will cast our sins into the depths of the sea." And again, specifying the place of His advent, he says: "The Lord hath spoken from Zion, and He has uttered His voice from Jerusalem." And that it is from that region which is towards the south of the inheritance of Judah that the Son of God shall come, who is God, and who was from Bethlehem, where the Lord was born [and] will send out His praise through all the earth, thus says the prophet Habakkuk: "God shall come from the south, and the Holy One from Mount Effrem. His power covered the heavens over, and the earth is full of His praise. Before His face shall go forth the Word, and His feet shall advance in the plains." Thus he indicates in clear terms that He is God, and that His advent was [to take place] in Bethlehem, and from Mount Effrem which is towards the south of the inheritance, and that [He is] man. For he says, "His feet shall advance in the plains:" and this is an indication proper to man.

Chapter XXI.—A vindication of the prophecy in Isa. vii. 14 against the misinterpretations of Theodotion, Aquila, the Ebionites, and the Jews. Authority of the Septuagint version. Arguments in proof that Christ was born of a virgin.

1. God, then, was made man, and the Lord did Himself save us, giving us the token of the Virgin. But not as some allege, among those now presuming to expound the Scripture, [thus:] "Behold, a young woman shall conceive, and bring forth a son," as Theodotion the Ephesian has interpreted, and Aquila of Pontus, both Jewish proselytes. The Ebionites, following these, assert that He was begotten by Joseph; thus destroying, as far as in them lies, such a marvellous dispensation of God,

and setting aside the testimony of the prophets which proceeded from God. For truly this prediction was uttered before the removal of the people to Babylon; that is, anterior to the supremacy acquired by the Medes and Persians. But it was interpreted into Greek by the Jews themselves, much before the period of our Lord's advent, that there might remain no suspicion that perchance the Jews, complying with our humour, did put this interpretation upon these words. They indeed, had they been cognizant of our future existence, and that we should use these proofs from the Scriptures, would themselves never have hesitated to burn their own Scriptures, which do declare that all other nations partake of [eternal] life, and show that they who boast themselves as being the house of Jacob and the people of Israel, are disinherited from the grace of God.

2. For before the Romans possessed their kingdom, while as yet the Macedonians held Asia, Ptolemy the son of Lagus, being anxious to adorn the library which he had founded in Alexandria, with a collection of the writings of all men, which were [works] of merit, made request to the people of Jerusalem, that they should have their Scriptures translated into the Greek language. And they—for at that time they were still subject to the Macedonians—sent to Ptolemy seventy of their elders, who were thoroughly skilled in the Scriptures and in both the languages, to carry out what he had desired. But he, wishing to test them individually, and fearing lest they might perchance, by taking counsel together, conceal the truth in the Scriptures, by their interpretation, separated them from each other, and commanded them all to write the same translation. He did this with respect to all the books. But when they came together in the same place before Ptolemy, and each of them compared his own interpretation with that of every other, God was indeed glorified, and the Scriptures were acknowledged as truly divine. For all of them read out the common translation [which they had prepared] in the very same words and the very same names, from beginning to end, so that even the Gentiles present perceived that the Scriptures had been interpreted by the inspiration of God. And there was nothing astonishing in God having done this,—He who, when, during the captivity of the people under Nebuchadnezzar, the Scriptures had been corrupted, and when, after seventy years, the Jews had returned to their own land, then, in the times of Artaxerxes king of the Persians, inspired Esdras the priest, of the tribe of Levi, to recast all the

words of the former prophets, and to re-establish with the people the Mosaic legislation.

3. Since, therefore, the Scriptures have been interpreted with such fidelity, and by the grace of God, and since from these God has prepared and formed again our faith towards His Son, and has preserved to us the unadulterated Scriptures in Egypt, where the house of Jacob flourished, fleeing from the famine in Canaan; where also our Lord was preserved when He fled from the persecution set on foot by Herod; and [since] this interpretation of these Scriptures was made prior to our Lord's descent [to earth], and came into being before the Christians appeared —for our Lord was born about the forty-first year of the reign of Augustus; but Ptolemy was much earlier, under whom the Scriptures were interpreted;—[since these things are so, I say,] truly these men are proved to be impudent and presumptuous, who would now show a desire to make different translations, when we refute them out of these Scriptures, and shut them up to a belief in the advent of the Son of God. But our faith is stedfast, unfeigned, and the only true one, having clear proof from these Scriptures, which were interpreted in the way I have related; and the preaching of the Church is without interpolation. For the apostles, since they are of more ancient date than all these [heretics], agree with this aforesaid translation; and the translation harmonizes with the tradition of the apostles. For Peter, and John, and Matthew, and Paul, and the rest successively, as well as their followers, did set forth all prophetical [announcements], just as the interpretation of the elders contains them.

4. For the one and the same Spirit of God, who proclaimed by the prophets what and of what sort the advent of the Lord should be, did by these elders give a just interpretation of what had been truly prophesied; and He did Himself, by the apostles, announce that the fulness of the times of the adoption had arrived, that the kingdom of heaven had drawn nigh, and that He was dwelling within those that believe on Him who was born Emmanuel of the Virgin. To this effect they testify, [saying,] that before Joseph had come together with Mary, while she therefore remained in virginity, "she was found with child of the Holy Ghost;" and that the angel Gabriel said unto her, "The Holy Ghost shall come upon thee, and the power of the Highest shall overshadow thee; therefore also that holy thing which shall be born of

thee shall be called the Son of God;" and that the angel said to Joseph in a dream, "Now this was done, that it might be fulfilled which was spoken by Isaiah the prophet, Behold, a virgin shall be with child." But the elders have thus interpreted what Esaias said: "And the Lord, moreover, said unto Ahaz, Ask for thyself a sign from the Lord thy God out of the depth below, or from the height above. And Ahaz said, I will not ask, and I will not tempt the Lord. And he said, It is not a small thing for you to weary men; and how does the Lord weary them? Therefore the Lord himself shall give you a sign; Behold, a virgin shall conceive, and bear a son; and ye shall call His name Emmanuel. Butter and honey shall He eat: before He knows or chooses out things that are evil, He shall exchange them for what is good; for before the child knows good or evil, He shall not consent to evil, that He may choose that which is good." Carefully, then, has the Holy Ghost pointed out, by what has been said, His birth from a virgin, and His essence, that He is God (for the name Emmanuel indicates this). And He shows that He is a man, when He says, "Butter and honey shall He eat;" and in that He terms Him a child also, [in saying,] "before He knows good and evil;" for these are all the tokens of a human infant. But that He "will not consent to evil, that He may choose that which is good,"—this is proper to God; that by the fact, that He shall eat butter and honey, we should not understand that He is a mere man only, nor, on the other hand, from the name Emmanuel, should suspect Him to be God without flesh.

5. And when He says, "Hear, O house of David," He performed the part of one indicating that He whom God promised David that He would raise up from the fruit of his belly (ventris) an eternal King, is the same who was born of the Virgin, herself of the lineage of David. For on this account also, He promised that the King should be "of the fruit of his belly," which was the appropriate [term to use with respect] to a virgin conceiving, and not "of the fruit of his loins," nor "of the fruit of his reins," which expression is appropriate to a generating man, and a woman conceiving by a man. In this promise, therefore, the Scripture excluded all virile influence; yet it certainly is not mentioned that He who was born was not from the will of man. But it has fixed and established "the fruit of the belly," that it might declare the generation of Him who should be [born] from the Virgin, as Elisabeth testified when filled with the Holy Ghost, saying to Mary, "Blessed art thou among women, and blessed is the fruit of thy belly;" the Holy Ghost pointing out to those willing to hear, that the promise which God had

made, of raising up a King from the fruit of [David's] belly, was fulfilled in the birth from the Virgin, that is, from Mary. Let those, therefore, who alter the passage of Isaiah thus, "Behold, a young woman shall conceive," and who will have Him to be Joseph's son, also alter the form of the promise which was given to David, when God promised him to raise up, from the fruit of his belly, the horn of Christ the King. But they did not understand, otherwise they would have presumed to alter even this passage also.

6. But what Isaiah said, "From the height above, or from the depth beneath," was meant to indicate, that "He who descended was the same also who ascended." But in this that he said, "The Lord Himself shall give you a sign," he declared an unlooked-for thing with regard to His generation, which could have been accomplished in no other way than by God the Lord of all, God Himself giving a sign in the house of David. For what great thing or what sign should have been in this, that a young woman conceiving by a man should bring forth,—a thing which happens to all women that produce offspring? But since an unlooked-for salvation was to be provided for men through the help of God, so also was the unlooked-for birth from a virgin accomplished; God giving this sign, but man not working it out.

7. On this account also, Daniel, foreseeing His advent, said that a stone, cut out without hands, came into this world. For this is what "without hands" means, that His coming into this world was not by the operation of human hands, that is, of those men who are accustomed to stone-cutting; that is, Joseph taking no part with regard to it, but Mary alone co-operating with the pre-arranged plan. For this stone from the earth derives existence from both the power and the wisdom of God. Wherefore also Isaiah says: "Thus saith the Lord, Behold, I deposit in the foundations of Zion a stone, precious, elect, the chief, the corner-one, to be had in honour." So, then, we understand that His advent in human nature was not by the will of a man, but by the will of God.

8. Wherefore also Moses giving a type, cast his rod upon the earth, in order that it, by becoming flesh, might expose and swallow up all the opposition of the Egyptians, which was lifting itself up against the pre-arranged plan of God; that the Egyptians themselves might testify that

it is the finger of God which works salvation for the people, and not the son of Joseph. For if He were the son of Joseph, how could He be greater than Solomon, or greater than Jonah, or greater than David, when He was generated from the same seed, and was a descendant of these men? And how was it that He also pronounced Peter blessed, because he acknowledged Him to be the Son of the living God?

9. But besides, if indeed He had been the son of Joseph, He could not, according to Jeremiah, be either king or heir. For Joseph is shown to be the son of Joachim and Jechoniah, as also Matthew sets forth in his pedigree. But Jechoniah, and all his posterity, were disinherited from the kingdom; Jeremiah thus declaring, "As I live, saith the Lord, if Jechoniah the son of Joachim king of Judah had been made the signet of my right hand, I would pluck him thence, and deliver him into the hand of those seeking thy life." And again: "Jechoniah is dishonoured as a useless vessel, for he has been cast into a land which he knew not. Earth, hear the word of the Lord: Write this man a disinherited person; for none of his seed, sitting on the throne of David, shall prosper, or be a prince in Judah." And again, God speaks of Joachim his father: "Therefore thus saith the Lord concerning Joachim his father, king of Judea, There shall be from him none sitting upon the throne of David: and his dead body shall be cast out in the heat of day, and in the frost of night. And I will look upon him, and upon his sons, and will bring upon them, and upon the inhabitants of Jerusalem, upon the land of Judah, all the evils that I have pronounced against them." Those, therefore, who say that He was begotten of Joseph, and that they have hope in Him, do cause themselves to be disinherited from the kingdom, failing under the curse and rebuke directed against Jechoniah and his seed. Because for this reason have these things been spoken concerning Jechoniah, the [Holy] Spirit foreknowing the doctrines of the evil teachers; that they may learn that from his seed—that is, from Joseph—He was not to be born but that, according to the promise of God, from David's belly the King eternal is raised up, who sums up all things in Himself, and has gathered into Himself the ancient formation [of man].

10. For as by one man's disobedience sin entered, and death obtained [a place] through sin; so also by the obedience of one man, righteousness having been introduced, shall cause life to fructify in those persons who in times past were dead. And as the protoplast himself Adam, had his

substance from untilled and as yet virgin soil ("for God had not yet sent rain, and man had not tilled the ground"), and was formed by the hand of God, that is, by the Word of God, for "all things were made by Him," and the Lord took dust from the earth and formed man; so did He who is the Word, recapitulating Adam in Himself, rightly receive a birth, enabling Him to gather up Adam [into Himself], from Mary, who was as yet a virgin. If, then, the first Adam had a man for his father, and was born of human seed, it were reasonable to say that the second Adam was begotten of Joseph. But if the former was taken from the dust, and God was his Maker, it was incumbent that the latter also, making a recapitulation in Himself, should be formed as man by God, to have an analogy with the former as respects His origin. Why, then, did not God again take dust, but wrought so that the formation should be made of Mary? It was that there might not be another formation called into being, nor any other which should [require to] be saved, but that the very same formation should be summed up [in Christ as had existed in Adam], the analogy having been preserved.

Chapter XXII.—Christ assumed actual flesh, conceived and born of the Virgin.

1. Those, therefore, who allege that He took nothing from the Virgin do greatly err, [since,] in order that they may cast away the inheritance of the flesh, they also reject the analogy [between Him and Adam]. For if the one [who sprang] from the earth had indeed formation and substance from both the hand and workmanship of God, but the other not from the hand and workmanship of God, then He who was made after the image and likeness of the former did not, in that case, preserve the analogy of man, and He must seem an inconsistent piece of work, not having wherewith He may show His wisdom. But this is to say, that He also appeared putatively as man when He was not man, and that He was made man while taking nothing from man. For if He did not receive the substance of flesh from a human being, He neither was made man nor the Son of man; and if He was not made what we were, He did no great thing in what He suffered and endured. But every one will allow that we are [composed of] a body taken from the earth, and a soul receiving spirit from God. This, therefore, the Word of God was made, recapitulating in Himself His own handiwork; and on this account does He confess Himself the Son of man, and blesses "the meek, because they shall inherit the earth." The Apostle Paul, moreover, in the Epistle to the Galatians, declares plainly, "God sent His Son, made of a

woman." And again, in that to the Romans, he says, "Concerning His Son, who was made of the seed of David according to the flesh, who was predestinated as the Son of God with power, according to the spirit of holiness, by the resurrection from the dead, Jesus Christ our Lord."

2. Superfluous, too, in that case is His descent into Mary; for why did He come down into her if He were to take nothing of her? Still further, if He had taken nothing of Mary, He would never have availed Himself of those kinds of food which are derived from the earth, by which that body which has been taken from the earth is nourished; nor would He have hungered, fasting those forty days, like Moses and Elias, unless His body was craving after its own proper nourishment; nor, again, would John His disciple have said, when writing of Him, "But Jesus, being wearied with the journey, was sitting [to rest];" nor would David have proclaimed of Him beforehand, "They have added to the grief of my wounds;" nor would He have wept over Lazarus, nor have sweated great drops of blood; nor have declared, "My soul is exceeding sorrowful;" nor, when His side was pierced, would there have come forth blood and water. For all these are tokens of the flesh which had been derived from the earth, which He had recapitulated in Himself, bearing salvation to His own handiwork.

3. Wherefore Luke points out that the pedigree which traces the generation of our Lord back to Adam contains seventy-two generations, connecting the end with the beginning, and implying that it is He who has summed up in Himself all nations dispersed from Adam downwards, and all languages and generations of men, together with Adam himself. Hence also was Adam himself termed by Paul "the figure of Him that was to come," because the Word, the Maker of all things, had formed beforehand for Himself the future dispensation of the human race, connected with the Son of God; God having predestined that the first man should be of an animal nature, with this view, that he might be saved by the spiritual One. For inasmuch as He had a pre-existence as a saving Being, it was necessary that what might be saved should also be called into existence, in order that the Being who saves should not exist in vain.

4. In accordance with this design, Mary the Virgin is found obedient, saying, "Behold the handmaid of the Lord; be it unto me according to thy word." But Eve was disobedient; for she did not obey when as yet she was a virgin. And even as she, having indeed a husband, Adam, but being nevertheless as yet a virgin (for in Paradise "they were both naked, and were not ashamed," inasmuch as they, having been created a short time previously, had no understanding of the procreation of children: for it was necessary that they should first come to adult age, and then multiply from that time onward), having become disobedient, was made the cause of death, both to herself and to the entire human race; so also did Mary, having a man betrothed [to her], and being nevertheless a virgin, by yielding obedience, become the cause of salvation, both to herself and the whole human race. And on this account does the law term a woman betrothed to a man, the wife of him who had betrothed her, although she was as yet a virgin; thus indicating the back-reference from Mary to Eve, because what is joined together could not otherwise be put asunder than by inversion of the process by which these bonds of union had arisen; so that the former ties be cancelled by the latter, that the latter may set the former again at liberty. And it has, in fact, happened that the first compact looses from the second tie, but that the second tie takes the position of the first which has been cancelled. For this reason did the Lord declare that the first should in truth be last, and the last first. And the prophet, too, indicates the same, saying, "instead of fathers, children have been born unto thee." For the Lord, having been born "the First-begotten of the dead," and receiving into His bosom the ancient fathers, has regenerated them into the life of God, He having been made Himself the beginning of those that live, as Adam became the beginning of those who die. Wherefore also Luke, commencing the genealogy with the Lord, carried it back to Adam, indicating that it was He who regenerated them into the Gospel of life, and not they Him. And thus also it was that the knot of Eve's disobedience was loosed by the obedience of Mary. For what the virgin Eve had bound fast through unbelief, this did the virgin Mary set free through faith.

Chapter XXIII.—Arguments in opposition to Tatian, showing that it was consonant to divine justice and mercy that the first Adam should first partake in that salvation offered to all by Christ.

1. It was necessary, therefore, that the Lord, coming to the lost sheep, and making recapitulation of so comprehensive a dispensation, and

seeking after His own handiwork, should save that very man who had been created after His image and likeness, that is, Adam, filling up the times of His condemnation, which had been incurred through disobedience,—[times] "which the Father had placed in His own power." [This was necessary,] too, inasmuch as the whole economy of salvation regarding man came to pass according to the good pleasure of the Father, in order that God might not be conquered, nor His wisdom lessened, [in the estimation of His creatures.] For if man, who had been created by God that he might live, after losing life, through being injured by the serpent that had corrupted him, should not any more return to life, but should be utterly [and for ever] abandoned to death, God would [in that case] have been conquered, and the wickedness of the serpent would have prevailed over the will of God. But inasmuch as God is invincible and long- suffering, He did indeed show Himself to be long-suffering in the matter of the correction of man and the probation of all, as I have already observed; and by means of the second man did He bind the strong man, and spoiled his goods, and abolished death, vivifying that man who had been in a state of death. For at the first Adam became a vessel in his (Satan's) possession, whom he did also hold under his power, that is, by bringing sin on him iniquitously, and under colour of immortality entailing death upon him. For, while promising that they should be as gods, which was in no way possible for him to be, he wrought death in them: wherefore he who had led man captive, was justly captured in his turn by God; but man, who had been led captive, was loosed from the bonds of condemnation.

2. But this is Adam, if the truth should be told, the first formed man, of whom the Scripture says that the Lord spake, "Let Us make man after Our own image and likeness;" and we are all from him: and as we are from him, therefore have we all inherited his title. But inasmuch as man is saved, it is fitting that he who was created the original man should be saved. For it is too absurd to maintain, that he who was so deeply injured by the enemy, and was the first to suffer captivity, was not rescued by Him who conquered the enemy, but that his children were, —those whom he had begotten in the same captivity. Neither would the enemy appear to be as yet conquered, if the old spoils remained with him. To give an illustration: If a hostile force had overcome certain [enemies], had bound them, and led them away captive, and held them for a long time in servitude, so that they begat children among them; and somebody, compassionating those who had been made slaves, should

overcome this same hostile force; he certainly would not act equitably, were he to liberate the children of those who had been led captive, from the sway of those who had enslaved their fathers, but should leave these latter, who had suffered the act of capture, subject to their enemies,— those, too, on whose very account he had proceeded to this retaliation,— the children succeeding to liberty through the avenging of their fathers' cause, but not so that their fathers, who suffered the act of capture itself, should be left [in bondage]. For God is neither devoid of power nor of justice, who has afforded help to man, and restored him to His own liberty.

3. It was for this reason, too, that immediately after Adam had transgressed, as the Scripture relates, He pronounced no curse against Adam personally, but against the ground, in reference to his works, as a certain person among the ancients has observed: "God did indeed transfer the curse to the earth, that it might not remain in man." But man received, as the punishment of his transgression, the toilsome task of tilling the earth, and to eat bread in the sweat of his face, and to return to the dust from whence he was taken. Similarly also did the woman [receive] toil, and labour, and groans, and the pangs of parturition, and a state of subjection, that is, that she should serve her husband; so that they should neither perish altogether when cursed by God, nor, by remaining unreprimanded, should be led to despise God. But the curse in all its fulness fell upon the serpent, which had beguiled them. "And God," it is declared, "said to the serpent: Because thou hast done this, cursed art thou above all cattle, and above all the beasts of the earth." And this same thing does the Lord also say in the Gospel, to those who are found upon the left hand: "Depart from me, ye cursed, into everlasting fire, which my Father hath prepared for the devil and his angels;" indicating that eternal fire was not originally prepared for man, but for him who beguiled man, and caused him to offend—for him, I say, who is chief of the apostasy, and for those angels who became apostates along with him; which [fire], indeed, they too shall justly feel, who, like him, persevere in works of wickedness, without repentance, and without retracing their steps.

4. [These act] as Cain [did, who], when he was counselled by God to keep quiet, because he had not made an equitable division of that share to which his brother was entitled, but with envy and malice thought that

he could domineer over him, not only did not acquiesce, but even added sin to sin, indicating his state of mind by his action. For what he had planned, that did he also put in practice: he tyrannized over and slew him; God subjecting the just to the unjust, that the former might be proved as the just one by the things which he suffered, and the latter detected as the unjust by those which he perpetrated. And he was not softened even by this, nor did he stop short with that evil deed; but being asked where his brother was, he said, "I know not; am I my brother's keeper?" extending and aggravating [his] wickedness by his answer. For if it is wicked to slay a brother, much worse is it thus insolently and irreverently to reply to the omniscient God as if he could battle Him. And for this he did himself bear a curse about with him, because he gratuitously brought an offering of sin, having had no reverence for God, nor being put to confusion by the act of fratricide.

5. The case of Adam, however, had no analogy with this, but was altogether different. For, having been beguiled by another under the pretext of immortality, he is immediately seized with terror, and hides himself; not as if he were able to escape from God; but, in a state of confusion at having transgressed His command, he feels unworthy to appear before and to hold converse with God. Now, "the fear of the Lord is the beginning of wisdom;" the sense of sin leads to repentance, and God bestows His compassion upon those who are penitent. For [Adam] showed his repentance by his conduct, through means of the girdle [which he used], covering himself with fig-leaves, while there were many other leaves, which would have irritated his body in a less degree. He, however, adopted a dress conformable to his disobedience, being awed by the fear of God; and resisting the erring, the lustful propensity of his flesh (since he had lost his natural disposition and child-like mind, and had come to the knowledge of evil things), he girded a bridle of continence upon himself and his wife, fearing God, and waiting for His coming, and indicating, as it were, some such thing [as follows]: Inasmuch as, he says, I have by disobedience lost that robe of sanctity which I had from the Spirit, I do now also acknowledge that I am deserving of a covering of this nature, which affords no gratification, but which gnaws and frets the body. And he would no doubt have retained this clothing for ever, thus humbling himself, if God, who is merciful, had not clothed them with tunics of skins instead of fig-leaves. For this purpose, too, He interrogates them, that the blame might light upon the woman; and again, He interrogates her, that she might convey

the blame to the serpent. For she related what had occurred. "The serpent," says she, "beguiled me, and I did eat." But He put no question to the serpent; for He knew that he had been the prime mover in the guilty deed; but He pronounced the curse upon him in the first instance, that it might fall upon man with a mitigated rebuke. For God detested him who had led man astray, but by degrees, and little by little, He showed compassion to him who had been beguiled.

6. Wherefore also He drove him out of Paradise, and removed him far from the tree of life, not because He envied him the tree of life, as some venture to assert, but because He pitied him, [and did not desire] that he should continue a sinner for ever, nor that the sin which surrounded him should be immortal, and evil interminable and irremediable. But He set a bound to his [state of] sin, by interposing death, and thus causing sin to cease, putting an end to it by the dissolution of the flesh, which should take place in the earth, so that man, ceasing at length to live to sin, and dying to it, might begin to live to God.

7. For this end did He put enmity between the serpent and the woman and her seed, they keeping it up mutually: He, the sole of whose foot should be bitten, having power also to tread upon the enemy's head; but the other biting, killing, and impeding the steps of man, until the seed did come appointed to tread down his head,— which was born of Mary, of whom the prophet speaks: "Thou shalt tread upon the asp and the basilisk; thou shalt trample down the lion and the dragon;"—indicating that sin, which was set up and spread out against man, and which rendered him subject to death, should be deprived of its power, along with death, which rules [over men]; and that the lion, that is, antichrist, rampant against mankind in the latter days, should be trampled down by Him; and that He should bind "the dragon, that old serpent" and subject him to the power of man, who had been conquered so that all his might should be trodden down. Now Adam had been conquered, all life having been taken away from him: wherefore, when the foe was conquered in his turn, Adam received new life; and the last enemy, death, is destroyed, which at the first had taken possession of man. Therefore, when man has been liberated, "what is written shall come to pass, Death is swallowed up in victory. O death, where is thy sting?" This could not be said with justice, if that man, over whom death did first obtain dominion, were not set free. For his salvation is death's

destruction. When therefore the Lord vivifies man, that is, Adam, death is at the same time destroyed.

8. All therefore speak falsely who disallow his (Adam's) salvation, shutting themselves out from life for ever, in that they do not believe that the sheep which had perished has been found. For if it has not been found, the whole human race is still held in a state of perdition. False, therefore, is that, man who first started this idea, or rather, this ignorance and blindness—Tatian. As I have already indicated, this man entangled himself with all the heretics. This dogma, however, has been invented by himself, in order that, by introducing something new, independently of the rest, and by speaking vanity, he might acquire for himself hearers void of faith, affecting to be esteemed a teacher, and endeavouring from time to time to employ sayings of this kind often [made use of] by Paul: "In Adam we all die;" ignorant, however, that "where sin abounded, grace did much more abound." Since this, then, has been clearly shown, let all his disciples be put to shame, and let them wrangle about Adam, as if some great gain were to accrue to them if he be not saved; when they profit nothing more [by that], even as the serpent also did not profit when persuading man [to sin], except to this effect, that he proved him a transgressor, obtaining man as the first-fruits of his own apostasy. But he did not know God's power. Thus also do those who disallow Adam's salvation gain nothing, except this, that they render themselves heretics and apostates from the truth, and show themselves patrons of the serpent and of death.

Chapter XXIV.—Recapitulation of the various arguments adduced against Gnostic impiety under all its aspects. The heretics, tossed about by every blast of doctrine, are opposed by the uniform teaching of the Church, which remains so always, and is consistent with itself.

1. Thus, then, have all these men been exposed, who bring in impious doctrines regarding our Maker and Framer, who also formed this world, and above whom there is no other God; and those have been overthrown by their own arguments who teach falsehoods regarding the substance of our Lord, and the dispensation which He fulfilled for the sake of His own creature man. But [it has, on the other hand, been shown], that the preaching of the Church is everywhere consistent, and

continues in an even course, and receives testimony from the prophets, the apostles, and all the disciples—as I have proved— through [those in] the beginning, the middle, and the end, and through the entire dispensation of God, and that well-grounded system which tends to man's salvation, namely, our faith; which, having been received from the Church, we do preserve, and which always, by the Spirit of God, renewing its youth, as if it were some precious deposit in an excellent vessel, causes the vessel itself containing it to renew its youth also. For this gift of God has been entrusted to the Church, as breath was to the first created man, for this purpose, that all the members receiving it may be vivified; and the [means of] communion with Christ has been distributed throughout it, that is, the Holy Spirit, the earnest of incorruption, the means of confirming our faith, and the ladder of ascent to God. "For in the Church," it is said, "God hath set apostles, prophets, teachers," and all the other means through which the Spirit works; of which all those are not partakers who do not join themselves to the Church, but defraud themselves of life through their perverse opinions and infamous behaviour. For where the Church is, there is the Spirit of God; and where the Spirit of God is, there is the Church, and every kind of grace; but the Spirit is truth. Those, therefore, who do not partake of Him, are neither nourished into life from the mother's breasts, nor do they enjoy that most limpid fountain which issues from the body of Christ; but they dig for themselves broken cisterns out of earthly trenches, and drink putrid water out of the mire, fleeing from the faith of the Church lest they be convicted; and rejecting the Spirit, that they may not be instructed.

2. Alienated thus from the truth, they do deservedly wallow in all error, tossed to and fro by it, thinking differently in regard to the same things at different times, and never attaining to a well-grounded knowledge, being more anxious to be sophists of words than disciples of the truth. For they have not been founded upon the one rock, but upon the sand, which has in itself a multitude of stones. Wherefore they also imagine many gods, and they always have the excuse of searching [after truth] (for they are blind), but never succeed in finding it. For they blaspheme the Creator, Him who is truly God, who also furnishes power to find [the truth]; imagining that they have discovered another god beyond God, or another Pleroma, or another dispensation. Wherefore also the light which is from God does not illumine them, because they have dishonoured and despised God, holding Him of small account, because,

through His love and infinite benignity, He has come within reach of human knowledge (knowledge, however, not with regard to His greatness, or with regard to His essence—for that has no man measured or handled—but after this sort: that we should know that He who made, and formed, and breathed in them the breath of life, and nourishes us by means of the creation, establishing all things by His Word, and binding them together by His Wisdom— this is He who is the only true God); but they dream of a non-existent being above Him, that they may be regarded as having found out the great God, whom nobody, [they hold,] can recognise holding communication with the human race, or as directing mundane matters: that is to say, they find out the god of Epicurus, who does nothing either for himself or others; that is, he exercises no providence at all.

Chapter XXV.—This world is ruled by the providence of one God, who is both endowed with infinite justice to punish the wicked, and with infinite goodness to bless the pious, and impart to them salvation.

1. God does, however, exercise a providence over all things, and therefore He also gives counsel; and when giving counsel, He is present with those who attend to moral discipline. It follows then of course, that the things which are watched over and governed should be acquainted with their ruler; which things are not irrational or vain, but they have understanding derived from the providence of God. And, for this reason certain of the Gentiles, who were less addicted to [sensual] allurements and voluptuousness, and were not led away to such a degree of superstition with regard to idols, being moved, though but slightly, by His providence, were nevertheless convinced that they should call the Maker of this universe the Father, who exercises a providence over all things, and arranges the affairs of our world.

2. Again, that they might remove the rebuking and judicial power from the Father, reckoning that as unworthy of God, and thinking that they had found out a God both without anger and [merely] good, they have alleged that one [God] judges, but that another saves, unconsciously taking away the intelligence and justice of both deities. For if the judicial one is not also good, to bestow favours upon the deserving, and to direct reproofs against those requiring them, he will appear neither a just nor

a wise judge. On the other hand, the good God, if he is merely good, and not one who tests those upon whom he shall send his goodness, will be out of the range of justice and goodness; and his goodness will seem imperfect, as not saving all; [for it should do so,] if it be not accompanied with judgment.

3. Marcion, therefore, himself, by dividing God into two, maintaining one to be good and the other judicial, does in fact, on both sides, put an end to deity. For he that is the judicial one, if he be not good, is not God, because he from whom goodness is absent is no God at all; and again, he who is good, if he has no judicial power, suffers the same [loss] as the former, by being deprived of his character of deity. And how can they call the Father of all wise, if they do not assign to Him a judicial faculty? For if He is wise, He is also one who tests [others]; but the judicial power belongs to him who tests, and justice follows the judicial faculty, that it may reach a just conclusion; justice calls forth judgment, and judgment, when it is executed with justice, will pass on to wisdom. Therefore the Father will excel in wisdom all human and angelic wisdom, because He is Lord, and Judge, and the Just One, and Ruler over all. For He is good, and merciful, and patient, and saves whom He ought: nor does goodness desert Him in the exercise of justice, nor is His wisdom lessened; for He saves those whom He should save, and judges those worthy of judgment. Neither does He show Himself unmercifully just; for His goodness, no doubt, goes on before, and takes precedency.

4. The God, therefore, who does benevolently cause His sun to rise upon all, and sends rain upon the just and unjust, shall judge those who, enjoying His equally distributed kindness, have led lives not corresponding to the dignity of His bounty; but who have spent their days in wantonness and luxury, in opposition to His benevolence, and have, moreover, even blasphemed Him who has conferred so great benefits upon them.

5. Plato is proved to be more religious than these men, for he allowed that the same God was both just and good, having power over all things, and Himself executing judgment, expressing himself thus, "And God indeed, as He is also the ancient Word, possessing the beginning, the

end, and the mean of all existing things, does everything rightly, moving round about them according to their nature; but retributive justice always follows Him against those who depart from the divine law." Then, again, he points out that the Maker and Framer of the universe is good. "And to the good," he says, "no envy ever springs up with regard to anything;" thus establishing the goodness of God, as the beginning and the cause of the creation of the world, but not ignorance, nor an erring Æon, nor the consequence of a defect, nor the Mother weeping and lamenting, nor another God or Father.

6. Well may their Mother bewail them, as capable of conceiving and inventing such things for they have worthily uttered this falsehood against themselves, that their Mother is beyond the Pleroma, that is beyond the knowledge of God, and that their entire multitude became a shapeless and crude abortion: for it apprehends nothing of the truth; it falls into void and darkness: for their wisdom (Sophia) was void, and wrapped up in darkness; and Horos did not permit her to enter the Pleroma: for the Spirit (Achamoth) did not receive them into the place of refreshment. For their father, by begetting ignorance, wrought in them the sufferings of death. We do not misrepresent [their opinions on] these points; but they do themselves confirm, they do themselves teach, they do glory in them, they imagine a lofty [mystery] about their Mother, whom they represent as having been begotten without a father, that is, without God, a female from a female, that is, corruption from error.

7. We do indeed pray that these men may not remain in the pit which they themselves have dug, but separate themselves from a Mother of this nature, and depart from Bythus, and stand away from the void, and relinquish the shadow; and that they, being converted to the Church of God, may be lawfully begotten, and that Christ may be formed in them, and that they may know the Framer and Maker of this universe, the only true God and Lord of all. We pray for these things on their behalf, loving them better than they seem to love themselves. For our love, inasmuch as it is true, is salutary to them, if they will but receive it. It may be compared to a severe remedy, extirpating the proud and sloughing flesh of a wound; for it puts an end to their pride and haughtiness. Wherefore it shall not weary us, to endeavour with all our might to stretch out the hand unto them. Over and above what has been already stated, I have

deferred to the following book, to adduce the words of the Lord; if, by convincing some among them, through means of the very instruction of Christ, I may succeed in persuading them to abandon such error, and to cease from blaspheming their Creator, who is both God alone, and the Father of our Lord Jesus Christ. Amen.

BOOK V

Preface.

In the four preceding books, my very dear friend, which I put forth to thee, all the heretics have been exposed, and their doctrines brought to light, and these men refuted who have devised irreligious opinions. [I have accomplished this by adducing] something from the doctrine peculiar to each of these men, which they have left in their writings, as well as by using arguments of a more general nature, and applicable to them all. Then I have pointed out the truth, and shown the preaching of the Church, which the prophets proclaimed (as I have already demonstrated), but which Christ brought to perfection, and the apostles have handed down, from whom the Church, receiving [these truths], and throughout all the world alone preserving them in their integrity (bene), has transmitted them to her sons. Then also—having disposed of all questions which the heretics propose to us, and having explained the doctrine of the apostles, and clearly set forth many of those things which were said and done by the Lord in parables—I shall endeavour, in this the fifth book of the entire work which treats of the exposure and refutation of knowledge falsely so called, to exhibit proofs from the rest of the Lord's doctrine and the apostolical epistles: [thus] complying with thy demand, as thou didst request of me (since indeed I have been assigned a place in the ministry of the word); and, labouring by every means in my power to furnish thee with large assistance against the contradictions of the heretics, as also to reclaim the wanderers and convert them to the Church of God, to confirm at the same time the minds of the neophytes, that they may preserve stedfast the faith which they have received, guarded by the Church in its integrity, in order that they be in no way perverted by those who endeavour to teach them false doctrines, and lead them away from the truth. It will be incumbent upon thee, however, and all who may happen to read this writing, to peruse with great attention what I have already said, that thou mayest obtain a knowledge of the subjects against which I am contending. For it is thus that thou wilt both controvert them in a legitimate manner, and wilt be prepared to receive the proofs brought forward against them, casting away their doctrines as filth by means of the celestial faith; but following the only true and stedfast Teacher, the Word of God, our Lord Jesus Christ, who did, through His transcendent love, become what we are, that He might bring us to be even what He is Himself.

Chapter I.—Christ alone is able to teach divine things, and to redeem us: He, the same, took flesh of the Virgin Mary, not merely in appearance, but actually, by the operation of the Holy Spirit, in order to renovate us. Strictures on the conceits of Valentinus and Ebion.

1. For in no other way could we have learned the things of God, unless our Master, existing as the Word, had become man. For no other being had the power of revealing to us the things of the Father, except His own proper Word. For what other person "knew the mind of the Lord," or who else "has become His counsellor?" Again, we could have learned in no other way than by seeing our Teacher, and hearing His voice with our own ears, that, having become imitators of His works as well as doers of His words, we may have communion with Him, receiving increase from the perfect One, and from Him who is prior to all creation. We —who were but lately created by the only best and good Being, by Him also who has the gift of immortality, having been formed after His likeness (predestinated, according to the prescience of the Father, that we, who had as yet no existence, might come into being), and made the first-fruits of creation—have received, in the times known beforehand, [the blessings of salvation] according to the ministration of the Word, who is perfect in all things, as the mighty Word, and very man, who, redeeming us by His own blood in a manner consonant to reason, gave Himself as a redemption for those who had been led into captivity. And since the apostasy tyrannized over us unjustly, and, though we were by nature the property of the omnipotent God, alienated us contrary to nature, rendering us its own disciples, the Word of God, powerful in all things, and not defective with regard to His own justice, did righteously turn against that apostasy, and redeem from it His own property, not by violent means, as the [apostasy] had obtained dominion over us at the beginning, when it insatiably snatched away what was not its own, but by means of persuasion, as became a God of counsel, who does not use violent means to obtain what He desires; so that neither should justice be infringed upon, nor the ancient handiwork of God go to destruction. Since the Lord thus has redeemed us through His own blood, giving His soul for our souls, and His flesh for our flesh, and has also poured out the Spirit of the Father for the union and communion of God and man, imparting indeed God to men by means of the Spirit, and, on the other hand, attaching man to God by His own incarnation, and bestowing upon us at His coming immortality durably

and truly, by means of communion with God,— all the doctrines of the heretics fall to ruin.

2. Vain indeed are those who allege that He appeared in mere seeming. For these things were not done in appearance only, but in actual reality. But if He did appear as a man, when He was not a man, neither could the Holy Spirit have rested upon Him,—an occurrence which did actually take place—as the Spirit is invisible; nor, [in that case], was there any degree of truth in Him, for He was not that which He seemed to be. But I have already remarked that Abraham and the other prophets beheld Him after a prophetical manner, foretelling in vision what should come to pass. If, then, such a being has now appeared in outward semblance different from what he was in reality, there has been a certain prophetical vision made to men; and another advent of His must be looked forward to, in which He shall be such as He has now been seen in a prophetic manner. And I have proved already, that it is the same thing to say that He appeared merely to outward seeming, and [to affirm] that He received nothing from Mary. For He would not have been one truly possessing flesh and blood, by which He redeemed us, unless He had summed up in Himself the ancient formation of Adam. Vain therefore are the disciples of Valentinus who put forth this opinion, in order that they my exclude the flesh from salvation, and cast aside what God has fashioned.

Christ was born of a virgin to redeem us

3. Vain also are the Ebionites, who do not receive by faith into their soul the union of God and man, but who remain in the old leaven of [the natural] birth, and who do not choose to understand that the Holy Ghost came upon Mary, and the power of the Most High did overshadow her: wherefore also what was generated is a holy thing, and the Son of the Most High God the Father of all, who effected the incarnation of this being, and showed forth a new [kind of] generation; that as by the former generation we inherited death, so by this new generation we might inherit life. Therefore do these men reject the commixture of the heavenly wine, and wish it to be water of the world only, not receiving God so as to have union with Him, but they remain in that Adam who had been conquered and was expelled from Paradise: not considering that as, at the beginning of our formation in Adam, that breath of life which proceeded from God, having been united to what had been fashioned, animated the man, and manifested him as a being

endowed with reason; so also, in [the times of] the end, the Word of the Father and the Spirit of God, having become united with the ancient substance of Adam's formation, rendered man living and perfect, receptive of the perfect Father, in order that as in the natural [Adam] we all were dead, so in the spiritual we may all be made alive. For never at any time did Adam escape the hands of God, to whom the Father speaking, said, "Let Us make man in Our image, after Our likeness." And for this reason in the last times (fine), not by the will of the flesh, nor by the will of man, but by the good pleasure of the Father, His hands formed a living man, in order that Adam might be created [again] after the image and likeness of God.

Chapter II.—When Christ visited us in His grace, He did not come to what did not belong to Him: also, by shedding His true blood for us, and exhibiting to us His true flesh in the Eucharist, He conferred upon our flesh the capacity of salvation.

1. And vain likewise are those who say that God came to those things which did not belong to Him, as if covetous of another's property; in order that He might deliver up that man who had been created by another, to that God who had neither made nor formed anything, but who also was deprived from the beginning of His own proper formation of men. The advent, therefore, of Him whom these men represent as coming to the things of others, was not righteous; nor did He truly redeem us by His own blood, if He did not really become man, restoring to His own handiwork what was said [of it] in the beginning, that man was made after the image and likeness of God; not snatching away by stratagem the property of another, but taking possession of His own in a righteous and gracious manner. As far as concerned the apostasy, indeed, He redeems us righteously from it by His own blood; but as regards us who have been redeemed, [He does this] graciously. For we have given nothing to Him previously, nor does He desire anything from us, as if He stood in need of it; but we do stand in need of fellowship with Him. And for this reason it was that He graciously poured Himself out, that He might gather us into the bosom of the Father.

2. But vain in every respect are they who despise the entire dispensation of God, and disallow the salvation of the flesh, and treat with contempt

its regeneration, maintaining that it is not capable of incorruption. But if this indeed do not attain salvation, then neither did the Lord redeem us with His blood, nor is the cup of the Eucharist the communion of His blood, nor the bread which we break the communion of His body. For blood can only come from veins and flesh, and whatsoever else makes up the substance of man, such as the Word of God was actually made. By His own blood he redeemed us, as also His apostle declares, "In whom we have redemption through His blood, even the remission of sins." And as we are His members, we are also nourished by means of the creation (and He Himself grants the creation to us, for He causes His sun to rise, and sends rain when He wills). He has acknowledged the cup (which is a part of the creation) as His own blood, from which He bedews our blood; and the bread (also a part of the creation) He has established as His own body, from which He gives increase to our bodies.

3. When, therefore, the mingled cup and the manufactured bread receives the Word of God, and the Eucharist of the blood and the body of Christ is made, from which things the substance of our flesh is increased and supported, how can they affirm that the flesh is incapable of receiving the gift of God, which is life eternal, which [flesh] is nourished from the body and blood of the Lord, and is a member of Him?—even as the blessed Paul declares in his Epistle to the Ephesians, that "we are members of His body, of His flesh, and of His bones." He does not speak these words of some spiritual and invisible man, for a spirit has not bones nor flesh; but [he refers to] that dispensation [by which the Lord became] an actual man, consisting of flesh, and nerves, and bones,—that [flesh] which is nourished by the cup which is His blood, and receives increase from the bread which is His body. And just as a cutting from the vine planted in the ground fructifies in its season, or as a corn of wheat falling into the earth and becoming decomposed, rises with manifold increase by the Spirit of God, who contains all things, and then, through the wisdom of God, serves for the use of men, and having received the Word of God, becomes the Eucharist, which is the body and blood of Christ; so also our bodies, being nourished by it, and deposited in the earth, and suffering decomposition there, shall rise at their appointed time, the Word of God granting them resurrection to the glory of God, even the Father, who freely gives to this mortal immortality, and to this corruptible incorruption, because the strength of God is made perfect in weakness, in order that we may never become

puffed up, as if we had life from ourselves, and exalted against God, our minds becoming ungrateful; but learning by experience that we possess eternal duration from the excelling power of this Being, not from our own nature, we may neither undervalue that glory which surrounds God as He is, nor be ignorant of our own nature, but that we may know what God can effect, and what benefits man receives, and thus never wander from the true comprehension of things as they are, that is, both with regard to God and with regard to man. And might it not be the case, perhaps, as I have already observed, that for this purpose God permitted our resolution into the common dust of mortality, that we, being instructed by every mode, may be accurate in all things for the future, being ignorant neither of God nor of ourselves?

Chapter III.—The power and glory of God shine forth in the weakness of human flesh, as He will render our body a participator of the resurrection and of immortality, although He has formed it from the dust of the earth; He will also bestow upon it the enjoyment of immortality, just as He grants it this short life in common with the soul.

In the
weaknes
of Man
man
encounter
God

1. The Apostle Paul has, moreover, in the most lucid manner, pointed out that man has been delivered over to his own infirmity, lest, being uplifted, he might fall away from the truth. Thus he says in the second [Epistle] to the Corinthians: "And lest I should be lifted up by the sublimity of the revelations, there was given unto me a thorn in the flesh, the messenger of Satan to buffet me. And upon this I besought the Lord three times, that it might depart from me. But he said unto me, My grace is sufficient for thee; for strength is made perfect in weakness. Gladly therefore shall I rather glory in infirmities, that the power of Christ may dwell in me." What, therefore? (as some may exclaim:) did the Lord wish, in that case, that His apostles should thus undergo buffeting, and that he should endure such infirmity? Even so it was; the word says it. For strength is made perfect in weakness, rendering him a better man who by means of his infirmity becomes acquainted with the power of God. For how could a man have learned that he is himself an infirm being, and mortal by nature, but that God is immortal and powerful, unless he had learned by experience what is in both? For there is nothing evil in learning one's infirmities by endurance; yea, rather, it has even the beneficial effect of preventing him from forming an undue opinion of his own nature (non aberrare in natura sua). But the being lifted up

against God, and taking His glory to one's self, rendering man ungrateful, has brought much evil upon him. [And thus, I say, man must learn both things by experience], that he may not be destitute of truth and love either towards himself or his Creator. But the experience of both confers upon him the true knowledge as to God and man, and increases his love towards God. Now, where there exists an increase of love, there a greater glory is wrought out by the power of God for those who love Him.

2. Those men, therefore, set aside the power of God, and do not consider what the word declares, when they dwell upon the infirmity of the flesh, but do not take into consideration the power of Him who raises it up from the dead. For if He does not vivify what is mortal, and does not bring back the corruptible to incorruption, He is not a God of power. But that He is powerful in all these respects, we ought to perceive from our origin, inasmuch as God, taking dust from the earth, formed man. And surely it is much more difficult and incredible, from non-existent bones, and nerves, and veins, and the rest of man's organization, to bring it about that all this should be, and to make man an animated and rational creature, than to reintegrate again that which had been created and then afterwards decomposed into earth (for the reasons already mentioned), having thus passed into those [elements] from which man, who had no previous existence, was formed. For He who in the beginning caused him to have being who as yet was not, just when He pleased, shall much more reinstate again those who had a former existence, when it is His will [that they should inherit] the life granted by Him. And that flesh shall also be found fit for and capable of receiving the power of God, which at the beginning received the skilful touches of God; so that one part became the eye for seeing; another, the ear for hearing; another, the hand for feeling and working; another, the sinews stretched out everywhere, and holding the limbs together; another, arteries and veins, passages for the blood and the air; another, the various internal organs; another, the blood, which is the bond of union between soul and body. But why go [on in this strain]? Numbers would fail to express the multiplicity of parts in the human frame, which was made in no other way than by the great wisdom of God. But those things which partake of the skill and wisdom of God, do also partake of His power.

3. The flesh, therefore, is not destitute [of participation] in the constructive wisdom and power of God. But if the power of Him who is the bestower of life is made perfect in weakness —that is, in the flesh—let them inform us, when they maintain the incapacity of flesh to receive the life granted by God, whether they do say these things as being living men at present, and partakers of life, or acknowledge that, having no part in life whatever, they are at the present moment dead men. And if they really are dead men, how is it that they move about, and speak, and perform those other functions which are not the actions of the dead, but of the living? But if they are now alive, and if their whole body partakes of life, how can they venture the assertion that the flesh is not qualified to be a partaker of life, when they do confess that they have life at the present moment? It is just as if anybody were to take up a sponge full of water, or a torch on fire, and to declare that the sponge could not possibly partake of the water, or the torch of the fire. In this very manner do those men, by alleging that they are alive and bear life about in their members, contradict themselves afterwards, when they represent these members as not being capable of [receiving] life. But if the present temporal life, which is of such an inferior nature to eternal life, can nevertheless effect so much as to quicken our mortal members, why should not eternal life, being much more powerful than this, vivify the flesh, which has already held converse with, and been accustomed to sustain, life? For that the flesh can really partake of life, is shown from the fact of its being alive; for it lives on, as long as it is God's purpose that it should do so. It is manifest, too, that God has the power to confer life upon it, inasmuch as He grants life to us who are in existence. And, therefore, since the Lord has power to infuse life into what He has fashioned, and since the flesh is capable of being quickened, what remains to prevent its participating in incorruption, which is a blissful and never-ending life granted by God?

The flesh will be renewed when God renew it.

Chapter IV.—Those persons are deceived who feign another God the Father besides the Creator of the world; for he must have been feeble and useless, or else malignant and full of envy, if he be either unable or unwilling to extend external life to our bodies.

1. Those persons who feign the existence of another Father beyond the Creator, and who term him the good God, do deceive themselves; for they introduce him as a feeble, worthless, and negligent being, not to say malign and full of envy, inasmuch as they affirm that our bodies are not quickened by him. For when they say of things which it is manifest to

all do remain immortal, such as the spirit and the soul, and such other things, that they are quickened by the Father, but that another thing [viz. the body] which is quickened in no different manner than by God granting [life] to it, is abandoned by life,—[they must either confess] that this proves their Father to be weak and powerless, or else envious and malignant. For since the Creator does even here quicken our mortal bodies, and promises them resurrection by the prophets, as I have pointed out; who [in that case] is shown to be more powerful, stronger, or truly good? Whether is it the Creator who vivifies the whole man, or is it their Father, falsely so called? He feigns to be the quickener of those things which are immortal by nature, to which things life is always present by their very nature; but he does not benevolently quicken those things which required his assistance, that they might live, but leaves them carelessly to fall under the power of death. Whether is it the case, then, that their Father does not bestow life upon them when he has the power of so doing, or is it that he does not possess the power? If, on the one hand, it is because he cannot, he is, upon that supposition, not a powerful being, nor is he more perfect than the Creator; for the Creator grants, as we must perceive, what He is unable to afford. But if, on the other hand, [it be that he does not grant this] when he has the power of so doing, then he is proved to be not a good, but an envious and malignant Father.

2. If, again, they refer to any cause on account of which their Father does not impart life to bodies, then that cause must necessarily appear superior to the Father, since it restrains Him from the exercise of His benevolence; and His benevolence will thus be proved weak, on account of that cause which they bring forward. Now every one must perceive that bodies are capable of receiving life. For they live to the extent that God pleases that they should live; and that being so, the [heretics] cannot maintain that [these bodies] are utterly incapable of receiving life. If, therefore, on account of necessity and any other cause, those [bodies] which are capable of participating in life are not vivified, their Father shall be the slave of necessity and that cause, and not therefore a free agent, having His will under His own control.

Chapter V.—The prolonged life of the ancients, the translation of Elijah and of Enoch in their own bodies, as well as the preservation of Jonah,

 examples from the Bible that God can raise bodies

of Shadrach, Meshach, and Abednego, in the midst of extreme peril, are clear demonstrations that God can raise up our bodies to life eternal.

1. [In order to learn] that bodies did continue in existence for a lengthened period, as long as it was God's good pleasure that they should flourish, let [these heretics] read the Scriptures, and they will find that our predecessors advanced beyond seven hundred, eight hundred, and nine hundred years of age; and that their bodies kept pace with the protracted length of their days, and participated in life as long as God willed that they should live. But why do I refer to these men? For Enoch, when he pleased God, was translated in the same body in which he did please Him, thus pointing out by anticipation the translation of the just. Elijah, too, was caught up [when he was yet] in the substance of the [natural] form; thus exhibiting in prophecy the assumption of those who are spiritual, and that nothing stood in the way of their body being translated and caught up. For by means of the very same hands through which they were moulded at the beginning, did they receive this translation and assumption. For in Adam the hands of God had become accustomed to set in order, to rule, and to sustain His own workmanship, and to bring it and place it where they pleased. Where, then, was the first man placed? In paradise certainly, as the Scripture declares "And God planted a garden [paradisum] eastward in Eden, and there He placed the man whom He had formed." And then afterwards when [man] proved disobedient, he was cast out thence into this world. Wherefore also the elders who were disciples of the apostles tell us that those who were translated were transferred to that place (for paradise has been prepared for righteous men, such as have the Spirit; in which place also Paul the apostle, when he was caught up, heard words which are unspeakable as regards us in our present condition), and that there shall they who have been translated remain until the consummation [of all things], as a prelude to immortality.

2. If, however, any one imagine it impossible that men should survive for such a length of time, and that Elias was not caught up in the flesh, but that his flesh was consumed in the fiery chariot, let him consider that Jonah, when he had been cast into the deep, and swallowed down into the whale's belly, was by the command of God again thrown out safe upon the land. And then, again, when Ananias, Azarias, and Misaël were cast into the furnace of fire sevenfold heated, they sustained no

harm whatever, neither was the smell of fire perceived upon them. As, therefore, the hand of God was present with them, working out marvellous things in their case—[things] impossible [to be accomplished] by man's nature—what wonder was it, if also in the case of those who were translated it performed something wonderful, working in obedience to the will of God, even the Father? Now this is the Son of God, as the Scripture represents Nebuchadnezzar the king as having said, "Did not we cast three men bound into the furnace? and, lo, I do see four walking in the midst of the fire, and the fourth is like the Son of God." Neither the nature of any created thing, therefore, nor the weakness of the flesh, can prevail against the will of God. For God is not subject to created things, but created things to God; and all things yield obedience to His will. Wherefore also the Lord declares, "The things which are impossible with men, are possible with God." As, therefore, it might seem to the men of the present day, who are ignorant of God's appointment, to be a thing incredible and impossible that any man could live for such a number of years, yet those who were before us did live [to such an age], and those who were translated do live as an earnest of the future length of days; and [as it might also appear impossible] that from the whale's belly and from the fiery furnace men issued forth unhurt, yet they nevertheless did so, led forth as it were by the hand of God, for the purpose of declaring His power: so also now, although some, not knowing the power and promise of God, may oppose their own salvation, deeming it impossible for God, who raises up the dead; to have power to confer upon them eternal duration, yet the scepticism of men of this stamp shall not render the faithfulness of God of none effect.

Chapter VI.—God will bestow salvation upon the whole nature of man, consisting of body and soul in close union, since the Word took it upon Him, and adorned with the gifts of the Holy Spirit, of whom our bodies are, and are termed, the temples.

1. Now God shall be glorified in His handiwork, fitting it so as to be conformable to, and modelled after, His own Son. For by the hands of the Father, that is, by the Son and the Holy Spirit, man, and not [merely] a part of man, was made in the likeness of God. Now the soul and the spirit are certainly a part of the man, but certainly not the man; for the perfect man consists in the commingling and the union of the soul receiving the spirit of the Father, and the admixture of that fleshly nature which was moulded after the image of God. For this reason does the

apostle declare, "We speak wisdom among them that are perfect," terming those persons "perfect" who have received the Spirit of God, and who through the Spirit of God do speak in all languages, as he used Himself also to speak. In like manner we do also hear many brethren in the Church, who possess prophetic gifts, and who through the Spirit speak all kinds of languages, and bring to light for the general benefit the hidden things of men, and declare the mysteries of God, whom also the apostle terms "spiritual," they being spiritual because they partake of the Spirit, and not because their flesh has been stripped off and taken away, and because they have become purely spiritual. For if any one take away the substance of flesh, that is, of the handiwork [of God], and understand that which is purely spiritual, such then would not be a spiritual man but would be the spirit of a man, or the Spirit of God. But when the spirit here blended with the soul is united to [God's] handiwork, the man is rendered spiritual and perfect because of the outpouring of the Spirit, and this is he who was made in the image and likeness of God. But if the Spirit be wanting to the soul, he who is such is indeed of an animal nature, and being left carnal, shall be an imperfect being, possessing indeed the image [of God] in his formation (in plasmate), but not receiving the similitude through the Spirit; and thus is this being imperfect. Thus also, if any one take away the image and set aside the handiwork, he cannot then understand this as being a man, but as either some part of a man, as I have already said, or as something else than a man. For that flesh which has been moulded is not a perfect man in itself, but the body of a man, and part of a man. Neither is the soul itself, considered apart by itself, the man; but it is the soul of a man, and part of a man. Neither is the spirit a man, for it is called the spirit, and not a man; but the commingling and union of all these constitutes the perfect man. And for this cause does the apostle, explaining himself, make it clear that the saved man is a complete man as well as a spiritual man; saying thus in the first Epistle to the Thessalonians, "Now the God of peace sanctify you perfect (perfectos); and may your spirit, and soul, and body be preserved whole without complaint to the coming of the Lord Jesus Christ." Now what was his object in praying that these three—that is, soul, body, and spirit—might be preserved to the coming of the Lord, unless he was aware of the [future] reintegration and union of the three, and [that they should be heirs of] one and the same salvation? For this cause also he declares that those are "the perfect" who present unto the Lord the three [component parts] without offence. Those, then, are the perfect who have had the Spirit of God remaining in them, and have preserved their souls and bodies blameless, holding fast the faith of God, that is, that faith which is [directed] towards God, and maintaining righteous dealings with respect to their neighbours.

2. Whence also he says, that this handiwork is "the temple of God," thus declaring: "Know ye not that ye are the temple of God, and that the Spirit of God dwelleth in you? If any man, therefore, will defile the temple of God, him will God destroy: for the temple of God is holy, which [temple] ye are." Here he manifestly declares the body to be the temple in which the Spirit dwells. As also the Lord speaks in reference to Himself, "Destroy this temple, and in three days I will raise it up. He spake this, however," it is said, "of the temple of His body." And not only does he (the apostle) acknowledge our bodies to be a temple, but even the temple of Christ, saying thus to the Corinthians, "Know ye not that your bodies are members of Christ? Shall I then take the members of Christ, and make them the members of an harlot?" He speaks these things, not in reference to some other spiritual man; for a being of such a nature could have nothing to do with an harlot: but he declares "our body," that is, the flesh which continues in sanctity and purity, to be "the members of Christ;" but that when it becomes one with an harlot, it becomes the members of an harlot. And for this reason he said, "If any man defile the temple of God, him will God destroy." How then is it not the utmost blasphemy to allege, that the temple of God, in which the Spirit of the Father dwells, and the members of Christ, do not partake of salvation, but are reduced to perdition? Also, that our bodies are raised not from their own substance, but by the power of God, he says to the Corinthians, "Now the body is not for fornication, but for the Lord, and the Lord for the body. But God hath both raised up the Lord, and shall raise us up by His own power."

Chapter VII.—Inasmuch as Christ did rise in our flesh, it follows that we shall be also raised in the same; since the resurrection promised to us should not be referred to spirits naturally immortal, but to bodies in themselves mortal.

1. In the same manner, therefore, as Christ did rise in the substance of flesh, and pointed out to His disciples the mark of the nails and the opening in His side (now these are the tokens of that flesh which rose from the dead), so "shall He also," it is said, "raise us up by His own

power." And again to the Romans he says, "But if the Spirit of Him that raised up Jesus from the dead dwell in you, He that raised up Christ from the dead shall also quicken your mortal bodies." What, then, are mortal bodies? Can they be souls? Nay, for souls are incorporeal when put in comparison with mortal bodies; for God "breathed into the face of man the breath of life, and man became a living soul." Now the breath of life is an incorporeal thing. And certainly they cannot maintain that the very breath of life is mortal. Therefore David says, "My soul also shall live to Him," just as if its substance were immortal. Neither, on the other hand, can they say that the spirit is the mortal body. What therefore is there left to which we may apply the term "mortal body," unless it be the thing that was moulded, that is, the flesh, of which it is also said that God will vivify it? For this it is which dies and is decomposed, but not the soul or the spirit. For to die is to lose vital power, and to become henceforth breathless, inanimate, and devoid of motion, and to melt away into those [component parts] from which also it derived the commencement of [its] substance. But this event happens neither to the soul, for it is the breath of life; nor to the spirit, for the spirit is simple and not composite, so that it cannot be decomposed, and is itself the life of those who receive it. We must therefore conclude that it is in reference to the flesh that death is mentioned; which [flesh], after the soul's departure, becomes breathless and inanimate, and is decomposed gradually into the earth from which it was taken. This, then, is what is mortal. And it is this of which he also says, "He shall also quicken your mortal bodies." And therefore in reference to it he says, in the first [Epistle] to the Corinthians: "So also is the resurrection of the dead: it is sown in corruption, it rises in incorruption." For he declares, "That which thou sowest cannot be quickened, unless first it die."

2. But what is that which, like a grain of wheat, is sown in the earth and decays, unless it be the bodies which are laid in the earth, into which seeds are also cast? And for this reason he said, "It is sown in dishonour, it rises in glory." For what is more ignoble than dead flesh? Or, on the other hand, what is more glorious than the same when it arises and partakes of incorruption? "It is sown in weakness, it is raised in power:" in its own weakness certainly, because since it is earth it goes to earth; but [it is quickened] by the power of God, who raises it from the dead. "It is sown an animal body, it rises a spiritual body." He has taught, beyond all doubt, that such language was not used by him, either with

reference to the soul or to the spirit, but to bodies that have become corpses. For these are animal bodies, that is, [bodies] which partake of life, which when they have lost, they succumb to death; then, rising through the Spirit's instrumentality, they become spiritual bodies, so that by the Spirit they possess a perpetual life. "For now," he says, "we know in part, and we prophesy in part, but then face to face." And this it is which has been said also by Peter: "Whom having not seen, ye love; in whom now also, not seeing, ye believe; and believing, ye shall rejoice with joy unspeakable." For our face shall see the face of the Lord and shall rejoice with joy unspeakable,—that is to say, when it shall behold its own Delight.

Chapter VIII.—The gifts of the Holy Spirit which we receive prepare us for incorruption, render us spiritual, and separate us from carnal men. These two classes are signified by the clean and unclean animals in the legal dispensation.

1. But we do now receive a certain portion of His Spirit, tending towards perfection, and preparing us for incorruption, being little by little accustomed to receive and bear God; which also the apostle terms "an earnest," that is, a part of the honour which has been promised us by God, where he says in the Epistle to the Ephesians, "In which ye also, having heard the word of truth, the Gospel of your salvation, believing in which we have been sealed with the Holy Spirit of promise, which is the earnest of our inheritance." This earnest, therefore, thus dwelling in us, renders us spiritual even now, and the mortal is swallowed up by immortality. "For ye," he declares, "are not in the flesh, but in the Spirit, if so be that the Spirit of God dwell in you." This, however does not take place by a casting away of the flesh, but by the impartation of the Spirit. For those to whom he was writing were not without flesh, but they were those who had received the Spirit of God, "by which we cry, Abba, Father." If therefore, at the present time, having the earnest, we do cry, "Abba, Father," what shall it be when, on rising again, we behold Him face to face; when all the members shall burst out into a continuous hymn of triumph, glorifying Him who raised them from the dead, and gave the gift of eternal life? For if the earnest, gathering man into itself, does even now cause him to cry, "Abba, Father," what shall the complete grace of the Spirit effect, which shall be given to men by God?

The Holy Spirit Shapes us to Perfection

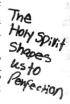

It will render us like unto Him, and accomplish the will of the Father; for it shall make man after the image and likeness of God.

2. Those persons, then, who possess the earnest of the Spirit, and who are not enslaved by the lusts of the flesh, but are subject to the Spirit, and who in all things walk according to the light of reason, does the apostle properly term "spiritual," because the Spirit of God dwells in them. Now, spiritual men shall not be incorporeal spirits; but our substance, that is, the union of flesh and spirit, receiving the Spirit of God, makes up the spiritual man. But those who do indeed reject the Spirit's counsel, and are the slaves of fleshly lusts, and lead lives contrary to reason, and who, without restraint, plunge headlong into their own desires, having no longing after the Divine Spirit, do live after the manner of swine and of dogs; these men, [I say], does the apostle very properly term "carnal," because they have no thought of anything else except carnal things.

3. For the same reason, too, do the prophets compare them to irrational animals, on account of the irrationality of their conduct, saying, "They have become as horses raging for the females; each one of them neighing after his neighbour's wife." And again, "Man, when he was in honour, was made like unto cattle." This denotes that, for his own fault, he is likened to cattle, by rivalling their irrational life. And we also, as the custom is, do designate men of this stamp as cattle and irrational beasts.

4. Now the law has figuratively predicted all these, delineating man by the [various] animals: whatsoever of these, says [the Scripture], have a double hoof and ruminate, it proclaims as clean; but whatsoever of them do not possess one or other of these [properties], it sets aside by themselves as unclean. Who then are the clean? Those who make their way by faith steadily towards the Father and the Son; for this is denoted by the steadiness of those which divide the hoof; and they meditate day and night upon the words of God, that they may be adorned with good works: for this is the meaning of the ruminants. The unclean, however, are those which do neither divide the hoof nor ruminate; that is, those persons who have neither faith in God, nor do meditate on His words: and such is the abomination of the Gentiles. But as to those animals which do indeed chew the cud, but have not the double hoof, and are

themselves unclean, we have in them a figurative description of the Jews, who certainly have the words of God in their mouth, but who do not fix their rooted stedfastness in the Father and in the Son; wherefore they are an unstable generation. For those animals which have the hoof all in one piece easily slip; but those which have it divided are more sure-footed, their cleft hoofs succeeding each other as they advance, and the one hoof supporting the other. In like manner, too, those are unclean which have the double hoof but do not ruminate: this is plainly an indication of all heretics, and of those who do not meditate on the words of God, neither are adorned with works of righteousness; to whom also the Lord says, "Why call ye Me Lord, Lord, and do not the things which I say to you?" For men of this stamp do indeed say that they believe in the Father and the Son, but they never meditate as they should upon the things of God, neither are they adorned with works of righteousness; but, as I have already observed, they have adopted the lives of swine and of dogs, giving themselves over to filthiness, to gluttony, and recklessness of all sorts. Justly, therefore, did the apostle call all such "carnal" and "animal," —[all those, namely], who through their own unbelief and luxury do not receive the Divine Spirit, and in their various phases cast out from themselves the life-giving Word, and walk stupidly after their own lusts: the prophets, too, spake of them as beasts of burden and wild beasts; custom likewise has viewed them in the light of cattle and irrational creatures; and the law has pronounced them unclean.

Chapter IX.—Showing how that passage of the apostle which the heretics pervert, should be understood; viz., "Flesh and blood shall not possess the kingdom of God."

1. Among the other [truths] proclaimed by the apostle, there is also this one, "That flesh and blood cannot inherit the kingdom of God." This is [the passage] which is adduced by all the heretics in support of their folly, with an attempt to annoy us, and to point out that the handiwork of God is not saved. They do not take this fact into consideration, that there are three things out of which, as I have shown, the complete man is composed—flesh, soul, and spirit. One of these does indeed preserve and fashion [the man]—this is the spirit; while as to another it is united and formed—that is the flesh; then [comes] that which is between these two—that is the soul, which sometimes indeed, when it follows the spirit, is raised up by it, but sometimes it sympathizes with the flesh, and falls into carnal lusts. Those then, as many as they be, who have not that

which saves and forms [us] into life [eternal], shall be, and shall be called, [mere] flesh and blood; for these are they who have not the Spirit of God in themselves. Wherefore men of this stamp are spoken of by the Lord as "dead;" for, says He, "Let the dead bury their dead," because they have not the Spirit which quickens man.

2. On the other hand, as many as fear God and trust in His Son's advent, and who through faith do establish the Spirit of God in their hearts,—such men as these shall be properly called both "pure," and "spiritual," and "those living to God," because they possess the Spirit of the Father, who purifies man, and raises him up to the life of God. For as the Lord has testified that "the flesh is weak," so [does He also say] that "the spirit is willing." For this latter is capable of working out its own suggestions. If, therefore, any one admix the ready inclination of the Spirit to be, as it were, a stimulus to the infirmity of the flesh, it inevitably follows that what is strong will prevail over the weak, so that the weakness of the flesh will be absorbed by the strength of the Spirit; and that the man in whom this takes place cannot in that case be carnal, but spiritual, because of the fellowship of the Spirit. Thus it is, therefore, that the martyrs bear their witness, and despise death, not after the infirmity of the flesh, but because of the readiness of the Spirit. For when the infirmity of the flesh is absorbed, it exhibits the Spirit as powerful; and again, when the Spirit absorbs the weakness [of the flesh], it possesses the flesh as an inheritance in itself, and from both of these is formed a living man,— living, indeed, because he partakes of the Spirit, but man, because of the substance of flesh.

3. The flesh, therefore, when destitute of the Spirit of God, is dead, not having life, and cannot possess the kingdom of God: [it is as] irrational blood, like water poured out upon the ground. And therefore he says, "As is the earthy, such are they that are earthy." But where the Spirit of the Father is, there is a living man; [there is] the rational blood preserved by God for the avenging [of those that shed it]; [there is] the flesh possessed by the Spirit, forgetful indeed of what belongs to it, and adopting the quality of the Spirit, being made conformable to the Word of God. And on this account he (the apostle) declares, "As we have borne the image of him who is of the earth, we shall also bear the image of Him who is from heaven." What, therefore, is the earthly? That which was fashioned. And what is the heavenly? The Spirit. As therefore he

says, when we were destitute of the celestial Spirit, we walked in former times in the oldness of the flesh, not obeying God; so now let us, receiving the Spirit, walk in newness of life, obeying God. Inasmuch, therefore, as without the Spirit of God we cannot be saved, the apostle exhorts us through faith and chaste conversation to preserve the Spirit of God, lest, having become non-participators of the Divine Spirit, we lose the kingdom of heaven; and he exclaims, that flesh in itself, and blood, cannot possess the kingdom of God.

4. If, however, we must speak strictly, [we would say that] the flesh does not inherit, but is inherited; as also the Lord declares, "Blessed are the meek, for they shall possess the earth by inheritance;" as if in the [future] kingdom, the earth, from whence exists the substance of our flesh, is to be possessed by inheritance. This is the reason for His wishing the temple (i.e., the flesh) to be clean, that the Spirit of God may take delight therein, as a bridegroom with a bride. As, therefore, the bride cannot [be said] to wed, but to be wedded, when the bridegroom comes and takes her, so also the flesh cannot by itself possess the kingdom of God by inheritance; but it can be taken for an inheritance into the kingdom of God. For a living person inherits the goods of the deceased; and it is one thing to inherit, another to be inherited. The former rules, and exercises power over, and orders the things inherited at his will; but the latter things are in a state of subjection, are under order, and are ruled over by him who has obtained the inheritance. What, therefore, is it that lives? The Spirit of God, doubtless. What, again, are the possessions of the deceased? The various parts of the man, surely, which rot in the earth. But these are inherited by the Spirit when they are translated into the kingdom of heaven. For this cause, too, did Christ die, that the Gospel covenant being manifested and known to the whole world, might in the first place set free His slaves; and then afterwards, as I have already shown, might constitute them heirs of His property, when the Spirit possesses them by inheritance. For he who lives inherits, but the flesh is inherited. In order that we may not lose life by losing that Spirit which possesses us, the apostle, exhorting us to the communion of the Spirit, has said, according to reason, in those words already quoted, "That flesh and blood cannot inherit the kingdom of God." Just as if he were to say, "Do not err; for unless the Word of God dwell with, and the Spirit of the Father be in you, and if ye shall live frivolously and carelessly as if ye were this only, viz., mere flesh and blood, ye cannot inherit the kingdom of God."

Chapter X.—By a comparison drawn from the wild olive-tree, whose quality but not whose nature is changed by grafting, he proves more important things; he points out also that man without the Spirit is not capable of bringing forth fruit, or of inheriting the kingdom of God.

1. This truth, therefore, [he declares], in order that we may not reject the engrafting of the Spirit while pampering the flesh. "But thou, being a wild olive-tree," he says, "hast been grafted into the good olive-tree, and been made a partaker of the fatness of the olive-tree." As, therefore, when the wild olive has been engrafted, if it remain in its former condition, viz., a wild olive, it is "cut off, and cast into the fire;" but if it takes kindly to the graft, and is changed into the good olive-tree, it becomes a fruit-bearing olive, planted, as it were, in a king's park (paradiso): so likewise men, if they do truly progress by faith towards better things, and receive the Spirit of God, and bring forth the fruit thereof, shall be spiritual, as being planted in the paradise of God. But if they cast out the Spirit, and remain in their former condition, desirous of being of the flesh rather than of the Spirit, then it is very justly said with regard to men of this stamp, "That flesh and blood shall not inherit the kingdom of God;" just as if any one were to say that the wild olive is not received into the paradise of God. Admirably therefore does the apostle exhibit our nature, and God's universal appointment, in his discourse about flesh and blood and the wild olive. For as the good olive, if neglected for a certain time, if left to grow wild and to run to wood, does itself become a wild olive; or again, if the wild olive be carefully tended and grafted, it naturally reverts to its former fruit-bearing condition: so men also, when they become careless, and bring forth for fruit the lusts of the flesh like woody produce, are rendered, by their own fault, unfruitful in righteousness. For when men sleep, the enemy sows the material of tares; and for this cause did the Lord command His disciples to be on the watch. And again, those persons who are not bringing forth the fruits of righteousness, and are, as it were, covered over and lost among brambles, if they use diligence, and receive the word of God as a graft, arrive at the pristine nature of man—that which was created after the image and likeness of God.

2. But as the engrafted wild olive does not certainly lose the substance of its wood, but changes the quality of its fruit, and receives another name, being now not a wild olive, but a fruit-bearing olive, and is called

so; so also, when man is grafted in by faith and receives the Spirit of God, he certainly does not lose the substance of flesh, but changes the quality of the fruit [brought forth, i.e.,] of his works, and receives another name, showing that he has become changed for the better, being now not [mere] flesh and blood, but a spiritual man, and is called such. Then, again, as the wild olive, if it be not grafted in, remains useless to its lord because of its woody quality, and is cut down as a tree bearing no fruit, and cast into the fire; so also man, if he does not receive through faith the engrafting of the Spirit, remains in his old condition, and being [mere] flesh and blood, he cannot inherit the kingdom of God. Rightly therefore does the apostle declare, "Flesh and blood cannot inherit the kingdom of God;" and, "Those who are in the flesh cannot please God:" not repudiating [by these words] the substance of flesh, but showing that into it the Spirit must be infused. And for this reason, he says, "This mortal must put on immortality, and this corruptible must put on incorruption." And again he declares, "But ye are not in the flesh, but in the Spirit, if so be that the Spirit of God dwell in you." He sets this forth still more plainly, where he says, "The body indeed is dead, because of sin; but the Spirit is life, because of righteousness. But if the Spirit of Him who raised up Jesus from the dead dwell in you, He that raised up Christ from the dead shall also quicken your mortal bodies, because of His Spirit dwelling in you." And again he says, in the Epistle to the Romans, "For if ye live after the flesh, ye shall die." [Now by these words] he does not prohibit them from living their lives in the flesh, for he was himself in the flesh when he wrote to them; but he cuts away the lusts of the flesh, those which bring death upon a man. And for this reason he says in continuation, "But if ye through the Spirit do mortify the works of the flesh, ye shall live. For whosoever are led by the Spirit of God, these are the sons of God."

Chapter XI.—Treats upon the actions of carnal and of spiritual persons; also, that the spiritual cleansing is not to be referred to the substance of our bodies, but to the manner of our former life.

1. [The apostle], foreseeing the wicked speeches of unbelievers, has particularized the works which he terms carnal; and he explains himself, lest any room for doubt be left to those who do dishonestly pervert his meaning, thus saying in the Epistle to the Galatians: "Now the works of the flesh are manifest, which are adulteries, fornications, uncleanness, luxuriousness, idolatries, witchcrafts, hatreds, contentions jealousies, wraths, emulations, animosities, irritable speeches, dissensions, heresies,

envyings, drunkenness, carousings, and such like; of which I warn you, as also I have warned you, that they who do such things shall not inherit the kingdom of God." Thus does he point out to his hearers in a more explicit manner what it is [he means when he declares], "Flesh and blood shall not inherit the kingdom of God." For they who do these things, since they do indeed walk after the flesh, have not the power of living unto God. And then, again, he proceeds to tell us the spiritual actions which vivify a man, that is, the engrafting of the Spirit; thus saying, "But the fruit of the Spirit is love, joy, peace, long-suffering, goodness, benignity, faith, meekness, continence, chastity: against these there is no law." As, therefore, he who has gone forward to the better things, and has brought forth the fruit of the Spirit, is saved altogether because of the communion of the Spirit; so also he who has continued in the aforesaid works of the flesh, being truly reckoned as carnal, because he did not receive the Spirit of God, shall not have power to inherit the kingdom of heaven. As, again, the same apostle testifies, saying to the Corinthians, "Know ye not that the unrighteous shall not inherit the kingdom of God? Do not err," he says: "neither fornicators, nor idolaters, nor adulterers, nor effeminate, nor abusers of themselves with mankind, nor thieves, nor covetous, nor revilers, nor rapacious persons, shall inherit the kingdom of God. And these ye indeed have been; but ye have been washed, but ye have been sanctified, but ye have been justified in the name of the Lord Jesus Christ, and in the Spirit of our God." He shows in the clearest manner through what things it is that man goes to destruction, if he has continued to live after the flesh; and then, on the other hand, [he points out] through what things he is saved. Now he says that the things which save are the name of our Lord Jesus Christ, and the Spirit of our God.

2. Since, therefore, in that passage he recounts those works of the flesh which are without the Spirit, which bring death [upon their doers], he exclaimed at the end of his Epistle, in accordance with what he had already declared, "And as we have borne the image of him who is of the earth, we shall also bear the image of Him who is from heaven. For this I say, brethren, that flesh and blood cannot inherit the kingdom of God." Now this which he says, "as we have borne the image of him who is of the earth," is analogous to what has been declared, "And such indeed ye were; but ye have been washed, but ye have been sanctified, but ye have been justified in the name of our Lord Jesus Christ, and in the Spirit of our God." When, therefore, did we bear the image of him

who is of the earth? Doubtless it was when those actions spoken of as "works of the flesh" used to be wrought in us. And then, again, when [do we bear] the image of the heavenly? Doubtless when he says, "Ye have been washed," believing in the name of the Lord, and receiving His Spirit. Now we have washed away, not the substance of our body, nor the image of our [primary] formation, but the former vain conversation. In these members, therefore, in which we were going to destruction by working the works of corruption, in these very members are we made alive by working the works of the Spirit.

Chapter XII.—Of the difference between life and death; of the breath of life and the vivifying Spirit: also how it is that the substance of flesh revives which once was dead.

1. For as the flesh is capable of corruption, so is it also of incorruption; and as it is of death, so is it also of life. These two do mutually give way to each other; and both cannot remain in the same place, but one is driven out by the other, and the presence of the one destroys that of the other. If, then, when death takes possession of a man, it drives life away from him, and proves him to be dead, much more does life, when it has obtained power over the man, drive out death, and restore him as living unto God. For if death brings mortality, why should not life, when it comes, vivify man? Just as Esaias the prophet says, "Death devoured when it had prevailed." And again, "God has wiped away every tear from every face." Thus that former life is expelled, because it was not given by the Spirit, but by the breath.

2. For the breath of life, which also rendered man an animated being, is one thing, and the vivifying Spirit another, which also caused him to become spiritual. And for this reason Isaiah said, "Thus saith the Lord, who made heaven and established it, who founded the earth and the things therein, and gave breath to the people upon it, and Spirit to those walking upon it;" thus telling us that breath is indeed given in common to all people upon earth, but that the Spirit is theirs alone who tread down earthly desires. And therefore Isaiah himself, distinguishing the things already mentioned, again exclaims, "For the Spirit shall go forth from Me, and I have made every breath." Thus does he attribute the Spirit as peculiar to God which in the last times He pours forth upon the human race by the adoption of sons; but [he shows] that breath was common throughout the creation, and points it out as something

created. Now what has been made is a different thing from him who makes it. The breath, then, is temporal, but the Spirit eternal. The breath, too, increases [in strength] for a short period, and continues for a certain time; after that it takes its departure, leaving its former abode destitute of breath. But when the Spirit pervades the man within and without, inasmuch as it continues there, it never leaves him. "But that is not first which is spiritual," says the apostle, speaking this as if with reference to us human beings; "but that is first which is animal, afterwards that which is spiritual," in accordance with reason. For there had been a necessity that, in the first place, a human being should be fashioned, and that what was fashioned should receive the soul; afterwards that it should thus receive the communion of the Spirit. Wherefore also "the first Adam was made" by the Lord "a living soul, the second Adam a quickening spirit." As, then, he who was made a living soul forfeited life when he turned aside to what was evil, so, on the other hand, the same individual, when he reverts to what is good, and receives the quickening Spirit, shall find life.

If one forsakes earthly pleasures they will find life.

3. For it is not one thing which dies and another which is quickened, as neither is it one thing which is lost and another which is found, but the Lord came seeking for that same sheep which had been lost. What was it, then, which was dead? Undoubtedly it was the substance of the flesh; the same, too, which had lost the breath of life, and had become breathless and dead. This same, therefore, was what the Lord came to quicken, that as in Adam we do all die, as being of an animal nature, in Christ we may all live, as being spiritual, not laying aside God's handiwork, but the lusts of the flesh, and receiving the Holy Spirit; as the apostle says in the Epistle to the Colossians: "Mortify, therefore, your members which are upon the earth." And what these are he himself explains: "Fornication, uncleanness, inordinate affection, evil concupiscence; and covetousness, which is idolatry." The laying aside of these is what the apostle preaches; and he declares that those who do such things, as being merely flesh and blood, cannot inherit the kingdom of heaven. For their soul, tending towards what is worse, and descending to earthly lusts, has become a partaker in the same designation which belongs to these [lusts, viz., "earthly"], which, when the apostle commands us to lay aside, he says in the same Epistle, "Cast ye off the old man with his deeds." But when he said this, he does not remove away the ancient formation [of man]; for in that case it would be incumbent on us to rid ourselves of its company by committing suicide.

4. But the apostle himself also, being one who had been formed in a womb, and had issued thence, wrote to us, and confessed in his Epistle to the Philippians that "to live in the flesh was the fruit of [his] work;" thus expressing himself. Now the final result of the work of the Spirit is the salvation of the flesh. For what other visible fruit is there of the invisible Spirit, than the rendering of the flesh mature and capable of incorruption? If then [he says], "To live in the flesh, this is the result of labour to me," he did not surely contemn the substance of flesh in that passage where he said, "Put ye off the old man with his works;" but he points out that we should lay aside our former conversation, that which waxes old and becomes corrupt; and for this reason he goes on to say, "And put ye on the new man, that which is renewed in knowledge, after the image of Him who created him." In this, therefore, that he says, "which is renewed in knowledge," he demonstrates that he, the selfsame man who was in ignorance in times past, that is, in ignorance of God, is renewed by that knowledge which has respect to Him. For the knowledge of God renews man. And when he says, "after the image of the Creator," he sets forth the recapitulation of the same man, who was at the beginning made after the likeness of God.

5. And that he, the apostle, was the very same person who had been born from the womb, that is, of the ancient substance of flesh, he does himself declare in the Epistle to the Galatians: "But when it pleased God, who separated me from my mother's womb, and called me by His grace, to reveal His Son in me, that I might preach Him among the Gentiles," it was not, as I have already observed, one person who had been born from the womb, and another who preached the Gospel of the Son of God; but that same individual who formerly was ignorant, and used to persecute the Church, when the revelation was made to him from heaven, and the Lord conferred with him, as I have pointed out in the third book, preached the Gospel of Jesus Christ the Son of God, who was crucified under Pontius Pilate, his former ignorance being driven out by his subsequent knowledge: just as the blind men whom the Lord healed did certainly lose their blindness, but received the substance of their eyes perfect, and obtained the power of vision in the very same eyes with which they formerly did not see; the darkness being merely driven away by the power of vision, while the substance of the eyes was retained, in order that, by means of those eyes through which they had not seen, exercising again the visual power, they might give

The body is Part of the resurrection

thanks to Him who had restored them again to sight. And thus, also, he whose withered hand was healed, and all who were healed generally, did not change those parts of their bodies which had at their birth come forth from the womb, but simply obtained these anew in a healthy condition.

6. For the Maker of all things, the Word of God, who did also from the beginning form man, when He found His handiwork impaired by wickedness, performed upon it all kinds of healing. At one time [He did so], as regards each separate member, as it is found in His own handiwork; and at another time He did once for all restore man sound and whole in all points, preparing him perfect for Himself unto the resurrection. For what was His object in healing [different] portions of the flesh, and restoring them to their original condition, if those parts which had been healed by Him were not in a position to obtain salvation? For if it was [merely] a temporary benefit which He conferred, He granted nothing of importance to those who were the subjects of His healing. Or how can they maintain that the flesh is incapable of receiving the life which flows from Him, when it received healing from Him? For life is brought about through healing, and incorruption through life. He, therefore, who confers healing, the same does also confer life; and He [who gives] life, also surrounds His own handiwork with incorruption.

Chapter XIII.—In the dead who were raised by Christ we possess the highest proof of the resurrection; and our hearts are shown to be capable of life eternal, because they can now receive the Spirit of God.

1. Let our opponents—that is, they who speak against their own salvation—inform us [as to this point]: The deceased daughter of the high priest; the widow's dead son, who was being carried out [to burial] near the gate [of the city]; and Lazarus, who had lain four days in the tomb,—in what bodies did they rise again? In those same, no doubt, in which they had also died. For if it were not in the very same, then certainly those same individuals who had died did not rise again. For [the Scripture] says, "The Lord took the hand of the dead man, and said to him, Young man, I say unto thee, Arise. And the dead man sat up, and He commanded that something should be given him to eat; and He delivered him to his mother." Again, He called Lazarus "with a loud voice, saying, Lazarus, come forth; and he that was dead came forth

bound with bandages, feet and hands." This was symbolical of that man who had been bound in sins. And therefore the Lord said, "Loose him, and let him depart." As, therefore, those who were healed were made whole in those members which had in times past been afflicted; and the dead rose in the identical bodies, their limbs and bodies receiving health, and that life which was granted by the Lord, who prefigures eternal things by temporal, and shows that it is He who is Himself able to extend both healing and life to His handiwork, that His words concerning its [future] resurrection may also be believed; so also at the end, when the Lord utters His voice "by the last trumpet," the dead shall be raised, as He Himself declares: "The hour shall come, in which all the dead which are in the tombs shall hear the voice of the Son of man, and shall come forth; those that have done good to the resurrection of life, and those that have done evil to the resurrection of judgment."

2. Vain, therefore, and truly miserable, are those who do not choose to see what is so manifest and clear, but shun the light of truth, blinding themselves like the tragic Œdipus. And as those who are not practised in wrestling, when they contend with others, laying hold with a determined grasp of some part of [their opponent's] body, really fall by means of that which they grasp, yet when they fall, imagine that they are gaining the victory, because they have obstinately kept their hold upon that part which they seized at the outset, and besides falling, become subjects of ridicule; so is it with respect to that [favourite] expression of the heretics: "Flesh and blood cannot inherit the kingdom of God;" while taking two expressions of Paul's, without having perceived the apostle's meaning, or examined critically the force of the terms, but keeping fast hold of the mere expressions by themselves, they die in consequence of their influence (περὶ αὐτάς), overturning as far as in them lies the entire dispensation of God.

3. For thus they will allege that this passage refers to the flesh strictly so called, and not to fleshly works, as I have pointed out, so representing the apostle as contradicting himself. For immediately following, in the same Epistle, he says conclusively, speaking thus in reference to the flesh: "For this corruptible must put on incorruption, and this mortal must put on immortality. So, when this mortal shall have put on immortality, then shall be brought to pass the saying which is written, Death is swallowed up in victory. O death, where is thy sting? O death,

where is thy victory?" Now these words shall be appropriately said at the time when this mortal and corruptible flesh, which is subject to death, which also is pressed down by a certain dominion of death, rising up into life, shall put on incorruption and immortality. For then, indeed, shall death be truly vanquished, when that flesh which is held down by it shall go forth from under its dominion. And again, to the Philippians he says: "But our conversation is in heaven, from whence also we look for the Saviour, the Lord Jesus, who shall transfigure the body of our humiliation conformable to the body of His glory, even as He is able (ita ut possit) according to the working of His own power." What, then, is this "body of humiliation" which the Lord shall transfigure, [so as to be] conformed to "the body of His glory?" Plainly it is this body composed of flesh, which is indeed humbled when it falls into the earth. Now its transformation [takes place thus], that while it is mortal and corruptible, it becomes immortal and incorruptible, not after its own proper substance, but after the mighty working of the Lord, who is able to invest the mortal with immortality, and the corruptible with incorruption. And therefore he says, "that mortality may be swallowed up of life. He who has perfected us for this very thing is God, who also has given unto us the earnest of the Spirit." He uses these words most manifestly in reference to the flesh; for the soul is not mortal, neither is the spirit. Now, what is mortal shall be swallowed up of life, when the flesh is dead no longer, but remains living and incorruptible, hymning the praises of God, who has perfected us for this very thing. In order, therefore, that we may be perfected for this, aptly does he say to the Corinthians, "Glorify God in your body." Now God is He who gives rise to immortality.

4. That he uses these words with respect to the body of flesh, and to none other, he declares to the Corinthians manifestly, indubitably, and free from all ambiguity: "Always bearing about in our body the dying of Jesus, that also the life of Jesus Christ might be manifested in our body. For if we who live are delivered unto death for Jesus' sake, it is that the life of Jesus may also be manifested in our mortal flesh." And that the Spirit lays hold on the flesh, he says in the same Epistle, "That ye are the epistle of Christ, ministered by us, inscribed not with ink, but with the Spirit of the living God, not in tables of stone, but in the fleshly tables of the heart." If, therefore, in the present time, fleshly hearts are made partakers of the Spirit, what is there astonishing if, in the resurrection, they receive that life which is granted by the Spirit? Of

which resurrection the apostle speaks in the Epistle to the Philippians: "Having been made conformable to His death, if by any means I might attain to the resurrection which is from the dead." In what other mortal flesh, therefore, can life be understood as being manifested, unless in that substance which is also put to death on account of that confession which is made of God? —as he has himself declared, "If, as a man, I have fought with beasts at Ephesus, what advantageth it me if the dead rise not? For if the dead rise not, neither has Christ risen. Now, if Christ has not risen, our preaching is vain, and your faith is vain. In that case, too, we are found false witnesses for God, since we have testified that He raised up Christ, whom [upon that supposition] He did not raise up. For if the dead rise not, neither has Christ risen. But if Christ be not risen, your faith is vain, since ye are yet in your sins. Therefore those who have fallen asleep in Christ have perished. If in this life only we have hope in Christ, we are more miserable than all men. But now Christ has risen from the dead, the first-fruits of those that sleep; for as by man [came] death, by man also [came] the resurrection of the dead."

5. In all these passages, therefore, as I have already said, these men must either allege that the apostle expresses opinions contradicting himself, with respect to that statement, "Flesh and blood cannot inherit the kingdom of God;" or, on the other hand, they will be forced to make perverse and crooked interpretations of all the passages, so as to overturn and alter the sense of the words. For what sensible thing can they say, if they endeavour to interpret otherwise this which he writes: "For this corruptible must put on incorruption, and this mortal put on immortality;" and, "That the life of Jesus may be made manifest in our mortal flesh;" and all the other passages in which the apostle does manifestly and clearly declare the resurrection and incorruption of the flesh? And thus shall they be compelled to put a false interpretation upon passages such as these, they who do not choose to understand one correctly.

Chapter XIV.—Unless the flesh were to be saved, the Word would not have taken upon Him flesh of the same substance as ours: from this it would follow that neither should we have been reconciled by Him.

1. And inasmuch as the apostle has not pronounced against the very substance of flesh and blood, that it cannot inherit the kingdom of God, the same apostle has everywhere adopted the term "flesh and blood"

with regard to the Lord Jesus Christ, partly indeed to establish His human nature (for He did Himself speak of Himself as the Son of man), and partly that He might confirm the salvation of our flesh. For if the flesh were not in a position to be saved, the Word of God would in no wise have become flesh. And if the blood of the righteous were not to be inquired after, the Lord would certainly not have had blood [in His composition]. But inasmuch as blood cries out (vocalis est) from the beginning [of the world], God said to Cain, when he had slain his brother, "The voice of thy brother's blood crieth to Me." And as their blood will be inquired after, He said to those with Noah, "For your blood of your souls will I require, [even] from the hand of all beasts;" and again, "Whosoever will shed man's blood, it shall be shed for his blood." In like manner, too, did the Lord say to those who should afterwards shed His blood, "All righteous blood shall be required which is shed upon the earth, from the blood of righteous Abel to the blood of Zacharias the son of Barachias, whom ye slew between the temple and the altar. Verily I say unto you, All these things shall come upon this generation." He thus points out the recapitulation that should take place in his own person of the effusion of blood from the beginning, of all the righteous men and of the prophets, and that by means of Himself there should be a requisition of their blood. Now this [blood] could not be required unless it also had the capability of being saved; nor would the Lord have summed up these things in Himself, unless He had Himself been made flesh and blood after the way of the original formation [of man], saving in his own person at the end that which had in the beginning perished in Adam.

2. But if the Lord became incarnate for any other order of things, and took flesh of any other substance, He has not then summed up human nature in His own person, nor in that case can He be termed flesh. For flesh has been truly made [to consist in] a transmission of that thing moulded originally from the dust. But if it had been necessary for Him to draw the material [of His body] from another substance, the Father would at the beginning have moulded the material [of flesh] from a different substance [than from what He actually did]. But now the case stands thus, that the Word has saved that which really was [created, viz.,] humanity which had perished, effecting by means of Himself that communion which should be held with it, and seeking out its salvation. But the thing which had perished possessed flesh and blood. For the Lord, taking dust from the earth, moulded man; and it was upon his

behalf that all the dispensation of the Lord's advent took place. He had Himself, therefore, flesh and blood, recapitulating in Himself not a certain other, but that original handiwork of the Father, seeking out that thing which had perished. And for this cause the apostle, in the Epistle to the Colossians, says, "And though ye were formerly alienated, and enemies to His knowledge by evil works, yet now ye have been reconciled in the body of His flesh, through His death, to present yourselves holy and chaste, and without fault in His sight." He says, "Ye have been reconciled in the body of His flesh," because the righteous flesh has reconciled that flesh which was being kept under bondage in sin, and brought it into friendship with God.

3. If, then, any one allege that in this respect the flesh of the Lord was different from ours, because it indeed did not commit sin, neither was deceit found in His soul, while we, on the other hand, are sinners, he says what is the fact. But if he pretends that the, Lord possessed another substance of flesh, the sayings respecting reconciliation will not agree with that man. For that thing is reconciled which had formerly been in enmity. Now, if the Lord had taken flesh from another substance, He would not, by so doing, have reconciled that one to God which had become inimical through transgression. But now, by means of communion with Himself, the Lord has reconciled man to God the Father, in reconciling us to Himself by the body of His own flesh, and redeeming us by His own blood, as the apostle says to the Ephesians, "In whom we have redemption through His blood, the remission of sins;" and again to the same he says, "Ye who formerly were far off have been brought near in the blood of Christ;" and again, "Abolishing in His flesh the enmities, [even] the law of commandments [contained] in ordinances." And in every Epistle the apostle plainly testifies, that through the flesh of our Lord, and through His blood, we have been saved.

4. If, therefore, flesh and blood are the things which procure for us life, it has not been declared of flesh and blood, in the literal meaning (proprie) of the terms, that they cannot inherit the kingdom of God; but [these words apply] to those carnal deeds already mentioned, which, perverting man to sin, deprive him of life. And for this reason he says, in the Epistle to the Romans: "Let not sin, therefore, reign in your mortal body, to be under its control: neither yield ye your members

instruments of unrighteousness unto sin; but yield yourselves to God, as being alive from the dead, and your members as instruments of righteousness unto God." In these same members, therefore, in which we used to serve sin, and bring forth fruit unto death, does He wish us to [be obedient] unto righteousness, that we may bring forth fruit unto life. Remember, therefore, my beloved friend, that thou hast been redeemed by the flesh of our Lord, re- established by His blood; and "holding the Head, from which the whole body of the Church, having been fitted together, takes increase"—that is, acknowledging the advent in the flesh of the Son of God, and [His] divinity (deum), and looking forward with constancy to His human nature (hominem), availing thyself also of these proofs drawn from Scripture—thou dost easily overthrow, as I have pointed out, all those notions of the heretics which were concocted afterwards.

Chapter XV.—Proofs of the resurrection from Isaiah and Ezekiel; the same God who created us will also raise us up.

1. Now, that He who at the beginning created man, did promise him a second birth after his dissolution into earth, Esaias thus declares: "The dead shall rise again, and they who are in the tombs shall arise, and they who are in the earth shall rejoice. For the dew which is from Thee is health to them." And again: "I will comfort you, and ye shall be comforted in Jerusalem: and ye shall see, and your heart shall rejoice, and your bones shall flourish as the grass; and the hand of the Lord shall be known to those who worship Him." And Ezekiel speaks as follows: "And the hand of the Lord came upon me, and the Lord led me forth in the Spirit, and set me down in the midst of the plain, and this place was full of bones. And He caused me to pass by them round about: and, behold, there were many upon the surface of the plain very dry. And He said unto me, Son of man, can these bones live? And I said, Lord, Thou who hast made them dost know. And He said unto me, Prophesy upon these bones, and thou shalt say to them, Ye dry bones, hear the word of the Lord. Thus saith the Lord to these bones, Behold, I will cause the spirit of life to come upon you, and I will lay sinews upon you, and bring up flesh again upon you, and I will stretch skin upon you, and will put my Spirit into you, and ye shall live; and ye shall know that I am the Lord. And I prophesied as the Lord had commanded me. And it came to pass, when I was prophesying, that, behold, an earthquake, and the bones were drawn together, each one to its own articulation: and I beheld, and, lo, the sinews and flesh were produced upon them, and the

skins rose upon them round about, but there was no breath in them. And He said unto me, Prophesy to the breath, son of man, and say to the breath, These things saith the Lord, Come from the four winds (spiritibus), and breathe upon these dead, that they may live. So I prophesied as the Lord had commanded me, and the breath entered into them; and they did live, and stood upon their feet, an exceeding great gathering." And again he says, "Thus saith the Lord, Behold, I will set your graves open, and cause you to come out of your graves, and bring you into the land of Israel; and ye shall know that I am the Lord, when I shall open your sepulchres, that I may bring my people again out of the sepulchres: and I will put my Spirit into you, and ye shall live; and I will place you in your land, and ye shall know that I am the Lord. I have said, and I will do, saith the Lord." As we at once perceive that the Creator (Demiurgo) is in this passage represented as vivifying our dead bodies, and promising resurrection to them, and resuscitation from their sepulchres and tombs, conferring upon them immortality also (He says, "For as the tree of life, so shall their days be"), He is shown to be the only God who accomplishes these things, and as Himself the good Father, benevolently conferring life upon those who have not life from themselves.

2. And for this reason did the Lord most plainly manifest Himself and the Father to His disciples, lest, forsooth, they might seek after another God besides Him who formed man, and who gave him the breath of life; and that men might not rise to such a pitch of madness as to feign another Father above the Creator. And thus also He healed by a word all the others who were in a weakly condition because of sin; to whom also He said, "Behold, thou art made whole, sin no more, lest a worse thing come upon thee:" pointing out by this, that, because of the sin of disobedience, infirmities have come upon men. To that man, however, who had been blind from his birth, He gave sight, not by means of a word, but by an outward action; doing this not without a purpose, or because it so happened, but that He might show forth the hand of God, that which at the beginning had moulded man. And therefore, when His disciples asked Him for what cause the man had been born blind, whether for his own or his parents' fault, He replied, "Neither hath this man sinned, nor his parents, but that the works of God should be made manifest in him." Now the work of God is the fashioning of man. For, as the Scripture says, He made [man] by a kind of process: "And the Lord took clay from the earth, and formed man." Wherefore also the

Lord spat on the ground and made clay, and smeared it upon the eyes, pointing out the original fashioning [of man], how it was effected, and manifesting the hand of God to those who can understand by what [hand] man was formed out of the dust. For that which the artificer, the Word, had omitted to form in the womb, [viz., the blind man's eyes], He then supplied in public, that the works of God might be manifested in him, in order that we might not be seeking out another hand by which man was fashioned, nor another Father; knowing that this hand of God which formed us at the beginning, and which does form us in the womb, has in the last times sought us out who were lost, winning back His own, and taking up the lost sheep upon His shoulders, and with joy restoring it to the fold of life.

3. Now, that the Word of God forms us in the womb, He says to Jeremiah, "Before I formed thee in the womb, I knew thee; and before thou wentest forth from the belly, I sanctified thee, and appointed thee a prophet among the nations." And Paul, too, says in like manner, "But when it pleased God, who separated me from my mother's womb, that I might declare Him among the nations." As, therefore, we are by the Word formed in the womb, this very same Word formed the visual power in him who had been blind from his birth; showing openly who it is that fashions us in secret, since the Word Himself had been made manifest to men: and declaring the original formation of Adam, and the manner in which he was created, and by what hand he was fashioned, indicating the whole from a part. For the Lord who formed the visual powers is He who made the whole man, carrying out the will of the Father. And inasmuch as man, with respect to that formation which, was after Adam, having fallen into transgression, needed the laver of regeneration, [the Lord] said to him [upon whom He had conferred sight], after He had smeared his eyes with the clay, "Go to Siloam, and wash;" thus restoring to him both [his perfect] confirmation, and that regeneration which takes place by means of the laver. And for this reason when he was washed he came seeing, that he might both know Him who had fashioned him, and that man might learn [to know] Him who has conferred upon him life.

4. All the followers of Valentinus, therefore, lose their case, when they say that man was not fashioned out of this earth, but from a fluid and diffused substance. For, from the earth out of which the Lord formed

eyes for that man, from the same earth it is evident that man was also fashioned at the beginning. For it were incompatible that the eyes should indeed be formed from one source and the rest of the body from another; as neither would it be compatible that one [being] fashioned the body, and another the eyes. But He, the very same who formed Adam at the beginning, with whom also the Father spake, [saying], "Let Us make man after Our image and likeness," revealing Himself in these last times to men, formed visual organs (visionem) for him who had been blind [in that body which he had derived] from Adam. Wherefore also the Scripture, pointing out what should come to pass, says, that when Adam had hid himself because of his disobedience, the Lord came to him at eventide, called him forth, and said, "Where art thou?" That means that in the last times the very same Word of God came to call man, reminding him of his doings, living in which he had been hidden from the Lord. For just as at that time God spake to Adam at eventide, searching him out; so in the last times, by means of the same voice, searching out his posterity, He has visited them.

Chapter XVI.—Since our bodies return to the earth, it follows that they have their substance from it; also, by the advent of the Word, the image of God in us appeared in a clearer light.

1. And since Adam was moulded from this earth to which we belong, the Scripture tells us that God said to him, "In the sweat of thy face shall thou eat thy bread, until thou turnest again to the dust from whence thou wert taken." If then, after death, our bodies return to any other substance, it follows that from it also they have their substance. But if it be into this very [earth], it is manifest that it was also from it that man's frame was created; as also the Lord clearly showed, when from this very substance He formed eyes for the man [to whom He gave sight]. And thus was the hand of God plainly shown forth, by which Adam was fashioned, and we too have been formed; and since there is one and the same Father, whose voice from the beginning even to the end is present with His handiwork, and the substance from which we were formed is plainly declared through the Gospel, we should therefore not seek after another Father besides Him, nor [look for] another substance from which we have been formed, besides what was mentioned beforehand, and shown forth by the Lord; nor another hand of God besides that which, from the beginning even to the end, forms us and prepares us for life, and is present with His handiwork, and perfects it after the image and likeness of God.

2. And then, again, this Word was manifested when the Word of God was made man, assimilating Himself to man, and man to Himself, so that by means of his resemblance to the Son, man might become precious to the Father. For in times long past, it was said that man was created after the image of God, but it was not [actually] shown; for the Word was as yet invisible, after whose image man was created, Wherefore also he did easily lose the similitude. When, however, the Word of God became flesh, He confirmed both these: for He both showed forth the image truly, since He became Himself what was His image; and He re-established the similitude after a sure manner, by assimilating man to the invisible Father through means of the visible Word.

3. And not by the aforesaid things alone has the Lord manifested Himself, but [He has done this] also by means of His passion. For doing away with [the effects of] that disobedience of man which had taken place at the beginning by the occasion of a tree, "He became obedient unto death, even the death of the cross;" rectifying that disobedience which had occurred by reason of a tree, through that obedience which was [wrought out] upon the tree [of the cross]. Now He would not have come to do away, by means of that same [image], the disobedience which had been incurred towards our Maker if He proclaimed another Father. But inasmuch as it was by these things that we disobeyed God, and did not give credit to His word, so was it also by these same that He brought in obedience and consent as respects His Word; by which things He clearly shows forth God Himself, whom indeed we had offended in the first Adam, when he did not perform His commandment. In the second Adam, however, we are reconciled, being made obedient even unto death. For we were debtors to none other but to Him whose commandment we had transgressed at the beginning.

Chapter XVII.—There is but one Lord and one God, the Father and Creator of all things, who has loved us in Christ, given us commandments, and remitted our sins; whose Son and Word Christ proved Himself to be, when He forgave our sins.

1. Now this being is the Creator (Demiurgus), who is, in respect of His love, the Father; but in respect of His power, He is Lord; and in respect

of His wisdom, our Maker and Fashioner; by transgressing whose commandment we became His enemies. And therefore in the last times the Lord has restored us into friendship through His incarnation, having become "the Mediator between God and men;" propitiating indeed for us the Father against whom we had sinned, and cancelling (consolatus) our disobedience by His own obedience; conferring also upon us the gift of communion with, and subjection to, our Maker. For this reason also He has taught us to say in prayer, "And forgive us our debts;" since indeed He is our Father, whose debtors we were, having transgressed His commandments. But who is this Being? Is He some unknown one, and a Father who gives no commandment to any one? Or is He the God who is proclaimed in the Scriptures, to whom we were debtors, having transgressed His commandment? Now the commandment was given to man by the Word. For Adam, it is said, "heard the voice of the Lord God." Rightly then does His Word say to man, "Thy sins are forgiven thee;" He, the same against whom we had sinned in the beginning, grants forgiveness of sins in the end. But if indeed we had disobeyed the command of any other, while it was a different being who said, "Thy sins are forgiven thee;" such an one is neither good, nor true, nor just. For how can he be good, who does not give from what belongs to himself? Or how can he be just, who snatches away the goods of another? And in what way can sins be truly remitted, unless that He against whom we have sinned has Himself granted remission "through the bowels of mercy of our God," in which "He has visited us" through His Son?

2. And therefore, when He had healed the man sick of the palsy, [the evangelist] says "The people upon seeing it glorified God, who gave such power unto men." What God, then, did the bystanders glorify? Was it indeed that unknown Father invented by the heretics? And how could they glorify him who was altogether unknown to them? It is evident, therefore, that the Israelites glorified Him who has been proclaimed as God by the law and the prophets, who is also the Father of our Lord; and therefore He taught men, by the evidence of their senses through those signs which He accomplished, to give glory to God. If, however, He Himself had come from another Father, and men glorified a different Father when they beheld His miracles, He [in that case] rendered them ungrateful to that Father who had sent the gift of healing. But as the only-begotten Son had come for man's salvation from Him who is God, He did both stir up the incredulous by the

miracles which He was in the habit of working, to give glory to the Father; and to the Pharisees, who did not admit the advent of His Son, and who consequently did not believe in the remission [of sins] which was conferred by Him, He said, "That ye may know that the Son of man hath power to forgive sins." And when He had said this, He commanded the paralytic man to take up the pallet upon which he was lying, and go into his house. By this work of His He confounded the unbelievers, and showed that He is Himself the voice of God, by which man received commandments, which he broke, and became a sinner; for the paralysis followed as a consequence of sins.

3. Therefore, by remitting sins, He did indeed heal man, while He also manifested Himself who He was. For if no one can forgive sins but God alone, while the Lord remitted them and healed men, it is plain that He was Himself the Word of God made the Son of man, receiving from the Father the power of remission of sins; since He was man, and since He was God, in order that since as man He suffered for us, so as God He might have compassion on us, and forgive us our debts, in which we were made debtors to God our Creator. And therefore David said beforehand, "Blessed are they whose iniquities are forgiven, and whose sins are covered. Blessed is the man to whom the Lord has not imputed sin;" pointing out thus that remission of sins which follows upon His advent, by which "He has destroyed the handwriting" of our debt, and "fastened it to the cross;" so that as by means of a tree we were made debtors to God, [so also] by means of a tree we may obtain the remission of our debt.

4. This fact has been strikingly set forth by many others, and especially through means of Elisha the prophet. For when his fellow- prophets were hewing wood for the construction of a tabernacle, and when the iron [head], shaken loose from the axe, had fallen into the Jordan and could not be found by them, upon Elisha's coming to the place, and learning what had happened, he threw some wood into the water. Then, when he had done this, the iron part of the axe floated up, and they took up from the surface of the water what they had previously lost. By this action the prophet pointed out that the sure word of God, which we had negligently lost by means of a tree, and were not in the way of finding again, we should receive anew by the dispensation of a tree, [viz., the cross of Christ]. For that the word of God is likened to an axe, John

the Baptist declares [when he says] in reference to it, "But now also is the axe laid to the root of the trees." Jeremiah also says to the same purport: "The word of God cleaveth the rock as an axe." This word, then, what was hidden from us, did the dispensation of the tree make manifest, as I have already remarked. For as we lost it by means of a tree, by means of a tree again was it made manifest to all, showing the height, the length, the breadth, the depth in itself; and, as a certain man among our predecessors observed, "Through the extension of the hands of a divine person, gathering together the two peoples to one God." For these were two hands, because there were two peoples scattered to the ends of the earth; but there was one head in the middle, as there is but one God, who is above all, and through all, and in us all.

Chapter XVIII.—God the Father and His Word have formed all created things (which They use) by Their own power and wisdom, not out of defect or ignorance. The Son of God, who received all power from the Father, would otherwise never have taken flesh upon Him.

1. And such or so important a dispensation He did not bring about by means of the creations of others, but by His own; neither by those things which were created out of ignorance and defect, but by those which had their substance from the wisdom and power of His Father. For He was neither unrighteous, so that He should covet the property of another; nor needy, that He could not by His own means impart life to His own, and make use of His own creation for the salvation of man. For indeed the creation could not have sustained Him [on the cross], if He had sent forth [simply by commission] what was the fruit of ignorance and defect. Now we have repeatedly shown that the incarnate Word of God was suspended upon a tree, and even the very heretics do acknowledge that He was crucified. How, then, could the fruit of ignorance and defect sustain Him who contains the knowledge of all things, and is true and perfect? Or how could that creation which was concealed from the Father, and far removed from Him, have sustained His Word? And if this world were made by the angels (it matters not whether we suppose their ignorance or their cognizance of the Supreme God), when the Lord declared, "For I am in the Father, and the Father in Me," how could this workmanship of the angels have borne to be burdened at once with the Father and the Son? How, again, could that creation which is beyond the Pleroma have contained Him who contains the entire Pleroma? Inasmuch, then, as all these things are impossible and incapable of proof, that preaching of the Church is alone true [which proclaims] that

His own creation bare Him, which subsists by the power, the skill, and the wisdom of God; which is sustained, indeed, after an invisible manner by the Father, but, on the contrary, after a visible manner it bore His Word: and this is the true [Word].

2. For the Father bears the creation and His own Word simultaneously, and the Word borne by the Father grants the Spirit to all as the Father wills. To some He gives after the manner of creation what is made; but to others [He gives] after the manner of adoption, that is, what is from God, namely generation. And thus one God the Father is declared, who is above all, and through all, and in all. The Father is indeed above all, and He is the Head of Christ; but the Word is through all things, and is Himself the Head of the Church; while the Spirit is in us all, and He is the living water, which the Lord grants to those who rightly believe in Him, and love Him, and who know that "there is one Father, who is above all, and through all, and in us all." And to these things does John also, the disciple of the Lord, bear witness, when he speaks thus in the Gospel: "In the beginning was the Word, and the Word was with God, and the Word was God. This was in the beginning with God. All things were made by Him, and without Him was nothing made." And then he said of the Word Himself: "He was in the world, and the world was made by Him, and the world knew Him not. To His own things He came, and His own people received Him not. However, as many as did receive Him, to these gave He power to become the sons of God, to those that believe in His name." And again, showing the dispensation with regard to His human nature, John said: "And the Word was made flesh, and dwelt among us." And in continuation he says, "And we beheld His glory, the glory as of the Only-begotten by the Father, full of grace and truth." He thus plainly points out to those willing to hear, that is, to those having ears, that there is one God, the Father over all, and one Word of God, who is through all, by whom all things have been made; and that this world belongs to Him, and was made by Him, according to the Father's will, and not by angels; nor by apostasy, defect, and ignorance; nor by any power of Prunicus, whom certain of them also call "the Mother;" nor by any other maker of the world ignorant of the Father.

3. For the Creator of the world is truly the Word of God: and this is our Lord, who in the last times was made man, existing in this world, and

who in an invisible manner contains all things created, and is inherent in the entire creation, since the Word of God governs and arranges all things; and therefore He came to His own in a visible manner, and was made flesh, and hung upon the tree, that He might sum up all things in Himself. "And His own peculiar people did not receive Him," as Moses declared this very thing among the people: "And thy life shall be hanging before thine eyes, and thou wilt not believe thy life." Those therefore who did not receive Him did not receive life. "But to as many as received Him, to them gave He power to become the sons of God." For it is He who has power from the Father over all things, since He is the Word of God, and very man, communicating with invisible beings after the manner of the intellect, and appointing a law observable to the outward senses, that all things should continue each in its own order; and He reigns manifestly over things visible and pertaining to men; and brings in just judgment and worthy upon all; as David also, clearly pointing to this, says, "Our God shall openly come, and will not keep silence." Then he shows also the judgment which is brought in by Him, saying, "A fire shall burn in His sight, and a strong tempest shall rage round about Him. He shall call upon the heaven from above, and the earth, to judge His people."

Chapter XIX.—A comparison is instituted between the disobedient and sinning Eve and the Virgin Mary, her patroness. Various and discordant heresies are mentioned.

1. That the Lord then was manifestly coming to His own things, and was sustaining them by means of that creation which is supported by Himself, and was making a recapitulation of that disobedience which had occurred in connection with a tree, through the obedience which was [exhibited by Himself when He hung] upon a tree, [the effects] also of that deception being done away with, by which that virgin Eve, who was already espoused to a man, was unhappily misled,— was happily announced, through means of the truth [spoken] by the angel to the Virgin Mary, who was [also espoused] to a man. For just as the former was led astray by the word of an angel, so that she fled from God when she had transgressed His word; so did the latter, by an angelic communication, receive the glad tidings that she should sustain (portaret) God, being obedient to His word. And if the former did disobey God, yet the latter was persuaded to be obedient to God, in order that the Virgin Mary might become the patroness (advocata) of the virgin Eve. And thus, as the human race fell into bondage to death

by means of a virgin, so is it rescued by a virgin; virginal disobedience having been balanced in the opposite scale by virginal obedience. For in the same way the sin of the first created man (protoplasti) receives amendment by the correction of the First- begotten, and the coming of the serpent is conquered by the harmlessness of the dove, those bonds being unloosed by which we had been fast bound to death.

2. The heretics being all unlearned and ignorant of God's arrangements, and not acquainted with that dispensation by which He took upon Him human nature (inscii ejus quæ est secundum hominem dispensationis), inasmuch as they blind themselves with regard to the truth, do in fact speak against their own salvation. Some of them introduce another Father besides the Creator; some, again, say that the world and its substance was made by certain angels; certain others [maintain] that it was widely separated by Horos from him whom they represent as being the Father—that it sprang forth (floruisse) of itself, and from itself was born. Then, again, others [of them assert] that it obtained substance in those things which are contained by the Father, from defect and ignorance; others still, despise the advent of the Lord manifest [to the senses], for they do not admit His incarnation; while others, ignoring the arrangement [that He should be born] of a virgin, maintain that He was begotten by Joseph. And still further, some affirm that neither their soul nor their body can receive eternal life, but merely the inner man. Moreover, they will have it that this [inner man] is that which is the understanding (sensum) in them, and which they decree as being the only thing to ascend to "the perfect." Others [maintain], as I have said in the first book, that while the soul is saved, their body does not participate in the salvation which comes from God; in which [book] I have also set forward the hypotheses of all these men, and in the second have pointed out their weakness and inconsistency.

Chapter XX.—Those pastors are to be heard to whom the apostles committed the Churches, possessing one and the same doctrine of salvation; the heretics, on the other hand, are to be avoided. We must think soberly with regard to the mysteries of the faith.

1. Now all these [heretics] are of much later date than the bishops to whom the apostles committed the Churches; which fact I have in the third book taken all pains to demonstrate. It follows, then, as a matter of course, that these heretics aforementioned, since they are blind to the

truth, and deviate from the [right] way, will walk in various roads; and therefore the footsteps of their doctrine are scattered here and there without agreement or connection. But the path of those belonging to the Church circumscribes the whole world, as possessing the sure tradition from the apostles, and gives unto us to see that the faith of all is one and the same, since all receive one and the same God the Father, and believe in the same dispensation regarding the incarnation of the Son of God, and are cognizant of the same gift of the Spirit, and are conversant with the same commandments, and preserve the same form of ecclesiastical constitution, and expect the same advent of the Lord, and await the same salvation of the complete man, that is, of the soul and body. And undoubtedly the preaching of the Church is true and stedfast, in which one and the same way of salvation is shown throughout the whole world. For to her is entrusted the light of God; and therefore the "wisdom" of God, by means of which she saves all men, "is declared in [its] going forth; it uttereth [its voice] faithfully in the streets, is preached on the tops of the walls, and speaks continually in the gates of the city." For the Church preaches the truth everywhere, and she is the seven- branched candlestick which bears the light of Christ.

2. Those, therefore, who desert the preaching of the Church, call in question the knowledge of the holy presbyters, not taking into consideration of how much greater consequence is a religious man, even in a private station, than a blasphemous and impudent sophist. Now, such are all the heretics, and those who imagine that they have hit upon something more beyond the truth, so that by following those things already mentioned, proceeding on their way variously, inharmoniously, and foolishly, not keeping always to the same opinions with regard to the same things, as blind men are led by the blind, they shall deservedly fall into the ditch of ignorance lying in their path, ever seeking and never finding out the truth. It behoves us, therefore, to avoid their doctrines, and to take careful heed lest we suffer any injury from them; but to flee to the Church, and be brought up in her bosom, and be nourished with the Lord's Scriptures. For the Church has been planted as a garden (paradisus) in this world; therefore says the Spirit of God, "Thou mayest freely eat from every tree of the garden," that is, Eat ye from every Scripture of the Lord; but ye shall not eat with an uplifted mind, nor touch any heretical discord. For these men do profess that they have themselves the knowledge of good and evil; and they set their own

impious minds above the God who made them. They therefore form opinions on what is beyond the limits of the understanding. For this cause also the apostle says, "Be not wise beyond what it is fitting to be wise, but be wise prudently," that we be not cast forth by eating of the "knowledge" of these men (that knowledge which knows more than it should do) from the paradise of life. Into this paradise the Lord has introduced those who obey His call, "summing up in Himself all things which are in heaven, and which are on earth;" but the things in heaven are spiritual, while those on earth constitute the dispensation in human nature (secundum hominem est dispositio). These things, therefore, He recapitulated in Himself: by uniting man to the Spirit, and causing the Spirit to dwell in man, He is Himself made the head of the Spirit, and gives the Spirit to be the head of man: for through Him (the Spirit) we see, and hear, and speak.

Chapter XXI.—Christ is the head of all things already mentioned. It was fitting that He should be sent by the Father, the Creator of all things, to assume human nature, and should be tempted by Satan, that He might fulfil the promises, and carry off a glorious and perfect victory.

1. He has therefore, in His work of recapitulation, summed up all things, both waging war against our enemy, and crushing him who had at the beginning led us away captives in Adam, and trampled upon his head, as thou canst perceive in Genesis that God said to the serpent, "And I will put enmity between thee and the woman, and between thy seed and her seed; He shall be on the watch for (observabit) thy head, and thou on the watch for His heel." For from that time, He who should be born of a woman, [namely] from the Virgin, after the likeness of Adam, was preached as keeping watch for the head of the serpent. This is the seed of which the apostle says in the Epistle to the Galatians, "that the law of works was established until the seed should come to whom the promise was made." This fact is exhibited in a still clearer light in the same Epistle, where he thus speaks: "But when the fulness of time was come, God sent forth His Son, made of a woman." For indeed the enemy would not have been fairly vanquished, unless it had been a man [born] of a woman who conquered him. For it was by means of a woman that he got the advantage over man at first, setting himself up as man's opponent. And therefore does the Lord profess Himself to be the Son of man, comprising in Himself that original man out of whom the

woman was fashioned (ex quo ea quæ secundum mulierem est plasmatio facta est), in order that, as our species went down to death through a vanquished man, so we may ascend to life again through a victorious one; and as through a man death received the palm [of victory] against us, so again by a man we may receive the palm against death.

2. Now the Lord would not have recapitulated in Himself that ancient and primary enmity against the serpent, fulfilling the promise of the Creator (Demiurgi), and performing His command, if He had come from another Father. But as He is one and the same, who formed us at the beginning, and sent His Son at the end, the Lord did perform His command, being made of a woman, by both destroying our adversary, and perfecting man after the image and likeness of God. And for this reason He did not draw the means of confounding him from any other source than from the words of the law, and made use of the Father's commandment as a help towards the destruction and confusion of the apostate angel. Fasting forty days, like Moses and Elias, He afterwards hungered, first, in order that we may perceive that He was a real and substantial man—for it belongs to a man to suffer hunger when fasting; and secondly, that His opponent might have an opportunity of attacking Him. For as at the beginning it was by means of food that [the enemy] persuaded man, although not suffering hunger, to transgress God's commandments, so in the end he did not succeed in persuading Him that was an hungered to take that food which proceeded from God. For, when tempting Him, he said, "If thou be the Son of God, command that these stones be made bread." But the Lord repulsed him by the commandment of the law, saying, "It is written, Man doth not live by bread alone." As to those words [of His enemy,] "If thou be the Son of God," [the Lord] made no remark; but by thus acknowledging His human nature He baffled His adversary, and exhausted the force of his first attack by means of His Father's word. The corruption of man, therefore, which occurred in paradise by both [of our first parents] eating, was done away with by [the Lord's] want of food in this world. But he, being thus vanquished by the law, endeavoured again to make an assault by himself quoting a commandment of the law. For, bringing Him to the highest pinnacle of the temple, he said to Him, "If thou art the Son of God, cast thyself down. For it is written, That God shall give His angels charge concerning thee, and in their hands they shall bear thee up, lest perchance thou dash thy foot against a stone;" thus concealing a falsehood under the guise of Scripture, as is done by all the

heretics. For that was indeed written, [namely], "That He hath given His angels charge concerning Him;" but "cast thyself down from hence" no Scripture said in reference to Him: this kind of persuasion the devil produced from himself. The Lord therefore confuted him out of the law, when He said, "It is written again, Thou shalt not tempt the Lord thy God;" pointing out by the word contained in the law that which is the duty of man, that he should not tempt God; and in regard to Himself, since He appeared in human form, [declaring] that He would not tempt the Lord his God. The pride of reason, therefore, which was in the serpent, was put to nought by the humility found in the man [Christ], and now twice was the devil conquered from Scripture, when he was detected as advising things contrary to God's commandment, and was shown to be the enemy of God by [the expression of] his thoughts. He then, having been thus signally defeated, and then, as it were, concentrating his forces, drawing up in order all his available power for falsehood, in the third place "showed Him all the kingdoms of the world, and the glory of them," saying, as Luke relates, "All these will I give thee,— for they are delivered to me; and to whom I will, I give them,—if thou wilt fall down and worship me." The Lord then, exposing him in his true character, says, "Depart, Satan; for it is written, Thou shalt worship the Lord thy God, and Him only shalt thou serve." He both revealed him by this name, and showed [at the same time] who He Himself was. For the Hebrew word "Satan" signifies an apostate. And thus, vanquishing him for the third time, He spurned him from Him finally as being conquered out of the law; and there was done away with that infringement of God's commandment which had occurred in Adam, by means of the precept of the law, which the Son of man observed, who did not transgress the commandment of God.

3. Who, then, is this Lord God to whom Christ bears witness, whom no man shall tempt, whom all should worship, and serve Him alone? It is, beyond all manner of doubt, that God who also gave the law. For these things had been predicted in the law, and by the words (sententiam) of the law the Lord showed that the law does indeed declare the Word of God from the Father; and the apostate angel of God is destroyed by its voice, being exposed in his true colours, and vanquished by the Son of man keeping the commandment of God. For as in the beginning he enticed man to transgress his Maker's law, and thereby got him into his power; yet his power consists in transgression and apostasy, and with these he bound man [to himself]; so again, on the other hand, it was

necessary that through man himself he should, when conquered, be bound with the same chains with which he had bound man, in order that man, being set free, might return to his Lord, leaving to him (Satan) those bonds by which he himself had been fettered, that is, sin. For when Satan is bound, man is set free; since "none can enter a strong man's house and spoil his goods, unless he first bind the strong man himself." The Lord therefore exposes him as speaking contrary to the word of that God who made all things, and subdues him by means of the commandment. Now the law is the commandment of God. The Man proves him to be a fugitive from and a transgressor of the law, an apostate also from God. After [the Man had done this], the Word bound him securely as a fugitive from Himself, and made spoil of his goods,—namely, those men whom he held in bondage, and whom he unjustly used for his own purposes. And justly indeed is he led captive, who had led men unjustly into bondage; while man, who had been led captive in times past, was rescued from the grasp of his possessor, according to the tender mercy of God the Father, who had compassion on His own handiwork, and gave to it salvation, restoring it by means of the Word—that is, by Christ—in order that men might learn by actual proof that he receives incorruptibility not of himself, but by the free gift of God.

Chapter XXII.—The true Lord and the one God is declared by the law, and manifested by Christ His Son in the Gospel; whom alone we should adore, and from Him we must look for all good things, not from Satan.

1. Thus then does the Lord plainly show that it was the true Lord and the one God who had been set forth by the law; for Him whom the law proclaimed as God, the same did Christ point out as the Father, whom also it behoves the disciples of Christ alone to serve. By means of the statements of the law, He put our adversary to utter confusion; and the law directs us to praise God the Creator (Demiurgum), and to serve Him alone. Since this is the case, we must not seek for another Father besides Him, or above Him, since there is one God who justifies the circumcision by faith, and the uncircumcision through faith. For if there were any other perfect Father above Him, He (Christ) would by no means have overthrown Satan by means of His words and commandments. For one ignorance cannot be done away with by means of another ignorance, any more than one defect by another defect. If, therefore, the law is due to ignorance and defect, how could the

statements contained therein bring to nought the ignorance of the devil, and conquer the strong man? For a strong man can be conquered neither by an inferior nor by an equal, but by one possessed of greater power. But the Word of God is the superior above all, He who is loudly proclaimed in the law: "Hear, O Israel, the Lord thy God is one God;" and, "Thou shalt love the Lord thy God with all thy heart;" and, "Him shall thou adore, and Him alone shall thou serve." Then in the Gospel, casting down the apostasy by means of these expressions, He did both overcome the strong man by His Father's voice, and He acknowledges the commandment of the law to express His own sentiments, when He says, "Thou shall not tempt the Lord thy God." For He did not confound the adversary by the saying of any other, but by that belonging to His own Father, and thus overcame the strong man.

2. He taught by His commandment that we who have been set free should, when hungry, take that food which is given by God; and that, when placed in the exalted position of every grace [that can be received], we should not, either by trusting to works of righteousness, or when adorned with super-eminent [gifts of] ministration, by any means be lifted up with pride, nor should we tempt God, but should feel humility in all things, and have ready to hand [this saying], "Thou shall not tempt the Lord thy God." As also the apostle taught, saying, "Minding not high things, but consenting to things of low estate;" that we should neither be ensnared with riches, nor mundane glory, nor present fancy, but should know that we must "worship the Lord thy God, and serve Him alone," and give no heed to him who falsely promised things not his own, when he said, "All these will I give thee, if, falling down, thou wilt worship me." For he himself confesses that to adore him, and to do his will, is to fall from the glory of God. And in what thing either pleasant or good can that man who has fallen participate? Or what else can such a person hope for or expect, except death? For death is next neighbour to him who has fallen. Hence also it follows that he will not give what he has promised. For how can he make grants to him who has fallen? Moreover, since God rules over men and him too, and without the will of our Father in heaven not even a sparrow falls to the ground, it follows that his declaration, "All these things are delivered unto me, and to whomsoever I will I give them," proceeds from him when puffed up with pride. For the creation is not subjected to his power, since indeed he is himself but one among created things. Nor shall he give away the rule over men to men; but both all other things, and all human

affairs, are arranged according to God the Father's disposal. Besides, the Lord declares that "the devil is a liar from the beginning, and the truth is not in him." If then he be a liar and the truth be not in him, he certainly did not speak truth, but a lie, when he said, "For all these things are delivered to me, and to whomsoever I will I give them."

Chapter XXIII.—The devil is well practised in falsehood, by which Adam having been led astray, sinned on the sixth day of the creation, in which day also he has been renewed by Christ.

1. He had indeed been already accustomed to lie against God, for the purpose of leading men astray. For at the beginning, when God had given to man a variety of things for food, while He commanded him not to eat of one tree only, as the Scripture tells us that God said to Adam: "From every tree which is in the garden thou shalt eat food; but from the tree of knowledge of good and evil, from this ye shall not eat: for in the day that ye shall eat of it, ye shall die by death;" he then, lying against the Lord, tempted man, as the Scripture says that the serpent said to the woman: "Has God indeed said this, Ye shall not eat from every tree of the garden?" And when she had exposed the falsehood, and simply related the command, as He had said, "From every tree of the garden we shall eat; but of the fruit of the tree which is in the midst of the garden, God hath said, Ye shall not eat of it, neither shall ye touch it, lest ye die:" when he had [thus] learned from the woman the command of God, having brought his cunning into play, he finally deceived her by a falsehood, saying, "Ye shall not die by death; for God knew that in the day ye shall eat of it your eyes shall be opened, and ye shall be as gods, knowing good and evil." In the first place, then, in the garden of God he disputed about God, as if God was not there, for he was ignorant of the greatness of God; and then, in the next place, after he had learned from the woman that God had said that they should die if they tasted the aforesaid tree, opening his mouth, he uttered the third falsehood, "Ye shall not die by death." But that God was true, and the serpent a liar, was proved by the result, death having passed upon them who had eaten. For along with the fruit they did also fall under the power of death, because they did eat in disobedience; and disobedience to God entails death. Wherefore, as they became forfeit to death, from that [moment] they were handed over to it.

2. Thus, then, in the day that they did eat, in the same did they die, and became death's debtors, since it was one day of the creation. For it is said, "There was made in the evening, and there was made in the morning, one day." Now in this same day that they did eat, in that also did they die. But according to the cycle and progress of the days, after which one is termed first, another second, and another third, if anybody seeks diligently to learn upon what day out of the seven it was that Adam died, he will find it by examining the dispensation of the Lord. For by summing up in Himself the whole human race from the beginning to the end, He has also summed up its death. From this it is clear that the Lord suffered death, in obedience to His Father, upon that day on which Adam died while he disobeyed God. Now he died on the same day in which he did eat. For God said, "In that day on which ye shall eat of it, ye shall die by death." The Lord, therefore, recapitulating in Himself this day, underwent His sufferings upon the day preceding the Sabbath, that is, the sixth day of the creation, on which day man was created; thus granting him a second creation by means of His passion, which is that [creation] out of death. And there are some, again, who relegate the death of Adam to the thousandth year; for since "a day of the Lord is as a thousand years," he did not overstep the thousand years, but died within them, thus bearing out the sentence of his sin. Whether, therefore, with respect to disobedience, which is death; whether [we consider] that, on account of that, they were delivered over to death, and made debtors to it; whether with respect to [the fact that on] one and the same day on which they ate they also died (for it is one day of the creation); whether [we regard this point], that, with respect to this cycle of days, they died on the day in which they did also eat, that is, the day of the preparation, which is termed "the pure supper," that is, the sixth day of the feast, which the Lord also exhibited when He suffered on that day; or whether [we reflect] that he (Adam) did not overstep the thousand years, but died within their limit,—it follows that, in regard to all these significations, God is indeed true. For they died who tasted of the tree; and the serpent is proved a liar and a murderer, as the Lord said of him: "For he is a murderer from the beginning, and the truth is not in him."

Chapter XXIV.—Of the constant falsehood of the devil, and of the powers and governments of the world, which we ought to obey, inasmuch as they are appointed of God, not of the devil.

1. As therefore the devil lied at the beginning, so did he also in the end, when he said, "All these are delivered unto me, and to whomsoever I will I give them." For it is not he who has appointed the kingdoms of this world, but God; for "the heart of the king is in the hand of God." And the Word also says by Solomon, "By me kings do reign, and princes administer justice. By me chiefs are raised up, and by me kings rule the earth." Paul the apostle also says upon this same subject: "Be ye subject to all the higher powers; for there is no power but of God: now those which are have been ordained of God." And again, in reference to them he says, "For he beareth not the sword in vain; for he is the minister of God, the avenger for wrath to him who does evil." Now, that he spake these words, not in regard to angelical powers, nor of invisible rulers—as some venture to expound the passage—but of those of actual human authorities, [he shows when] he says, "For this cause pay ye tribute also: for they are God's ministers, doing service for this very thing." This also the Lord confirmed, when He did not do what He was tempted to by the devil; but He gave directions that tribute should be paid to the tax-gatherers for Himself and Peter; because "they are the ministers of God, serving for this very thing."

2. For since man, by departing from God, reached such a pitch of fury as even to look upon his brother as his enemy, and engaged without fear in every kind of restless conduct, and murder, and avarice; God imposed upon mankind the fear of man, as they did not acknowledge the fear of God, in order that, being subjected to the authority of men, and kept under restraint by their laws, they might attain to some degree of justice, and exercise mutual forbearance through dread of the sword suspended full in their view, as the apostle says: "For he beareth not the sword in vain; for he is the minister of God, the avenger for wrath upon him who does evil." And for this reason too, magistrates themselves, having laws as a clothing of righteousness whenever they act in a just and legitimate manner, shall not be called in question for their conduct, nor be liable to punishment. But whatsoever they do to the subversion of justice, iniquitously, and impiously, and illegally, and tyrannically, in these things shall they also perish; for the just judgment of God comes equally upon all, and in no case is defective. Earthly rule, therefore, has been appointed by God for the benefit of nations, and not by the devil, who is never at rest at all, nay, who does not love to see even nations conducting themselves after a quiet manner, so that under the fear of human rule, men may not eat each other up like fishes; but that, by

means of the establishment of laws, they may keep down an excess of wickedness among the nations. And considered from this point of view, those who exact tribute from us are "God's ministers, serving for this very purpose."

3. As, then, "the powers that be are ordained of God," it is clear that the devil lied when he said, "These are delivered unto me; and to whomsoever I will, I give them." For by the law of the same Being as calls men into existence are kings also appointed, adapted for those men who are at the time placed under their government. Some of these [rulers] are given for the correction and the benefit of their subjects, and for the preservation of justice; but others, for the purposes of fear and punishment and rebuke: others, as [the subjects] deserve it, are for deception, disgrace, and pride; while the just judgment of God, as I have observed already, passes equally upon all. The devil, however, as he is the apostate angel, can only go to this length, as he did at the beginning, [namely] to deceive and lead astray the mind of man into disobeying the commandments of God, and gradually to darken the hearts of those who would endeavour to serve him, to the forgetting of the true God, but to the adoration of himself as God.

4. Just as if any one, being an apostate, and seizing in a hostile manner another man's territory, should harass the inhabitants of it, in order that he might claim for himself the glory of a king among those ignorant of his apostasy and robbery; so likewise also the devil, being one among those angels who are placed over the spirit of the air, as the Apostle Paul has declared in his Epistle to the Ephesians, becoming envious of man, was rendered an apostate from the divine law: for envy is a thing foreign to God. And as his apostasy was exposed by man, and man became the [means of] searching out his thoughts (et examinatio sententiæ ejus, homo factus est), he has set himself to this with greater and greater determination, in opposition to man, envying his life, and wishing to involve him in his own apostate power. The Word of God, however, the Maker of all things, conquering him by means of human nature, and showing him to be an apostate, has, on the contrary, put him under the power of man. For He says, "Behold, I confer upon you the power of treading upon serpents and scorpions, and upon all the power of the enemy," in order that, as he obtained dominion over man by apostasy,

so again his apostasy might be deprived of power by means of man turning back again to God.

Chapter XXV.—The fraud, pride, and tyrannical kingdom of Antichrist, as described by Daniel and Paul.

1. And not only by the particulars already mentioned, but also by means of the events which shall occur in the time of Antichrist is it shown that he, being an apostate and a robber, is anxious to be adored as God; and that, although a mere slave, he wishes himself to be proclaimed as a king. For he (Antichrist) being endued with all the power of the devil, shall come, not as a righteous king, nor as a legitimate king, [i.e., one] in subjection to God, but an impious, unjust, and lawless one; as an apostate, iniquitous and murderous; as a robber, concentrating in himself [all] satanic apostasy, and setting aside idols to persuade [men] that he himself is God, raising up himself as the only idol, having in himself the multifarious errors of the other idols. This he does, in order that they who do [now] worship the devil by means of many abominations, may serve himself by this one idol, of whom the apostle thus speaks in the second Epistle to the Thessalonians: "Unless there shall come a failing away first, and the man of sin shall be revealed, the son of perdition, who opposeth and exalteth himself above all that is called God, or that is worshipped; so that he sitteth in the temple of God, showing himself as if he were God." The apostle therefore clearly points out his apostasy, and that he is lifted up above all that is called God, or that is worshipped—that is, above every idol —for these are indeed so called by men, but are not [really] gods; and that he will endeavour in a tyrannical manner to set himself forth as God.

2. Moreover, he (the apostle) has also pointed out this which I have shown in many ways, that the temple in Jerusalem was made by the direction of the true God. For the apostle himself, speaking in his own person, distinctly called it the temple of God. Now I have shown in the third book, that no one is termed God by the apostles when speaking for themselves, except Him who truly is God, the Father of our Lord, by whose directions the temple which is at Jerusalem was constructed for those purposes which I have already mentioned; in which [temple] the enemy shall sit, endeavouring to show himself as Christ, as the Lord also declares: "But when ye shall see the abomination of desolation, which has been spoken of by Daniel the prophet, standing in the holy

place (let him that readeth understand), then let those who are in Judea flee into the mountains; and he who is upon the house-top, let him not come down to take anything out of his house: for there shall then be great hardship, such as has not been from the beginning of the world until now, nor ever shall be."

3. Daniel too, looking forward to the end of the last kingdom, i.e., the ten last kings, amongst whom the kingdom of those men shall be partitioned, and upon whom the son of perdition shall come, declares that ten horns shall spring from the beast, and that another little horn shall arise in the midst of them, and that three of the former shall be rooted up before his face. He says: "And, behold, eyes were in this horn as the eyes of a man, and a mouth speaking great things, and his look was more stout than his fellows. I was looking, and this horn made war against the saints, and prevailed against them, until the Ancient of days came and gave judgment to the saints of the most high God, and the time came, and the saints obtained the kingdom." Then, further on, in the interpretation of the vision, there was said to him: "The fourth beast shall be the fourth kingdom upon earth, which shall excel all other kingdoms, and devour the whole earth, and tread it down, and cut it in pieces. And its ten horns are ten kings which shall arise; and after them shall arise another, who shall surpass in evil deeds all that were before him, and shall overthrow three kings; and he shall speak words against the most high God, and wear out the saints of the most high God, and shall purpose to change times and laws; and [everything] shall be given into his hand until a time of times and a half time," that is, for three years and six months, during which time, when he comes, he shall reign over the earth. Of whom also the Apostle Paul again, speaking in the second [Epistle] to the Thessalonians, and at the same time proclaiming the cause of his advent, thus says: "And then shall the wicked one be revealed, whom the Lord Jesus shall slay with the spirit of His mouth, and destroy by the presence of His coming; whose coming [i.e., the wicked one's] is after the working of Satan, in all power, and signs, and portents of lies, and with all deceivableness of wickedness for those who perish; because they did not receive the love of the truth, that they might be saved. And therefore God will send them the working of error, that they may believe a lie; that they all may be judged who did not believe the truth, but gave consent to iniquity,"

4. The Lord also spoke as follows to those who did not believe in Him: "I have come in my Father's name, and ye have not received Me: when another shall come in his own name, him ye will receive," calling Antichrist "the other," because he is alienated from the Lord. This is also the unjust judge, whom the Lord mentioned as one "who feared not God, neither regarded man," to whom the widow fled in her forgetfulness of God,—that is, the earthly Jerusalem,—to be avenged of her adversary. Which also he shall do in the time of his kingdom: he shall remove his kingdom into that [city], and shall sit in the temple of God, leading astray those who worship him, as if he were Christ. To this purpose Daniel says again: "And he shall desolate the holy place; and sin has been given for a sacrifice, and righteousness been cast away in the earth, and he has been active (fecit), and gone on prosperously." And the angel Gabriel, when explaining his vision, states with regard to this person: "And towards the end of their kingdom a king of a most fierce countenance shall arise, one understanding [dark] questions, and exceedingly powerful, full of wonders; and he shall corrupt, direct, influence (faciet), and put strong men down, the holy people likewise; and his yoke shall be directed as a wreath [round their neck]; deceit shall be in his hand, and he shall be lifted up in his heart: he shall also ruin many by deceit, and lead many to perdition, bruising them in his hand like eggs." And then he points out the time that his tyranny shall last, during which the saints shall be put to flight, they who offer a pure sacrifice unto God: "And in the midst of the week," he says, "the sacrifice and the libation shall be taken away, and the abomination of desolation [shall be brought] into the temple: even unto the consummation of the time shall the desolation be complete." Now three years and six months constitute the half-week.

5. From all these passages are revealed to us, not merely the particulars of the apostasy, and [the doings] of him who concentrates in himself every satanic error, but also, that there is one and the same God the Father, who was declared by the prophets, but made manifest by Christ. For if what Daniel prophesied concerning the end has been confirmed by the Lord, when He said, "When ye shall see the abomination of desolation, which has been spoken of by Daniel the prophet" (and the angel Gabriel gave the interpretation of the visions to Daniel, and he is the archangel of the Creator (Demiurgi), who also proclaimed to Mary the visible coming and the incarnation of Christ), then one and the same

God is most manifestly pointed out, who sent the prophets, and made promise of the Son, and called us into His knowledge.

Chapter XXVI.—John and Daniel have predicted the dissolution and desolation of the Roman Empire, which shall precede the end of the world and the eternal kingdom of Christ. The Gnostics are refuted, those tools of Satan, who invent another Father different from the Creator.

1. In a still clearer light has John, in the Apocalypse, indicated to the Lord's disciples what shall happen in the last times, and concerning the ten kings who shall then arise, among whom the empire which now rules [the earth] shall be partitioned. He teaches us what the ten horns shall be which were seen by Daniel, telling us that thus it had been said to him: "And the ten horns which thou sawest are ten kings, who have received no kingdom as yet, but shall receive power as if kings one hour with the beast. These have one mind, and give their strength and power to the beast. These shall make war with the Lamb, and the Lamb shall overcome them, because He is the Lord of lords and the King of kings." It is manifest, therefore, that of these [potentates], he who is to come shall slay three, and subject the remainder to his power, and that he shall be himself the eighth among them. And they shall lay Babylon waste, and burn her with fire, and shall give their kingdom to the beast, and put the Church to flight. After that they shall be destroyed by the coming of our Lord. For that the kingdom must be divided, and thus come to ruin, the Lord [declares when He] says: "Every kingdom divided against itself is brought to desolation, and every city or house divided against itself shall not stand." It must be, therefore, that the kingdom, the city, and the house be divided into ten; and for this reason He has already foreshadowed the partition and division [which shall take place]. Daniel also says particularly, that the end of the fourth kingdom consists in the toes of the image seen by Nebuchadnezzar, upon which came the stone cut out without hands; and as he does himself say: "The feet were indeed the one part iron, the other part clay, until the stone was cut out without hands, and struck the image upon the iron and clay feet, and dashed them into pieces, even to the end." Then afterwards, when interpreting this, he says: "And as thou sawest the feet and the toes, partly indeed of clay, and partly of iron, the kingdom shall be divided, and there shall be in it a root of iron, as thou sawest iron mixed with baked clay. And the toes were indeed the one part iron, but the other part clay." The ten toes, therefore, are these ten kings, among whom the kingdom shall be

partitioned, of whom some indeed shall be strong and active, or energetic; others, again, shall be sluggish and useless, and shall not agree; as also Daniel says: "Some part of the kingdom shall be strong, and part shall be broken from it. As thou sawest the iron mixed with the baked clay, there shall be minglings among the human race, but no cohesion one with the other, just as iron cannot be welded on to pottery ware." And since an end shall take place, he says: "And in the days of these kings shall the God of heaven raise up a kingdom which shall never decay, and His kingdom shall not be left to another people. It shall break in pieces and shatter all kingdoms, and shall itself be exalted for ever. As thou sawest that the stone was cut without hands from the mountain, and brake in pieces the baked clay, the iron, the brass, the silver, and the gold, God has pointed out to the king what shall come to pass after these things; and the dream is true, and the interpretation trustworthy."

2. If therefore the great God showed future things by Daniel, and confirmed them by His Son; and if Christ is the stone which is cut out without hands, who shall destroy temporal kingdoms, and introduce an eternal one, which is the resurrection of the just; as he declares, "The God of heaven shall raise up a kingdom which shall never be destroyed,"—let those thus confuted come to their senses, who reject the Creator (Demiurgum), and do not agree that the prophets were sent beforehand from the same Father from whom also the Lord came, but who assert that prophecies originated from diverse powers. For those things which have been predicted by the Creator alike through all the prophets has Christ fulfilled in the end, ministering to His Father's will, and completing His dispensations with regard to the human race. Let those persons, therefore, who blaspheme the Creator, either by openly expressed words, such as the disciples of Marcion, or by a perversion of the sense [of Scripture], as those of Valentinus and all the Gnostics falsely so called, be recognised as agents of Satan by all those who worship God; through whose agency Satan now, and not before, has been seen to speak against God, even Him who has prepared eternal fire for every kind of apostasy. For he did not venture to blaspheme his Lord openly of himself; as also in the beginning he led man astray through the instrumentality of the serpent, concealing himself as it were from God. Truly has Justin remarked: That before the Lord's appearance Satan never dared to blaspheme God, inasmuch as he did not yet know his own sentence, because it was contained in parables and allegories; but that after the Lord's appearance, when he had clearly ascertained

from the words of Christ and His apostles that eternal fire has been prepared for him as he apostatized from God of his own free-will, and likewise for all who unrepentant continue in the apostasy, he now blasphemes, by means of such men, the Lord who brings judgment [upon him] as being already condemned, and imputes the guilt of his apostasy to his Maker, not to his own voluntary disposition. Just as it is with those who break the laws, when punishment overtakes them: they throw the blame upon those who frame the laws, but not upon themselves. In like manner do those men, filled with a satanic spirit, bring innumerable accusations against our Creator, who has both given to us the spirit of life, and established a law adapted for all; and they will not admit that the judgment of God is just. Wherefore also they set about imagining some other Father who neither cares about nor exercises a providence over our affairs, nay, one who even approves of all sins.

Chapter XXVII.—The future judgment by Christ. Communion with and separation from the divine being. The eternal punishment of unbelievers.

1. If the Father, then, does not exercise judgment, [it follows] that judgment does not belong to Him, or that He consents to all those actions which take place; and if He does not judge, all persons will be equal, and accounted in the same condition. The advent of Christ will therefore be without an object, yea, absurd, inasmuch as [in that case] He exercises no judicial power. For "He came to divide a man against his father, and the daughter against the mother, and the daughter-in- law against the mother-in-law;" and when two are in one bed, to take the one, and to leave the other; and of two women grinding at the mill, to take one and leave the other: [also] at the time of the end, to order the reapers to collect first the tares together, and bind them in bundles, and burn them with unquenchable fire, but to gather up the wheat into the barn; and to call the lambs into the kingdom prepared for them, but to send the goats into everlasting fire, which has been prepared by His Father for the devil and his angels. And why is this? Has the Word come for the ruin and for the resurrection of many? For the ruin, certainly, of those who do not believe Him, to whom also He has threatened a greater damnation in the judgment-day than that of Sodom and Gomorrah; but for the resurrection of believers, and those who do the will of His Father in heaven. If then the advent of the Son comes indeed alike to all, but is for the purpose of judging, and separating the believing

from the unbelieving, since, as those who believe do His will agreeably to their own choice, and as, [also] agreeably to their own choice, the disobedient do not consent to His doctrine; it is manifest that His Father has made all in a like condition, each person having a choice of his own, and a free understanding; and that He has regard to all things, and exercises a providence over all, "making His sun to rise upon the evil and on the good, and sending rain upon the just and unjust."

2. And to as many as continue in their love towards God, does He grant communion with Him. But communion with God is life and light, and the enjoyment of all the benefits which He has in store. But on as many as, according to their own choice, depart from God, He inflicts that separation from Himself which they have chosen of their own accord. But separation from God is death, and separation from light is darkness; and separation from God consists in the loss of all the benefits which He has in store. Those, therefore, who cast away by apostasy these forementioned things, being in fact destitute of all good, do experience every kind of punishment. God, however, does not punish them immediately of Himself, but that punishment falls upon them because they are destitute of all that is good. Now, good things are eternal and without end with God, and therefore the loss of these is also eternal and never-ending. It is in this matter just as occurs in the case of a flood of light: those who have blinded themselves, or have been blinded by others, are for ever deprived of the enjoyment of light. It is not, [however], that the light has inflicted upon them the penalty of blindness, but it is that the blindness itself has brought calamity upon them: and therefore the Lord declared, "He that believeth in Me is not condemned," that is, is not separated from God, for he is united to God through faith. On the other hand, He says, "He that believeth not is condemned already, because he has not believed in the name of the only-begotten Son of God;" that is, he separated himself from God of his own accord. "For this is the condemnation, that light is come into this world, and men have loved darkness rather than light. For every one who doeth evil hateth the light, and cometh not to the light, lest his deeds should be reproved. But he that doeth truth cometh to the light, that his deeds may be made manifest, that he has wrought them in God."

Chapter XXVIII.—The distinction to be made between the righteous and the wicked. The future apostasy in the time of Antichrist, and the end of the world.

1. Inasmuch, then, as in this world (αἰῶνι) some persons betake themselves to the light, and by faith unite themselves with God, but others shun the light, and separate themselves from God, the Word of God comes preparing a fit habitation for both. For those indeed who are in the light, that they may derive enjoyment from it, and from the good things contained in it; but for those in darkness, that they may partake in its calamities. And on this account He says, that those upon the right hand are called into the kingdom of heaven, but that those on the left He will send into eternal fire for they have deprived themselves of all good.

2. And for this reason the apostle says: "Because they received not the love of God, that they might be saved, therefore God shall also send them the operation of error, that they may believe a lie, that they all may be judged who have not believed the truth, but consented to unrighteousness." For when he (Antichrist) is come, and of his own accord concentrates in his own person the apostasy, and accomplishes whatever he shall do according to his own will and choice, sitting also in the temple of God, so that his dupes may adore him as the Christ; wherefore also shall he deservedly "be cast into the lake of fire:" [this will happen according to divine appointment], God by His prescience foreseeing all this, and at the proper time sending such a man, "that they may believe a lie, that they all may be judged who did not believe the truth, but consented to unrighteousness;" whose coming John has thus described in the Apocalypse: "And the beast which I had seen was like unto a leopard, and his feet as of a bear, and his mouth as the mouth of a lion; and the dragon conferred his own power upon him, and his throne, and great might. And one of his heads was as it were slain unto death; and his deadly wound was healed, and all the world wondered after the beast. And they worshipped the dragon because he gave power to the beast; and they worshipped the beast, saying, Who is like unto this beast, and who is able to make war with him? And there was given unto him a mouth speaking great things, and blasphemy and power was given to him during forty and two months. And he opened his mouth for blasphemy against God, to blaspheme His name and His tabernacle, and those who dwell in heaven. And power was given him over every tribe, and people, and tongue, and nation. And all who dwell upon the

earth worshipped him, [every one] whose name was not written in the book of the Lamb slain from the foundation of the world. If any one have ears, let him hear. If any one shall lead into captivity, he shall go into captivity. If any shall slay with the sword, he must be slain with the sword. Here is the endurance and the faith of the saints." After this he likewise describes his armour-bearer, whom he also terms a false prophet: "He spake as a dragon, and exercised all the power of the first beast in his sight, and caused the earth, and those that dwell therein, to adore the first beast, whose deadly wound was healed. And he shall perform great wonders, so that he can even cause fire to descend from heaven upon the earth in the sight of men, and he shall lead the inhabitants of the earth astray." Let no one imagine that he performs these wonders by divine power, but by the working of magic. And we must not be surprised if, since the demons and apostate spirits are at his service, he through their means performs wonders, by which he leads the inhabitants of the earth astray. John says further: "And he shall order an image of the beast to be made, and he shall give breath to the image, so that the image shall speak; and he shall cause those to be slain who will not adore it." He says also: "And he will cause a mark [to be put] in the forehead and in the right hand, that no one may be able to buy or sell, unless he who has the mark of the name of the beast or the number of his name; and the number is six hundred and sixty-six," that is, six times a hundred, six times ten, and six units. [He gives this] as a summing up of the whole of that apostasy which has taken place during six thousand years.

3. For in as many days as this world was made, in so many thousand years shall it be concluded. And for this reason the Scripture says: "Thus the heaven and the earth were finished, and all their adornment. And God brought to a conclusion upon the sixth day the works that He had made; and God rested upon the seventh day from all His works." This is an account of the things formerly created, as also it is a prophecy of what is to come. For the day of the Lord is as a thousand years; and in six days created things were completed: it is evident, therefore, that they will come to an end at the sixth thousand year.

4. And therefore throughout all time, man, having been moulded at the beginning by the hands of God, that is, of the Son and of the Spirit, is made after the image and likeness of God: the chaff, indeed, which is

the apostasy, being cast away; but the wheat, that is, those who bring forth fruit to God in faith, being gathered into the barn. And for this cause tribulation is necessary for those who are saved, that having been after a manner broken up, and rendered fine, and sprinkled over by the patience of the Word of God, and set on fire [for purification], they may be fitted for the royal banquet. As a certain man of ours said, when he was condemned to the wild beasts because of his testimony with respect to God: "I am the wheat of Christ, and am ground by the teeth of the wild beasts, that I may be found the pure bread of God."

Chapter XXIX.—All things have been created for the service of man. The deceits, wickedness, and apostate power of Antichrist. This was prefigured at the deluge, as afterwards by the persecution of Shadrach, Meshach, and Abednego.

1. In the previous books I have set forth the causes for which God permitted these things to be made, and have pointed out that all such have been created for the benefit of that human nature which is saved, ripening for immortality that which is [possessed] of its own free will and its own power, and preparing and rendering it more adapted for eternal subjection to God. And therefore the creation is suited to [the wants of] man; for man was not made for its sake, but creation for the sake of man. Those nations however, who did not of themselves raise up their eyes unto heaven, nor returned thanks to their Maker, nor wished to behold the light of truth, but who were like blind mice concealed in the depths of ignorance, the word justly reckons "as waste water from a sink, and as the turning-weight of a balance—in fact, as nothing;" so far useful and serviceable to the just, as stubble conduces towards the growth of the wheat, and its straw, by means of combustion, serves for working gold. And therefore, when in the end the Church shall be suddenly caught up from this, it is said, "There shall be tribulation such as has not been since the beginning, neither shall be." For this is the last contest of the righteous, in which, when they overcome they are crowned with incorruption.

2. And there is therefore in this beast, when he comes, a recapitulation made of all sorts of iniquity and of every deceit, in order that all apostate power, flowing into and being shut up in him, may be sent into the furnace of fire. Fittingly, therefore, shall his name possess the number six hundred and sixty-six, since he sums up in his own person all the

commixture of wickedness which took place previous to the deluge, due to the apostasy of the angels. For Noah was six hundred years old when the deluge came upon the earth, sweeping away the rebellious world, for the sake of that most infamous generation which lived in the times of Noah. And [Antichrist] also sums up every error of devised idols since the flood, together with the slaying of the prophets and the cutting off of the just. For that image which was set up by Nebuchadnezzar had indeed a height of sixty cubits, while the breadth was six cubits; on account of which Ananias, Azarias, and Misaël, when they did not worship it, were cast into a furnace of fire, pointing out prophetically, by what happened to them, the wrath against the righteous which shall arise towards the [time of the] end. For that image, taken as a whole, was a prefiguring of this man's coming, decreeing that he should undoubtedly himself alone be worshipped by all men. Thus, then, the six hundred years of Noah, in whose time the deluge occurred because of the apostasy, and the number of the cubits of the image for which these just men were sent into the fiery furnace, do indicate the number of the name of that man in whom is concentrated the whole apostasy of six thousand years, and unrighteousness, and wickedness, and false prophecy, and deception; for which things' sake a cataclysm of fire shall also come [upon the earth].

Chapter XXX.—Although certain as to the number of the name of Antichrist, yet we should come to no rash conclusions as to the name itself, because this number is capable of being fitted to many names. Reasons for this point being reserved by the Holy Spirit. Antichrist's reign and death.

1. Such, then, being the state of the case, and this number being found in all the most approved and ancient copies [of the Apocalypse], and those men who saw John face to face bearing their testimony [to it]; while reason also leads us to conclude that the number of the name of the beast, [if reckoned] according to the Greek mode of calculation by the [value of] the letters contained in it, will amount to six hundred and sixty and six; that is, the number of tens shall be equal to that of the hundreds, and the number of hundreds equal to that of the units (for that number which [expresses] the digit six being adhered to throughout, indicates the recapitulations of that apostasy, taken in its full extent, which occurred at the beginning, during the intermediate periods, and which shall take place at the end),—I do not know how it is that some have erred following the ordinary mode of speech, and have vitiated the

middle number in the name, deducting the amount of fifty from it, so that instead of six decads they will have it that there is but one. [I am inclined to think that this occurred through the fault of the copyists, as is wont to happen, since numbers also are expressed by letters; so that the Greek letter which expresses the number sixty was easily expanded into the letter Iota of the Greeks.] Others then received this reading without examination; some in their simplicity, and upon their own responsibility, making use of this number expressing one decad; while some, in their inexperience, have ventured to seek out a name which should contain the erroneous and spurious number. Now, as regards those who have done this in simplicity, and without evil intent, we are at liberty to assume that pardon will be granted them by God. But as for those who, for the sake of vainglory, lay it down for certain that names containing the spurious number are to be accepted, and affirm that this name, hit upon by themselves, is that of him who is to come; such persons shall not come forth without loss, because they have led into error both themselves and those who confided in them. Now, in the first place, it is loss to wander from the truth, and to imagine that as being the case which is not; then again, as there shall be no light punishment [inflicted] upon him who either adds or subtracts anything from the Scripture, under that such a person must necessarily fall. Moreover, another danger, by no means trifling, shall overtake those who falsely presume that they know the name of Antichrist. For if these men assume one [number], when this [Antichrist] shall come having another, they will be easily led away by him, as supposing him not to be the expected one, who must be guarded against.

2. These men, therefore, ought to learn [what really is the state of the case], and go back to the true number of the name, that they be not reckoned among false prophets. But, knowing the sure number declared by Scripture, that is, six hundred sixty and six, let them await, in the first place, the division of the kingdom into ten; then, in the next place, when these kings are reigning, and beginning to set their affairs in order, and advance their kingdom, [let them learn] to acknowledge that he who shall come claiming the kingdom for himself, and shall terrify those men of whom we have been speaking, having a name containing the aforesaid number, is truly the abomination of desolation. This, too, the apostle affirms: "When they shall say, Peace and safety, then sudden destruction shall come upon them." And Jeremiah does not merely point out his sudden coming, but he even indicates the tribe from which he shall

come, where he says, "We shall hear the voice of his swift horses from Dan; the whole earth shall be moved by the voice of the neighing of his galloping horses: he shall also come and devour the earth, and the fulness thereof, the city also, and they that dwell therein." This, too, is the reason that this tribe is not reckoned in the Apocalypse along with those which are saved.

3. It is therefore more certain, and less hazardous, to await the fulfilment of the prophecy, than to be making surmises, and casting about for any names that may present themselves, inasmuch as many names can be found possessing the number mentioned; and the same question will, after all, remain unsolved. For if there are many names found possessing this number, it will be asked which among them shall the coming man bear. It is not through a want of names containing the number of that name that I say this, but on account of the fear of God, and zeal for the truth: for the name Evanthas (ΕΥΑΝΘΑΣ) contains the required number, but I make no allegation regarding it. Then also Lateinos (ΛΑΤΕΙΝΟΣ) has the number six hundred and sixty-six; and it is a very probable [solution], this being the name of the last kingdom [of the four seen by Daniel]. For the Latins are they who at present bear rule: I will not, however, make any boast over this [coincidence]. Teitan too, (TEITAN, the first syllable being written with the two Greek vowels ε and ι, among all the names which are found among us, is rather worthy of credit. For it has in itself the predicted number, and is composed of six letters, each syllable containing three letters; and [the word itself] is ancient, and removed from ordinary use; for among our kings we find none bearing this name Titan, nor have any of the idols which are worshipped in public among the Greeks and barbarians this appellation. Among many persons, too, this name is accounted divine, so that even the sun is termed "Titan" by those who do now possess [the rule]. This word, too, contains a certain outward appearance of vengeance, and of one inflicting merited punishment because he (Antichrist) pretends that he vindicates the oppressed. And besides this, it is an ancient name, one worthy of credit, of royal dignity, and still further, a name belonging to a tyrant. Inasmuch, then, as this name "Titan" has so much to recommend it, there is a strong degree of probability, that from among the many [names suggested], we infer, that perchance he who is to come shall be called "Titan." We will not, however, incur the risk of pronouncing positively as to the name of Antichrist; for if it were necessary that his name should be distinctly revealed in this present time,

it would have been announced by him who beheld the apocalyptic vision. For that was seen no very long time since, but almost in our day, towards the end of Domitian's reign.

4. But he indicates the number of the name now, that when this man comes we may avoid him, being aware who he is: the name, however, is suppressed, because it is not worthy of being proclaimed by the Holy Spirit. For if it had been declared by Him, he (Antichrist) might perhaps continue for a long period. But now as "he was, and is not, and shall ascend out of the abyss, and goes into perdition," as one who has no existence; so neither has his name been declared, for the name of that which does not exist is not proclaimed. But when this Antichrist shall have devastated all things in this world, he will reign for three years and six months, and sit in the temple at Jerusalem; and then the Lord will come from heaven in the clouds, in the glory of the Father, sending this man and those who follow him into the lake of fire; but bringing in for the righteous the times of the kingdom, that is, the rest, the hallowed seventh day; and restoring to Abraham the promised inheritance, in which kingdom the Lord declared, that "many coming from the east and from the west should sit down with Abraham, Isaac, and Jacob."

Chapter XXXI.—The preservation of our bodies is confirmed by the resurrection and ascension of Christ: the souls of the saints during the intermediate period are in a state of expectation of that time when they shall receive their perfect and consummated glory.

1. Since, again, some who are reckoned among the orthodox go beyond the pre-arranged plan for the exaltation of the just, and are ignorant of the methods by which they are disciplined beforehand for incorruption, they thus entertain heretical opinions. For the heretics, despising the handiwork of God, and not admitting the salvation of their flesh, while they also treat the promise of God contemptuously, and pass beyond God altogether in the sentiments they form, affirm that immediately upon their death they shall pass above the heavens and the Demiurge, and go to the Mother (Achamoth) or to that Father whom they have feigned. Those persons, therefore, who disallow a resurrection affecting the whole man (universam reprobant resurrectionem), and as far as in them lies remove it from the midst [of the Christian scheme], how can they be wondered at, if again they know nothing as to the plan of the resurrection? For they do not choose to understand, that if these things

are as they say, the Lord Himself, in whom they profess to believe, did not rise again upon the third day; but immediately upon His expiring on the cross, undoubtedly departed on high, leaving His body to the earth. But the case was, that for three days He dwelt in the place where the dead were, as the prophet says concerning Him: "And the Lord remembered His dead saints who slept formerly in the land of sepulture; and He descended to them, to rescue and save them." And the Lord Himself says, "As Jonas remained three days and three nights in the whale's belly, so shall the Son of man be in the heart of the earth." Then also the apostle says, "But when He ascended, what is it but that He also descended into the lower parts of the earth?" This, too, David says when prophesying of Him, "And thou hast delivered my soul from the nethermost hell;" and on His rising again the third day, He said to Mary, who was the first to see and to worship Him, "Touch Me not, for I have not yet ascended to the Father; but go to the disciples, and say unto them, I ascend unto My Father, and unto your Father."

2. If, then, the Lord observed the law of the dead, that He might become the first-begotten from the dead, and tarried until the third day "in the lower parts of the earth;" then afterwards rising in the flesh, so that He even showed the print of the nails to His disciples, He thus ascended to the Father;—[if all these things occurred, I say], how must these men not be put to confusion, who allege that "the lower parts" refer to this world of ours, but that their inner man, leaving the body here, ascends into the super-celestial place? For as the Lord "went away in the midst of the shadow of death," where the souls of the dead were, yet afterwards arose in the body, and after the resurrection was taken up [into heaven], it is manifest that the souls of His disciples also, upon whose account the Lord underwent these things, shall go away into the invisible place allotted to them by God, and there remain until the resurrection, awaiting that event; then receiving their bodies, and rising in their entirety, that is bodily, just as the Lord arose, they shall come thus into the presence of God. "For no disciple is above the Master, but every one that is perfect shall be as his Master." As our Master, therefore, did not at once depart, taking flight [to heaven], but awaited the time of His resurrection prescribed by the Father, which had been also shown forth through Jonas, and rising again after three days was taken up [to heaven]; so ought we also to await the time of our resurrection prescribed by God and foretold by the prophets, and so,

rising, be taken up, as many as the Lord shall account worthy of this [privilege].

Chapter XXXII.—In that flesh in which the saints have suffered so many afflictions, they shall receive the fruits of their labours; especially since all creation waits for this, and God promises it to Abraham and his seed.

1. Inasmuch, therefore, as the opinions of certain [orthodox persons] are derived from heretical discourses, they are both ignorant of God's dispensations, and of the mystery of the resurrection of the just, and of the [earthly] kingdom which is the commencement of incorruption, by means of which kingdom those who shall be worthy are accustomed gradually to partake of the divine nature (capere Deum); and it is necessary to tell them respecting those things, that it behoves the righteous first to receive the promise of the inheritance which God promised to the fathers, and to reign in it, when they rise again to behold God in this creation which is renovated, and that the judgment should take place afterwards. For it is just that in that very creation in which they toiled or were afflicted, being proved in every way by suffering, they should receive the reward of their suffering; and that in the creation in which they were slain because of their love to God, in that they should be revived again; and that in the creation in which they endured servitude, in that they should reign. For God is rich in all things, and all things are His. It is fitting, therefore, that the creation itself, being restored to its primeval condition, should without restraint be under the dominion of the righteous; and the apostle has made this plain in the Epistle to the Romans, when he thus speaks: "For the expectation of the creature waiteth for the manifestation of the sons of God. For the creature has been subjected to vanity, not willingly, but by reason of him who hath subjected the same in hope; since the creature itself shall also be delivered from the bondage of corruption into the glorious liberty of the sons of God."

2. Thus, then, the promise of God, which He gave to Abraham, remains stedfast. For thus He said: "Lift up thine eyes, and look from this place where now thou art, towards the north and south, and east and west. For all the earth which thou seest, I will give to thee and to thy seed, even for ever." And again He says, "Arise, and go through the length and breadth of the land, since I will give it unto thee;" and [yet] he did

not receive an inheritance in it, not even a footstep, but was always a stranger and a pilgrim therein. And upon the death of Sarah his wife, when the Hittites were willing to bestow upon him a place where he might bury her, he declined it as a gift, but bought the burying-place (giving for it four hundred talents of silver) from Ephron the son of Zohar the Hittite. Thus did he await patiently the promise of God, and was unwilling to appear to receive from men, what God had promised to give him, when He said again to him as follows: "I will give this land to thy seed, from the river of Egypt even unto the great river Euphrates." If, then, God promised him the inheritance of the land, yet he did not receive it during all the time of his sojourn there, it must be, that together with his seed, that is, those who fear God and believe in Him, he shall receive it at the resurrection of the just. For his seed is the Church, which receives the adoption to God through the Lord, as John the Baptist said: "For God is able from the stones to raise up children to Abraham." Thus also the apostle says in the Epistle to the Galatians: "But ye, brethren, as Isaac was, are the children of the promise." And again, in the same Epistle, he plainly declares that they who have believed in Christ do receive Christ, the promise to Abraham thus saying, "The promises were spoken to Abraham, and to his seed. Now He does not say, And of seeds, as if [He spake] of many, but as of one, And to thy seed, which is Christ." And again, confirming his former words, he says, "Even as Abraham believed God, and it was accounted to him for righteousness. Know ye therefore, that they which are of faith are the children of Abraham. But the Scripture, foreseeing that God would justify the heathen through faith, declared to Abraham beforehand, That in thee shall all nations be blessed. So then they which are of faith shall be blessed with faithful Abraham." Thus, then, they who are of faith shall be blessed with faithful Abraham, and these are the children of Abraham. Now God made promise of the earth to Abraham and his seed; yet neither Abraham nor his seed, that is, those who are justified by faith, do now receive any inheritance in it; but they shall receive it at the resurrection of the just. For God is true and faithful; and on this account He said, "Blessed are the meek, for they shall inherit the earth."

Chapter XXXIII.—Further proofs of the same proposition, drawn from the promises made by Christ, when He declared that He would drink of the fruit of the vine with His disciples in His Father's kingdom, while at the same time He promised to reward them an hundred-fold, and to make them partake of banquets. The blessing pronounced by Jacob had pointed out this already, as Papias and the elders have interpreted it.

1. For this reason, when about to undergo His sufferings, that He might declare to Abraham and those with him the glad tidings of the inheritance being thrown open, [Christ], after He had given thanks while holding the cup, and had drunk of it, and given it to the disciples, said to them: "Drink ye all of it: this is My blood of the new covenant, which shall be shed for many for the remission of sins. But I say unto you, I will not drink henceforth of the fruit of this vine, until that day when I will drink it new with you in my Father's kingdom." Thus, then, He will Himself renew the inheritance of the earth, and will re-organize the mystery of the glory of [His] sons; as David says, "He who hath renewed the face of the earth." He promised to drink of the fruit of the vine with His disciples, thus indicating both these points: the inheritance of the earth in which the new fruit of the vine is drunk, and the resurrection of His disciples in the flesh. For the new flesh which rises again is the same which also received the new cup. And He cannot by any means be understood as drinking of the fruit of the vine when settled down with his [disciples] above in a super-celestial place; nor, again, are they who drink it devoid of flesh, for to drink of that which flows from the vine pertains to flesh, and not spirit.

2. And for this reason the Lord declared, "When thou makest a dinner or a supper, do not call thy friends, nor thy neighbours, nor thy kinsfolk, lest they ask thee in return, and so repay thee. But call the lame, the blind, and the poor, and thou shall be blessed, since they cannot recompense thee, but a recompense shall be made thee at the resurrection of the just." And again He says, "Whosoever shall have left lands, or houses, or parents, or brethren, or children because of Me, he shall receive in this world an hundred-fold, and in that to come he shall inherit eternal life." For what are the hundred-fold [rewards] in this word, the entertainments given to the poor, and the suppers for which a return is made? These are [to take place] in the times of the kingdom, that is, upon the seventh day, which has been sanctified, in which God rested from all the works which He created, which is the true Sabbath of the righteous, which they shall not be engaged in any earthly

occupation; but shall have a table at hand prepared for them by God, supplying them with all sorts of dishes.

3. The blessing of Isaac with which he blessed his younger son Jacob has the same meaning, when he says, "Behold, the smell of my son is as the smell of a full field which the Lord has blessed." But "the field is the world." And therefore he added, "God give to thee of the dew of heaven, and of the fatness of the earth, plenty of corn and wine. And let the nations serve thee, and kings bow down to thee; and be thou lord over thy brother, and thy father's sons shall bow down to thee: cursed shall be he who shall curse thee, and blessed shall be he who shall bless thee." If any one, then, does not accept these things as referring to the appointed kingdom, he must fall into much contradiction and contrariety, as is the case with the Jews, who are involved in absolute perplexity. For not only did not the nations in this life serve this Jacob; but even after he had received the blessing, he himself going forth [from his home], served his uncle Laban the Syrian for twenty years; and not only was he not made lord of his brother, but he did himself bow down before his brother Esau, upon his return from Mesopotamia to his father, and offered many gifts to him. Moreover, in what way did he inherit much corn and wine here, he who emigrated to Egypt because of the famine which possessed the land in which he was dwelling, and became subject to Pharaoh, who was then ruling over Egypt? The predicted blessing, therefore, belongs unquestionably to the times of the kingdom, when the righteous shall bear rule upon their rising from the dead; when also the creation, having been renovated and set free, shall fructify with an abundance of all kinds of food, from the dew of heaven, and from the fertility of the earth: as the elders who saw John, the disciple of the Lord, related that they had heard from him how the Lord used to teach in regard to these times, and say: The days will come, in which vines shall grow, each having ten thousand branches, and in each branch ten thousand twigs, and in each true twig ten thousand shoots, and in each one of the shoots ten thousand clusters, and on every one of the clusters ten thousand grapes, and every grape when pressed will give five and twenty metretes of wine. And when any one of the saints shall lay hold of a cluster, another shall cry out, "I am a better cluster, take me; bless the Lord through me." In like manner [the Lord declared] that a grain of wheat would produce ten thousand ears, and that every ear should have ten thousand grains, and every grain would yield ten pounds (quinque bilibres) of clear, pure, fine flour; and that all other

fruit- bearing trees, and seeds and grass, would produce in similar proportions (secundum congruentiam iis consequentem); and that all animals feeding [only] on the productions of the earth, should [in those days] become peaceful and harmonious among each other, and be in perfect subjection to man.

4. And these things are borne witness to in writing by Papias, the hearer of John, and a companion of Polycarp, in his fourth book; for there were five books compiled (συντεταγμένα) by him. And he says in addition, "Now these things are credible to believers." And he says that, "when the traitor Judas did not give credit to them, and put the question, 'How then can things about to bring forth so abundantly be wrought by the Lord?' the Lord declared, 'They who shall come to these [times] shall see.' " When prophesying of these times, therefore, Esaias says: "The wolf also shall feed with the lamb, and the leopard shall take his rest with the kid; the calf also, and the bull, and the lion shall eat together; and a little boy shall lead them. The ox and the bear shall feed together, and their young ones shall agree together; and the lion shall eat straw as well as the ox. And the infant boy shall thrust his hand into the asp's den, into the nest also of the adder's brood; and they shall do no harm, nor have power to hurt anything in my holy mountain." And again he says, in recapitulation, "Wolves and lambs shall then browse together, and the lion shall eat straw like the ox, and the serpent earth as if it were bread; and they shall neither hurt nor annoy anything in my holy mountain, saith the Lord." I am quite aware that some persons endeavour to refer these words to the case of savage men, both of different nations and various habits, who come to believe, and when they have believed, act in harmony with the righteous. But although this is [true] now with regard to some men coming from various nations to the harmony of the faith, nevertheless in the resurrection of the just [the words shall also apply] to those animals mentioned. For God is rich in all things. And it is right that when the creation is restored, all the animals should obey and be in subjection to man, and revert to the food originally given by God (for they had been originally subjected in obedience to Adam), that is, the productions of the earth. But some other occasion, and not the present, is [to be sought] for showing that the lion shall [then] feed on straw. And this indicates the large size and rich quality of the fruits. For if that animal, the lion, feeds upon straw [at that period], of what a quality must the wheat itself be whose straw shall serve as suitable food for lions?

Chapter XXXIV.—He fortifies his opinions with regard to the temporal and earthly kingdom of the saints after their resurrection, by the various testimonies of Isaiah, Ezekiel, Jeremiah, and Daniel; also by the parable of the servants watching, to whom the Lord promised that He would minister.

1. Then, too, Isaiah himself has plainly declared that there shall be joy of this nature at the resurrection of the just, when he says: "The dead shall rise again; those, too, who are in the tombs shall arise, and those who are in the earth shall rejoice. For the dew from Thee is health to them." And this again Ezekiel also says: "Behold, I will open your tombs, and will bring you forth out of your graves; when I will draw my people from the sepulchres, and I will put breath in you, and ye shall live; and I will place you on your own land, and ye shall know that I am the Lord." And again the same speaks thus: "These things saith the Lord, I will gather Israel from all nations whither they have been driven, and I shall be sanctified in them in the sight of the sons of the nations: and they shall dwell in their own land, which I gave to my servant Jacob. And they shall dwell in it in peace; and they shall build houses, and plant vineyards, and dwell in hope, when I shall cause judgment to fall among all who have dishonoured them, among those who encircle them round about; and they shall know that I am the Lord their God, and the God of their fathers." Now I have shown a short time ago that the church is the seed of Abraham; and for this reason, that we may know that He who in the New Testament "raises up from the stones children unto Abraham," is He who will gather, according to the Old Testament, those that shall be saved from all the nations, Jeremiah says: "Behold, the days come, saith the Lord, that they shall no more say, The Lord liveth, who led the children of Israel from the north, and from every region whither they had been driven; He will restore them to their own land which He gave to their fathers."

2. That the whole creation shall, according to God's will, obtain a vast increase, that it may bring forth and sustain fruits such [as we have mentioned], Isaiah declares: "And there shall be upon every high mountain, and upon every prominent hill, water running everywhere in that day, when many shall perish, when walls shall fall. And the light of the moon shall be as the light of the sun, seven times that of the day, when He shall heal the anguish of His people, and do away with the pain

of His stroke." Now "the pain of the stroke" means that inflicted at the beginning upon disobedient man in Adam, that is, death; which [stroke] the Lord will heal when He raises us from the dead, and restores the inheritance of the fathers, as Isaiah again says: "And thou shall be confident in the Lord, and He will cause thee to pass over the whole earth, and feed thee with the inheritance of Jacob thy father." This is what the Lord declared: "Happy are those servants whom the Lord when He cometh shall find watching. Verily I say unto you, that He shall gird Himself, and make them to sit down [to meat], and will come forth and serve them. And if He shall come in the evening watch, and find them so, blessed are they, because He shall make them sit down, and minister to them; or if this be in the second, or it be in the third, blessed are they." Again John also says the very same in the Apocalypse: "Blessed and holy is he who has part in the first resurrection." Then, too, Isaiah has declared the time when these events shall occur; he says: "And I said, Lord, how long? Until the cities be wasted without inhabitant, and the houses be without men, and the earth be left a desert. And after these things the Lord shall remove us men far away (longe nos faciet Deus homines), and those who shall remain shall multiply upon the earth." Then Daniel also says this very thing: "And the kingdom and dominion, and the greatness of those under the heaven, is given to the saints of the Most High God, whose kingdom is everlasting, and all dominions shall serve and obey Him." And lest the promise named should be understood as referring to this time, it was declared to the prophet: "And come thou, and stand in thy lot at the consummation of the days."

3. Now, that the promises were not announced to the prophets and the fathers alone, but to the Churches united to these from the nations, whom also the Spirit terms "the islands" (both because they are established in the midst of turbulence, suffer the storm of blasphemies, exist as a harbour of safety to those in peril, and are the refuge of those who love the height [of heaven], and strive to avoid Bythus, that is, the depth of error), Jeremiah thus declares: "Hear the word of the Lord, ye nations, and declare it to the isles afar off; say ye, that the Lord will scatter Israel, He will gather him, and keep him, as one feeding his flock of sheep. For the Lord hath redeemed Jacob, and rescued him from the hand of one stronger than he. And they shall come and rejoice in Mount Zion, and shall come to what is good, and into a land of wheat, and wine, and fruits, of animals and of sheep; and their soul shall be as a tree

bearing fruit, and they shall hunger no more. At that time also shall the virgins rejoice in the company of the young men: the old men, too, shall be glad, and I will turn their sorrow into joy; and I will make them exult, and will magnify them, and satiate the souls of the priests the sons of Levi; and my people shall be satiated with my goodness." Now, in the preceding book I have shown that all the disciples of the Lord are Levites and priests, they who used in the temple to profane the Sabbath, but are blameless. Promises of such a nature, therefore, do indicate in the clearest manner the feasting of that creation in the kingdom of the righteous, which God promises that He will Himself serve.

4. Then again, speaking of Jerusalem, and of Him reigning there, Isaiah declares, "Thus saith the Lord, Happy is he who hath seed in Zion, and servants in Jerusalem. Behold, a righteous king shall reign, and princes shall rule with judgment." And with regard to the foundation on which it shall be rebuilt, he says: "Behold, I will lay in order for thee a carbuncle stone, and sapphire for thy foundations; and I will lay thy ramparts with jasper, and thy gates with crystal, and thy wall with choice stones: and all thy children shall be taught of God, and great shall be the peace of thy children; and in righteousness shalt thou be built up." And yet again does he say the same thing: "Behold, I make Jerusalem a rejoicing, and my people [a joy]; for the voice of weeping shall be no more heard in her, nor the voice of crying. Also there shall not be there any immature [one], nor an old man who does not fulfil his time: for the youth shall be of a hundred years; and the sinner shall die a hundred years old, yet shall be accursed. And they shall build houses, and inhabit them themselves; and shall plant vineyards, and eat the fruit of them themselves, and shall drink wine. And they shall not build, and others inhabit; neither shall they prepare the vineyard, and others eat. For as the days of the tree of life shall be the days of the people in thee; for the works of their hands shall endure."

Chapter XXXV.—He contends that these testimonies already alleged cannot be understood allegorically of celestial blessings, but that they shall have their fulfilment after the coming of Antichrist, and the resurrection, in the terrestrial Jerusalem. To the former prophecies he subjoins others drawn from Isaiah, Jeremiah, and the Apocalypse of John.

1. If, however, any shall endeavour to allegorize [prophecies] of this kind, they shall not be found consistent with themselves in all points, and shall be confuted by the teaching of the very expressions [in question]. For example: "When the cities" of the Gentiles "shall be desolate, so that they be not inhabited, and the houses so that there shall be no men in them and the land shall be left desolate." "For, behold," says Isaiah, "the day of the Lord cometh past remedy, full of fury and wrath, to lay waste the city of the earth, and to root sinners out of it." And again he says, "Let him be taken away, that he behold not the glory of God." And when these things are done, he says, "God will remove men far away, and those that are left shall multiply in the earth." "And they shall build houses, and shall inhabit them themselves: and plant vineyards, and eat of them themselves." For all these and other words were unquestionably spoken in reference to the resurrection of the just, which takes place after the coming of Antichrist, and the destruction of all nations under his rule; in [the times of] which [resurrection] the righteous shall reign in the earth, waxing stronger by the sight of the Lord: and through Him they shall become accustomed to partake in the glory of God the Father, and shall enjoy in the kingdom intercourse and communion with the holy angels, and union with spiritual beings; and [with respect to] those whom the Lord shall find in the flesh, awaiting Him from heaven, and who have suffered tribulation, as well as escaped the hands of the Wicked one. For it is in reference to them that the prophet says: "And those that are left shall multiply upon the earth," And Jeremiah the prophet has pointed out, that as many believers as God has prepared for this purpose, to multiply those left upon earth, should both be under the rule of the saints to minister to this Jerusalem, and that [His] kingdom shall be in it, saying, "Look around Jerusalem towards the east, and behold the joy which comes to thee from God Himself. Behold, thy sons shall come whom thou hast sent forth: they shall come in a band from the east even unto the west, by the word of that Holy One, rejoicing in that splendour which is from thy God. O Jerusalem, put off thy robe of mourning and of affliction, and put on that beauty of eternal splendour from thy God. Gird thyself with the double garment of that righteousness proceeding from thy God; place the mitre of eternal glory upon thine head. For God will show thy glory to the whole earth under heaven. For thy name shall for ever be called by God Himself, the peace of righteousness and glory to him that worships God. Arise, Jerusalem, stand on high, and look towards the east, and behold thy sons from the rising of the sun, even to the west, by the Word of that Holy One, rejoicing in the very remembrance of

God. For the footmen have gone forth from thee, while they were drawn away by the enemy. God shall bring them in to thee, being borne with glory as the throne of a kingdom. For God has decreed that every high mountain shall be brought low, and the eternal hills, and that the valleys be filled, so that the surface of the earth be rendered smooth, that Israel, the glory of God, may walk in safety. The woods, too, shall make shady places, and every sweet-smelling tree shall be for Israel itself by the command of God. For God shall go before with joy in the light of His splendour, with the pity and righteousness which proceeds from Him."

2. Now all these things being such as they are, cannot be understood in reference to super-celestial matters; "for God," it is said, "will show to the whole earth that is under heaven thy glory." But in the times of the kingdom, the earth has been called again by Christ [to its pristine condition], and Jerusalem rebuilt after the pattern of the Jerusalem above, of which the prophet Isaiah says, "Behold, I have depicted thy walls upon my hands, and thou art always in my sight." And the apostle, too, writing to the Galatians, says in like manner, "But the Jerusalem which is above is free, which is the mother of us all." He does not say this with any thought of an erratic Æon, or of any other power which departed from the Pleroma, or of Prunicus, but of the Jerusalem which has been delineated on [God's] hands. And in the Apocalypse John saw this new [Jerusalem] descending upon the new earth. For after the times of the kingdom, he says, "I saw a great white throne, and Him who sat upon it, from whose face the earth fled away, and the heavens; and there was no more place for them." And he sets forth, too, the things connected with the general resurrection and the judgment, mentioning "the dead, great and small." "The sea," he says, "gave up the dead which it had in it, and death and hell delivered up the dead that they contained; and the books were opened. Moreover," he says, "the book of life was opened, and the dead were judged out of those things that were written in the books, according to their works; and death and hell were sent into the lake of fire, the second death." Now this is what is called Gehenna, which the Lord styled eternal fire. "And if any one," it is said, "was not found written in the book of life, he was sent into the lake of fire." And after this, he says, "I saw a new heaven and a new earth, for the first heaven and earth have passed away; also there was no more sea. And I saw the holy city, new Jerusalem, coming down from heaven, as a bride adorned for her husband." "And I heard," it is said, "a great voice from

the throne, saying, Behold, the tabernacle of God is with men, and He will dwell with them; and they shall be His people, and God Himself shall be with them as their God. And He will wipe away every tear from their eyes; and death shall be no more, neither sorrow, nor crying, neither shall there be any more pain, because the former things have passed away." Isaiah also declares the very same: "For there shall be a new heaven and a new earth; and there shall be no remembrance of the former, neither shall the heart think about them, but they shall find in it joy and exultation." Now this is what has been said by the apostle: "For the fashion of this world passeth away." To the same purpose did the Lord also declare, "Heaven and earth shall pass away." When these things, therefore, pass away above the earth, John, the Lord's disciple, says that the new Jerusalem above shall [then] descend, as a bride adorned for her husband; and that this is the tabernacle of God, in which God will dwell with men. Of this Jerusalem the former one is an image—that Jerusalem of the former earth in which the righteous are disciplined beforehand for incorruption and prepared for salvation. And of this tabernacle Moses received the pattern in the mount; and nothing is capable of being allegorized, but all things are stedfast, and true, and substantial, having been made by God for righteous men's enjoyment. For as it is God truly who raises up man, so also does man truly rise from the dead, and not allegorically, as I have shown repeatedly. And as he rises actually, so also shall he be actually disciplined beforehand for incorruption, and shall go forwards and flourish in the times of the kingdom, in order that he may be capable of receiving the glory of the Father. Then, when all things are made new, he shall truly dwell in the city of God. For it is said, "He that sitteth on the throne said, Behold, I make all things new. And the Lord says, Write all this; for these words are faithful and true. And He said to me, They are done." And this is the truth of the matter.

Chapter XXXVI.—Men shall be actually raised: the world shall not be annihilated; but there shall be various mansions for the saints, according to the rank allotted to each individual. All things shall be subject to God the Father, and so shall He be all in all.

1. For since there are real men, so must there also be a real establishment (plantationem), that they vanish not away among non- existent things, but progress among those which have an actual existence. For neither is the substance nor the essence of the creation annihilated (for faithful and true is He who has established it), but "the fashion of the world

passeth away;" that is, those things among which transgression has occurred, since man has grown old in them. And therefore this [present] fashion has been formed temporary, God foreknowing all things; as I have pointed out in the preceding book, and have also shown, as far as was possible, the cause of the creation of this world of temporal things. But when this [present] fashion [of things] passes away, and man has been renewed, and flourishes in an incorruptible state, so as to preclude the possibility of becoming old, [then] there shall be the new heaven and the new earth, in which the new man shall remain [continually], always holding fresh converse with God. And since (or, that) these things shall ever continue without end, Isaiah declares, "For as the new heavens and the new earth which I do make, continue in my sight, saith the Lord, so shall your seed and your name remain." And as the presbyters say, Then those who are deemed worthy of an abode in heaven shall go there, others shall enjoy the delights of paradise, and others shall possess the splendour of the city; for everywhere the Saviour shall be seen according as they who see Him shall be worthy.

2. [They say, moreover], that there is this distinction between the habitation of those who produce an hundred-fold, and that of those who produce sixty-fold, and that of those who produce thirty-fold: for the first will be taken up into the heavens, the second will dwell in paradise, the last will inhabit the city; and that was on this account the Lord declared, "In My Father's house are many mansions." For all things belong to God, who supplies all with a suitable dwelling- place; even as His Word says, that a share is allotted to all by the Father, according as each person is or shall be worthy. And this is the couch on which the guests shall recline, having been invited to the wedding. The presbyters, the disciples of the apostles, affirm that this is the gradation and arrangement of those who are saved, and that they advance through steps of this nature; also that they ascend through the Spirit to the Son, and through the Son to the Father, and that in due time the Son will yield up His work to the Father, even as it is said by the apostle, "For He must reign till He hath put all enemies under His feet. The last enemy that shall be destroyed is death." For in the times of the kingdom, the righteous man who is upon the earth shall then forget to die. "But when He saith, All things shall be subdued unto Him, it is manifest that He is excepted who did put all things under Him. And when all things shall be subdued unto Him, then shall the Son also Himself be subject unto Him who put all things under Him, that God may be all in all."

3. John, therefore, did distinctly foresee the first "resurrection of the just," and the inheritance in the kingdom of the earth; and what the prophets have prophesied concerning it harmonize [with his vision]. For the Lord also taught these things, when He promised that He would have the mixed cup new with His disciples in the kingdom. The apostle, too, has confessed that the creation shall be free from the bondage of corruption, [so as to pass] into the liberty of the sons of God. And in all these things, and by them all, the same God the Father is manifested, who fashioned man, and gave promise of the inheritance of the earth to the fathers, who brought it (the creature) forth [from bondage] at the resurrection of the just, and fulfils the promises for the kingdom of His Son; subsequently bestowing in a paternal manner those things which neither the eye has seen, nor the ear has heard, nor has [thought concerning them] arisen within the heart of man, For there is the one Son, who accomplished His Father's will; and one human race also in which the mysteries of God are wrought, "which the angels desire to look into;" and they are not able to search out the wisdom of God, by means of which His handiwork, confirmed and incorporated with His Son, is brought to perfection; that His offspring, the First-begotten Word, should descend to the creature (facturam), that is, to what had been moulded (plasma), and that it should be contained by Him; and, on the other hand, the creature should contain the Word, and ascend to Him, passing beyond the angels, and be made after the image and likeness of God.

EXHORTATION TO THE GREEKS

Clement of Alexandria

TRANSLATED BY ALEXANDER ROBERTS AND JAMES DONALDSON

CHAP. I.--EXHORTATION TO ABANDON THE IMPIOUS MYSTERIES OF IDOLATRY FOR THE ADORATION OF THE DIVINE WORD AND GOD THE FATHER.

AMPHION of Thebes and Arion of Methymna were both minstrels, and both were renowned in story. They are celebrated in song to this day in the chorus of the Greeks; the one for having allured the fishes, and the other for having surrounded Thebes with walls by the power of music. Another, a Thracian, a cunning master of his art (he also is the subject of a Hellenic legend), tamed the wild beasts by the mere might of song; and transplanted trees--oaks--by music. I might tell you also the story of another, a brother to these--the subject of a myth, and a minstrel--Eunomos the Locrian and the Pythic grasshopper. A solemn Hellenic assembly had met at Pytho, to celebrate the death of the Pythic serpent, when Eunomos sang the reptile's epitaph. Whether his ode was a hymn in praise of the serpent, or a dirge, I am not able to say. But there was a contest, and Eunomos was playing the lyre in the summer time: it was when the grasshoppers, warmed by the sun, were chirping beneath the leaves along the hills; but they were singing not to that dead dragon, but to God All-wise,--a lay unfettered by rule, better than the numbers of Eunomos. The Locrian breaks a string. The grasshopper sprang on the neck of the instrument, and sang on it as on a branch; and the minstrel, adapting his strain to the grasshopper's song, made up for the want of the missing string. The grasshopper then was attracted by the song of Eunomos, as the fable represents, according to which also a brazen statue of Eunomos with his lyre, and the Locrian's ally in the contest, was erected at Pytho. But of its own accord it flew to the lyre, and of its own accord sang, and was regarded by the Greeks as a musical performer.

How, let me ask, have you believed vain fables and supposed animals to be charmed by music while Truth's shining face alone, as would seem appears to you disguised, and is looked on with incredulous eyes? And so Cithaeron, and Helicon, and the mountains of the Odrysi, and the initiatory rites of the Thracians, mysteries of deceit, are hallowed and celebrated in hymns. For me, I am pained at such calamities as form the subjects of tragedy, though but myths; but by you the records of miseries are turned into dramatic compositions.

But the dramas and the raving poets, now quite intoxicated, let us crown with ivy; and distracted outright as they are, in Bacchic fashion, with the satyrs, and the frenzied rabble, and the rest of the demon crew, let us confine to Cithaeron and Helicon, now antiquated.

But let us bring from above out of heaven, Truth, with Wisdom in all its brightness, and the sacred prophetic choir, down to the holy mount of God; and let Truth, darting her light to the most distant points, cast her rays all around on those that are involved in darkness, and deliver men from delusion, stretching out her very strong right hand, which is wisdom, for their salvation. And raising their eyes, and looking above, let them abandon Helicon and Cithaeron, and take up their abode in Sion. "For out of Sion shall go forth the law, and the word of the LORD from Jerusalem, --the celestial Word, the true athlete crowned in the theatre of the whole universe. What my Eunomos sings is not the measure of Terpander, nor that of Capito, nor the Phrygian, nor Lydian, nor Dorian, but the immortal measure of the new harmony which bears God's name--the new, the Levitical song.

"Soother of pain, calmer of wrath, producing forgetfulness of all ills."

Sweet and true is the charm of persuasion which blends with this strain.

To me, therefore, that Thracian Orpheus, that Theban, and that Methymnaean,--men, and yet unworthy of the name,--seem to have been deceivers, who, under the pretence of poetry corrupting human life, possessed by a spirit of artful sorcery for purposes of destruction, celebrating crimes in their orgies, and making human woes the materials of religious worship, were the first to entice men to idols; nay, to build up the stupidity of the nations with blocks of wood and stone,--that is, statues and images,--subjecting to the yoke of extremest bondage the truly noble freedom of those who lived as free citizens under heaven by their songs and incantations. But not such is my song, which has come to loose, and that speedily, the bitter bondage of tyrannizing demons; and leading us back to the mild and loving yoke of piety, recalls to heaven those that had been cast prostrate to the earth. It alone has tamed men, the most intractable of animals; the frivolous among them answering to the fowls of the air, deceivers to reptiles, the irascible to lions, the voluptuous to swine, the rapacious to wolves. The silly are stocks and stones, and still more senseless than stones is a man who is steeped in ignorance. As our witness, let us adduce the voice of prophecy accordant with truth, and bewailing those who are crushed in ignorance and folly: "For God is able of these stones to raise up children to Abraham;" and He, commiserating their great ignorance and hardness of heart who are petrified against the truth, has raised up a seed of piety, sensitive to virtue, of those stones--of the nations, that is, who trusted in stones. Again, therefore, some venomous and false hypocrites, who plotted against righteousness, He once called "a brood of vipers." But if one of those serpents even is willing to repent, and follows the Word, he becomes a man of God.

Others he figuratively calls wolves, clothed in sheep-skins, meaning thereby monsters of rapacity in human form. And so all such most savage beasts, and all such blocks of stone, the celestial song has transformed into tractable men. "For even we ourselves were sometime foolish, disobedient, deceived, serving divers lusts and pleasures, living in malice and envy, hateful, hating one another." Thus speaks the apostolic Scripture: "But after that the kindness and love of God our saviour to man appeared, not by works of righteousness which we have done, but according to His mercy, He saved us."

Behold the might of the new song! It has made men out of stones, men out of beasts. Those, moreover, that were as dead, not being partakers of the true life, have come to life again, simply by becoming listeners to this song. It also composed the universe into melodious order, and tuned the discord of the elements to harmonious arrangement, so that the whole world might become harmony. It let loose the fluid ocean, and yet has prevented it from encroaching on the land. The earth, again, which had been in a state of commotion, it has established, and fixed the sea as its boundary. The violence of fire it has softened by the atmosphere, as the Dorian is blended with the Lydian strain; and the harsh cold of the air it has moderated by the embrace of fire, harmoniously arranging these the extreme tones of the universe. And this deathless strain,the support of the whole and the harmony of all,--reaching from the centre to the circumference, and from the extremities to the central part, has harmonized this universal frame of things, not according to the Thracian music, which is like that invented by Jubal, but according to the paternal counsel of God, which fired the zeal of David. And He who is of David, and yet before him, the Word of God, despising the lyre and harp, which are but lifeless instruments, and having tuned by the Holy Spirit the universe, and especially man,--who, composed of body and soul, is a universe in miniature,makes melody to God on this instrument of many tones; and to this intrument--I mean man-- he sings accordant: "For thou art my harp, and pipe, and temple." -- a harp for harmony--a pipe by reason of the Spirit a temple by reason of the word; so that the first may sound, the second breathe, the third contain the Lord. And David the king, the harper whom we mentioned a little above, who exhorted to the truth and dissuaded from idols, was so far from celebrating demons in song, that in reality they were driven away by his music. Thus, when Saul was plagued with a demon, he cured him by merely playing. A beautiful breathing instrument of music the Lord made man, after His own image. And He Himself also, surely, who is the supramundane Wisdom, the celestial Word, is the all-harmonious, melodious, holy instrument of God. What, then, does this instrument--the Word of God, the Lord, the New Song--desire? To open the eyes of the blind, and unstop the ears of the deaf, and to lead the lame or the erring to righteousness, to exhibit God to the foolish, to put a stop to corruption, to conquer death, to reconcile disobedient children to their father. The instrument of God loves mankind. The Lord pities, instructs, exhorts, admonishes, saves, shields, and of His bounty promises us the kingdom of heaven as a reward for learning; and the only advantage He reaps is, that we are saved. For wickedness feeds on men's destruction; but truth, like the bee, harming nothing, delights only in the salvation of men.

You have, then, God's promise; you have His love: become partaker of His grace. And do not suppose the song of salvation to be new, as a vessel or a house is new. For "before the morning star it was;" 'and "in the beginning was the Word, and the Word was with God, and the Word was God." Error seems old, but truth seems a new thing.

Whether, then, the Phrygians are shown to be the most ancient people by the goats of the fable; or, on the other hand, the Arcadians by the poets, who describe them as older than the moon; or, finally, the Egyptians by those who dream that this land first gave birth to gods and men: yet none of these at least existed before the world. But before the foundation of the world were we, who, because destined to be in Him, pre-existed in the eye of God before,--we the rational creatures of the Word of God, on whose account we date from the beginning; for "in the beginning was the Word." Well, inasmuch as the Word was from the first, He was and is the divine source of all things; but inasmuch as He has now assumed the name Christ, consecrated of old, and worthy of power, he has been called by me the New Song. This Word, then, the Christ, the cause of both our being at first (for He was in God) and of our well-being, this very Word has now appeared as man, He alone being both, both God and man--the Author of all blessings to us; by whom we, being taught to live well, are sent on our way to life eternal. For, according to that inspired apostle of the Lord, "the grace of God which bringeth salvation hath appeared to all men, teaching us, that, denying ungodliness and worldly lusts, we should live soberly, righteously, and godly, in this present world; looking for the blessed hope, and appearing of the glory of the great God and our Saviour Jesus Christ."

This is the New Song, the manifestation of the Word that was in the beginning, and before the beginning. The Saviour, who existed before, has in recent days appeared. He, who is in Him that truly is, has appeared; for the Word, who "was with God," and by whom all things were created, has appeared as our Teacher. The Word, who in the beginning bestowed on us life as Creator when He formed us, taught us to live well when He appeared as our Teacher; that as God He might afterwards conduct us to the life which never ends. He did not now for the first time pity us for our error; but He pitied us from the first, from the beginning. But now, at His appearance, lost as we already were, He accomplished our salvation. For that wicked reptile monster, by his enchantments, enslaves and plagues men even till now; inflicting, as seems to me, such barbarous vengeance on them as those who are said to bind the captives to corpses till they rot together. This wicked tyrant and serpent, accordingly, binding fast with the miserable chain of superstition whomsoever he can draw to his side from their birth, to stones, and stocks, and images, and such like idols, may with truth be said to have taken and buried living men with those dead idols, till both suffer corruption together.

Therefore (for the seducer is one and the same) he that at the beginning brought Eve down to death, now brings thither the rest of mankind. Our ally and helper, too, is one and the same--the Lord, who from the beginning gave revelations by prophecy, but now plainly calls to salvation. In obedience to the apostolic injunction, therefore, let us flee from "the prince of the power of the air, the spirit that now worketh in the children of disobedience," and let us run to the Lord the saviour, who now exhorts to salvation, as He has ever done, as He did by signs and wonders in Egypt and the desert, both by the bush and the cloud, which, through the favour of divine love, attended the Hebrews like a handmaid. By the fear which these inspired He addressed the hard-hearted; while by Moses, learned in all wisdom, and Isaiah, lover of truth, and the whole prophetic choir, in a way appealing more to reason, He turns to the Word those who have ears to hear. Sometimes He upbraids, and sometimes He threatens. Some men He mourns over, others He addresses with the voice of song, just as a good physician treats some of his patients with cataplasms, some with rubbing, some with fomentations; in one case cuts open with the lancet, in another cauterizes, in another amputates, in order if possible to cure the patient's diseased part or member. The Saviour has many tones of voice, and many methods for the salvation of men; by threatening He admonishes, by upbraiding He converts, by bewailing He pities, by the voice of song He cheers. He spake by the burning bush, for the men of that day needed signs and wonders.

He awed men by the fire when He made flame to burst from the pillar of cloud--a token at once of grace and fear: if you obey, there is the light; if you disobey, there is the fire; but. since humanity is nobler than the pillar or the bush, after them the prophets uttered their voice,--the Lord Himself speaking in Isaiah, in Elias,--speaking Himself by the mouth of the prophets. But if thou dost not believe the prophets, but supposest both the men and the fire a myth, the Lord Himself shall speak to thee, "who, being in the form of God, thought it not robbery to be equal with God, but humbled Himself," --He, the merciful God, exerting Himself to save man. And now the Word Himself clearly speaks to thee, Shaming thy unbelief; yea, I say, the Word of God became man, that thou mayest learn from man how man may become God. Is it not then monstrous, my friends, that while God is ceaselessly exhorting us to virtue, we should spurn His kindness and reject salvation?

Does not John also invite to salvation, and is he not entirely a voice of exhortation? Let us then ask him, "Who of men art thou, and whence?" He will not say Elias. He will deny that he is Christ, but will profess himself to be "a voice crying in the wilderness." Who, then, is John? In a word, we may say, "The beseeching voice of the Word crying in the wilderness." What criest thou, O voice? Tell us also. "Make straight the paths of the LORD." John is the forerunner, and that voice the precursor of the Word; an inviting voice, preparing for salvation,--a voice urging men on to the inheritance of the heavens, and through which the barren and the desolate is childless no more. This fecundity the angel's voice foretold; and this voice was also the precursor of the Lord preaching glad tidings to the barren woman, as John did to the wilderness. By reason of this voice of the Word, therefore, the barren woman bears children, and the desert becomes fruitful. The two voices which heralded the Lord's--that of the angel and that of John--intimate, as I think, the salvation in store for us to be, that on the appearance of this Word we should reap, as the fruit of this productiveness, eternal life. The Scripture makes this all clear, by referring both the voices to the same thing: "Let her hear who has not brought forth, and let her who has not had the pangs of childbirth utter her voice: for more are the children of the desolate, than of her who hath an husband."

The angel announced to us the glad tidings of a husband. John entreated us to recognise the husbandman, to seek the husband. For this husband of the barren woman, and this husbandman of the desert--who filled with divine power the barren woman and the desert--is one and the same. For because many were the children of the mother of noble rule, yet the Hebrew woman, once blessed with many children, was made childless because of unbelief: the barren woman receives the husband, and the desert the husbandman; then both become mothers through the word, the one of fruits, the other of believers. But to the Unbelieving the barren and the desert are still reserved. For this reason John, the herald of the Word, besought men to make themselves ready against the coming of the Christ Of God. And it was this which was signified by the dumbness of Zacharias, which waited for fruit in the person of the harbinger of Christ, that the Word, the light of truth, by becoming the Gospel, might break the mystic silence of the prophetic enigmas. But if thou desirest truly to see God, take to thyself means of purification worthy of Him, not leaves of laurel fillets interwoven. with wool and purple; but wreathing thy brows with righteousness, and encircling them with the leaves of temperance, set thyself earnestly to find Christ. "For I am," He says, "the door," which we who desire to understand God must discover, that He may throw heaven's gates wide open to. us. For the gates of the Word being intellectual, are opened by the key of faith. No one knows God but the Son, and he to whom the Son shall reveal Him. And I know well that He who has opened the door hitherto shut, will afterwards reveal what is within; and will show what we could not have known before, had we not entered in by Christ, through whom alone God is beheld.

CHAP. II.--THE ABSURDITY AND IMPIETY OF THE HEATHEN MYSTERIES AND FABLES ABOUT THE BIRTH AND DEATH OF THEIR GODS.

Explore not then too curiously the shrines of impiety, or the mouths of caverns full of monstrosity, or the Thesprotian caldron, or the Cirrhaean tripod, or the Dodonian copper. The Gerandryon, once regarded sacred in the midst of desert sands, and the oracle there gone to decay with the oak itself, consigned to the region of antiquated fables. The fountain of Castalia is silent, and the other fountain of Colophon; and, in like manner, all the rest of the springs of divination are dead, and stripped of their vainglory, although at a late date, are shown with their fabulous legends to have run dry. Recount to us also the useless oracles of that other kind of divination, or rather madness, the Clarian, the Pythian, the Didymaean, that of Amphiaraus, of Apollo, of Amphilochus; and if you will, couple with them the expounders of prodigies, the augurs, and the interpreters of dreams. And bring and place beside the Pythian those that divine by flour, and those that divine by barley, and the ventriloquists still held in honour by many. Let the secret shrines of the Egyptians and the necromancies of the Etruscans be consigned to darkness. Insane devices truly are they all of unbelieving men. Goats, too, have been confederates in this art of soothsaying, trained to divination; and crows taught by men to give oracular responses to men.

And what if I go over the mysteries? I will not divulge them in mockery, as they say Alcibiades did, but I will expose right well by the word of truth the sorcery hidden in them; and those so-called gods of yours, whose are the mystic rites, I shall display, as it were, on the stage of life, to the spectators of truth. The bacchanals hold their orgies in honour of the frenzied Dionysus, celebrating their sacred frenzy by the eating of raw flesh, and go through the distribution of the parts of butchered victims, crowned with snakes, shrieking out the name of that Eva by whom error came into the world. The symbol of the Bacchic orgies. is a consecrated serpent. Moreover, according to the strict interpretation of the Hebrew term, the name Hevia, aspirated, signifies a female serpent.

Demeter and Proserpine have become the heroines of a mystic drama; and their wanderings, and seizure, and grief, Eleusis celebrates by torchlight processions. I think that the derivation of orgies and mysteries ought to be traced, the former to the wrath (orgh) of Demeter against Zeus, the latter to the nefarious wickedness (musos) relating to Dionysus; but if from Myus of Attica, who Pollodorus says was killed in hunting--no matter, I don't grudge your mysteries the glory of funeral honours. You may understand mysteria in another way, as mytheria (hunting fables), the letters of the two words being interchanged; for certainly fables of this sort hunt after the most barbarous of the Thracians, the most senseless of the Phrygians, and the superstitious among the Greeks.

Perish, then, the man who was the author of this imposture among men, be he Dardanus, who taught the mysteries of the mother of the gods, or Eetion, who instituted the orgies and mysteries of the Samothracians, or that Phrygian Midas who, having learned the cunning imposture from Odrysus, communicated it to his subjects. For I will never be persuaded by that Cyprian Islander Cinyras, who dared to bring forth from night to the light of day the lewd orgies of Aphrodite in his eagerness to deify a strumpet of his own country. Others say that Melampus the son of Amythaon imported the festivals of Ceres from Egypt into Greece, celebrating her grief in song.

These I would instance as the prime authors of evil, the parents of impious fables and of deadly superstition, who sowed in human life that seed of evil and ruin--the mysteries.

And now, for it is time, I will prove their orgies to be full of imposture and quackery. And if you have been initiated, you will laugh all the more at these fables of yours which have been held in honour. I publish without reserve what has been involved in secrecy, not ashamed to tell what you are not ashamed to worship.

There is then the foam-born and Cyprus-born, the darling of Cinyras,--I mean Aphrodite, lover of the virilia, because sprung from them, even from those of Uranus, that were cut off,--those lustful members, that, after being cut off, offered violence to the waves. Of members so lewd a worthy fruit--Aphrodite--is born. In the rites which celebrate this enjoyment of the sea, as a symbol of her birth a lump of suit and the phallus are handed to those who are initiated into the art of uncleanness. And those initiated bring a piece of money to her, as a courtesan's paramours do to her, Then there are the mysteries of Demeter, and Zeus's wanton embraces of his mother, and the wrath of Demeter; I know not what for the future I shall call her, mother or wife, on which account it is that she is called Brimo, as is said; also the entreaties of Zeus, and the drink of gall, the plucking out of the hearts of sacrifices, and deeds that we dare not name. Such rites the Phrygians perform in honour of Attis and Cybele and the Corybantes. And the story goes, that

Zeus, having torn away the orchites of a ram, brought them out and cast them at the breasts of Demeter, paying thus a fraudulent penalty for his violent embrace, pretending to have cut out his own. The symbols of initiation into these rites, when set before you in a vacant hour, I know will excite your laughter, although on account of the exposure by no means inclined to laugh. "I have eaten out of the drum, I have drunk out of the cymbal, I have carried the Cernos, I have slipped into the bedroom." Are not these tokens a disgrace? Are not the mysteries absurdity?

What if I add the rest? Demeter becomes a mother, Core is reared up to womanhood. And, in course of time, he who begot her,--this same Zeus has intercourse with his own daughter Pherephatta,--after Ceres, the mother,--forgetting his former abominable wickedness. Zeus is both the father and the seducer of Core, and shamefully courts her in the shape of a dragon; his identity, however, was discovered. The token of the Sabazian mysteries to the initiated is "the deity gliding over the breast,"--the deity being this serpent crawling over the breasts of the initiated. Proof surely this of the unbridled lust of Zeus.

Pherephatta has a child, though, to be sure, in the form of a bull, as an idolatrous poet says,- "The bull The dragon's father, and the father of the bull the dragon, On shill the herdsman's hidden ox-goad,"- alluding, as I believe, under the name of the herdsman's ox-goad, to the reed wielded by bacchanals. Do you wish me to go into the story of Persephatta's gathering of flowers, her basket, and her seizure by Pluto (Aidoneus), and the rent in the earth, and the swine of Eubouleus that were swallowed up with the two goddesses; for which reason, in the Thesmophoria, speaking the Megaric tongue, they thrust out swine? This mythological story the women celebrate variously in different cities in the festivals called Thesmophoria and Scirophoria; dramatizing in many forms the rape of Pherephatta or Persephatta (Proserpine).

The mysteries of Dionysus are wholly inhuman; for while still a child, and the Curetes danced around [his cradle] clashing their weapons, and the Titans having come upon them by stealth, and having beguiled him with childish toys, these very Titans tore him limb from limb when but a child, as the bard of this mystery, the Thracian Orpheus, says:- "Cone, and spinning-top, and limb-moving rattles, And fair golden apples from the clear-toned Hesperides."

And the useless symbols of this mystic rite it will not be useless to exhibit for condemnation. These are dice, ball, hoop, apples, top, looking-glass, tuft of wool.

Athene (Minerva), to resume our account, having abstracted the heart of Dionysus, was called Pallas, from the vibrating of the heart; and the Titans who had torn him limb from limb, setting a caldron on a tripod, and throwing into it the members of Dionysus, first boiled them down, and then fixing them on spits, "held them over the fire." But Zeus having appeared, since he was a god, having speedily perceived the savour of the pieces of flesh that were being cooked,-- that savour which your gods agree to have assigned to them as their perquisite,assails the Titans with his thunderbolt, and consigns the members of Dionysus to his son Apollo to be interred. And he—for he did not disobey Zeus--bore the dismembered corpse to Parnassus, and there deposited it.

If you wish to inspect the orgies of the Corybantes, then know that, having killed their third brother, they covered the head of the dead body with a purple cloth, crowned it, and carrying it on the point of a spear, buried it under the roots of Olympus. These mysteries are, in short, murders and funerals. And the priests of these rites, who are called kings of the sacred rites by those whose business it is to name them, give additional strangeness to the tragic occurrence, by forbidding parsley with the roots from being placed on the table, for they think that parsley grew from the Corybantic blood that flowed forth; just as the women, in celebrating the Thesmophoria, abstain from eating the seeds of the pomegranate which have fallen on the ground, from the idea that pomegranates sprang from the drops of the blood of Dionysus. Those Corybantes also they call Cabiric; and the ceremony itself they announce as the Cabiric mystery.

For those two identical fratricides, having abstracted the box in which the phallus of Bacchus was deposited, took it to Etruria-- dealers in honourable wares truly. They lived there as exiles, employing themselves in communicating the precious teaching of their superstition, and presenting phallic symbols and the box for the Tyrrhenians to worship. And some will have it, not improbably, that for this reason Dionysus was called Attis, because he was mutilated. And what is surprising at the Tyrrhenians, who were barbarians, being thus initiated into these foul indignities, when among the Athenians, and in the whole of Greece--I blush to say it--the shameful legend about Demeter holds its ground? For Demeter, wandering in quest of her daughter Core, broke down with fatigue near Eleusis, a place in Attica, and sat down on a well overwhelmed with grief. This is even now prohibited to those who are initiated, lest they should appear to mimic the weeping goddess. The indigenous inhabitants then occupied Eleusis: their names were Baubo, and Dusaules, and Triptolemus; and besides, Eumolpus and Eubouleus. Triptolemus was a herdsman, Eumolpus a shepherd, and Eubouleus a swineherd; from whom came the race of the Eumolpidae and that of the Heralds--a race of Hierophants--who flourished at Athens.

Well, then (for I shall not refrain from the recital), Baubo having received Demeter hospitably, reaches to her a refreshing draught; and on her refusing it, not having any inclination to drink (for she was very sad), and Baubo having become annoyed, thinking herself slighted, uncovered her shame, and exhibited her nudity to the goddess. Demeter is delighted at the sight, and takes, though with difficulty, the draught-pleased, I repeat, at the spectacle. These are the secret mysteries of the Athenians; these Orpheus records. I shall produce the very words of Orpheus, that you may have the great authority on the mysteries himself, as evidence for this piece of turpitude:- "Having thus spoken, she drew aside her garments, And showed all that shape of the body which it is improper to name, And with her own hand Baubo stripped herself under the breasts.

Blandly then the goddess laughed and laughed in her mind, And received the glancing cup in which was the draught."

And the following is the token of the Eleusinian mysteries: I have fasted, I have drunk the cup; I have received from the box; having done, I put it into the basket, and out of the basket into the chest. Fine sights truly, and becoming a goddess; mysteries worthy of the night, and flame, and the magnanimous or rather silly people of the Erechthidae, and the other Greeks besides, "whom a fate they hope not for awaits after death." And in truth against these Heraclitus the Ephesian prophesies, as "the night-walkers, the magi, the bacchanals, the Lenaean revellers, the initiated." These he threatens with what will follow death, and predicts for them fire. For what are regarded among men as mysteries, they celebrate sacrilegiously. Law, then, and opinion, are nugatory. And the mysteries of the dragon are an imposture, which celebrates religiously mysteries that are no mysteries at all, and observes with a spurious piety profane rites. What are these mystic chests?--for I must expose their sacred things, and divulge things not fit for speech. Are they not sesame cakes, and pyramidal cakes, and globular and flat cakes, embossed all over, and lumps of salt, and a serpent the symbol of Dionysus Bassareus? And besides these, are they not pomegranates, and branches, and rods, and ivy leaves? and besides, round cakes and poppy seeds? And further, there are the unmentionable symbols of Themis, marjoram, a lamp, a sword, a woman's comb, which is a euphemism and mystic expression for the muliebria.

O unblushing shamelessness! Once on a time night was silent, a veil for the pleasure of temperate men; but now for the initiated, the holy night is the tell-tale of the rites of licentiousness; and the glare of torches reveals vicious indulgences. Quench the flame, O Hierophant; reverence, O Torch-bearer, the torches. That light exposes Iacchus; let thy mysteries be honoured, and command the orgies to be hidden in night and darkness.

The fire dissembles not; it exposes and punishes what it is bidden.

Such are the mysteries of the Atheists. And with reason I call those Atheists who know not the true God, and pay shameless worship to a boy torn in pieces by the Titans, and a woman in distress, and to parts of the body that in truth cannot be mentioned for shame, held fast as they are in the double impiety, first in that they know not God, not acknowledging as God Him who truly is; the other and second is the error of regarding those who exist not, as existing and calling those gods that have no real existence, or rather no existence at all, who have nothing but a name. Wherefore the apostle reproves us, saying, "And ye were strangers to the covenants of promise, having no hope, and without God in the world."

All honour to that king of the Scythians, whoever Anacharsis was, who shot with an arrow one of his subjects who imitated among the Scythians the mystery of the Mother of the gods, as practised by the inhabitants of Cyzicus, beating a drum and sounding a cymbal strung from his neck like a priest of Cybele, condemning him as having become effeminate among the Greeks, and a teacher of the disease of effeminacy to the rest of the Cythians.

Wherefore (for I must by no means conceal it) I cannot help wondering how Euhemerus of Agrigentum, and Nicanor of Cyprus, and Diagoras, and Hippo of Melos, and besides these, that Cyrenian of the name of Theodorus, and numbers of others, who lived a sober life, and had a clearer insight than the rest of the world into the prevailing error respecting those gods, were called Atheists; for if they did not arrive at the knowledge of the truth, they certainly suspected the error of the common opinion; which suspicion is no insignificant seed, and becomes the germ of true wisdom. One of these charges the Egyptians thus: "If you believe them to be gods, do not mourn or bewail them; and if you mourn and bewail them, do not any more regard them as gods." And another, taking an image of Hercules made of wood (for he happened most likely to be cooking something at home), said, "Come now, Hercules; now is the time to undergo for us this thirteenth labour, as you did the twelve for Eurystheus, and make this ready for Diagoras," and so cast it into the fire as a log of wood. For the extremes of ignorance are atheism and superstition, from which we must endeavour to keep. And do you not see Moses, the hierophant of the truth, enjoining that no eunuch, or emasculated man, or son of a harlot, should enter the congregation? By the two first he alludes to the impious custom by which men were deprived both of divine energy and of their virility; and by the third, to him who, in place of the only real God, assumes many gods falsely so called,--as the son of a harlot, in ignorance of his true father, may claim many putative fathers.

There was an innate original communion between men and heaven, obscured through ignorance, but which now at length has leapt forth instantaneously from the darkness, and shines resplendent; as has been expressed by one in the following lines:- "See'st thou this lofty, this boundless ether, Holding the earth in the embrace of its humid arms."

And in these:- "O Thou, who makest the earth Thy chariot, and in the earth hast Thy seat, Whoever Thou be, baffling our efforts to behold Thee."

And whatever else the sons of the poets sing.

But sentiments erroneous, and deviating from what is right, and certainly pernicious, have turned man, a creature of heavenly origin, away from the heavenly life, and stretched him on the earth, by inducing him to cleave to earthly objects. For some, beguiled by the contemplation of the heavens, and trusting to their sight alone, while they looked on the motions of the stars, straightway were seized with admiration, and deified them, calling the stars gods from their motion (qeos from qein); and worshipped the sun,--as, for example, the Indians; and the moon, as the Phrygians. Others, plucking the benignant fruits of earth-born plants, called grain Demeter, as the Athenians, and the vine Dionysus, as the Thebans. Others, considering the penalties of wickedness, deified them, worshipping various forms of retribution and calamity. Hence the Erinnyes, and the Eumenides, and the piacular deities, and the judges and avengers of crime, are the creations of the tragic poets. And some even of the philosophers, after the poets, make idols of forms of the affections in your breasts,--such as fear, and love, and joy, and hope; as, to be sure, Epimenides of old, who raised ar Athens the altars of Insult and Impudence. Other objects deified by men take their rise from events, and are fashioned in bodily shape, such as a Dike, a Clotho, and Lachesis, and Atropos, and Heimarmene, and Auxo, and Thallo, which are Attic goddesses. There is a sixth mode of introducing error and of manufacturing gods, according to which they number the twelve gods, whose birth is the theme of which Hesiod sings in his Theogony, and of whom Homer speaks in all that he says of the gods. The last mode remains (for there are seven in all)--that which takes its rise from the divine beneficence towards men. For, not understanding that it is God that does us good, they have invented saviours in the persons of the Dioscuri, and Hercules the averter of evil, and Asclepius the healer. These are the slippery and hurtful deviations from the truth which draw man down from heaven, and cast him into the abyss. I wish to show thoroughly what like these gods of yours are, that now at length you may abandon your delusion, and speed your flight back to heaven. "For we also were once children of wrath, even as others; but God, being rich in mercy, for the great love wherewith He loved us, when we were now dead in trespasses, quickened us together with Christ." For the Word is living, and having been buried with Christ, is exalted with God. But those who are still unbelieving are called children of wrath, reared for wrath. We who have been rescued from error, and restored to the truth, are no longer the nurslings of wrath. Thus, therefore, we who were once the children of lawlessness, have through the philanthropy of the Word now become the sons of God.

But to you a poet of your own, Empedocles of Agrigentum, comes and says:- "Wherefore, distracted with grievous evils, You will never ease your soul of its miserable woes."

The most of what is told of your gods is fabled and invented; and those things which are supposed to have taken place, are recorded of vile men who lived licentious lives:- "You walk in pride and madness, And leaving the right and straight path, you have gone away Through thorns and briars. Why do ye wander?

Cease, foolish men, from mortals; Leave the darkness of night, and lay hold on the light." These counsels the Sibyl, who is at once prophetic and poetic, enjoins on us; and truth enjoins them on us too, stripping the crowd of deities of those terrifying and threatening masks of theirs, disproving the rash opinions formed of them by showing the similarity of names. For there are those who reckon three Jupiters: him of Aether in Arcadia, and the other two sons of Kronos; and of these, one in Crete, and the others again in Arcadia. And there are those that reckon five Athenes: the Athenian, the daughter of Hephaestus; the second, the Egyptian, the daughter of Nilus; the third the inventor of war, the daughter of Kronos; the fourth, the daughter of Zeus, whom the Messenians have named Coryphasia, from her mother; above all, the daughter of Pallas and Titanis, the daughter of Oceanus, who, having wickedly killed her father, adorned herself with her father's skin, as if it had been the fleece of a sheep. Further, Aristotle calls the first Apollo, the son of Hephaestus and Athene (consequently Athene is no more a virgin); the second, that in Crete, the son of Corybas; the third, the son Zeus; the fourth, the Arcadian, the son of Silenus (this one is called by the Arcadians Nomius); and in addition to these, he specifies the Libyan Apollo, the son of Ammon; and to these Didymus the grammarian adds a sixth, the son of Magnes. And now how many Apollos are there? They are numberless, mortal men, all helpers of their fellow-men who similarly with those already mentioned have been so called. And what were I to mention the many Asclepiuses, or all the Mercuries that are reckoned up, or the Vulcans of fable? Shall I not appear extravagant, deluging your ears with these numerous names?

At any rate, the native countries of your gods, and their arts and lives, and besides especially their sepulchres, demonstrate them to have been men. Mars, accordingly, who by the poets is held in the highest possible honour:- "Mars, Mars, bane of men, blood-stained stormer of walls," - this deity, always changing sides, and implacable, as Epicharmus says, was a Spartan; Sophocles knew him for a Thracian; others say he was an Arcadian. This god, Homer says, was bound thirteen months:- "Mars had his suffering; by Aloeus' sons, Otus and Ephialtes, strongly bound, He thirteen months in brazen fetters lay."

Good luck attend the Carians, who sacrifice dogs to him! And may the Scythians never leave off sacrificing asses, as Apollodorus and Callimachus relate:- "Phoebus rises propitious to the Hyperboreans, Then they offer sacrifices of asses to him."

And the same in another place:- "Fat sacrifices of asses' flesh delight Phoebus."

Hephaestus, whom Jupiter cast from Olympus, from its divine threshold, having fallen on Lemnos, practised the art of working in brass, maimed in his feet:- "His tottering knees were bowed beneath his weight."

You have also a doctor, and not only a brass-worker among the gods. And the doctor was greedy of gold; Asclepius was his name. I shall produce as a witness your own poet, the Boeotian Pindar:- "Him even the gold glittering in his hands, Amounting to a splendid fee, persuaded To rescue a man, already death's capture, from his grasp; But Saturnian Jove, having shot his bolt through both, Quickly took the breath from their breasts, And his flaming thunderbolt sealed their doom."

And Euripides:- "For Zeus was guilty of the murder of my son Asclepius, by casting the lightning flame at his breast."

He therefore lies struck with lightning in the regions of Cynosuris. Philochorus also says, that Poseidon was worshipped as a physician in Tenos; and that Kronos settled in Sicily, and there was buried. Patroclus the Thurian, and Sophocles the younger, in three tragedies, have told the story of the Dioscuri; and these Dioscuri were only two mortals, if Homer is worthy of of credit:- " . . . . . . but they beneath the teeming earth, In Lacedaemon lay, their native land." And, in addition, he who wrote the Cyprian poems says Castor was mortal, and death was decreed to him by fate; but Pollux was immortal, being the progeny of Mars. This he has poetically fabled. But Homer is more worthy of credit, who spoke as above of both the Dioscuri; and, besides, proved Herucles to be a mere phantom:- "The man Hercules, expert in mighty deeds."

Hercules, therefore, was known by Homer himself as only a mortal man. And Hieronymus the philosopher describes the make of his body, as tall, bristling-haired, robust; and Dicaearchus says that he was square-built, muscular, dark, hook-nosed, with greyish eyes and long hair. This Hercules, accordingly, after living fifty-two years, came to his end, and was burned in a funeral pyre in OEta. As for the Muses, whom Alcander calls the daughters of Zeus and Mnemosyne, and the rest of the poets and authors deify and worship,-those Muses, in honour of whom whole states have already erected museums, being handmaids, were hired by Megaclo, the daughter of Macar. This Macar reigned over the Lesbians, and was always quarrelling with his wife; and Megaclo was vexed for her mother's sake. What would she not do on her account? Accordingly she hires those handmaids, being so many in number, and calls them Mysae, according to the dialect of the Aeolians. These she taught to sing deeds of the olden time, and play melodiously on the lyre. And they, by assiduously playing the lyre, and singing sweetly to it, soothed Macar, and put a stop to his ill-temper. Wherefore Megaclo, as a token of gratitude to them, on her mother's account erected brazen pillars, and ordered them to be held in honour in all the temples. Such, then, are the Muses. This account is in Myrsilus of Lesbos.

And now, then, hear the loves of your gods, and the incredible tales of their licentiousness, and their wounds, and their bonds, and their laughings, and their fights, their servitudes too, and their banquets; and furthermore, their embraces, and tears, and sufferings, and lewd delights. Call me Poseidon, and the troop of damsels deflowered by him, Amphitrite Amymone, Alope, Melanippe, Alcyone, Hippothoe, Chione, and myriads of others; with whom, though so many, the passions of your Poseidon were not satiated.

Call me Apollo; this is Phoebus, both a holy prophet and a good adviser. But Sterope will not say that, nor Aethousa, nor Arsinoe, nor Zeuxippe, nor Prothoe, nor Marpissa, nor Hypsipyle. For Daphne alone escaped the prophet and seduction.

And, above all, let the father of gods and men, according to you, himself come, who was so given to sexual pleasure, as to lust after all, and indulge his lust on all, like the goats of the Thmuitae. And thy poems, O Homer, fill me with admiration!

"He said, and nodded with his shadowy brows; Waved on the immortal head the ambrosial locks, And all Olympus trembled at his nod."

Thou makest Zeus venerable, O Homer; and the nod which thou dost ascribe to him is most reverend. But show him only a woman's girdle, and Zeus is exposed, and his locks are dishonoured. To what a pitch of licentiousness did that Zeus of yours proceed, who spent so many nights in voluptuousness with Alcmene? For not even these nine nights were long to this insatiable monster. But, on the contrary, a whole lifetime were short enough for his lust; that he might beget for us the evil-averting god.

Hercules, the son of Zeus--a true son of Zeus--was the offspring of that long night, who with hard toil accomplished the twelve labours in a long time, but in one night deflowered the fifty daughters of Thestius, and thus was at once the debaucher and the bridegroom of so many virgins. It is not, then, without reason that the poets call him a cruel wretch and a nefarious scoundrel. It were tedious to recount his adulteries of all sorts, and debauching of boys. For your gods did not even abstain from boys, one having loved Hylas, another Hyacinthus, another Pelops, another Chrysippus, and another Ganymede. Let such gods as these be worshipped by your wives, and let them pray that their husbands be such as these--so temperate; that, emulating them in the same practices, they may be like the gods. Such gods let your boys be trained to worship, that they may grow up to be men with the accursed likeness of fornication on them received from the gods.

But it is only the male deities, perhaps, that are impetuous in sexual indulgence.

"The female deities stayed each in the house, for shame," says Homer; the goddesses blushing, for modesty's sake, to look on Aphrodite when she had been guilty of adultery. But these are more passionately licentious, bound in the chains of adultery; Eos having disgraced herself with Tithonus, Selene with Endymion, Nereis with Aeacus, Thetis with Peleus, Demeter with Jason, Persephatta with Adonis. And Aphrodite having disgraced herself with Ares, crossed over to Cinyra and married Anchises, and laid snares for Phaethon, and loved Adonis. She contended with the ox-eyed Juno; and the goddesses un-robed for the sake of the apple, and presented themselves naked before the shepherd, that he might decide which was the fairest.

The gods Sexual Sins

But come, let us briefly go the round of the games, and do away with those solemn assemblages at tombs, the Isthmian, Nemean, and Pythian, and finally the Olympian. At Pytho the Pythian dragon is worshipped, and the festival-assemblage of the serpent is called by the name Pythia. At the Isthmus the sea spit out a piece of miserable refuse; and the Isthmian games bewail Melicerta.

At Nemea another--a little boy, Archemorus--was buried; and the funeral games of the child are called Nemea. Pisa is the grave of the Phrygian charioteer, O Hellenes of all tribes; and the Olympian games, which are nothing else than the funeral sacrifices of Pelops, the Zeus of Phidias claims for himself. The mysteries were then, as is probable, games held in honour of the dead; so also were the oracles, and both became public. But the mysteries at Sagra and in Alimus of Attica were confined to Athens. But those contests and phalloi consecrated to Dionysus were a world's shame, pervading life with their deadly influence. For Dionysus, eagerly desiring to descend to Hades, did not know the way; a man, by name Prosymnus, offers to tell him, not without reward. The reward was a disgraceful one, though not so in the opinion of Dionysus: it was an Aphrodisian favour that was asked of Dionysus as a reward. The god was not reluctant to grant the request made to him, and promises to fulfil it should he return, and confirms his promise with an oath. Having learned the way, he departed and again returned: he did not find Prosymnus, for he had died. In order to acquit himself of his promise to his lover, he rushes to his tomb, and burns with unnatural lust. Cutting a fig-branch that came to his hand, he shaped the phallus, and so performed his promise to the dead man. As a mystic memorial of this incident, phalloi are raised aloft in honour of Dionysus through the various cities. "For did they not make a procession in honour of Dionysus, and sing most shameless songs in honour of the pudenda, all would go wrong," says Heraclitus. This is that Pluto and Dionysus in whose honour they give themselves up to frenzy, and play the bacchanal,--not so much, in my opinion, for the sake of intoxication, as for the sake of the shameless ceremonial practised. With reason, therefore, such as have become slaves of their passions are your gods!

Furthermore, like the Helots among the Lacedemonians, Apollo came under the yoke of slavery to Admetus in Pherae, Hercules to Omphale in Sardis. Poseidon--was a drudge to Laomedon; and so was Apollo, who, like a good-for-nothing servant, was unable to obtain his freedom from his former master; and at that time the walls of Troy were built by them for the Phrygian. And Homer is not ashamed to speak of Athene as appearing to Ulysses with a golden lamp in her hand. And we read of Aphrodite, like a wanton serving- wench, taking and setting a seat for Helen opposite the adulterer, in order to entice him.

Panyasis, too, tells us of gods in plenty besides those who acted as servants, writing thus:- "Demeter underwent servitude, and so did the famous lame god; Poseidon underwent it, and Apollo too, of the silver bow, With a mortal man for a year. And fierce Mars Underwent it at the compulsion of his father."

And so on.

Agreeably to this, it remains for me to bring before you those amatory and sensuous deities of yours, as in every respect having human feelings.

"For theirs was a mortal body."

This Homer most distinctly shows, by introducing Aphrodite uttering loud and shrill cries on account of her wound; and describing the most warlike Ares himself as wounded in the stomach by Diomede. Polemo, too, says that Athene was wounded by Ornytus; nay, Homer says that Pluto even was struck with an arrow by Hercules; and Panyasis relates that the beams of Sol were struck by the arrows of Hercules; and the same Panyasis relates, that by the same Hercules Hera the goddess of marriage was wounded in sandy Pylos. Sosibius, too, relates that Hercules was wounded in the hand by the sons of Hippocoon. And if there are wounds, there is blood. For the ichor of the poets is more repulsive than blood; for the putrefaction of blood is called ichor. Wherefore cures and means of sustenance of which they stand in need must be furnished. Accordingly mention is made of tables, and potations, and laughter, and intercourse; for men would not devote themselves to love, or beget children, or sleep, if they were immortal, and had no wants, and never grew old. Jupiter himself, when the guest of Lycaon the Arcadian, partook of a human table among the Ethiopians--a table rather inhuman and forbidden. For he satiated himself with human flesh unwittingly; for the god did not know that Lycaon the Arcadian, his entertainer, had slain his son (his name was Nyctimus), and served him up cooked before Zeus.

This is Jupiter the good, the prophetic, the patron of hospitality, the protector of suppliants, the benign, the author of omens, the avenger of wrongs; rather the unjust, the violater of right and of law, the impious, the inhuman, the violent, the seducer, the adulterer, the amatory. But perhaps when he was such he was a man; but now these fables seem to have grown old on our hands. Zeus is no longer a serpent, a swan, nor an eagle, nor a licentious man; the god no longer flies, nor loves boys, nor kisses, nor offers violence, although there are still many beautiful women, more comely than Leda, more blooming than Semele, and boys of better looks and manners than the Phrygian herdsman. Where is now that eagle? where now that swan? where now is Zeus himself? He has grown old with his feathers; for as yet he does not repent of his amatory exploits, nor is he taught continence. The fable is exposed before you: Leda is dead, the swan is dead. Seek your Jupiter. Ransack not heaven, but earth. The Cretan, in whose country he was buried, will show him to you,-

-I mean Callimachus, in his hymns:- "For thy tomb, O king, The Cretans fashioned!"

For Zeus is dead, be not distressed, as Leda is dead, and the swan, and the eagle, and the libertine, and the serpent. And now even the superstitious seem, although reluctantly, yet truly, to have come to understand their error respecting the Gods.

"For not from an ancient oak, nor from a rock, But from men, is thy descent."

But shortly after this, they will be found to be but oaks and stones. One Agamemnon is said by Staphylus to be worshipped as a Jupiter in Sparta; and Phanocles, in his book of the Brave and Fair, relates that Agamemnon king of the Hellenes erected the temple of Argennian Aphrodite, in honour of Argennus his friend. An Artemis, named the Strangled, is worshipped by the Arcadians, as Callimachus says in his Book of Causes; and at Methymna another Artemis had divine honours paid her, viz., Artemis Con dylitis. There is also the temple of another Artemis--Artemis Podagra (or, the gout)--in Laconica, as Sosibius says. Polemo tells of an image of a yawning Apollo; and again of another image, reverenced in Elis, of the guzzling Apollo. Then the Eleans sacrifice to Zeus, the averter of flies; and the Romans sacrifice to Hercules, the averter of flies; and to Fever, and to Terror, whom also they reckon among the attendants of Hercules. (I pass over the Argives, who worshipped Aphrodite, opener of graves.) The Argives and Spartans reverence Artemis Chelytis, or the cougher, from keluttein, which in their speech signifies to cough.

Do you imagine from what source these details have been quoted? Only such as are furnished by yourselves are here adduced; and you do not seem to recognise your own writers, whom I call as witnesses against your unbelief. Poor wretches that ye are, who have filled with unholy jesting the whole compass of your life--a life in reality devoid of life!

Is not Zeus the Baldhead worshipped in Argos; and another Zeus, the avenger, in Cyprus? Do not the Argives sacrifice to Aphrodite Peribaso (the protectress), and the Athenians to Aphrodite Hetsera (the courtesan), and the Syracusans to Aphrodite Kallipygos, whom Nicander has somewhere called Kalliglutos (with beautiful rump). I pass over in silence just now Dionysus Choiropsales. The Sicyonians reverence this deity, whom they have constituted the god of the muliebria--the patron of filthiness--and religiously honour as the author of licentiousness. Such, then, are their gods; such are they also who make mockery of the gods, or rather mock and insult themselves. How much better are the Egyptians, who in their towns and villages pay divine honours to the irrational creatures, than the Greeks, who worship such gods as these?

For if they are beasts, they are not adulterous or libidinous, and seek pleasure in nothing that is contrary to nature. And of what sort these deities are, what need is there further to say, as they have been already sufficiently exposed? Furthermore, the Egyptians whom I have now mentioned are divided in their objects of worship. The Syenites worship the braize-fish; and the maiotes--this is another fish--is worshipped by those who inhabit Elephantine: the Oxyrinchites likewise worship a fish which takes its name from their country. Again, the Heraclitopolites worship the ichneumon, the inhab, itants of Sais and of Thebes a sheep, the Leucopolites a wolf, the Cynopolites a dog, the Memphites Apis, the Mendesians a goat. And you, who are altogether better than the Egyptians (I shrink from saying worse)., who never cease laughing every day of your lives at the Egyptians, what are some of you, too, with regard to brute beasts? For of your number the Thessalians pay divine homage to storks, in accordance with ancient custom; and the Thebans to weasels, for their assistance at the birth of Hercules. And again, are not the Thessalians reported to worship ants, since they have learned that Zeus in the likeness of an ant had intercourse with Eurymedusa, the daughter of Cletor, and begot Myrmidon? Polemo, too, relates that the people who inhabit the Troad worship the mice of the country, which they call Sminthoi, because they gnawed the strings of their enemies' bows; and from those mice Apollo has received his epithet of Sminthian. Heraclides, in his work, Regarding the Building of Temples in Acarnania, says that, at the place where the promontory of Actium is, and the temple of Apollo of Actium, they offer to the flies the sacrifice of an ox.

Nor shall I forget the Samians: the Samians, as Euphorion says, reverence the sheep. Nor shall I forget the Syrians, who inhabit Phoenicia, of whom some revere doves, and others fishes, with as excessive veneration as the Eleans do Zeus. Well, then, since those you worship are not gods, it seems to me requisite to ascertain if those are really demons who are ranked, as you say, in this second order [next the gods]. For if the lickerish and impure are demons, indigenous demons who have obtained sacred honours may be discovered in crowds throughout your cities: Menedemus among the Cythnians; among the Tenians, Callistagoras; among the Delians, Anius; among the Laconians, Astrabacus; at Phalerus, a hero affixed to the prow of ships is worshipped; and the Pythian priestess enjoined the Plataeans to sacrifice to Androcrates and Democrates, and Cyclaeus and Leuco while the Median war was at its height. Other demons in plenty may be brought to light by any one who can look about him a little.

"For thrice ten thousand are there in the all-nourishing earth Of demons immortal, the guardians of articulate-speaking men."

Who these guardians are, do not grudge, O Boeotian, to tell. Is it not clear that they are those we have mentioned, and those of more renown, the great demons, Apollo, Artemis, Leto, Demeter, Core, Pluto, Hercules, and Zeus himself?

But it is from running away that they guard us, O Ascraean, or perhaps it is from sinning, as forsooth they have never tried their hand at sin themselves! In that case verily the proverb may fitly be uttered:- "The father who took no admonition admonishes his son." If these are our guardians, it is not because they have any ardour of kindly feeling towards us, but intent on your ruin, after the manner of flatterers, they prey on your substance, enticed by, the smoke. These demons themselves indeed confess their own gluttony, saying:- "For with drink-offerings due, and fat of lambs, My altar still hath at their hands been fed; Such honour hath to us been ever paid. "

What other speech would they utter, if indeed the gods of the Egyptians, such as cats and weasels, should receive the faculty of speech, than that Homeric and poetic one which proclaims their liking for savoury odours and cookery? Such are your demons and gods, and demigods, if there are any so called, as there are demi-asses (mules); for you have no want of terms to make up compound names of impiety.

CHAP. III.--THE CRUELTY OF THE SACRIFICES TO THE GODS.

Well, now, let us say in addition, what inhuman demons, and hostile to the human race, your gods were, not only delighting in the insanity of men, but gloating over human slaughter,--now in the armed contests for superiority in the stadia, and now in the numberless contests for renown in the wars providing for themselves the means of pleasure, that they might be able abundantly to satiate themselves with the murder of human beings.

And now, like plagues invading cities and nations, they demanded cruel oblations. Thus Aristomenes the Messenian slew three hundred human beings in honour of Ithometan Zeus thinking that hecatombs of such a number and quality would give good omens; among whom was Theopompos, king of the Lacedemonians, a noble victim.

The Taurians, the people who inhabit the Tauric Chersonese, sacrifice to the Tauric Artemis forthwith whatever strangers they lay hands on on their coasts who have been east adrift on the sea. These sacrifices Euripides represents in tragedies on the stage. Monimus relates, in his treatise on marvels, that at Pella, in Thessaly, a man of Achaia was slain in sacrifice to Peleus and Chiron. That the Lyctii, who are a Cretan race, slew men in sacrifice to Zeus, Anticlides shows in his Homeward Journeys; and that the Lesbians offered the like sacrifice to Dionysus, is said by Dosidas. The Phocaeans also (for I will not pass over such as they are), Pytho cles informs us in his third book, On Concord, offer a man as a burn-sacrifice to the Taurian Artemis.

Erechtheus of Attica and Marius the Roman sacrificed their daughters,--the former to Pherephatta, as Demaratus mentions in his first book on Tragic Streets; the latter to the evil-averting deities, as Dorotheus relates in his first book of Italian Affairs. Philanthropic, assuredly, the demons appear, from these examples; and how shall those who revere the demons not be correspondingly pious? The former are called by the fair name of saviours; and the latter ask for safety from those who plot against their safety, imagining that they sacrifice with good omens to them, and forget that they themselves are slaying men. For a murder does not become a sacrifice by being committed in a particular spot. You are not to call it a sacred sacrifice, if one slays a man either at the altar or on the highway to Artemis or Zeus, any more than if he slew him for anger or covetousness,--other demons very like the former; but a sacrifice of this kind is murder and human butchery. Then why is it, O men, wisest of all creatures, that you avoid wild beasts, and get out of the way of the savage animals, if you fall in with a bear or lion?

" . . . ..As when some traveller spies, Coiled in his path upon the mountain side, A deadly snake, back he recoils in haste,- His limbs all trembling, and his cheek all pale,"

But though you perceive and understand demons to be deadly and wicked, plotters, haters of the human race, and destroyers, why do you not turn out of their way, or turn them out of yours? What truth can the wicked tell, or what good can they do any one?

I can then readily demonstrate that man is better than these gods of yours, who are but demons; and can show, for instance, that Cyrus and Solon were superior to oracular Apollo. Your Phoebus was a lover of gifts, but not a lover of men. 'He betrayed his friend Croesus, and forgetting the reward he had got (so careful was he of his fame), led him across the Halys to the stake.

The demons love men in such a way as to bring them to the fire [unquenchable].

But O man, who lovest the human race better, and art truer than Apollo, pity him that is bound on the pyre. Do thou, O Solon, declare truth; and thou, O Cyrus, command the fire to be extinguished. Be wise, then, at last, O

Croesus, taught by suffering. He whom you worship is an ingrate; he accepts your reward, and after taking the gold plays false. "Look again to the end, O

Solon. It is not the demon, but the man that tells you this. It is not ambiguous oracles that Solon utters. You shall easily take him up. Nothing but true, O Barbarian, shall you find by proof this oracle to be, when you are placed on the pyre. Whence I cannot help wondering, by what plausible reasons those who first went astray were impelled to preach superstition to men, when they exhorted them to worship wicked demons, whether it was Phoroneus or Merops, or whoever else that raised temples and altars to them; and besides, as is fabled, were the first to offer sacrifices to them. But, unquestionably, in succeeding ages men invented for themselves gods to worship. It is beyond doubt that this Eros, who is said to be among the oldest of the gods, was worshipped by no one till Charmus took a little boy and raised an altar to him in Academia, --a thing more seemly, than the lust he had gratified; and the lewdness of vice men called by the name of Eros, deifying thus unbridled lust. The Athenians, again, knew not who Pan was till Philippides told them.

Superstition, then, as was to be expected, having taken its rise thus, became the fountain of insensate wickedness; and not being subsequently checked, but having gone on augmenting and rushing along in full flood, it became the originator of many demons, and was displayed in sacrificing hecatombs, appointing solemn assemblies, setting up images, and building temples, which were in reality tombs: for I will not pass these over in silence, but make a thorough exposure of them, though called by the august name of temples; that is, the tombs which got the name of temples. But do ye now at length quite give up your superstition, feeling ashamed to regard sepulchres with religious veneration. In the temple of Athene in Larissa, on the Acropolis, is the grave of Acrisius; and at Athens, on the Acropolis, is that of Cecrops, as Antiochus says in the ninth book of his Histories. What of Erichthonius? was he not buried in the temple of Polias? And Immarus, the son of Eumolpus and Daira, were they not buried in the precincts of the Elusinium, which is under the Acropolis; and the daughters of Celeus, were they not interred in Eleusis? Why should I enumerate to you the wives of the Hyperboreans? They were called Hyperoche and Laodice; they were buried in the Artemisium in Delos, which is in the temple of the Delian Apollo. Leandrius says that Clearchus was buried in Miletus, in the Didymaeum. Following the Myndian Zeno, it were unsuitable in this connection to pass over the sepulchre of Leucophryne, who was buried in the temple of Artemis in Magnesia; or the altar of Apollo in Telmessus, which is reported to be the tomb of Telmisseus the seer. Further, Ptolemy the son of Agesarchus, in his first book about Philopator, says that Cinyras and the descendants of Cinyras were interred in the temple of Aphrodite in Paphos. But all time would not be sufficient for me, were I to go over the tombs which are held sacred by you, And if no shame for these audacious impieties steals over you, it comes to this, that you are completely dead, putting, as really you do, your trust in the dead. "

Poor wretches, what misery is this you suffer?

Your heads axe enveloped in the darkness of night."

CHAP. IV.--THE ABSURDITY AND SHAMEFULNESS OF THE IMAGES BY WHICH THE GODS ARE WORSHIPPED.

If, in addition, I take and set before you for inspection these very images, you will, as you go over them, find how truly silly is the custom in which you have been reared, of worshipping the senseless works of men's hands.

Anciently, then, the Scythians worshipped their sabres, the Arabs stones, the Persians rivers. And some, belonging to other races still more ancient, set up blocks of wood in conspicuous situations, and erected pillars of stone, which were called Xoana, from the carving of the material of which they were made. The image of Artemis in Icarus was doubtless unwrought wood, and that of the Cithaeronian Here was a felled tree-trunk; and that of the Samian Here, as Aethlius says, was at first a plank, and was afterwards during the government of Proclus carved into human shape. And when the Xoana began to be made in the likeness of men, they got the name of Brete,a term derived from Brotos (man). In Rome, the historian Varro says that in ancient times the Xoaron of Mars--the idol by which he was worshipped--was a spear, artists not having yet applied themselves to this specious pernicious art; but when art flourished, error increased. That of stones and stocks--and, to speak briefly, of dead matte--you have made images of human form,

The gods were fashioned by human hands (idols)

by which you have produced a counterfeit of piety, and slandered the truth, is now as clear as can be; but such proof as the point may demand must not be declined.

That the statue of Zeus at Olympia, and that of Polias at Athens, were executed of gold and ivory by Phidias, is known by everybody; and that the image of Here in Samos was formed by the chisel of Euclides, Olympichus relates in his Samiaca. Do not, then, entertain any doubt, that of the gods called at Athens venerable, Scopas made two of the stone called Lychnis, and Calos the one which they are reported to have had placed between them, as Polemon shows in the fourth of his books addressed to

Timaeus. Nor need you doubt respecting the images of Zeus and Apollo at Patara, in Lycia, which Phidias executed, as well as the lions that recline with them; and if, as some say, they were the work of Bryxis, I do not dispute,--you have in him another maker of images. Whichever of these you like, write down. Furthermore, the statues nine cubits in height of Poseidon and Amphitrite, worshipped in Tenos are the work of Telesius the Athenian, as we are told by Philochorus. Demetrius, in the second book of his Argolics, writes of the image of Here in Tiryns, both that the material was pear-tree and the artist was Argus.

Many, perhaps, may be surprised to learn that the Palladium which is called the Diopetes--that is, fallen from heaven--which Diomede and Ulysses are related to have carried off from Troy and deposited at Demophoon, was made of the bones of Pelops, as the Olympian Jove of other bones--those of the Indian wild beast. I adduce as my authority Dionysius, who relates this in the fifth part of his Cycle. And Apellas, in the Delphics, says that there were two Palladia, and that both were fashioned by men. But that one may suppose that I have passed over them through ignorance, I shall add that the image of Dionysus Morychus at Athens was made of the stones called Phellata, and was the work of Simon the son of Eupalamus, as Polemo says in a letter. There were also two other sculptors of Crete, as I think: they were called Scyles and Dipoenus; and these executed the statues of the Dioscuri in Argos, and the image of Hercules in Tiryns, and the effigy of the Munychian Artemis in Sicyon. Why should I linger over these, when I can point out to you the great deity himself, and show you who he was,--whom indeed, conspicuously above all, we hear to have been considered worthy of veneration? Him they have dared to speak of as made without hands--I mean the Egyptian Serapis. For some relate that he was sent as a present by the people of Sinope to Ptolemy Philadelphus, king of the Egyptians, who won their favour by sending them corn from Egypt when they were perishing with famine; and that this idol was an image of Pluto; and Ptolemy, having received the statue, placed it on the promontory which is now called Racotis; where the temple of Serapis was held in honour, and the sacred enclosure borders on the Spot; and that Blistichis the courtesan having died in Canopus, Ptolemy had her conveyed there, and buried beneath the forementioned shrine.

Others say that the Serapis was a Pontic idol, and was transported with solemn pomp to Alexandria. Isidore alone says that it was brought from the Seleucians, near Antioch, who also had been visited with a dearth of corn, and had been fed by Ptolemy. But Athenodorns the son of Sandon, while wishing to make out the Serapis to be ancient, has somehow slipped into the mistake of proving it to be an image fashioned by human hands. He says that Sesostris the Egyptian king, having subjugated the most of the Hellenic races, on his return to Egypt brought a number of craftsmen with him. Accordingly he ordered a statue of Osiris, his ancestor, to be executed in sumptuous style; and the work was done by the artist Bryaxis, not the Athenian, but another of the same name, who employed in its execution a mixture of various materials. For he had filings of gold, and silver, and lead, and in addition, tin; and of Egyptian stones not one was wanting, and there were fragments of sapphire, and hematite, and emerald, and topaz. Having ground down and mixed together all these ingredients, he gave to the composition a blue colour, whence the darkish hue of the image; and having mixed the whole with the colouring matter that was left over from the funeral of Osiris and Apis, moulded the Serapis, the name of which points to its connection with sepulture and its construction from funeral materials, compounded as it is of Osiris and Apis, which together make Osirapis Another new deity was added to the number with great religious pomp in Egypt, and was near being so in Greece by the king of the Romans, who deified Antinous, whom he loved as Zeus loved Ganymede, and whose beauty was of a very rare order: for lust is not easily restrained, destitute as it is of fear; and men now observe the sacred nights of Antinous, the shameful character of which the lover who spent them with him knew well. Why reckon him among the gods, who is honoured on account of uncleanness? And why do you command him to be lamented as a son? And why should you enlarge on his beauty? Beauty blighted by vice is loathsome. Do not play the tyrant, O man, over beauty, nor offer foul insult to youth in its bloom. Keep beauty pure, that it may be truly fair. Be king over beauty, not its tyrant. Remain free, and then I shall acknowledge thy beauty, because thou hast kept its image pure: then will I worship that true beauty which is the archetype of all who are beautiful. Now the grave of the debauched boy is the temple and town of Antinous. For just as temples are held in reverence, so also are sepulchres, and pyramids, and mausoleums, and labyrinths, which are temples of the dead, as the others are sepulchres of the gods. As teacher on this point, I shall produce to you the Sibyl prophetess:- "Not the oracular lie of Phoebus, Whom silly men called God, and falsely termed Prophet; But the oracles of the great God, who was not made by men's hands, Like dumb idols of Sculptured stone."

She also predicts the ruin of the temple, foretelling that that of the Ephesian Artemis would be engulphed by earthquakes and rents in the ground, as follows:- "Prostrate on the ground Ephesus shall wail, weeping by the shore, And seeking a temple that has no longer an inhabit ant."

She says also that the temple of Isis and Serapis would be demolished and burned:- "Isis, thrice-wretched goddess, thou shalt linger by the streams of the Nile; Solitary, frenzied, silent, on the sands of Acheron."

Then she proceeds:- "And thou, Serapis, covered with a heap of white stones, Shalt lie a huge ruin in thrice-wretched Egypt."

But if you attend not to the prophetess, hear at least your own philosopher, the Ephesian Heraclitus, upbraiding images with their senselessness: "And to these images they pray, with the same result as if one were to talk to the Walls of his house." For are they not to be wondered at who worship stones, and place them before the doors, as if capable of activity? They worship Hermes as a god, and place Aguieus as a doorkeeper. For if people upbraid them with being devoid of sensation, why worship them as gods? And if they are thought to be endowed with sensation, why place them before the door? The Romans, who ascribed their greatest successes to Fortune, and regarded her as a very great deity, took her statue to the privy, and erected it there, assigning to the goddess as a fitting temple--the necessary. But senseless wood and stone, and rich gold, care not a whir for either savoury odour, or blood, or smoke, by which, being at once honoured and fumigated, they are blackened; no more do they for honour or insult. And these images are more worthless than any animal. I am at a loss to conceive how objects devoid of sense were deified, and feel compelled to pity as miserable wretches those that wander in the mazes of this folly: for if some living creatures have not all the senses, as worms and caterpillars, and such as even from the first appear imperfect, as moles and the shrew-mouse, which Nicander says is blind and uncouth; yet are they superior to those utterly senseless idols and images. For they have some one sense,--say, for example, hearing, or touching, or something analogous to smell or taste; while images do not possess even one sense. There are many creatures that have neither sight, nor hearing, nor speech, such as the genus of oysters, which yet live and grow, and are affected by the changes of the moon. But images, being motionless, inert, and senseless, are bound, nailed, glued,--are melted, filed, sawed, polished, carved. The senseless earth is dishonoured by the makers of images, who change it by their art from its proper nature, and induce men to worship it; and the makers of gods worship not gods and demons, but in my view earth and art, which go to make up images. For, in sooth, the image is only dead matter shaped by the craftsman's hand. But we have no sensible image of sensible matter, but an image that is perceived by the mind alone,-- God, who alone is truly God.

And again, when involved in calamities, the superstitious worshippers of stones, though they have learned by the event that senseless matter is not to be worshipped, yet, yielding to the pressure of misfortune, become the victims of their superstition; and though despising the images, yet not wishing to appear wholly to neglect them, are found fault with by those gods by whose names the images are called.

For Dionysius the tyrant, the younger, having stripped off the golden mantle from the statue of Jupiter in Sicily, ordered him to be clothed in a woollen one, remarking facetiously that the latter was better than the golden one, being lighter in summer and warmer in winter. And Antiochus of Cyzicus, being in difficulties for money, ordered the golden statue of Zeus, fifteen cubits in height, to be melted; and one like it, of less valuable material, plated with gold, to be erected in place of it. And the swallows and most birds fly to these statues, and void their excrement on them, paying no respect either to Olympian Zeus, or Epidaurian Asclepius, or even to Athene Polias, or the Egyptian Serapis; but not even from them have you learned the senselessness of images. But it has happened that miscreants or enemies have assailed and set fire to temples, and plundered them of their votive gifts, and melted even the images themselves, from base greed of gain. And if a Cambyses or a Darius, or any other madman, has made such attempts, and if one has killed the Egyptian Apis, I laugh at him killing their god, while pained at the outrage being perpetrated for the sake of gain. I will therefore willingly forget such villany, looking on acts like these more as deeds of covetousness, than as a proof of the impotence of idols. But fire and earthquakes are shrewd enough not to feel shy or frightened at either demons or idols, any more than at pebbles heaped by the waves on the shore.

I know fire to be capable of exposing and curing superstition. If thou art willing to abandon this folly, the element of fire shall light thy way. This same fire burned the temple in Argos, with Chrysis the priestess; and that of Artemis in Ephesus the second time after the Amazons.

And the Capitol in Rome was often wrapped in flames; nor did the fire spare the temple of Serapis, in the city of the Alexandrians. At Athens it demolished the temple of the Eleutherian Dionysus; and as to the temple of Apollo at Delphi, first a storm assailed it, and then the discerning fire utterly destroyed it. This is told as the preface of what the fire promises. And the makers of images, do they not shame those of you who are wise into despising matter? The Athenian Phidias inscribed on the finger of the Olympian Jove, Pantarkes is beautiful. It was not Zeus that was beautiful in his eyes, but the man he loved. And Praxiteles, as Posidippus relates in his book about Cnidus, when he fashioned the statue of Aphrodite of Cnidus, made it like the form of Cratine, of whom he was enamoured, that the miserable people might have the paramour of Praxiteles to worship. And when Phryne the courtesan, the Thespian, was in her bloom, all the painters made their pictures of Aphrodite copies of the beauty of Phryne; as, again, the sculptors at Athens made their Mercuries like Alcibiades. It remains for you to judge whether you ought to worship cour-tesans. Moved, as I believe, by such facts, and despising such fables, the ancient kings unblushingly proclaimed themselves gods, as this involved no danger from men, and thus taught that on account of their glory they were made immortal. Ceux, the son of Eolus, was styled Zeus by his wife Alcyone; Alcyone, again, being by her husband styled Hera. Ptolemy the Fourth was called Dionysus; and Mithridates of Pontus was also called Dionysus; and Alexander wished to be considered the son of Ammon, and to have his statue made horned by the sculptors--eager to disgrace the beauty of the human form by the addition of a horn. And not kings only, but private persons dignified themselves with the names of deities, as Menecrates the physician, who took the name of Zeus. What need is there for me to instance Alexarchus? He, having been by profession a grammarian, assumed the character of the sun-god, as Aristus of Salamis relates. And why mention Nicagorus? He was a native of Zela [in Pontus], and lived in the days of Alexander. Nicagorus was styled Hermes, and used the dress of Hermes, as he himself testifies. And whilst whole nations, and cities with all their inhabitants, sinking into self-flattery, treat the myths about the gods with contempt, at the same time men themselves, assuming the air of equality with the gods, and being puffed up with vainglory, vote themselves extravagant honours. There is the case of the Macedonian Philip of Pella, the son of Amyntor, to whom they decreed divine worship in Cynosargus, although his collar-bone was broken, and he had a lame leg, and had one of his eyes knocked out. And again that of Demetrius, who was raised to the rank of the gods; and where he alighted from his horse on his entrance into Athens is the temple of Demetrius the Alighter; and altars were raised to him everywhere, and nuptials with Athene assigned to him by the Athenians. But he disdained the goddess, as he could not marry the statue; and taking the courtesan Lamia, he ascended the Acropolis, and lay with her on the couch of Athene, showing to the old virgin the postures of the young courtesan. There is no cause for indignation, then, at Hippo, who immortalized his own death. For this Hippo ordered the following elegy to be inscribed on his tomb:- "This is the sepulchre of Hippo, whom Destiny Made, through death, equal to the immortal gods."

Well done, Hippo! thou showest to us the delusion of men. If they did not believe thee speaking, now that thou art dead, let them become thy disciples. This is the oracle of Hippo; let us consider it. The objects of your worship were once men, and in process of time died; and fable and time have raised them to honour. For somehow, what is present is wont to be despised through familiarity; but what is past, being separated through the obscurity of time from the temporary censure that attached to it, is invested with honour by fiction, so that the present is viewed with distrust, the past with admiration. Exactly in this way is it, then, that the dead men of antiquity, being reverenced through the long prevalence of delusion respecting them, are regarded as gods by posterity. As grounds of your belief in these, there are your mysteries, your solemn assemblies, bonds and wounds, and weeping deities.

"Woe, woe! that fate decrees my best-belov'd, Sarpedon, by Patroclus' hand to fall."

The will of Zeus was overruled; and Zeus being worsted, laments for Sarpedon. With rcason, therefore, have you yourselves called them shades and demons, since Homer, paying Athene and the other divinities sinister honour, has styled them demons:- "She her heavenward course pursued To join the immortals in the abode of Jove."

How, then, can shades and demons be still reckoned gods, being in reality unclean and impure spirits, acknowledged by all to be of an earthly and watery nature, sinking downwards by their own weight, and flitting about graves and tombs, about which they appear dimly, being but shadowy phantasms? Such things are your gods--shades and shadows; and to these add those maimed, wrinkled, squinting divinities the Litae, daughters of Thersites rather than of Zeus. So that Bion--wittily, as I think--says, How in reason could men pray Zeus for a beautiful progeny,--a thing he could not obtain for himself? The incorruptible being, as far as in you lies, you sink in the earth; and that pure and holy essence you have buried in the grave, robbing the divine of its true nature.

Why, I pray you, have you assigned the prerogatives of God to what are no gods? Why, let me ask, have you forsaken heaven to pay divine honour to earth? What else is gold, or silver, or steel, or iron, or brass, or ivory, or precious stones? Are they not earth, and of the earth?

Are not all these things which you look on the progeny of one mother--the earth?

Why, then, foolish and silly men (for I will repeat it), have you, defaming the supercelestial region, dragged religion to the ground, by fashioning to yourselves gods of earth, and by going after those created objects, instead of the uncreated Deity, have sunk into deepest darkness?

The Parian stone is beautiful, but it is not yet Poseidon. The ivory is beautiful, but it is not yet the Olympian Zeus. Matter always needs art to fashion it, but the deity needs nothing. Art has come forward to do its work, and the matter is clothed with its shape; and while the preciousness of the material makes it capable of being turned to profitable account, it is only on account of its form that it comes to be deemed worthy of veneration. Thy image, if considered as to its origin, is gold, it is wood, it is stone, it is earth, which has received shape from the artist's hand. But I have been in the habit of walking on the earth, not of worshipping it. For I hold it wrong to entrust my spirit's hopes to things destitute of the breath of life. We must therefore approach as close as possible to the images. How peculiarly inherent deceit is in them, is manifest from their very look. For the forms of the images are plainly stamped with the characteristic nature of demons. If one go round and inspect the pictures and images, he will at a glance recognise your gods from their shameful forms: Dionysus from his robe; Hephaestus from his art; Demeter from her calamity; Ino from her head-dress; Poseidon from his trident; Zeus from the swan; the pyre indicates Heracles; and if one sees a statue of a naked woman without an inscription, he understands it to be the golden Aphrodite. Thus that Cyprian Pygmalion became enamoured of an image of ivory: the image was Aphrodite, and it was nude. The Cyprian is made a conquest of by the mere shape, and embraces the image.

This is related by Philostephanus. A different Aphrodite in Cnidus was of stone, and beautiful. Another person became enamoured of it, and shamefully embraced the stone. Posidippus relates this. The former of these authors, in his book on Cyprus, and the latter in his book on Cnidus. So powerful is art to delude, by seducing amorous men into the pit. Art is powerful, but it cannot deceive reason, nor those who live agreeably to reason. The doves on the picture were represented so to the life by the painter's art, that the pigeons flew to them; and horses have neighed to well-executed pictures of mares. They say that a girl became enamoured of an image, and a comely youth of the statue at Cnidus. But it was the eyes of the spectators that were deceived by art; for no one in his senses ever would have embraced a goddess, or entombed himself with a lifeless paramour, or become enamoured of a demon and a stone. But it is with a different kind of spell that art deludes you, if it leads you not to the indulgence of amorous affections: it leads you to pay religious honour and worship to images and pictures.

The picture is like. Well and good! Let art receive its meed of praise, but let it not deceive man by passing itself off for truth. The horse stands quiet; the dove flutters not, its wing is motionless. But the cow of Daedalus, made of wood, allured the savage bull; and art having deceived him, compelled him to meet a woman full of licentious passion. Such frenzy have mischief--working arts created in the minds of the insensate. On the other hand, apes are admired by those who feed and care for them, because nothing in the shape of images and girls' ornaments of wax or clay deceives them. You then will show yourselves inferior to apes by cleaving to stone, and wood, and gold, and ivory images, and to pictures. Your makers of such mischievous toys-- the sculptors and makers of images, the painters and workers in metal, and the poets--have introduced a motley crowd of divinities: in the fields, Satyrs and Pans; in the woods, Nymphs, and Oreads, and Hamadryads; and besides, in the waters, the rivers, and fountains, the Naiads; and in the sea the Nereids. And now the Magi boast that the demons are the ministers of their impiety, reckoning them among the number of their domestics, and by their charms compelling them to be their slaves.

Besides, the nuptials of the deities, their begetting and bringing forth of children that are recounted, their adulteries celebrated in song, their carousals represented in comedy, and bursts of laughter over their cups, which your authors introduce, urge me to cry out, though I would fain be silent. Oh the godlessness! You have turned heaven into a stage; sluggard, as a fountain thy harvest shall come," the "Word of the Father, the benign light, the Lord that bringeth light, faith to all, and salvation." For "the LORD who created the earth by His power," as Jeremiah says, "has raised up the world by His wisdom;" for wisdom, which is His word, raises us up to the truth, who have fallen prostrate before idols, and is itself the first resurrection from our fall. Whence Moses, the man of God, dissuading from all idolatry, beautifully exclaims, "Hear, O Israel, the LORD thy God is one LORD; and thou shall worship the LORD thy God, and Him only shall thou serve." "Now therefore be wise, O men," according to that blessed psalmist David; "lay hold on instruction, lest the Lord be angry, and ye perish from the way of righteousness, when His wrath has quickly kindled. Blessed are all they who put their trust in Him." But already the Lord, in His surpassing pity, has inspired the song of salvation, sounding like a battle march, "Sons of men, how long will ye be slow of heart? Why do you love vanity, and seek after a lie?" What, then, is the vanity, and what the lie? The holy apostle of the Lord, reprehending the Greeks, will show thee: "Because that, when they knew God, they glorified Him not as God, neither were thankful; but became vain in their imaginations, and changed the glory of God into the likeness of corruptible man, and worshipped and served the creature more than the Creator." And verily this is the God who "in the beginning made the heaven and the earth." But you do not know God, and worship the heaven, and how shall you escape the guilt of impiety? Hear again the prophet speaking: "The sun, shall suffer eclipse, and the heaven be darkened; but the Almighty shall shine for ever: while the powers of the heavens shall be shaken, and the heavens stretched out and drawn together shall be rolled as a parchment-skin (for these are the prophetic expressions), and the earth shall flee away from before the face of the Lord."

CHAP. IX.--"THAT THOSE GRIEVOUSLY SIN WHO DESPISE OR NEGLECT GOD'S GRACIOUS CALLING."

I could adduce ten thousand Scriptures of which not "one tittle shall pass away," without being fulfilled; for the mouth of the Lord the Holy Spirit hath spoken these things. "Do not any longer," he says, "my son, despise the chastening of the LORD, nor faint when thou art rebuked of Him." O surpassing love for man! Not as a teacher speaking to his pupils, not as a master to his domestics, nor as God to men, but as a father, does the Lord gently admonish his children. Thus Moses confesses that "he was filled with quaking and terror" while he listened to God speaking concerning the Word. And art not thou afraid as thou hearest the voice of the Divine Word? Art not thou distressed? Do you not fear, and hasten to learn of Him,--that is, to salvation,--dreading wrath, loving grace, eagerly striving after the hope set before us, that you may shun the judgment threatened? Come, come, O my young people! For if you become not again as little children, and be born again, as saith the Scripture, you shall not receive the truly existent Father, nor shall you ever enter into the kingdom of heaven. For in what way is a stranger permitted to enter? Well, as I take it, then, when he is enrolled and made a citizen, and receives one to stand to him in the relation of father, then will he be occupied with the Father's concerns, then shall he be deemed worthy to be made His heir, then will he share the kingdom of the Father with His own dear Son. For this is the first-born Church, composed of many good children; these are "the first-born enrolled in heaven, who hold high festival with so many myriads of angels." We, too, are first-born sons, who are reared by God, who are the genuine friends of the First-born, who first of all other men attained to the knowledge of God, who first were wrenched away from our sins, first severed from the devil. And now the more benevolent God is, the more impious men are; for He desires us from slaves to become sons, while they scorn to become sons. O the prodigious folly of being ashamed of the Lord! He often freedom, you flee into bondage; He bestows salvation, you sink down into destruction; He confers everlasting life, you wait for punishment, and prefer the fire which the Lord "has prepared for the devil and his angels." Wherefore the blessed apostle says: "I testify in the Lord, that ye walk no longer as the Gentiles walk, in the vanity of their mind; having their understanding darkened, being alienated from the life of God through the ignorance that is in them, because of the hardness of their heart: who, being past feeling, have given themselves over to lasciviousness, to work all uncleanness and concupiscence." After the accusation of such a witness, and his invocation of God, what else remains for the unbelieving than judgment and condemnation? And the Lord, with ceaseless assiduity, exhorts, terrifies, urges, rouses, admonishes; He awakes from the sleep of darkness, and raises up those who have wandered in error. "Awake," He says, "thou that sleepest, and arise from the dead, and Christ shall give thee light," -- Christ, the Sun of the Resurrection, He "who was born before the morning star," and with His beams bestows life. Let no one then despise the Word, lest he unwittingly despise himself. For the Scripture somewhere says, "To-day, if ye will hear His voice, harden not your hearts, as in the provocation, in the day of temptation in the wilderness, when your fathers proved Me by trial." And what was the trim? If you wish to learn, the Holy Spirit will show you: "And saw my works," He says, "forty years. Wherefore I was grieved with that generation, and said, They do always err in heart, and have not known My ways. So I sware in my wrath, they shall not enter into My rest." Look to the threatening! Look to the exhortation! Look to the punishment! Why, then, should we any longer change grace into wrath, and not receive the word with open ears, and entertain God as a guest in pure spirits? For great is the grace of His promise, "if to-day we hear His voice." And that to-day is lengthened out day by day, while it is called to-day. And to the end the to-day and the instruction continue; and then the true to-day, the never-ending day of God, extends over eternity. Let us then ever obey the voice of the divine word. For the to-day signifies eternity. And day is the symbol of light; and the light of men is the Word, by whom we behold God. Rightly, then, to those that have believed and obey, grace will superabound; while with those that have been unbelieving, and err in heart, and have not known the Lord's ways, which John commanded to make straight and to prepare, God is incensed, and those He threatens.

And, indeed, the old Hebrew wanderers in the desert received typically the end of the threatening; for they are said not to have entered into the rest, because of unbelief, till, having followed the successor of Moses, they learned by experience, though late, that they could not be saved otherwise than by believing on Jesus. But the Lord, in His love to man, invites all men to the knowledge of the truth, and for this end sends the Paraclete. What, then, is this knowledge? Godliness; and "godliness," according to Paul, "is profitable for all things, having the promise of the life that now is, and of that which is to come." If eternal salvation were to be sold, for how much, O men, would you propose to purchase it? Were one to estimate the value of the whole of Pactolus, the fabulous river of gold, he would not have reckoned up a price equivalent to salvation.

Do not, however, faint. You may, if you choose, purchase salvation, though of inestimable value, with your own resources, love and living faith, which will be reckoned a suitable price. This recompense God cheerfully accepts; "for we trust in the living God, who is the Saviour of all men, especially of those who believe."

But the rest, round whom the world's growths have fastened, as the rocks on the sea-shore are covered over with sea-weed, make light of immortality, like the old man of Ithaca, eagerly longing to see, not the truth, not the fatherland in heaven, not the true light, but smoke. But godliness, that makes man as far as can be like God, designates God as our suitable teacher, who alone can worthily assimilate man to God. This teaching the apostle knows as truly divine. "Thou, O Timothy," he says, "from a child hast known the holy letters, which are able to make thee wise unto salvation, through faith that is in Christ Jesus." For truly holy are those letters that sanctify and deify; and the writings or volumes that consist of those holy letters and syllables, the same apostle consequently calls "inspired of God, being profitable for doctrine, for reproof, for correction, for instruction in righteousness, that the man of God may be perfect, thoroughly furnished to every good work." No one will be so impressed by the exhortations of any of the saints, as he is by the words of the Lord Himself, the lover of man. For this, and nothing but this, is His only work--the salvation of man. Therefore He Himself, urging them on to salvation, cries, "The kingdom of heaven is at hand." Those men that draw near through fear, He converts. Thus also the apostle of the Lord, beseeching the Macedonians, becomes the interpreter of the divine voice, when he says, "The Lord is at hand; take care that ye be not apprehended empty." But are ye so devoid of fear, or rather of faith, as not to believe the Lord Himself, or Paul, who in Christ's stead thus entreats:

"Taste and see that Christ is God?" Faith will lead you in; experience will teach you; Scripture will train you, for it says, "Come hither, O children; listen to me, and I will teach you the fear of the LORD." Then, as to those who already believe, it briefly adds, "What man is he that desireth life, that loveth to see good days?" It is we, we shall say--we who are the devotees of good, we who eagerly desire good things. Hear, then, ye who are far off, hear ye who are near: the word has not been hidden from any; light is common, it shines "on all men." No one is a Cimmerian in respect to the word. Let us haste to salvation, to regeneration; let us who are many haste that we may be brought together into one love, according to the union of the essential unity; and let us, by being made good, conformably follow after union, seeking after the good Monad.

a single unit

The union of many in one, issuing in the production of divine harmony out of a medley of sounds and division, becomes one symphony following one choir-leader and teacher, the Word, reaching and resting in the same truth, and crying Abba, Father. This, the true utterance of His children, God accepts with gracious welcome--the first-fruits He receives from them.

CHAP. X.-- ANSWER TO THE OBJECTION OF THE HEATHEN, THAT IT WAS NOT RIGHT TO ABANDON THE CUSTOMS OF THEIR FATHERS.

But you say it is not creditable to subvert the customs handed down to us from our fathers. And why, then, do we not still use our first nourishment, milk, to which our nurses accustomed us from the time of our birth? Why do we increase or diminish our patrimony, and not keep it exactly the same as we got it? Why do we not still vomit on our parents' breasts, or still do the things for which, when infants, and nursed by our mothers, we were laughed at, but have corrected ourselves, even if we did not fall in with good instructors? Then, if excesses in the indulgence of the passions, though pernicious and dangerous, yet are accompanied with pleasure, why do we not in the conduct of life abandon that usage which is evil, and provocative of passion, and godless, even should our fathers feel hurt, and betake ourselves to the truth, and seek Him who is truly our Father, rejecting custom as a deleterious drug? For of all that I have undertaken to do, the task I now attempt is the noblest, viz., to demonstrate to you how inimical this insane and most wretched custom is to godliness. For a boon so great, the greatest ever given by God to the human race, would never have been hated and rejected, had not you been carried away by custom, and then shut your ears against us; and just as unmanageable horses throw off the reins, and take the bit between their teeth, you rush away from the arguments addressed to you, in your eager desire to shake yourselves clear of us, who seek to guide the chariot of your life, and, impelled by your folly, dash towards the precipices of destruction, and regard the holy word of God as an accursed thing. The reward of your choice, therefore, as described by Sophocles, follows:- "The mind a blank, useless ears, vain thoughts."

And you know not that, of all truths, this is the truest, that the good and godly shall obtain the good reward, inasmuch as they held goodness in high esteem; while, on the other hand, the wicked shall receive meet punishment. For the author of evil, torment has been prepared; and so the prophet Zecharias threatens him: "He that hath chosen Jerusalem rebuke thee; lo, is not this a brand plucked from the fire?" What an infatuated desire, then, for voluntary death is this, rooted in men's minds! Why do they flee to this fatal brand, with which they shall be burned, when it is within their power to live nobly according to God, and not according to custom? For God bestows life freely; but evil custom, after our departure from this world, brings on the sinner unavailing remorse with punishment. By sad experience, even a child knows how superstition destroys and piety saves. Let any of you look at those who minister before the idols, their hair matted, their persons disgraced with filthy and tattered clothes; who never come near a bath, and let their nails grow to an extraordinary length, like wild beasts; many of them castrated, who show the idol's temples to be in reality graves or prisons. These appear to me to bewail the gods, not to worship them, and their sufferings to be worthy of pity rather than piety. And seeing these things, do you still continue blind, and will you not look up to the Ruler of all, the Lord of the universe? And will you not escape from those dungeons, and flee to the mercy that comes down from heaven? For God, of His great love to man, comes to the help of man, as the mother-bird flies to one of her young that has fallen out of the nest; and if a serpent open its mouth to swallow the little bird, "the mother flutters round, uttering cries of grief over her dear progeny;" and God the Father seeks His creature, and heals his transgression, and pursues the serpent, and recovers the young one, and incites it to fly up to the nest.

Thus dogs that have strayed, track out their master by the scent; and horses that have thrown their riders, come to their master's call if he but whistle. "The ox," it is said, "knoweth his owner, and the ass his master's crib; but Israel hath not known Me." What, then, of the Lord? He remembers not our ill desert; He still pities, He still urges us to repentance.

And I would ask you, if it does not appear to you monstrous, that you men who are God's handiwork, who have received your souls from Him, and belong wholly to God, should be subject to another master, and, what is more, serve the tyrant instead of the rightful King--the evil one instead of the good? For, in the name of truth, what man in his senses turns his back on good, and attaches himself to evil? What, then, is he who flees from God to consort with demons? Who, that may become a son of God, prefers to be in bondage? Or who is he that pursues his way to Erebus, when it is in his power to be a citizen of heaven, and to cultivate Paradise, and walk about in heaven and partake

great analogy!

of the tree of life and immortality, and, cleaving his way through the sky in the track of the luminous cloud, behold, like Elias, the rain of salvation? Some there are, who, like worms wallowing in marshes and mud in the streams of pleasure, feed on foolish and useless delights--swinish men. For swine, it is said, like mud better than pure water; and, according to Democritus, "doat upon dirt."

Let us not then be enslaved or become swinish; but, as true children of the light, let us raise our eyes and look on the light, lest the Lord discover us to be spurious, as the sun does the eagles. Let us therefore repent, and pass from ignorance to knowledge, from foolishness to wisdom, from licentiousness to self-restraint, from unrighteousness to righteousness, from godlessness to God. It is an enterprise of noble daring to take our way to God; and the enjoyment of many other good things is within the reach of the lovers of righteousness, who pursue eternal life, specially those things to which God Himself alludes, speaking by Isaiah: "There is an inheritance for those who serve the LORD." Noble and desirable is this inheritance: not gold, not silver, not raiment, which the moth assails, and things of earth which are assailed by the robber, whose eye is dazzled by worldly wealth; but it is that treasure of salvation to which we must hasten, by becoming lovers of the Word. Thence praise-worthy works descend to us, and fly with us on the wing of truth. This is the inheritance with Which the eternal covenant of God invests us, conveying the everlasting gift of grace; and thus our loving Father-- the true Father--ceases not to exhort, admonish, train, love us. For He ceases not to save, and advises the best course: "Become righteous," says the Lord. Ye that thirst, come to the water; and ye that have no money, come, and buy and drink without money. He invites to the layer, to salvation, to illumination, all but crying out and saying, The land I give thee, and the sea, my child, and heaven too; and all the living creatures in them I freely bestow upon thee. Only, O child, thirst for thy Father; God shall be revealed to thee without price; the truth is not made merchandise of. He gives thee all creatures that fly and swim, and those on the land. These the Father has created for thy thankful enjoyment. What the bastard, who is a son of perdition, foredoomed to be the slave of mammon, has to buy for money, He assigns to thee as thine own, even to His own son who loves the Father; for whose sake He still works, and to whom alone He promises, saying, "The land shall not be sold in perpetuity," for it is not destined to corruption. "For the whole land is mine;" and it is thine too, if thou receive God. Wherefore the Scripture, as might have been expected, proclaims good news to those who have believed. "The saints of the Lord shall inherit the glory of God and His power." What glory, tell me, O blessed One, which "eye hath not seen, nor ear heard, nor hath it entered into the heart of man;" and "they shall be glad in the kingdom of their Lord for ever and ever! Amen." You have, O men, the divine promise of grace; you have heard, on the other hand, the threatening of punishment: by these the Lord saves, teaching men by fear and grace. Why do we delay? Why do we not shun the punishment? Why do we not receive the free gift?

Why, in fine. do we not choose the better part, God instead of the evil one, and prefer wisdom to idolatry, and take life in exchange for death? "Behold,"

He says, "I have set before your face death and life." The Lord tries you, that "you may choose life." He counsels yon as a father to obey God. "For if ye hear Me," He says, "and be willing, ye shall eat the good things of the land:" this is the grace attached to obedience. "But if ye obey Me not, and are unwilling, the sword and fire shall devour you:" this is the penalty of disobedience. For the mouth of the Lord-

-the law of truth, the word of the Lord--hath spoken these things. Are you willing that I should be your good counsellor? Well, do you hear. I, if possible, will explain. You ought, O men, when reflecting on the Good, to have brought forward a witness inborn and competent, viz, faith, which of itself, and from its own resources, chooses at once what is best, instead of occupying yourselves in painfully inquiring whether what is best ought to be followed. For, allow me to tell you, you ought to doubt whether you should get drunk, but you get drunk before reflecting on the matter; and whether you ought to do an injury, but you do injury with the utmost readiness. The only thing you make the subject of question is, whether God should be worshipped, and whether this wise God and Christ should be followed: and this you think requires deliberation and doubt, and know not what is worthy of God. Have faith in us, as you have in drunkenness, that you may be wise; have faith in us, as you have in injury, that you may live. But if, acknowledging the conspicuous trustworthiness of the virtues, you wish to trust them, come and I will set before you in abundance, materials of persuasion respecting the Word. But do you--for your ancestral customs, by which your minds are preoccupied, divert you from the truth,--do you now hear what is the real state of the case as follows.

And let not any shame of this name preoccupy you, which does great harm to men, and seduces them from salvation. Let us then openly strip for the contest, and nobly strive in the arena of truth, the holy Word being the judge, and the Lord of the universe prescribing the contest. For 'tis no insignificant prize, the guerdon of immortality which is set before us. Pay no more regard, then, if you are rated by some of the low rabble who lead the dance of impiety, and are driven on to the same pit by their folly and insanity, makers of idols and worshippers of stones. For these have dared to deify men,-- Alexander of Macedon, for example, whom they canonized as the thirteenth god, whose pretensions Babylon confuted, which showed him dead. I admire, therefore, the divine sophist. Theocritus was his name. After Alexander's death, Theocritus, holding up the vain opinions entertained by men respecting the gods, to ridicule before his fellow-citizens, said: "Men, keep up your hearts as long as you see the gods dying sooner than men." And, truly, he who worships gods that are visible, and the promiscuous rabble of creatures begotten and born, and attaches himself to them, is a far more wretched object than the very demons. For God is by no manner of means unrighteous, as the demons are, but in the very highest degree righteous; and nothing more resembles God than one of us when he becomes righteous in the highest possible degree:- "Go into the way, the whole tribe of you handicrafts-men, Who worship Jove's fierce- eyed daughter, the working goddess, With fans duly placed, fools that ye are"- fashioners of stones, and worshippers of them. Let your Phidias, and Polycletus, and your Praxiteles and Apelles too, come, and all that are engaged in mechanical arts, who, being themselves of the earth, are workers of the earth. "For then," says a certain prophecy, "the affairs here turn out unfortunately, when men put their trust in images." Let the meaner artists, too--for I will not stop calling--come. None of these ever made a breathing image, or out of earth moulded soft flesh. Who liquefied the marrow? or who solidified the bones? Who stretched the nerves? who distended the veins? Who poured the blood into them? Or who spread the skin? Who ever could have made eyes capable of seeing? Who breathed spirit into the lifeless form? Who bestowed righteousness? Who promised immortality? The Maker of the universe alone; the Great Artist and Father has formed us, such a living image as man is. But your Olympian Jove, the image of an image, greatly out of harmony with truth, is the senseless work of Attic hands. For the image of God is His Word, the genuine Son of Mind, the Divine Word, the archetypal light of light; and the image of the Word is the true man, the mind which is in man, who is therefore said to have been made "in the image and likeness of God," assimilated to the Divine Word in the affections of the soul, and therefore rational; but effigies sculptured in human form, the earthly image of that part of man which is visible and earth-born, are but a perishable impress of humanity, manifestly wide of the truth. That life, then, which is occupied with so much earnestness about matter, seems to me to be nothing else than full of insanity. And custom, which has made you taste bondage and unreasonable care, is fostered by vain opinion; and ignorance, which has proved to the human race the cause of unlawful rites and delusive shows, and also of deadly plagues and hateful images, has, by devising many shapes of demons, stamped on all that follow it the mark of long-continued death.

Receive, then, the water of the word; wash, ye polluted ones; purify yourselves from custom, by sprinkling yourselves with the drops of truth.

The pure must ascend to heaven. Thou art a man, if we look to that which is most common to thee and others--seek Him who created thee; thou art a son, if we look to that which is thy peculiar prerogative--acknowledge thy Father. But do you still continue in your sins, engrossed with pleasures? To whom shall the Lord say, "Yours is the kingdom of heaven?" Yours, whose choice is set on God, if you will; yours, if you will only believe, and comply with the brief terms of the announcement; which the Ninevites having obeyed, instead of the destruction they looked for, obtained a signal deliverance. How, then, may I ascend to heaven, is it said? The Lord is the way; a strait way, but leading from heaven, strait in truth, but leading back to heaven, strait, despised on earth; broad, adored in heaven.

Then, he that is uninstructed in the word, has ignorance as the excuse of his error; but as for him into whose ears instruction has been poured, and who deliberately maintains his incredulity in his soul, the wiser he appears to be, the more harm will his understanding do him; for he has his own sense as his accuser for not having chosen the best part. For man has been otherwise constituted by nature, so as to have fellowship with God. As, then, we do not compel the horse to plough, or the bull to hunt, but set each animal to that for which it is by nature fitted; so, placing our finger on what is man's peculiar and distinguishing characteristic above other creatures, we invite him-- born, as he is, for the contemplation of heaven, and being, as he is, a truly heavenly plant--to the knowledge of God, counselling him to furnish himself with what is his sufficient provision for eternity, namely piety. Practise husbandry, we say, if you are a husbandman; but while you till your fields, know God. Sail the sea, you who are devoted to navigation, yet call the whilst on the heavenly Pilot. Has knowledge taken hold of you while engaged in military service? Listen to the commander, who orders what is right. As those, then, who have been overpowered with sleep and drunkenness, do ye awake; and using your eyes a little, consider what mean those stones which you worship, and the expenditure you frivolously lavish on matter. Your means and substance you squander on ignorance, even as you throw away your lives to death, having found no other end of your vain hope than this. Not only unable to pity yourselves, you are incapable even of yielding to the persuasions of those who commiserate you; enslaved as you are to evil custom, and, clinging to it voluntarily till your last breath, you are hurried to destruction: "because light is come into the world, and men have loved the darkness rather than the light," while they could sweep away those hindrances to salvation, pride, and wealth, and fear, repeating this poetic utterance:- "Whither do I bear these abundant riches? and whither Do I myself wander?"

If you wish, then, to cast aside these vain phantasies, and bid adieu to evil custom, say to vain opinion:- "Lying dreams, farewell; you were then nothing."

For what, think you, O men, is the Hermes of Typho, and that of Andocides, and that of Amyetus? Is it not evident to all that they are stones, as is the veritable Hermes himself? As the Halo is not a god, and as the Iris is not a god, but are states of the atmosphere and of the clouds; and as, likewise, a day is not a god, nor a year, nor time, which is made up of these, so neither is sun nor moon, by which each of those mentioned above is determined. Who, then, in his right senses, can imagine Correction, and Punishment, and Justice, and Retribution to be gods? For neither the Furies, nor the Fates, nor Destiny are gods, since neither Government, nor Glory, nor Wealth are gods, which last [as Plutus] painters represent as blind. But if you deify Modesty, and Love, and Venus, let these be followed by Infamy, and Passion, and Beauty, and Intercourse. Therefore Sleep and Death cannot reasonably any more be regarded as twin deities, being merely changes which take place naturally in living creatures; no more will you with propriety call Fortune, or Destiny, or the Fates goddesses. And if Strife and Battle be not gods, no more are Ares and Enyo. Still further, if the lightnings, and thunderbolts, and rains are not gods, how can fire and water be gods? how can shooting stars and comets, which are produced by atmospheric changes? He who calls Fortune a god, let him also so call Action. If, then, none of these, nor of the images formed by human hands, and destitute of feeling, is held to be a God, while a providence exercised about us is evidently the result of a divine power, it remains only to acknowledge this, that He alone who is truly God, only truly is and subsists. But those who are insensible to this are like men who have drunk mandrake or some other drug. May God grant that you may at length awake from this slumber, and know God; and that neither Gold, nor Stone, nor Tree, nor Action, nor Suffering, nor Disease, nor Fear, may appear in your eyes as a god. For there are, in sooth, "on the fruitful earth thrice ten thousand" demons, not immortal, nor indeed mortal; for they are not endowed with sensation, so as to render them capable of death, but only things of wood and stone, that hold despotic sway over men insulting and violating life through the force of custom. "The earth is the LORD'S," it is said, "and the fulness thereof." Then why darest thou, while luxuriating in the bounties of the Lord, to ignore the Sovereign Ruler? "Leave my earth," the Lord will say to thee. "Touch not the water which I bestow. Partake not of the fruits of the earth produced by my hus bandry." Give to God recompense for your sustenance; acknowledge thy Master. Thou art God's creature. What belongs to Him, how can it with justice be alienated? For that which is alienated, being deprived of the properties that belonged to it, is also deprived of truth. For, after the fashion of Niobe, or, to express myself more mystically, like the Hebrew woman called by the ancients Lot's wife, are ye not turned into a state of insensibility? This woman we have heard, was turned into stone for her love of Sodore. And those who are godless, addicted to impiety, hard-hearted and foolish are Sodomites. Believe that these utterances are addressed to you from God. For think not that stones, and stocks, and birds, and serpents are sacred things, and men are not; but, on the contrary, regard men as truly sacred, and take beasts and stones for what they are. For there are miserable wretches of human kind, who consider that God utters His voice by the raven and the jackdaw, but says nothing by man; and honour the raven as a messenger of God. But the man of God, who croaks not, nor chatters, but speaks rationally and instructs lovingly, alas, they persecute; and while he is inviting them to cultivate righteousness, they try inhumanly to slay him, neither welcoming the grace which, comes from above, nor fearing the penalty. For they believe not God, nor understand His power, whose love to man is ineffable; and His hatred of evil is inconceivable. His anger augments punishment against sin; His love bestows bless-rags on repentance. It is the height of wretchedness to be deprived of the help which comes from God. Hence this blindness of eyes and dulness of hearing are more grievous than other inflictions of the evil one; for the one deprives them of heavenly vision, the other robs them of divine instruction. But ye, thus maimed as respects the truth, blind in mind, deaf in understanding, are not grieved, are not pained, have had no desire to see heaven and the Maker of heaven, nor, by fixing your choice on salvation, have sought to hear the Creator of the universe, and to learn of Him; for no hindrance stands in the way of him who is bent on the knowledge of God. Neither childlessness, nor poverty, nor obscurity, nor want, can hinder him who eagerly strives after the knowledge of God; nor does any one who has conquered by brass or iron the true wisdom for himself choose to exchange it, for it is vastly preferred to everything else. Christ is able to save in every place. For he that is fired with ardour and admiration for righteousness, being the lover of One who needs nothing, needs himself but little, having treasured up his bliss in nothing but himself and God, where is neither moth, robber, nor pirate, but the eternal Giver of good. With justice, then, have you been compared to those serpents who shut their ears against the charmers. For "their mind," says the Scripture, "is like the serpent, like the deaf adder, which stoppeth her ear, and will not hear the voice of the charmers." But allow yourselves to feel the influence of the charming strains of sanctity, and receive that mild word of ours, and reject the deadly poison, that it may be granted to you to divest yourselves as much as possible of destruction, as they s have been divested of old age. Hear me, and do not stop your ears; do not block up the avenues of hearing, but lay to heart what is said. Excellent is the medicine of immortality! Stop at length your grovelling reptile motions. "For the enemies of the Lord," says Scripture, "shall lick the dust." Raise your eyes from earth to the skies, look up to heaven, admire the sight, cease watching with outstretched head the heel of the righteous, and hindering the way of truth. Be wise and harmless.

Perchance the Lord will endow you with the wing of simplicity (for He has resolved to give wings to those that are earth-born), that you may leave your holes and dwell in heaven. Only let us with our whole heart repent, that we may be able with our whole heart to contain God. "Trust in Him, all ye assembled people; pour out all your hearts before Him." He says to those that have newly abandoned wickedness, "He pities them, and fills them with righteousness." Believe Him who is man and God; believe, O man. Believe, O man, the living God, who suffered and is adored. Believe, ye slaves, Him who died; believe, all ye of human kind, Him who alone is God of all men.

Believe, and receive salvation as your reward. Seek God, and your soul shall live. He who seeks God is busying himself about his own salvation. Hast thou found God?--then thou hast life. Let us then seek, in order that we may live.

The reward of seeking is life with God. "Let all who seek Thee be glad and rejoice in Thee; and let them say continually, God be magnified." A noble hymn of God is an immortal man, established in righteousness, in whom the oracles of truth are engraved. For where but in a soul that is wise can you write truth? where love? where reverence? where meekness? Those who have had these divine characters impressed on them, ought, I think, to regard wisdom as a fair port whence to embark, to whatever lot in life they turn; and likewise to deem it the calm haven of salvation: wisdom, by which those who have betaken themselves to the Father, have proved good fathers to their children; and good parents to their sons, those who have known the Son; and good husbands to their wives, those who remember the Bridegroom; and good masters to their servants, those who have been redeemed from utter slavery. Oh, happier far the beasts than men involved in error! who live in ignorance as you, but do not counterfeit the truth. There are no tribes of flatterers among them. Fishes have no superstition: the birds worship not a single image; only they look with admiration on heaven, since, deprived as they are of reason, they are unable to know God. So are you not ashamed for living through so many periods of life in impiety, making yourselves more irrational than irrational creatures? You were boys, then striplings, then youths, then men, but never as yet were you good. If you have respect for old age, be wise, now that you have reached life's sunset; and albeit at the close of life, acquire the knowledge of God, that the end of life may to you prove the beginning of salvation. You have become old in superstition; as young, enter on the practice of piety. God regards you as innocent children. Let, then, the Athenian follow the laws of Solon, and the Argive those of Phoroneus, and the Spartan those of Lycurgus: but if thou enrol thyself as one of God's people, heaven is thy country, God thy lawgiver. And what are the laws? "Thou shalt not kill; thou shalt not commit adultery; thou shalt not seduce boys; thou shalt not steal; thou shalt not bear false witness; thou shalt love the Lord thy God." And the complements of these are those laws. of reason and words of sanctity which are inscribed on men's hearts: "Thou shalt love thy neighbour as thyself; to him who strikes thee on the cheek, present also the other;" "thou shalt not lust, for by lust alone thou hast committed adultery." How much better, therefore, is it for men from the beginning not to wish to desire things forbidden, than to obtain their desires! But

Severity of Manner

ye are not able to endure the austerity of salvation; but as we delight in sweet' things, and prize them higher for the agreeableness of the pleasure they yield, while, on the other hand, those bitter things which are distasteful to the palate are curative and healing, and the harshness of medicines strengthens people of weak stomach, thus custom pleases and, tickles; but custom pushes into the abyss, while truth conducts to heaven. Harsh it is at first, but a good nurse of youth; and it is at once the decorous place where the household maids and matrons dwell together, and the sage council-chamber. Nor is it difficult to approach, or impossible to attain, but is very near us in our very homes; as Moses, endowed with all wisdom, says, while referring to it, it has its abode in three departments of our constitution--in the hands, the mouth, and the heart: a meet emblem this of truth, which is embraced by these three things in all--will, action, speech. And be not afraid lest the multitude of pleasing objects which rise before you withdraw you from wisdom. You yourself will spontaneously surmount the frivolousness of custom, as boys when they have become men throw aside their toys. For with a celerity unsurpassable, and a benevolence to which we have ready access, the divine power, casting its radiance on the earth, hath filled the universe with the seed of salvation. For it was not without divine care that so great a work was accomplished in so brief a space by the Lord, who, though despised as to appearance, was in reality adored, the expiator of sin, the Saviour, the clement, the Divine Word, He that is truly most manifest Deity, He that is made equal to the Lord of the universe; because He was His Son, and the Word was in God, not disbelieved in by all when He was first preached, nor altogether unknown when, assuming the character of man, and fashioning Himself in flesh, He enacted the drama of human salvation: for He was a true champion and a fellow-champion with the creature. And being communicated most speedily to men, having dawned from His Father's counsel quicker than the sun, with the most perfect ease He made God shine on us. Whence He was and what He was, He showed by what He taught and exhibited, manifesting Himself as the Herald of the Covenant, the Reconciler, our Saviour, the Word, the Fount of life, the Giver of peace, diffused over the whole face of the earth; by whom, so to speak, the universe has already become an ocean of blessings.

CHAP. XI.--HOW GREAT ARE THE BENEFITS CONFERRED ON MAN THROUGH THE ADVENT OF

Contemplate a little, if agreeable to you, the divine beneficence. The first man, when in Paradise, sported free, because he was the child of God; but when he succumbed to pleasure (for the serpent allegorically signifies pleasure crawling on its belly, earthly wickedness nour ished for fuel to the flames), was as a child seduced by lusts, and grew old in disobedience; and by disobeying his Father, dishonoured God. Such was the influence of pleasure. Man, that had been free by reason of simplicity, was found fettered to sins. The Lord then wished to release him from his bonds, and clothing Himself with flesh--O divine mystery!--vanquished the serpent, and enslaved the tyrant death; and, most marvellous of all, man that had been deceived by pleasure, and bound fast by corruption, had his hands unloosed, and was set free. O mystic wonder! The Lord was laid low, and man rose up; and he that fell from Paradise receives as the reward of obedience something greater [than Paradise]--namely, heaven itself. Wherefore, since the Word Himself has come to us from heaven, we need not, I reckon, go any more in search of human learning to Athens and the rest of Greece, and to Ionia. For if we have as our teacher Him that filled the universe with His holy energies in creation, salvation, beneficence, legislation, prophecy, teaching, we have the Teacher from whom all instruction comes; and the whole world, with Athens and Greece, has already become the domain of the Word. For you, who believed the poetical fable which designated Minos the Cretan as the bosom friend of Zeus, will not refuse to believe that we who have become the disciples of God have received the only true wisdom; and that which the chiefs of philosophy only guessed at, the disciples of Christ have both apprehended and proclaimed. And the one whole Christ is not divided: "There is neither barbarian, nor Jew, nor Greek, neither male nor female, but a new man," transformed by God's Holy Spirit. Further, the other counsels and precepts are unimportant, and respect particular things,--as, for example, if one may marry, take part in public affairs, beget children; but the only command that is universal, and over the whole course of existence, at all times and in all circumstances, tends to the highest end, viz., life, is piety, --all that is necessary, in order that we may live for ever, being that we live in accordance with it. Philosophy, however, as the ancients say, is "a long-lived exhortation, wooing the eternal love of wisdom;" while the commandment of the Lord is far-shining, "enlightening the eyes." Receive Christ, receive sight, receive thy light, "In order that you may know well both God and man."

"Sweet is the Word that gives us light, precious above gold and gems; it is to be desired above honey and the honey-comb."

For how can it be other than desirable, since it has filled with light the mind which had been buried in darkness, and given keenness to the "light-bringing eyes" of the soul? For just as, had the sun not been in existence, night would have brooded over the universe notwithstanding the other luminaries of heaven; so, had we nor known the Word, and been illuminated by Him; we should have been nowise different from fowls that are being fed, fattened in darkness, and nourished for death. Let us then admit the light, that we may admit God; let us admit the light, and become disciples to the Lord. This, too, He has been promised to the Father: "I will declare Thy name to my brethren; in the midst of the Church will I praise Thee."

Praise and declare to me Thy Father God; Thy utterances save; Thy hymn teaches that hitherto I have wandered in error, seeking God. But since Thou leadest me to the light, O Lord, and I find God through Thee, and receive the Father from Thee, I become "Thy fellow-heir," since Thou "weft not ashamed of me as Thy brother." Let us put away, then, let us put away oblivion of the truth, viz., ignorance; and removing the darkness which obstructs, as dimness of sight, let us contemplate the only true God, first raising our voice in this hymn of praise: Hail, O light! For in us, buried in darkness, shut up in the shadow of death, light has shone forth from heaven, purer than the sun, sweeter than life here below. That light is eternal life; and whatever partakes of it lives. But night fears the light, and hiding itself in terror, gives place to the day of the Lord. Sleepless light is now over all, and the west has given credence to the east. For this was the end of the new creation. For "the Sun of Righteousness," who drives His chariot over all, pervades equally all humanity, like "His Father, who makes His sun to rise on all men," and distils on them the dew of the truth. He hath changed sunset into sunrise, and through the cross brought death to life; and having wrenched man from destruction, He hath raised him to the skies, transplanting mortality into immortality, and translating earth to heaven--He, the husbandman of God, "Pointing out the favourable signs and rousing the nations To good works, putting them in mind of the true sustenance;" having bestowed on us the truly great, divine, and inalienable inheritance of the Father, deifying man by heavenly teaching, putting His laws into our minds, and writing them on our hearts. What laws does He inscribe? "That all shall know God, from small to great;" and, "I will be merciful to them," says God, "and will not remember their sins." Let us receive the laws of life, let us comply with God's

strong disprove

expostulations; let us become acquainted with Him, that He may be gracious. And though God needs nothing let us render to Him the grateful recompense of a thankful heart and of piety, as a kind of house-rent for our dwelling here below.

"Gold for brass, A hundred oxen's worth for that of nine;" that is, for your little faith He gives you the earth of so great extent to till, water to drink and also to sail on, air to breathe, fire to do your work, a world to dwell in; and He has permitted you to conduct a colony from here to heaven: with these important works of His hand, and benefits in such numbers, He has rewarded your little faith. Then, those who have put faith in necromancers, receive from them amulets and charms, to ward off evil forsooth; and will you not allow the heavenly Word, the Saviour, to be bound on to you as an amulet, and, by trusting in God's own charm, be delivered from passions which are the diseases of the mind, and rescued from sin?--for sin is eternal death. Surely utterly dull and blind, and, like moles, doing nothing but eat, you spend your lives in darkness, surrounded with corruption. But it is truth which cries, "The light shall shine forth from the darkness." Let the light then shine in the hidden part of man, that is, the heart; and let the beams of knowledge arise to reveal and irradiate the hidden inner man, the disciple of the Light, the familiar friend and fellow-heir of Christ; especially now that we have come to know the most precious and venerable name of the good Father, who to a pious and good child gives gentle counsels, and commands what is salutary for His child. He who obeys Him has the advantage in all things, follows God, obeys the Father, knows Him through wandering, loves God, loves his neighbour, fulfils the commandment, seeks the prize, claims the promise. But it has been God's fixed and constant purpose to save the flock of men: for this end the good God sent the good Shepherd. And the Word, having unfolded the truth, showed to men the height of salvation, that either repenting they might be saved, or refusing to obey, they might be judged. This is the proclamation of righteousness: to those that obey, glad tidings; to those that disobey, judgment. The loud trumpet, when sounded, collects the soldiers, and proclaims war. And shall not Christ, breathing a strain of peace to the ends of the earth, gather together His own soldiers, the soldiers of peace? Well, by His blood, and by the word, He has gathered the bloodless host of peace, and assigned to them the kingdom of heaven. The trumpet of Christ is His Gospel. He hath blown it, and we have heard. "Let us array ourselves in the armour of peace, putting on the breastplate of righteousness, and taking the shield of faith, and binding our brows with the helmet, of salvation; and the sword of the

Spirit, which is the word of God," let us sharpen. So the apostle in the spirit of peace commands. These are our invulnerable weapons: armed with these, let us face the evil one; "the fiery darts of the evil one" let us quench with the sword-points dipped in water, that, have been baptized by the Word, returning grateful thanks for the benefits we have received, and honouring God through the Divine Word. "For while thou art yet speaking," it is said, "He will say, Behold, I am beside thee." O this holy and blessed power, by which God has fellowship with men! Better far, then, is it to become at once the imitator and the servant of the best of all beings; for only by holy service will any one be able to imitate God, and to serve and worship Him only by imitating Him. The heavenly and truly divine love comes to men thus, when in the soul itself the spark of true goodness, kindled in the soul by the Divine Word, is able to burst forth into flame; and, what is of the highest importance, salvation runs parallel with sincere willingness-- choice and life being, so to speak, yoked together. Wherefore this exhortation of the truth alone, like the most faithful of our friends, abides with us till our last breath, and is to the whole and perfect spirit of the soul the kind attendant on our ascent to heaven. What, then, is the exhortation I give you? I urge you to be saved. This Christ desires. In one word. He freely bestows life on you. And who is He? Briefly learn. The Word of truth, the Word of incorruption, that regenerates man by bringing him back to the truth-- the goad that urges to salvation t He who expels destruction and pursues death-- He who builds up the temple of God in men, that He may cause God to take up His abode in men.

Cleanse the temple; and pleasures and amusements abandon to the winds and the fire, as a fading flower; but wisely cultivate the fruits of self-command, and present thyself to God as an offering of first- fruits, that there may be not the work alone, but also the grace of God; and both are requisite, that the friend of Christ may be rendered worthy of the kingdom, and be counted worthy of the kingdom.

CHAP. XII.--EXHORTATION TO ABANDON THEIR OLD ERRORS AND LISTEN TO THE INSTRUCTIONS OF CHRIST.

Let us then avoid custom as we would a dangerous headland, or the threatening Charybdis, or the mythic sirens. It chokes man, turns him away from truth, leads him away from life: custom is a snare, a gulf, a pit, a mischievous winnowing fan.

"Urge the ship beyond that smoke and billow."

Let us shun, fellow-mariners, let us shun this billow; it vomits forth fire: it is a wicked island, heaped with bones and corpses, and in it sings a fair courtesan, Pleasure, delighting with music for the common ear.

"Hie thee hither, far-famed Ulysses, great glory of the Achaeans; Moor the ship, that thou mayest hears diviner voice."

[margin annotation: Pleasure analogous to an island]

She praises thee, O mariner, and calls the eillustrious; and the courtesan tries to win to herself the glory of the Greeks. Leave her to prey on the dead; a heavenly spirit comes to thy help: pass by Pleasure, she beguiles.

"Let not a woman with flowing train cheat you of your senses, With her flattering prattle seeking your hurt."

Sail past the song; it works death. Exert your will only, and you have overcome ruin; bound to the wood of the cross, thou shalt be freed from destruction: the word of God will be thy pilot, and the Holy Spirit will bring thee to anchor in the haven of heaven. Then shalt thou see my God, and be initiated into the sacred mysteries, and come to the fruition of those things which are laid up in heaven reserved for me, which "ear hath not heard, nor have they entered into the heart of any."

"And in sooth methinks I see two suns, And a double Thebes," said one frenzy-stricken in the worship of idols, intoxicated with mere ignorance. I would pity him in his frantic intoxication, and thus frantic I would invite him to the sobriety of salvation; for the Lord welcomes a sinner's repentance, and not his death. Come, O madman, not leaning on the thyrsus, not crowned with ivy; throw away the mitre, throw away the fawn-skin; come to thy senses. I will show thee the Word, and the mysteries of the Word, expounding them after thine own fashion. This is the mountain beloved of God, not the subject of tragedies like Cithaeron, but consecrated to dramas of the truth,--a mount of sobriety, shaded with forests of purity; and there revel on it not the Maenades, the sisters of Semele, who was struck by the thunderbolt, practising in their initiator rites unholy division of flesh, but the daughters of God, the fair lambs, who celebrate the holy rites of the Word, raising a sober choral dance. The righteous are the chorus; the music is a hymn of the King of the universe. The maidens strike the lyre, the angels praise, the prophets speak; the sound of music issues forth, they run and pursue the jubilant band; those that are called make haste, eagerly desiring to receive the Father.

Come thou also, O aged man, leaving Thebes, and casting away from thee both divination and Bacchic frenzy, allow thyself to be led to the truth. I give thee the staff [of the cross] on which to lean. Haste, Tiresias; believe, and thou wilt see. Christ, by whom the eyes of the blind recover sight, will shed on thee a light brighter than the sun; night will flee from thee, fire will fear, death will be gone; thou, old man, who saw not Thebes, shalt see the heavens. O truly sacred mysteries! O stainless light! My way is lighted with torches, and I survey the heavens and God; I become holy whilst I am initiated. The Lord is the hierophant, and seals while illuminating him who is initiated, and presents to the Father him who believes, to be kept safe for ever. Such are the reveries of my mysteries. If it is thy wish, be thou also initiated; and thou shall join the choir along with angels around the unbegotten and indestructible and the only true God, the Word of God, raising the hymn with us. This Jesus, who is eternal, the one great High Priest of the one God, and of His Father, prays for and exhorts men.

"Hear, ye myriad tribes, rather whoever among men are endowed with reason, both barbarians and Greeks. I call on the whole race of men, whose Creator I am, by the will of the Father. Come to Me, that you may be put in your due rank under the one God and the one Word of God; and do not only have the advantage of the irrational creatures in the possession of reason; for to you of all mortals I grant the enjoyment of immortality. For I want, I want to impart to you this grace, bestowing on you the perfect boon of immortality; and I confer on you both the Word and the knowledge of God, My complete self. This am I, this God wills, this is symphony, this the harmony of the Father, this is the Son, this is Christ, this the Word of God, the arm of the Lord, the power of the universe, the will of the Father; of which things there were images of old, but not all adequate. I desire to restore you according to the original model, that ye may become also like Me. I anoint you with the ungent of faith, by which you throw off corrup tion, and show you the naked form of righteousness by which you ascend to God. Come to Me, all ye that labour and are heavy laden, and I will give you rest. Take My yoke upon you, and learn of Me; for I am meek and lowly in heart: and ye shall find rest to your souls. For My yoke is easy, and My burden light."

Let us haste, let us run, my fellowmen--us, who are God-loving and God-like images of the Word. Let us haste, let us run, let us take His yoke, let us receive, to conduct us to immortality, the good charioteer of men. Let us love Christ. He led the colt with its parent; and having yoked the team of humanity to God, directs His chariot to immortality, hastening clearly to fulfil, by driving now into heaven, what He shadowed forth before by riding into Jerusalem. A spectacle most beautiful to the Father is the eternal Son crowned with victory. Let us aspire, then, after what is good; let us become God-loving men, and obtain the greatest of all things which are incapable of being harmed--God and life. Our helper is the Word; let us put confidence in Him; and never let us be visited with such a craving for silver and gold, and glory, as for the Word of truth Himself. For it will not, it will not be pleasing to God Himself if we value least those things which are worth most, and hold in the highest estimation the manifest enormities and the utter impiety of folly, and ignorance, and thoughtlessness, and idolatry. For not improperly the sons of the philosophers consider that the foolish are guilty of profanity and impiety in whatever they do; and describing ignorance itself as a species of madness, allege that the multitude are nothing but madmen. There is therefore no room to doubt, the Word will say, whether it is better to be sane or insane; but holding on to truth with our teeth, we must with all our might follow God, and in the exercise of wisdom regard all things to be, as they are, His; and besides, having learned that we are the most excellent of His possessions, let us commit ourselves to God, loving the Lord God, and regarding this as our business all our life long. And if what belongs to friends be reckoned common property, and man be the friend of God-for through the mediation of the Word has he been made the friend of God--then accordingly all things become man's, because all things are God's, and the common property of both the friends, God and man.

It is time, then, for us to say that the pious Christian alone is rich and wise, and of noble birth, and thus call and believe him to be God's image, and also His likeness, having become righteous and holy and wise by Jesus Christ, and so far already like God. Accordingly this grace is indicated by the prophet, when he says, "I said that ye are gods, and all sons of the Highest." For us, yea us, He has adopted, and wishes to be called the Father of us alone, not of the unbelieving. Such is then our position who are the attendants of Christ.

"As are men's wishes, so are their words; As are their words, so are their deeds; And as their works, such is their life."

Good is the whole life of those who have known Christ.

Enough, methinks, of words, though, impelled by love to man, I might have gone on to pour out what I had from God, that I might exhort to what is the greatest of blessings--salvation. For discourses concerning the life which has no end, are not readily brought to the end of their disclosures. To you still remains this conclusion, to choose which will profit you most--judgment or grace. For I do not think there is even room for doubt which of these is the better; nor is it allowable to compare life with destruction.

HISTORY OF THE CHURCH

Eusebius

TRANSLATED BY ARTHUR CUSHMAN MCGIFFERT

BOOK I

Chapter 1. The Plan of the Work.

1. It is my purpose to write an account of the successions of the holy apostles, as well as of the times which have elapsed from the days of our Saviour to our own; and to relate the many important events which are said to have occurred in the history of the Church; and to mention those who have governed and presided over the Church in the most prominent parishes, and those who in each generation have proclaimed the divine word either orally or in writing.

2. It is my purpose also to give the names and number and times of those who through love of innovation have run into the greatest errors, and, proclaiming themselves discoverers of knowledge falsely so-called 1 Timothy 6:20 have like fierce wolves unmercifully devastated the flock of Christ.

3. It is my intention, moreover, to recount the misfortunes which immediately came upon the whole Jewish nation in consequence of their plots against our Saviour, and to record the ways and the times in which the divine word has been attacked by the Gentiles, and to describe the character of those who at various periods have contended for it in the face of blood and of tortures, as well as the confessions which have been made in our own days, and finally the gracious and kindly succor which our Saviour has afforded them all. Since I propose to write of all these things I shall commence my work with the beginning of the dispensation of our Saviour and Lord Jesus Christ.

4. But at the outset I must crave for my work the indulgence of the wise, for I confess that it is beyond my power to produce a perfect and complete history, and since I am the first to enter upon the subject, I am attempting to traverse as it were a lonely and untrodden path. I pray that I may have God as my guide and the power of the Lord as my aid, since I am unable to find even the bare footsteps of those who have

traveled the way before me, except in brief fragments, in which some in one way, others in another, have transmitted to us particular accounts of the times in which they lived. From afar they raise their voices like torches, and they cry out, as from some lofty and conspicuous watchtower, admonishing us where to walk and how to direct the course of our work steadily and safely.

5. Having gathered therefore from the matters mentioned here and there by them whatever we consider important for the present work, and having plucked like flowers from a meadow the appropriate passages from ancient writers, we shall endeavor to embody the whole in an historical narrative, content if we preserve the memory of the successions of the apostles of our Saviour; if not indeed of all, yet of the most renowned of them in those churches which are the most noted, and which even to the present time are held in honor.

6. This work seems to me of especial importance because I know of no ecclesiastical writer who has devoted himself to this subject; and I hope that it will appear most useful to those who are fond of historical research.

7. I have already given an epitome of these things in the Chronological Canons which I have composed, but notwithstanding that, I have undertaken in the present work to write as full an account of them as I am able.

8. My work will begin, as I have said, with the dispensation of the Saviour Christ — which is loftier and greater than human conception

— and with a discussion of his divinity.

9. For it is necessary, inasmuch as we derive even our name from Christ, for one who proposes to write a history of the Church to begin with the very origin of Christ's dispensation, a dispensation more divine than many think.

Chapter 2. Summary View of the Pre-existence and Divinity of Our Saviour and Lord Jesus Christ.

1. Since in Christ there is a twofold nature, and the one — in so far as he is thought of as God — resembles the head of the body, while the other may be compared with the feet — in so far as he, for the sake of our salvation, put on human nature with the same passions as our own — the following work will be complete only if we begin with the chief

and lordliest events of all his history. In this way will the antiquity and divinity of Christianity be shown to those who suppose it of recent and foreign origin, and imagine that it appeared only yesterday.

2. No language is sufficient to express the origin and the worth, the being and the nature of Christ. Wherefore also the divine Spirit says in the prophecies, Who shall declare his generation? Isaiah 53:8 For none knows the Father except the Son, neither can any one know the Son adequately except the Father alone who has begotten him.

3. For who beside the Father could clearly understand the Light which was before the world, the intellectual and essential Wisdom which existed before the ages, the living Word which was in the beginning with the Father and which was God, the first and only begotten of God which was before every creature and creation visible and invisible, the commander-in-chief of the rational and immortal host of heaven, the messenger of the great counsel, the executor of the Father's unspoken will, the creator, with the Father, of all things, the second cause of the universe after the Father, the true and only- begotten Son of God, the Lord and God and King of all created things, the one who has received dominion and power, with divinity itself, and with might and honor from the Father; as it is said in regard to him in the mystical passages of Scripture which speak of his divinity: In the beginning was the Word, and the Word was with God, and the Word was God. John 1:1 All things were made by him; and without him was not anything made. John 1:3

4. This, too, the great Moses teaches, when, as the most ancient of all the prophets, he describes under the influence of the divine Spirit the creation and arrangement of the universe. He declares that the maker of the world and the creator of all things yielded to Christ himself, and to none other than his own clearly divine and first-born Word, the making of inferior things, and communed with him respecting the creation of man. For, says he, God said, Let us make man in our image and in our likeness. Genesis 1:26

5. And another of the prophets confirms this, speaking of God in his hymns as follows: He spoke and they were made, he commanded and they were created. He here introduces the Father and Maker as Ruler of all, commanding with a kingly nod, and second to him the divine Word, none other than the one who is proclaimed by us, as carrying out the Father's commands.

6. All that are said to have excelled in righteousness and piety since the creation of man, the great servant Moses and before him in the first

place Abraham and his children, and as many righteous men and prophets as afterward appeared, have contemplated him with the pure eyes of the mind, and have recognized him and offered to him the worship which is due him as Son of God.

7. But he, by no means neglectful of the reverence due to the Father, was appointed to teach the knowledge of the Father to them all. For instance, the Lord God, it is said, appeared as a common man to Abraham while he was sitting at the oak of Mambre. And he, immediately falling down, although he saw a man with his eyes, nevertheless worshipped him as God, and sacrificed to him as Lord, and confessed that he was not ignorant of his identity when he uttered the words, Lord, the judge of all the earth, will you not execute righteous judgment? Genesis 18:25

8. For if it is unreasonable to suppose that the unbegotten and immutable essence of the almighty God was changed into the form of man or that it deceived the eyes of the beholders with the appearance of some created thing, and if it is unreasonable to suppose, on the other hand, that the Scripture should falsely invent such things, when the God and Lord who judges all the earth and executes judgment is seen in the form of a man, who else can be called, if it be not lawful to call him the first cause of all things, than his only pre-existent Word? Concerning whom it is said in the Psalms, He sent his Word and healed them, and delivered them from their destructions.

9. Moses most clearly proclaims him second Lord after the Father, when he says, The Lord rained upon Sodom and Gomorrha brimstone and fire from the Lord. Genesis 19:24 The divine Scripture also calls him God, when he appeared again to Jacob in the form of a man, and said to Jacob, Your name shall be called no more Jacob, but Israel shall be your name, because you have prevailed with God. Genesis 32:28 Wherefore also Jacob called the name of that place Vision of God, saying, For I have seen God face to face, and my life is preserved. Genesis 32:30

10. Nor is it admissible to suppose that the theophanies recorded were appearances of subordinate angels and ministers of God, for whenever any of these appeared to men, the Scripture does not conceal the fact, but calls them by name not God nor Lord, but angels, as it is easy to prove by numberless testimonies.

11. Joshua, also, the successor of Moses, calls him, as leader of the heavenly angels and archangels and of the supramundane powers, and

as lieutenant of the Father, entrusted with the second rank of sovereignty and rule over all, captain of the host of the Lord, although he saw him not otherwise than again in the form and appearance of a man. For it is written:

12. And it came to pass when Joshua was at Jericho that he looked and saw a man standing over against him with his sword drawn in his hand, and Joshua went unto him and said, Are you for us or for our adversaries? And he said unto him, As captain of the host of the Lord am I now come. And Joshua fell on his face to the earth and said unto him, Lord, what do you command your servant? And the captain of the Lord said unto Joshua, Loose your shoe from off your feet, for the place whereon you stand is holy.

13. You will perceive also from the same words that this was no other than he who talked with Moses. For the Scripture says in the same words and with reference to the same one, When the Lord saw that he drew near to see, the Lord called to him out of the bush and said, Moses, Moses. And he said, What is it? And he said, Draw not near hither; loose your shoe from off your feet, for the place whereon you stand is holy ground. And he said unto him, I am the God of your fathers, the God of Abraham, and the God of Isaac, and the God of Jacob.

14. And that there is a certain substance which lived and subsisted before the world, and which ministered unto the Father and God of the universe for the formation of all created things, and which is called the Word of God and Wisdom, we may learn, to quote other proofs in addition to those already cited, from the mouth of Wisdom herself, who reveals most clearly through Solomon the following mysteries concerning herself: I, Wisdom, have dwelt with prudence and knowledge, and I have invoked understanding. Through me kings reign, and princes ordain righteousness. Through me the great are magnified, and through me sovereigns rule the earth.

15. To which she adds: The Lord created me in the beginning of his ways, for his works; before the world he established me, in the beginning, before he made the earth, before he made the depths, before the mountains were settled, before all hills he begot me. When he prepared the heavens I was present with him, and when he established the fountains of the region under heaven I was with him, disposing. I was the one in whom he delighted; daily I rejoiced before him at all times when he was rejoicing at having completed the world.

16. That the divine Word, therefore, pre-existed and appeared to some, if not to all, has thus been briefly shown by us.

17. But why the Gospel was not preached in ancient times to all men and to all nations, as it is now, will appear from the following considerations. The life of the ancients was not of such a kind as to permit them to receive the all-wise and all-virtuous teaching of Christ.

18. For immediately in the beginning, after his original life of blessedness, the first man despised the command of God, and fell into this mortal and perishable state, and exchanged his former divinely inspired luxury for this curse-laden earth. His descendants having filled our earth, showed themselves much worse, with the exception of one here and there, and entered upon a certain brutal and insupportable mode of life.

19. They thought neither of city nor state, neither of arts nor sciences. They were ignorant even of the name of laws and of justice, of virtue and of philosophy. As nomads, they passed their lives in deserts, like wild and fierce beasts, destroying, by an excess of voluntary wickedness, the natural reason of man, and the seeds of thought and of culture implanted in the human soul. They gave themselves wholly over to all kinds of profanity, now seducing one another, now slaying one another, now eating human flesh, and now daring to wage war with the Gods and to undertake those battles of the giants celebrated by all; now planning to fortify earth against heaven, and in the madness of ungoverned pride to prepare an attack upon the very God of all.

20. On account of these things, when they conducted themselves thus, the all-seeing God sent down upon them floods and conflagrations as upon a wild forest spread over the whole earth. He cut them down with continuous famines and plagues, with wars, and with thunderbolts from heaven, as if to check some terrible and obstinate disease of souls with more severe punishments.

21. Then, when the excess of wickedness had overwhelmed nearly all the race, like a deep fit of drunkenness, beclouding and darkening the minds of men, the first-born and first-created wisdom of God, the pre-existent Word himself, induced by his exceeding love for man, appeared to his servants, now in the form of angels, and again to one and another of those ancients who enjoyed the favor of God, in his own person as the saving power of God, not otherwise, however, than in the shape of man, because it was impossible to appear in any other way.

22. And as by them the seeds of piety were sown among a multitude of men and the whole nation, descended from the Hebrews, devoted themselves persistently to the worship of God, he imparted to them through the prophet Moses, as to multitudes still corrupted by their ancient practices, images and symbols of a certain mystic Sabbath and of circumcision, and elements of other spiritual principles, but he did not grant them a complete knowledge of the mysteries themselves.

23. But when their law became celebrated, and, like a sweet odor, was diffused among all men, as a result of their influence the dispositions of the majority of the heathen were softened by the lawgivers and philosophers who arose on every side, and their wild and savage brutality was changed into mildness, so that they enjoyed deep peace, friendship, and social intercourse. Then, finally, at the time of the origin of the Roman Empire, there appeared again to all men and nations throughout the world, who had been, as it were, previously assisted, and were now fitted to receive the knowledge of the Father, that same teacher of virtue, the minister of the Father in all good things, the divine and heavenly Word of God, in a human body not at all differing in substance from our own. He did and suffered the things which had been prophesied. For it had been foretold that one who was at the same time man and God should come and dwell in the world, should perform wonderful works, and should show himself a teacher to all nations of the piety of the Father. The marvelous nature of his birth, and his new teaching, and his wonderful works had also been foretold; so likewise the manner of his death, his resurrection from the dead, and, finally, his divine ascension into heaven.

24. For instance, Daniel the prophet, under the influence of the divine Spirit, seeing his kingdom at the end of time, was inspired thus to describe the divine vision in language fitted to human comprehension: For I beheld, he says, until thrones were placed, and the Ancient of Days did sit, whose garment was white as snow and the hair of his head like pure wool; his throne was a flame of fire and his wheels burning fire. A river of fire flowed before him. Thousand thousands ministered unto him, and ten thousand times ten thousand stood before him. He appointed judgment, and the books were opened. Daniel 7:9-10

25. And again, I saw, says he, and behold, one like the Son of man came with the clouds of heaven, and he hastened unto the Ancient of Days and was brought into his presence, and there was given him the dominion and the glory and the kingdom; and all peoples, tribes, and

tongues serve him. His dominion is an everlasting dominion which shall not pass away, and his kingdom shall not be destroyed. Daniel 7:13-14

26. It is clear that these words can refer to no one else than to our Saviour, the God Word who was in the beginning with God, and who was called the Son of man because of his final appearance in the flesh.

27. But since we have collected in separate books the selections from the prophets which relate to our Saviour Jesus Christ, and have arranged in a more logical form those things which have been revealed concerning him, what has been said will suffice for the present.

Chapter 3. The Name Jesus and also the Name Christ were known from the Beginning, and were honored by the Inspired Prophets.

1. It is now the proper place to show that the very name Jesus and also the name Christ were honored by the ancient prophets beloved of God.

2. Moses was the first to make known the name of Christ as a name especially august and glorious. When he delivered types and symbols of heavenly things, and mysterious images, in accordance with the oracle which said to him, Look that you make all things according to the pattern which was shown you in the mount, Exodus 25:40 he consecrated a man high priest of God, in so far as that was possible, and him he called Christ. And thus to this dignity of the high priesthood, which in his opinion surpassed the most honorable position among men, he attached for the sake of honor and glory the name of Christ.

3. He knew so well that in Christ was something divine. And the same one foreseeing, under the influence of the divine Spirit, the name Jesus, dignified it also with a certain distinguished privilege. For the name of Jesus, which had never been uttered among men before the time of Moses, he applied first and only to the one who he knew would receive after his death, again as a type and symbol, the supreme command.

4. His successor, therefore, who had not hitherto borne the name Jesus, but had been called by another name, Auses, which had been given him by his parents, he now called Jesus, bestowing the name upon him as a gift of honor, far greater than any kingly diadem. For Jesus himself, the son of Nave, bore a resemblance to our Saviour in the fact that he alone, after Moses and after the completion of the symbolic worship which had been transmitted by him, succeeded to the government of the true and pure religion.

5. Thus Moses bestowed the name of our Saviour, Jesus Christ, as a mark of the highest honor, upon the two men who in his time surpassed all the rest of the people in virtue and glory; namely, upon the high priest and upon his own successor in the government.

6. And the prophets that came after also clearly foretold Christ by name, predicting at the same time the plots which the Jewish people would form against him, and the calling of the nations through him. Jeremiah, for instance, speaks as follows: The Spirit before our face, Christ the Lord, was taken in their destructions; of whom we said, under his shadow we shall live among the nations. Lamentations 4:20 And David, in perplexity, says, Why did the nations rage and the people imagine vain things? The kings of the earth set themselves in array, and the rulers were gathered together against the Lord and against his Christ; to which he adds, in the person of Christ himself, The Lord said unto me, You are my Son, this day have I begotten you. Ask of me, and I will give you the nations for your inheritance, and the uttermost parts of the earth for your possession.

7. And not only those who were honored with the high priesthood, and who for the sake of the symbol were anointed with especially prepared oil, were adorned with the name of Christ among the Hebrews, but also the kings whom the prophets anointed under the influence of the divine Spirit, and thus constituted, as it were, typical Christs. For they also bore in their own persons types of the royal and sovereign power of the true and only Christ, the divine Word who rules over all.

8. And we have been told also that certain of the prophets themselves became, by the act of anointing, Christs in type, so that all these have reference to the true Christ, the divinely inspired and heavenly Word, who is the only high priest of all, and the only King of every creature, and the Father's only supreme prophet of prophets.

9. And a proof of this is that no one of those who were of old symbolically anointed, whether priests, or kings, or prophets, possessed so great a power of inspired virtue as was exhibited by our Saviour and Lord Jesus, the true and only Christ.

10. None of them at least, however superior in dignity and honor they may have been for many generations among their own people, ever gave to their followers the name of Christians from their own typical name of Christ. Neither was divine honor ever rendered to any one of them by their subjects; nor after their death was the disposition of their followers such that they were ready to die for the one whom they

honored. And never did so great a commotion arise among all the nations of the earth in respect to any one of that age; for the mere symbol could not act with such power among them as the truth itself which was exhibited by our Saviour.

11. He, although he received no symbols and types of high priesthood from any one, although he was not born of a race of priests, although he was not elevated to a kingdom by military guards, although he was not a prophet like those of old, although he obtained no honor nor pre-eminence among the Jews, nevertheless was adorned by the Father with all, if not with the symbols, yet with the truth itself.

12. And therefore, although he did not possess like honors with those whom we have mentioned, he is called Christ more than all of them. And as himself the true and only Christ of God, he has filled the whole earth with the truly august and sacred name of Christians, committing to his followers no longer types and images, but the uncovered virtues themselves, and a heavenly life in the very doctrines of truth.

13. And he was not anointed with oil prepared from material substances, but, as befits divinity, with the divine Spirit himself, by participation in the unbegotten deity of the Father. And this is taught also again by Isaiah, who exclaims, as if in the person of Christ himself, The Spirit of the Lord is upon me; therefore has he anointed me. He has sent me to preach the Gospel to the poor, to proclaim deliverance to captives, and recovery of sight to the blind.

14. And not only Isaiah, but also David addresses him, saying, Your throne, O God, is forever and ever. A scepter of equity is the scepter of your kingdom. You have loved righteousness and have hated iniquity. Therefore God, your God, has anointed you with the oil of gladness above your fellows. Here the Scripture calls him God in the first verse, in the second it honors him with a royal scepter.

15. Then a little farther on, after the divine and royal power, it represents him in the third place as having become Christ, being anointed not with oil made of material substances, but with the divine oil of gladness. It thus indicates his special honor, far superior to and different from that of those who, as types, were of old anointed in a more material way.

16. And elsewhere the same writer speaks of him as follows: The Lord said unto my Lord, Sit at my right hand until I make your enemies your footstool; and, Out of the womb, before the morning star, have I

begotten you. The Lord has sworn and he will not repent. You are a priest forever after the order of Melchizedec.

17. But this Melchizedec is introduced in the Holy Scriptures as a priest of the most high God, not consecrated by any anointing oil, especially prepared, and not even belonging by descent to the priesthood of the Jews. Wherefore after his order, but not after the order of the others, who received symbols and types, was our Saviour proclaimed, with an appeal to an oath, Christ and priest.

18. History, therefore, does not relate that he was anointed corporeally by the Jews, nor that he belonged to the lineage of priests, but that he came into existence from God himself before the morning star, that is before the organization of the world, and that he obtained an immortal and undecaying priesthood for eternal ages.

19. But it is a great and convincing proof of his incorporeal and divine unction that he alone of all those who have ever existed is even to the present day called Christ by all men throughout the world, and is confessed and witnessed to under this name, and is commemorated both by Greeks and Barbarians and even to this day is honored as a King by his followers throughout the world, and is admired as more than a prophet, and is glorified as the true and only high priest of God. And besides all this, as the pre-existent Word of God, called into being before all ages, he has received august honor from the Father, and is worshipped as God.

20. But most wonderful of all is the fact that we who have consecrated ourselves to him, honor him not only with our voices and with the sound of words, but also with complete elevation of soul, so that we choose to give testimony unto him rather than to preserve our own lives.

21. I have of necessity prefaced my history with these matters in order that no one, judging from the date of his incarnation, may think that our Saviour and Lord Jesus, the Christ, has but recently come into being.

Chapter 4. The Religion Proclaimed by Him to All Nations Was Neither New Nor Strange.

1. But that no one may suppose that his doctrine is new and strange, as if it were framed by a man of recent origin, differing in no respect from other men, let us now briefly consider this point also.

2. It is admitted that when in recent times the appearance of our Saviour Jesus Christ had become known to all men there immediately made its appearance a new nation; a nation confessedly not small, and not dwelling in some corner of the earth, but the most numerous and pious of all nations, indestructible and unconquerable, because it always receives assistance from God. This nation, thus suddenly appearing at the time appointed by the inscrutable counsel of God, is the one which has been honored by all with the name of Christ.

3. One of the prophets, when he saw beforehand with the eye of the Divine Spirit that which was to be, was so astonished at it that he cried out, Who has heard of such things, and who has spoken thus? Hath the earth brought forth in one day, and has a nation been born at once? Isaiah 66:8 And the same prophet gives a hint also of the name by which the nation was to be called, when he says, Those that serve me shall be called by a new name, which shall be blessed upon the earth. Isaiah 65:15-16

4. But although it is clear that we are new and that this new name of Christians has really but recently been known among all nations, nevertheless our life and our conduct, with our doctrines of religion, have not been lately invented by us, but from the first creation of man, so to speak, have been established by the natural understanding of divinely favored men of old. That this is so we shall show in the following way.

5. That the Hebrew nation is not new, but is universally honored on account of its antiquity, is known to all. The books and writings of this people contain accounts of ancient men, rare indeed and few in number, but nevertheless distinguished for piety and righteousness and every other virtue. Of these, some excellent men lived before the flood, others of the sons and descendants of Noah lived after it, among them Abraham, whom the Hebrews celebrate as their own founder and forefather.

6. If any one should assert that all those who have enjoyed the testimony of righteousness, from Abraham himself back to the first man, were Christians in fact if not in name, he would not go beyond the truth.

7. For that which the name indicates, that the Christian man, through the knowledge and the teaching of Christ, is distinguished for temperance and righteousness, for patience in life and manly virtue, and for a profession of piety toward the one and only God over all— all that was zealously practiced by them not less than by us.

8. They did not care about circumcision of the body, neither do we. They did not care about observing Sabbaths, nor do we. They did not avoid certain kinds of food, neither did they regard the other distinctions which Moses first delivered to their posterity to be observed as symbols; nor do Christians of the present day do such things. But they also clearly knew the very Christ of God; for it has already been shown that he appeared unto Abraham, that he imparted revelations to Isaac, that he talked with Jacob, that he held converse with Moses and with the prophets that came after.

9. Hence you will find those divinely favored men honored with the name of Christ, according to the passage which says of them, Touch not my Christs, and do my prophets no harm.

10. So that it is clearly necessary to consider that religion, which has lately been preached to all nations through the teaching of Christ, the first and most ancient of all religions, and the one discovered by those divinely favored men in the age of Abraham.

11. If it is said that Abraham, a long time afterward, was given the command of circumcision, we reply that nevertheless before this it was declared that he had received the testimony of righteousness through faith; as the divine word says, Abraham believed in God, and it was counted unto him for righteousness. Genesis 15:6

12. And indeed unto Abraham, who was thus before his circumcision a justified man, there was given by God, who revealed himself unto him (but this was Christ himself, the word of God), a prophecy in regard to those who in coming ages should be justified in the same way as he. The prophecy was in the following words: And in you shall all the tribes of the earth be blessed. Genesis 12:3 And again, He shall become a nation great and numerous; and in him shall all the nations of the earth be blessed. Genesis 18:18

13. It is permissible to understand this as fulfilled in us. For he, having renounced the superstition of his fathers, and the former error of his life, and having confessed the one God over all, and having worshipped him with deeds of virtue, and not with the service of the law which was afterward given by Moses, was justified by faith in Christ, the Word of God, who appeared unto him. To him, then, who was a man of this character, it was said that all the tribes and all the nations of the earth should be blessed in him.

14. But that very religion of Abraham has reappeared at the present time, practiced in deeds, more efficacious than words, by Christians alone throughout the world.

15. What then should prevent the confession that we who are of Christ practice one and the same mode of life and have one and the same religion as those divinely favored men of old? Whence it is evident that the perfect religion committed to us by the teaching of Christ is not new and strange, but, if the truth must be spoken, it is the first and the true religion. This may suffice for this subject.

Chapter 5. The Time of his Appearance among Men.

1. And now, after this necessary introduction to our proposed history of the Church, we can enter, so to speak, upon our journey, beginning with the appearance of our Saviour in the flesh. And we invoke God, the Father of the Word, and him, of whom we have been speaking, Jesus Christ himself our Saviour and Lord, the heavenly Word of God, as our aid and fellow-laborer in the narration of the truth.

2. It was in the forty-second year of the reign of Augustus and the twenty-eighth after the subjugation of Egypt and the death of Antony and Cleopatra, with whom the dynasty of the Ptolemies in Egypt came to an end, that our Saviour and Lord Jesus Christ was born in Bethlehem of Judea, according to the prophecies which had been uttered concerning him. Micah 5:2 His birth took place during the first census, while Cyrenius was governor of Syria.

3. Flavius Josephus, the most celebrated of Hebrew historians, also mentions this census, which was taken during Cyrenius' term of office. In the same connection he gives an account of the uprising of the Galileans, which took place at that time, of which also Luke, among our writers, has made mention in the Acts, in the following words: After this man rose up Judas of Galilee in the days of the taxing, and drew away a multitude after him: he also perished; and all, even as many as obeyed him, were dispersed. Acts 5:37

4. The above-mentioned author, in the eighteenth book of his Antiquities, in agreement with these words, adds the following, which we quote exactly: Cyrenius, a member of the senate, one who had held other offices and had passed through them all to the consulship, a man also of great dignity in other respects, came to Syria with a small retinue,

being sent by Cæsar to be a judge of the nation and to make an assessment of their property.

5. And after a little he says: But Judas, a Gaulonite, from a city called Gamala, taking with him Sadduchus, a Pharisee, urged the people to revolt, both of them saying that the taxation meant nothing else than downright slavery, and exhorting the nation to defend their liberty.

6. And in the second book of his History of the Jewish War, he writes as follows concerning the same man: At this time a certain Galilean, whose name was Judas, persuaded his countrymen to revolt, declaring that they were cowards if they submitted to pay tribute to the Romans, and if they endured, besides God, masters who were mortal. These things are recorded by Josephus.

Chapter 6. About the Time of Christ, in accordance with Prophecy, the Rulers who had governed the Jewish Nation in Regular Succession from the Days of Antiquity came to an End, and Herod, the First Foreigner, Became King.

1. When Herod, the first ruler of foreign blood, became King, the prophecy of Moses received its fulfillment, according to which there should not be wanting a prince of Judah, nor a ruler from his loins, until he come for whom it is reserved. The latter, he also shows, was to be the expectation of the nations.

2. This prediction remained unfulfilled so long as it was permitted them to live under rulers from their own nation, that is, from the time of Moses to the reign of Augustus. Under the latter, Herod, the first foreigner, was given the Kingdom of the Jews by the Romans. As Josephus relates, he was an Idumean on his father's side and an Arabian on his mother's. But Africanus, who was also no common writer, says that they who were more accurately informed about him report that he was a son of Antipater, and that the latter was the son of a certain Herod of Ascalon, one of the so-called servants of the temple of Apollo.

3. This Antipater, having been taken a prisoner while a boy by Idumean robbers, lived with them, because his father, being a poor man, was unable to pay a ransom for him. Growing up in their practices he was afterward befriended by Hyrcanus, the high priest of the Jews. A son of his was that Herod who lived in the times of our Saviour.

4. When the Kingdom of the Jews had devolved upon such a man the expectation of the nations was, according to prophecy, already at the

door. For with him their princes and governors, who had ruled in regular succession from the time of Moses came to an end.

5. Before their captivity and their transportation to Babylon they were ruled by Saul first and then by David, and before the kings leaders governed them who were called Judges, and who came after Moses and his successor Jesus.

6. After their return from Babylon they continued to have without interruption an aristocratic form of government, with an oligarchy. For the priests had the direction of affairs until Pompey, the Roman general, took Jerusalem by force, and defiled the holy places by entering the very innermost sanctuary of the temple. Aristobulus, who, by the right of ancient succession, had been up to that time both king and high priest, he sent with his children in chains to Rome; and gave to Hyrcanus, brother of Aristobulus, the high priesthood, while the whole nation of the Jews was made tributary to the Romans from that time.

7. But Hyrcanus, who was the last of the regular line of high priests, was very soon afterward taken prisoner by the Parthians, and Herod, the first foreigner, as I have already said, was made King of the Jewish nation by the Roman senate and by Augustus.

8. Under him Christ appeared in bodily shape, and the expected Salvation of the nations and their calling followed in accordance with prophecy. From this time the princes and rulers of Judah, I mean of the Jewish nation, came to an end, and as a natural consequence the order of the high priesthood, which from ancient times had proceeded regularly in closest succession from generation to generation, was immediately thrown into confusion.

9. Of these things Josephus is also a witness, who shows that when Herod was made King by the Romans he no longer appointed the high priests from the ancient line, but gave the honor to certain obscure persons. A course similar to that of Herod in the appointment of the priests was pursued by his son Archelaus, and after him by the Romans, who took the government into their own hands.

10. The same writer shows that Herod was the first that locked up the sacred garment of the high priest under his own seal and refused to permit the high priests to keep it for themselves. The same course was followed by Archelaus after him, and after Archelaus by the Romans.

11. These things have been recorded by us in order to show that another prophecy has been fulfilled in the appearance of our Saviour Jesus

Christ. For the Scripture, in the Book of Daniel, Daniel 9:26 having expressly mentioned a certain number of weeks until the coming of Christ, of which we have treated in other books, most clearly prophesies, that after the completion of those weeks the unction among the Jews should totally perish. And this, it has been clearly shown, was fulfilled at the time of the birth of our Saviour Jesus Christ. This has been necessarily premised by us as a proof of the correctness of the time.

Chapter 7. The Alleged Discrepancy in the Gospels in regard to the Genealogy of Christ.

1. Matthew and Luke in their gospels have given us the genealogy of Christ differently, and many suppose that they are at variance with one another. Since as a consequence every believer, in ignorance of the truth, has been zealous to invent some explanation which shall harmonize the two passages, permit us to subjoin the account of the matter which has come down to us, and which is given by Africanus, who was mentioned by us just above, in his epistle to Aristides, where he discusses the harmony of the gospel genealogies. After refuting the opinions of others as forced and deceptive, he give the account which he had received from tradition in these words:

2. For whereas the names of the generations were reckoned in Israel either according to nature or according to law—according to nature by the succession of legitimate offspring, and according to law whenever another raised up a child to the name of a brother dying childless; for because a clear hope of resurrection was not yet given they had a representation of the future promise by a kind of mortal resurrection, in order that the name of the one deceased might be perpetuated—

3. whereas then some of those who are inserted in this genealogical table succeeded by natural descent, the son to the father, while others, though born of one father, were ascribed by name to another, mention was made of both of those who were progenitors in fact and of those who were so only in name.

4. Thus neither of the gospels is in error, for one reckons by nature, the other by law. For the line of descent from Solomon and that from Nathan were so involved, the one with the other, by the raising up of children to the childless and by second marriages, that the same persons are justly considered to belong at one time to one, at another time to another; that is, at one time to the reputed fathers, at another to the

actual fathers. So that both these accounts are strictly true and come down to Joseph with considerable intricacy indeed, yet quite accurately.

5. But in order that what I have said may be made clear I shall explain the interchange of the generations. If we reckon the generations from David through Solomon, the third from the end is found to be Matthan, who begot Jacob the father of Joseph. But if, with Luke, we reckon them from Nathan the son of David, in like manner the third from the end is Melchi, whose son Eli was the father of Joseph. For Joseph was the son of Eli, the son of Melchi.

6. Joseph therefore being the object proposed to us, it must be shown how it is that each is recorded to be his father, both Jacob, who derived his descent from Solomon, and Eli, who derived his from Nathan; first how it is that these two, Jacob and Eli, were brothers, and then how it is that their fathers, Matthan and Melchi, although of different families, are declared to be grandfathers of Joseph.

7. Matthan and Melchi having married in succession the same woman, begot children who were uterine brothers, for the law did not prohibit a widow, whether such by divorce or by the death of her husband, from marrying another.

8. By Estha then (for this was the woman's name according to tradition) Matthan, a descendant of Solomon, first begot Jacob. And when Matthan was dead, Melchi, who traced his descent back to Nathan, being of the same tribe but of another family, married her as before said, and begot a son Eli.

9. Thus we shall find the two, Jacob and Eli, although belonging to different families, yet brethren by the same mother. Of these the one, Jacob, when his brother Eli had died childless, took the latter's wife and begot by her a son Joseph, his own son by nature and in accordance with reason. Wherefore also it is written: 'Jacob begot Joseph.' Matthew 1:6 But according to law he was the son of Eli, for Jacob, being the brother of the latter, raised up seed to him.

10. Hence the genealogy traced through him will not be rendered void, which the evangelist Matthew in his enumeration gives thus: 'Jacob begot Joseph.' But Luke, on the other hand, says: 'Who was the son, as was supposed' (for this he also adds), 'of Joseph, the son of Eli, the son of Melchi'; for he could not more clearly express the generation according to law. And the expression 'he begot' he has omitted in his genealogical table up to the end, tracing the genealogy back to Adam the

son of God. This interpretation is neither incapable of proof nor is it an idle conjecture.

11. For the relatives of our Lord according to the flesh, whether with the desire of boasting or simply wishing to state the fact, in either case truly, have handed down the following account: Some Idumean robbers, having attacked Ascalon, a city of Palestine, carried away from a temple of Apollo which stood near the walls, in addition to other booty, Antipater, son of a certain temple slave named Herod. And since the priest was not able to pay the ransom for his son, Antipater was brought up in the customs of the Idumeans, and afterward was befriended by Hyrcanus, the high priest of the Jews.

12. And having been sent by Hyrcanus on an embassy to Pompey, and having restored to him the kingdom which had been invaded by his brother Aristobulus, he had the good fortune to be named procurator of Palestine. But Antipater having been slain by those who were envious of his great good fortune was succeeded by his son Herod, who was afterward, by a decree of the senate, made King of the Jews under Antony and Augustus. His sons were Herod and the other tetrarchs. These accounts agree also with those of the Greeks.

13. But as there had been kept in the archives up to that time the genealogies of the Hebrews as well as of those who traced their lineage back to proselytes, such as Achior the Ammonite and Ruth the Moabitess, and to those who were mingled with the Israelites and came out of Egypt with them, Herod, inasmuch as the lineage of the Israelites contributed nothing to his advantage, and since he was goaded with the consciousness of his own ignoble extraction, burned all the genealogical records, thinking that he might appear of noble origin if no one else were able, from the public registers, to trace back his lineage to the patriarchs or proselytes and to those mingled with them, who were called Georae.

14. A few of the careful, however, having obtained private records of their own, either by remembering the names or by getting them in some other way from the registers, pride themselves on preserving the memory of their noble extraction. Among these are those already mentioned, called Desposyni, on account of their connection with the family of the Saviour. Coming from Nazara and Cochaba, villages of Judea, into other parts of the world, they drew the aforesaid genealogy from memory and from the book of daily records as faithfully as possible.

15. Whether then the case stand thus or not no one could find a clearer explanation, according to my own opinion and that of every candid person. And let this suffice us, for, although we can urge no testimony in its support, we have nothing better or truer to offer. In any case the Gospel states the truth. And at the end of the same epistle he adds these words: Matthan, who was descended from Solomon, begot Jacob. And when Matthan was dead, Melchi, who was descended from Nathan begot Eli by the same woman. Eli and Jacob were thus uterine brothers. Eli having died childless, Jacob raised up seed to him, begetting Joseph, his own son by nature, but by law the son of Eli. Thus Joseph was the son of both.

17. Thus far Africanus. And the lineage of Joseph being thus traced, Mary also is virtually shown to be of the same tribe with him, since, according to the law of Moses, intermarriages between different tribes were not permitted. For the command is to marry one of the same family and lineage, so that the inheritance may not pass from tribe to tribe. This may suffice here.

Chapter 8. The Cruelty of Herod toward the Infants, and the Manner of his Death.

1. When Christ was born, according to the prophecies, in Bethlehem of Judea, at the time indicated, Herod was not a little disturbed by the enquiry of the magi who came from the east, asking where he who was born King of the Jews was to be found—for they had seen his star, and this was their reason for taking so long a journey; for they earnestly desired to worship the infant as God, — for he imagined that his kingdom might be endangered; and he enquired therefore of the doctors of the law, who belonged to the Jewish nation, where they expected Christ to be born. When he learned that the prophecy of Micah Micah 5:2 announced that Bethlehem was to be his birthplace he commanded, in a single edict, all the male infants in Bethlehem, and all its borders, that were two years of age or less, according to the time which he had accurately ascertained from the magi, to be slain, supposing that Jesus, as was indeed likely, would share the same fate as the others of his own age.

2. But the child anticipated the snare, being carried into Egypt by his parents, who had learned from an angel that appeared unto them what was about to happen. These things are recorded by the Holy Scriptures in the Gospel. Matthew 2

3. It is worth while, in addition to this, to observe the reward which Herod received for his daring crime against Christ and those of the same age. For immediately, without the least delay, the divine vengeance overtook him while he was still alive, and gave him a foretaste of what he was to receive after death.

4. It is not possible to relate here how he tarnished the supposed felicity of his reign by successive calamities in his family, by the murder of wife and children, and others of his nearest relatives and dearest friends. The account, which casts every other tragic drama into the shade, is detailed at length in the histories of Josephus.

5. How, immediately after his crime against our Saviour and the other infants, the punishment sent by God drove him on to his death, we can best learn from the words of that historian who, in the seventeenth book of his Antiquities of the Jews, writes as follows concerning his end:

6. But the disease of Herod grew more severe, God inflicting punishment for his crimes. For a slow fire burned in him which was not so apparent to those who touched him, but augmented his internal distress; for he had a terrible desire for food which it was not possible to resist. He was affected also with ulceration of the intestines, and with especially severe pains in the colon, while a watery and transparent humor settled about his feet.

7. He suffered also from a similar trouble in his abdomen. Nay more, his privy member was putrefied and produced worms. He found also excessive difficulty in breathing, and it was particularly disagreeable because of the offensiveness of the odor and the rapidity of respiration.

8. He had convulsions also in every limb, which gave him uncontrollable strength. It was said, indeed, by those who possessed the power of divination and wisdom to explain such events, that God had inflicted this punishment upon the King on account of his great impiety.

9. The writer mentioned above recounts these things in the work referred to. And in the second book of his History he gives a similar account of the same Herod, which runs as follows: The disease then seized upon his whole body and distracted it by various torments. For he had a slow fever, and the itching of the skin of his whole body was insupportable. He suffered also from continuous pains in his colon, and there were swellings on his feet like those of a person suffering from dropsy, while his abdomen was inflamed and his privy member so putrefied as to produce worms. Besides this he could breathe only in an

upright posture, and then only with difficulty, and he had convulsions in all his limbs, so that the diviners said that his diseases were a punishment.

10. But he, although wrestling with such sufferings, nevertheless clung to life and hoped for safety, and devised methods of cure. For instance, crossing over Jordan he used the warm baths at Callirhoë, which flow into the Lake Asphaltites, but are themselves sweet enough to drink.

11. His physicians here thought that they could warm his whole body again by means of heated oil. But when they had let him down into a tub filled with oil, his eyes became weak and turned up like the eyes of a dead person. But when his attendants raised an outcry, he recovered at the noise; but finally, despairing of a cure, he commanded about fifty drachms to be distributed among the soldiers, and great sums to be given to his generals and friends.

12. Then returning he came to Jericho, where, being seized with melancholy, he planned to commit an impious deed, as if challenging death itself. For, collecting from every town the most illustrious men of all Judea, he commanded that they be shut up in the so-called hippodrome.

13. And having summoned Salome, his sister, and her husband, Alexander, he said: 'I know that the Jews will rejoice at my death. But I may be lamented by others and have a splendid funeral if you are willing to perform my commands. When I shall expire surround these men, who are now under guard, as quickly as possible with soldiers, and slay them, in order that all Judea and every house may weep for me even against their will.'

14. And after a little Josephus says, And again he was so tortured by want of food and by a convulsive cough that, overcome by his pains, he planned to anticipate his fate. Taking an apple he asked also for a knife, for he was accustomed to cut apples and eat them. Then looking round to see that there was no one to hinder, he raised his right hand as if to stab himself.

15. In addition to these things the same writer records that he slew another of his own sons before his death, the third one slain by his command, and that immediately afterward he breathed his last, not without excessive pain.

16. Such was the end of Herod, who suffered a just punishment for his slaughter of the children of Bethlehem, which was the result of his plots against our Saviour.

17. After this an angel appeared in a dream to Joseph in Egypt and commanded him to go to Judea with the child and its mother, revealing to him that those who had sought the life of the child were dead. To this the evangelist adds, But when he heard that Archelaus did reign in the room of his father Herod he was afraid to go there; notwithstanding being warned of God in a dream he turned aside into the parts of Galilee. Matthew 2:22

Chapter 9. The Times of Pilate.

1. The historian already mentioned agrees with the evangelist in regard to the fact that Archelaus succeeded to the government after Herod. He records the manner in which he received the kingdom of the Jews by the will of his father Herod and by the decree of Cæsar Augustus, and how, after he had reigned ten years, he lost his kingdom, and his brothers Philip and Herod the younger, with Lysanias, still ruled their own tetrarchies. The same writer, in the eighteenth book of his Antiquities, says that about the twelfth year of the reign of Tiberius, who had succeeded to the empire after Augustus had ruled fifty-seven years, Pontius Pilate was entrusted with the government of Judea, and that he remained there ten full years, almost until the death of Tiberius.

2. Accordingly the forgery of those who have recently given currency to acts against our Saviour is clearly proved. For the very date given in them shows the falsehood of their fabricators.

3. For the things which they have dared to say concerning the passion of the Saviour are put into the fourth consulship of Tiberius, which occurred in the seventh year of his reign; at which time it is plain that Pilate was not yet ruling in Judea, if the testimony of Josephus is to be believed, who clearly shows in the above-mentioned work that Pilate was made procurator of Judea by Tiberius in the twelfth year of his reign.

Chapter 10. The High Priests of the Jews under whom Christ taught.

1. It was in the fifteenth year of the reign of Tiberius, according to the evangelist, and in the fourth year of the governorship of Pontius Pilate,

while Herod and Lysanias and Philip were ruling the rest of Judea, that our Saviour and Lord, Jesus the Christ of God, being about thirty years of age, came to John for baptism and began the promulgation of the Gospel.

2. The Divine Scripture says, moreover, that he passed the entire time of his ministry under the high priests Annas and Caiaphas, showing that in the time which belonged to the priesthood of those two men the whole period of his teaching was completed. Since he began his work during the high priesthood of Annas and taught until Caiaphas held the office, the entire time does not comprise quite four years.

3. For the rites of the law having been already abolished since that time, the customary usages in connection with the worship of God, according to which the high priest acquired his office by hereditary descent and held it for life, were also annulled and there were appointed to the high priesthood by the Roman governors now one and now another person who continued in office not more than one year.

4. Josephus relates that there were four high priests in succession from Annas to Caiaphas. Thus in the same book of the Antiquities he writes as follows: Valerius Gratus having put an end to the priesthood of Ananus appoints Ishmael, the son of Fabi, high priest. And having removed him after a little he appoints Eleazer, the son of Ananus the high priest, to the same office. And having removed him also at the end of a year he gives the high priesthood to Simon, the son of Camithus. But he likewise held the honor no more than a year, when Josephus, called also Caiaphas, succeeded him. Accordingly the whole time of our Saviour's ministry is shown to have been not quite four full years, four high priests, from Annas to the accession of Caiaphas, having held office a year each. The Gospel therefore has rightly indicated Caiaphas as the high priest under whom the Saviour suffered. From which also we can see that the time of our Saviour's ministry does not disagree with the foregoing investigation.

5. Our Saviour and Lord, not long after the beginning of his ministry, called the twelve apostles, and these alone of all his disciples he named apostles, as a special honor. And again he appointed seventy others whom he sent out two by two before his face into every place and city whither he himself was about to come.

Chapter 11. Testimonies in Regard to John the Baptist and Christ.

1. Not long after this John the Baptist was beheaded by the younger Herod, as is stated in the Gospels. Josephus also records the same fact, making mention of Herodias by name, and stating that, although she was the wife of his brother, Herod made her his own wife after divorcing his former lawful wife, who was the daughter of Aretas, king of Petra, and separating Herodias from her husband while he was still alive.

2. It was on her account also that he slew John, and waged war with Aretas, because of the disgrace inflicted on the daughter of the latter. Josephus relates that in this war, when they came to battle, Herod's entire army was destroyed, and that he suffered this calamity on account of his crime against John.

3. The same Josephus confesses in this account that John the Baptist was an exceedingly righteous man, and thus agrees with the things written of him in the Gospels. He records also that Herod lost his kingdom on account of the same Herodias, and that he was driven into banishment with her, and condemned to live at Vienne in Gaul.

4. He relates these things in the eighteenth book of the Antiquities, where he writes of John in the following words: It seemed to some of the Jews that the army of Herod was destroyed by God, who most justly avenged John called the Baptist.

5. For Herod slew him, a good man and one who exhorted the Jews to come and receive baptism, practicing virtue and exercising righteousness toward each other and toward God; for baptism would appear acceptable unto Him when they employed it, not for the remission of certain sins, but for the purification of the body, as the soul had been already purified in righteousness.

6. And when others gathered about him (for they found much pleasure in listening to his words), Herod feared that his great influence might lead to some sedition, for they appeared ready to do whatever he might advise. He therefore considered it much better, before any new thing should be done under John's influence, to anticipate it by slaying him, than to repent after revolution had come, and when he found himself in the midst of difficulties. On account of Herod's suspicion John was sent in bonds to the above-mentioned citadel of Machæra, and there slain.

7. After relating these things concerning John, he makes mention of our Saviour in the same work, in the following words: And there lived at that time Jesus, a wise man, if indeed it be proper to call him a man. For he was a doer of wonderful works, and a teacher of such men as receive

the truth in gladness. And he attached to himself many of the Jews, and many also of the Greeks. He was the Christ.

8. When Pilate, on the accusation of our principal men, condemned him to the cross, those who had loved him in the beginning did not cease loving him. For he appeared unto them again alive on the third day, the divine prophets having told these and countless other wonderful things concerning him. Moreover, the race of Christians, named after him, continues down to the present day.

9. Since an historian, who is one of the Hebrews themselves, has recorded in his work these things concerning John the Baptist and our Saviour, what excuse is there left for not convicting them of being destitute of all shame, who have forged the acts against them? But let this suffice here.

Chapter 12. The Disciples of our Saviour.

1. The names of the apostles of our Saviour are known to every one from the Gospels. But there exists no catalogue of the seventy disciples. Barnabas, indeed, is said to have been one of them, of whom the Acts of the Apostles makes mention in various places, and especially Paul in his Epistle to the Galatians.

2. They say that Sosthenes also, who wrote to the Corinthians with Paul, was one of them. This is the account of Clement in the fifth book of his Hypotyposes, in which he also says that Cephas was one of the seventy disciples, a man who bore the same name as the apostle Peter, and the one concerning whom Paul says, When Cephas came to Antioch I withstood him to his face. Galatians 2:11

3. Matthias, also, who was numbered with the apostles in the place of Judas, and the one who was honored by being made a candidate with him, are likewise said to have been deemed worthy of the same calling with the seventy. They say that Thaddeus also was one of them, concerning whom I shall presently relate an account which has come down to us. And upon examination you will find that our Saviour had more than seventy disciples, according to the testimony of Paul, who says that after his resurrection from the dead he appeared first to Cephas, then to the twelve, and after them to above five hundred brethren at once, of whom some had fallen asleep; but the majority were still living at the time he wrote.

4. Afterwards he says he appeared unto James, who was one of the so-called brethren of the Saviour. But, since in addition to these, there were many others who were called apostles, in imitation of the Twelve, as was Paul himself, he adds: Afterward he appeared to all the apostles. 1 Corinthians 15:7 So much in regard to these persons. But the story concerning Thaddeus is as follows.

Chapter 13. Narrative concerning the Prince of the Edessenes.

1. The divinity of our Lord and Saviour Jesus Christ being noised abroad among all men on account of his wonder-working power, he attracted countless numbers from foreign countries lying far away from Judea, who had the hope of being cured of their diseases and of all kinds of sufferings.

2. For instance the King Abgarus, who ruled with great glory the nations beyond the Euphrates, being afflicted with a terrible disease which it was beyond the power of human skill to cure, when he heard of the name of Jesus, and of his miracles, which were attested by all with one accord sent a message to him by a courier and begged him to heal his disease.

3. But he did not at that time comply with his request; yet he deemed him worthy of a personal letter in which he said that he would send one of his disciples to cure his disease, and at the same time promised salvation to himself and all his house.

4. Not long afterward his promise was fulfilled. For after his resurrection from the dead and his ascent into heaven, Thomas, one of the twelve apostles, under divine impulse sent Thaddeus, who was also numbered among the seventy disciples of Christ, to Edessa, as a preacher and evangelist of the teaching of Christ.

5. And all that our Saviour had promised received through him its fulfillment. You have written evidence of these things taken from the archives of Edessa, which was at that time a royal city. For in the public registers there, which contain accounts of ancient times and the acts of Abgarus, these things have been found preserved down to the present time. But there is no better way than to hear the epistles themselves which we have taken from the archives and have literally translated from the Syriac language in the following manner.

Copy of an epistle written by Abgarus the ruler to Jesus, and sent to him at Jerusalem by Ananias the swift courier.

6. Abgarus, ruler of Edessa, to Jesus the excellent Saviour who has appeared in the country of Jerusalem, greeting. I have heard the reports of you and of your cures as performed by you without medicines or herbs. For it is said that you make the blind to see and the lame to walk, that you cleanse lepers and cast out impure spirits and demons, and that you heal those afflicted with lingering disease, and raise the dead.

7. And having heard all these things concerning you, I have concluded that one of two things must be true: either you are God, and having come down from heaven you do these things, or else you, who does these things, are the Son of God. faith in who Christ is

8. I have therefore written to you to ask you if you would take the trouble to come to me and heal the disease which I have. For I have heard that the Jews are murmuring against you and are plotting to injure you. But I have a very small yet noble city which is great enough for us both. This might be true *

The answer of Jesus to the ruler Abgarus by the courier Ananias.

9. Blessed are you who hast believed in me without having seen me. For it is written concerning me, that they who have seen me will not believe in me, and that they who have not seen me will believe and be saved. But in regard to what you have written me, that I should come to you, it is necessary for me to fulfill all things here for which I have been sent, and after I have fulfilled them thus to be taken up again to him that sent me. But after I have been taken up I will send to you one of my disciples, that he may heal your disease and give life to you and yours.

Further accounts

10. To these epistles there was added the following account in the Syriac language. After the ascension of Jesus, Judas, who was also called Thomas, sent to him Thaddeus, an apostle, one of the Seventy. When he had come he lodged with Tobias, the son of Tobias. When the report of him got abroad, it was told Abgarus that an apostle of Jesus had come, as he had written him.

11. Thaddeus began then in the power of God to heal every disease and infirmity, insomuch that all wondered. And when Abgarus heard of the great and wonderful things which he did and of the cures which he performed, he began to suspect that he was the one of whom Jesus had

written him, saying, 'After I have been taken up I will send to you one of my disciples who will heal you.'

12. Therefore, summoning Tobias, with whom Thaddeus lodged, he said, I have heard that a certain man of power has come and is lodging in your house. Bring him to me. And Tobias coming to Thaddeus said to him, The ruler Abgarus summoned me and told me to bring you to him that you might heal him. And Thaddeus said, I will go, for I have been sent to him with power.

13. Tobias therefore arose early on the following day, and taking Thaddeus came to Abgarus. And when he came, the nobles were present and stood about Abgarus. And immediately upon his entrance a great vision appeared to Abgarus in the countenance of the apostle Thaddeus. When Abgarus saw it he prostrated himself before Thaddeus, while all those who stood about were astonished; for they did not see the vision, which appeared to Abgarus alone.

14. He then asked Thaddeus if he were in truth a disciple of Jesus the Son of God, who had said to him, 'I will send you one of my disciples, who shall heal you and give you life.' And Thaddeus said, Because you have mightily believed in him that sent me, therefore have I been sent unto you. And still further, if you believe in him, the petitions of your heart shall be granted you as you believe.

15. And Abgarus said to him, So much have I believed in him that I wished to take an army and destroy those Jews who crucified him, had I not been deterred from it by reason of the dominion of the Romans. And Thaddeus said, Our Lord has fulfilled the will of his Father, and having fulfilled it has been taken up to his Father. And Abgarus said to him, I too have believed in him and in his Father.

16. And Thaddeus said to him, Therefore I place my hand upon you in his name. And when he had done it, immediately Abgarus was cured of the disease and of the suffering which he had.

17. And Abgarus marvelled, that as he had heard concerning Jesus, so he had received in very deed through his disciple Thaddeus, who healed him without medicines and herbs, and not only him, but also Abdus the son of Abdus, who was afflicted with the gout; for he too came to him and fell at his feet, and having received a benediction by the imposition of his hands, he was healed. The same Thaddeus cured also many other inhabitants of the city, and did wonders and marvelous works, and preached the word of God.

18. And afterward Abgarus said, You, O Thaddeus, do these things with the power of God, and we marvel. But, in addition to these things, I pray you to inform me in regard to the coming of Jesus, how he was born; and in regard to his power, by what power he performed those deeds of which I have heard.

19. And Thaddeus said, Now indeed will I keep silence, since I have been sent to proclaim the word publicly. But tomorrow assemble for me all your citizens, and I will preach in their presence and sow among them the word of God, concerning the coming of Jesus, how he was born; and concerning his mission, for what purpose he was sent by the Father; and concerning the power of his works, and the mysteries which he proclaimed in the world, and by what power he did these things; and concerning his new preaching, and his abasement and humiliation, and how he humbled himself, and died and debased his divinity and was crucified, and descended into Hades, and burst the bars which from eternity had not been broken, and raised the dead; for he descended alone, but rose with many, and thus ascended to his Father.

20. Abgarus therefore commanded the citizens to assemble early in the morning to hear the preaching of Thaddeus, and afterward he ordered gold and silver to be given him. But he refused to take it, saying, If we have forsaken that which was our own, how shall we take that which is another's? These things were done in the three hundred and fortieth year. I have inserted them here in their proper place, translated from the Syriac literally, and I hope to good purpose.

BOOK II

Introduction.

1. We have discussed in the preceding book those subjects in ecclesiastical history which it was necessary to treat by way of introduction, and have accompanied them with brief proofs. Such were the divinity of the saving Word, and the antiquity of the doctrines which we teach, as well as of that evangelical life which is led by Christians, together with the events which have taken place in connection with Christ's recent appearance, and in connection with his passion and with the choice of the apostles.

2. In the present book let us examine the events which took place after his ascension, confirming some of them from the divine Scriptures, and others from such writings as we shall refer to from time to time.

Chapter 1. The Course pursued by the Apostles after the Ascension of Christ.

1. First, then, in the place of Judas, the betrayer, Matthias, who, as has been shown was also one of the Seventy, was chosen to the apostolate. And there were appointed to the diaconate, for the service of the congregation, by prayer and the laying on of the hands of the apostles, approved men, seven in number, of whom Stephen was one. He first, after the Lord, was stoned to death at the time of his ordination by the slayers of the Lord, as if he had been promoted for this very purpose. And thus he was the first to receive the crown, corresponding to his name, which belongs to the martyrs of Christ, who are worthy of the meed of victory.

2. Then James, whom the ancients surnamed the Just on account of the excellence of his virtue, is recorded to have been the first to be made bishop of the church of Jerusalem. This James was called the brother of the Lord because he was known as a son of Joseph, and Joseph was supposed to be the father of Christ, because the Virgin, being betrothed to him, was found with child by the Holy Ghost before they came together, Matthew 1:18 as the account of the holy Gospels shows.

3. But Clement in the sixth book of his Hypotyposes writes thus: For they say that Peter and James and John after the ascension of our Saviour, as if also preferred by our Lord, strove not after honor, but chose James the Just bishop of Jerusalem.

4. But the same writer, in the seventh book of the same work, relates also the following things concerning him: The Lord after his resurrection imparted knowledge to James the Just and to John and Peter, and they imparted it to the rest of the apostles, and the rest of the apostles to the seventy, of whom Barnabas was one. But there were two Jameses: one called the Just, who was thrown from the pinnacle of the temple and was beaten to death with a club by a fuller, and another who was beheaded. Paul also makes mention of the same James the Just, where he writes, Other of the apostles saw I none, save James the Lord's brother. Galatians 1:19

5. At that time also the promise of our Saviour to the king of the Osrhœnians was fulfilled. For Thomas, under a divine impulse, sent Thaddeus to Edessa as a preacher and evangelist of the religion of Christ, as we have shown a little above from the document found there.

7. When he came to that place he healed Abgarus by the word of Christ; and after bringing all the people there into the right attitude of mind by means of his works, and leading them to adore the power of Christ, he made them disciples of the Saviour's teaching. And from that time down to the present the whole city of the Edessenes has been devoted to the name of Christ, offering no common proof of the beneficence of our Saviour toward them also.

8. These things have been drawn from ancient accounts; but let us now turn again to the divine Scripture. When the first and greatest persecution was instigated by the Jews against the church of Jerusalem in connection with the martyrdom of Stephen, and when all the disciples, except the Twelve, were scattered throughout Judea and Samaria, some, as the divine Scripture says, went as far as Phœnicia and Cyprus and Antioch, but could not yet venture to impart the word of faith to the nations, and therefore preached it to the Jews alone.

9. During this time Paul was still persecuting the church, and entering the houses of believers was dragging men and women away and committing them to prison.

10. Philip also, one of those who with Stephen had been entrusted with the diaconate, being among those who were scattered abroad, went down to Samaria, and being filled with the divine power, he first preached the word to the inhabitants of that country. And divine grace worked so mightily with him that even Simon Magus with many others was attracted by his words.

11. Simon was at that time so celebrated, and had acquired, by his jugglery, such influence over those who were deceived by him, that he was thought to be the great power of God. But at this time, being amazed at the wonderful deeds wrought by Philip through the divine power, he feigned and counterfeited faith in Christ, even going so far as to receive baptism.

12. And what is surprising, the same thing is done even to this day by those who follow his most impure heresy. For they, after the manner of their forefather, slipping into the Church, like a pestilential and leprous disease greatly afflict those into whom they are able to infuse the deadly and terrible poison concealed in themselves. The most of these have been expelled as soon as they have been caught in their wickedness, as Simon himself, when detected by Peter, received the merited punishment.

13. But as the preaching of the Saviour's Gospel was daily advancing, a certain providence led from the land of the Ethiopians an officer of the queen of that country, for Ethiopia even to the present day is ruled, according to ancestral custom, by a woman. He, first among the Gentiles, received of the mysteries of the divine word from Philip in consequence of a revelation, and having become the first-fruits of believers throughout the world, he is said to have been the first on returning to his country to proclaim the knowledge of the God of the universe and the life-giving sojourn of our Saviour among men; so that through him in truth the prophecy obtained its fulfillment, which declares that Ethiopia stretches out her hand unto God.

14. In addition to these, Paul, that chosen vessel, Acts 9:15 not of men neither through men, but by the revelation of Jesus Christ himself and of God the Father who raised him from the dead, Galatians 1:1 was appointed an apostle, being made worthy of the call by a vision and by a voice which was uttered in a revelation from heaven.

Chapter 2. How Tiberius was affected when informed by Pilate concerning Christ.

1. And when the wonderful resurrection and ascension of our Saviour were already noised abroad, in accordance with an ancient custom which prevailed among the rulers of the provinces, of reporting to the emperor the novel occurrences which took place in them, in order that nothing might escape him, Pontius Pilate informed Tiberius of the reports which

were noised abroad through all Palestine concerning the resurrection of our Saviour Jesus from the dead.

2. He gave an account also of other wonders which he had learned of him, and how, after his death, having risen from the dead, he was now believed by many to be a God. They say that Tiberius referred the matter to the Senate, but that they rejected it, ostensibly because they had not first examined into the matter (for an ancient law prevailed that no one should be made a God by the Romans except by a vote and decree of the Senate), but in reality because the saving teaching of the divine Gospel did not need the confirmation and recommendation of men.

3. But although the Senate of the Romans rejected the proposition made in regard to our Saviour, Tiberius still retained the opinion which he had held at first, and contrived no hostile measures against Christ.

4. These things are recorded by Tertullian, a man well versed in the laws of the Romans, and in other respects of high repute, and one of those especially distinguished in Rome. In his apology for the Christians, which was written by him in the Latin language, and has been translated into Greek, he writes as follows:

5. But in order that we may give an account of these laws from their origin, it was an ancient decree that no one should be consecrated a God by the emperor until the Senate had expressed its approval. Marcus Aurelius did thus concerning a certain idol, Alburnus. And this is a point in favor of our doctrine, that among you divine dignity is conferred by human decree. If a God does not please a man he is not made a God. Thus, according to this custom, it is necessary for man to be gracious to God.

6. Tiberius, therefore, under whom the name of Christ made its entry into the world, when this doctrine was reported to him from Palestine, where it first began, communicated with the Senate, making it clear to them that he was pleased with the doctrine. But the Senate, since it had not itself proved the matter, rejected it. But Tiberius continued to hold his own opinion, and threatened death to the accusers of the Christians. Heavenly providence had wisely instilled this into his mind in order that the doctrine of the Gospel, unhindered at its beginning, might spread in all directions throughout the world.

Chapter 3. The Doctrine of Christ soon spread throughout All the World.

1. Thus, under the influence of heavenly power, and with the divine co-operation, the doctrine of the Saviour, like the rays of the sun, quickly illumined the whole world; and straightway, in accordance with the divine Scriptures, the voice of the inspired evangelists and apostles went forth through all the earth, and their words to the end of the world.

2. In every city and village, churches were quickly established, filled with multitudes of people like a replenished threshing-floor. And those whose minds, in consequence of errors which had descended to them from their forefathers, were fettered by the ancient disease of idolatrous superstition, were, by the power of Christ operating through the teaching and the wonderful works of his disciples, set free, as it were, from terrible masters, and found a release from the most cruel bondage. They renounced with abhorrence every species of demoniacal polytheism, and confessed that there was only one God, the creator of all things, and him they honored with the rites of true piety, through the inspired and rational worship which has been planted by our Saviour among men.

3. But the divine grace being now poured out upon the rest of the nations, Cornelius, of Cæsarea in Palestine, with his whole house, through a divine revelation and the agency of Peter, first received faith in Christ; and after him a multitude of other Greeks in Antioch, to whom those who were scattered by the persecution of Stephen had preached the Gospel. When the church of Antioch was now increasing and abounding, and a multitude of prophets from Jerusalem were on the ground, among them Barnabas and Paul and in addition many other brethren, the name of Christians first sprang up there, as from a fresh and life-giving fountain.

4. And Agabus, one of the prophets who was with them, uttered a prophecy concerning the famine which was about to take place, and Paul and Barnabas were sent to relieve the necessities of the brethren.

Chapter 4. After the Death of Tiberius, Caius appointed Agrippa King of the Jews, having punished Herod with Perpetual Exile.

1. Tiberius died, after having reigned about twenty-two years, and Caius succeeded him in the empire. He immediately gave the government of the Jews to Agrippa, making him king over the tetrarchies of Philip and of Lysanias; in addition to which he bestowed upon him, not long afterward, the tetrarchy of Herod, having punished Herod (the one

under whom the Saviour suffered) and his wife Herodias with perpetual exile on account of numerous crimes. Josephus is a witness to these facts.

2. Under this emperor, Philo became known; a man most celebrated not only among many of our own, but also among many scholars without the Church. He was a Hebrew by birth, but was inferior to none of those who held high dignities in Alexandria. How exceedingly he labored in the Scriptures and in the studies of his nation is plain to all from the work which he has done. How familiar he was with philosophy and with the liberal studies of foreign nations, it is not necessary to say, since he is reported to have surpassed all his contemporaries in the study of Platonic and Pythagorean philosophy, to which he particularly devoted his attention.

Chapter 5. Philo's Embassy to Caius in Behalf of the Jews.

1. Philo has given us an account, in five books, of the misfortunes of the Jews under Caius. He recounts at the same time the madness of Caius: how he called himself a god, and performed as emperor innumerable acts of tyranny; and he describes further the miseries of the Jews under him, and gives a report of the embassy upon which he himself was sent to Rome in behalf of his fellow-countrymen in Alexandria; how when he appeared before Caius in behalf of the laws of his fathers he received nothing but laughter and ridicule, and almost incurred the risk of his life.

2. Josephus also makes mention of these things in the eighteenth book of his Antiquities, in the following words: A sedition having arisen in Alexandria between the Jews that dwell there and the Greeks, three deputies were chosen from each faction and went to Caius.

3. One of the Alexandrian deputies was Apion, who uttered many slanders against the Jews; among other things saying that they neglected the honors due to Cæsar. For while all other subjects of Rome erected altars and temples to Caius, and in all other respects treated him just as they did the gods, they alone considered it disgraceful to honor him with statues and to swear by his name.

4. And when Apion had uttered many severe charges by which he hoped that Caius would be aroused, as indeed was likely, Philo, the chief of the Jewish embassy, a man celebrated in every respect, a brother of

Alexander the Alabarch, and not unskilled in philosophy, was prepared to enter upon a defense in reply to his accusations.

5. But Caius prevented him and ordered him to leave, and being very angry, it was plain that he meditated some severe measure against them. And Philo departed covered with insult and told the Jews that were with him to be of good courage; for while Caius was raging against them he was in fact already contending with God.

6. Thus far Josephus. And Philo himself, in the work On the Embassy which he wrote, describes accurately and in detail the things which were done by him at that time. But I shall omit the most of them and record only those things which will make clearly evident to the reader that the misfortunes of the Jews came upon them not long after their daring deeds against Christ and on account of the same.

7. And in the first place he relates that at Rome in the reign of Tiberius, Sejanus, who at that time enjoyed great influence with the emperor, made every effort to destroy the Jewish nation utterly; and that in Judea, Pilate, under whom the crimes against the Saviour were committed, attempted something contrary to the Jewish law in respect to the temple, which was at that time still standing in Jerusalem, and excited them to the greatest tumults.

Chapter 6. The Misfortunes which overwhelmed the Jews after their Presumption against Christ.

1. After the death of Tiberius, Caius received the empire, and, besides innumerable other acts of tyranny against many people, he greatly afflicted especially the whole nation of the Jews. These things we may learn briefly from the words of Philo, who writes as follows:

2. So great was the caprice of Caius in his conduct toward all, and especially toward the nation of the Jews. The latter he so bitterly hated that he appropriated to himself their places of worship in the other cities, and beginning with Alexandria he filled them with images and statues of himself (for in permitting others to erect them he really erected them himself). The temple in the holy city, which had hitherto been left untouched, and had been regarded as an inviolable asylum, he altered and transformed into a temple of his own, that it might be called the temple of the visible Jupiter, the younger Caius.

3. Innumerable other terrible and almost indescribable calamities which came upon the Jews in Alexandria during the reign of the same emperor,

are recorded by the same author in a second work, to which he gave the title, On the Virtues. With him agrees also Josephus, who likewise indicates that the misfortunes of the whole nation began with the time of Pilate, and with their daring crimes against the Saviour.

4. Hear what he says in the second book of his Jewish War, where he writes as follows: Pilate being sent to Judea as procurator by Tiberius, secretly carried veiled images of the emperor, called ensigns, to Jerusalem by night. The following day this caused the greatest disturbance among the Jews. For those who were near were confounded at the sight, beholding their laws, as it were, trampled under foot. For they allow no image to be set up in their city.

5. Comparing these things with the writings of the evangelists, you will see that it was not long before there came upon them the penalty for the exclamation which they had uttered under the same Pilate, when they cried out that they had no other king than Cæsar. John 19:15

6. The same writer further records that after this another calamity overtook them. He writes as follows: After this he stirred up another tumult by making use of the holy treasure, which is called Corban, in the construction of an aqueduct three hundred stadia in length.

7. The multitude were greatly displeased at it, and when Pilate was in Jerusalem they surrounded his tribunal and gave utterance to loud complaints. But he, anticipating the tumult, had distributed through the crowd armed soldiers disguised in citizen's clothing, forbidding them to use the sword, but commanding them to strike with clubs those who should make an outcry. To them he now gave the preconcerted signal from the tribunal. And the Jews being beaten, many of them perished in consequence of the blows, while many others were trampled under foot by their own countrymen in their flight, and thus lost their lives. But the multitude, overawed by the fate of those who were slain, held their peace.

8. In addition to these the same author records many other tumults which were stirred up in Jerusalem itself, and shows that from that time seditions and wars and mischievous plots followed each other in quick succession, and never ceased in the city and in all Judea until finally the siege of Vespasian overwhelmed them. Thus the divine vengeance overtook the Jews for the crimes which they dared to commit against Christ.

Chapter 7. Pilate's Suicide.

It is worthy of note that Pilate himself, who was governor in the time of our Saviour, is reported to have fallen into such misfortunes under Caius, whose times we are recording, that he was forced to become his own murderer and executioner; and thus divine vengeance, as it seems, was not long in overtaking him. This is stated by those Greek historians who have recorded the Olympiads, together with the respective events which have taken place in each period.

Chapter 8. The Famine which took Place in the Reign of Claudius.

1. Caius had held the power not quite four years, when he was succeeded by the emperor Claudius. Under him the world was visited with a famine, which writers that are entire strangers to our religion have recorded in their histories. And thus the prediction of Agabus recorded in the Acts of the Apostles, Acts 11:28 according to which the whole world was to be visited by a famine, received its fulfillment.

2. And Luke, in the Acts, after mentioning the famine in the time of Claudius, and stating that the brethren of Antioch, each according to his ability, sent to the brethren of Judea by the hands of Paul and Barnabas, Acts 11:29-30 adds the following account.

Chapter 9. The Martyrdom of James the Apostle.

1. Acts 12:1-2 Now about that time (it is clear that he means the time of Claudius) Herod the King stretched forth his hands to vex certain of the Church. And he killed James the brother of John with the sword.

2. And concerning this James, Clement, in the seventh book of his Hypotyposes, relates a story which is worthy of mention; telling it as he received it from those who had lived before him. He says that the one who led James to the judgment-seat, when he saw him bearing his testimony, was moved, and confessed that he was himself also a Christian.

3. They were both therefore, he says, led away together; and on the way he begged James to forgive him. And he, after considering a little, said, Peace be with you, and kissed him. And thus they were both beheaded at the same time.

4. And then, as the divine Scripture says, Acts 12:3sqq Herod, upon the death of James, seeing that the deed pleased the Jews, attacked Peter also and committed him to prison, and would have slain him if he had not, by the divine appearance of an angel who came to him by night, been wonderfully released from his bonds, and thus liberated for the service of the Gospel. Such was the providence of God in respect to Peter.

Chapter 10. Agrippa, who was also called Herod, having persecuted the Apostles, immediately experienced the Divine Vengeance.

1. The consequences of the king's undertaking against the apostles were not long deferred, but the avenging minister of divine justice overtook him immediately after his plots against them, as the Book of Acts records. For when he had journeyed to Cæsarea, on a notable feast-day, clothed in a splendid and royal garment, he delivered an address to the people from a lofty throne in front of the tribunal. And when all the multitude applauded the speech, as if it were the voice of a god and not of a man, the Scripture relates that an angel of the Lord smote him, and being eaten of worms he gave up the ghost. Acts 12:23

2. We must admire the account of Josephus for its agreement with the divine Scriptures in regard to this wonderful event; for he clearly bears witness to the truth in the nineteenth book of his Antiquities, where he relates the wonder in the following words:

3. He had completed the third year of his reign over all Judea when he came to Cæsarea, which was formerly called Strato's Tower. There he held games in honor of Cæsar, learning that this was a festival observed in behalf of Cæsar's safety. At this festival was collected a great multitude of the highest and most honorable men in the province.

4. And on the second day of the games he proceeded to the theater at break of day, wearing a garment entirely of silver and of wonderful texture. And there the silver, illuminated by the reflection of the sun's earliest rays, shone marvelously, gleaming so brightly as to produce a sort of fear and terror in those who gazed upon him.

5. And immediately his flatterers, some from one place, others from another, raised up their voices in a way that was not for his good, calling him a god, and saying, 'Be merciful; if up to this time we have feared you as a man, henceforth we confess that you are superior to the nature of mortals.'

6. The king did not rebuke them, nor did he reject their impious flattery. But after a little, looking up, he saw an angel sitting above his head. And this he quickly perceived would be the cause of evil as it had once been the cause of good fortune, and he was smitten with a heart-piercing pain.

7. And straightway distress, beginning with the greatest violence, seized his bowels. And looking upon his friends he said, 'I, your god, am now commanded to depart this life; and fate thus on the spot disproves the lying words you have just uttered concerning me. He who has been called immortal by you is now led away to die; but our destiny must be accepted as God has determined it. For we have passed our life by no means ingloriously, but in that splendor which is called happiness.'

8. And when he had said this he labored with an increase of pain. He was accordingly carried in haste to the palace, while the report spread among all that the king would undoubtedly soon die. But the multitude, with their wives and children, sitting on sackcloth after the custom of their fathers, implored God in behalf of the king, and every place was filled with lamentation and tears. And the king as he lay in a lofty chamber, and saw them below lying prostrate on the ground, could not refrain from weeping himself.

9. And after suffering continually for five days with pain in the bowels, he departed this life, in the fifty-fourth year of his age, and in the seventh year of his reign. Four years he ruled under the Emperor Caius— three of them over the tetrarchy of Philip, to which was added in the fourth year that of Herod — and three years during the reign of the Emperor Claudius.

10. I marvel greatly that Josephus, in these things as well as in others, so fully agrees with the divine Scriptures. But if there should seem to anyone to be a disagreement in respect to the name of the king, the time at least and the events show that the same person is meant, whether the change of name has been caused by the error of a copyist, or is due to the fact that he, like so many, bore two names.

Chapter 11. The Impostor Theudas and his Followers.

1. Luke, in the Acts, introduces Gamaliel as saying, at the consultation which was held concerning the apostles, that at the time referred to, rose up Theudas boasting himself to be somebody; who was slain; and all, as many as obeyed him, were scattered. Acts 5:36 Let us therefore add the

account of Josephus concerning this man. He records in the work mentioned just above, the following circumstances:

2. While Fadus was procurator of Judea a certain impostor called Theudas persuaded a very great multitude to take their possessions and follow him to the river Jordan. For he said that he was a prophet, and that the river should be divided at his command, and afford them an easy passage.

3. And with these words he deceived many. But Fadus did not permit them to enjoy their folly, but sent a troop of horsemen against them, who fell upon them unexpectedly and slew many of them and took many others alive, while they took Theudas himself captive, and cut off his head and carried it to Jerusalem. Besides this he also makes mention of the famine, which took place in the reign of Claudius, in the following words.

Chapter 12. Helen, the Queen of the Osrhœnians.

1. And at this time it came to pass that the great famine took place in Judea, in which the queen Helen, having purchased grain from Egypt with large sums, distributed it to the needy.

2. You will find this statement also in agreement with the Acts of the Apostles, where it is said that the disciples at Antioch, each according to his ability, determined to send relief to the brethren that dwelt in Judea; which also they did, and sent it to the elders by the hands of Barnabas and Paul.

3. But splendid monuments of this Helen, of whom the historian has made mention, are still shown in the suburbs of the city which is now called Ælia. But she is said to have been queen of the Adiabeni.

Chapter 13. Simon Magus.

1. But faith in our Saviour and Lord Jesus Christ having now been diffused among all men, the enemy of man's salvation contrived a plan for seizing the imperial city for himself. He conducted there the above-mentioned Simon, aided him in his deceitful arts, led many of the inhabitants of Rome astray, and thus brought them into his own power.

2. This is stated by Justin, one of our distinguished writers who lived not long after the time of the apostles. Concerning him I shall speak in the

proper place. Take and read the work of this man, who in the first Apology which he addressed to Antonine in behalf of our religion writes as follows:

3. And after the ascension of the Lord into heaven the demons put forward certain men who said they were gods, and who were not only allowed by you to go unpersecuted, but were even deemed worthy of honors. One of them was Simon, a Samaritan of the village of Gitto, who in the reign of Claudius Cæsar performed in your imperial city some mighty acts of magic by the art of demons operating in him, and was considered a god, and as a god was honored by you with a statue, which was erected in the river Tiber, between the two bridges, and bore this inscription in the Latin tongue, Simoni Deo Sancto, that is, To Simon the Holy God.

4. And nearly all the Samaritans and a few even of other nations confess and worship him as the first God. And there went around with him at that time a certain Helena who had formerly been a prostitute in Tyre of Phœnicia; and her they call the first idea that proceeded from him.

5. Justin relates these things, and Irenæus also agrees with him in the first book of his work, Against Heresies, where he gives an account of the man and of his profane and impure teaching. It would be superfluous to quote his account here, for it is possible for those who wish to know the origin and the lives and the false doctrines of each of the heresiarchs that have followed him, as well as the customs practiced by them all, to find them treated at length in the above- mentioned work of Irenæus.

6. We have understood that Simon was the author of all heresy. From his time down to the present those who have followed his heresy have feigned the sober philosophy of the Christians, which is celebrated among all on account of its purity of life. But they nevertheless have embraced again the superstitions of idols, which they seemed to have renounced; and they fall down before pictures and images of Simon himself and of the above-mentioned Helena who was with him; and they venture to worship them with incense and sacrifices and libations.

7. But those matters which they keep more secret than these, in regard to which they say that one upon first hearing them would be astonished, and, to use one of the written phrases in vogue among them, would be confounded, are in truth full of amazing things, and of madness and folly, being of such a sort that it is impossible not only to commit them

to writing, but also for modest men even to utter them with the lips on account of their excessive baseness and lewdness.

8. For whatever could be conceived of, viler than the vilest thing— all that has been outdone by this most abominable sect, which is composed of those who make a sport of those miserable females that are literally overwhelmed with all kinds of vices.

Chapter 14. The Preaching of the Apostle Peter in Rome.

1. The evil power, who hates all that is good and plots against the salvation of men, constituted Simon at that time the father and author of such wickedness, as if to make him a mighty antagonist of the great, inspired apostles of our Saviour.

2. For that divine and celestial grace which co-operates with its ministers, by their appearance and presence, quickly extinguished the kindled flame of evil, and humbled and cast down through them every high thing that exalted itself against the knowledge of God. 2 Corinthians 10:5

3. Wherefore neither the conspiracy of Simon nor that of any of the others who arose at that period could accomplish anything in those apostolic times. For everything was conquered and subdued by the splendors of the truth and by the divine word itself which had but lately begun to shine from heaven upon men, and which was then flourishing upon earth, and dwelling in the apostles themselves.

4. Immediately the above-mentioned impostor was smitten in the eyes of his mind by a divine and miraculous flash, and after the evil deeds done by him had been first detected by the apostle Peter in Judea, he fled and made a great journey across the sea from the East to the West, thinking that only thus could he live according to his mind.

5. And coming to the city of Rome, by the mighty co-operation of that power which was lying in wait there, he was in a short time so successful in his undertaking that those who dwelt there honored him as a god by the erection of a statue.

6. But this did not last long. For immediately, during the reign of Claudius, the all-good and gracious Providence, which watches over all things, led Peter, that strongest and greatest of the apostles, and the one who on account of his virtue was the speaker for all the others, to Rome against this great corrupter of life. He like a noble commander of God,

clad in divine armor, carried the costly merchandise of the light of the understanding from the East to those who dwelt in the West, proclaiming the light itself, and the word which brings salvation to souls, and preaching the kingdom of heaven.

Chapter 15. The Gospel according to Mark.

1. And thus when the divine word had made its home among them, the power of Simon was quenched and immediately destroyed, together with the man himself. And so greatly did the splendor of piety illumine the minds of Peter's hearers that they were not satisfied with hearing once only, and were not content with the unwritten teaching of the divine Gospel, but with all sorts of entreaties they besought Mark, a follower of Peter, and the one whose Gospel is extant, that he would leave them a written monument of the doctrine which had been orally communicated to them. Nor did they cease until they had prevailed with the man, and had thus become the occasion of the written Gospel which bears the name of Mark.

2. And they say that Peter — when he had learned, through a revelation of the Spirit, of that which had been done — was pleased with the zeal of the men, and that the work obtained the sanction of his authority for the purpose of being used in the churches. Clement in the eighth book of his Hypotyposes gives this account, and with him agrees the bishop of Hierapolis named Papias. And Peter makes mention of Mark in his first epistle which they say that he wrote in Rome itself, as is indicated by him, when he calls the city, by a figure, Babylon, as he does in the following words: The church that is at Babylon, elected together with you, salutes you; and so does Marcus my son.

Chapter 16. Mark first proclaimed Christianity to the Inhabitants of Egypt.

1. And they say that this Mark was the first that was sent to Egypt, and that he proclaimed the Gospel which he had written, and first established churches in Alexandria.

2. And the multitude of believers, both men and women, that were collected there at the very outset, and lived lives of the most philosophical and excessive asceticism, was so great, that Philo thought it worth while to describe their pursuits, their meetings, their entertainments, and their whole manner of life.

Chapter 17. Philo's Account of the Ascetics of Egypt.

1. It is also said that Philo in the reign of Claudius became acquainted at Rome with Peter, who was then preaching there. Nor is this indeed improbable, for the work of which we have spoken, and which was composed by him some years later, clearly contains those rules of the Church which are even to this day observed among us.

2. And since he describes as accurately as possible the life of our ascetics, it is clear that he not only knew, but that he also approved, while he venerated and extolled, the apostolic men of his time, who were as it seems of the Hebrew race, and hence observed, after the manner of the Jews, the most of the customs of the ancients.

3. In the work to which he gave the title, On a Contemplative Life or on Suppliants, after affirming in the first place that he will add to those things which he is about to relate nothing contrary to truth or of his own invention, he says that these men were called Therapeutæ and the women that were with them Therapeutrides. He then adds the reasons for such a name, explaining it from the fact that they applied remedies and healed the souls of those who came to them, by relieving them like physicians, of evil passions, or from the fact that they served and worshipped the Deity in purity and sincerity.

4. Whether Philo himself gave them this name, employing an epithet well suited to their mode of life, or whether the first of them really called themselves so in the beginning, since the name of Christians was not yet everywhere known, we need not discuss here.

5. He bears witness, however, that first of all they renounce their property. When they begin the philosophical mode of life, he says, they give up their goods to their relatives, and then, renouncing all the cares of life, they go forth beyond the walls and dwell in lonely fields and gardens, knowing well that intercourse with people of a different character is unprofitable and harmful. They did this at that time, as seems probable, under the influence of a spirited and ardent faith, practicing in emulation the prophets' mode of life.

6. For in the Acts of the Apostles, a work universally acknowledged as authentic, it is recorded that all the companions of the apostles sold their possessions and their property and distributed to all according to the necessity of each one, so that no one among them was in want. For as many as were possessors of lands or houses, as the account says, sold

them and brought the prices of the things that were sold, and laid them at the apostles' feet, so that distribution was made unto every man according as he had need. Acts 2:45

7. Philo bears witness to facts very much like those here described and then adds the following account: Everywhere in the world is this race found. For it was fitting that both Greek and Barbarian should share in what is perfectly good. But the race particularly abounds in Egypt, in each of its so-called nomes, and especially about Alexandria.

8. The best men from every quarter emigrate, as if to a colony of the Therapeutæ's fatherland, to a certain very suitable spot which lies above the Lake Maria upon a low hill excellently situated on account of its security and the mildness of the atmosphere.

9. And then a little further on, after describing the kind of houses which they had, he speaks as follows concerning their churches, which were scattered about here and there: In each house there is a sacred apartment which is called a sanctuary and monastery, where, quite alone, they perform the mysteries of the religious life. They bring nothing into it, neither drink nor food, nor any of the other things which contribute to the necessities of the body, but only the laws, and the inspired oracles of the prophets, and hymns and such other things as augment and make perfect their knowledge and piety.

10. And after some other matters he says: The whole interval, from morning to evening, is for them a time of exercise. For they read the holy Scriptures, and explain the philosophy of their fathers in an allegorical manner, regarding the written words as symbols of hidden truth which is communicated in obscure figures.

11. They have also writings of ancient men, who were the founders of their sect, and who left many monuments of the allegorical method. These they use as models, and imitate their principles.

12. These things seem to have been stated by a man who had heard them expounding their sacred writings. But it is highly probable that the works of the ancients, which he says they had, were the Gospels and the writings of the apostles, and probably some expositions of the ancient prophets, such as are contained in the Epistle to the Hebrews, and in many others of Paul's Epistles.

13. Then again he writes as follows concerning the new psalms which they composed: So that they not only spend their time in meditation, but they also compose songs and hymns to God in every variety of

metre and melody, though they divide them, of course, into measures of more than common solemnity.

14. The same book contains an account of many other things, but it seemed necessary to select those facts which exhibit the characteristics of the ecclesiastical mode of life.

15. But if any one thinks that what has been said is not peculiar to the Gospel polity, but that it can be applied to others besides those mentioned, let him be convinced by the subsequent words of the same author, in which, if he is unprejudiced, he will find undisputed testimony on this subject. Philo's words are as follows:

16. Having laid down temperance as a sort of foundation in the soul, they build upon it the other virtues. None of them may take food or drink before sunset, since they regard philosophizing as a work worthy of the light, but attention to the wants of the body as proper only in the darkness, and therefore assign the day to the former, but to the latter a small portion of the night.

17. But some, in whom a great desire for knowledge dwells, forget to take food for three days; and some are so delighted and feast so luxuriously upon wisdom, which furnishes doctrines richly and without stint, that they abstain even twice as long as this, and are accustomed, after six days, scarcely to take necessary food. These statements of Philo we regard as referring clearly and indisputably to those of our communion.

18. But if after these things any one still obstinately persists in denying the reference, let him renounce his incredulity and be convinced by yet more striking examples, which are to be found nowhere else than in the evangelical religion of the Christians.

19. For they say that there were women also with those of whom we are speaking, and that the most of them were aged virgins who had preserved their chastity, not out of necessity, as some of the priestesses among the Greeks, but rather by their own choice, through zeal and a desire for wisdom. And that in their earnest desire to live with it as their companion they paid no attention to the pleasures of the body, seeking not mortal but immortal progeny, which only the pious soul is able to bear of itself.

20. Then after a little he adds still more emphatically: They expound the Sacred Scriptures figuratively by means of allegories. For the whole law seems to these men to resemble a living organism, of which the spoken

words constitute the body, while the hidden sense stored up within the words constitutes the soul. This hidden meaning has first been particularly studied by this sect, which sees, revealed as in a mirror of names, the surpassing beauties of the thoughts.

21. Why is it necessary to add to these things their meetings and the respective occupations of the men and of the women during those meetings, and the practices which are even to the present day habitually observed by us, especially such as we are accustomed to observe at the feast of the Saviour's passion, with fasting and night watching and study of the divine Word.

22. These things the above-mentioned author has related in his own work, indicating a mode of life which has been preserved to the present time by us alone, recording especially the vigils kept in connection with the great festival, and the exercises performed during those vigils, and the hymns customarily recited by us, and describing how, while one sings regularly in time, the others listen in silence, and join in chanting only the close of the hymns; and how, on the days referred to they sleep on the ground on beds of straw, and to use his own words, taste no wine at all, nor any flesh, but water is their only drink, and the reish with their bread is salt and hyssop.

23. In addition to this Philo describes the order of dignities which exists among those who carry on the services of the church, mentioning the diaconate, and the office of bishop, which takes the precedence over all the others. But whosoever desires a more accurate knowledge of these matters may get it from the history already cited.

24. But that Philo, when he wrote these things, had in view the first heralds of the Gospel and the customs handed down from the beginning by the apostles, is clear to every one.

Chapter 18. The Works of Philo that have come down to us.

1. Copious in language, comprehensive in thought, sublime and elevated in his views of divine Scripture, Philo has produced manifold and various expositions of the sacred books. On the one hand, he expounds in order the events recorded in Genesis in the books to which he gives the title Allegories of the Sacred Laws; on the other hand, he makes successive divisions of the chapters in the Scriptures which are the subject of investigation, and gives objections and solutions, in the books

which he quite suitably calls Questions and Answers on Genesis and Exodus.

2. There are, besides these, treatises expressly worked out by him on certain subjects, such as the two books On Agriculture, and the same number On Drunkenness; and some others distinguished by different titles corresponding to the contents of each; for instance, Concerning the Things Which the Sober Mind Desires and Execrates, On the Confusion of Tongues, On Flight and Discovery, On Assembly for the Sake of Instruction, On the Question, 'Who is Heir to Things Divine?' or On the Division of Things into Equal and Unequal, and still further the work On the Three Virtues Which With Others Have Been Described by Moses.

3. In addition to these is the work On Those Whose Names Have Been Changed and Why They Have Been Changed, in which he says that he had written also two books On Covenants.

4. And there is also a work of his On Emigration, and one On the Life of a Wise Man Made Perfect in Righteousness, or On Unwritten Laws; and still further the work On Giants or On the Immutability of God, and a first, second, third, fourth and fifth book On the Proposition, That Dreams According to Moses are Sent by God. These are the books on Genesis that have come down to us.

5. But on Exodus we are acquainted with the first, second, third, fourth and fifth books of Questions and Answers; also with that On the Tabernacle, and that On the Ten Commandments, and the four books On the Laws Which Refer Especially to the Principal Divisions of the Ten Commandments, and another On Animals Intended for Sacrifice and On the Kinds of Sacrifice, and another On the Rewards Fixed in the Law for the Good, and on the Punishments and Curses Fixed for the Wicked.

6. In addition to all these there are extant also some single-volumed works of his; as for instance, the work On Providence, and the book composed by him On the Jews, and The Statesman; and still further, Alexander, or On the Possession of Reason by the Irrational Animals. Besides these there is a work On the Proposition that Every Wicked Man is a Slave, to which is subjoined the work On the Proposition that Every Good Man is Free.

7. After these was composed by him the work On the Contemplative Life, or On Suppliants, from which we have drawn the facts concerning

the life of the apostolic men; and still further, the Interpretation of the Hebrew Names in the Law and in the Prophets are said to be the result of his industry.

8. And he is said to have read in the presence of the whole Roman Senate during the reign of Claudius the work which he had written, when he came to Rome under Caius, concerning Caius' hatred of the gods, and to which, with ironical reference to its character, he had given the title On the Virtues. And his discourses were so much admired as to be deemed worthy of a place in the libraries.

9. At this time, while Paul was completing his journey from Jerusalem and round about unto Illyricum, Romans 15:19 Claudius drove the Jews out of Rome; and Aquila and Priscilla, leaving Rome with the other Jews, came to Asia, and there abode with the apostle Paul, who was confirming the churches of that region whose foundations he had newly laid. The sacred book of the Acts informs us also of these things.

Chapter 19. The Calamity which befell the Jews in Jerusalem on the Day of the Passover.

1. While Claudius was still emperor, it happened that so great a tumult and disturbance took place in Jerusalem at the feast of the Passover, that thirty thousand of those Jews alone who were forcibly crowded together at the gate of the temple perished, being trampled under foot by one another. Thus the festival became a season of mourning for all the nation, and there was weeping in every house. These things are related literally by Josephus.

2. But Claudius appointed Agrippa, son of Agrippa, king of the Jews, having sent Felix as procurator of the whole country of Samaria and Galilee, and of the land called Perea. And after he had reigned thirteen years and eight months he died, and left Nero as his successor in the empire.

Chapter 20. The Events which took Place in Jerusalem during the Reign of Nero.

1. Josephus again, in the twentieth book of his Antiquities, relates the quarrel which arose among the priests during the reign of Nero, while Felix was procurator of Judea.

2. His words are as follows : There arose a quarrel between the high priests on the one hand and the priests and leaders of the people of Jerusalem on the other. And each of them collected a body of the boldest and most restless men, and put himself at their head, and whenever they met they hurled invectives and stones at each other. And there was no one that would interpose; but these things were done at will as if in a city destitute of a ruler.

3. And so great was the shamelessness and audacity of the high priests that they dared to send their servants to the threshing-floors to seize the tithes due to the priests; and thus those of the priests that were poor were seen to be perishing of want. In this way did the violence of the factions prevail over all justice.

4. And the same author again relates that about the same time there sprang up in Jerusalem a certain kind of robbers, who by day, as he says, and in the middle of the city slew those who met them.

5. For, especially at the feasts, they mingled with the multitude, and with short swords, which they concealed under their garments, they stabbed the most distinguished men. And when they fell, the murderers themselves were among those who expressed their indignation. And thus on account of the confidence which was reposed in them by all, they remained undiscovered.

6. The first that was slain by them was Jonathan the high priest; and after him many were killed every day, until the fear became worse than the evil itself, each one, as in battle, hourly expecting death.

Chapter 21. The Egyptian, who is mentioned also in the Acts of the Apostles.

1. After other matters he proceeds as follows: But the Jews were afflicted with a greater plague than these by the Egyptian false prophet. For there appeared in the land an impostor who aroused faith in himself as a prophet, and collected about thirty thousand of those whom he had deceived, and led them from the desert to the so-called Mount of Olives whence he was prepared to enter Jerusalem by force and to overpower the Roman garrison and seize the government of the people, using those who made the attack with him as body guards.

2. But Felix anticipated his attack, and went out to meet him with the Roman legionaries, and all the people joined in the defense, so that when

the battle was fought the Egyptian fled with a few followers, but the most of them were destroyed or taken captive.

3. Josephus relates these events in the second book of his History. But it is worth while comparing the account of the Egyptian given here with that contained in the Acts of the Apostles. In the time of Felix it was said to Paul by the centurion in Jerusalem, when the multitude of the Jews raised a disturbance against the apostle, Are you not he who before these days made an uproar, and led out into the wilderness four thousand men that were murderers? Acts 21:38 These are the events which took place in the time of Felix.

Chapter 22. Paul having been sent bound from Judea to Rome, made his Defense, and was acquitted of every Charge.

1. Festus was sent by Nero to be Felix's successor. Under him Paul, having made his defense, was sent bound to Rome. Aristarchus was with him, whom he also somewhere in his epistles quite naturally calls his fellow-prisoner. Colossians 4:10 And Luke, who wrote the Acts of the Apostles, brought his history to a close at this point, after stating that Paul spent two whole years at Rome as a prisoner at large, and preached the word of God without restraint.

2. Thus after he had made his defense it is said that the apostle was sent again upon the ministry of preaching, and that upon coming to the same city a second time he suffered martyrdom. In this imprisonment he wrote his second epistle to Timothy, in which he mentions his first defense and his impending death.

3. But hear his testimony on these matters: At my first answer, he says, no man stood with me, but all men forsook me: I pray God that it may not be laid to their charge. Notwithstanding the Lord stood with me, and strengthened me; that by me the preaching might be fully known, and that all the Gentiles might hear: and I was delivered out of the mouth of the lion. 2 Timothy 4:16-17

4. He plainly indicates in these words that on the former occasion, in order that the preaching might be fulfilled by him, he was rescued from the mouth of the lion, referring, in this expression, to Nero, as is probable on account of the latter's cruelty. He did not therefore afterward add the similar statement, He will rescue me from the mouth of the lion; for he saw in the spirit that his end would not be long delayed.

5. Wherefore he adds to the words, And he delivered me from the mouth of the lion, this sentence: The Lord shall deliver me from every evil work, and will preserve me unto his heavenly kingdom, 2 Timothy 4:18 indicating his speedy martyrdom; which he also foretells still more clearly in the same epistle, when he writes, For I am now ready to be offered, and the time of my departure is at hand.

6. In his second epistle to Timothy, moreover, he indicates that Luke was with him when he wrote, but at his first defense not even he. Whence it is probable that Luke wrote the Acts of the Apostles at that time, continuing his history down to the period when he was with Paul.

7. But these things have been adduced by us to show that Paul's martyrdom did not take place at the time of that Roman sojourn which Luke records.

8. It is probable indeed that as Nero was more disposed to mildness in the beginning, Paul's defense of his doctrine was more easily received; but that when he had advanced to the commission of lawless deeds of daring, he made the apostles as well as others the subjects of his attacks.

Chapter 23. The Martyrdom of James, who was called the Brother of the Lord.

1. But after Paul, in consequence of his appeal to Cæsar, had been sent to Rome by Festus, the Jews, being frustrated in their hope of entrapping him by the snares which they had laid for him, turned against James, the brother of the Lord, to whom the episcopal seat at Jerusalem had been entrusted by the apostles. The following daring measures were undertaken by them against him.

2. Leading him into their midst they demanded of him that he should renounce faith in Christ in the presence of all the people. But, contrary to the opinion of all, with a clear voice, and with greater boldness than they had anticipated, he spoke out before the whole multitude and confessed that our Saviour and Lord Jesus is the Son of God. But they were unable to bear longer the testimony of the man who, on account of the excellence of ascetic virtue and of piety which he exhibited in his life, was esteemed by all as the most just of men, and consequently they slew him. Opportunity for this deed of violence was furnished by the prevailing anarchy, which was caused by the fact that Festus had died

just at this time in Judea, and that the province was thus without a governor and head.

3. The manner of James' death has been already indicated by the above-quoted words of Clement, who records that he was thrown from the pinnacle of the temple, and was beaten to death with a club. But Hegesippus, who lived immediately after the apostles, gives the most accurate account in the fifth book of his Memoirs. He writes as follows:

4. James, the brother of the Lord, succeeded to the government of the Church in conjunction with the apostles. He has been called the Just by all from the time of our Saviour to the present day; for there were many that bore the name of James.

5. He was holy from his mother's womb; and he drank no wine nor strong drink, nor did he eat flesh. No razor came upon his head; he did not anoint himself with oil, and he did not use the bath.

6. He alone was permitted to enter into the holy place; for he wore not woolen but linen garments. And he was in the habit of entering alone into the temple, and was frequently found upon his knees begging forgiveness for the people, so that his knees became hard like those of a camel, in consequence of his constantly bending them in his worship of God, and asking forgiveness for the people.

7. Because of his exceeding great justice he was called the Just, and Oblias, which signifies in Greek, 'Bulwark of the people' and 'Justice,' in accordance with what the prophets declare concerning him.

8. Now some of the seven sects, which existed among the people and which have been mentioned by me in the Memoirs, asked him, 'What is the gate of Jesus?' and he replied that he was the Saviour.

9. On account of these words some believed that Jesus is the Christ. But the sects mentioned above did not believe either in a resurrection or in one's coming to give to every man according to his works. But as many as believed did so on account of James.

10. Therefore when many even of the rulers believed, there was a commotion among the Jews and Scribes and Pharisees, who said that there was danger that the whole people would be looking for Jesus as the Christ. Coming therefore in a body to James they said, 'We entreat you, restrain the people; for they are gone astray in regard to Jesus, as if he were the Christ. We entreat you to persuade all that have come to the feast of the Passover concerning Jesus; for we all have confidence in

you. For we bear you witness, as do all the people, that you are just, and do not respect persons. Matthew 22:16

11. Therefore, persuade the multitude not to be led astray concerning Jesus. For the whole people, and all of us also, have confidence in you. Stand therefore upon the pinnacle of the temple, that from that high position you may be clearly seen, and that your words may be readily heard by all the people. For all the tribes, with the Gentiles also, have come together on account of the Passover.'

12. The aforesaid Scribes and Pharisees therefore placed James upon the pinnacle of the temple, and cried out to him and said: 'You just one, in whom we ought all to have confidence, forasmuch as the people are led astray after Jesus, the crucified one, declare to us, what is the gate of Jesus.'

13. And he answered with a loud voice, 'Why do you ask me concerning Jesus, the Son of Man? He himself sits in heaven at the right hand of the great Power, and is about to come upon the clouds of heaven.'

14. And when many were fully convinced and gloried in the testimony of James, and said, 'Hosanna to the Son of David,' these same Scribes and Pharisees said again to one another, 'We have done badly in supplying such testimony to Jesus. But let us go up and throw him down, in order that they may be afraid to believe him.'

15. And they cried out, saying, 'Oh! Oh! The just man is also in error.' And they fulfilled the Scripture written in Isaiah, 'Let us take away the just man, because he is troublesome to us: therefore they shall eat the fruit of their doings.'

16. So they went up and threw down the just man, and said to each other, 'Let us stone James the Just.' And they began to stone him, for he was not killed by the fall; but he turned and knelt down and said, 'I entreat you, Lord God our Father, forgive them, for they know not what they do.' Luke 23:34

17. And while they were thus stoning him one of the priests of the sons of Rechab, the son of the Rechabites, who are mentioned by Jeremiah the prophet, cried out, saying, 'Stop. What are you doing? The just one prays for you.'

18. And one of them, who was a fuller, took the club with which he beat out clothes and struck the just man on the head. And thus he suffered martyrdom. And they buried him on the spot, by the temple, and his monument still remains by the temple. He became a true witness, both

to Jews and Greeks, that Jesus is the Christ. And immediately Vespasian besieged them.

19. These things are related at length by Hegesippus, who is in agreement with Clement. James was so admirable a man and so celebrated among all for his justice, that the more sensible even of the Jews were of the opinion that this was the cause of the siege of Jerusalem, which happened to them immediately after his martyrdom for no other reason than their daring act against him.

20. Josephus, at least, has not hesitated to testify this in his writings, where he says, These things happened to the Jews to avenge James the Just, who was a brother of Jesus, that is called the Christ. For the Jews slew him, although he was a most just man.

21. And the same writer records his death also in the twentieth book of his Antiquities in the following words: But the emperor, when he learned of the death of Festus, sent Albinus to be procurator of Judea. But the younger Ananus, who, as we have already said, had obtained the high priesthood, was of an exceedingly bold and reckless disposition. He belonged, moreover, to the sect of the Sadducees, who are the most cruel of all the Jews in the execution of judgment, as we have already shown.

22. Ananus, therefore, being of this character, and supposing that he had a favorable opportunity on account of the fact that Festus was dead, and Albinus was still on the way, called together the Sanhedrin, and brought before them the brother of Jesus, the so-called Christ, James by name, together with some others, and accused them of violating the law, and condemned them to be stoned.

23. But those in the city who seemed most moderate and skilled in the law were very angry at this, and sent secretly to the king, requesting him to order Ananus to cease such proceedings. For he had not done right even this first time. And certain of them also went to meet Albinus, who was journeying from Alexandria, and reminded him that it was not lawful for Ananus to summon the Sanhedrin without his knowledge.

24. And Albinus, being persuaded by their representations, wrote in anger to Ananus, threatening him with punishment. And the king, Agrippa, in consequence, deprived him of the high priesthood, which he had held three months, and appointed Jesus, the son of Damnæus.

25. These things are recorded in regard to James, who is said to be the author of the first of the so-called catholic epistles. But it is to be

observed that it is disputed; at least, not many of the ancients have mentioned it, as is the case likewise with the epistle that bears the name of Jude, which is also one of the seven so-called catholic epistles. Nevertheless we know that these also, with the rest, have been read publicly in very many churches.

Chapter 24. Annianus the First Bishop of the Church of Alexandria after Mark.

1. When Nero was in the eighth year of his reign, Annianus succeeded Mark the Evangelist in the administration of the parish of Alexandria.

Chapter 25. The Persecution under Nero in which Paul and Peter were honored at Rome with Martyrdom in Behalf of Religion.

1. When the government of Nero was now firmly established, he began to plunge into unholy pursuits, and armed himself even against the religion of the God of the universe.

2. To describe the greatness of his depravity does not lie within the plan of the present work. As there are many indeed that have recorded his history in most accurate narratives, every one may at his pleasure learn from them the coarseness of the man's extraordinary madness, under the influence of which, after he had accomplished the destruction of so many myriads without any reason, he ran into such blood-guiltiness that he did not spare even his nearest relatives and dearest friends, but destroyed his mother and his brothers and his wife, with very many others of his own family as he would private and public enemies, with various kinds of deaths.

3. But with all these things this particular in the catalogue of his crimes was still wanting, that he was the first of the emperors who showed himself an enemy of the divine religion.

4. The Roman Tertullian is likewise a witness of this. He writes as follows: Examine your records. There you will find that Nero was the first that persecuted this doctrine, particularly then when after subduing all the east, he exercised his cruelty against all at Rome. We glory in having such a man the leader in our punishment. For whoever knows him can understand that nothing was condemned by Nero unless it was something of great excellence.

5. Thus publicly announcing himself as the first among God's chief enemies, he was led on to the slaughter of the apostles. It is, therefore, recorded that Paul was beheaded in Rome itself, and that Peter likewise was crucified under Nero. This account of Peter and Paul is substantiated by the fact that their names are preserved in the cemeteries of that place even to the present day.

6. It is confirmed likewise by Caius, a member of the Church, who arose under Zephyrinus, bishop of Rome. He, in a published disputation with Proclus, the leader of the Phrygian heresy, speaks as follows concerning the places where the sacred corpses of the aforesaid apostles are laid:

7. But I can show the trophies of the apostles. For if you will go to the Vatican or to the Ostian way, you will find the trophies of those who laid the foundations of this church.

8. And that they both suffered martyrdom at the same time is stated by Dionysius, bishop of Corinth, in his epistle to the Romans, in the following words: You have thus by such an admonition bound together the planting of Peter and of Paul at Rome and Corinth. For both of them planted and likewise taught us in our Corinth. And they taught together in like manner in Italy, and suffered martyrdom at the same time. I have quoted these things in order that the truth of the history might be still more confirmed.

Chapter 26. The Jews, afflicted with Innumerable Evils, commenced the Last War Against the Romans.

1. Josephus again, after relating many things in connection with the calamity which came upon the whole Jewish nation, records, in addition to many other circumstances, that a great many of the most honorable among the Jews were scourged in Jerusalem itself and then crucified by Florus. It happened that he was procurator of Judea when the war began to be kindled, in the twelfth year of Nero.

2. Josephus says that at that time a terrible commotion was stirred up throughout all Syria in consequence of the revolt of the Jews, and that everywhere the latter were destroyed without mercy, like enemies, by the inhabitants of the cities, so that one could see cities filled with unburied corpses, and the dead bodies of the aged scattered about with the bodies of infants, and women without even a covering for their nakedness, and the whole province full of indescribable calamities, while the dread of those things that were threatened was greater than the sufferings

themselves which they anywhere endured. Such is the account of Josephus; and such was the condition of the Jews at that time.

BOOK III

Chapter 1. The Parts of the World in which the Apostles preached Christ.

1. Such was the condition of the Jews. Meanwhile the holy apostles and disciples of our Saviour were dispersed throughout the world. Parthia, according to tradition, was allotted to Thomas as his field of labor, Scythia to Andrew, and Asia to John, who, after he had lived some time there, died at Ephesus.

2. Peter appears to have preached in Pontus, Galatia, Bithynia, Cappadocia, and Asia to the Jews of the dispersion. And at last, having come to Rome, he was crucified head-downwards; for he had requested that he might suffer in this way. What do we need to say concerning Paul, who preached the Gospel of Christ from Jerusalem to Illyricum, and afterwards suffered martyrdom in Rome under Nero? These facts are related by Origen in the third volume of his Commentary on Genesis.

Chapter 2. The First Successor to St. Peter in Rome.

1. After the martyrdom of Paul and of Peter, Linus was the first to obtain the episcopate of the church at Rome. Paul mentions him, when writing to Timothy from Rome, in the salutation at the end of the epistle.

Chapter 3. The Epistles of the Apostles.

1. One epistle of Peter, that called the first, is acknowledged as genuine. And this the ancient elders used freely in their own writings as an undisputed work. But we have learned that his extant second Epistle does not belong to the canon; yet, as it has appeared profitable to many, it has been used with the other Scriptures.

2. The so-called Acts of Peter, however, and the Gospel which bears his name, and the Preaching and the Apocalypse, as they are called, we know have not been universally accepted, because no ecclesiastical writer, ancient or modern, has made use of testimonies drawn from them.

3. But in the course of my history I shall be careful to show, in addition to the official succession, what ecclesiastical writers have from time to

time made use of any of the disputed works, and what they have said in regard to the canonical and accepted writings, as well as in regard to those which are not of this class.

4. Such are the writings that bear the name of Peter, only one of which I know to be genuine and acknowledged by the ancient elders.

5. Paul's fourteen epistles are well known and undisputed. It is not indeed right to overlook the fact that some have rejected the Epistle to the Hebrews, saying that it is disputed by the church of Rome, on the ground that it was not written by Paul. But what has been said concerning this epistle by those who lived before our time I shall quote in the proper place. In regard to the so-called Acts of Paul, I have not found them among the undisputed writings.

6. But as the same apostle, in the salutations at the end of the Epistle to the Romans, has made mention among others of Hermas, to whom the book called The Shepherd is ascribed, it should be observed that this too has been disputed by some, and on their account cannot be placed among the acknowledged books; while by others it is considered quite indispensable, especially to those who need instruction in the elements of the faith. Hence, as we know, it has been publicly read in churches, and I have found that some of the most ancient writers used it.

7. This will serve to show the divine writings that are undisputed as well as those that are not universally acknowledged.

Chapter 4. The First Successors of the Apostles.

1. That Paul preached to the Gentiles and laid the foundations of the churches from Jerusalem round about even unto Illyricum, is evident both from his own words, Romans 15:19 and from the account which Luke has given in the Acts.

2. And in how many provinces Peter preached Christ and taught the doctrine of the new covenant to those of the circumcision is clear from his own words in his epistle already mentioned as undisputed, in which he writes to the Hebrews of the dispersion in Pontus, Galatia, Cappadocia, Asia, and Bithynia. 1 Peter 1:1

3. But the number and the names of those among them that became true and zealous followers of the apostles, and were judged worthy to tend the churches founded by them, it is not easy to tell, except those mentioned in the writings of Paul.

4. For he had innumerable fellow-laborers, or fellow-soldiers, as he called them, and most of them were honored by him with an imperishable memorial, for he gave enduring testimony concerning them in his own epistles.

5. Luke also in the Acts speaks of his friends, and mentions them by name.

6. Timothy, so it is recorded, was the first to receive the episcopate of the parish in Ephesus, Titus of the churches in Crete.

7. But Luke, who was of Antiochian parentage and a physician by profession, and who was especially intimate with Paul and well acquainted with the rest of the apostles, has left us, in two inspired books, proofs of that spiritual healing art which he learned from them. One of these books is the Gospel, which he testifies that he wrote as those who were from the beginning eyewitnesses and ministers of the word delivered unto him, all of whom, as he says, he followed accurately from the first. Luke 1:2-3 The other book is the Acts of the Apostles which he composed not from the accounts of others, but from what he had seen himself.

8. And they say that Paul meant to refer to Luke's Gospel wherever, as if speaking of some gospel of his own, he used the words, according to my Gospel.

9. As to the rest of his followers, Paul testifies that Crescens was sent to Gaul; but Linus, whom he mentions in the Second Epistle to Timothy 2 Timothy 4:21 as his companion at Rome, was Peter's successor in the episcopate of the church there, as has already been shown.

10. Clement also, who was appointed third bishop of the church at Rome, was, as Paul testifies, his co-laborer and fellow-soldier.

11. Besides these, that Areopagite, named Dionysius, who was the first to believe after Paul's address to the Athenians in the Areopagus (as recorded by Luke in the Acts) is mentioned by another Dionysius, an ancient writer and pastor of the parish in Corinth, as the first bishop of the church at Athens.

12. But the events connected with the apostolic succession we shall relate at the proper time. Meanwhile let us continue the course of our history.

Chapter 5. The Last Siege of the Jews after Christ.

1. After Nero had held the power thirteen years, and Galba and Otho had ruled a year and six months, Vespasian, who had become distinguished in the campaigns against the Jews, was proclaimed sovereign in Judea and received the title of Emperor from the armies there. Setting out immediately, therefore, for Rome, he entrusted the conduct of the war against the Jews to his son Titus.

2. For the Jews after the ascension of our Saviour, in addition to their crime against him, had been devising as many plots as they could against his apostles. First Stephen was stoned to death by them, and after him James, the son of Zebedee and the brother of John, was beheaded, and finally James, the first that had obtained the episcopal seat in Jerusalem after the ascension of our Saviour, died in the manner already described. But the rest of the apostles, who had been incessantly plotted against with a view to their destruction, and had been driven out of the land of Judea, went unto all nations to preach the Gospel, relying upon the power of Christ, who had said to them, Go and make disciples of all the nations in my name.

3. But the people of the church in Jerusalem had been commanded by a revelation, vouchsafed to approved men there before the war, to leave the city and to dwell in a certain town of Perea called Pella. And when those that believed in Christ had come there from Jerusalem, then, as if the royal city of the Jews and the whole land of Judea were entirely destitute of holy men, the judgment of God at length overtook those who had committed such outrages against Christ and his apostles, and totally destroyed that generation of impious men.

4. But the number of calamities which everywhere fell upon the nation at that time; the extreme misfortunes to which the inhabitants of Judea were especially subjected, the thousands of men, as well as women and children, that perished by the sword, by famine, and by other forms of death innumerable—all these things, as well as the many great sieges which were carried on against the cities of Judea, and the excessive sufferings endured by those that fled to Jerusalem itself, as to a city of perfect safety, and finally the general course of the whole war, as well as its particular occurrences in detail, and how at last the abomination of desolation, proclaimed by the prophets, Daniel 9:27 stood in the very temple of God, so celebrated of old, the temple which was now awaiting its total and final destruction by fire — all these things any one that wishes may find accurately described in the history written by Josephus.

5. But it is necessary to state that this writer records that the multitude of those who were assembled from all Judea at the time of the Passover, to the number of three million souls, were shut up in Jerusalem as in a prison, to use his own words.

6. For it was right that in the very days in which they had inflicted suffering upon the Saviour and the Benefactor of all, the Christ of God, that in those days, shut up as in a prison, they should meet with destruction at the hands of divine justice.

7. But passing by the particular calamities which they suffered from the attempts made upon them by the sword and by other means, I think it necessary to relate only the misfortunes which the famine caused, that those who read this work may have some means of knowing that God was not long in executing vengeance upon them for their wickedness against the Christ of God.

Chapter 6. The Famine which oppressed them.

1. Taking the fifth book of the History of Josephus again in our hands, let us go through the tragedy of events which then occurred.

2. For the wealthy, he says, it was equally dangerous to remain. For under pretense that they were going to desert, men were put to death for their wealth. The madness of the seditions increased with the famine and both the miseries were inflamed more and more day by day.

3. Nowhere was food to be seen; but, bursting into the houses men searched them thoroughly, and whenever they found anything to eat they tormented the owners on the ground that they had denied that they had anything; but if they found nothing, they tortured them on the ground that they had more carefully concealed it.

4. The proof of their having or not having food was found in the bodies of the poor wretches. Those of them who were still in good condition they assumed were well supplied with food, while those who were already wasted away they passed by, for it seemed absurd to slay those who were on the point of perishing for want.

5. Many, indeed, secretly sold their possessions for one measure of wheat, if they belonged to the wealthier class, of barley if they were poorer. Then shutting themselves up in the innermost parts of their houses, some ate the grain uncooked on account of their terrible want, while others baked it according as necessity and fear dictated.

6. Nowhere were tables set, but, snatching the yet uncooked food from the fire, they tore it in pieces. Wretched was the fare, and a lamentable spectacle it was to see the more powerful secure an abundance while the weaker mourned.

7. Of all evils, indeed, famine is the worst, and it destroys nothing so effectively as shame. For that which under other circumstances is worthy of respect, in the midst of famine is despised. Thus women snatched the food from the very mouths of their husbands and children, from their fathers, and what was most pitiable of all, mothers from their babes. And while their dearest ones were wasting away in their arms, they were not ashamed to take away from them the last drops that supported life.

8. And even while they were eating thus they did not remain undiscovered. But everywhere the rioters appeared, to rob them even of these portions of food. For whenever they saw a house shut up, they regarded it as a sign that those inside were taking food. And immediately bursting open the doors they rushed in and seized what they were eating, almost forcing it out of their very throats.

9. Old men who clung to their food were beaten, and if the women concealed it in their hands, their hair was torn for so doing. There was pity neither for gray hairs nor for infants, but, taking up the babes that clung to their morsels of food, they dashed them to the ground. But to those that anticipated their entrance and swallowed what they were about to seize, they were still more cruel, just as if they had been wronged by them.

10. And they devised the most terrible modes of torture to discover food, stopping up the privy passages of the poor wretches with bitter herbs, and piercing their seats with sharp rods. And men suffered things horrible even to hear of, for the sake of compelling them to confess to the possession of one loaf of bread, or in order that they might be made to disclose a single drachm of barley which they had concealed. But the tormentors themselves did not suffer hunger.

11. Their conduct might indeed have seemed less barbarous if they had been driven to it by necessity; but they did it for the sake of exercising their madness and of providing sustenance for themselves for days to come.

12. And when any one crept out of the city by night as far as the outposts of the Romans to collect wild herbs and grass, they went to meet him;

and when he thought he had already escaped the enemy, they seized what he had brought with him, and even though oftentimes the man would entreat them, and, calling upon the most awful name of God, adjure them to give him a portion of what he had obtained at the risk of his life, they would give him nothing back. Indeed, it was fortunate if the one that was plundered was not also slain.

13. To this account Josephus, after relating other things, adds the following: The possibility of going out of the city being brought to an end, all hope of safety for the Jews was cut off. And the famine increased and devoured the people by houses and families. And the rooms were filled with dead women and children, the lanes of the city with the corpses of old men.

14. Children and youths, swollen with the famine, wandered about the marketplaces like shadows, and fell down wherever the death agony overtook them. The sick were not strong enough to bury even their own relatives, and those who had the strength hesitated because of the multitude of the dead and the uncertainty as to their own fate. Many, indeed, died while they were burying others, and many betook themselves to their graves before death came upon them.

15. There was neither weeping nor lamentation under these misfortunes; but the famine stifled the natural affections. Those that were dying a lingering death looked with dry eyes upon those that had gone to their rest before them. Deep silence and death-laden night encircled the city.

16. But the robbers were more terrible than these miseries; for they broke open the houses, which were now mere sepulchres, robbed the dead and stripped the covering from their bodies, and went away with a laugh. They tried the points of their swords in the dead bodies, and some that were lying on the ground still alive they thrust through in order to test their weapons. But those that prayed that they would use their right hand and their sword upon them, they contemptuously left to be destroyed by the famine. Every one of these died with eyes fixed upon the temple; and they left the seditious alive.

17. These at first gave orders that the dead should be buried out of the public treasury, for they could not endure the stench. But afterward, when they were not able to do this, they threw the bodies from the walls into the trenches.

18. And as Titus went around and saw the trenches filled with the dead, and the thick blood oozing out of the putrid bodies, he groaned aloud, and, raising his hands, called God to witness that this was not his doing.

19. After speaking of some other things, Josephus proceeds as follows: I cannot hesitate to declare what my feelings compel me to. I suppose, if the Romans had longer delayed in coming against these guilty wretches, the city would have been swallowed up by a chasm, or overwhelmed with a flood, or struck with such thunderbolts as destroyed Sodom. For it had brought forth a generation of men much more godless than were those that suffered such punishment. By their madness indeed was the whole people brought to destruction.

20. And in the sixth book he writes as follows: Of those that perished by famine in the city the number was countless, and the miseries they underwent unspeakable. For if so much as the shadow of food appeared in any house, there was war, and the dearest friends engaged in hand-to-hand conflict with one another, and snatched from each other the most wretched supports of life.

21. Nor would they believe that even the dying were without food; but the robbers would search them while they were expiring, lest any one should feign death while concealing food in his bosom. With mouths gaping for want of food, they stumbled and staggered along like mad dogs, and beat the doors as if they were drunk, and in their impotence they would rush into the same houses twice or thrice in one hour.

22. Necessity compelled them to eat anything they could find, and they gathered and devoured things that were not fit even for the filthiest of irrational beasts. Finally they did not abstain even from their girdles and shoes, and they stripped the hides off their shields and devoured them. Some used even wisps of old hay for food, and others gathered stubble and sold the smallest weight of it for four Attic drachmæ.

23. But why should I speak of the shamelessness which was displayed during the famine toward inanimate things? For I am going to relate a fact such as is recorded neither by Greeks nor Barbarians; horrible to relate, incredible to hear. And indeed I should gladly have omitted this calamity, that I might not seem to posterity to be a teller of fabulous tales, if I had not innumerable witnesses to it in my own age. And besides, I should render my country poor service if I suppressed the account of the sufferings which she endured.

24. There was a certain woman named Mary that dwelt beyond Jordan, whose father was Eleazer, of the village of Bathezor (which signifies the house of hyssop). She was distinguished for her family and her wealth, and had fled with the rest of the multitude to Jerusalem and was shut up there with them during the siege.

25. The tyrants had robbed her of the rest of the property which she had brought with her into the city from Perea. And the remnants of her possessions and whatever food was to be seen the guards rushed in daily and snatched away from her. This made the woman terribly angry, and by her frequent reproaches and imprecations she aroused the anger of the rapacious villains against herself.

26. But no one either through anger or pity would slay her; and she grew weary of finding food for others to eat. The search, too, was already become everywhere difficult, and the famine was piercing her bowels and marrow, and resentment was raging more violently than famine. Taking, therefore, anger and necessity as her counsellors, she proceeded to do a most unnatural thing.

27. Seizing her child, a boy which was sucking at her breast, she said, Oh, wretched child, in war, in famine, in sedition, for what do I preserve you? Slaves among the Romans we shall be even if we are allowed to live by them. But even slavery is anticipated by the famine, and the rioters are more cruel than both. Come, be food for me, a fury for these rioters, and a bye-word to the world, for this is all that is wanting to complete the calamities of the Jews.

28. And when she had said this she slew her son; and having roasted him, she ate one half herself, and covering up the remainder, she kept it. Very soon the rioters appeared on the scene, and, smelling the nefarious odor, they threatened to slay her immediately unless she should show them what she had prepared. She replied that she had saved an excellent portion for them, and with that she uncovered the remains of the child.

29. They were immediately seized with horror and amazement and stood transfixed at the sight. But she said, This is my own son, and the deed is mine. Eat for I too have eaten. Be not more merciful than a woman, nor more compassionate than a mother. But if you are too pious and shrink from my sacrifice, I have already eaten of it; let the rest also remain for me.

30. At these words the men went out trembling, in this one case being affrighted; yet with difficulty did they yield that food to the mother. Forthwith the whole city was filled with the awful crime, and as all pictured the terrible deed before their own eyes, they trembled as if they had done it themselves.

31. Those that were suffering from the famine now longed for death; and blessed were they that had died before hearing and seeing miseries like these.

32. Such was the reward which the Jews received for their wickedness and impiety, against the Christ of God.

Chapter 7. The Predictions of Christ.

1. It is fitting to add to these accounts the true prediction of our Saviour in which he foretold these very events.

2. His words are as follows: Woe unto them that are with child, and to them that give suck in those days! But pray that your flight be not in the winter, neither on the Sabbath day. For there shall be great tribulation, such as was not since the beginning of the world to this time, no, nor ever shall be.

3. The historian, reckoning the whole number of the slain, says that eleven hundred thousand persons perished by famine and sword, and that the rest of the rioters and robbers, being betrayed by each other after the taking of the city, were slain. But the tallest of the youths and those that were distinguished for beauty were preserved for the triumph. Of the rest of the multitude, those that were over seventeen years of age were sent as prisoners to labor in the works of Egypt, while still more were scattered through the provinces to meet their death in the theaters by the sword and by beasts. Those under seventeen years of age were carried away to be sold as slaves, and of these alone the number reached ninety thousand.

4. These things took place in this manner in the second year of the reign of Vespasian, in accordance with the prophecies of our Lord and Saviour Jesus Christ, who by divine power saw them beforehand as if they were already present, and wept and mourned according to the statement of the holy evangelists, who give the very words which he uttered, when, as if addressing Jerusalem herself, he said:

5. If you had known, even you, in this day, the things which belong unto your peace! But now they are hid from your eyes. For the days shall come upon you, that your enemies shall cast a rampart about you, and compass you round, and keep you in on every side, and shall lay you and your children even with the ground.

6. And then, as if speaking concerning the people, he says, For there shall be great distress in the land, and wrath upon this people. And they shall fall by the edge of the sword, and shall be led away captive into all nations. And Jerusalem shall be trodden down of the Gentiles, until the times of the Gentiles be fulfilled. And again: When you shall see Jerusalem compassed with armies, then know that the desolation thereof is near.

7. If any one compares the words of our Saviour with the other accounts of the historian concerning the whole war, how can one fail to wonder, and to admit that the foreknowledge and the prophecy of our Saviour were truly divine and marvellously strange.

8. Concerning those calamities, then, that befell the whole Jewish nation after the Saviour's passion and after the words which the multitude of the Jews uttered, when they begged the release of the robber and murderer, but besought that the Prince of Life should be taken from their midst, it is not necessary to add anything to the account of the historian.

9. But it may be proper to mention also those events which exhibited the graciousness of that all-good Providence which held back their destruction full forty years after their crime against Christ—during which time many of the apostles and disciples, and James himself the first bishop there, the one who is called the brother of the Lord, were still alive, and dwelling in Jerusalem itself, remained the surest bulwark of the place. Divine Providence thus still proved itself long- suffering toward them in order to see whether by repentance for what they had done they might obtain pardon and salvation; and in addition to such long-suffering, Providence also furnished wonderful signs of the things which were about to happen to them if they did not repent.

10. Since these matters have been thought worthy of mention by the historian already cited, we cannot do better than to recount them for the benefit of the readers of this work.

Chapter 8. The Signs which preceded the War.

1. Taking, then, the work of this author, read what he records in the sixth book of his History. His words are as follows: Thus were the miserable people won over at this time by the impostors and false prophets; but they did not heed nor give credit to the visions and signs that foretold the approaching desolation. On the contrary, as if struck by lightning, and as if possessing neither eyes nor understanding, they slighted the proclamations of God.

2. At one time a star, in form like a sword, stood over the city, and a comet, which lasted for a whole year; and again before the revolt and before the disturbances that led to the war, when the people were gathered for the feast of unleavened bread, on the eighth of the month Xanthicus, at the ninth hour of the night, so great a light shone about the altar and the temple that it seemed to be bright day; and this continued for half an hour. This seemed to the unskillful a good sign, but was interpreted by the sacred scribes as portending those events which very soon took place.

3. And at the same feast a cow, led by the high priest to be sacrificed, brought forth a lamb in the midst of the temple.

4. And the eastern gate of the inner temple, which was of bronze and very massive, and which at evening was closed with difficulty by twenty men, and rested upon iron-bound beams, and had bars sunk deep in the ground, was seen at the sixth hour of the night to open of itself.

5. And not many days after the feast, on the twenty-first of the month Artemisium, a certain marvelous vision was seen which passes belief. The prodigy might seem fabulous were it not related by those who saw it, and were not the calamities which followed deserving of such signs. For before the setting of the sun chariots and armed troops were seen throughout the whole region in mid-air, wheeling through the clouds and encircling the cities.

6. And at the feast which is called Pentecost, when the priests entered the temple at night, as was their custom, to perform the services, they said that at first they perceived a movement and a noise, and afterward a voice as of a great multitude, saying, 'Let us go hence.'

7. But what follows is still more terrible; for a certain Jesus, the son of Ananias, a common countryman, four years before the war, when the city was particularly prosperous and peaceful, came to the feast, at which it was customary for all to make tents at the temple to the honor of God, and suddenly began to cry out: 'A voice from the east, a voice from the

west, a voice from the four winds, a voice against Jerusalem and the temple, a voice against bridegrooms and brides, a voice against all the people.' Day and night he went through all the alleys crying thus.

8. But certain of the more distinguished citizens, vexed at the ominous cry, seized the man and beat him with many stripes. But without uttering a word in his own behalf, or saying anything in particular to those that were present, he continued to cry out in the same words as before.

9. And the rulers, thinking, as was true, that the man was moved by a higher power, brought him before the Roman governor. And then, though he was scourged to the bone, he neither made supplication nor shed tears, but, changing his voice to the most lamentable tone possible, he answered each stroke with the words, 'Woe, woe unto Jerusalem.'

10. The same historian records another fact still more wonderful than this. He says that a certain oracle was found in their sacred writings which declared that at that time a certain person should go forth from their country to rule the world. He himself understood that this was fulfilled in Vespasian.

11. But Vespasian did not rule the whole world, but only that part of it which was subject to the Romans. With better right could it be applied to Christ; to whom it was said by the Father, Ask of me, and I will give you the heathen for your inheritance, and the ends of the earth for your possession. At that very time, indeed, the voice of his holy apostles went throughout all the earth, and their words to the end of the world.

Chapter 9. Josephus and the Works which he has left.

1. After all this it is fitting that we should know something in regard to the origin and family of Josephus, who has contributed so much to the history in hand. He himself gives us information on this point in the following words: Josephus, the son of Mattathias, a priest of Jerusalem, who himself fought against the Romans in the beginning and was compelled to be present at what happened afterward.

2. He was the most noted of all the Jews of that day, not only among his own people, but also among the Romans, so that he was honored by the erection of a statue in Rome, and his works were deemed worthy of a place in the library.

3. He wrote the whole of the Antiquities of the Jews in twenty books, and a history of the war with the Romans which took place in his time,

in seven books. He himself testifies that the latter work was not only written in Greek, but that it was also translated by himself into his native tongue. He is worthy of credit here because of his truthfulness in other matters.

4. There are extant also two other books of his which are worth reading. They treat of the antiquity of the Jews, and in them he replies to Apion the Grammarian, who had at that time written a treatise against the Jews, and also to others who had attempted to vilify the hereditary institutions of the Jewish people.

5. In the first of these books he gives the number of the canonical books of the so-called Old Testament. Apparently drawing his information from ancient tradition, he shows what books were accepted without dispute among the Hebrews. His words are as follows.

Chapter 10. The Manner in which Josephus mentions the Divine Books.

1. We have not, therefore, a multitude of books disagreeing and conflicting with one another; but we have only twenty-two, which contain the record of all time and are justly held to be divine.

2. Of these, five are by Moses, and contain the laws and the tradition respecting the origin of man, and continue the history down to his own death. This period embraces nearly three thousand years.

3. From the death of Moses to the death of Artaxerxes, who succeeded Xerxes as king of Persia, the prophets that followed Moses wrote the history of their own times in thirteen books. The other four books contain hymns to God, and precepts for the regulation of the life of men.

4. From the time of Artaxerxes to our own day all the events have been recorded, but the accounts are not worthy of the same confidence that we repose in those which preceded them, because there has not been during this time an exact succession of prophets.

5. How much we are attached to our own writings is shown plainly by our treatment of them. For although so great a period has already passed by, no one has ventured either to add to or to take from them, but it is inbred in all Jews from their very birth to regard them as the teachings of God, and to abide by them, and, if necessary, cheerfully to die for them.

These remarks of the historian I have thought might advantageously be introduced in this connection.

6. Another work of no little merit has been produced by the same writer, On the Supremacy of Reason, which some have called Maccabaicum, because it contains an account of the struggles of those Hebrews who contended manfully for the true religion, as is related in the books called Maccabees.

7. And at the end of the twentieth book of his Antiquities Josephus himself intimates that he had purposed to write a work in four books concerning God and his existence, according to the traditional opinions of the Jews, and also concerning the laws, why it is that they permit some things while prohibiting others. And the same writer also mentions in his own works other books written by himself.

8. In addition to these things it is proper to quote also the words that are found at the close of his Antiquities, in confirmation of the testimony which we have drawn from his accounts. In that place he attacks Justus of Tiberias, who, like himself, had attempted to write a history of contemporary events, on the ground that he had not written truthfully. Having brought many other accusations against the man, he continues in these words:

9. I indeed was not afraid in respect to my writings as you were, but, on the contrary, I presented my books to the emperors themselves when the events were almost under men's eyes. For I was conscious that I had preserved the truth in my account, and hence was not disappointed in my expectation of obtaining their attestation.

10. And I presented my history also to many others, some of whom were present at the war, as, for instance, King Agrippa and some of his relatives.

11. For the Emperor Titus desired so much that the knowledge of the events should be communicated to men by my history alone, that he endorsed the books with his own hand and commanded that they should be published. And King Agrippa wrote sixty-two epistles testifying to the truthfulness of my account. Of these epistles Josephus subjoins two. But this will suffice in regard to him. Let us now proceed with our history.

Chapter 11. Symeon rules the Church of Jerusalem after James.

1. After the martyrdom of James and the conquest of Jerusalem which immediately followed, it is said that those of the apostles and disciples of the Lord that were still living came together from all directions with those that were related to the Lord according to the flesh (for the majority of them also were still alive) to take counsel as to who was worthy to succeed James.

2. They all with one consent pronounced Symeon, the son of Clopas, of whom the Gospel also makes mention; to be worthy of the episcopal throne of that parish. He was a cousin, as they say, of the Saviour. For Hegesippus records that Clopas was a brother of Joseph.

Chapter 12. Vespasian commands the Descendants of David to be sought.

He also relates that Vespasian after the conquest of Jerusalem gave orders that all that belonged to the lineage of David should be sought out, in order that none of the royal race might be left among the Jews; and in consequence of this a most terrible persecution again hung over the Jews.

Chapter 13. Anencletus, the Second Bishop of Rome.

After Vespasian had reigned ten years Titus, his son, succeeded him. In the second year of his reign, Linus, who had been bishop of the church of Rome for twelve years, delivered his office to Anencletus. But Titus was succeeded by his brother Domitian after he had reigned two years and the same number of months.

Chapter 14. Abilius, the Second Bishop of Alexandria.

In the fourth year of Domitian, Annianus, the first bishop of the parish of Alexandria, died after holding office twenty-two years, and was succeeded by Abilius, the second bishop.

Chapter 15. Clement, the Third Bishop of Rome.

In the twelfth year of the same reign Clement succeeded Anencletus after the latter had been bishop of the church of Rome for twelve years. The apostle in his Epistle to the Philippians informs us that this Clement was his fellow-worker. His words are as follows: With Clement and the rest of my fellow-laborers whose names are in the book of life.

Chapter 16. The Epistle of Clement.

There is extant an epistle of this Clement which is acknowledged to be genuine and is of considerable length and of remarkable merit. He wrote it in the name of the church of Rome to the church of Corinth, when a sedition had arisen in the latter church. We know that this epistle also has been publicly used in a great many churches both in former times and in our own. And of the fact that a sedition did take place in the church of Corinth at the time referred to Hegesippus is a trustworthy witness.

Chapter 17. The Persecution under Domitian.

Domitian, having shown great cruelty toward many, and having unjustly put to death no small number of well-born and notable men at Rome, and having without cause exiled and confiscated the property of a great many other illustrious men, finally became a successor of Nero in his hatred and enmity toward God. He was in fact the second that stirred up a persecution against us, although his father Vespasian had undertaken nothing prejudicial to us.

It was under the reign of Domitian that John saw the vision

Chapter 18. The Apostle John and the Apocalypse.

1. It is said that in this persecution the apostle and evangelist John, who was still alive, was condemned to dwell on the island of Patmos in consequence of his testimony to the divine word.

2. Irenæus, in the fifth book of his work Against Heresies, where he discusses the number of the name of Antichrist which is given in the so-called Apocalypse of John, speaks as follows concerning him:

3. If it were necessary for his name to be proclaimed openly at the present time, it would have been declared by him who saw the revelation. For it was seen not long ago, but almost in our own generation, at the end of the reign of Domitian.

4. To such a degree, indeed, did the teaching of our faith flourish at that time that even those writers who were far from our religion did not

hesitate to mention in their histories the persecution and the martyrdoms which took place during it.

5. And they, indeed, accurately indicated the time. For they recorded that in the fifteenth year of Domitian Flavia Domitilla, daughter of a sister of Flavius Clement, who at that time was one of the consuls of Rome, was exiled with many others to the island of Pontia in consequence of testimony borne to Christ.

Chapter 19. Domitian commands the Descendants of David to be slain.

But when this same Domitian had commanded that the descendants of David should be slain, an ancient tradition says that some of the heretics brought accusation against the descendants of Jude (said to have been a brother of the Saviour according to the flesh), on the ground that they were of the lineage of David and were related to Christ himself. Hegesippus relates these facts in the following words.

Chapter 20. The Relatives of our Saviour.

1. Of the family of the Lord there were still living the grandchildren of Jude, who is said to have been the Lord's brother according to the flesh.

2. Information was given that they belonged to the family of David, and they were brought to the Emperor Domitian by the Evocatus.

3. For Domitian feared the coming of Christ as Herod also had feared it. And he asked them if they were descendants of David, and they confessed that they were. Then he asked them how much property they had, or how much money they owned. And both of them answered that they had only nine thousand denarii, half of which belonged to each of them.

4. And this property did not consist of silver, but of a piece of land which contained only thirty-nine acres, and from which they raised their taxes and supported themselves by their own labor.

5. Then they showed their hands, exhibiting the hardness of their bodies and the callousness produced upon their hands by continuous toil as evidence of their own labor.

6. And when they were asked concerning Christ and his kingdom, of what sort it was and where and when it was to appear, they answered that it was not a temporal nor an earthly kingdom, but a heavenly and

angelic one, which would appear at the end of the world, when he should come in glory to judge the quick and the dead, and to give unto every one according to his works.

7. Upon hearing this, Domitian did not pass judgment against them, but, despising them as of no account, he let them go, and by a decree put a stop to the persecution of the Church.

8. But when they were released they ruled the churches because they were witnesses and were also relatives of the Lord. And peace being established, they lived until the time of Trajan. These things are related by Hegesippus.

9. Tertullian also has mentioned Domitian in the following words: Domitian also, who possessed a share of Nero's cruelty, attempted once to do the same thing that the latter did. But because he had, I suppose, some intelligence, he very soon ceased, and even recalled those whom he had banished.

10. But after Domitian had reigned fifteen years, and Nerva had succeeded to the empire, the Roman Senate, according to the writers that record the history of those days, voted that Domitian's honors should be cancelled, and that those who had been unjustly banished should return to their homes and have their property restored to them.

11. It was at this time that the apostle John returned from his banishment in the island and took up his abode at Ephesus, according to an ancient Christian tradition.

Chapter 21. Cerdon becomes the Third Ruler of the Church of Alexandria.

1. After Nerva had reigned a little more than a year he was succeeded by Trajan. It was during the first year of his reign that Abilius, who had ruled the church of Alexandria for thirteen years, was succeeded by Cerdon.

2. He was the third that presided over that church after Annianus, who was the first. At that time Clement still ruled the church of Rome, being also the third that held the episcopate there after Paul and Peter.

3. Linus was the first, and after him came Anencletus.

Chapter 22. Ignatius, the Second Bishop of Antioch.

At this time Ignatius was known as the second bishop of Antioch, Evodius having been the first. Symeon likewise was at that time the second ruler of the church of Jerusalem, the brother of our Saviour having been the first.

Chapter 23. Narrative Concerning John the Apostle.

1. At that time the apostle and evangelist John, the one whom Jesus loved, was still living in Asia, and governing the churches of that region, having returned after the death of Domitian from his exile on the island.

2. And that he was still alive at that time may be established by the testimony of two witnesses. They should be trustworthy who have maintained the orthodoxy of the Church; and such indeed were Irenæus and Clement of Alexandria.

3. The former in the second book of his work Against Heresies, writes as follows: And all the elders that associated with John the disciple of the Lord in Asia bear witness that John delivered it to them. For he remained among them until the time of Trajan.

4. And in the third book of the same work he attests the same thing in the following words: But the church in Ephesus also, which was founded by Paul, and where John remained until the time of Trajan, is a faithful witness of the apostolic tradition.

5. Clement likewise in his book entitled What Rich Man can be saved? indicates the time, and subjoins a narrative which is most attractive to those that enjoy hearing what is beautiful and profitable. Take and read the account which runs as follows:

6. Listen to a tale, which is not a mere tale, but a narrative concerning John the apostle, which has been handed down and treasured up in memory. For when, after the tyrant's death, he returned from the isle of Patmos to Ephesus, he went away upon their invitation to the neighboring territories of the Gentiles, to appoint bishops in some places, in other places to set in order whole churches, elsewhere to choose to the ministry some one of those that were pointed out by the Spirit.

7. When he had come to one of the cities not far away (the name of which is given by some), and had consoled the brethren in other matters, he finally turned to the bishop that had been appointed, and seeing a youth of powerful physique, of pleasing appearance, and of

ardent temperament, he said, 'This one I commit to you in all earnestness in the presence of the Church and with Christ as witness.' And when the bishop had accepted the charge and had promised all, he repeated the same injunction with an appeal to the same witnesses, and then departed for Ephesus.

8. But the presbyter taking home the youth committed to him, reared, kept, cherished, and finally baptized him. After this he relaxed his stricter care and watchfulness, with the idea that in putting upon him the seal of the Lord he had given him a perfect protection.

9. But some youths of his own age, idle and dissolute, and accustomed to evil practices, corrupted him when he was thus prematurely freed from restraint. At first they enticed him by costly entertainments; then, when they went forth at night for robbery, they took him with them, and finally they demanded that he should unite with them in some greater crime.

10. He gradually became accustomed to such practices, and on account of the positiveness of his character, leaving the right path, and taking the bit in his teeth like a hard-mouthed and powerful horse, he rushed the more violently down into the depths.

11. And finally despairing of salvation in God, he no longer meditated what was insignificant, but having committed some great crime, since he was now lost once for all, he expected to suffer a like fate with the rest. Taking them, therefore, and forming a band of robbers, he became a bold bandit-chief, the most violent, most bloody, most cruel of them all.

12. Time passed, and some necessity having arisen, they sent for John. But he, when he had set in order the other matters on account of which he had come, said, 'Come, O bishop, restore us the deposit which both I and Christ committed to you, the church, over which you preside, being witness.'

13. But the bishop was at first confounded, thinking that he was falsely charged in regard to money which he had not received, and he could neither believe the accusation respecting what he had not, nor could he disbelieve John. But when he said, 'I demand the young man and the soul of the brother,' the old man, groaning deeply and at the same time bursting into tears, said, 'He is dead.' 'How and what kind of death?' 'He is dead to God,' he said; 'for he turned wicked and abandoned, and at

last a robber. And now, instead of the church, he haunts the mountain with a band like himself.'

14. But the Apostle rent his clothes, and beating his head with great lamentation, he said, 'A fine guard I left for a brother's soul! But let a horse be brought me, and let some one show me the way.' He rode away from the church just as he was, and coming to the place, he was taken prisoner by the robbers' outpost.

Wow! John forgave the Robber and Pursued him

15. He, however, neither fled nor made entreaty, but cried out, 'For this did I come; lead me to your captain.'

16. The latter, meanwhile, was waiting, armed as he was. But when he recognized John approaching, he turned in shame to flee.

17. But John, forgetting his age, pursued him with all his might, crying out, 'Why, my son, do you flee from me, your own father, unarmed, aged? Pity me, my son; fear not; you have still hope of life. I will give account to Christ for you. If need be, I will willingly endure your death as the Lord suffered death for us. For you will I give up my life. Stand, believe; Christ has sent me.'

18. And he, when he heard, first stopped and looked down; then he threw away his arms, and then trembled and wept bitterly. And when the old man approached, he embraced him, making confession with lamentations as he was able, baptizing himself a second time with tears, and concealing only his right hand.

19. But John, pledging himself, and assuring him on oath that he would find forgiveness with the Saviour, besought him, fell upon his knees, kissed his right hand itself as if now purified by repentance, and led him back to the church. And making intercession for him with copious prayers, and struggling together with him in continual fastings, and subduing his mind by various utterances, he did not depart, as they say, until he had restored him to the church, furnishing a great example of true repentance and a great proof of regeneration, a trophy of a visible resurrection.

Chapter 24. The Order of the Gospels.

1. This extract from Clement I have inserted here for the sake of the history and for the benefit of my readers. Let us now point out the undisputed writings of this apostle.

2. And in the first place his Gospel, which is known to all the churches under heaven, must be acknowledged as genuine. That it has with good reason been put by the ancients in the fourth place, after the other three Gospels, may be made evident in the following way.

3. Those great and truly divine men, I mean the apostles of Christ, were purified in their life, and were adorned with every virtue of the soul, but were uncultivated in speech. They were confident indeed in their trust in the divine and wonder-working power which was granted unto them by the Saviour, but they did not know how, nor did they attempt to proclaim the doctrines of their teacher in studied and artistic language, but employing only the demonstration of the divine Spirit, which worked with them, and the wonder-working power of Christ, which was displayed through them, they published the knowledge of the kingdom of heaven throughout the whole world, paying little attention to the composition of written works.

4. And this they did because they were assisted in their ministry by one greater than man. Paul, for instance, who surpassed them all in vigor of expression and in richness of thought, committed to writing no more than the briefest epistles, although he had innumerable mysterious matters to communicate, for he had attained even unto the sights of the third heaven, had been carried to the very paradise of God, and had been deemed worthy to hear unspeakable utterances there.

5. And the rest of the followers of our Saviour, the twelve apostles, the seventy disciples, and countless others besides, were not ignorant of these things. Nevertheless, of all the disciples of the Lord, only Matthew and John have left us written memorials, and they, tradition says, were led to write only under the pressure of necessity.

6. For Matthew, who had at first preached to the Hebrews, when he was about to go to other peoples, committed his Gospel to writing in his native tongue, and thus compensated those whom he was obliged to leave for the loss of his presence.

7. And when Mark and Luke had already published their Gospels, they say that John, who had employed all his time in proclaiming the Gospel orally, finally proceeded to write for the following reason. The three Gospels already mentioned having come into the hands of all and into his own too, they say that he accepted them and bore witness to their truthfulness; but that there was lacking in them an account of the deeds done by Christ at the beginning of his ministry.

8. And this indeed is true. For it is evident that the three evangelists recorded only the deeds done by the Saviour for one year after the imprisonment of John the Baptist, and indicated this in the beginning of their account.

9. For Matthew, after the forty days' fast and the temptation which followed it, indicates the chronology of his work when he says: Now when he heard that John was delivered up he withdrew from Judea into Galilee. Matthew 4:12

10. Mark likewise says: Now after that John was delivered up Jesus came into Galilee. Mark 1:14 And Luke, before commencing his account of the deeds of Jesus, similarly marks the time, when he says that Herod, adding to all the evil deeds which he had done, shut up John in prison. Luke 3:20

11. They say, therefore, that the apostle John, being asked to do it for this reason, gave in his Gospel an account of the period which had been omitted by the earlier evangelists, and of the deeds done by the Saviour during that period; that is, of those which were done before the imprisonment of the Baptist. And this is indicated by him, they say, in the following words: This beginning of miracles did Jesus; and again when he refers to the Baptist, in the midst of the deeds of Jesus, as still baptizing in Ænon near Salim; John 3:23 where he states the matter clearly in the words: For John was not yet cast into prison.

12. John accordingly, in his Gospel, records the deeds of Christ which were performed before the Baptist was cast into prison, but the other three evangelists mention the events which happened after that time.

13. One who understands this can no longer think that the Gospels are at variance with one another, inasmuch as the Gospel according to John contains the first acts of Christ, while the others give an account of the latter part of his life. And the genealogy of our Saviour according to the flesh John quite naturally omitted, because it had been already given by Matthew and Luke, and began with the doctrine of his divinity, which had, as it were, been reserved for him, as their superior, by the divine Spirit.

14. These things may suffice, which we have said concerning the Gospel of John. The cause which led to the composition of the Gospel of Mark has been already stated by us.

15. But as for Luke, in the beginning of his Gospel, he states himself the reasons which led him to write it. He states that since many others had

more rashly undertaken to compose a narrative of the events of which he had acquired perfect knowledge, he himself, feeling the necessity of freeing us from their uncertain opinions, delivered in his own Gospel an accurate account of those events in regard to which he had learned the full truth, being aided by his intimacy and his stay with Paul and by his acquaintance with the rest of the apostles.

16. So much for our own account of these things. But in a more fitting place we shall attempt to show by quotations from the ancients, what others have said concerning them.

17. But of the writings of John, not only his Gospel, but also the former of his epistles, has been accepted without dispute both now and in ancient times. But the other two are disputed.

18. In regard to the Apocalypse, the opinions of most men are still divided. But at the proper time this question likewise shall be decided from the testimony of the ancients.

Chapter 25. The Divine Scriptures that are accepted and those that are not.

1. Since we are dealing with this subject it is proper to sum up the writings of the New Testament which have been already mentioned. First then must be put the holy quaternion of the Gospels; following them the Acts of the Apostles.

2. After this must be reckoned the epistles of Paul; next in order the extant former epistle of John, and likewise the epistle of Peter, must be maintained. After them is to be placed, if it really seem proper, the Apocalypse of John, concerning which we shall give the different opinions at the proper time. These then belong among the accepted writings.

3. Among the disputed writings, which are nevertheless recognized by many, are extant the so-called epistle of James and that of Jude, also the second epistle of Peter, and those that are called the whether they belong to the evangelist or to another person of the same name.

4. Among the rejected writings must be reckoned also the Acts of Paul, and the so-called Shepherd, and the Apocalypse of Peter, and in addition to these the extant epistle of Barnabas, and the so-called Teachings of the Apostles; and besides, as I said, the Apocalypse of John, if it seem

proper, which some, as I said, reject, but which others class with the accepted books.

5. And among these some have placed also the Gospel according to the Hebrews, with which those of the Hebrews that have accepted Christ are especially delighted. And all these may be reckoned among the disputed books.

6. But we have nevertheless felt compelled to give a catalogue of these also, distinguishing those works which according to ecclesiastical tradition are true and genuine and commonly accepted, from those others which, although not canonical but disputed, are yet at the same time known to most ecclesiastical writers— we have felt compelled to give this catalogue in order that we might be able to know both these works and those that are cited by the heretics under the name of the apostles, including, for instance, such books as the Gospels of Peter, of Thomas, of Matthias, or of any others besides them, and the Acts of Andrew and John and the other apostles, which no one belonging to the succession of ecclesiastical writers has deemed worthy of mention in his writings.

7. And further, the character of the style is at variance with apostolic usage, and both the thoughts and the purpose of the things that are related in them are so completely out of accord with true orthodoxy that they clearly show themselves to be the fictions of heretics. Wherefore they are not to be placed even among the rejected writings, but are all of them to be cast aside as absurd and impious.

Let us now proceed with our history.

Chapter 26. Menander the Sorcerer.

1. Menander, who succeeded Simon Magus, showed himself in his conduct another instrument of diabolical power, not inferior to the former. He also was a Samaritan and carried his sorceries to no less an extent than his teacher had done, and at the same time reveled in still more marvelous tales than he.

2. For he said that he was himself the Saviour, who had been sent down from invisible æons for the salvation of men; and he taught that no one could gain the mastery over the world-creating angels themselves unless he had first gone through the magical discipline imparted by him and had received baptism from him. Those who were deemed worthy of this would partake even in the present life of perpetual immortality, and

would never die, but would remain here forever, and without growing old become immortal. These facts can be easily learned from the works of Irenæus.

3. And Justin, in the passage in which he mentions Simon, gives an account of this man also, in the following words: And we know that a certain Menander, who was also a Samaritan, from the village of Capparattea, was a disciple of Simon, and that he also, being driven by the demons, came to Antioch and deceived many by his magical art. And he persuaded his followers that they should not die. And there are still some of them that assert this.

4. And it was indeed an artifice of the devil to endeavor, by means of such sorcerers, who assumed the name of Christians, to defame the great mystery of godliness by magic art, and through them to make ridiculous the doctrines of the Church concerning the immortality of the soul and the resurrection of the dead. But they that have chosen these men as their saviours have fallen away from the true hope.

Chapter 27. The Heresy of the Ebionites.

1. The evil demon, however, being unable to tear certain others from their allegiance to the Christ of God, yet found them susceptible in a different direction, and so brought them over to his own purposes. The ancients quite properly called these men Ebionites, because they held poor and mean opinions concerning Christ.

2. For they considered him a plain and common man, who was justified only because of his superior virtue, and who was the fruit of the intercourse of a man with Mary. In their opinion the observance of the ceremonial law was altogether necessary, on the ground that they could not be saved by faith in Christ alone and by a corresponding life.

3. There were others, however, besides them, that were of the same name, but avoided the strange and absurd beliefs of the former, and did not deny that the Lord was born of a virgin and of the Holy Spirit. But nevertheless, inasmuch as they also refused to acknowledge that he pre-existed, being God, Word, and Wisdom, they turned aside into the impiety of the former, especially when they, like them, endeavored to observe strictly the bodily worship of the law.

4. These men, moreover, thought that it was necessary to reject all the epistles of the apostle, whom they called an apostate from the law; and

they used only the so-called Gospel according to the Hebrews and made small account of the rest.

5. The Sabbath and the rest of the discipline of the Jews they observed just like them, but at the same time, like us, they celebrated the Lord's days as a memorial of the resurrection of the Saviour.

6. Wherefore, in consequence of such a course they received the name of Ebionites, which signified the poverty of their understanding. For this is the name by which a poor man is called among the Hebrews.

Chapter 28. Cerinthus the Heresiarch.

1. We have understood that at this time Cerinthus, the author of another heresy, made his appearance. Caius, whose words we quoted above, in the Disputation which is ascribed to him, writes as follows concerning this man:

2. But Cerinthus also, by means of revelations which he pretends were written by a great apostle, brings before us marvelous things which he falsely claims were shown him by angels; and he says that after the resurrection the kingdom of Christ will be set up on earth, and that the flesh dwelling in Jerusalem will again be subject to desires and pleasures. And being an enemy of the Scriptures of God, he asserts, with the purpose of deceiving men, that there is to be a period of a thousand years for marriage festivals.

3. And Dionysius, who was bishop of the parish of Alexandria in our day, in the second book of his work On the Promises, where he says some things concerning the Apocalypse of John which he draws from tradition, mentions this same man in the following words:

4. But (they say that) Cerinthus, who founded the sect which was called, after him, the Cerinthian, desiring reputable authority for his fiction, prefixed the name. For the doctrine which he taught was this: that the kingdom of Christ will be an earthly one.

5. And as he was himself devoted to the pleasures of the body and altogether sensual in his nature, he dreamed that that kingdom would consist in those things which he desired, namely, in the delights of the belly and of sexual passion, that is to say, in eating and drinking and marrying, and in festivals and sacrifices and the slaying of victims, under the guise of which he thought he could indulge his appetites with a better grace.

6. These are the words of Dionysius. But Irenæus, in the first book of his work Against Heresies, gives some more abominable false doctrines of the same man, and in the third book relates a story which deserves to be recorded. He says, on the authority of Polycarp, that the apostle John once entered a bath to bathe; but, learning that Cerinthus was within, he sprang from the place and rushed out of the door, for he could not bear to remain under the same roof with him. And he advised those that were with him to do the same, saying, Let us flee, lest the bath fall; for Cerinthus, the enemy of the truth, is within.

Chapter 29. Nicolaus and the Sect named after him.

1. At this time the so-called sect of the Nicolaitans made its appearance and lasted for a very short time. Mention is made of it in the Apocalypse of John. They boasted that the author of their sect was Nicolaus, one of the deacons who, with Stephen, were appointed by the apostles for the purpose of ministering to the poor. Clement of Alexandria, in the third book of his Stromata, relates the following things concerning him.

2. They say that he had a beautiful wife, and after the ascension of the Saviour, being accused by the apostles of jealousy, he led her into their midst and gave permission to any one that wished to marry her. For they say that this was in accord with that saying of his, that one ought to abuse the flesh. And those that have followed his heresy, imitating blindly and foolishly that which was done and said, commit fornication without shame.

3. But I understand that Nicolaus had to do with no other woman than her to whom he was married, and that, so far as his children are concerned, his daughters continued in a state of virginity until old age, and his son remained uncorrupt. If this is so, when he brought his wife, whom he jealously loved, into the midst of the apostles, he was evidently renouncing his passion; and when he used the expression, 'to abuse the flesh,' he was inculcating self-control in the face of those pleasures that are eagerly pursued. For I suppose that, in accordance with the command of the Saviour, he did not wish to serve two masters, pleasure and the Lord.

4. But they say that Matthias also taught in the same manner that we ought to fight against and abuse the flesh, and not give way to it for the sake of pleasure, but strengthen the soul by faith and knowledge. So

much concerning those who then attempted to pervert the truth, but in less time than it has taken to tell it became entirely extinct.

Chapter 30. The Apostles that were Married.

1. Clement, indeed, whose words we have just quoted, after the above-mentioned facts gives a statement, on account of those who rejected marriage, of the apostles that had wives. Or will they, says he, reject even the apostles? For Peter and Philip begot children; and Philip also gave his daughters in marriage. And Paul does not hesitate, in one of his epistles, to greet his wife, whom he did not take about with him, that he might not be inconvenienced in his ministry.

2. And since we have mentioned this subject it is not improper to subjoin another account which is given by the same author and which is worth reading. In the seventh book of his Stromata he writes as follows: They say, accordingly, that when the blessed Peter saw his own wife led out to die, he rejoiced because of her summons and her return home, and called to her very encouragingly and comfortingly, addressing her by name, and saying, 'Remember the Lord.' Such was the marriage of the blessed, and their perfect disposition toward those dearest to them. This account being in keeping with the subject in hand, I have related here in its proper place.

Chapter 31. The Death of John and Philip.

1. The time and the manner of the death of Paul and Peter as well as their burial places, have been already shown by us.

2. The time of John's death has also been given in a general way, but his burial place is indicated by an epistle of Polycrates (who was bishop of the parish of Ephesus), addressed to Victor, bishop of Rome. In this epistle he mentions him together with the apostle Philip and his daughters in the following words:

3. For in Asia also great lights have fallen asleep, which shall rise again on the last day, at the coming of the Lord, when he shall come with glory from heaven and shall seek out all the saints. Among these are Philip, one of the twelve apostles, who sleeps in Hierapolis, and his two aged virgin daughters, and another daughter who lived in the Holy Spirit and now rests at Ephesus; and moreover John, who was both a witness

and a teacher, who reclined upon the bosom of the Lord, and being a priest wore the sacerdotal plate. He also sleeps at Ephesus.

4. So much concerning their death. And in the Dialogue of Caius which we mentioned a little above, Proclus, against whom he directed his disputation, in agreement with what has been quoted, speaks thus concerning the death of Philip and his daughters: After him there were four prophetesses, the daughters of Philip, at Hierapolis in Asia. Their tomb is there and the tomb of their father. Such is his statement.

5. But Luke, in the Acts of the Apostles, mentions the daughters of Philip who were at that time at Cæsarea in Judea with their father, and were honored with the gift of prophecy. His words are as follows: We came unto Cæsarea; and entering into the house of Philip the evangelist, who was one of the seven, we abode with him. Now this man had four daughters, virgins, which did prophesy.

6. We have thus set forth in these pages what has come to our knowledge concerning the apostles themselves and the apostolic age, and concerning the sacred writings which they have left us, as well as concerning those which are disputed, but nevertheless have been publicly used by many in a great number of churches, and moreover, concerning those that are altogether rejected and are out of harmony with apostolic orthodoxy. Having done this, let us now proceed with our history.

Chapter 32. Symeon, Bishop of Jerusalem, suffers Martyrdom.

1. It is reported that after the age of Nero and Domitian, under the emperor whose times we are now recording, a persecution was stirred up against us in certain cities in consequence of a popular uprising. In this persecution we have understood that Symeon, the son of Clopas, who, as we have shown, was the second bishop of the church of Jerusalem, suffered martyrdom.

2. Hegesippus, whose words we have already quoted in various places, is a witness to this fact also. Speaking of certain heretics he adds that Symeon was accused by them at this time; and since it was clear that he was a Christian, he was tortured in various ways for many days, and astonished even the judge himself and his attendants in the highest degree, and finally he suffered a death similar to that of our Lord.

3. But there is nothing like hearing the historian himself, who writes as follows: Certain of these heretics brought accusation against Symeon,

the son of Clopas, on the ground that he was a descendant of David and a Christian; and thus he suffered martyrdom, at the age of one hundred and twenty years, while Trajan was emperor and Atticus governor.

4. And the same writer says that his accusers also, when search was made for the descendants of David, were arrested as belonging to that family. And it might be reasonably assumed that Symeon was one of those that saw and heard the Lord, judging from the length of his life, and from the fact that the Gospel makes mention of Mary, the wife of Clopas, who was the father of Symeon, as has been already shown.

5. The same historian says that there were also others, descended from one of the so-called brothers of the Saviour, whose name was Judas, who, after they had borne testimony before Domitian, as has been already recorded, in behalf of faith in Christ, lived until the same reign.

6. He writes as follows: They came, therefore, and took the lead of every church as witnesses and as relatives of the Lord. And profound peace being established in every church, they remained until the reign of the Emperor Trajan, and until the above-mentioned Symeon, son of Clopas, an uncle of the Lord, was informed against by the heretics, and was himself in like manner accused for the same cause before the governor Atticus. And after being tortured for many days he suffered martyrdom, and all, including even the proconsul, marveled that, at the age of one hundred and twenty years, he could endure so much. And orders were given that he should be crucified.

7. In addition to these things the same man, while recounting the events of that period, records that the Church up to that time had remained a pure and uncorrupted virgin, since, if there were any that attempted to corrupt the sound norm of the preaching of salvation, they lay until then concealed in obscure darkness.

8. But when the sacred college of apostles had suffered death in various forms, and the generation of those that had been deemed worthy to hear the inspired wisdom with their own ears had passed away, then the league of godless error took its rise as a result of the folly of heretical teachers, who, because none of the apostles was still living, attempted henceforth, with a bold face, to proclaim, in opposition to the preaching of the truth, the 'knowledge which is falsely so-called.'

Chapter 33. Trajan forbids the Christians to be sought after.

1. So great a persecution was at that time opened against us in many places that Plinius Secundus, one of the most noted of governors, being disturbed by the great number of martyrs, communicated with the emperor concerning the multitude of those that were put to death for their faith. At the same time, he informed him in his communication that he had not heard of their doing anything profane or contrary to the laws—except that they arose at dawn and sang hymns to Christ as a God; but that they renounced adultery and murder and like criminal offenses, and did all things in accordance with the laws.

2. In reply to this Trajan made the following decree: that the race of Christians should not be sought after, but when found should be punished. On account of this the persecution which had threatened to be a most terrible one was to a certain degree checked, but there were still left plenty of pretexts for those who wished to do us harm. Sometimes the people, sometimes the rulers in various places, would lay plots against us, so that, although no great persecutions took place, local persecutions were nevertheless going on in particular provinces, and many of the faithful endured martyrdom in various forms.

3. We have taken our account from the Latin Apology of Tertullian which we mentioned above. The translation runs as follows: And indeed we have found that search for us has been forbidden. For when Plinius Secundus, the governor of a province, had condemned certain Christians and deprived them of their dignity, he was confounded by the multitude, and was uncertain what further course to pursue. He therefore communicated with Trajan the emperor, informing him that, aside from their unwillingness to sacrifice, he had found no impiety in them.

4. And he reported this also, that the Christians arose early in the morning and sang hymns unto Christ as a God, and for the purpose of preserving their discipline forbade murder, adultery, avarice, robbery, and the like. In reply to this Trajan wrote that the race of Christians should not be sought after, but when found should be punished. Such were the events which took place at that time.

Chapter 34. Evarestus, the Fourth Bishop of the Church of Rome.

1. In the third year of the reign of the emperor mentioned above, Clement committed the episcopal government of the church of Rome

to Evarestus, and departed this life after he had superintended the teaching of the divine word nine years in all.

Chapter 35. Justus, the Third Bishop of Jerusalem.

1. But when Symeon also had died in the manner described, a certain Jew by the name of Justus succeeded to the episcopal throne in Jerusalem. He was one of the many thousands of the circumcision who at that time believed in Christ.

Chapter 36. Ignatius and His Epistles.

1. At that time Polycarp, a disciple of the apostles, was a man of eminence in Asia, having been entrusted with the episcopate of the church of Smyrna by those who had seen and heard the Lord.

2. And at the same time Papias, bishop of the parish of Hierapolis, became well known, as did also Ignatius, who was chosen bishop of Antioch, second in succession to Peter, and whose fame is still celebrated by a great many.

3. Report says that he was sent from Syria to Rome, and became food for wild beasts on account of his testimony to Christ.

4. And as he made the journey through Asia under the strictest military surveillance, he fortified the parishes in the various cities where he stopped by oral homilies and exhortations, and warned them above all to be especially on their guard against the heresies that were then beginning to prevail, and exhorted them to hold fast to the tradition of the apostles. Moreover, he thought it necessary to attest that tradition in writing, and to give it a fixed form for the sake of greater security.

5. So when he came to Smyrna, where Polycarp was, he wrote an epistle to the church of Ephesus, in which he mentions Onesimus, its pastor; and another to the church of Magnesia, situated upon the Mæander, in which he makes mention again of a bishop Damas; and finally one to the church of Tralles, whose bishop, he states, was at that time Polybius.

6. In addition to these he wrote also to the church of Rome, entreating them not to secure his release from martyrdom, and thus rob him of his earnest hope. In confirmation of what has been said it is proper to quote briefly from this epistle.

7. He writes as follows: From Syria even unto Rome I fight with wild beasts, by land and by sea, by night and by day, being bound amidst ten leopards that is, a company of soldiers who only become worse when they are well treated. In the midst of their wrongdoings, however, I am more fully learning discipleship, but I am not thereby justified.

8. May I have joy of the beasts that are prepared for me; and I pray that I may find them ready; I will even coax them to devour me quickly that they may not treat me as they have some whom they have refused to touch through fear. And if they are unwilling, I will compel them. Forgive me.

9. I know what is expedient for me. Now do I begin to be a disciple. May nothing of things visible and things invisible envy me; that I may attain unto Jesus Christ. Let fire and cross and attacks of wild beasts, let wrenching of bones, cutting of limbs, crushing of the whole body, tortures of the devil—let all these come upon me if only I may attain unto Jesus Christ.

10. These things he wrote from the above-mentioned city to the churches referred to. And when he had left Smyrna he wrote again from Troas to the Philadelphians and to the church of Smyrna; and particularly to Polycarp, who presided over the latter church. And since he knew him well as an apostolic man, he commended to him, like a true and good shepherd, the flock at Antioch, and besought him to care diligently for it.

11. And the same man, writing to the Smyrnæans, used the following words concerning Christ, taken I know not whence: But I know and believe that he was in the flesh after the resurrection. And when he came to Peter and his companions he said to them, Take, handle me, and see that I am not an incorporeal spirit. And immediately they touched him and believed.

12. Irenæus also knew of his martyrdom and mentions his epistles in the following words: As one of our people said, when he was condemned to the beasts on account of his testimony unto God, I am God's wheat, and by the teeth of wild beasts am I ground, that I may be found pure bread.

13. Polycarp also mentions these letters in the epistle to the Philippians which is ascribed to him. His words are as follows: I exhort all of you, therefore, to be obedient and to practice all patience such as you saw with your own eyes not only in the blessed Ignatius and Rufus and

Zosimus, but also in others from among yourselves as well as in Paul himself and the rest of the apostles; being persuaded that all these ran not in vain, but in faith and righteousness, and that they are gone to their rightful place beside the Lord, with whom also they suffered. For they loved not the present world, but him that died for our sakes and was raised by God for us.

14. And afterwards he adds: You have written to me, both you and Ignatius, that if any one go to Syria he may carry with him the letters from you. And this I will do if I have a suitable opportunity, either I myself or one whom I send to be an ambassador for you also.

15. The epistles of Ignatius which were sent to us by him and the others which we had with us we sent to you as you gave charge. They are appended to this epistle, and from them you will be able to derive great advantage. For they comprise faith and patience, and every kind of edification that pertains to our Lord. So much concerning Ignatius. But he was succeeded by Heros in the episcopate of the church of Antioch.

Chapter 37. The Evangelists that were still Eminent at that Time.

1. Among those that were celebrated at that time was Quadratus, who, report says, was renowned along with the daughters of Philip for his prophetical gifts. And there were many others besides these who were known in those days, and who occupied the first place among the successors of the apostles. And they also, being illustrious disciples of such great men, built up the foundations of the churches which had been laid by the apostles in every place, and preached the Gospel more and more widely and scattered the saving seeds of the kingdom of heaven far and near throughout the whole world.

2. For indeed most of the disciples of that time, animated by the divine word with a more ardent love for philosophy, had already fulfilled the command of the Saviour, and had distributed their goods to the needy. Then starting out upon long journeys they performed the office of evangelists, being filled with the desire to preach Christ to those who had not yet heard the word of faith, and to deliver to them the divine Gospels.

3. And when they had only laid the foundations of the faith in foreign places, they appointed others as pastors, and entrusted them with the nurture of those that had recently been brought in, while they themselves went on again to other countries and nations, with the grace

and the co-operation of God. For a great many wonderful works were done through them by the power of the divine Spirit, so that at the first hearing whole multitudes of men eagerly embraced the religion of the Creator of the universe.

4. But since it is impossible for us to enumerate the names of all that became shepherds or evangelists in the churches throughout the world in the age immediately succeeding the apostles, we have recorded, as was fitting, the names of those only who have transmitted the apostolic doctrine to us in writings still extant.

Chapter 38. The Epistle of Clement and the Writings falsely ascribed to him.

1. Thus Ignatius has done in the epistles which we have mentioned, and Clement in his epistle which is accepted by all, and which he wrote in the name of the church of Rome to the church of Corinth. In this epistle he gives many thoughts drawn from the Epistle to the Hebrews, and also quotes verbally some of its expressions, thus showing most plainly that it is not a recent production.

2. Wherefore it has seemed reasonable to reckon it with the other writings of the apostle. For as Paul had written to the Hebrews in his native tongue, some say that the evangelist Luke, others that this Clement himself, translated the epistle.

3. The latter seems more probable, because the epistle of Clement and that to the Hebrews have a similar character in regard to style, and still further because the thoughts contained in the two works are not very different.

4. But it must be observed also that there is said to be a second epistle of Clement. But we do not know that this is recognized like the former, for we do not find that the ancients have made any use of it.

5. And certain men have lately brought forward other wordy and lengthy writings under his name, containing dialogues of Peter and Apion. But no mention has been made of these by the ancients; for they do not even preserve the pure stamp of apostolic orthodoxy. The acknowledged writing of Clement is well known. We have spoken also of the works of Ignatius and Polycarp.

Chapter 39. The Writings of Papias.

1. There are extant five books of Papias, which bear the title Expositions of Oracles of the Lord. Irenæus makes mention of these as the only works written by him, in the following words: These things are attested by Papias, an ancient man who was a hearer of John and a companion of Polycarp, in his fourth book. For five books have been written by him. These are the words of Irenæus.

2. But Papias himself in the preface to his discourses by no means declares that he was himself a hearer and eye-witness of the holy apostles, but he shows by the words which he uses that he received the doctrines of the faith from those who were their friends.

3. He says: But I shall not hesitate also to put down for you along with my interpretations whatsoever things I have at any time learned carefully from the elders and carefully remembered, guaranteeing their truth. For I did not, like the multitude, take pleasure in those that speak much, but in those that teach the truth; not in those that relate strange commandments, but in those that deliver the commandments given by the Lord to faith, and springing from the truth itself.

4. If, then, any one came, who had been a follower of the elders, I questioned him in regard to the words of the elders— what Andrew or what Peter said, or what was said by Philip, or by Thomas, or by James, or by John, or by Matthew, or by any other of the disciples of the Lord, and what things Aristion and the presbyter John, the disciples of the Lord, say. For I did not think that what was to be gotten from the books would profit me as much as what came from the living and abiding voice.

5. It is worth while observing here that the name John is twice enumerated by him. The first one he mentions in connection with Peter and James and Matthew and the rest of the apostles, clearly meaning the evangelist; but the other John he mentions after an interval, and places him among others outside of the number of the apostles, putting Aristion before him, and he distinctly calls him a presbyter.

6. This shows that the statement of those is true, who say that there were two persons in Asia that bore the same name, and that there were two tombs in Ephesus, each of which, even to the present day, is called John's. It is important to notice this. For it is probable that it was the second, if one is not willing to admit that it was the first that saw the Revelation, which is ascribed by name to John.

7. And Papias, of whom we are now speaking, confesses that he received the words of the apostles from those that followed them, but says that he was himself a hearer of Aristion and the presbyter John. At least he mentions them frequently by name, and gives their traditions in his writings. These things, we hope, have not been uselessly adduced by us.

8. But it is fitting to subjoin to the words of Papias which have been quoted, other passages from his works in which he relates some other wonderful events which he claims to have received from tradition.

9. That Philip the apostle dwelt at Hierapolis with his daughters has been already stated. But it must be noted here that Papias, their contemporary, says that he heard a wonderful tale from the daughters of Philip. For he relates that in his time one rose from the dead. And he tells another wonderful story of Justus, surnamed Barsabbas: that he drank a deadly poison, and yet, by the grace of the Lord, suffered no harm.

10. The Book of Acts records that the holy apostles after the ascension of the Saviour, put forward this Justus, together with Matthias, and prayed that one might be chosen in place of the traitor Judas, to fill up their number. The account is as follows: And they put forward two, Joseph, called Barsabbas, who was surnamed Justus, and Matthias; and they prayed and said. Acts 1:23

11. The same writer gives also other accounts which he says came to him through unwritten tradition, certain strange parables and teachings of the Saviour, and some other more mythical things.

12. To these belong his statement that there will be a period of some thousand years after the resurrection of the dead, and that the kingdom of Christ will be set up in material form on this very earth. I suppose he got these ideas through a misunderstanding of the apostolic accounts, not perceiving that the things said by them were spoken mystically in figures.

13. For he appears to have been of very limited understanding, as one can see from his discourses. But it was due to him that so many of the Church Fathers after him adopted a like opinion, urging in their own support the antiquity of the man; as for instance Irenæus and anyone else that may have proclaimed similar views.

14. Papias gives also in his own work other accounts of the words of the Lord on the authority of Aristion who was mentioned above, and traditions as handed down by the presbyter John; to which we refer

those who are fond of learning. But now we must add to the words of his which we have already quoted the tradition which he gives in regard to Mark, the author of the Gospel.

15. This also the presbyter said: Mark, having become the interpreter of Peter, wrote down accurately, though not in order, whatsoever he remembered of the things said or done by Christ. For he neither heard the Lord nor followed him, but afterward, as I said, he followed Peter, who adapted his teaching to the needs of his hearers, but with no intention of giving a connected account of the Lord's discourses, so that Mark committed no error while he thus wrote some things as he remembered them. For he was careful of one thing, not to omit any of the things which he had heard, and not to state any of them falsely. These things are related by Papias concerning Mark.

16. But concerning Matthew he writes as follows: So then Matthew wrote the oracles in the Hebrew language, and every one interpreted them as he was able. And the same writer uses testimonies from the first Epistle of John and from that of Peter likewise. And he relates another story of a woman, who was accused of many sins before the Lord, which is contained in the Gospel according to the Hebrews. These things we have thought it necessary to observe in addition to what has been already stated.

BOOK IV

Chapter 1. The Bishops of Rome and of Alexandria during the Reign of Trajan.

1. About the twelfth year of the reign of Trajan the above-mentioned bishop of the parish of Alexandria died, and Primus, the fourth in succession from the apostles, was chosen to the office.

2. At that time also Alexander, the fifth in the line of succession from Peter and Paul, received the episcopate at Rome, after Evarestus had held the office eight years.

Chapter 2. The Calamities of the Jews during Trajan's Reign.

1. The teaching and the Church of our Saviour flourished greatly and made progress from day to day; but the calamities of the Jews increased, and they underwent a constant succession of evils. In the eighteenth year of Trajan's reign there was another disturbance of the Jews, through which a great multitude of them perished.

2. For in Alexandria and in the rest of Egypt, and also in Cyrene, as if incited by some terrible and factious spirit, they rushed into seditious measures against their fellow-inhabitants, the Greeks. The insurrection increased greatly, and in the following year, while Lupus was governor of all Egypt, it developed into a war of no mean magnitude.

3. In the first attack it happened that they were victorious over the Greeks, who fled to Alexandria and imprisoned and slew the Jews that were in the city. But the Jews of Cyrene, although deprived of their aid, continued to plunder the land of Egypt and to devastate its districts, under the leadership of Lucuas. Against them the emperor sent Marcius Turbo with a foot and naval force and also with a force of cavalry.

4. He carried on the war against them for a long time and fought many battles, and slew many thousands of Jews, not only of those of Cyrene, but also of those who dwelt in Egypt and had come to the assistance of their king Lucuas.

5. But the emperor, fearing that the Jews in Mesopotamia would also make an attack upon the inhabitants of that country, commanded Lucius Quintus to clear the province of them. And he having marched against them slew a great multitude of those that dwelt there; and in consequence of his success he was made governor of Judea by the

emperor. These events are recorded also in these very words by the Greek historians that have written accounts of those times.

Chapter 3. The Apologists that wrote in Defense of the Faith during the Reign of Adrian.

1. After Trajan had reigned for nineteen and a half years Ælius Adrian became his successor in the empire. To him Quadratus addressed a discourse containing an apology for our religion, because certain wicked men had attempted to trouble the Christians. The work is still in the hands of a great many of the brethren, as also in our own, and furnishes clear proofs of the man's understanding and of his apostolic orthodoxy.

2. He himself reveals the early date at which he lived in the following words: But the works of our Saviour were always present, for they were genuine:— those that were healed, and those that were raised from the dead, who were seen not only when they were healed and when they were raised, but were also always present; and not merely while the Saviour was on earth, but also after his death, they were alive for quite a while, so that some of them lived even to our day. Such then was Quadratus.

3. Aristides also, a believer earnestly devoted to our religion, left, like Quadratus, an apology for the faith, addressed to Adrian. His work, too, has been preserved even to the present day by a great many persons.

Chapter 4. The Bishops of Rome and of Alexandria under the Same Emperor.

In the third year of the same reign, Alexander, bishop of Rome, died after holding office ten years. His successor was Xystus. About the same time Primus, bishop of Alexandria, died in the twelfth year of his episcopate, and was succeeded by Justus.

Chapter 5. The Bishops of Jerusalem from the Age of our Saviour to the Period under Consideration

1. The chronology of the bishops of Jerusalem I have nowhere found preserved in writing; for tradition says that they were all short lived.

2. But I have learned this much from writings, that until the siege of the Jews, which took place under Adrian, there were fifteen bishops in succession there, all of whom are said to have been of Hebrew descent, and to have received the knowledge of Christ in purity, so that they were approved by those who were able to judge of such matters, and were deemed worthy of the episcopate. For their whole church consisted then of believing Hebrews who continued from the days of the apostles until the siege which took place at this time; in which siege the Jews, having again rebelled against the Romans, were conquered after severe battles.

3. But since the bishops of the circumcision ceased at this time, it is proper to give here a list of their names from the beginning. The first, then, was James, the so-called brother of the Lord; the second, Symeon; the third, Justus; the fourth, Zacchæus; the fifth, Tobias; the sixth, Benjamin; the seventh, John; the eighth, Matthias; the ninth, Philip; the

tenth, Seneca; the eleventh, Justus; the twelfth, Levi; the thirteenth, Ephres; the fourteenth, Joseph; and finally, the fifteenth, Judas.

4. These are the bishops of Jerusalem that lived between the age of the apostles and the time referred to, all of them belonging to the circumcision.

5. In the twelfth year of the reign of Adrian, Xystus, having completed the tenth year of his episcopate, was succeeded by Telesphorus, the seventh in succession from the apostles. In the meantime, after the lapse of a year and some months, Eumenes, the sixth in order, succeeded to the leadership of the Alexandrian church, his predecessor having held office eleven years.

Chapter 6. The Last Siege of the Jews under Adrian.

1. As the rebellion of the Jews at this time grew much more serious, Rufus, governor of Judea, after an auxiliary force had been sent him by the emperor, using their madness as a pretext, proceeded against them without mercy, and destroyed indiscriminately thousands of men and women and children, and in accordance with the laws of war reduced their country to a state of complete subjection.

2. The leader of the Jews at this time was a man by the name of Barcocheba (which signifies a star), who possessed the character of a robber and a murderer, but nevertheless, relying upon his name, boasted to them, as if they were slaves, that he possessed wonderful powers; and he pretended that he was a star that had come down to them out of heaven to bring them light in the midst of their misfortunes.

3. The war raged most fiercely in the eighteenth year of Adrian, at the city of Bithara, which was a very secure fortress, situated not far from Jerusalem. When the siege had lasted a long time, and the rebels had been driven to the last extremity by hunger and thirst, and the instigator of the rebellion had suffered his just punishment, the whole nation was prohibited from this time on by a decree, and by the commands of Adrian, from ever going up to the country about Jerusalem. For the emperor gave orders that they should not even see from a distance the land of their fathers. Such is the account of Aristo of Pella.

4. And thus, when the city had been emptied of the Jewish nation and had suffered the total destruction of its ancient inhabitants, it was colonized by a different race, and the Roman city which subsequently arose changed its name and was called Ælia, in honor of the emperor

Ælius Adrian. And as the church there was now composed of Gentiles, the first one to assume the government of it after the bishops of the circumcision was Marcus.

Chapter 7. The Persons that became at that Time Leaders of Knowledge falsely so-called.

1. As the churches throughout the world were now shining like the most brilliant stars, and faith in our Saviour and Lord Jesus Christ was flourishing among the whole human race, the demon who hates everything that is good, and is always hostile to the truth, and most bitterly opposed to the salvation of man, turned all his arts against the Church. In the beginning he armed himself against it with external persecutions.

2. But now, being shut off from the use of such means, he devised all sorts of plans, and employed other methods in his conflict with the Church, using base and deceitful men as instruments for the ruin of souls and as ministers of destruction. Instigated by him, impostors and deceivers, assuming the name of our religion, brought to the depth of ruin such of the believers as they could win over, and at the same time, by means of the deeds which they practiced, turned away from the path which leads to the word of salvation those who were ignorant of the faith.

3. Accordingly there proceeded from that Menander, whom we have already mentioned as the successor of Simon, a certain serpent-like power, double-tongued and two-headed, which produced the leaders of two different heresies, Saturninus, an Antiochian by birth, and Basilides, an Alexandrian. The former of these established schools of godless heresy in Syria, the latter in Alexandria.

4. Irenæus states that the false teaching of Saturninus agreed in most respects with that of Menander, but that Basilides, under the pretext of unspeakable mysteries, invented monstrous fables, and carried the fictions of his impious heresy quite beyond bounds.

5. But as there were at that time a great many members of the Church who were fighting for the truth and defending apostolic and ecclesiastical doctrine with uncommon eloquence, so there were some also that furnished posterity through their writings with means of defense against the heresies to which we have referred.

6. Of these there has come down to us a most powerful refutation of Basilides by Agrippa Castor, one of the most renowned writers of that day, which shows the terrible imposture of the man.

7. While exposing his mysteries he says that Basilides wrote twenty- four books upon the Gospel, and that he invented prophets for himself named Barcabbas and Barcoph, and others that had no existence, and that he gave them barbarous names in order to amaze those who marvel at such things; that he taught also that the eating of meat offered to idols and the unguarded renunciation of the faith in times of persecution were matters of indifference; and that he enjoined upon his followers, like Pythagoras, a silence of five years.

8. Other similar things the above-mentioned writer has recorded concerning Basilides, and has ably exposed the error of his heresy.

9. Irenæus also writes that Carpocrates was a contemporary of these men, and that he was the father of another heresy, called the heresy of the Gnostics, who did not wish to transmit any longer the magic arts of Simon, as that one had done, in secret, but openly. For they boasted — as of something great — of love potions that were carefully prepared by them, and of certain demons that sent them dreams and lent them their protection, and of other similar agencies; and in accordance with these things they taught that it was necessary for those who wished to enter fully into their mysteries, or rather into their abominations, to practice all the worst kinds of wickedness, on the ground that they could escape the cosmic powers, as they called them, in no other way than by discharging their obligations to them all by infamous conduct.

10. Thus it came to pass that the malignant demon, making use of these ministers, on the one hand enslaved those that were so pitiably led astray by them to their own destruction, while on the other hand he furnished to the unbelieving heathen abundant opportunities for slandering the divine word, inasmuch as the reputation of these men brought infamy upon the whole race of Christians.

11. In this way, therefore, it came to pass that there was spread abroad in regard to us among the unbelievers of that age, the infamous and most absurd suspicion that we practiced unlawful commerce with mothers and sisters, and enjoyed impious feasts.

12. He did not, however, long succeed in these artifices, as the truth established itself and in time shone with great brilliancy.

13. For the machinations of its enemies were refuted by its power and speedily vanished. One new heresy arose after another, and the former ones always passed away, and now at one time, now at another, now in one way, now in other ways, were lost in ideas of various kinds and various forms. But the splendor of the catholic and only true Church, which is always the same, grew in magnitude and power, and reflected its piety and simplicity and freedom, and the modesty and purity of its inspired life and philosophy to every nation both of Greeks and of Barbarians.

14. At the same time the slanderous accusations which had been brought against the whole Church also vanished, and there remained our teaching alone, which has prevailed over all, and which is acknowledged to be superior to all in dignity and temperance, and in divine and philosophical doctrines. So that none of them now ventures to affix a base calumny upon our faith, or any such slander as our ancient enemies formerly delighted to utter.

15. Nevertheless, in those times the truth again called forth many champions who fought in its defense against the godless heresies, refuting them not only with oral, but also with written arguments.

Chapter 8. Ecclesiastical Writers.

1. Among these Hegesippus was well known. We have already quoted his words a number of times, relating events which happened in the time of the apostles according to his account.

2. He records in five books the true tradition of apostolic doctrine in a most simple style, and he indicates the time in which he flourished when he writes as follows concerning those that first set up idols: To whom they erected cenotaphs and temples, as is done to the present day. Among whom is also Antinoüs, a slave of the Emperor Adrian, in whose honor are celebrated also the Antinoian games, which were instituted in our day. For he [i.e. Adrian] also founded a city named after Antinoüs, and appointed prophets.

3. At the same time also Justin, a genuine lover of the true philosophy, was still continuing to busy himself with Greek literature. He indicates this time in the Apology which he addressed to Antonine, where he writes as follows: We do not think it out of place to mention here Antinoüs also, who lived in our day, and whom all were driven by fear

to worship as a god, although they knew who he was and whence he came.

4. The same writer, speaking of the Jewish war which took place at that time, adds the following: For in the late Jewish war Barcocheba, the leader of the Jewish rebellion, commanded that Christians alone should be visited with terrible punishments unless they would deny and blaspheme Jesus Christ.

5. And in the same work he shows that his conversion from Greek philosophy to Christianity was not without reason, but that it was the result of deliberation on his part. His words are as follows: For I myself, while I was delighted with the doctrines of Plato, and heard the Christians slandered, and saw that they were afraid neither of death nor of anything else ordinarily looked upon as terrible, concluded that it was impossible that they could be living in wickedness and pleasure. For what pleasure-loving or intemperate man, or what man that counts it good to feast on human flesh, could welcome death that he might be deprived of his enjoyments, and would not rather strive to continue permanently his present life, and to escape the notice of the rulers, instead of giving himself up to be put to death?

6. The same writer, moreover, relates that Adrian having received from Serennius Granianus, a most distinguished governor, a letter in behalf of the Christians, in which he stated that it was not just to slay the Christians without a regular accusation and trial, merely for the sake of gratifying the outcries of the populace, sent a rescript to Minucius Fundanus, proconsul of Asia, commanding him to condemn no one without an indictment and a well-grounded accusation.

7. And he gives a copy of the epistle, preserving the original Latin in which it was written, and prefacing it with the following words: Although from the epistle of the greatest and most illustrious Emperor Adrian, your father, we have good ground to demand that you order judgment to be given as we have desired, yet we have asked this not because it was ordered by Adrian, but rather because we know that what we ask is just. And we have subjoined the copy of Adrian's epistle that you may know that we are speaking the truth in this matter also. And this is the copy.

8. After these words the author referred to gives the rescript in Latin, which we have translated into Greek as accurately as we could. It reads as follows:

Chapter 9. The Epistle of Adrian, decreeing that we should not be punished without a Trial.

1. To Minucius Fundanus. I have received an epistle, written to me by Serennius Granianus, a most illustrious man, whom you have succeeded. It does not seem right to me that the matter should be passed by without examination, lest the men be harassed and opportunity be given to the informers for practicing villainy.

2. If, therefore, the inhabitants of the province can clearly sustain this petition against the Christians so as to give answer in a court of law, let them pursue this course alone, but let them not have resort to men's petitions and outcries. For it is far more proper, if any one wishes to make an accusation, that you should examine into it.

3. If any one therefore accuses them and shows that they are doing anything contrary to the laws, do you pass judgment according to the heinousness of the crime. But, by Hercules! If any one bring an accusation through mere calumny, decide in regard to his criminality, and see to it that you inflict punishment.

Such are the contents of Adrian's rescript.

Chapter 10. The Bishops of Rome and of Alexandria during the Reign of Antoninus.

Adrian having died after a reign of twenty-one years, was succeeded in the government of the Romans by Antoninus, called the Pious. In the first year of his reign Telesphorus died in the eleventh year of his episcopate, and Hyginus became bishop of Rome. Irenæus records that Telesphorus' death was made glorious by martyrdom, and in the same connection he states that in the time of the above-mentioned Roman bishop Hyginus, Valentinus, the founder of a sect of his own, and Cerdon, the author of Marcion's error, were both well known at Rome. He writes as follows:

Chapter 11. The Heresiarchs of that Age.

1. For Valentinus came to Rome under Hyginus, flourished under Pius, and remained until Anicetus. Cerdon also, Marcion's predecessor, entered the Church in the time of Hyginus, the ninth bishop, and made confession, and continued in this way, now teaching in secret, now making confession again, and now denounced for corrupt doctrine and withdrawing from the assembly of the brethren.

2. These words are found in the third book of the work Against Heresies. And again in the first book he speaks as follows concerning Cerdon: A certain Cerdon, who had taken his system from the followers of Simon, and had come to Rome under Hyginus, the ninth in the episcopal succession from the apostles, taught that the God proclaimed by the law and prophets was not the father of our Lord Jesus Christ. For the former was known, but the latter unknown; and the former was just, but the latter good. Marcion of Pontus succeeded Cerdon and developed his doctrine, uttering shameless blasphemies.

3. The same Irenæus unfolds with the greatest vigor the unfathomable abyss of Valentinus' errors in regard to matter, and reveals his wickedness, secret and hidden like a serpent lurking in its nest.

4. And in addition to these men he says that there was also another that lived in that age, Marcus by name, who was remarkably skilled in magic arts. And he describes also their unholy initiations and their abominable mysteries in the following words:

5. For some of them prepare a nuptial couch and perform a mystic rite with certain forms of expression addressed to those who are being initiated, and they say that it is a spiritual marriage which is celebrated by them, after the likeness of the marriages above. But others lead them to water, and while they baptize them they repeat the following words: Into the name of the unknown father of the universe, into truth, the mother of all things, into the one that descended upon Jesus. Others repeat Hebrew names in order the better to confound those who are being initiated.

6. But Hyginus having died at the close of the fourth year of his episcopate, Pius succeeded him in the government of the church of Rome. In Alexandria Marcus was appointed pastor, after Eumenes had filled the office thirteen years in all. And Marcus having died after holding office ten years was succeeded by Celadion in the government of the church of Alexandria.

7. And in Rome Pius died in the fifteenth year of his episcopate, and Anicetus assumed the leadership of the Christians there. Hegesippus records that he himself was in Rome at this time, and that he remained there until the episcopate of Eleutherus.

8. But Justin was especially prominent in those days. In the guise of a philosopher he preached the divine word, and contended for the faith in his writings. He wrote also a work against Marcion, in which he states that the latter was alive at the time he wrote.

9. He speaks as follows: And there is a certain Marcion of Pontus, who is even now still teaching his followers to think that there is some other God greater than the Creator. And by the aid of the demons he has persuaded many of every race of men to utter blasphemy, and to deny that the maker of this universe is the father of Christ, and to confess that some other, greater than he, was the creator. And all who followed them are, as we have said, called Christians, just as the name of philosophy is given to philosophers, although they may have no doctrines in common.

10. To this he adds: And we have also written a work against all the heresies that have existed, which we will give you if you wish to read it.

11. But this same Justin contended most successfully against the Greeks, and addressed discourses containing an apology for our faith to the Emperor Antoninus, called Pius, and to the Roman senate. For he lived

at Rome. But who and whence he was he shows in his Apology in the following words.

Chapter 12. The Apology of Justin addressed to Antoninus.

To the Emperor Titus Ælius Adrian Antoninus Pius Cæsar Augustus, and to Verissimus his son, the philosopher, and to Lucius the philosopher, own son of Cæsar and adopted son of Pius, a lover of learning, and to the sacred senate and to the whole Roman people, I, Justin, son of Priscus and grandson of Bacchius, of Flavia Neapolis in Palestine, Syria, present this address and petition in behalf of those men of every nation who are unjustly hated and persecuted, I myself being one of them. And the same emperor having learned also from other brethren in Asia of the injuries of all kinds which they were suffering from the inhabitants of the province, thought it proper to address the following ordinance to the Common Assembly of Asia.

Chapter 13. The Epistle of Antoninus to the Common Assembly of Asia in Regard to our Doctrine.

1. The Emperor Cæsar Marcus Aurelius Antoninus Augustus, Armenicus, Pontifex Maximus, for the fifteenth time Tribune, for the third time Consul, to the Common Assembly of Asia, Greeting.

2. I know that the gods also take care that such persons do not escape detection. For they would much rather punish those who will not worship them than you would.

3. But you throw them into confusion, and while you accuse them of atheism you only confirm them in the opinion which they hold. It would indeed be more desirable for them, when accused, to appear to die for their God, than to live. Wherefore also they come off victorious when they give up their lives rather than yield obedience to your commands.

4. And in regard to the earthquakes which have been and are still taking place, it is not improper to admonish you who lose heart whenever they occur, and nevertheless are accustomed to compare your conduct with theirs.

5. They indeed become the more confident in God, while you, during the whole time, neglect, in apparent ignorance, the other gods and the worship of the Immortal, and oppress and persecute even unto death the Christians who worship him.

6. But in regard to these persons, many of the governors of the provinces wrote also to our most divine father, to whom he wrote in reply that they should not trouble these people unless it should appear that they were attempting something affecting the Roman government. And to me also many have sent communications concerning these men, but I have replied to them in the same way that my father did.

7. But if any one still persists in bringing accusations against any of these people as such, the person who is accused shall be acquitted of the charge, even if it appear that he is one of them, but the accuser shall be punished. Published in Ephesus in the Common Assembly of Asia.

8. To these things Melito, bishop of the church of Sardis, and a man well known at that time, is a witness, as is clear from his words in the Apology which he addressed to the Emperor Verus in behalf of our doctrine.

Chapter 14. The Circumstances related of Polycarp, a Friend of the Apostles.

1. At this time, while Anicetus was at the head of the church of Rome, Irenæus relates that Polycarp, who was still alive, was at Rome, and that he had a conference with Anicetus on a question concerning the day of the paschal feast.

2. And the same writer gives another account of Polycarp which I feel constrained to add to that which has been already related in regard to him. The account is taken from the third book of Irenæus' work Against Heresies, and is as follows:

3. But Polycarp also was not only instructed by the apostles, and acquainted with many that had seen Christ, but was also appointed by apostles in Asia bishop of the church of Smyrna.

4. We too saw him in our early youth; for he lived a long time, and died, when a very old man, a glorious and most illustrious martyr's death, having always taught the things which he had learned from the apostles, which the Church also hands down, and which alone are true.

5. To these things all the Asiatic churches testify, as do also those who, down to the present time, have succeeded Polycarp, who was a much more trustworthy and certain witness of the truth than Valentinus and Marcion and the rest of the heretics. He also was in Rome in the time of Anicetus and caused many to turn away from the above-mentioned heretics to the Church of God, proclaiming that he had received from

the apostles this one and only system of truth which has been transmitted by the Church.

6. And there are those that heard from him that John, the disciple of the Lord, going to bathe in Ephesus and seeing Cerinthus within, ran out of the bath-house without bathing, crying, 'Let us flee, lest even the bath fall, because Cerinthus, the enemy of the truth, is within.'

7. And Polycarp himself, when Marcion once met him and said, 'Do you know us? replied, 'I know the first born of Satan.' Such caution did the apostles and their disciples exercise that they might not even converse with any of those who perverted the truth; as Paul also said, 'A man that is a heretic, after the first and second admonition, reject; knowing he that is such is subverted, and sins, being condemned of himself.' Titus 3:10-11

8. There is also a very powerful epistle of Polycarp written to the Philippians, from which those that wish to do so, and that are concerned for their own salvation, may learn the character of his faith and the preaching of the truth. Such is the account of Irenæus.

9. But Polycarp, in his above-mentioned epistle to the Philippians, which is still extant, has made use of certain testimonies drawn from the First Epistle of Peter.

10. And when Antoninus, called Pius, had completed the twenty- second year of his reign, Marcus Aurelius Verus, his son, who was also called Antoninus, succeeded him, together with his brother Lucius.

Chapter 15. Under Verus, Polycarp with Others suffered Martyrdom at Smyrna.

1. At this time, when the greatest persecutions were exciting Asia, Polycarp ended his life by martyrdom. But I consider it most important that his death, a written account of which is still extant, should be recorded in this history.

2. There is a letter, written in the name of the church over which he himself presided, to the parishes in Pontus, which relates the events that befell him, in the following words:

3. The church of God which dwells in Philomelium, and to all the parishes of the holy Catholic Church in every place; mercy and peace and love from God the Father be multiplied. We write unto you, brethren, an account of what happened to those that suffered

martyrdom and to the blessed Polycarp, who put an end to the persecution, having, as it were, sealed it by his martyrdom.

4. After these words, before giving the account of Polycarp, they record the events which befell the rest of the martyrs, and describe the great firmness which they exhibited in the midst of their pains. For they say that the bystanders were struck with amazement when they saw them lacerated with scourges even to the innermost veins and arteries, so that the hidden inward parts of the body, both their bowels and their members, were exposed to view; and then laid upon sea-shells and certain pointed spits, and subjected to every species of punishment and of torture, and finally thrown as food to wild beasts.

5. And they record that the most noble Germanicus especially distinguished himself, overcoming by the grace of God the fear of bodily death implanted by nature. When indeed the proconsul wished to persuade him, and urged his youth, and besought him, as he was very young and vigorous, to take compassion on himself, he did not hesitate, but eagerly lured the beast toward himself, all but compelling and irritating him, in order that he might the sooner be freed from their unrighteous and lawless life.

6. After his glorious death the whole multitude, marveling at the bravery of the God-beloved martyr and at the fortitude of the whole race of Christians, began to cry out suddenly, Away with the atheists; let Polycarp be sought.

7. And when a very great tumult arose in consequence of the cries, a certain Phrygian, Quintus by name, who was newly come from Phrygia, seeing the beasts and the additional tortures, was smitten with cowardice and gave up the attainment of salvation.

8. But the above-mentioned epistle shows that he, too hastily and without proper discretion, had rushed forward with others to the tribunal, but when seized had furnished a clear proof to all, that it is not right for such persons rashly and recklessly to expose themselves to danger. Thus did matters turn out in connection with them.

9. But the most admirable Polycarp, when he first heard of these things, continued undisturbed, preserved a quiet and unshaken mind, and determined to remain in the city. But being persuaded by his friends who entreated and exhorted him to retire secretly, he went out to a farm not far distant from the city and abode there with a few companions, night and day doing nothing but wrestle with the Lord in prayer, beseeching

and imploring, and asking peace for the churches throughout the whole world. For this was always his custom.

10. And three days before his arrest, while he was praying, he saw in a vision at night the pillow under his head suddenly seized by fire and consumed; and upon this awakening he immediately interpreted the vision to those that were present, almost foretelling that which was about to happen, and declaring plainly to those that were with him that it would be necessary for him for Christ's sake to die by fire.

11. Then, as those who were seeking him pushed the search with vigor, they say that he was again constrained by the solicitude and love of the brethren to go to another farm. Thither his pursuers came after no long time, and seized two of the servants there, and tortured one of them for the purpose of learning from him Polycarp's hiding- place.

12. And coming late in the evening, they found him lying in an upper room, whence he might have gone to another house, but he would not, saying, The will of God be done.

13. And when he learned that they were present, as the account says, he went down and spoke to them with a very cheerful and gentle countenance, so that those who did not already know the man thought that they beheld a miracle when they observed his advanced age and the gravity and firmness of his bearing, and they marveled that so much effort should be made to capture a man like him.

14. But he did not hesitate, but immediately gave orders that a table should be spread for them. Then he invited them to partake of a bounteous meal, and asked of them one hour that he might pray undisturbed. And when they had given permission, he stood up and prayed, being full of the grace of the Lord, so that those who were present and heard him praying were amazed, and many of them now repented that such a venerable and godly old man was about to be put to death.

15. In addition to these things the narrative concerning him contains the following account: But when at length he had brought his prayer to an end, after remembering all that had ever come into contact with him, small and great, famous and obscure, and the whole Catholic Church throughout the world, the hour of departure having come, they put him upon an ass and brought him to the city, it being a great Sabbath. And he was met by Herod, the captain of police, and by his father Nicetes, who took him into their carriage, and sitting beside him endeavored to

persuade him, saying, 'For what harm is there in saying, Lord Cæsar, and sacrificing and saving your life?' He at first did not answer; but when they persisted, he said, 'I am not going to do what you advise me.'

16. And when they failed to persuade him, they uttered dreadful words, and thrust him down with violence, so that as he descended from the carriage he lacerated his shin. But without turning round, he went on his way promptly and rapidly, as if nothing had happened to him, and was taken to the stadium.

17. But there was such a tumult in the stadium that not many heard a voice from heaven, which came to Polycarp as he was entering the place: 'Be strong, Polycarp, and play the man.' And no one saw the speaker, but many of our people heard the voice.

18. And when he was led forward, there was a great tumult, as they heard that Polycarp was taken. Finally, when he came up, the proconsul asked if he were Polycarp. And when he confessed that he was, he endeavored to persuade him to deny, saying, 'Have regard for your age,' and other like things, which it is their custom to say: 'Swear by the genius of Cæsar; repent and say, Away with the Atheists.'

19. But Polycarp, looking with dignified countenance upon the whole crowd that was gathered in the stadium, waved his hand to them, and groaned, and raising his eyes toward heaven, said, 'Away with the Atheists.'

20. But when the magistrate pressed him, and said, 'Swear, and I will release you; revile Christ,' Polycarp said, 'Fourscore and six years have I been serving him, and he has done me no wrong; how then can I blaspheme my king who saved me?'

21. But when he again persisted, and said, 'Swear by the genius of Cæsar,' Polycarp replied, 'If you vainly suppose that I will swear by the genius of Cæsar, as you say, feigning to be ignorant who I am, hear plainly: I am a Christian. But if you desire to learn the doctrine of Christianity, assign a day and hear.'

22. The proconsul said, 'Persuade the people.' But Polycarp said, 'As for you, I thought you worthy of an explanation; for we have been taught to render to princes and authorities ordained by God the honor that is due, so long as it does not injure us; but as for these, I do not esteem them the proper persons to whom to make my defense.'

23. But the proconsul said, 'I have wild beasts; I will throw you to them unless you repent.' But he said, 'Call them; for repentance from better

to worse is a change we cannot make. But it is a noble thing to turn from wickedness to righteousness.'

24. But he again said to him, 'If you despise the wild beasts, I will cause you to be consumed by fire, unless you repent.' But Polycarp said, 'You threaten a fire which burns for an hour, and after a little is quenched; for you know not the fire of the future judgment and of the eternal punishment which is reserved for the impious. But why do you delay? Do what you will.'

25. Saying these and other words besides, he was filled with courage and joy, and his face was suffused with grace, so that not only was he not terrified and dismayed by the words that were spoken to him, but, on the contrary, the proconsul was amazed, and sent his herald to proclaim three times in the midst of the stadium: 'Polycarp has confessed that he is a Christian.'

26. And when this was proclaimed by the herald, the whole multitude, both of Gentiles and of Jews, who dwelt in Smyrna, cried out with ungovernable wrath and with a great shout, 'This is the teacher of Asia, the father of the Christians, the overthrower of our gods, who teaches many not to sacrifice nor to worship.'

27. When they had said this, they cried out and asked the Asiarch Philip to let a lion loose upon Polycarp. But he said that it was not lawful for him, since he had closed the games. Then they thought fit to cry out with one accord that Polycarp should be burned alive.

28. For it was necessary that the vision should be fulfilled which had been shown him concerning his pillow, when he saw it burning while he was praying, and turned and said prophetically to the faithful that were with him, 'I must needs be burned alive.'

29. These things were done with great speed — more quickly than they were said — the crowds immediately collecting from the workshops and baths timber and fagots, the Jews being especially zealous in the work, as is their wont.

30. But when the pile was ready, taking off all his upper garments, and loosing his girdle, he attempted also to remove his shoes, although he had never before done this, because of the effort which each of the faithful always made to touch his skin first; for he had been treated with all honor on account of his virtuous life even before his gray hairs came.

31. Forthwith then the materials prepared for the pile were placed about him; and as they were also about to nail him to the stake, he said, 'Leave

me thus; for he who has given me strength to endure the fire, will also grant me strength to remain in the fire unmoved without being secured by you with nails.' So they did not nail him, but bound him.

32. And he, with his hands behind him, and bound like a noble ram taken from a great flock, an acceptable burnt-offering unto God omnipotent, said,

33. 'Father of your beloved and blessed Son Jesus Christ, through whom we have received the knowledge of you, the God of angels and of powers and of the whole creation and of the entire race of the righteous who live in your presence, I bless you that you have deemed me worthy of this day and hour, that I might receive a portion in the number of the martyrs, in the cup of Christ, unto resurrection of eternal life, both of soul and of body, in the immortality of the Holy Spirit.

34. Among these may I be received before you this day, in a rich and acceptable sacrifice, as you, the faithful and true God, have beforehand prepared and revealed, and have fulfilled.

35. Wherefore I praise you also for everything; I bless you, I glorify you, through the eternal high priest, Jesus Christ, your beloved Son, through whom, with him, in the Holy Spirit, be glory unto you, both now and for the ages to come, Amen.'

36. When he had offered up his Amen and had finished his prayer, the firemen lighted the fire and as a great flame blazed out, we, to whom it was given to see, saw a wonder, and we were preserved that we might relate what happened to the others.

37. For the fire presented the appearance of a vault, like the sail of a vessel filled by the wind, and made a wall about the body of the martyr, and it was in the midst not like flesh burning, but like gold and silver refined in a furnace. For we perceived such a fragrant odor, as of the fumes of frankincense or of some other precious spices.

38. So at length the lawless men, when they saw that the body could not be consumed by the fire, commanded an executioner to approach and pierce him with the sword.

39. And when he had done this there came forth a quantity of blood so that it extinguished the fire; and the whole crowd marveled that there should be such a difference between the unbelievers and the elect, of whom this man also was one, the most wonderful teacher in our times, apostolic and prophetic, who was bishop of the Catholic Church in

Smyrna. For every word which came from his mouth was accomplished and will be accomplished.

40. But the jealous and envious Evil One, the adversary of the race of the righteous, when he saw the greatness of his martyrdom, and his blameless life from the beginning, and when he saw him crowned with the crown of immortality and bearing off an incontestable prize, took care that not even his body should be taken away by us, although many desired to do it and to have communion with his holy flesh.

41. Accordingly certain ones secretly suggested to Nicetes, the father of Herod and brother of Alce, that he should plead with the magistrate not to give up his body, 'lest,' it was said, 'they should abandon the crucified One and begin to worship this man.' They said these things at the suggestion and impulse of the Jews, who also watched as we were about to take it from the fire, not knowing that we shall never be able either to forsake Christ, who suffered for the salvation of the whole world of those that are saved, or to worship any other.

42. For we worship him who is the Son of God, but the martyrs, as disciples and imitators of the Lord, we love as they deserve on account of their matchless affection for their own king and teacher. May we also be made partakers and fellow-disciples with them.

43. The centurion, therefore, when he saw the contentiousness exhibited by the Jews, placed him in the midst and burned him, as was their custom. And so we afterwards gathered up his bones, which were more valuable than precious stones and more to be esteemed than gold, and laid them in a suitable place.

44. There the Lord will permit us to come together as we are able, in gladness and joy to celebrate the birthday of his martyrdom, for the commemoration of those who have already fought and for the training and preparation of those who shall hereafter do the same.

45. Such are the events that befell the blessed Polycarp, who suffered martyrdom in Smyrna with the eleven from Philadelphia. This one man is remembered more than the others by all, so that even by the heathen he is talked about in every place.

46. Of such an end was the admirable and apostolic Polycarp deemed worthy, as recorded by the brethren of the church of Smyrna in their epistle which we have mentioned. In the same volume concerning him are subjoined also other martyrdoms which took place in the same city, Smyrna, about the same period of time with Polycarp's martyrdom.

Among them also Metrodorus, who appears to have been a proselyte of the Marcionitic sect, suffered death by fire.

47. A celebrated martyr of those times was a certain man named Pionius. Those who desire to know his several confessions, and the boldness of his speech, and his apologies in behalf of the faith before the people and the rulers, and his instructive addresses and, moreover, his greetings to those who had yielded to temptation in the persecution, and the words of encouragement which he addressed to the brethren who came to visit him in prison, and the tortures which he endured in addition, and besides these the sufferings and the nailings, and his firmness on the pile, and his death after all the extraordinary trials, — those we refer to that epistle which has been given in the Martyrdoms of the Ancients, collected by us, and which contains a very full account of him.

48. And there are also records extant of others that suffered martyrdom in Pergamus, a city of Asia—of Carpus and Papylus, and a woman named Agathonice, who, after many and illustrious testimonies, gloriously ended their lives.

Chapter 16. Justin the Philosopher preaches the Word of Christ in Rome and suffers Martyrdom.

1. About this time Justin, who was mentioned by us just above, after he had addressed a second work in behalf of our doctrines to the rulers already named, was crowned with divine martyrdom, in consequence of a plot laid against him by Crescens, a philosopher who emulated the life and manners of the Cynics, whose name he bore. After Justin had frequently refuted him in public discussions he won by his martyrdom the prize of victory, dying in behalf of the truth which he preached.

2. And he himself, a man most learned in the truth, in his Apology already referred to clearly predicts how this was about to happen to him, although it had not yet occurred.

3. His words are as follows: I, too, therefore, expect to be plotted against and put in the stocks by some one of those whom I have named, or perhaps by Crescens, that unphilosophical and vainglorious man. For the man is not worthy to be called a philosopher who publicly bears witness against those concerning whom he knows nothing, declaring, for the sake of captivating and pleasing the multitude, that the Christians are atheistical and impious.

4. Doing this he errs greatly. For if he assails us without having read the teachings of Christ, he is thoroughly depraved, and is much worse than the illiterate, who often guard against discussing and bearing false witness about matters which they do not understand. And if he has read them and does not understand the majesty that is in them, or, understanding it, does these things in order that he may not be suspected of being an adherent, he is far more base and totally depraved, being enslaved to vulgar applause and irrational fear.

5. For I would have you know that when I proposed certain questions of the sort and asked him in regard to them, I learned and proved that he indeed knows nothing. And to show that I speak the truth I am ready, if these disputations have not been reported to you, to discuss the questions again in your presence. And this indeed would be an act worthy of an emperor.

6. But if my questions and his answers have been made known to you, it is obvious to you that he knows nothing about our affairs; or if he knows, but does not dare to speak because of those who hear him, he shows himself to be, as I have already said, not a philosopher, but a vainglorious man, who indeed does not even regard that most admirable saying of Socrates. These are the words of Justin.

7. And that he met his death as he had predicted that he would, in consequence of the machinations of Crescens, is stated by Tatian, a man who early in life lectured upon the sciences of the Greeks and won no little fame in them, and who has left a great many monuments of himself in his writings. He records this fact in his work against the Greeks, where he writes as follows: And that most admirable Justin declared with truth that the aforesaid persons were like robbers.

8. Then, after making some remarks about the philosophers, he continues as follows: Crescens, indeed, who made his nest in the great city, surpassed all in his unnatural lust, and was wholly devoted to the love of money.

9. And he who taught that death should be despised, was himself so greatly in fear of it that he endeavored to inflict death, as if it were a great evil, upon Justin, because the latter, when preaching the truth, had proved that the philosophers were gluttons and impostors. And such was the cause of Justin's martyrdom.

Chapter 17. The Martyrs whom Justin mentions in his Own Work.

1. The same man, before his conflict, mentions in his first Apology others that suffered martyrdom before him, and most fittingly records the following events.

2. He writes thus: A certain woman lived with a dissolute husband; she herself, too, having formerly been of the same character. But when she came to the knowledge of the teachings of Christ, she became temperate, and endeavored to persuade her husband likewise to be temperate, repeating the teachings, and declaring the punishment in eternal fire which shall come upon those who do not live temperately and conformably to right reason.

3. But he, continuing in the same excesses, alienated his wife by his conduct. For she finally, thinking it wrong to live as a wife with a man who, contrary to the law of nature and right, sought every possible means of pleasure, desired to be divorced from him.

4. And when she was earnestly entreated by her friends, who counseled her still to remain with him, on the ground that her husband might some time give hope of amendment, she did violence to herself and remained.

5. But when her husband had gone to Alexandria, and was reported to be conducting himself still worse, she— in order that she might not, by continuing in wedlock, and by sharing his board and bed, become a partaker in his lawlessness and impiety— gave him what we call a bill of divorce and left him.

6. But her noble and excellent husband—instead of rejoicing, as he ought to have done, that she had given up those actions which she had formerly recklessly committed with the servants and hirelings, when she delighted in drunkenness and in every vice, and that she desired him likewise to give them up—when she had gone from him contrary to his wish, brought an accusation concerning her, declaring that she was a Christian.

7. And she petitioned you, the emperor, that she might be permitted first to set her affairs in order, and afterwards, after the settlement of her affairs, to make her defense against the accusation. And this you granted.

8. But he who had once been her husband, being no longer able to prosecute her, directed his attacks against a certain Ptolemæus, who had been her teacher in the doctrines of Christianity, and whom Urbicius had punished. Against him he proceeded in the following manner:

9. He persuaded a centurion who was his friend to cast Ptolemæus into prison, and to take him and ask him this only: was he a Christian? And when Ptolemæus, who was a lover of truth, and not of a deceitful and false disposition, confessed that he was a Christian, the centurion bound him and punished him for a long time in the prison.

10. And finally, when the man was brought before Urbicius he was likewise asked this question only: was he a Christian? And again, conscious of the benefits which he enjoyed through the teaching of Christ, he confessed his schooling in divine virtue.

11. For whoever denies that he is a Christian, either denies because he despises Christianity, or he avoids confession because he is conscious that he is unworthy and an alien to it; neither of which is the case with the true Christian.

12. And when Urbicius commanded that he be led away to punishment, a certain Lucius, who was also a Christian, seeing judgment so unjustly passed, said to Urbicius, 'Why have you punished this man who is not an adulterer, nor a fornicator, nor a murderer, nor a thief, nor a robber, nor has been convicted of committing any crime at all, but has confessed that he bears the name of Christian? You do not judge, O Urbicius, in a manner befitting the Emperor Pius, or the philosophical son of Cæsar, or the sacred senate.'

13. And without making any other reply, he said to Lucius, 'You also seem to me to be one.' And when Lucius said, 'Certainly,' he again commanded that he too should be led away to punishment. But he professed his thanks, for he was liberated, he added, from such wicked rulers and was going to the good Father and King, God. And still a third having come forward was condemned to be punished.

14. To this, Justin fittingly and consistently adds the words which we quoted above, saying, I, too, therefore expect to be plotted against by some one of those whom I have named, etc.

Chapter 18. The Works of Justin which have come down to us.

1. This writer has left us a great many monuments of a mind educated and practiced in divine things, which are replete with profitable matter of every kind. To them we shall refer the studious, noting as we proceed those that have come to our knowledge.

2. There is a certain discourse of his in defense of our doctrine addressed to Antoninus surnamed the Pious, and to his sons, and to the Roman senate. Another work contains his second Apology in behalf of our faith, which he offered to him who was the successor of the emperor mentioned and who bore the same name, Antoninus Verus, the one whose times we are now recording.

3. Also another work against the Greeks, in which he discourses at length upon most of the questions at issue between us and the Greek philosophers, and discusses the nature of demons. It is not necessary for me to add any of these things here.

4. And still another work of his against the Greeks has come down to us, to which he gave the title Refutation. And besides these another, On the Sovereignty of God, which he establishes not only from our Scriptures, but also from the books of the Greeks.

5. Still further, a work entitled Psaltes, and another disputation On the Soul, in which, after propounding various questions concerning the problem under discussion, he gives the opinions of the Greek philosophers, promising to refute it, and to present his own view in another work.

6. He composed also a dialogue against the Jews, which he held in the city of Ephesus with Trypho, a most distinguished man among the Hebrews of that day. In it he shows how the divine grace urged him on to the doctrine of the faith, and with what earnestness he had formerly pursued philosophical studies, and how ardent a search he had made for the truth.

7. And he records of the Jews in the same work, that they were plotting against the teaching of Christ, asserting the same things against Trypho: Not only did you not repent of the wickedness which you had committed, but you selected at that time chosen men, and you sent them out from Jerusalem through all the land, to announce that the godless heresy of the Christians had made its appearance, and to accuse them of those things which all that are ignorant of us say against us, so that you become the causes not only of your own injustice, but also of all other men's.

8. He writes also that even down to his time prophetic gifts shone in the Church. And he mentions the Apocalypse of John, saying distinctly that it was the apostle's. He also refers to certain prophetic declarations, and accuses Trypho on the ground that the Jews had cut them out of the

Scripture. A great many other works of his are still in the hands of many of the brethren.

9. And the discourses of the man were thought so worthy of study even by the ancients, that Irenæus quotes his words: for instance, in the fourth book of his work Against Heresies, where he writes as follows: And Justin well says in his work against Marcion, that he would not have believed the Lord himself if he had preached another God besides the Creator; and again in the fifth book of the same work he says: And Justin well said that before the coming of the Lord, Satan never dared to blaspheme God, because he did not yet know his condemnation.

10. These things I have deemed it necessary to say for the sake of stimulating the studious to peruse his works with diligence. So much concerning him.

Chapter 19. The Rulers of the Churches of Rome and Alexandria during the Reign of Verus.

1. In the eighth year of the above-mentioned reign Soter succeeded Anicetus as bishop of the church of Rome, after the latter had held office eleven years in all. But when Celadion had presided over the church of Alexandria for fourteen years he was succeeded by Agripinnus.

Chapter 20. The Rulers of the Church of Antioch.

1. At that time also in the church of Antioch, Theophilus was well known as the sixth from the apostles. For Cornelius, who succeeded Hero, was the fourth, and after him Eros, the fifth in order, had held the office of bishop.

Chapter 21. The Ecclesiastical Writers that flourished in Those Days.

1. At that time there flourished in the Church Hegesippus, whom we know from what has gone before, and Dionysius, bishop of Corinth, and another bishop, Pinytus of Crete, and besides these, Philip, and Apolinarius, and Melito, and Musanus, and Modestus, and finally, Irenæus. From them has come down to us in writing, the sound and orthodox faith received from apostolic tradition.

Chapter 22. Hegesippus and the Events which he mentions.

1. Hegesippus in the five books of Memoirs which have come down to us has left a most complete record of his own views. In them he states that on a journey to Rome he met a great many bishops, and that he received the same doctrine from all. It is fitting to hear what he says after making some remarks about the epistle of Clement to the Corinthians.

2. His words are as follows: And the church of Corinth continued in the true faith until Primus was bishop in Corinth. I conversed with them on my way to Rome, and abode with the Corinthians many days, during which we were mutually refreshed in the true doctrine.

3. And when I had come to Rome I remained there until Anicetus, whose deacon was Eleutherus. And Anicetus was succeeded by Soter, and he by Eleutherus. In every succession, and in every city that is held which is preached by the law and the prophets and the Lord.

4. The same author also describes the beginnings of the heresies which arose in his time, in the following words: And after James the Just had suffered martyrdom, as the Lord had also on the same account, Symeon, the son of the Lord's uncle, Clopas, was appointed the next bishop. All proposed him as second bishop because he was a cousin of the Lord. Therefore, they called the Church a virgin, for it was not yet corrupted by vain discourses.

5. But Thebuthis, because he was not made bishop, began to corrupt it. He also was sprung from the seven sects among the people, like Simon, from whom came the Simonians, and Cleobius, from whom came the Cleobians, and Dositheus, from whom came the Dositheans, and Gorthæus, from whom came the Goratheni, and Masbotheus, from whom came the Masbothæans. From them sprang the Menandrianists, and Marcionists, and Carpocratians, and Valentinians, and Basilidians, and Saturnilians. Each introduced privately and separately his own peculiar opinion. From them came false Christs, false prophets, false apostles, who divided the unity of the Church by corrupt doctrines uttered against God and against his Christ.

6. The same writer also records the ancient heresies which arose among the Jews, in the following words: There were, moreover, various opinions in the circumcision, among the children of Israel. The following were those that were opposed to the tribe of Judah and the

Christ: Essenes, Galileans, Hemerobaptists, Masbothæans, Samaritans, Sadducees, Pharisees.

7. And he wrote of many other matters, which we have in part already mentioned, introducing the accounts in their appropriate places. And from the Syriac Gospel according to the Hebrews he quotes some passages in the Hebrew tongue, showing that he was a convert from the Hebrews, and he mentions other matters as taken from the unwritten tradition of the Jews.

8. And not only he, but also Irenæus and the whole company of the ancients, called the Proverbs of Solomon All-virtuous Wisdom. And when speaking of the books called Apocrypha, he records that some of them were composed in his day by certain heretics. But let us now pass on to another.

Chapter 23. Dionysius, Bishop of Corinth, and the Epistles which he wrote.

1. And first we must speak of Dionysius, who was appointed bishop of the church in Corinth, and communicated freely of his inspired labors not only to his own people, but also to those in foreign lands, and rendered the greatest service to all in the catholic epistles which he wrote to the churches.

2. Among these is the one addressed to the Lacedæmonians, containing instruction in the orthodox faith and an admonition to peace and unity; the one also addressed to the Athenians, exciting them to faith and to the life prescribed by the Gospel, which he accuses them of esteeming lightly, as if they had almost apostatized from the faith since the martyrdom of their ruler Publius, which had taken place during the persecutions of those days.

3. He mentions Quadratus also, stating that he was appointed their bishop after the martyrdom of Publius, and testifying that through his zeal they were brought together again and their faith revived. He records, moreover, that Dionysius the Areopagite, who was converted to the faith by the apostle Paul, according to the statement in the Acts of the Apostles, first obtained the episcopate of the church at Athens.

4. And there is extant another epistle of his addressed to the Nicomedians, in which he attacks the heresy of Marcion, and stands fast by the canon of the truth.

5. Writing also to the church that is in Gortyna, together with the other parishes in Crete, he commends their bishop Philip, because of the many acts of fortitude which are testified to as performed by the church under him, and he warns them to be on their guard against the aberrations of the heretics.

6. And writing to the church that is in Amastris, together with those in Pontus, he refers to Bacchylides and Elpistus, as having urged him to write, and he adds explanations of passages of the divine Scriptures, and mentions their bishop Palmas by name. He gives them much advice also in regard to marriage and chastity, and commands them to receive those who come back again after any fall, whether it be delinquency or heresy.

7. Among these is inserted also another epistle addressed to the Cnosians, in which he exhorts Pinytus, bishop of the parish, not to lay upon the brethren a grievous and compulsory burden in regard to chastity, but to have regard to the weakness of the multitude.

8. Pinytus, replying to this epistle, admires and commends Dionysius, but exhorts him in turn to impart some time more solid food, and to feed the people under him, when he wrote again, with more advanced teaching, that they might not be fed continually on these milky doctrines and imperceptibly grow old under a training calculated for children. In this epistle also Pinytus' orthodoxy in the faith and his care for the welfare of those placed under him, his learning and his comprehension of divine things, are revealed as in a most perfect image.

9. There is extant also another epistle written by Dionysius to the Romans, and addressed to Soter, who was bishop at that time. We cannot do better than to subjoin some passages from this epistle, in which he commends the practice of the Romans which has been retained down to the persecution in our own days. His words are as follows:

10. For from the beginning it has been your practice to do good to all the brethren in various ways, and to send contributions to many churches in every city. Thus relieving the want of the needy, and making provision for the brethren in the mines by the gifts which you have sent from the beginning, you Romans keep up the hereditary customs of the Romans, which your blessed bishop Soter has not only maintained, but also added to, furnishing an abundance of supplies to the saints, and encouraging the brethren from abroad with blessed words, as a loving father his children.

11. In this same epistle he makes mention also of Clement's epistle to the Corinthians, showing that it had been the custom from the beginning to read it in the church. His words are as follows: Today we have passed the Lord's holy day, in which we have read your epistle. From it, whenever we read it, we shall always be able to draw advice, as also from the former epistle, which was written to us through Clement.

12. The same writer also speaks as follows concerning his own epistles, alleging that they had been mutilated: As the brethren desired me to write epistles, I wrote. And these epistles the apostles of the devil have filled with tares, cutting out some things and adding others. For them a woe is reserved. It is, therefore, not to be wondered at if some have attempted to adulterate the Lord's writings also, since they have formed designs even against writings which are of less account.

There is extant, in addition to these, another epistle of Dionysius, written to Chrysophora, a most faithful sister. In it he writes what is suitable, and imparts to her also the proper spiritual food. So much concerning Dionysius.

Chapter 24. Theophilus Bishop of Antioch.

1. Of Theophilus, whom we have mentioned as bishop of the church of Antioch, three elementary works addressed to Autolycus are extant; also another writing entitled Against the Heresy of Hermogenes, in which he makes use of testimonies from the Apocalypse of John, and finally certain other catechetical books.

2. And as the heretics, no less then than at other times, were like tares, destroying the pure harvest of apostolic teaching, the pastors of the churches everywhere hastened to restrain them as wild beasts from the fold of Christ, at one time by admonitions and exhortations to the brethren, at another time by contending more openly against them in oral discussions and refutations, and again by correcting their opinions with most accurate proofs in written works.

3. And that Theophilus also, with the others, contended against them, is manifest from a certain discourse of no common merit written by him against Marcion. This work too, with the others of which we have spoken, has been preserved to the present day.

Maximinus, the seventh from the apostles, succeeded him as bishop of the church of Antioch.

Chapter 25. Philip and Modestus.

Philip who, as we learn from the words of Dionysius, was bishop of the parish of Gortyna, likewise wrote a most elaborate work against Marcion, as did also Irenæus and Modestus. The last named has exposed the error of the man more clearly than the rest to the view of all. There are a number of others also whose works are still presented by a great many of the brethren.

Chapter 26. Melito and the Circumstances which he records.

1. In those days also Melito, bishop of the parish in Sardis, and Apolinarius, bishop of Hierapolis, enjoyed great distinction. Each of them on his own part addressed apologies in behalf of the faith to the above-mentioned emperor of the Romans who was reigning at that time.

2. The following works of these writers have come to our knowledge. Of Melito, the two books On the Passover, and one On the Conduct of Life and the Prophets, the discourse On the Church, and one On the Lord's Day, still further one On the Faith of Man, and one On his Creation, another also On the Obedience of Faith, and one On the Senses; besides these the work On the Soul and Body, and that On Baptism, and the one On Truth, and On the Creation and Generation of Christ; his discourse also On Prophecy, and that On Hospitality; still further, The Key, and the books On the Devil and the Apocalypse of John, and the work On the Corporeality of God, and finally the book addressed to Antoninus.

3. In the books On the Passover he indicates the time at which he wrote, beginning with these words: While Servilius Paulus was proconsul of Asia, at the time when Sagaris suffered martyrdom, there arose in Laodicea a great strife concerning the Passover, which fell according to rule in those days; and these were written.

4. And Clement of Alexandria refers to this work in his own discourse On the Passover, which, he says, he wrote on occasion of Melito's work.

5. But in his book addressed to the emperor he records that the following events happened to us under him: For, what never before happened, the race of the pious is now suffering persecution, being driven about in Asia by new decrees. For the shameless informers and

coveters of the property of others, taking occasion from the decrees, openly carry on robbery night and day, despoiling those who are guilty of no wrong. And a little further on he says: If these things are done by your command, well and good. For a just ruler will never take unjust measures; and we indeed gladly accept the honor of such a death.

6. But this request alone we present to you, that you would yourself first examine the authors of such strife, and justly judge whether they be worthy of death and punishment, or of safety and quiet. But if, on the other hand, this counsel and this new decree, which is not fit to be executed even against barbarian enemies, be not from you, much more do we beseech you not to leave us exposed to such lawless plundering by the populace.

7. Again he adds the following: For our philosophy formerly flourished among the Barbarians; but having sprung up among the nations under your rule, during the great reign of your ancestor Augustus, it became to your empire especially a blessing of auspicious omen. For from that time the power of the Romans has grown in greatness and splendor. To this power you have succeeded, as the desired possessor, and such shall you continue with your son, if you guard the philosophy which grew up with the empire and which came into existence with Augustus; that philosophy which your ancestors also honored along with the other religions.

8. And a most convincing proof that our doctrine flourished for the good of an empire happily begun, is this — that there has no evil happened since Augustus' reign, but that, on the contrary, all things have been splendid and glorious, in accordance with the prayers of all.

9. Nero and Domitian, alone, persuaded by certain calumniators, have wished to slander our doctrine, and from them it has come to pass that the falsehood has been handed down, in consequence of an unreasonable practice which prevails of bringing slanderous accusations against the Christians.

10. But your pious fathers corrected their ignorance, having frequently rebuked in writing many who dared to attempt new measures against them. Among them your grandfather Adrian appears to have written to many others, and also to Fundanus, the proconsul and governor of Asia. And your father, when you also were ruling with him, wrote to the cities, forbidding them to take any new measures against us; among the rest to the Larissæans, to the Thessalonians, to the Athenians, and to all the Greeks.

11. And as for you—since your opinions respecting the Christians are the same as theirs, and indeed much more benevolent and philosophic — we are the more persuaded that you will do all that we ask of you. These words are found in the above-mentioned work.

12. But in the Extracts made by him the same writer gives at the beginning of the introduction a catalogue of the acknowledged books of the Old Testament, which it is necessary to quote at this point. He writes as follows:

13. Melito to his brother Onesimus, greeting: Since you have often, in your zeal for the word, expressed a wish to have extracts made from the Law and the Prophets concerning the Saviour and concerning our entire faith, and has also desired to have an accurate statement of the ancient book, as regards their number and their order, I have endeavored to perform the task, knowing your zeal for the faith, and your desire to gain information in regard to the word, and knowing that you, in your yearning after God, esteem these things above all else, struggling to attain eternal salvation.

14. Accordingly when I went East and came to the place where these things were preached and done, I learned accurately the books of the Old Testament, and send them to you as written below. Their names are as follows: Of Moses, five books: Genesis, Exodus, Numbers, Leviticus, Deuteronomy; Jesus Nave, Judges, Ruth; of Kings, four books; of Chronicles, two; the Psalms of David, the Proverbs of Solomon, Wisdom also, Ecclesiastes, Song of Songs, Job; of Prophets, Isaiah, Jeremiah; of the twelve prophets, one book ; Daniel, Ezekiel, Esdras. From which also I have made the extracts, dividing them into six books. Such are the words of Melito.

Chapter 27. Apolinarius, Bishop of the Church of Hierapolis.

A number of works of Apolinarius have been preserved by many, and the following have reached us: the Discourse addressed to the above-mentioned emperor, five books Against the Greeks, On Truth, a first and second book, and those which he subsequently wrote against the heresy of the Phrygians, which not long afterwards came out with its innovations, but at that time was, as it were, in its incipiency, since Montanus, with his false prophetesses, was then laying the foundations of his error.

Chapter 28. Musanus and His Writings.

And as for Musanus, whom we have mentioned among the foregoing writers, a certain very elegant discourse is extant, which was written by him against some brethren that had gone over to the heresy of the so-called Encratites, which had recently sprung up, and which introduced a strange and pernicious error. It is said that Tatian was the author of this false doctrine.

Chapter 29. The Heresy of Tatian.

1. He is the one whose words we quoted a little above in regard to that admirable man, Justin, and whom we stated to have been a disciple of the martyr. Irenæus declares this in the first book of his work Against Heresies, where he writes as follows concerning both him and his heresy:

2. Those who are called Encratites, and who sprung from Saturninus and Marcion, preached celibacy, setting aside the original arrangement of God and tacitly censuring him who made male and female for the propagation of the human race. They introduced also abstinence from the things called by them animate, thus showing ingratitude to the God who made all things. And they deny the salvation of the first man.

3. But this has been only recently discovered by them, a certain Tatian being the first to introduce this blasphemy. He was a hearer of Justin, and expressed no such opinion while he was with him, but after the martyrdom of the latter he left the Church, and becoming exalted with the thought of being a teacher, and puffed up with the idea that he was superior to others, he established a peculiar type of doctrine of his own, inventing certain invisible æons like the followers of Valentinus, while, like Marcion and Saturninus, he pronounced marriage to be corruption and fornication. His argument against the salvation of Adam, however, he devised for himself. Irenæus at that time wrote thus.

4. But a little later a certain man named Severus put new strength into the aforesaid heresy, and thus brought it about that those who took their origin from it were called, after him, Severians.

5. They, indeed, use the Law and Prophets and Gospels, but interpret in their own way the utterances of the Sacred Scriptures. And they abuse Paul the apostle and reject his epistles, and do not accept even the Acts of the Apostles.

6. But their original founder, Tatian, formed a certain combination and collection of the Gospels, I know not how, to which he gave the title Diatessaron, and which is still in the hands of some. But they say that he ventured to paraphrase certain words of the apostle, in order to improve their style.

7. He has left a great many writings. Of these the one most in use among many persons is his celebrated Address to the Greeks, which also appears to be the best and most useful of all his works. In it he deals with the most ancient times, and shows that Moses and the Hebrew prophets were older than all the celebrated men among the Greeks. So much in regard to these men.

Chapter 30. Bardesanes the Syrian and his Extant Works.

1. In the same reign, as heresies were abounding in the region between the rivers, a certain Bardesanes, a most able man and a most skillful disputant in the Syriac tongue, having composed dialogues against Marcion's followers and against certain others who were authors of various opinions, committed them to writing in his own language, together with many other works. His pupils, of whom he had very many (for he was a powerful defender of the faith), translated these productions from the Syriac into Greek.

2. Among them there is also his most able dialogue On Fate, addressed to Antoninus, and other works which they say he wrote on occasion of the persecution which arose at that time.

3. He indeed was at first a follower of Valentinus, but afterward, having rejected his teaching and having refuted most of his fictions, he fancied that he had come over to the more correct opinion. Nevertheless he did not entirely wash off the filth of the old heresy.

About this time also Soter, bishop of the Church of Rome, departed this life.

BOOK V

Introduction.

1. Soter, bishop of the church of Rome, died after an episcopate of eight years, and was succeeded by Eleutherus, the twelfth from the apostles. In the seventeenth year of the Emperor Antoninus Verus, the persecution of our people was rekindled more fiercely in certain districts on account of an insurrection of the masses in the cities; and judging by the number in a single nation, myriads suffered martyrdom throughout the world. A record of this was written for posterity, and in truth it is worthy of perpetual remembrance.

2. A full account, containing the most reliable information on the subject, is given in our Collection of Martyrdoms, which constitutes a narrative instructive as well as historical. I will repeat here such portions of this account as may be needful for the present purpose.

3. Other writers of history record the victories of war and trophies won from enemies, the skill of generals, and the manly bravery of soldiers, defiled with blood and with innumerable slaughters for the sake of children and country and other possessions.

4. But our narrative of the government of God will record in ineffaceable letters the most peaceful wars waged in behalf of the peace of the soul, and will tell of men doing brave deeds for truth rather than country, and for piety rather than dearest friends. It will hand down to imperishable remembrance the discipline and the much-tried fortitude of the athletes of religion, the trophies won from demons, the victories over invisible enemies, and the crowns placed upon all their heads.

Chapter 1. The Number of those who fought for Religion in Gaul Under Verus and the Nature of their Conflicts.

1. The country in which the arena was prepared for them was Gaul, of which Lyons and Vienne are the principal and most celebrated cities. The Rhone passes through both of them, flowing in a broad stream through the entire region.

2. The most celebrated churches in that country sent an account of the witnesses to the churches in Asia and Phrygia, relating in the following manner what was done among them.

I will give their own words.

3. The servants of Christ residing at Vienne and Lyons, in Gaul, to the brethren through out Asia and Phrygia, who hold the same faith and hope of redemption, peace and grace and glory from God the Father and Christ Jesus our Lord.

4. Then, having related some other matters, they begin their account in this manner: The greatness of the tribulation in this region, and the fury of the heathen against the saints, and the sufferings of the blessed witnesses, we cannot recount accurately, nor indeed could they possibly be recorded.

5. For with all his might the adversary fell upon us, giving us a foretaste of his unbridled activity at his future coming. He endeavored in every manner to practice and exercise his servants against the servants of God, not only shutting us out from houses and baths and markets, but forbidding any of us to be seen in any place whatever.

6. But the grace of God led the conflict against him, and delivered the weak, and set them as firm pillars, able through patience to endure all the wrath of the Evil One. And they joined battle with him, undergoing all kinds of shame and injury; and regarding their great sufferings as little, they hastened to Christ, manifesting truly that 'the sufferings of this present time are not worthy to be compared with the glory which shall be revealed to us afterward.' Romans 8:18

7. First of all, they endured nobly the injuries heaped upon them by the populace; clamors and blows and draggings and robberies and stonings and imprisonments, and all things which an infuriated mob delight in inflicting on enemies and adversaries.

8. Then, being taken to the forum by the chiliarch and the authorities of the city, they were examined in the presence of the whole multitude, and having confessed, they were imprisoned until the arrival of the governor.

9. When, afterwards, they were brought before him, and he treated us with the utmost cruelty, Vettius Epagathus, one of the brethren, and a man filled with love for God and his neighbor, interfered. His life was so consistent that, although young, he had attained a reputation equal to that of the elder Zacharias: for he 'walked in all the commandments and ordinances of the Lord blameless,' Luke 1:6 and was untiring in every good work for his neighbor, zealous for God and fervent in spirit. Such being his character, he could not endure the unreasonable judgment against us, but was filled with indignation, and asked to be permitted to

testify in behalf of his brethren, that there is among us nothing ungodly or impious.

10. But those about the judgment seat cried out against him, for he was a man of distinction; and the governor refused to grant his just request, and merely asked if he also were a Christian. And he, confessing this with a loud voice, was himself taken into the order of the witnesses, being called the Advocate of the Christians, but having the Advocate in himself, the Spirit more abundantly than Zacharias. He showed this by the fullness of his love, being well pleased even to lay down his life in defense of the brethren. For he was and is a true disciple of Christ, 'following the Lamb wherever he goes.' Revelation 14:4

11. Then the others were divided, and the proto-witnesses were manifestly ready, and finished their confession with all eagerness. But some appeared unprepared and untrained, weak as yet, and unable to endure so great a conflict. About ten of these proved abortions, causing us great grief and sorrow beyond measure, and impairing the zeal of the others who had not yet been seized, but who, though suffering all kinds of affliction, continued constantly with the witnesses and did not forsake them.

12. Then all of us feared greatly on account of uncertainty as to their confession; not because we dreaded the sufferings to be endured, but because we looked to the end, and were afraid that some of them might fall away.

13. But those who were worthy were seized day by day, filling up their number, so that all the zealous persons, and those through whom especially our affairs had been established, were collected together out of the two churches.

14. And some of our heathen servants also were seized, as the governor had commanded that all of us should be examined publicly. These, being ensnared by Satan, and fearing for themselves the tortures which they beheld the saints endure, and being also urged on by the soldiers, accused us falsely of Thyestean banquets and Œdipodean intercourse, and of deeds which are not only unlawful for us to speak of or to think, but which we cannot believe were ever done by men.

15. When these accusations were reported, all the people raged like wild beasts against us, so that even if any had before been moderate on account of friendship, they were now exceedingly furious and gnashed their teeth against us. And that which was spoken by our Lord was

fulfilled: 'The time will come when whosoever kills you will think that he does God service.' John 16:2

16. Then finally the holy witnesses endured sufferings beyond description, Satan striving earnestly that some of the slanders might be uttered by them also.

17. But the whole wrath of the populace, and governor, and soldiers was aroused exceedingly against Sanctus, the deacon from Vienne, and Maturus, a late convert, yet a noble combatant, and against Attalus, a native of Pergamos where he had always been a pillar and foundation, and Blandina, through whom Christ showed that things which appear mean and obscure and despicable to men are with God of great glory, 1 Corinthians 1:27-28 through love toward him manifested in power, and not boasting in appearance.

18. For while we all trembled, and her earthly mistress, who was herself also one of the witnesses, feared that on account of the weakness of her body, she would be unable to make bold confession, Blandina was filled with such power as to be delivered and raised above those who were torturing her by turns from morning till evening in every manner, so that they acknowledged that they were conquered, and could do nothing more to her. And they were astonished at her endurance, as her entire body was mangled and broken; and they testified that one of these forms of torture was sufficient to destroy life, not to speak of so many and so great sufferings.

19. But the blessed woman, like a noble athlete, renewed her strength in her confession; and her comfort and recreation and relief from the pain of her sufferings was in exclaiming, 'I am a Christian, and there is nothing vile done by us.'

20. But Sanctus also endured marvelously and superhumanly all the outrages which he suffered. While the wicked men hoped, by the continuance and severity of his tortures to wring something from him which he ought not to say, he girded himself against them with such firmness that he would not even tell his name, or the nation or city to which he belonged, or whether he was bond or free, but answered in the Roman tongue to all their questions, 'I am a Christian.' He confessed this instead of name and city and race and everything besides, and the people heard from him no other word.

21. There arose therefore on the part of the governor and his tormentors a great desire to conquer him; but having nothing more that they could

do to him, they finally fastened red-hot brazen plates to the most tender parts of his body.

22. And these indeed were burned, but he continued unbending and unyielding, firm in his confession, and refreshed and strengthened by the heavenly fountain of the water of life, flowing from the bowels of Christ.

23. And his body was a witness of his sufferings, being one complete wound and bruise, drawn out of shape, and altogether unlike a human form. Christ, suffering in him, manifested his glory, delivering him from his adversary, and making him an ensample for the others, showing that nothing is fearful where the love of the Father is, and nothing painful where there is the glory of Christ.

24. For when the wicked men tortured him a second time after some days, supposing that with his body swollen and inflamed to such a degree that he could not bear the touch of a hand, if they should again apply the same instruments, they would overcome him, or at least by his death under his sufferings others would be made afraid, not only did not this occur, but, contrary to all human expectation, his body arose and stood erect in the midst of the subsequent torments, and resumed its original appearance and the use of its limbs, so that, through the grace of Christ, these second sufferings became to him, not torture, but healing.

25. But the devil, thinking that he had already consumed Biblias, who was one of those who had denied Christ, desiring to increase her condemnation through the utterance of blasphemy, brought her again to the torture, to compel her, as already feeble and weak, to report impious things concerning us.

26. But she recovered herself under the suffering, and as if awaking from a deep sleep, and reminded by the present anguish of the eternal punishment in hell, she contradicted the blasphemers. 'How,' she said, 'could those eat children who do not think it lawful to taste the blood even of irrational animals?' And thenceforward she confessed herself a Christian, and was given a place in the order of the witnesses.

27. But as the tyrannical tortures were made by Christ of none effect through the patience of the blessed, the devil invented other contrivances—confinement in the dark and most loathsome parts of the prison, stretching of the feet to the fifth hole in the stocks, and the other outrages which his servants are accustomed to inflict upon the prisoners

when furious and filled with the devil. A great many were suffocated in prison, being chosen by the Lord for this manner of death, that he might manifest in them his glory.

28. For some, though they had been tortured so cruelly that it seemed impossible that they could live, even with the most careful nursing, yet, destitute of human attention, remained in the prison, being strengthened by the Lord, and invigorated both in body and soul; and they exhorted and encouraged the rest. But such as were young, and arrested recently, so that their bodies had not become accustomed to torture, were unable to endure the severity of their confinement, and died in prison.

29. The blessed Pothinus, who had been entrusted with the bishopric of Lyons, was dragged to the judgment seat. He was more than ninety years of age, and very infirm, scarcely indeed able to breathe because of physical weakness; but he was strengthened by spiritual zeal through his earnest desire for martyrdom. Though his body was worn out by old age and disease, his life was preserved that Christ might triumph in it.

30. When he was brought by the soldiers to the tribunal, accompanied by the civil magistrates and a multitude who shouted against him in every manner as if he were Christ himself, he bore noble witness.

31. Being asked by the governor, Who was the God of the Christians, he replied, 'If you are worthy, you shall know.' Then he was dragged away harshly, and received blows of every kind. Those near him struck him with their hands and feet, regardless of his age; and those at a distance hurled at him whatever they could seize; all of them thinking that they would be guilty of great wickedness and impiety if any possible abuse were omitted. For thus they thought to avenge their own deities. Scarcely able to breathe, he was cast into prison and died after two days.

32. Then a certain great dispensation of God occurred, and the compassion of Jesus appeared beyond measure, in a manner rarely seen among the brotherhood, but not beyond the power of Christ.

33. For those who had recanted at their first arrest were imprisoned with the others, and endured terrible sufferings, so that their denial was of no profit to them even for the present. But those who confessed what they were were imprisoned as Christians, no other accusation being brought against them. But the first were treated afterwards as murderers and defiled, and were punished twice as severely as the others.

34. For the joy of martyrdom, and the hope of the promises, and love for Christ, and the Spirit of the Father supported the latter; but their

consciences so greatly distressed the former that they were easily distinguishable from all the rest by their very countenances when they were led forth.

35. For the first went out rejoicing, glory and grace being blended in their faces, so that even their bonds seemed like beautiful ornaments, as those of a bride adorned with variegated golden fringes; and they were perfumed with the sweet savor of Christ, so that some supposed they had been anointed with earthly ointment. But the others were downcast and humble and dejected and filled with every kind of disgrace, and they were reproached by the heathen as ignoble and weak, bearing the accusation of murderers, and having lost the one honorable and glorious and life-giving Name. The rest, beholding this, were strengthened, and when apprehended, they confessed without hesitation, paying no attention to the persuasions of the devil.

36. After certain other words they continue:

After these things, finally, their martyrdoms were divided into every form. For plaiting a crown of various colors and of all kinds of flowers, they presented it to the Father. It was proper therefore that the noble athletes, having endured a manifold strife, and conquered grandly, should receive the crown, great and incorruptible.

37. Maturus, therefore, and Sanctus and Blandina and Attalus were led to the amphitheater to be exposed to the wild beasts, and to give to the heathen public a spectacle of cruelty, a day for fighting with wild beasts being specially appointed on account of our people.

38. Both Maturus and Sanctus passed again through every torment in the amphitheater, as if they had suffered nothing before, or rather, as if, having already conquered their antagonist in many contests, they were now striving for the crown itself. They endured again the customary running of the gauntlet and the violence of the wild beasts, and everything which the furious people called for or desired, and at last, the iron chair in which their bodies being roasted, tormented them with the fumes.

39. And not with this did the persecutors cease, but were yet more mad against them, determined to overcome their patience. But even thus they did not hear a word from Sanctus except the confession which he had uttered from the beginning.

40. These, then, after their life had continued for a long time through the great conflict, were at last sacrificed, having been made throughout that day a spectacle to the world, in place of the usual variety of combats.

41. But Blandina was suspended on a stake, and exposed to be devoured by the wild beasts who should attack her. And because she appeared as if hanging on a cross, and because of her earnest prayers, she inspired the combatants with great zeal. For they looked on her in her conflict, and beheld with their outward eyes, in the form of their sister, him who was crucified for them, that he might persuade those who believe in him, that every one who suffers for the glory of Christ has fellowship always with the living God.

42. As none of the wild beasts at that time touched her, she was taken down from the stake, and cast again into prison. She was preserved thus for another contest, that, being victorious in more conflicts, she might make the punishment of the crooked serpent irrevocable; and, though small and weak and despised, yet clothed with Christ the mighty and conquering Athlete, she might arouse the zeal of the brethren, and, having overcome the adversary many times might receive, through her conflict, the crown incorruptible.

43. But Attalus was called for loudly by the people, because he was a person of distinction. He entered the contest readily on account of a good conscience and his genuine practice in Christian discipline, and as he had always been a witness for the truth among us.

44. He was led around the amphitheater, a tablet being carried before him on which was written in the Roman language 'This is Attalus the Christian,' and the people were filled with indignation against him. But when the governor learned that he was a Roman, he commanded him to be taken back with the rest of those who were in prison concerning whom he had written to Cæsar, and whose answer he was awaiting.

45. But the intervening time was not wasted nor fruitless to them; for by their patience the measureless compassion of Christ was manifested. For through their continued life the dead were made alive, and the witnesses showed favor to those who had failed to witness. And the virgin mother had much joy in receiving alive those whom she had brought forth as dead.

46. For through their influence many who had denied were restored, and re-begotten, and rekindled with life, and learned to confess. And being made alive and strengthened, they went to the judgment seat to

be again interrogated by the governor; God, who desires not the death of the sinner, Ezekiel 33:11 but mercifully invites to repentance, treating them with kindness.

47. For Cæsar commanded that they should be put to death, but that any who might deny should be set free. Therefore, at the beginning of the public festival which took place there, and which was attended by crowds of men from all nations, the governor brought the blessed ones to the judgment seat, to make of them a show and spectacle for the multitude. Wherefore also he examined them again, and beheaded those who appeared to possess Roman citizenship, but he sent the others to the wild beasts.

48. And Christ was glorified greatly in those who had formerly denied him, for, contrary to the expectation of the heathen, they confessed. For they were examined by themselves, as about to be set free; but confessing, they were added to the order of the witnesses. But some continued without, who had never possessed a trace of faith, nor any apprehension of the wedding garment, Matthew 22:11 nor an understanding of the fear of God; but, as sons of perdition, they blasphemed the Way through their apostasy.

49. But all the others were added to the Church. While these were being examined, a certain Alexander, a Phrygian by birth, and physician by profession, who had resided in Gaul for many years, and was well known to all on account of his love to God and boldness of speech (for he was not without a share of apostolic grace), standing before the judgment seat, and by signs encouraging them to confess, appeared to those standing by as if in travail.

50. But the people being enraged because those who formerly denied now confessed, cried out against Alexander as if he were the cause of this. Then the governor summoned him and inquired who he was. And when he answered that he was a Christian, being very angry he condemned him to the wild beasts. And on the next day he entered along with Attalus. For to please the people, the governor had ordered Attalus again to the wild beasts.

51. And they were tortured in the amphitheater with all the instruments contrived for that purpose, and having endured a very great conflict, were at last sacrificed. Alexander neither groaned nor murmured in any manner, but communed in his heart with God.

52. But when Attalus was placed in the iron seat, and the fumes arose from his burning body, he said to the people in the Roman language: 'Lo! This which you do is devouring men; but we do not devour men; nor do any other wicked thing.' And being asked, what name God has, he replied, 'God has not a name as man has.'

53. After all these, on the last day of the contests, Blandina was again brought in, with Ponticus, a boy about fifteen years old. They had been brought every day to witness the sufferings of the others, and had been pressed to swear by the idols. But because they remained steadfast and despised them, the multitude became furious, so that they had no compassion for the youth of the boy nor respect for the sex of the woman.

54. Therefore they exposed them to all the terrible sufferings and took them through the entire round of torture, repeatedly urging them to swear, but being unable to effect this; for Ponticus, encouraged by his sister so that even the heathen could see that she was confirming and strengthening him, having nobly endured every torture, gave up the ghost.

55. But the blessed Blandina, last of all, having, as a noble mother, encouraged her children and sent them before her victorious to the King, endured herself all their conflicts and hastened after them, glad and rejoicing in her departure as if called to a marriage supper, rather than cast to wild beasts.

56. And, after the scourging, after the wild beasts, after the roasting seat, she was finally enclosed in a net, and thrown before a bull. And having been tossed about by the animal, but feeling none of the things which were happening to her, on account of her hope and firm hold upon what had been entrusted to her, and her communion with Christ, she also was sacrificed. And the heathen themselves confessed that never among them had a woman endured so many and such terrible tortures.

57. But not even thus was their madness and cruelty toward the saints satisfied. For, incited by the Wild Beast, wild and barbarous tribes were not easily appeased, and their violence found another peculiar opportunity in the dead bodies.

58. For, through their lack of manly reason, the fact that they had been conquered did not put them to shame, but rather the more enkindled their wrath as that of a wild beast, and aroused alike the hatred of governor and people to treat us unjustly; that the Scripture might be

fulfilled: 'He that is lawless, let him be lawless still, and he that is righteous, let him be righteous still.'

59. For they cast to the dogs those who had died of suffocation in the prison, carefully guarding them by night and day, lest any one should be buried by us. And they exposed the remains left by the wild beasts and by fire, mangled and charred, and placed the heads of the others by their bodies, and guarded them in like manner from burial by a watch of soldiers for many days.

60. And some raged and gnashed their teeth against them, desiring to execute more severe vengeance upon them; but others laughed and mocked at them, magnifying their own idols, and imputed to them the punishment of the Christians. Even the more reasonable, and those who had seemed to sympathize somewhat, reproached them often, saying, 'Where is their God, and what has their religion, which they have chosen rather than life, profited them?'

61. So various was their conduct toward us; but we were in deep affliction because we could not bury the bodies. For neither did night avail us for this purpose, nor did money persuade, nor entreaty move to compassion; but they kept watch in every way, as if the prevention of the burial would be of some great advantage to them.

In addition, they say after other things:

62. The bodies of the martyrs, having thus in every manner been exhibited and exposed for six days, were afterward burned and reduced to ashes, and swept into the Rhone by the wicked men, so that no trace of them might appear on the earth.

63. And this they did, as if able to conquer God, and prevent their new birth; 'that,' as they said, 'they may have no hope of a resurrection, through trust in which they bring to us this foreign and new religion, and despise terrible things, and are ready even to go to death with joy. Now let us see if they will rise again, and if their God is able to help them, and to deliver them out of our hands.'

Chapter 2. The Martyrs, beloved of God, kindly ministered unto those who fell in the Persecution.

1. Such things happened to the churches of Christ under the above-mentioned emperor, from which we may reasonably conjecture the occurrences in the other provinces. It is proper to add other selections

from the same letter, in which the moderation and compassion of these witnesses is recorded in the following words:

2. They were also so zealous in their imitation of Christ—'who, being in the form of God, counted it not a prize to be on an equality with God,' Philippians 2:6 — that, though they had attained such honor, and had borne witness, not once or twice, but many times—having been brought back to prison from the wild beasts, covered with burns and scars and wounds—yet they did not proclaim themselves witnesses, nor did they suffer us to address them by this name. If any one of us, in letter or conversation, spoke of them as witnesses, they rebuked him sharply.

3. For they conceded cheerfully the appellation of Witness to Christ 'the faithful and true Witness,' Revelation 3:14 and 'firstborn of the dead,' Revelation 1:5 and prince of the life of God; and they reminded us of the witnesses who had already departed, and said, 'They are already witnesses whom Christ has deemed worthy to be taken up in their confession, having sealed their testimony by their departure; but we are lowly and humble confessors.' And they besought the brethren with tears that earnest prayers should be offered that they might be made perfect.

4. They showed in their deeds the power of 'testimony,' manifesting great boldness toward all the brethren, and they made plain their nobility through patience and fearlessness and courage, but they refused the title of Witnesses as distinguishing them from their brethren, being filled with the fear of God.

5. A little further on they say: They humbled themselves under the mighty hand, by which they are now greatly exalted. They defended all, but accused none. They absolved all, but bound none. And they prayed for those who had inflicted cruelties upon them, even as Stephen, the perfect witness, 'Lord, lay not this sin to their charge.' Acts 7:60 But if he prayed for those who stoned him, how much more for the brethren!

6. And again after mentioning other matters, they say: For, through the genuineness of their love, their greatest contest with him was that the Beast, being choked, might cast out alive those whom he supposed he had swallowed. For they did not boast over the fallen, but helped them in their need with those things in which they themselves abounded, having the compassion of a mother, and shedding many tears on their account before the Father.

7. They asked for life, and he gave it to them, and they shared it with their neighbors. Victorious over everything, they departed to God. Having always loved peace, and having commended peace to us they went in peace to God, leaving no sorrow to their mother, nor division or strife to the brethren, but joy and peace and concord and love.

8. This record of the affection of those blessed ones toward the brethren that had fallen may be profitably added on account of the inhuman and unmerciful disposition of those who, after these events, acted unsparingly toward the members of Christ.

Chapter 3. The Vision which appeared in a Dream to the Witness Attalus.

1. The same letter of the above-mentioned witnesses contains another account worthy of remembrance. No one will object to our bringing it to the knowledge of our readers.

2. It runs as follows: For a certain Alcibiades, who was one of them, led a very austere life, partaking of nothing whatever but bread and water. When he endeavored to continue this same sort of life in prison, it was revealed to Attalus after his first conflict in the amphitheater that Alcibiades was not doing well in refusing the creatures of God and placing a stumbling-block before others.

3. And Alcibiades obeyed, and partook of all things without restraint, giving thanks to God. For they were not deprived of the grace of God, but the Holy Ghost was their counselor. Let this suffice for these matters.

4. The followers of Montanus, Alcibiades and Theodotus in Phrygia were now first giving wide circulation to their assumption in regard to prophecy—for the many other miracles that, through the gift of God, were still wrought in the different churches caused their prophesying to be readily credited by many—and as dissension arose concerning them, the brethren in Gaul set forth their own prudent and most orthodox judgment in the matter, and published also several epistles from the witnesses that had been put to death among them. These they sent, while they were still in prison, to the brethren throughout Asia and Phrygia, and also to Eleutherus, who was then bishop of Rome, negotiating for the peace of the churches.

Chapter 4. Irenæus commended by the Witnesses in a Letter.

1. The same witnesses also recommended Irenæus, who was already at that time a presbyter of the parish of Lyons, to the above- mentioned bishop of Rome, saying many favorable things in regard to him, as the following extract shows:

2. We pray, father Eleutherus, that you may rejoice in God in all things and always. We have requested our brother and comrade Irenæus to carry this letter to you, and we ask you to hold him in esteem, as zealous for the covenant of Christ. For if we thought that office could confer righteousness upon any one, we should commend him among the first as a presbyter of the church, which is his position.

3. Why should we transcribe the catalogue of the witnesses given in the letter already mentioned, of whom some were beheaded, others cast to the wild beasts, and others fell asleep in prison, or give the number of confessors still surviving at that time? For whoever desires can readily find the full account by consulting the letter itself, which, as I have said, is recorded in our Collection of Martyrdoms. Such were the events which happened under Antoninus.

Chapter 5. God sent Rain from Heavenfor Marcus Aurelius Cæsar in Answer to the Prayers of our People.

1. It is reported that Marcus Aurelius Cæsar, brother of Antoninus, being about to engage in battle with the Germans and Sarmatians, was in great trouble on account of his army suffering from thirst. But the soldiers of the so-called Melitene legion, through the faith which has given strength from that time to the present, when they were drawn up before the enemy, kneeled on the ground, as is our custom in prayer, and engaged in supplications to God.

2. This was indeed a strange sight to the enemy, but it is reported that a stranger thing immediately followed. The lightning drove the enemy to flight and destruction, but a shower refreshed the army of those who had called on God, all of whom had been on the point of perishing with thirst.

3. This story is related by non-Christian writers who have been pleased to treat the times referred to, and it has also been recorded by our own people. By those historians who were strangers to the faith, the marvel is mentioned, but it is not acknowledged as an answer to our prayers.

But by our own people, as friends of the truth, the occurrence is related in a simple and artless manner.

4. Among these is Apolinarius, who says that from that time the legion through whose prayers the wonder took place received from the emperor a title appropriate to the event, being called in the language of the Romans the Thundering Legion.

5. Tertullian is a trustworthy witness of these things. In the Apology for the Faith, which he addressed to the Roman Senate, and which work we have already mentioned, he confirms the history with greater and stronger proofs.

6. He writes that there are still extant letters of the most intelligent Emperor Marcus in which he testifies that his army, being on the point of perishing with thirst in Germany, was saved by the prayers of the Christians. And he says also that this emperor threatened death to those who brought accusation against us.

7. He adds further: What kind of laws are those which impious, unjust, and cruel persons use against us alone? Which Vespasian, though he had conquered the Jews, did not regard; which Trajan partially annulled, forbidding Christians to be sought after; which neither Adrian, though inquisitive in all matters, nor he who was called Pius sanctioned. But let any one treat these things as he chooses; we must pass on to what followed.

8. Pothinus having died with the other martyrs in Gaul at ninety years of age, Irenæus succeeded him in the episcopate of the church at Lyons. We have learned that, in his youth, he was a hearer of Polycarp.

9. In the third book of his work Against Heresies he has inserted a list of the bishops of Rome, bringing it down as far as Eleutherus (whose times we are now considering), under whom he composed his work. He writes as follows:

Chapter 6. Catalogue of the Bishops of Rome.

1. The blessed apostles having founded and established the church, entrusted the office of the episcopate to Linus. Paul speaks of this Linus in his Epistles to Timothy. 2 Timothy 4:21

2. Anencletus succeeded him, and after Anencletus, in the third place from the apostles, Clement received the episcopate. He had seen and conversed with the blessed apostles, and their preaching was still

sounding in his ears, and their tradition was still before his eyes. Nor was he alone in this, for many who had been taught by the apostles yet survived.

3. In the times of Clement, a serious dissension having arisen among the brethren in Corinth, the church of Rome sent a most suitable letter to the Corinthians, reconciling them in peace, renewing their faith, and proclaiming the doctrine lately received from the apostles.

4. A little farther on he says: Evarestus succeeded Clement, and Alexander, Evarestus. Then Xystus, the sixth from the apostles, was appointed. After him Telesphorus, who suffered martyrdom gloriously; then Hyginus; then Pius; and after him Anicetus; Soter succeeded Anicetus; and now, in the twelfth place from the apostles, Eleutherus holds the office of bishop.

5. In the same order and succession the tradition in the Church and the preaching of the truth has descended from the apostles unto us.

Chapter 7. Even down to those Times Miracles were performed by the Faithful.

1. These things Irenæus, in agreement with the accounts already given by us, records in the work which comprises five books, and to which he gave the title Refutation and Overthrow of the Knowledge Falsely So-called. In the second book of the same treatise he shows that manifestations of divine and miraculous power continued to his time in some of the churches.

2. He says: But so far do they come short of raising the dead, as the Lord raised them, and the apostles through prayer. And oftentimes in the brotherhood, when, on account of some necessity, our entire Church has besought with fasting and much supplication, the spirit of the dead has returned, and the man has been restored through the prayers of the saints.

3. And again, after other remarks, he says: If they will say that even the Lord did these things in mere appearance, we will refer them to the prophetic writings, and show from them that all things were beforehand spoken of him in this manner, and were strictly fulfilled; and that he alone is the Son of God. Wherefore his true disciples, receiving grace from him, perform such works in his Name for the benefit of other men, as each has received the gift from him.

4. For some of them drive out demons effectually and truly, so that those who have been cleansed from evil spirits frequently believe and unite with the Church. Others have a foreknowledge of future events, and visions, and prophetic revelations. Still others heal the sick by the laying on of hands, and restore them to health. And, as we have said, even dead persons have been raised, and remained with us many years.

5. But why should we say more? It is not possible to recount the number of gifts which the Church, throughout all the world, has received from God in the name of Jesus Christ, who was crucified under Pontius Pilate, and exercises every day for the benefit of the heathen, never deceiving any nor doing it for money. For as she has received freely from God, freely also does she minister.

6. And in another place the same author writes:

As also we hear that many brethren in the Church possess prophetic gifts, and speak, through the Spirit, with all kinds of tongues, and bring to light the secret things of men for their good, and declare the mysteries of God.

So much in regard to the fact that various gifts remained among those who were worthy even until that time.

Chapter 8. The Statements of Irenæus in regard to the Divine Scriptures.

1. Since, in the beginning of this work, we promised to give, when needful, the words of the ancient presbyters and writers of the Church, in which they have declared those traditions which came down to them concerning the canonical books, and since Irenæus was one of them, we will now give his words and, first, what he says of the sacred Gospels:

2. Matthew published his Gospel among the Hebrews in their own language, while Peter and Paul were preaching and founding the church in Rome.

3. After their departure Mark, the disciple and interpreter of Peter, also transmitted to us in writing those things which Peter had preached; and Luke, the attendant of Paul, recorded in a book the Gospel which Paul had declared.

4. Afterwards John, the disciple of the Lord, who also reclined on his bosom, published his Gospel, while staying at Ephesus in Asia.

5. He states these things in the third book of his above-mentioned work. In the fifth book he speaks as follows concerning the Apocalypse of John, and the number of the name of Antichrist:

As these things are so, and this number is found in all the approved and ancient copies, and those who saw John face to face confirm it, and reason teaches us that the number of the name of the beast, according to the mode of calculation among the Greeks, appears in its letters....

6. And further on he says concerning the same: We are not bold enough to speak confidently of the name of Antichrist. For if it were necessary that his name should be declared clearly at the present time, it would have been announced by him who saw the revelation. For it was seen, not long ago, but almost in our generation, toward the end of the reign of Domitian.

7. He states these things concerning the Apocalypse in the work referred to. He also mentions the first Epistle of John, taking many proofs from it, and likewise the first Epistle of Peter. And he not only knows, but also receives, The Shepherd, writing as follows: Well did the Scripture speak, saying, 'First of all believe that God is one, who has created and completed all things,' etc.

8. And he uses almost the precise words of the Wisdom of Solomon, saying: The vision of God produces immortality, but immortality renders us near to God. He mentions also the memoirs of a certain apostolic presbyter, whose name he passes by in silence, and gives his expositions of the sacred Scriptures.

9. And he refers to Justin the Martyr, and to Ignatius, using testimonies also from their writings. Moreover, he promises to refute Marcion from his own writings, in a special work.

10. Concerning the translation of the inspired Scriptures by the Seventy, hear the very words which he writes: God in truth became man, and the Lord himself saved us, giving the sign of the virgin; but not as some say, who now venture to translate the Scripture, 'Behold, a young woman shall conceive and bring forth a son,' as Theodotion of Ephesus and Aquila of Pontus, both of them Jewish proselytes, interpreted; following whom, the Ebionites say that he was begotten by Joseph.

11. Shortly after he adds: For before the Romans had established their empire, while the Macedonians were still holding Asia, Ptolemy, the son of Lagus, being desirous of adorning the library which he had founded in Alexandria with the meritorious writings of all men, requested the

people of Jerusalem to have their Scriptures translated into the Greek language.

12. But, as they were then subject to the Macedonians, they sent to Ptolemy seventy elders, who were the most skilled among them in the Scriptures and in both languages. Thus God accomplished his purpose.

13. But wishing to try them individually, as he feared lest, by taking counsel together, they might conceal the truth of the Scriptures by their interpretation, he separated them from one another, and commanded all of them to write the same translation. He did this for all the books.

14. But when they came together in the presence of Ptolemy, and compared their several translations, God was glorified, and the Scriptures were recognized as truly divine. For all of them had rendered the same things in the same words and with the same names from beginning to end, so that the heathen perceived that the Scriptures had been translated by the inspiration of God.

15. And this was nothing wonderful for God to do, who, in the captivity of the people under Nebuchadnezzar, when the Scriptures had been destroyed, and the Jews had returned to their own country after seventy years, afterwards, in the time of Artaxerxes, king of the Persians, inspired Ezra the priest, of the tribe of Levi, to relate all the words of the former prophets, and to restore to the people the legislation of Moses.

Such are the words of Irenæus.

Chapter 9. The Bishops under Commodus.

1. After Antoninus had been emperor for nineteen years, Commodus received the government. In his first year Julian became bishop of the Alexandrian churches, after Agripinnus had held the office for twelve years.

Chapter 10. Pantænus the Philosopher.

1. About that time, Pantænus, a man highly distinguished for his learning, had charge of the school of the faithful in Alexandria. A school of sacred learning, which continues to our day, was established there in ancient times, and as we have been informed, was managed by men of great ability and zeal for divine things. Among these it is reported that

Pantænus was at that time especially conspicuous, as he had been educated in the philosophical system of those called Stoics.

2. They say that he displayed such zeal for the divine Word, that he was appointed as a herald of the Gospel of Christ to the nations in the East, and was sent as far as India. For indeed there were still many evangelists of the Word who sought earnestly to use their inspired zeal, after the examples of the apostles, for the increase and building up of the Divine Word.

3. Pantænus was one of these, and is said to have gone to India. It is reported that among persons there who knew of Christ, he found the Gospel according to Matthew, which had anticipated his own arrival. For Bartholomew, one of the apostles, had preached to them, and left with them the writing of Matthew in the Hebrew language, which they had preserved till that time.

4. After many good deeds, Pantænus finally became the head of the school at Alexandria, and expounded the treasures of divine doctrine both orally and in writing.

Chapter 11. Clement of Alexandria.

1. At this time Clement, being trained with him in the divine Scriptures at Alexandria, became well known. He had the same name as the one who anciently was at the head of the Roman church, and who was a disciple of the apostles.

2. In his Hypotyposes he speaks of Pantænus by name as his teacher. It seems to me that he alludes to the same person also in the first book of his Stromata, when, referring to the more conspicuous of the successors of the apostles whom he had met, he says:

3. This work is not a writing artfully constructed for display; but my notes are stored up for old age, as a remedy against forgetfulness; an image without art, and a rough sketch of those powerful and animated words which it was my privilege to hear, as well as of blessed and truly remarkable men.

4. Of these the one— the Ionian — was in Greece, the other in Magna Græcia; the one of them was from Cœle-Syria, the other from Egypt. There were others in the East, one of them an Assyrian, the other a Hebrew in Palestine. But when I met with the last, — in ability truly he

was first—having hunted him out in his concealment in Egypt, I found rest.

5. These men, preserving the true tradition of the blessed doctrine, directly from the holy apostles, Peter and James and John and Paul, the son receiving it from the father (but few were like the fathers), have come by God's will even to us to deposit those ancestral and apostolic seeds.

Chapter 12. The Bishops in Jerusalem.

1. At this time Narcissus was the bishop of the church at Jerusalem, and he is celebrated by many to this day. He was the fifteenth in succession from the siege of the Jews under Adrian. We have shown that from that time first the church in Jerusalem was composed of Gentiles, after those of the circumcision, and that Marcus was the first Gentile bishop that presided over them.

2. After him the succession in the episcopate was: first Cassianus; after him Publius; then Maximus; following them Julian; then Gaius; after him Symmachus and another Gaius, and again another Julian; after these Capito and Valens and Dolichianus; and after all of them Narcissus, the thirtieth in regular succession from the apostles.

Chapter 13. Rhodo and his Account of the Dissension of Marcion.

1. At this time Rhodo, a native of Asia, who had been instructed, as he himself states, by Tatian, with whom we have already become acquainted, having written several books, published among the rest one against the heresy of Marcion. He says that this heresy was divided in his time into various opinions; and while describing those who occasioned the division, he refutes accurately the falsehoods devised by each of them.

2. But hear what he writes:

Therefore also they disagree among themselves, maintaining an inconsistent opinion. For Apelles, one of the herd, priding himself on his manner of life and his age, acknowledges one principle, but says that the prophecies are from an opposing spirit, being led to this view by the responses of a maiden by name Philumene, who was possessed by a demon.

3. But others, among whom are Potitus and Basilicus, hold to two principles, as does the mariner Marcion himself.

4. These following the wolf of Pontus, and, like him, unable to fathom the division of things, became reckless, and without giving any proof asserted two principles. Others, again, drifting into a worse error, consider that there are not only two, but three natures. Of these, Syneros is the leader and chief, as those who defend his teaching say.

5. The same author writes that he engaged in conversation with Apelles. He speaks as follows:

For the old man Apelles, when conversing with us, was refuted in many things which he spoke falsely; whence also he said that it was not at all necessary to examine one's doctrine, but that each one should continue to hold what he believed. For he asserted that those who trusted in the Crucified would be saved, if only they were found doing good works. But as we have said before, his opinion concerning God was the most obscure of all. For he spoke of one principle, as also our doctrine does.

6. Then, after stating fully his own opinion, he adds:

When I said to him, Tell me how you know this or how can you assert that there is one principle, he replied that the prophecies refuted themselves, because they have said nothing true; for they are inconsistent, and false, and self-contradictory. But how there is one principle he said that he did not know, but that he was thus persuaded.

7. As I then adjured him to speak the truth, he swore that he did so when he said that he did not know how there is one unbegotten God, but that he believed it. Thereupon I laughed and reproved him because, though calling himself a teacher, he knew not how to confirm what he taught.

8. In the same work, addressing Callistio, the same writer acknowledges that he had been instructed at Rome by Tatian. And he says that a book of Problems had been prepared by Tatian, in which he promised to explain the obscure and hidden parts of the divine Scriptures. Rhodo himself promises to give in a work of his own solutions of Tatian's problems. There is also extant a Commentary of his on the Hexæmeron.

9. But this Apelles wrote many things, in an impious manner, of the law of Moses, blaspheming the divine words in many of his works, being, as it seemed, very zealous for their refutation and overthrow.

So much concerning these.

Chapter 14. The False Prophets of the Phrygians.

The enemy of God's Church, who is emphatically a hater of good and a lover of evil, and leaves untried no manner of craft against men, was again active in causing strange heresies to spring up against the Church. For some persons, like venomous reptiles, crawled over Asia and Phrygia, boasting that Montanus was the Paraclete, and that the women that followed him, Priscilla and Maximilla, were prophetesses of Montanus.

Chapter 15. The Schism of Blastus at Rome.

Others, of whom Florinus was chief, flourished at Rome. He fell from the presbyterate of the Church, and Blastus was involved in a similar fall. They also drew away many of the Church to their opinion, each striving to introduce his own innovations in respect to the truth.

Chapter 16. The Circumstances related of Montanus and his False Prophets.

1. Against the so-called Phrygian heresy, the power which always contends for the truth raised up a strong and invincible weapon, Apolinarius of Hierapolis, whom we have mentioned before, and with him many other men of ability, by whom abundant material for our history has been left.

2. A certain one of these, in the beginning of his work against them, first intimates that he had contended with them in oral controversies.

3. He commences his work in this manner:

Having for a very long and sufficient time, O beloved Avircius Marcellus, been urged by you to write a treatise against the heresy of those who are called after Miltiades, I have hesitated till the present time, not through lack of ability to refute the falsehood or bear testimony for the truth, but from fear and apprehension that I might seem to some to be making additions to the doctrines or precepts of the Gospel of the New Testament, which it is impossible for one who has chosen to live according to the Gospel, either to increase or to diminish.

4. But being recently in Ancyra in Galatia, I found the church there greatly agitated by this novelty, not prophecy, as they call it, but rather

false prophecy, as will be shown. Therefore, to the best of our ability, with the Lord's help, we disputed in the church many days concerning these and other matters separately brought forward by them, so that the church rejoiced and was strengthened in the truth, and those of the opposite side were for the time confounded, and the adversaries were grieved.

5. The presbyters in the place, our fellow presbyter Zoticus of Otrous also being present, requested us to leave a record of what had been said against the opposers of the truth. We did not do this, but we promised to write it out as soon as the Lord permitted us, and to send it to them speedily.

6. Having said this with other things, in the beginning of his work, he proceeds to state the cause of the above-mentioned heresy as follows: Their opposition and their recent heresy which has separated them from the Church arose on the following account.

7. There is said to be a certain village called Ardabau in that part of Mysia, which borders upon Phrygia. There first, they say, when Gratus was proconsul of Asia, a recent convert, Montanus by name, through his unquenchable desire for leadership, gave the adversary opportunity against him. And he became beside himself, and being suddenly in a sort of frenzy and ecstasy, he raved, and began to babble and utter strange things, prophesying in a manner contrary to the constant custom of the Church handed down by tradition from the beginning.

8. Some of those who heard his spurious utterances at that time were indignant, and they rebuked him as one that was possessed, and that was under the control of a demon, and was led by a deceitful spirit, and was distracting the multitude; and they forbade him to talk, remembering the distinction drawn by the Lord and his warning to guard watchfully against the coming of false prophets. Matthew 7:15 But others imagining themselves possessed of the Holy Spirit and of a prophetic gift, were elated and not a little puffed up; and forgetting the distinction of the Lord, they challenged the mad and insidious and seducing spirit, and were cheated and deceived by him. In consequence of this, he could no longer be held in check, so as to keep silence.

9. Thus by artifice, or rather by such a system of wicked craft, the devil, devising destruction for the disobedient, and being unworthily honored by them, secretly excited and inflamed their understandings which had already become estranged from the true faith. And he stirred up besides two women, and filled them with the false spirit, so that they talked

wildly and unreasonably and strangely, like the person already mentioned. And the spirit pronounced them blessed as they rejoiced and gloried in him, and puffed them up by the magnitude of his promises. But sometimes he rebuked them openly in a wise and faithful manner, that he might seem to be a reprover. But those of the Phrygians that were deceived were few in number.

And the arrogant spirit taught them to revile the entire universal Church under heaven, because the spirit of false prophecy received neither honor from it nor entrance into it.

10. For the faithful in Asia met often in many places throughout Asia to consider this matter, and examined the novel utterances and pronounced them profane, and rejected the heresy, and thus these persons were expelled from the Church and debarred from communion.

11. Having related these things at the outset, and continued the refutation of their delusion through his entire work, in the second book he speaks as follows of their end:

12. Since, therefore, they called us slayers of the prophets because we did not receive their loquacious prophets, who, they say, are those that the Lord promised to send to the people, Matthew 23:34 let them answer as in God's presence: Who is there, O friends, of these who began to talk, from Montanus and the women down, that was persecuted by the Jews, or slain by lawless men? None. Or has any of them been seized and crucified for the Name? Truly not. Or has one of these women ever been scourged in the synagogues of the Jews, or stoned? No; never anywhere.

13. But by another kind of death Montanus and Maximilla are said to have died. For the report is that, incited by the spirit of frenzy, they both hung themselves; not at the same time, but at the time which common report gives for the death of each. And thus they died, and ended their lives like the traitor Judas.

14. So also, as general report says, that remarkable person, the first steward, as it were, of their so-called prophecy, one Theodotus who, as if at sometime taken up and received into heaven, fell into trances, and entrusted himself to the deceitful spirit— was pitched like a quoit, and died miserably.

15. They say that these things happened in this manner. But as we did not see them, O friend, we do not pretend to know. Perhaps in such a

manner, perhaps not, Montanus and Theodotus and the above-mentioned woman died.

16. He says again in the same book that the holy bishops of that time attempted to refute the spirit in Maximilla, but were prevented by others who plainly co-operated with the spirit.

17. He writes as follows: And let not the spirit, in the same work of Asterius Urbanus, say through Maximilla, 'I am driven away from the sheep like a wolf. I am not a wolf. I am word and spirit and power.' But let him show clearly and prove the power in the spirit. And by the spirit let him compel those to confess him who were then present for the purpose of proving and reasoning with the talkative spirit,— those eminent men and bishops, Zoticus, from the village Comana, and Julian, from Apamea, whose mouths the followers of Themiso muzzled, refusing to permit the false and seductive spirit to be refuted by them.

18. Again in the same work, after saying other things in refutation of the false prophecies of Maximilla, he indicates the time when he wrote these accounts, and mentions her predictions in which she prophesied wars and anarchy. Their falsehood he censures in the following manner:

19. And has not this been shown clearly to be false? For it is today more than thirteen years since the woman died, and there has been neither a partial nor general war in the world; but rather, through the mercy of God, continued peace even to the Christians. These things are taken from the second book.

20. I will add also short extracts from the third book, in which he speaks thus against their boasts that many of them had suffered martyrdom: When therefore they are at a loss, being refuted in all that they say, they try to take refuge in their martyrs, alleging that they have many martyrs, and that this is sure evidence of the power of the so-called prophetic spirit that is with them. But this, as it appears, is entirely fallacious.

21. For some of the heresies have a great many martyrs; but surely we shall not on that account agree with them or confess that they hold the truth. And first, indeed, those called Marcionites, from the heresy of Marcion, say that they have a multitude of martyrs for Christ; yet they do not confess Christ himself in truth.

A little farther on he continues:

22. When those called to martyrdom from the Church for the truth of the faith have met with any of the so-called martyrs of the Phrygian heresy, they have separated from them, and died without any fellowship

with them, because they did not wish to give their assent to the spirit of Montanus and the women. And that this is true and took place in our own time in Apamea on the Mæander, among those who suffered martyrdom with Gaius and Alexander of Eumenia, is well known.

Chapter 17. Miltiades and His Works.

1. In this work he mentions a writer, Miltiades, stating that he also wrote a certain book against the above-mentioned heresy. After quoting some of their words, he adds: Having found these things in a certain work of theirs in opposition to the work of the brother Alcibiades, in which he shows that a prophet ought not to speak in ecstasy, I made an abridgment.

2. A little further on in the same work he gives a list of those who prophesied under the new covenant, among whom he enumerates a certain Ammia and Quadratus, saying: But the false prophet falls into an ecstasy, in which he is without shame or fear. Beginning with purposed ignorance, he passes on, as has been stated, to involuntary madness of soul.

3. They cannot show that one of the old or one of the new prophets was thus carried away in spirit. Neither can they boast of Agabus, or Judas, or Silas, or the daughters of Philip, or Ammia in Philadelphia, or Quadratus, or any others not belonging to them.

4. And again after a little he says: For if after Quadratus and Ammia in Philadelphia, as they assert, the women with Montanus received the prophetic gift, let them show who among them received it from Montanus and the women. For the apostle thought it necessary that the prophetic gift should continue in all the Church until the final coming. But they cannot show it, though this is the fourteenth year since the death of Maximilla.

5. He writes thus. But the Miltiades to whom he refers has left other monuments of his own zeal for the Divine Scriptures, in the discourses which he composed against the Greeks and against the Jews, answering each of them separately in two books. And in addition he addresses an apology to the earthly rulers, in behalf of the philosophy which he embraced.

Chapter 18. The Manner in which Apollonius refuted the Phrygians, and the Persons whom he Mentions.

1. As the so-called Phrygian heresy was still flourishing in Phrygia in his time, Apollonius also, an ecclesiastical writer, undertook its refutation, and wrote a special work against it, correcting in detail the false prophecies current among them and reproving the life of the founders of the heresy. But hear his own words respecting Montanus:

2. His actions and his teaching show who this new teacher is. This is he who taught the dissolution of marriage; who made laws for fasting; who named Pepuza and Tymion, small towns in Phrygia, Jerusalem, wishing to gather people to them from all directions; who appointed collectors of money; who contrived the receiving of gifts under the name of offerings; who provided salaries for those who preached his doctrine, that its teaching might prevail through gluttony.

3. He writes thus concerning Montanus; and a little farther on he writes as follows concerning his prophetesses: We show that these first prophetesses themselves, as soon as they were filled with the Spirit, abandoned their husbands. How falsely therefore they speak who call Prisca a virgin.

4. Afterwards he says: Does not all Scripture seem to you to forbid a prophet to receive gifts and money? When therefore I see the prophetess receiving gold and silver and costly garments, how can I avoid reproving her?

5. And again a little farther on he speaks thus concerning one of their confessors: So also Themiso, who was clothed with plausible covetousness, could not endure the sign of confession, but threw aside bonds for an abundance of possessions. Yet, though he should have been humble on this account, he dared to boast as a martyr, and in imitation of the apostle, he wrote a certain catholic epistle, to instruct those whose faith was better than his own, contending for words of empty sound, and blaspheming against the Lord and the apostles and the holy Church.

6. And again concerning others of those honored among them as martyrs, he writes as follows: Not to speak of many, let the prophetess herself tell us of Alexander, who called himself a martyr, with whom she is in the habit of banqueting, and who is worshipped by many. We need not mention his robberies and other daring deeds for which he was punished, but the archives contain them.

7. Which of these forgives the sins of the other? Does the prophet the robberies of the martyr, or the martyr the covetousness of the prophet? For although the Lord said, 'Provide neither gold, nor silver, neither two coats,' Matthew 10:9-10 these men, in complete opposition, transgress in respect to the possession of the forbidden things. For we will show that those whom they call prophets and martyrs gather their gain not only from rich men, but also from the poor, and orphans, and widows.

8. But if they are confident, let them stand up and discuss these matters, that if convicted they may hereafter cease transgressing. For the fruits of the prophet must be tried; 'for the tree is known by its fruit.' Matthew 12:33

9. But that those who wish may know concerning Alexander, he was tried by Æmilius Frontinus, proconsul at Ephesus; not on account of the Name, but for the robberies which he had committed, being already an apostate. Afterwards, having falsely declared for the name of the Lord, he was released, having deceived the faithful that were there. And his own parish, from which he came, did not receive him, because he was a robber. Those who wish to learn about him have the public records of Asia. And yet the prophet with whom he spent many years knows nothing about him!

10. Exposing him, through him we expose also the pretense of the prophet. We could show the same thing of many others. But if they are confident, let them endure the test.

11. Again, in another part of his work he speaks as follows of the prophets of whom they boast: If they deny that their prophets have received gifts, let them acknowledge this: that if they are convicted of receiving them, they are not prophets. And we will bring a multitude of proofs of this. But it is necessary that all the fruits of a prophet should be examined. Tell me, does a prophet dye his hair? Does a prophet stain his eyelids? Does a prophet delight in adornment? Does a prophet play with tables and dice? Does a prophet lend on usury? Let them confess whether these things are lawful or not; but I will show that they have been done by them.

12. This same Apollonius states in the same work that, at the time of his writing, it was the fortieth year since Montanus had begun his pretended prophecy.

13. And he says also that Zoticus, who was mentioned by the former writer, when Maximilla was pretending to prophesy in Pepuza, resisted

her and endeavored to refute the spirit that was working in her; but was prevented by those who agreed with her. He mentions also a certain Thraseas among the martyrs of that time.

He speaks, moreover, of a tradition that the Saviour commanded his apostles not to depart from Jerusalem for twelve years. He uses testimonies also from the Revelation of John, and he relates that a dead man had, through the Divine power, been raised by John himself in Ephesus. He also adds other things by which he fully and abundantly exposes the error of the heresy of which we have been speaking. These are the matters recorded by Apollonius.

Chapter 19. Serapion on the Heresy of the Phrygians.

1. Serapion, who, as report says, succeeded Maximinus at that time as bishop of the church of Antioch, mentions the works of Apolinarius against the above-mentioned heresy. And he alludes to him in a private letter to Caricus and Pontius, in which he himself exposes the same heresy, and adds the following words:

2. That you may see that the doings of this lying band of the new prophecy, so called, are an abomination to all the brotherhood throughout the world, I have sent you writings of the most blessed Claudius Apolinarius, bishop of Hierapolis in Asia.

3. In the same letter of Serapion the signatures of several bishops are found, one of whom subscribes himself as follows:

I, Aurelius Cyrenius, a witness, pray for your health. And another in this manner:

Ælius Publius Julius, bishop of Debeltum, a colony of Thrace. As God lives in the heavens, the blessed Sotas in Anchialus desired to cast the demon out of Priscilla, but the hypocrites did not permit him.

4. And the autograph signatures of many other bishops who agreed with them are contained in the same letter.

So much for these persons.

Chapter 20. The Writings of Irenæus against the Schismatics at Rome.

1. Irenæus wrote several letters against those who were disturbing the sound ordinance of the Church at Rome. One of them was to Blastus

On Schism; another to Florinus On Monarchy, or That God is not the Author of Evil. For Florinus seemed to be defending this opinion. And because he was being drawn away by the error of Valentinus, Irenæus wrote his work On the Ogdoad, in which he shows that he himself had been acquainted with the first successors of the apostles.

2. At the close of the treatise we have found a most beautiful note which we are constrained to insert in this work. It runs as follows:

I adjure you who may copy this book, by our Lord Jesus Christ, and by his glorious advent when he comes to judge the living and the dead, to compare what you shall write, and correct it carefully by this manuscript, and also to write this adjuration, and place it in the copy.

3. These things may be profitably read in his work, and related by us, that we may have those ancient and truly holy men as the best example of painstaking carefulness.

4. In the letter to Florinus, of which we have spoken, Irenæus mentions again his intimacy with Polycarp, saying:

These doctrines, O Florinus, to speak mildly, are not of sound judgment. These doctrines disagree with the Church, and drive into the greatest impiety those who accept them. These doctrines, not even the heretics outside of the Church, have ever dared to publish. These doctrines, the presbyters who were before us, and who were companions of the apostles, did not deliver to you.

5. For when I was a boy, I saw you in lower Asia with Polycarp, moving in splendor in the royal court, and endeavoring to gain his approbation.

6. I remember the events of that time more clearly than those of recent years. For what boys learn, growing with their mind, becomes joined with it; so that I am able to describe the very place in which the blessed Polycarp sat as he discoursed, and his goings out and his comings in, and the manner of his life, and his physical appearance, and his discourses to the people, and the accounts which he gave of his intercourse with John and with the others who had seen the Lord. And as he remembered their words, and what he heard from them concerning the Lord, and concerning his miracles and his teaching, having received them from eyewitnesses of the 'Word of life,' 1 John 1:1 Polycarp related all things in harmony with the Scriptures.

7. These things being told me by the mercy of God, I listened to them attentively, noting them down, not on paper, but in my heart. And continually, through God's grace, I recall them faithfully. And I am able

to bear witness before God that if that blessed and apostolic presbyter had heard any such thing, he would have cried out, and stopped his ears, and as was his custom, would have exclaimed, O good God, unto what times have you spared me that I should endure these things? And he would have fled from the place where, sitting or standing, he had heard such words.

8. And this can be shown plainly from the letters which he sent, either to the neighboring churches for their confirmation, or to some of the brethren, admonishing and exhorting them. Thus far Irenæus.

Chapter 21. How Appolonius suffered Martyrdom at Rome.

1. About the same time, in the reign of Commodus, our condition became more favorable, and through the grace of God the churches throughout the entire world enjoyed peace, and the word of salvation was leading every soul, from every race of man to the devout worship of the God of the universe. So that now at Rome many who were highly distinguished for wealth and family turned with all their household and relatives unto their salvation.

2. But the demon who hates what is good, being malignant in his nature, could not endure this, but prepared himself again for conflict, contriving many devices against us. And he brought to the judgment seat Apollonius, of the city of Rome, a man renowned among the faithful for learning and philosophy, having stirred up one of his servants, who was well fitted for such a purpose, to accuse him.

3. But this wretched man made the charge unseasonably, because by a royal decree it was unlawful that informers of such things should live. And his legs were broken immediately, Perennius the judge having pronounced this sentence upon him.

4. But the martyr, highly beloved of God, being earnestly entreated and requested by the judge to give an account of himself before the Senate, made in the presence of all an eloquent defense of the faith for which he was witnessing. And as if by decree of the Senate he was put to death by decapitation; an ancient law requiring that those who were brought to the judgment seat and refused to recant should not be liberated. Whoever desires to know his arguments before the judge and his answers to the questions of Perennius, and his entire defense before the Senate will find them in the records of the ancient martyrdoms which we have collected.

Chapter 22. The Bishops that were well known at this Time.

In the tenth year of the reign of Commodus, Victor succeeded Eleutherus, the latter having held the episcopate for thirteen years. In the same year, after Julian had completed his tenth year, Demetrius received the charge of the parishes at Alexandria. At this time the above-mentioned Serapion, the eighth from the apostles, was still well known as bishop of the church at Antioch. Theophilus presided at Cæsarea in Palestine; and Narcissus, whom we have mentioned before, still had charge of the church at Jerusalem. Bacchylus at the same time was bishop of Corinth in Greece, and Polycrates of the parish of Ephesus. And besides these a multitude of others, as is likely, were then prominent. But we have given the names of those alone, the soundness of whose faith has come down to us in writing.

Chapter 23. The Question then agitated concerning the Passover.

1. A question of no small importance arose at that time. For the parishes of all Asia, as from an older tradition, held that the fourteenth day of the moon, on which day the Jews were commanded to sacrifice the lamb, should be observed as the feast of the Saviour's passover. It was therefore necessary to end their fast on that day, whatever day of the week it should happen to be. But it was not the custom of the churches in the rest of the world to end it at this time, as they observed the practice which, from apostolic tradition, has prevailed to the present time, of terminating the fast on no other day than on that of the resurrection of our Saviour.

2. Synods and assemblies of bishops were held on this account, and all, with one consent, through mutual correspondence drew up an ecclesiastical decree, that the mystery of the resurrection of the Lord should be celebrated on no other but the Lord's day, and that we should observe the close of the paschal fast on this day only. There is still extant a writing of those who were then assembled in Palestine, over whom Theophilus, bishop of Cæsarea, and Narcissus, bishop of Jerusalem, presided. And there is also another writing extant of those who were assembled at Rome to consider the same question, which bears the name of Bishop Victor; also of the bishops in Pontus over whom Palmas, as the oldest, presided; and of the parishes in Gaul of which Irenæus was bishop, and of those in Osrhoëne and the cities there; and a personal

letter of Bacchylus, bishop of the church at Corinth, and of a great many others, who uttered the same opinion and judgment, and cast the same vote.

3. And that which has been given above was their unanimous decision.

Chapter 24. The Disagreement in Asia.

1. But the bishops of Asia, led by Polycrates, decided to hold to the old custom handed down to them. He himself, in a letter which he addressed to Victor and the church of Rome, set forth in the following words the tradition which had come down to him:

2. We observe the exact day; neither adding, nor taking away. For in Asia also great lights have fallen asleep, which shall rise again on the day of the Lord's coming, when he shall come with glory from heaven, and shall seek out all the saints. Among these are Philip, one of the twelve apostles, who fell asleep in Hierapolis; and his two aged virgin daughters, and another daughter, who lived in the Holy Spirit and now rests at Ephesus; and, moreover, John, who was both a witness and a teacher, who reclined upon the bosom of the Lord, and, being a priest, wore the sacerdotal plate.

3. He fell asleep at Ephesus.

4. And Polycarp in Smyrna, who was a bishop and martyr; and Thraseas, bishop and martyr from Eumenia, who fell asleep in Smyrna.

5. Why need I mention the bishop and martyr Sagaris who fell asleep in Laodicea, or the blessed Papirius, or Melito, the Eunuch who lived altogether in the Holy Spirit, and who lies in Sardis, awaiting the episcopate from heaven, when he shall rise from the dead?

6. All these observed the fourteenth day of the passover according to the Gospel, deviating in no respect, but following the rule of faith. And I also, Polycrates, the least of you all, do according to the tradition of my relatives, some of whom I have closely followed. For seven of my relatives were bishops; and I am the eighth. And my relatives always observed the day when the people put away the leaven.

7. I, therefore, brethren, who have lived sixty-five years in the Lord, and have met with the brethren throughout the world, and have gone through every Holy Scripture, am not affrighted by terrifying words. For those greater than I have said 'We ought to obey God rather than man.' Acts 5:29

8. He then writes of all the bishops who were present with him and thought as he did. His words are as follows:

I could mention the bishops who were present, whom I summoned at your desire; whose names, should I write them, would constitute a great multitude. And they, beholding my littleness, gave their consent to the letter, knowing that I did not bear my gray hairs in vain, but had always governed my life by the Lord Jesus.

9. Thereupon Victor, who presided over the church at Rome, immediately attempted to cut off from the common unity the parishes of all Asia, with the churches that agreed with them, as heterodox; and he wrote letters and declared all the brethren there wholly excommunicate.

10. But this did not please all the bishops. And they besought him to consider the things of peace, and of neighborly unity and love. Words of theirs are extant, sharply rebuking Victor.

11. Among them was Irenæus, who, sending letters in the name of the brethren in Gaul over whom he presided, maintained that the mystery of the resurrection of the Lord should be observed only on the Lord's day. He fittingly admonishes Victor that he should not cut off whole churches of God which observed the tradition of an ancient custom and after many other words he proceeds as follows:

12. For the controversy is not only concerning the day, but also concerning the very manner of the fast. For some think that they should fast one day, others two, yet others more; some, moreover, count their day as consisting of forty hours day and night.

13. And this variety in its observance has not originated in our time; but long before in that of our ancestors. It is likely that they did not hold to strict accuracy, and thus formed a custom for their posterity according to their own simplicity and peculiar mode. Yet all of these lived none the less in peace, and we also live in peace with one another; and the disagreement in regard to the fast confirms the agreement in the faith.

14. He adds to this the following account, which I may properly insert:

Among these were the presbyters before Soter, who presided over the church which you now rule. We mean Anicetus, and Pius, and Hyginus, and Telesphorus, and Xystus. They neither observed it themselves, nor did they permit those after them to do so. And yet though not observing it, they were none the less at peace with those who came to them from the parishes in which it was observed; although this observance was more opposed to those who did not observe it.

15. But none were ever cast out on account of this form; but the presbyters before you who did not observe it, sent the eucharist to those of other parishes who observed it.

16. And when the blessed Polycarp was at Rome in the time of Anicetus, and they disagreed a little about certain other things, they immediately made peace with one another, not caring to quarrel over this matter. For neither could Anicetus persuade Polycarp not to observe what he had always observed with John the disciple of our Lord, and the other apostles with whom he had associated; neither could Polycarp persuade Anicetus to observe it as he said that he ought to follow the customs of the presbyters that had preceded him.

17. But though matters were in this shape, they communed together, and Anicetus conceded the administration of the eucharist in the church to Polycarp, manifestly as a mark of respect. And they parted from each other in peace, both those who observed, and those who did not, maintaining the peace of the whole church.

18. Thus Irenæus, who truly was well named, became a peacemaker in this matter, exhorting and negotiating in this way in behalf of the peace of the churches. And he conferred by letter about this mooted question, not only with Victor, but also with most of the other rulers of the churches.

Chapter 25. How All came to an Agreement respecting the Passover.

1. Those in Palestine whom we have recently mentioned, Narcissus and Theophilus, and with them Cassius, bishop of the church of Tyre, and Clarus of the church of Ptolemais, and those who met with them, having stated many things respecting the tradition concerning the passover which had come to them in succession from the apostles, at the close of their writing add these words:

2. Endeavor to send copies of our letter to every church, that we may not furnish occasion to those who easily deceive their souls. We show you indeed that also in Alexandria they keep it on the same day that we do. For letters are carried from us to them and from them to us, so that in the same manner and at the same time we keep the sacred day.

Chapter 26. The Elegant Works of Irenæus which have come down to us.

Besides the works and letters of Irenæus which we have mentioned, a certain book of his On Knowledge, written against the Greeks, very concise and remarkably forcible, is extant; and another, which he dedicated to a brother Marcian, In Demonstration of the Apostolic Preaching; and a volume containing various Dissertations, in which he mentions the Epistle to the Hebrews and the so-called Wisdom of Solomon, making quotations from them. These are the works of Irenæus which have come to our knowledge.

Commodus having ended his reign after thirteen years, Severus became emperor in less than six months after his death, Pertinax having reigned during the intervening time.

Chapter 27. The Works of Others that flourished at that Time.

Numerous memorials of the faithful zeal of the ancient ecclesiastical men of that time are still preserved by many. Of these we would note particularly the writings of Heraclitus On the Apostle, and those of Maximus on the question so much discussed among heretics, the Origin of Evil, and on the Creation of Matter. Also those of Candidus on the Hexæmeron, and of Apion on the same subject; likewise of Sextus on the Resurrection, and another treatise of Arabianus, and writings of a multitude of others, in regard to whom, because we have no data, it is impossible to state in our work when they lived, or to give any account of their history. And works of many others have come down to us whose names we are unable to give, orthodox and ecclesiastical, as their interpretations of the Divine Scriptures show, but unknown to us, because their names are not stated in their writings.

Chapter 28. Those who first advanced the Heresy of Artemon; their Manner of Life, and how they dared to corrupt the Sacred Scriptures.

1. In a laborious work by one of these writers against the heresy of Artemon, which Paul of Samosata attempted to revive again in our day, there is an account appropriate to the history which we are now examining.

2. For he criticises, as a late innovation, the above-mentioned heresy which teaches that the Saviour was a mere man, because they were

attempting to magnify it as ancient. Having given in his work many other arguments in refutation of their blasphemous falsehood, he adds the following words:

3. For they say that all the early teachers and the apostles received and taught what they now declare, and that the truth of the Gospel was preserved until the times of Victor, who was the thirteenth bishop of Rome from Peter, but that from his successor, Zephyrinus, the truth had been corrupted.

4. And what they say might be plausible, if first of all the Divine Scriptures did not contradict them. And there are writings of certain brethren older than the times of Victor, which they wrote in behalf of the truth against the heathen, and against the heresies which existed in their day. I refer to Justin and Miltiades and Tatian and Clement and many others, in all of whose works Christ is spoken of as God.

5. For who does not know the works of Irenæus and of Melito and of others which teach that Christ is God and man? And how many psalms and hymns, written by the faithful brethren from the beginning, celebrate Christ the Word of God, speaking of him as Divine.

6. How then since the opinion held by the Church has been preached for so many years, can its preaching have been delayed as they affirm, until the times of Victor? And how is it that they are not ashamed to speak thus falsely of Victor, knowing well that he cut off from communion Theodotus, the cobbler, the leader and father of this God-denying apostasy, and the first to declare that Christ is mere man? For if Victor agreed with their opinions, as their slander affirms, how came he to cast out Theodotus, the inventor of this heresy?

7. So much in regard to Victor. His bishopric lasted ten years, and Zephyrinus was appointed his successor about the ninth year of the reign of Severus. The author of the above-mentioned book, concerning the founder of this heresy, narrates another event which occurred in the time of Zephyrinus, using these words:

8. I will remind many of the brethren of a fact which took place in our time, which, had it happened in Sodom, might, I think, have proved a warning to them. There was a certain confessor, Natalius, not long ago, but in our own day.

9. This man was deceived at one time by Asclepiodotus and another Theodotus, a money-changer. Both of them were disciples of Theodotus, the cobbler, who, as I have said, was the first person

excommunicated by Victor, bishop at that time, on account of this sentiment, or rather senselessness.

10. Natalius was persuaded by them to allow himself to be chosen bishop of this heresy with a salary, to be paid by them, of one hundred and fifty denarii a month.

11. When he had thus connected himself with them, he was warned oftentimes by the Lord through visions. For the compassionate God and our Lord Jesus Christ was not willing that a witness of his own sufferings, being cast out of the Church, should perish.

12. But as he paid little regard to the visions, because he was ensnared by the first position among them and by that shameful covetousness which destroys a great many, he was scourged by holy angels, and punished severely through the entire night. Thereupon having risen in the morning, he put on sackcloth and covered himself with ashes, and with great haste and tears he fell down before Zephyrinus, the bishop, rolling at the feet not only of the clergy, but also of the laity; and he moved with his tears the compassionate Church of the merciful Christ. And though he used much supplication, and showed the welts of the stripes which he had received, yet scarcely was he taken back into communion.

13. We will add from the same writer some other extracts concerning them, which run as follows:

They have treated the Divine Scriptures recklessly and without fear. They have set aside the rule of ancient faith; and Christ they have not known. They do not endeavor to learn what the Divine Scriptures declare, but strive laboriously after any form of syllogism which may be devised to sustain their impiety. And if any one brings before them a passage of Divine Scripture, they see whether a conjunctive or disjunctive form of syllogism can be made from it.

14. And as being of the earth and speaking of the earth, and as ignorant of him who comes from above, they forsake the holy writings of God to devote themselves to geometry. Euclid is laboriously measured by some of them; and Aristotle and Theophrastus are admired; and Galen, perhaps, by some is even worshipped.

15. But that those who use the arts of unbelievers for their heretical opinions and adulterate the simple faith of the Divine Scriptures by the craft of the godless, are far from the faith, what need is there to say?

Therefore they have laid their hands boldly upon the Divine Scriptures, alleging that they have corrected them.

16. That I am not speaking falsely of them in this matter, whoever wishes may learn. For if any one will collect their respective copies, and compare them one with another, he will find that they differ greatly.

17. Those of Asclepiades, for example, do not agree with those of Theodotus. And many of these can be obtained, because their disciples have assiduously written the corrections, as they call them, that is the corruptions, of each of them. Again, those of Hermophilus do not agree with these, and those of Apollonides are not consistent with themselves. For you can compare those prepared by them at an earlier date with those which they corrupted later, and you will find them widely different.

18. But how daring this offense is, it is not likely that they themselves are ignorant. For either they do not believe that the Divine Scriptures were spoken by the Holy Spirit, and thus are unbelievers, or else they think themselves wiser than the Holy Spirit, and in that case what else are they than demoniacs? For they cannot deny the commission of the crime, since the copies have been written by their own hands. For they did not receive such Scriptures from their instructors, nor can they produce any copies from which they were transcribed.

19. But some of them have not thought it worth while to corrupt them, but simply deny the law and the prophets, and thus through their lawless and impious teaching under pretense of grace, have sunk to the lowest depths of perdition.

Let this suffice for these things.

BOOK VI

Chapter 1. The Persecution under Severus.

When Severus began to persecute the churches, glorious testimonies were given everywhere by the athletes of religion. This was especially the case in Alexandria, to which city, as to a most prominent theater, athletes of God were brought from Egypt and all Thebais according to their merit, and won crowns from God through their great patience under many tortures and every mode of death. Among these was Leonides, who was called the father of Origen, and who was beheaded while his son was still young. How remarkable the predilection of this son was for the Divine Word, in consequence of his father's instruction, it will not be amiss to state briefly, as his fame has been very greatly celebrated by many.

Chapter 2. The Training of Origenfrom Childhood.

1. Many things might be said in attempting to describe the life of the man while in school; but this subject alone would require a separate treatise. Nevertheless, for the present, abridging most things, we shall state a few facts concerning him as briefly as possible, gathering them from certain letters, and from the statement of persons still living who were acquainted with him.

2. What they report of Origen seems to me worthy of mention, even, so to speak, from his swathing-bands.

It was the tenth year of the reign of Severus, while Lætus was governor of Alexandria and the rest of Egypt, and Demetrius had lately received the episcopate of the parishes there, as successor of Julian.

3. As the flame of persecution had been kindled greatly, and multitudes had gained the crown of martyrdom, such desire for martyrdom seized the soul of Origen, although yet a boy, that he went close to danger, springing forward and rushing to the conflict in his eagerness.

4. And truly the termination of his life had been very near had not the divine and heavenly Providence, for the benefit of many, prevented his desire through the agency of his mother.

5. For, at first, entreating him, she begged him to have compassion on her motherly feelings toward him; but finding, that when he had learned that his father had been seized and imprisoned, he was set the more resolutely, and completely carried away with his zeal for martyrdom, she hid all his clothing, and thus compelled him to remain at home.

6. But, as there was nothing else that he could do, and his zeal beyond his age would not suffer him to be quiet, he sent to his father an encouraging letter on martyrdom, in which he exhorted him, saying, Take heed not to change your mind on our account. This may be recorded as the first evidence of Origen's youthful wisdom and of his genuine love for piety.

7. For even then he had stored up no small resources in the words of the faith, having been trained in the Divine Scriptures from childhood. And he had not studied them with indifference, for his father, besides

giving him the usual liberal education, had made them a matter of no secondary importance.

8. First of all, before inducting him into the Greek sciences, he drilled him in sacred studies, requiring him to learn and recite every day.

9. Nor was this irksome to the boy, but he was eager and diligent in these studies. And he was not satisfied with learning what was simple and obvious in the sacred words, but sought for something more, and even at that age busied himself with deeper speculations. So that he puzzled his father with inquiries for the true meaning of the inspired Scriptures.

10. And his father rebuked him seemingly to his face, telling him not to search beyond his age, or further than the manifest meaning. But by himself he rejoiced greatly and thanked God, the author of all good, that he had deemed him worthy to be the father of such a child.

11. And they say that often, standing by the boy when asleep, he uncovered his breast as if the Divine Spirit were enshrined within it, and kissed it reverently; considering himself blessed in his goodly offspring. These and other things like them are related of Origen when a boy.

12. But when his father ended his life in martyrdom, he was left with his mother and six younger brothers when he was not quite seventeen years old.

13. And the property of his father being confiscated to the royal treasury, he and his family were in want of the necessaries of life. But he was deemed worthy of Divine care. And he found welcome and rest with a woman of great wealth, and distinguished in her manner of life and in other respects. She was treating with great honor a famous heretic then in Alexandria; who, however, was born in Antioch. He was with her as an adopted son, and she treated him with the greatest kindness.

14. But although Origen was under the necessity of associating with him, he nevertheless gave from this time on strong evidences of his orthodoxy in the faith. For when on account of the apparent skill in argument of Paul—for this was the man's name—a great multitude came to him, not only of heretics but also of our people, Origen could never be induced to join with him in prayer; for he held, although a boy, the rule of the Church, and abominated, as he somewhere expresses it, heretical teachings. Having been instructed in the sciences of the Greeks by his father, he devoted him after his death more assiduously and exclusively to the study of literature, so that he obtained considerable

preparation in philology and was able not long after the death of his father, by devoting himself to that subject, to earn a compensation amply sufficient for his needs at his age.

Chapter 3. While still very Young, he taught diligently the Word of Christ.

1. But while he was lecturing in the school, as he tells us himself, and there was no one at Alexandria to give instruction in the faith, as all were driven away by the threat of persecution, some of the heathen came to him to hear the word of God.

2. The first of them, he says, was Plutarch, who after living well, was honored with divine martyrdom. The second was Heraclas, a brother of Plutarch; who after he too had given with him abundant evidence of a philosophic and ascetic life, was esteemed worthy to succeed Demetrius in the bishopric of Alexandria.

3. He was in his eighteenth year when he took charge of the catechetical school. He was prominent also at this time, during the persecution under Aquila, the governor of Alexandria, when his name became celebrated among the leaders in the faith, through the kindness and goodwill which he manifested toward all the holy martyrs, whether known to him or strangers.

4. For not only was he with them while in bonds, and until their final condemnation, but when the holy martyrs were led to death, he was very bold and went with them into danger. So that as he acted bravely, and with great boldness saluted the martyrs with a kiss, oftentimes the heathen multitude round about them became infuriated, and were on the point of rushing upon him.

5. But through the helping hand of God, he escaped absolutely and marvelously. And this same divine and heavenly power, again and again, it is impossible to say how often, on account of his great zeal and boldness for the words of Christ, guarded him when thus endangered. So great was the enmity of the unbelievers toward him, on account of the multitude that were instructed by him in the sacred faith, that they placed bands of soldiers around the house where he abode.

6. Thus day by day the persecution burned against him, so that the whole city could no longer contain him; but he removed from house to house and was driven in every direction because of the multitude who attended upon the divine instruction which he gave. For his life also exhibited

right and admirable conduct according to the practice of genuine philosophy.

7. For they say that his manner of life was as his doctrine, and his doctrine as his life. Therefore, by the divine Power working with him he aroused a great many to his own zeal.

8. But when he saw yet more coming to him for instruction, and the catechetical school had been entrusted to him alone by Demetrius, who presided over the church, he considered the teaching of grammatical science inconsistent with training in divine subjects, and immediately he gave up his grammatical school as unprofitable and a hindrance to sacred learning.

9. Then, with becoming consideration, that he might not need aid from others, he disposed of whatever valuable books of ancient literature he possessed, being satisfied with receiving from the purchaser four oboli a day. For many years he lived philosophically in this manner, putting away all the incentives of youthful desires. Through the entire day he endured no small amount of discipline; and for the greater part of the night he gave himself to the study of the Divine Scriptures. He restrained himself as much as possible by a most philosophic life; sometimes by the discipline of fasting, again by limited time for sleep. And in his zeal he never lay upon a bed, but upon the ground.

10. Most of all, he thought that the words of the Saviour in the Gospel should be observed, in which he exhorts not to have two coats nor to use shoes nor to occupy oneself with cares for the future.

11. With a zeal beyond his age he continued in cold and nakedness; and, going to the very extreme of poverty, he greatly astonished those about him. And indeed he grieved many of his friends who desired to share their possessions with him, on account of the wearisome toil which they saw him enduring in the teaching of divine things.

12. But he did not relax his perseverance. He is said to have walked for a number of years never wearing a shoe, and, for a great many years, to have abstained from the use of wine, and of all other things beyond his necessary food; so that he was in danger of breaking down and destroying his constitution.

13. By giving such evidences of a philosophic life to those who saw him, he aroused many of his pupils to similar zeal; so that prominent men even of the unbelieving heathen and men that followed learning and philosophy were led to his instruction. Some of them having received

from him into the depth of their souls faith in the Divine Word, became prominent in the persecution then prevailing; and some of them were seized and suffered martyrdom.

Chapter 4. The pupils of Origen that became Martyrs.

1. The first of these was Plutarch, who was mentioned just above. As he was led to death, the man of whom we are speaking being with him at the end of his life, came near being slain by his fellow citizens, as if he were the cause of his death. But the providence of God preserved him at this time also.

2. After Plutarch, the second martyr among the pupils of Origen was Serenus, who gave through fire a proof of the faith which he had received.

3. The third martyr from the same school was Heraclides, and after him the fourth was Hero. The former of these was as yet a catechumen, and the latter had but recently been baptized. Both of them were beheaded. After them, the fifth from the same school proclaimed as an athlete of piety was another Serenus, who, it is reported, was beheaded, after a long endurance of tortures. And of women, Herais died while yet a catechumen, receiving baptism by fire, as Origen himself somewhere says.

Chapter 5. Potamiæna.

1. Basilides may be counted the seventh of these. He led to martyrdom the celebrated Potamiæna, who is still famous among the people of the country for the many things which she endured for the preservation of her chastity and virginity. For she was blooming in the perfection of her mind and her physical graces. Having suffered much for the faith of Christ, finally after tortures dreadful and terrible to speak of, she with her mother, Marcella, was put to death by fire.

2. They say that the judge, Aquila by name, having inflicted severe tortures upon her entire body, at last threatened to hand her over to the gladiators for bodily abuse. After a little consideration, being asked for her decision, she made a reply which was regarded as impious.

3. Thereupon she received sentence immediately, and Basilides, one of the officers of the army, led her to death. But as the people attempted to annoy and insult her with abusive words, he drove back her insulters,

showing her much pity and kindness. And perceiving the man's sympathy for her, she exhorted him to be of good courage, for she would supplicate her Lord for him after her departure, and he would soon receive a reward for the kindness he had shown her.

4. Having said this, she nobly sustained the issue, burning pitch being poured little by little, over various parts of her body, from the sole of her feet to the crown of her head. Such was the conflict endured by this famous maiden.

5. Not long after this Basilides, being asked by his fellow-soldiers to swear for a certain reason, declared that it was not lawful for him to swear at all, for he was a Christian, and he confessed this openly. At first they thought that he was jesting, but when he continued to affirm it, he was led to the judge, and, acknowledging his conviction before him, he was imprisoned. But the brethren in God coming to him and inquiring the reason of this sudden and remarkable resolution, he is reported to have said that Potamiæna, for three days after her martyrdom, stood beside him by night and placed a crown on his head and said that she had besought the Lord for him and had obtained what she asked, and that soon she would take him with her.

6. Thereupon the brethren gave him the seal of the Lord; and on the next day, after giving glorious testimony for the Lord, he was beheaded. And many others in Alexandria are recorded to have accepted speedily the word of Christ in those times.

7. For Potamiæna appeared to them in their dreams and exhorted them. But let this suffice in regard to this matter.

Chapter 6. Clement of Alexandria.

Clement having succeeded Pantænus, had charge at that time of the catechetical instruction in Alexandria, so that Origen also, while still a boy, was one of his pupils. In the first book of the work called Stromata, which Clement wrote, he gives a chronological table, bringing events down to the death of Commodus. So it is evident that that work was written during the reign of Severus, whose times we are now recording.

Chapter 7. The Writer, Judas.

At this time another writer, Judas, discoursing about the seventy weeks in Daniel, brings down the chronology to the tenth year of the reign of

Severus. He thought that the coming of Antichrist, which was much talked about, was then near. So greatly did the agitation caused by the persecution of our people at this time disturb the minds of many.

Chapter 8. Origen's Daring Deed.

1. At this time while Origen was conducting catechetical instruction at Alexandria, a deed was done by him which evidenced an immature and youthful mind, but at the same time gave the highest proof of faith and continence. For he took the words, There are eunuchs who have made themselves eunuchs for the kingdom of heaven's sake, Matthew 19:12 in too literal and extreme a sense. And in order to fulfill the Saviour's word, and at the same time to take away from the unbelievers all opportunity for scandal,— for, although young, he met for the study of divine things with women as well as men,— he carried out in action the word of the Saviour.

2. He thought that this would not be known by many of his acquaintances. But it was impossible for him, though desiring to do so, to keep such an action secret.

3. When Demetrius, who presided over that parish, at last learned of this, he admired greatly the daring nature of the act, and as he perceived his zeal and the genuineness of his faith, he immediately exhorted him to courage, and urged him the more to continue his work of catechetical instruction.

4. Such was he at that time. But soon afterward, seeing that he was prospering, and becoming great and distinguished among all men, the same Demetrius, overcome by human weakness, wrote of his deed as most foolish to the bishops throughout the world. But the bishops of Cesarea and Jerusalem, who were especially notable and distinguished among the bishops of Palestine, considering Origen worthy in the highest degree of the honor, ordained him a presbyter.

5. Thereupon his fame increased greatly, and his name became renowned everywhere, and he obtained no small reputation for virtue and wisdom. But Demetrius, having nothing else that he could say against him, save this deed of his boyhood, accused him bitterly, and dared to include with him in these accusations those who had raised him to the presbyterate.

6. These things, however, took place a little later. But at this time Origen continued fearlessly the instruction in divine things at Alexandria by day

and night to all who came to him; devoting his entire leisure without cessation to divine studies and to his pupils.

7. Severus, having held the government for eighteen years, was succeeded by his son, Antoninus. Among those who had endured courageously the persecution of that time, and had been preserved by the Providence of God through the conflicts of confession, was Alexander, of whom we have spoken already as bishop of the church in Jerusalem. On account of his pre-eminence in the confession of Christ he was thought worthy of that bishopric, while Narcissus, his predecessor, was still living.

Chapter 9. The Miracles of Narcissus.

1. The citizens of that parish mention many other miracles of Narcissus, on the tradition of the brethren who succeeded him; among which they relate the following wonder as performed by him.

2. They say that the oil once failed while the deacons were watching through the night at the great paschal vigil. Thereupon the whole multitude being dismayed, Narcissus directed those who attended to the lights, to draw water and bring it to him.

3. This being immediately done he prayed over the water, and with firm faith in the Lord, commanded them to pour it into the lamps. And when they had done so, contrary to all expectation by a wonderful and divine power, the nature of the water was changed into that of oil. A small portion of it has been preserved even to our day by many of the brethren there as a memento of the wonder.

4. They tell many other things worthy to be noted of the life of this man, among which is this. Certain base men being unable to endure the strength and firmness of his life, and fearing punishment for the many evil deeds of which they were conscious, sought by plotting to anticipate him, and circulated a terrible slander against him.

5. And to persuade those who heard of it, they confirmed their accusations with oaths: one invoked upon himself destruction by fire; another the wasting of his body by a foul disease; the third the loss of his eyes. But though they swore in this manner, they could not affect the mind of the believers; because the continence and virtuous life of Narcissus were well known to all.

6. But he could not in any wise endure the wickedness of these men; and as he had followed a philosophic life for a long time, he fled from the whole body of the Church, and hid himself in desert and secret places, and remained there many years.

7. But the great eye of judgment was not unmoved by these things, but soon looked down upon these impious men, and brought on them the curses with which they had bound themselves. The residence of the first, from nothing but a little spark falling upon it, was entirely consumed by night, and he perished with all his family. The second was speedily covered with the disease which he had imprecated upon himself, from the sole of his feet to his head.

8. But the third, perceiving what had happened to the others, and fearing the inevitable judgment of God, the ruler of all, confessed publicly what they had plotted together. And in his repentance he became so wasted by his great lamentations, and continued weeping to such an extent, that both his eyes were destroyed. Such were the punishments which these men received for their falsehood.

Chapter 10. The Bishops of Jerusalem.

Narcissus having departed, and no one knowing where he was, those presiding over the neighboring churches thought it best to ordain another bishop. His name was Dius. He presided but a short time, and Germanio succeeded him. He was followed by Gordius, in whose time Narcissus appeared again, as if raised from the dead. And immediately the brethren besought him to take the episcopate, as all admired him the more on account of his retirement and philosophy, and especially because of the punishment with which God had avenged him.

Chapter 11. Alexander.

1. But as on account of his great age Narcissus was no longer able to perform his official duties, the Providence of God called to the office with him, by a revelation given him in a night vision, the above-mentioned Alexander, who was then bishop of another parish.

2. Thereupon, as by Divine direction, he journeyed from the land of Cappadocia, where he first held the episcopate, to Jerusalem, in consequence of a vow and for the sake of information in regard to its places. They received him there with great cordiality, and would not

permit him to return, because of another revelation seen by them at night, which uttered the clearest message to the most zealous among them. For it made known that if they would go outside the gates, they would receive the bishop foreordained for them by God. And having done this, with the unanimous consent of the bishops of the neighboring churches, they constrained him to remain.

3. Alexander, himself, in private letters to the Antinoites, which are still preserved among us, mentions the joint episcopate of Narcissus and himself, writing in these words at the end of the epistle:

4. Narcissus salutes you, who held the episcopate here before me, and is now associated with me in prayers, being one hundred and sixteen years of age; and he exhorts you, as I do, to be of one mind.

These things took place in this manner. But, on the death of Serapion, Asclepiades, who had been himself distinguished among the confessors during the persecution, succeeded to the episcopate of the church at Antioch. Alexander alludes to his appointment, writing thus to the church at Antioch:

5. Alexander, a servant and prisoner of Jesus Christ, to the blessed church of Antioch, greeting in the Lord. The Lord has made my bonds during the time of my imprisonment light and easy, since I learned that, by the Divine Providence, Asclepiades, who in regard to the true faith is eminently qualified, has undertaken the bishopric of your holy church at Antioch.

6. He indicates that he sent this epistle by Clement, writing toward its close as follows:

My honored brethren, I have sent this letter to you by Clement, the blessed presbyter, a man virtuous and approved, whom you yourselves also know and will recognize. Being here, in the providence and oversight of the Master, he has strengthened and built up the Church of the Lord.

Chapter 12. Serapion and his Extant Works.

1. It is probable that others have preserved other memorials of Serapion's literary industry, but there have reached us only those addressed to a certain Domninus, who, in the time of persecution, fell away from faith in Christ to the Jewish will-worship; and those addressed to Pontius and Caricus, ecclesiastical men, and other letters

to different persons, and still another work composed by him on the so-called Gospel of Peter.

2. He wrote this last to refute the falsehoods which that Gospel contained, on account of some in the parish of Rhossus who had been led astray by it into heterodox notions. It may be well to give some brief extracts from his work, showing his opinion of the book. He writes as follows:

3. For we, brethren, receive both Peter and the other apostles as Christ; but we reject intelligently the writings falsely ascribed to them, knowing that such were not handed down to us.

4. When I visited you I supposed that all of you held the true faith, and as I had not read the Gospel which they put forward under the name of Peter, I said, If this is the only thing which occasions dispute among you, let it be read. But now having learned, from what has been told me, that their mind was involved in some heresy, I will hasten to come to you again. Therefore, brethren, expect me shortly.

5. But you will learn, brethren, from what has been written to you, that we perceived the nature of the heresy of Marcianus, and that, not understanding what he was saying, he contradicted himself.

6. For having obtained this Gospel from others who had studied it diligently, namely, from the successors of those who first used it, whom we call Docetæ; (for most of their opinions are connected with the teaching of that school) we have been able to read it through, and we find many things in accordance with the true doctrine of the Saviour, but some things added to that doctrine, which we have pointed out for you farther on. So much in regard to Serapion.

Chapter 13. The Writings of Clement.

1. All the eight Stromata of Clement are preserved among us, and have been given by him the following title: Titus Flavius Clement's Stromata of Gnostic Notes on the True Philosophy.

2. The books entitled Hypotyposes are of the same number. In them he mentions Pantænus by name as his teacher, and gives his opinions and traditions.

3. Besides these there is his Hortatory Discourse addressed to the Greeks; three books of a work entitled the Instructor; another with the title What Rich Man is Saved? the work on the Passover; discussions on

Fasting and on Evil Speaking; the Hortatory Discourse on Patience, or To Those Recently Baptized; and the one bearing the title Ecclesiastical Canon, or Against the Judaizers, which he dedicated to Alexander, the bishop mentioned above.

4. In the Stromata, he has not only treated extensively of the Divine Scripture, but he also quotes from the Greek writers whenever anything that they have said seems to him profitable.

5. He elucidates the opinions of many, both Greeks and barbarians. He also refutes the false doctrines of the heresiarchs, and besides this, reviews a large portion of history, giving us specimens of very various learning; with all the rest he mingles the views of philosophers. It is likely that on this account he gave his work the appropriate title of Stromata.

6. He makes use also in these works of testimonies from the disputed Scriptures, the so-called Wisdom of Solomon, and of Jesus, the son of Sirach, and the Epistle to the Hebrews, and those of Barnabas, and Clement and Jude.

7. He mentions also Tatian's Discourse to the Greeks, and speaks of Cassianus as the author of a chronological work. He refers to the Jewish authors Philo, Aristobulus, Josephus, Demetrius, and Eupolemus, as showing, all of them, in their works, that Moses and the Jewish race existed before the earliest origin of the Greeks.

8. These books abound also in much other learning. In the first of them the author speaks of himself as next after the successors of the apostles.

9. In them he promises also to write a commentary on Genesis. In his book on the Passover he acknowledges that he had been urged by his friends to commit to writing, for posterity, the traditions which he had heard from the ancient presbyters; and in the same work he mentions Melito and Irenæus, and certain others, and gives extracts from their writings.

Chapter 14. The Scriptures mentioned by Him.

1. To sum up briefly, he has given in the Hypotyposes abridged accounts of all canonical Scripture, not omitting the disputed books,

— I refer to Jude and the other Catholic epistles, and Barnabas and the so-called Apocalypse of Peter.

2. He says that the Epistle to the Hebrews is the work of Paul, and that it was written to the Hebrews in the Hebrew language; but that Luke translated it carefully and published it for the Greeks, and hence the same style of expression is found in this epistle and in the Acts.

3. But he says that the words, Paul the Apostle, were probably not prefixed, because, in sending it to the Hebrews, who were prejudiced and suspicious of him, he wisely did not wish to repel them at the very beginning by giving his name.

4. Farther on he says: But now, as the blessed presbyter said, since the Lord being the apostle of the Almighty, was sent to the Hebrews, Paul, as sent to the Gentiles, on account of his modesty did not subscribe himself an apostle of the Hebrews, through respect for the Lord, and because being a herald and apostle of the Gentiles he wrote to the Hebrews out of his superabundance.

5. Again, in the same books, Clement gives the tradition of the earliest presbyters, as to the order of the Gospels, in the following manner:

6. The Gospels containing the genealogies, he says, were written first. The Gospel according to Mark had this occasion. As Peter had preached the Word publicly at Rome, and declared the Gospel by the Spirit, many who were present requested that Mark, who had followed him for a long time and remembered his sayings, should write them out. And having composed the Gospel he gave it to those who had requested it.

7. When Peter learned of this, he neither directly forbade nor encouraged it. But, last of all, John, perceiving that the external facts had been made plain in the Gospel, being urged by his friends, and inspired by the Spirit, composed a spiritual Gospel. This is the account of Clement.

8. Again the above-mentioned Alexander, in a certain letter to Origen, refers to Clement, and at the same time to Pantænus, as being among his familiar acquaintances. He writes as follows:

For this, as you know, was the will of God, that the ancestral friendship existing between us should remain unshaken; nay, rather should be warmer and stronger.

9. For we know well those blessed fathers who have trodden the way before us, with whom we shall soon be; Pantænus, the truly blessed man and master, and the holy Clement, my master and benefactor, and if there is any other like them, through whom I became acquainted with you, the best in everything, my master and brother.

10. So much for these matters. But Adamantius, — for this also was a name of Origen—when Zephyrinus was bishop of Rome, visited Rome, desiring, as he himself somewhere says, to see the most ancient church of Rome.

11. After a short stay there he returned to Alexandria. And he performed the duties of catechetical instruction there with great zeal; Demetrius, who was bishop there at that time, urging and even entreating him to work diligently for the benefit of the brethren.

Chapter 15. Heraclas.

1. But when he saw that he had not time for the deeper study of divine things, and for the investigation and interpretation of the Sacred Scriptures, and also for the instruction of those who came to him—for coming, one after another, from morning till evening to be taught by him, they scarcely gave him time to breathe—he divided the multitude. And from those whom he knew well, he selected Heraclas, who was a zealous student of divine things, and in other respects a very learned man, not ignorant of philosophy, and made him his associate in the work of instruction. He entrusted to him the elementary training of beginners, but reserved for himself the teaching of those who were farther advanced.

Chapter 16. Origen's Earnest Study of the Divine Scriptures.

1. So earnest and assiduous was Origen's research into the divine words that he learned the Hebrew language, and procured as his own the original Hebrew Scriptures which were in the hands of the Jews. He investigated also the works of other translators of the Sacred Scriptures besides the Seventy. And in addition to the well-known translations of Aquila, Symmachus, and Theodotion, he discovered certain others which had been concealed from remote times—in what out-of-the-way corners I know not—and by his search he brought them to light.

2. Since he did not know the authors, he simply stated that he had found this one in Nicopolis near Actium and that one in some other place.

3. In the Hexapla of the Psalms, after the four prominent translations, he adds not only a fifth, but also a sixth and seventh. He states of one of these that he found it in a jar in Jericho in the time of Antoninus, the son of Severus.

4. Having collected all of these, he divided them into sections, and placed them opposite each other, with the Hebrew text itself. He thus left us the copies of the so-called Hexapla. He arranged also separately an edition of Aquila and Symmachus and Theodotion with the Septuagint, in the Tetrapla.

Chapter 17. The Translator Symmachus.

As to these translators it should be stated that Symmachus was an Ebionite. But the heresy of the Ebionites, as it is called, asserts that Christ was the son of Joseph and Mary, considering him a mere man, and insists strongly on keeping the law in a Jewish manner, as we have seen already in this history. Commentaries of Symmachus are still extant in which he appears to support this heresy by attacking the Gospel of Matthew. Origen states that he obtained these and other commentaries of Symmachus on the Scriptures from a certain Juliana, who, he says, received the books by inheritance from Symmachus himself.

Chapter 18. Ambrose.

1. About this time Ambrose, who held the heresy of Valentinus, was convinced by Origen's presentation of the truth, and, as if his mind were illumined by light, he accepted the orthodox doctrine of the Church.

2. Many others also, drawn by the fame of Origen's learning, which resounded everywhere, came to him to make trial of his skill in sacred literature. And a great many heretics, and not a few of the most distinguished philosophers, studied under him diligently, receiving instruction from him not only in divine things, but also in secular philosophy.

3. For when he perceived that any persons had superior intelligence he instructed them also in philosophic branches— in geometry, arithmetic, and other preparatory studies— and then advanced to the systems of the philosophers and explained their writings. And he made observations and comments upon each of them, so that he became celebrated as a great philosopher even among the Greeks themselves.

4. And he instructed many of the less learned in the common school branches, saying that these would be no small help to them in the study and understanding of the Divine Scriptures. On this account he

considered it especially necessary for himself to be skilled in secular and philosophic learning.

Chapter 19. Circumstances Related of Origen.

1. The Greek philosophers of his age are witnesses to his proficiency in these subjects. We find frequent mention of him in their writings. Sometimes they dedicated their own works to him; again, they submitted their labors to him as a teacher for his judgment.

2. Why need we say these things when even Porphyry, who lived in Sicily in our own times and wrote books against us, attempting to traduce the Divine Scriptures by them, mentions those who have interpreted them; and being unable in any way to find a base accusation against the doctrines, for lack of arguments turns to reviling and calumniating their interpreters, attempting especially to slander Origen, whom he says he knew in his youth.

3. But truly, without knowing it, he commends the man; telling the truth about him in some cases where he could not do otherwise; but uttering falsehoods where he thinks he will not be detected. Sometimes he accuses him as a Christian; again he describes his proficiency in philosophic learning. But hear his own words:

4. Some persons, desiring to find a solution of the baseness of the Jewish Scriptures rather than abandon them, have had recourse to explanations inconsistent and incongruous with the words written, which explanations, instead of supplying a defense of the foreigners, contain rather approval and praise of themselves. For they boast that the plain words of Moses are enigmas, and regard them as oracles full of hidden mysteries; and having bewildered the mental judgment by folly, they make their explanations. Farther on he says:

5. As an example of this absurdity take a man whom I met when I was young, and who was then greatly celebrated and still is, on account of the writings which he has left. I refer to Origen, who is highly honored by the teachers of these doctrines.

6. For this man, having been a hearer of Ammonius, who had attained the greatest proficiency in philosophy of any in our day, derived much benefit from his teacher in the knowledge of the sciences; but as to the correct choice of life, he pursued a course opposite to his.

7. For Ammonius, being a Christian, and brought up by Christian parents, when he gave himself to study and to philosophy straightway conformed to the life required by the laws. But Origen, having been educated as a Greek in Greek literature, went over to the barbarian recklessness. And carrying over the learning which he had obtained, he hawked it about, in his life conducting himself as a Christian and contrary to the laws, but in his opinions of material things and of the Deity being like a Greek, and mingling Grecian teachings with foreign fables.

8. For he was continually studying Plato, and he busied himself with the writings of Numenius and Cronius, Apollophanes, Longinus, Moderatus, and Nicomachus, and those famous among the Pythagoreans. And he used the books of Chæremon the Stoic, and of Cornutus. Becoming acquainted through them with the figurative interpretation of the Grecian mysteries, he applied it to the Jewish Scriptures.

9. These things are said by Porphyry in the third book of his work against the Christians. He speaks truly of the industry and learning of the man, but plainly utters a falsehood (for what will not an oppose of Christians do?) when he says that he went over from the Greeks, and that Ammonius fell from a life of piety into heathen customs.

10. For the doctrine of Christ was taught to Origen by his parents, as we have shown above. And Ammonius held the divine philosophy unshaken and unadulterated to the end of his life. His works yet extant show this, as he is celebrated among many for the writings which he has left. For example, the work entitled The Harmony of Moses and Jesus, and such others as are in the possession of the learned.

11. These things are sufficient to evince the slander of the false accuser, and also the proficiency of Origen in Grecian learning. He defends his diligence in this direction against some who blamed him for it, in a certain epistle, where he writes as follows:

12. When I devoted myself to the word, and the fame of my proficiency went abroad, and when heretics and persons conversant with Grecian learning, and particularly with philosophy, came to me, it seemed necessary that I should examine the doctrines of the heretics, and what the philosophers say concerning the truth.

13. And in this we have followed Pantænus, who benefited many before our time by his thorough preparation in such things, and also Heraclas,

who is now a member of the presbytery of Alexandria. I found him with the teacher of philosophic learning, with whom he had already continued five years before I began to hear lectures on those subjects.

14. And though he had formerly worn the common dress, he laid it aside and assumed and still wears the philosopher's garment; and he continues the earnest investigation of Greek works.

He says these things in defending himself for his study of Grecian literature.

15. About this time, while he was still at Alexandria, a soldier came and delivered a letter from the governor of Arabia to Demetrius, bishop of the parish, and to the prefect of Egypt who was in office at that time, requesting that they would with all speed send Origen to him for an interview. Being sent by them, he went to Arabia. And having in a short time accomplished the object of his visit, he returned to Alexandria.

16. But sometime after a considerable war broke out in the city, and he departed from Alexandria. And thinking that it would be unsafe for him to remain in Egypt, he went to Palestine and abode in Cæsarea. While there the bishops of the church in that country requested him to preach and expound the Scriptures publicly, although he had not yet been ordained as presbyter.

17. This is evident from what Alexander, bishop of Jerusalem and Theoctistus of Cæsarea, wrote to Demetrius in regard to the matter, defending themselves thus:

He has stated in his letter that such a thing was never heard of before, neither has hitherto taken place, that laymen should preach in the presence of bishops. I know not how he comes to say what is plainly untrue.

18. For whenever persons able to instruct the brethren are found, they are exhorted by the holy bishops to preach to the people. Thus in Laranda, Euelpis by Neon; and in Iconium, Paulinus by Celsus; and in Synada, Theodorus by Atticus, our blessed brethren. And probably this has been done in other places unknown to us.

He was honored in this manner while yet a young man, not only by his countrymen, but also by foreign bishops.

19. But Demetrius sent for him by letter, and urged him through members and deacons of the church to return to Alexandria. So he returned and resumed his accustomed duties.

Chapter 20. The Extant Works of the Writers of that Age.

1. There flourished many learned men in the Church at that time, whose letters to each other have been preserved and are easily accessible. They have been kept until our time in the library at Ælia, which was established by Alexander, who at that time presided over that church. We have been able to gather from that library material for our present work.

2. Among these Beryllus has left us, besides letters and treatises, various elegant works. He was bishop of Bostra in Arabia. Likewise also Hippolytus, who presided over another church, has left writings.

3. There has reached us also a dialogue of Caius, a very learned man, which was held at Rome under Zephyrinus, with Proclus, who contended for the Phrygian heresy. In this he curbs the rashness and boldness of his opponents in setting forth new Scriptures. He mentions only thirteen epistles of the holy apostle, not counting that to the Hebrews with the others. And unto our day there are some among the Romans who do not consider this a work of the apostle.

Chapter 21. The Bishops that were well known at that Time.

1. After Antoninus had reigned seven years and six months, Macrinus succeeded him. He held the government but a year, and was succeeded by another Antoninus. During his first year the Roman bishop, Zephyrinus, having held his office for eighteen years, died, and Callistus received the episcopate.

2. He continued for five years, and was succeeded by Urbanus. After this, Alexander became Roman emperor, Antoninus having reigned but four years. At this time Philetus also succeeded Asclepiades in the church of Antioch.

3. The mother of the emperor, Mammæa by name, was a most pious woman, if there ever was one, and of religious life. When the fame of Origen had extended everywhere and had come even to her ears, she desired greatly to see the man, and above all things to make trial of his celebrated understanding of divine things.

4. Staying for a time in Antioch, she sent for him with a military escort. Having remained with her a while and shown her many things which

were for the glory of the Lord and of the excellence of the divine teaching, he hastened back to his accustomed work.

Chapter 22. The Works of Hippolytus which have reached us.

1. At that time Hippolytus, besides many other treatises, wrote a work on the passover. He gives in this a chronological table, and presents a certain paschal canon of sixteen years, bringing the time down to the first year of the Emperor Alexander.

2. Of his other writings the following have reached us: On the Hexæmeron, On the Works after the Hexæmeron, Against Marcion, On the Song of Songs, On Portions of Ezekiel, On the Passover, Against All the Heresies; and you can find many other works preserved by many.

Chapter 23. Origen's Zeal and his Elevation to the Presbyterate.

1. At that time Origen began his commentaries on the Divine Scriptures, being urged thereto by Ambrose, who employed innumerable incentives, not only exhorting him by word, but also furnishing abundant means.

2. For he dictated to more than seven amanuenses, who relieved each other at appointed times. And he employed no fewer copyists, besides girls who were skilled in elegant writing. For all these Ambrose furnished the necessary expense in abundance, manifesting himself an inexpressible earnestness in diligence and zeal for the divine oracles, by which he especially pressed him on to the preparation of his commentaries.

3. While these things were in progress, Urbanus, who had been for eight years bishop of the Roman church, was succeeded by Pontianus, and Zebinus succeeded Philetus in Antioch.

4. At this time Origen was sent to Greece on account of a pressing necessity in connection with ecclesiastical affairs, and went through Palestine, and was ordained as presbyter in Cæsarea by the bishops of that country. The matters that were agitated concerning him on this account, and the decisions on these matters by those who presided over the churches, besides the other works concerning the divine word which he published while in his prime, demand a separate treatise. We have written of them to some extent in the second book of the Defense which we have composed in his behalf.

Chapter 24. The Commentaries which he prepared at Alexandria.

1. It may be well to add that in the sixth book of his exposition of the Gospel of John he states that he prepared the first five while in Alexandria. Of his work on the entire Gospel only twenty-two volumes have come down to us.

2. In the ninth of those on Genesis, of which there are twelve in all, he states that not only the preceding eight had been composed at Alexandria, but also those on the first twenty-five Psalms and on Lamentations. Of these last five volumes have reached us.

3. In them he mentions also his books On the Resurrection, of which there are two. He wrote also the books De Principiis before leaving Alexandria; and the discourses entitled Stromata, ten in number, he composed in the same city during the reign of Alexander, as the notes by his own hand preceding the volumes indicate.

Chapter 25. His Review of the Canonical Scriptures.

1. When expounding the first Psalm, he gives a catalogue of the sacred Scriptures of the Old Testament as follows:

It should be stated that the canonical books, as the Hebrews have handed them down, are twenty-two; corresponding with the number of their letters. Farther on he says:

2. The twenty-two books of the Hebrews are the following: That which is called by us Genesis, but by the Hebrews, from the beginning of the book, Bresith, which means, 'In the beginning'; Exodus, Welesmoth, that is, 'These are the names'; Leviticus, Wikra, 'And he called'; Numbers, Ammesphekodeim; Deuteronomy, Eleaddebareim, 'These are the words'; Jesus, the son of Nave, Josoue ben Noun; Judges and Ruth, among them in one book, Saphateim; the First and Second of Kings, among them one, Samouel, that is, 'The called of God'; the Third and Fourth of Kings in one, Wammelch David, that is, 'The kingdom of David'; of the Chronicles, the First and Second in one, Dabreïamein, that is, 'Records of days'; Esdras, First and Second in one, Ezra, that is, 'An assistant'; the book of Psalms, Spharthelleim; the Proverbs of Solomon, Meloth; Ecclesiastes, Koelth; the Song of Songs (not, as some suppose, Songs of Songs), Sir Hassirim; Isaiah, Jessia; Jeremiah, with Lamentations and the epistle in one, Jeremia; Daniel, Daniel; Ezekiel,

Jezekiel; Job, Job; Esther, Esther. And besides these there are the Maccabees, which are entitled Sarbeth Sabanaiel. He gives these in the above- mentioned work.

3. In his first book on Matthew's Gospel, maintaining the Canon of the Church, he testifies that he knows only four Gospels, writing as follows:

4. Among the four Gospels, which are the only indisputable ones in the Church of God under heaven, I have learned by tradition that the first was written by Matthew, who was once a publican, but afterwards an apostle of Jesus Christ, and it was prepared for the converts from Judaism, and published in the Hebrew language.

5. The second is by Mark, who composed it according to the instructions of Peter, who in his Catholic epistle acknowledges him as a son, saying, 'The church that is at Babylon elected together with you, salutes you, and so does Marcus, my son.' 1 Peter 5:13

6. And the third by Luke, the Gospel commended by Paul, and composed for Gentile converts. Last of all that by John.

7. In the fifth book of his Expositions of John's Gospel, he speaks thus concerning the epistles of the apostles: But he who was 'made sufficient to be a minister of the New Testament, not of the letter, but of the Spirit,' 2 Corinthians 3:6 that is, Paul, who 'fully preached the Gospel from Jerusalem and round about even unto Illyricum,' Romans 15:19 did not write to all the churches which he had instructed and to those to which he wrote he sent but few lines.

8. And Peter, on whom the Church of Christ is built, 'against which the gates of hell shall not prevail,' Matthew 16:18 has left one acknowledged epistle; perhaps also a second, but this is doubtful.

9. Why need we speak of him who reclined upon the bosom of Jesus, John, who has left us one Gospel, though he confessed that he might write so many that the world could not contain them? And he wrote also the Apocalypse, but was commanded to keep silence and not to write the words of the seven thunders.

10. He has left also an epistle of very few lines; perhaps also a second and third; but not all consider them genuine, and together they do not contain hundred lines.

11. In addition he makes the following statements in regard to the Epistle to the Hebrews in his Homilies upon it: That the verbal style of the epistle entitled 'To the Hebrews,' is not rude like the language of the

apostle, who acknowledged himself 'rude in speech' 2 Corinthians 11:6 that is, in expression; but that its diction is purer Greek, any one who has the power to discern differences of phraseology will acknowledge.

12. Moreover, that the thoughts of the epistle are admirable, and not inferior to the acknowledged apostolic writings, any one who carefully examines the apostolic text will admit.'

13. Farther on he adds: If I gave my opinion, I should say that the thoughts are those of the apostle, but the diction and phraseology are those of some one who remembered the apostolic teachings, and wrote down at his leisure what had been said by his teacher. Therefore if any church holds that this epistle is by Paul, let it be commended for this. For not without reason have the ancients handed it down as Paul's.

14. But who wrote the epistle, in truth, God knows. The statement of some who have gone before us is that Clement, bishop of the Romans, wrote the epistle, and of others that Luke, the author of the Gospel and the Acts, wrote it. But let this suffice on these matters.

Chapter 26. Heraclas becomes Bishop of Alexandria.

It was in the tenth year of the above-mentioned reign that Origen removed from Alexandria to Cæsarea, leaving the charge of the catechetical school in that city to Heraclas. Not long afterward Demetrius, bishop of the church of Alexandria, died, having held the office for forty-three full years, and Heraclas succeeded him. At this time Firmilianus, bishop of Cæsarea in Cappadocia, was conspicuous.

Chapter 27. How the Bishops regarded Origen.

He was so earnestly affected toward Origen, that he urged him to come to that country for the benefit of the churches, and moreover he visited him in Judea, remaining with him for some time, for the sake of improvement in divine things. And Alexander, bishop of Jerusalem, and Theoctistus, bishop of Cæsarea, attended on him constantly, as their only teacher, and allowed him to expound the Divine Scriptures, and to perform the other duties pertaining to ecclesiastical discourse.

Chapter 28. The Persecution under Maximinus.

The Roman emperor, Alexander, having finished his reign in thirteen years, was succeeded by Maximinus Cæsar. On account of his hatred toward the household of Alexander, which contained many believers, he began a persecution, commanding that only the rulers of the churches should be put to death, as responsible for the Gospel teaching. Thereupon Origen composed his work On Martyrdom, and dedicated it to Ambrose and Protoctetus, a presbyter of the parish of Cæsarea, because in the persecution there had come upon them both unusual hardships, in which it is reported that they were eminent in confession during the reign of Maximinus, which lasted but three years. Origen has noted this as the time of the persecution in the twenty-second book of his Commentaries on John, and in several epistles.

Chapter 29. Fabianus, who was wonderfully designated Bishop of Rome by God.

1. Gordianus succeeded Maximinus as Roman emperor; and Pontianus, who had been bishop of the church at Rome for six years, was succeeded by Anteros. After he had held the office for a month, Fabianus succeeded him.

2. They say that Fabianus having come, after the death of Anteros, with others from the country, was staying at Rome, and that while there he was chosen to the office through a most wonderful manifestation of divine and heavenly grace.

3. For when all the brethren had assembled to select by vote him who should succeed to the episcopate of the church, several renowned and honorable men were in the minds of many, but Fabianus, although present, was in the mind of none. But they relate that suddenly a dove flying down lighted on his head, resembling the descent of the Holy Spirit on the Saviour in the form of a dove.

4. Thereupon all the people, as if moved by one Divine Spirit, with all eagerness and unanimity cried out that he was worthy, and without delay they took him and placed him upon the episcopal seat.

5. About that time Zebinus, bishop of Antioch died, and Babylas succeeded him. And in Alexandria Heraclas, having received the episcopal office after Demetrius, was succeeded in the charge of the catechetical school by Dionysius, who had also been one of Origen's pupils.

Chapter 30. The Pupils of Origen.

While Origen was carrying on his customary duties in Cæsarea, many pupils came to him not only from the vicinity, but also from other countries. Among these Theodorus, the same that was distinguished among the bishops of our day under the name of Gregory, and his brother Athenodorus, we know to have been especially celebrated. Finding them deeply interested in Greek and Roman learning, he infused into them a love of philosophy, and led them to exchange their old zeal for the study of divinity. Remaining with him five years, they made such progress in divine things, that although they were still young, both of them were honored with a bishopric in the churches of Pontus.

Chapter 31. Africanus.

1. At this time also Africanus, the writer of the books entitled Cesti, was well known. There is extant an epistle of his to Origen, expressing doubts of the story of Susannah in Daniel, as being spurious and fictitious. Origen answered this very fully.

2. Other works of the same Africanus which have reached us are his five books on Chronology, a work accurately and laboriously prepared. He says in this that he went to Alexandria on account of the great fame of Heraclas, who excelled especially in philosophic studies and other Greek learning, and whose appointment to the bishopric of the church there we have already mentioned.

3. There is extant also another epistle from the same Africanus to Aristides on the supposed discrepancy between Matthew and Luke in the Genealogies of Christ. In this he shows clearly the agreement of the evangelists, from an account which had come down to him, which we have already given in its proper place in the first book of this work.

Chapter 32. The Commentaries which Origencomposed in Cæsarea in Palestine.

1. About this time Origen prepared his Commentaries on Isaiah and on Ezekiel. Of the former there have come down to us thirty books, as far as the third part of Isaiah, to the vision of the beasts in the desert; on Ezekiel twenty-five books, which are all that he wrote on the whole prophet.

2. Being at that time in Athens, he finished his work on Ezekiel and commenced his Commentaries on the Song of Songs, which he carried forward to the fifth book. After his return to Cæsarea, he completed these also, ten books in number.

3. But why should we give in this history an accurate catalogue of the man's works, which would require a separate treatise? we have furnished this also in our narrative of the life of Pamphilus, a holy martyr of our own time. After showing how great the diligence of Pamphilus was in divine things, we give in that a catalogue of the library which he collected of the works of Origen and of other ecclesiastical writers. Whoever desires may learn readily from this which of Origen's works have reached us. But we must proceed now with our history.

Chapter 33. The Error of Beryllus.

1. Beryllus, whom we mentioned recently as bishop of Bostra in Arabia, turned aside from the ecclesiastical standard and attempted to introduce ideas foreign to the faith. He dared to assert that our Saviour and Lord did not pre-exist in a distinct form of being of his own before his abode among men, and that he does not possess a divinity of his own, but only that of the Father dwelling in him.

2. Many bishops carried on investigations and discussions with him on this matter, and Origen having been invited with the others, went down at first for a conference with him to ascertain his real opinion. But when he understood his views, and perceived that they were erroneous, having persuaded him by argument, and convinced him by demonstration, he brought him back to the true doctrine, and restored him to his former sound opinion.

3. There are still extant writings of Beryllus and of the synod held on his account, which contain the questions put to him by Origen, and the discussions which were carried on in his parish, as well as all the things done at that time.

4. The elder brethren among us have handed down many other facts respecting Origen which I think proper to omit, as not pertaining to this work. But whatever it has seemed necessary to record about him can be found in the Apology in his behalf written by us and Pamphilus, the holy martyr of our day. We prepared this carefully and did the work jointly on account of faultfinders.

Chapter 34. Philip Cæsar.

Gordianus had been Roman emperor for six years when Philip, with his son Philip, succeeded him. It is reported that he, being a Christian, desired, on the day of the last paschal vigil, to share with the multitude in the prayers of the Church, but that he was not permitted to enter, by him who then presided, until he had made confession and had numbered himself among those who were reckoned as transgressors and who occupied the place of penance. For if he had not done this, he would never have been received by him, on account of the many crimes which he had committed. It is said that he obeyed readily, manifesting in his conduct a genuine and pious fear of God.

Chapter 35. Dionysius succeeds Heraclas in the Episcopate.

In the third year of this emperor, Heraclas died, having held his office for sixteen years, and Dionysius received the episcopate of the churches of Alexandria.

Chapter 36. Other Works of Origen.

1. At this time, as the faith extended and our doctrine was proclaimed boldly before all, Origen, being, as they say, over sixty years old, and having gained great facility by his long practice, very properly permitted his public discourses to be taken down by stenographers, a thing which he had never before allowed.

2. He also at this time composed a work of eight books in answer to that entitled True Discourse, which had been written against us by Celsus the Epicurean, and the twenty-five books on the Gospel of Matthew, besides those on the Twelve Prophets, of which we have found only twenty-five.

3. There is extant also an epistle of his to the Emperor Philip, and another to Severa his wife, with several others to different persons. We have arranged in distinct books to the number of one hundred, so that they might be no longer scattered, as many of these as we have been able to collect, which have been preserved here and there by different persons.

4. He wrote also to Fabianus, bishop of Rome, and to many other rulers of the churches concerning his orthodoxy. You have examples of these in the eighth book of the Apology which we have written in his behalf.

Chapter 37. The Dissension of the Arabians.

About the same time others arose in Arabia, putting forward a doctrine foreign to the truth. They said that during the present time the human soul dies and perishes with the body, but that at the time of the resurrection they will be renewed together. And at that time also a synod of considerable size assembled, and Origen, being again invited there, spoke publicly on the question with such effect that the opinions of those who had formerly fallen were changed.

Chapter 38. The Heresy of the Elkesites.

Another error also arose at this time, called the heresy of the Elkesites, which was extinguished in the very beginning. Origen speaks of it in this manner in a public homily on the eighty-second Psalm:

A certain man came just now, puffed up greatly with his own ability, proclaiming that godless and impious opinion which has appeared lately in the churches, styled 'of the Elkesites.' I will show you what evil things that opinion teaches, that you may not be carried away by it. It rejects certain parts of every scripture. Again it uses portions of the Old Testament and the Gospel, but rejects the apostle altogether. It says that to deny Christ is an indifferent matter, and that he who understands will, under necessity, deny with his mouth, but not in his heart. They produce a certain book which they say fell from heaven. They hold that whoever hears and believes this shall receive remission of sins, another remission than that which Jesus Christ has given. Such is the account of these persons.

Chapter 39. The Persecution under Decius, and the Sufferings of Origen.

1. After a reign of seven years Philip was succeeded by Decius. On account of his hatred of Philip, he commenced a persecution of the churches, in which Fabianus suffered martyrdom at Rome, and Cornelius succeeded him in the episcopate.

2. In Palestine, Alexander, bishop of the church of Jerusalem, was brought again on Christ's account before the governor's judgment seat in Cæsarea, and having acquitted himself nobly in a second confession was cast into prison, crowned with the hoary locks of venerable age.

3. And after his honorable and illustrious confession at the tribunal of the governor, he fell asleep in prison, and Mazabanes became his successor in the bishopric of Jerusalem.

4. Babylas in Antioch, having like Alexander passed away in prison after his confession, was succeeded by Fabius in the episcopate of that church.

5. But how many and how great things came upon Origen in the persecution, and what was their final result—as the demon of evil marshaled all his forces, and fought against the man with his utmost craft and power, assaulting him beyond all others against whom he contended at that time,— and what and how many things he endured for the word of Christ, bonds and bodily tortures and torments under the iron collar and in the dungeon; and how for many days with his feet stretched four spaces in the stocks he bore patiently the threats of fire and whatever other things were inflicted by his enemies; and how his sufferings terminated, as his judge strove eagerly with all his might not to end his life; and what words he left after these things, full of comfort to those needing aid, a great many of his epistles show with truth and accuracy.

Chapter 40. The Events which happened to Dionysius.

1. I shall quote from the epistle of Dionysius to Germanus an account of what befell the former. Speaking of himself, he writes as follows: I speak before God, and he knows that I do not lie. I did not flee on my own impulse nor without divine direction.

2. But even before this, at the very hour when the Decian persecution was commanded, Sabinus sent a frumentarius to search for me, and I remained at home four days awaiting his arrival.

3. But he went about examining all places—roads, rivers, and fields—where he thought I might be concealed or on the way. But he was smitten with blindness, and did not find the house, for he did not suppose, that being pursued, I would remain at home. And after the fourth day God commanded me to depart, and made a way for me in a wonderful manner; and I and my attendants and many of the brethren went away together. And that this occurred through the providence of God was made manifest by what followed, in which perhaps we were useful to some.

4. Farther on he relates in this manner what happened to him after his flight:

For about sunset, having been seized with those that were with me, I was taken by the soldiers to Taposiris, but in the providence of God, Timothy was not present and was not captured. But coming later, he found the house deserted and guarded by soldiers, and ourselves reduced to slavery.

5. After a little he says:

And what was the manner of his admirable management? For the truth shall be told. One of the country people met Timothy fleeing and disturbed, and inquired the cause of his haste. And he told him the truth.

6. And when the man heard it (he was on his way to a marriage feast, for it was customary to spend the entire night in such gatherings), he entered and announced it to those at the table. And they, as if on a preconcerted signal, arose with one impulse, and rushed out quickly and came and burst in upon us with a shout. Immediately the soldiers who were guarding us fled, and they came to us lying as we were upon the bare couches.

7. But I, God knows, thought at first that they were robbers who had come for spoil and plunder. So I remained upon the bed on which I was, clothed only in a linen garment, and offered them the rest of my clothing which was lying beside me. But they directed me to rise and come away quickly.

8. Then I understood why they had come, and I cried out, beseeching and entreating them to depart and leave us alone. And I requested them, if they desired to benefit me in any way, to anticipate those who were carrying me off, and cut off my head themselves. And when I had cried out in this manner, as my companions and partners in everything know, they raised me by force. But I threw myself on my back on the ground; and they seized me by the hands and feet and dragged me away.

9. And the witnesses of all these occurrences followed: Gaius, Faustus, Peter, and Paul. But they who had seized me carried me out of the village hastily, and placing me on an ass without a saddle, bore me away. Dionysius relates these things respecting himself.

Chapter 41. The Martyrs in Alexandria.

1. The same writer, in an epistle to Fabius, bishop of Antioch, relates as follows the sufferings of the martyrs in Alexandria under Decius:

The persecution among us did not begin with the royal decree, but preceded it an entire year. The prophet and author of evils to this city, whoever he was, previously moved and aroused against us the masses of the heathen, rekindling among them the superstition of their country.

2. And being thus excited by him and finding full opportunity for any wickedness, they considered this the only pious service of their demons, that they should slay us.

3. They seized first an old man named Metras, and commanded him to utter impious words. But as he would not obey, they beat him with clubs, and tore his face and eyes with sharp sticks, and dragged him out of the city and stoned him.

4. Then they carried to their idol temple a faithful woman, named Quinta, that they might force her to worship. And as she turned away in detestation, they bound her feet and dragged her through the entire city over the stone-paved streets, and dashed her against the millstones, and at the same time scourged her; then, taking her to the same place, they stoned her to death.

5. Then all with one impulse rushed to the homes of the pious, and they dragged forth whomsoever any one knew as a neighbor, and despoiled and plundered them. They took for themselves the more valuable property; but the poorer articles and those made of wood they scattered about and burned in the streets, so that the city appeared as if taken by an enemy.

6. But the brethren withdrew and went away, and 'took joyfully the spoiling of their goods,' like those to whom Paul bore witness. I know of no one unless possibly some one who fell into their hands, who, up to this time, denied the Lord.

7. Then they seized also that most admirable virgin, Apollonia, an old woman, and, smiting her on the jaws, broke out all her teeth. And they made a fire outside the city and threatened to burn her alive if she would not join with them in their impious cries. And she, supplicating a little, was released, when she leaped eagerly into the fire and was consumed.

8. Then they seized Serapion in his own house, and tortured him with harsh cruelties, and having broken all his limbs, they threw him headlong from an upper story. And there was no street, nor public road, nor lane open to us, by night or day; for always and everywhere, all of them cried

out that if any one would not repeat their impious words, he should immediately be dragged away and burned.

9. And matters continued thus for a considerable time. But a sedition and civil war came upon the wretched people and turned their cruelty toward us against one another. So we breathed for a little while as they ceased from their rage against us. But presently the change from that milder reign was announced to us, and great fear of what was threatened seized us.

10. For the decree arrived, almost like that most terrible time foretold by our Lord, which if it were possible would offend even the elect.

11. All truly were affrighted. And many of the more eminent in their fear came forward immediately; others who were in the public service were drawn on by their official duties; others were urged on by their acquaintances. And as their names were called they approached the impure and impious sacrifices. Some of them were pale and trembled as if they were not about to sacrifice, but to be themselves sacrifices and offerings to the idols; so that they were jeered at by the multitude who stood around, as it was plain to every one that they were afraid either to die or to sacrifice.

12. But some advanced to the altars more readily, declaring boldly that they had never been Christians. Of these the prediction of our Lord is most true that they shall 'hardly' be saved. Of the rest some followed the one, others the other of these classes, some fled and some were seized.

13. And of the latter some continued faithful until bonds and imprisonment, and some who had even been imprisoned for many days yet abjured the faith before they were brought to trial. Others having for a time endured great tortures finally retracted.

14. But the firm and blessed pillars of the Lord being strengthened by him, and having received vigor and might suitable and appropriate to the strong faith which they possessed, became admirable witnesses of his kingdom.

15. The first of these was Julian, a man who suffered so much with the gout that he was unable to stand or walk. They brought him forward with two others who carried him. One of these immediately denied. But the other, whose name was Cronion, and whose surname was Eunus, and the old man Julian himself, both of them having confessed the Lord, were carried on camels through the entire city, which, as you know, is a

very large one, and in this elevated position were beaten and finally burned in a fierce fire, surrounded by all the populace.

16. But a soldier, named Besas, who stood by them as they were led away rebuked those who insulted them. And they cried out against him, and this most manly warrior of God was arraigned, and having done nobly in the great contest for piety, was beheaded.

17. A certain other one, a Libyan by birth, but in name and blessedness a true Macar, was strongly urged by the judge to recant; but as he would not yield he was burned alive. After them Epimachus and Alexander, having remained in bonds for a long time, and endured countless agonies from scrapers and scourges, were also consumed in a fierce fire.

18. And with them there were four women. Ammonarium, a holy virgin, the judge tortured relentlessly and excessively, because she declared from the first that she would utter none of those things which he commanded; and having kept her promise truly, she was dragged away. The others were Mercuria, a very remarkable old woman, and Dionysia, the mother of many children, who did not love her own children above the Lord. As the governor was ashamed of torturing thus ineffectually, and being always defeated by women, they were put to death by the sword, without the trial of tortures. For the champion, Ammonarium, endured these in behalf of all.

19. The Egyptians, Heron and Ater and Isidorus, and with them Dioscorus, a boy about fifteen years old, were delivered up. At first the judge attempted to deceive the lad by fair words, as if he could be brought over easily, and then to force him by tortures, as one who would readily yield. But Dioscorus was neither persuaded nor constrained.

20. As the others remained firm, he scourged them cruelly and then delivered them to the fire. But admiring the manner in which Dioscorus had distinguished himself publicly, and his wise answers to his persuasions, he dismissed him, saying that on account of his youth he would give him time for repentance. And this most godly Dioscorus is among us now, awaiting a longer conflict and more severe contest.

21. But a certain Nemesion, who also was an Egyptian, was accused as an associate of robbers; but when he had cleared himself before the centurion of this charge most foreign to the truth, he was informed against as a Christian, and taken in bonds before the governor. And the most unrighteous magistrate inflicted on him tortures and scourgings double those which he executed on the robbers, and then burned him

between the robbers, thus honoring the blessed man by the likeness to Christ.

22. A band of soldiers, Ammon and Zeno and Ptolemy and Ingenes, and with them an old man, Theophilus, were standing close together before the tribunal. And as a certain person who was being tried as a Christian, seemed inclined to deny, they standing by gnashed their teeth, and made signs with their faces and stretched out their hands, and gestured with their bodies. And when the attention of all was turned to them, before any one else could seize them, they rushed up to the tribunal saying that they were Christians, so that the governor and his council were affrighted. And those who were on trial appeared most courageous in prospect of their sufferings, while their judges trembled. And they went exultingly from the tribunal rejoicing in their testimony; God himself having caused them to triumph gloriously.

Chapter 42. Others of whom Dionysius gives an Account.

1. Many others, in cities and villages, were torn asunder by the heathen, of whom I will mention one as an illustration. Ischyrion was employed as a steward by one of the rulers. His employer commanded him to sacrifice, and on his refusal insulted him, and as he remained firm, abused him. And as he still held out he seized a long staff and thrust it through his bowels and slew him.

2. Why need I speak of the multitude that wandered in the deserts and mountains, and perished by hunger, and thirst, and cold, and sickness, and robbers, and wild beasts? Those of them who survived are witnesses of their election and victory.

3. But I will relate one occurrence as an example. Chæremon, who was very old, was bishop of the city called Nilus. He fled with his wife to the Arabian mountain and did not return. And though the brethren searched diligently they could not find either them or their bodies.

4. And many who fled to the same Arabian mountain were carried into slavery by the barbarian Saracens. Some of them were ransomed with difficulty and at a large price; others have not been to the present time. I have related these things, my brother, not without an object, but that you may understand how many and great distresses came upon us. Those indeed will understand them the best who have had the largest experience of them.

5. A little further on he adds: These divine martyrs among us, who now are seated with Christ, and are sharers in his kingdom, partakers of his judgment and judges with him, received some of the brethren who had fallen away and become chargeable with the guilt of sacrificing. When they perceived that their conversion and repentance were sufficient to be acceptable with him who by no means desires the death of the sinner, but his repentance, having proved them they received them back and brought them together, and met with them and had fellowship with them in prayers and feasts.

6. What counsel then, brethren, do you give us concerning such persons? What should we do? Shall we have the same judgment and rule as theirs, and observe their decision and charity, and show mercy to those whom they pitied? Or, shall we declare their decision unrighteous, and set ourselves as judges of their opinion, and grieve mercy and overturn order? These words Dionysius very properly added when making mention of those who had been weak in the time of persecution.

Chapter 43. Novatus, his Manner of Life and his Heresy.

1. After this, Novatus, a presbyter of the church at Rome, being lifted up with arrogance against these persons, as if there was no longer for them a hope of salvation, not even if they should do all things pertaining to a genuine and pure conversion, became leader of the heresy of those who, in the pride of their imagination, call themselves Cathari.

2. There upon a very large synod assembled at Rome, of bishops in number sixty, and a great many more presbyters and deacons; while the pastors of the remaining provinces deliberated in their places privately concerning what ought to be done. A decree was confirmed by all, that Novatus and those who joined with him, and those who adopted his brother-hating and inhuman opinion, should be considered by the church as strangers; but that they should heal such of the brethren as had fallen into misfortune, and should minister to them with the medicines of repentance.

3. There have reached us epistles of Cornelius, bishop of Rome, to Fabius, of the church at Antioch, which show what was done at the synod at Rome, and what seemed best to all those in Italy and Africa and the regions thereabout. Also other epistles, written in the Latin language, of Cyprian and those with him in Africa, which show that they agreed as to the necessity of succoring those who had been tempted,

and of cutting off from the Catholic Church the leader of the heresy and all that joined with him.

4. Another epistle of Cornelius, concerning the resolutions of the synod, is attached to these; and yet others, on the conduct of Novatus, from which it is proper for us to make selections, that any one who sees this work may know about him.

5. Cornelius informs Fabius what sort of a man Novatus was, in the following words:

But that you may know that a long time ago this remarkable man desired the episcopate, but kept this ambitious desire to himself and concealed it—using as a cloak for his rebellion those confessors who had adhered to him from the beginning—I desire to speak.

6. Maximus, one of our presbyters, and Urbanus, who twice gained the highest honor by confession, with Sidonius, and Celerinus, a man who by the grace of God most heroically endured all kinds of torture, and by the strength of his faith overcame the weakness of the flesh, and mightily conquered the adversary—these men found him out and detected his craft and duplicity, his perjuries and falsehoods, his unsociability and cruel friendship. And they returned to the holy church and proclaimed in the presence of many, both bishops and presbyters and a large number of the laity, all his craft and wickedness, which for a long time he had concealed. And this they did with lamentations and repentance, because through the persuasions of the crafty and malicious beast they had left the church for the time. A little farther on he says:

7. How remarkable, beloved brother, the change and transformation which we have seen take place in him in a short time. For this most illustrious man, who bound himself with terrible oaths in nowise to seek the bishopric, suddenly appears a bishop as if thrown among us by some machine.

8. For this dogmatist, this defender of the doctrine of the Church, attempting to grasp and seize the episcopate, which had not been given him from above, chose two of his companions who had given up their own salvation. And he sent them to a small and insignificant corner of Italy, that there by some counterfeit argument he might deceive three bishops, who were rustic and very simple men. And they asserted positively and strongly that it was necessary that they should come quickly to Rome, in order that all the dissension which had arisen there might be appeased through their mediation, jointly with other bishops.

9. When they had come, being, as we have stated, very simple in the craft and artifice of the wicked, they were shut up with certain selected men like himself. And by the tenth hour, when they had become drunk and sick, he compelled them by force to confer on him the episcopate through a counterfeit and vain imposition of hands. Because it had not come to him, he avenged himself by craft and treachery.

10. One of these bishops shortly after came back to the church, lamenting and confessing his transgression. And we communed with him as with a layman, all the people present interceding for him. And we ordained successors of the other bishops, and sent them to the places where they were.

11. This avenger of the Gospel then did not know that there should be one bishop in a catholic church; yet he was not ignorant (for how could he be?) that in it there were forty-six presbyters, seven deacons, seven sub-deacons, forty-two acolyths, fifty-two exorcists, readers, and janitors, and over fifteen hundred widows and persons in distress, all of whom the grace and kindness of the Master nourish.

12. But not even this great multitude, so necessary in the church, nor those who, through God's providence, were rich and full, together with the very many, even innumerable people, could turn him from such desperation and presumption and recall him to the Church.

13. Again, farther on, he adds these words: Permit us to say further: On account of what works or conduct had he the assurance to contend for the episcopate? Was it that he had been brought up in the Church from the beginning, and had endured many conflicts in her behalf, and had passed through many and great dangers for religion? Truly this is not the fact.

14. But Satan, who entered and dwelt in him for a long time, became the occasion of his believing. Being delivered by the exorcists, he fell into a severe sickness; and as he seemed about to die, he received baptism by affusion, on the bed where he lay; if indeed we can say that such a one did receive it.

15. And when he was healed of his sickness he did not receive the other things which it is necessary to have according to the canon of the Church, even the being sealed by the bishop. And as he did not receive this, how could he receive the Holy Spirit?

16. Shortly after he says again:

In the time of persecution, through cowardice and love of life, he denied that he was a presbyter. For when he was requested and entreated by the deacons to come out of the chamber in which he had imprisoned himself and give aid to the brethren as far as was lawful and possible for a presbyter to assist those of the brethren who were in danger and needed help, he paid so little respect to the entreaties of the deacons that he went away and departed in anger. For he said that he no longer desired to be a presbyter, as he was an admirer of another philosophy.

17. Passing by a few things, he adds the following:

For this illustrious man forsook the Church of God, in which, when he believed, he was judged worthy of the presbyterate through the favor of the bishop who ordained him to the presbyterial office. This had been resisted by all the clergy and many of the laity; because it was unlawful that one who had been affused on his bed on account of sickness as he had been should enter into any clerical office; but the bishop requested that he might be permitted to ordain this one only.

18. He adds to these yet another, the worst of all the man's offenses, as follows:

For when he has made the offerings, and distributed a part to each man, as he gives it he compels the wretched man to swear in place of the blessing. Holding his hands in both of his own, he will not release him until he has sworn in this manner (for I will give his own words):

'Swear to me by the body and blood of our Lord Jesus Christ that you will never forsake me and turn to Cornelius.'

19. And the unhappy man does not taste until he has called down imprecations on himself; and instead of saying Amen, as he takes the bread, he says, I will never return to Cornelius. Farther on he says again:

20. But know that he has now been made bare and desolate; as the brethren leave him every day and return to the church. Moses also, the blessed martyr, who lately suffered among us a glorious and admirable martyrdom, while he was yet alive, beholding his boldness and folly, refused to commune with him and with the five presbyters who with him had separated themselves from the church.

21. At the close of his letter he gives a list of the bishops who had come to Rome and condemned the silliness of Novatus, with their names and the parish over which each of them presided.

22. He mentions also those who did not come to Rome, but who expressed by letters their agreement with the vote of these bishops, giving their names and the cities from which they severally sent them. Cornelius wrote these things to Fabius, bishop of Antioch.

Chapter 44. Dionysius' Account of Serapion.

1. To this same Fabius, who seemed to lean somewhat toward this schism, Dionysius of Alexandria also wrote an epistle. He writes in this many other things concerning repentance, and relates the conflicts of those who had lately suffered martyrdom at Alexandria. After the other account he mentions a certain wonderful fact, which deserves a place in this work. It is as follows:

2. I will give you this one example which occurred among us. There was with us a certain Serapion, an aged believer who had lived for a long time blamelessly, but had fallen in the trial. He besought often, but no one gave heed to him, because he had sacrificed. But he became sick, and for three successive days continued speechless and senseless.

3. Having recovered somewhat on the fourth day he sent for his daughter's son, and said, How long do you detain me, my child? I beseech you, make haste, and absolve me speedily. Call one of the presbyters to me. And when he had said this, he became again speechless. And the boy ran to the presbyter. But it was night and he was sick, and therefore unable to come.

4. But as I had commanded that persons at the point of death, if they requested it, and especially if they had asked for it previously, should receive remission, that they might depart with a good hope, he gave the boy a small portion of the eucharist, telling him to soak it and let the drops fall into the old man's mouth.

5. The boy returned with it, and as he drew near, before he entered, Serapion again arousing, said, 'You have come, my child, and the presbyter could not come; but do quickly what he directed, and let me depart.' Then the boy soaked it and dropped it into his mouth. And when he had swallowed a little, immediately he gave up the ghost.

6. Is it not evident that he was preserved and his life continued till he was absolved, and, his sin having been blotted out, he could be acknowledged for the many good deeds which he had done?

Dionysius relates these things.

Chapter 45. An Epistle of Dionysius to Novatus.

1. But let us see how the same man addressed Novatus when he was disturbing the Roman brotherhood. As he pretended that some of the brethren were the occasion of his apostasy and schism, as if he had been forced by them to proceed as he had, observe the manner in which he writes to him:

2. Dionysius to his brother Novatus, greeting. If, as you say, you have been led on unwillingly, you will prove this if you retire willingly. For it were better to suffer everything, rather than divide the Church of God. Even martyrdom for the sake of preventing division would not be less glorious than for refusing to worship idols. Nay, to me it seems greater. For in the one case a man suffers martyrdom for the sake of his own soul; in the other case in behalf of the entire Church. And now if you can persuade or induce the brethren to come to unanimity, your righteousness will be greater than your error, and this will not be counted, but that will be praised. But if you can not prevail with the disobedient, at least save your own soul. I pray that you may fare well, maintaining peace in the Lord. This he wrote to Novatus.

Chapter 46. Other Epistles of Dionysius.

1. He wrote also an epistle to the brethren in Egypt on Repentance. In this he sets forth what seemed proper to him in regard to those who had fallen, and he describes the classes of transgressions.

2. There is extant also a private letter on Repentance, which he wrote to Conon, bishop of the parish of Hermopolis, and another of an admonitory character, to his flock at Alexandria. Among them also is the one written to Origen on Martyrdom and to the brethren at Laodicea, of whom Thelymidres was bishop. He likewise sent one on Repentance to the brethren in Armenia, of whom Merozanes was bishop.

3. Besides all these, he wrote to Cornelius of Rome, when he had received from him an epistle against Novatus. He states in this that he had been invited by Helenus, bishop of Tarsus, in Cilicia, and the others who were with him, Firmilianus, bishop in Cappadocia, and Theoctistus, of Palestine, to meet them at the synod in Antioch, where some persons were endeavoring to establish the schism of Novatus.

4. Besides this he writes that he had been informed that Fabius had fallen asleep, and that Demetrianus had been appointed his successor in the episcopate of Antioch. He writes also in these words concerning the bishop of Jerusalem: For the blessed Alexander having been confined in prison, passed away happily.

5. In addition to this there is extant also a certain other diaconal epistle of Dionysius, sent to those in Rome through Hippolytus. And he wrote another to them on Peace, and likewise on Repentance; and yet another to the confessors there who still held to the opinion of Novatus. He sent two more to the same persons after they had returned to the Church. And he communicated with many others by letters, which he has left behind him as a benefit in various ways to those who now diligently study his writings.

BOOK VII

Introduction.

In this seventh book of the Church History, the great bishop of Alexandria, Dionysius, shall again assist us by his own words; relating the several affairs of his time in the epistles which he has left. I will begin with them.

Chapter 1. The Wickedness of Decius and Gallus.

When Decius had reigned not quite two years, he was slain with his children, and Gallus succeeded him. At this time Origen died, being sixty-nine years of age. Dionysius, writing to Hermammon, speaks as follows of Gallus:

Gallus neither recognized the wickedness of Decius, nor considered what had destroyed him; but stumbled on the same stone, though it lay before his eyes. For when his reign was prosperous and affairs were proceeding according to his mind, he attacked the holy men who were interceding with God for his peace and welfare. Therefore with them he persecuted also their prayers in his behalf. So much concerning him.

Chapter 2. The Bishops of Rome in those Times.

Cornelius, having held the episcopate in the city of Rome about three years, was succeeded by Lucius. He died in less than eight months, and transmitted his office to Stephen. Dionysius wrote to him the first of his letters on baptism, as no small controversy had arisen as to whether those who had turned from any heresy should be purified by baptism. For the ancient custom prevailed in regard to such, that they should receive only the laying on of hands with prayers.

Chapter 3. Cyprian, and the Bishops with him, first taught that it was necessary to purify by Baptism those converted from Heresy.

First of all, Cyprian, pastor of the parish of Carthage, maintained that they should not be received except they had been purified from their error by baptism. But Stephen considering it unnecessary to add any innovation contrary to the tradition which had been held from the beginning, was very indignant at this.

Chapter 4. The Epistles which Dionysius wrote on this Subject.

Dionysius, therefore, having communicated with him extensively on this question by letter, finally showed him that since the persecution had abated, the churches everywhere had rejected the novelty of Novatus, and were at peace among themselves. He writes as follows:

Chapter 5. The Peace following the Persecution.

1. But know now, my brethren, that all the churches throughout the East and beyond, which formerly were divided, have become united. And all the bishops everywhere are of one mind, and rejoice greatly in the peace which has come beyond expectation. Thus Demetrianus in Antioch, Theoctistus in Cæsarea, Mazabanes in Ælia, Marinus in Tyre (Alexander having fallen asleep), Heliodorus in Laodicea (Thelymidres being dead), Helenus in Tarsus, and all the churches of Cilicia, Firmilianus, and all Cappadocia. I have named only the more illustrious bishops, that I may not make my epistle too long and my words too burdensome.

2. And all Syria, and Arabia to which you send help when needed, and whither you have just written, Mesopotamia, Pontus, Bithynia, and in short all everywhere are rejoicing and glorifying God for the unanimity and brotherly love. Thus far Dionysius.

3. But Stephen, having filled his office two years, was succeeded by Xystus. Dionysius wrote him a second epistle on baptism, in which he shows him at the same time the opinion and judgment of Stephen and the other bishops, and speaks in this manner of Stephen:

4. He therefore had written previously concerning Helenus and Firmilianus, and all those in Cilicia and Cappadocia and Galatia and the neighboring nations, saying that he would not commune with them for this same cause; namely, that they re-baptized heretics. But consider the importance of the matter.

5. For truly in the largest synods of the bishops, as I learn, decrees have been passed on this subject, that those coming over from heresies should be instructed, and then should be washed and cleansed from the filth of the old and impure leaven. And I wrote entreating him concerning all these things. Further on he says:

6. I wrote also, at first in few words, recently in many, to our beloved fellow presbyters, Dionysius and Philemon, who formerly had held the

same opinion as Stephen, and had written to me on the same matters. So much in regard to the above-mentioned controversy.

Chapter 6. The Heresy of Sabellius.

He refers also in the same letter to the heretical teachings of Sabellius, which were in his time becoming prominent, and says:

For concerning the doctrine now agitated in Ptolemais of Pentapolis,—which is impious and marked by great blasphemy against the Almighty God, the Father, and our Lord Jesus Christ, and contains much unbelief respecting his Only Begotten Son and the first-born of every creature, the Word which became man, and a want of perception of the Holy Spirit—as there came to me communications from both sides and brethren discussing the matter, I wrote certain letters treating the subject as instructively as, by the help. of God, I was able. Of these I send you copies.

Chapter 7. The Abominable Error of the Heretics; the Divine Vision of Dionysius; and the Ecclesiastical Canon which he received.

1. In the third epistle on baptism which this same Dionysius wrote to Philemon, the Roman presbyter, he relates the following: But I examined the works and traditions of the heretics, defiling my mind for a little time with their abominable opinions, but receiving this benefit from them, that I refuted them by myself, and detested them all the more.

2. And when a certain brother among the presbyters restrained me, fearing that I should be carried away with the filth of their wickedness (for it would defile my soul)—in which also, as I perceived, he spoke the truth,— a vision sent from God came and strengthened me.

3. And the word which came to me commanded me, saying distinctly, 'Read everything which you can take in hand, for you are able to correct and prove all; and this has been to you from the beginning the cause of your faith.' I received the vision as agreeing with the apostolic word, which says to them that are stronger, 'Be skillful money-changers.'

4. Then after saying some things concerning all the heresies he adds: I received this rule and ordinance from our blessed father, Heraclas. For those who came over from heresies, although they had apostatized from the Church—or rather had not apostatized, but seemed to meet with

them, yet were charged with resorting to some false teacher—when he had expelled them from the Church he did not receive them back, though they entreated for it, until they had publicly reported all things which they had heard from their adversaries; but then he received them without requiring of them another baptism. For they had formerly received the Holy Spirit from him.

5. Again, after treating the question thoroughly, he adds: I have learned also that this is not a novel practice introduced in Africa alone, but that even long ago in the times of the bishops before us this opinion has been adopted in the most populous churches, and in synods of the brethren in Iconium and Synnada, and by many others. To overturn their counsels and throw them into strife and contention, I cannot endure. For it is said, 'You shall not remove your neighbor's landmark, which your fathers have set.' Deuteronomy 19:14

6. His fourth epistle on baptism was written to Dionysius of Rome, who was then a presbyter, but not long after received the episcopate of that church. It is evident from what is stated of him by Dionysius of Alexandria, that he also was a learned and admirable man. Among other things he writes to him as follows concerning Novatus:

Chapter 8. The Heterodoxy of Novatus.

For with good reason do we feel hatred toward Novatian, who has sundered the Church and drawn some of the brethren into impiety and blasphemy, and has introduced impious teaching concerning God, and has calumniated our most compassionate Lord Jesus Christ as unmerciful. And besides all this he rejects the holy baptism, and overturns the faith and confession which precede it, and entirely banishes from them the Holy Ghost, if indeed there was any hope that he would remain or return to them.

Chapter 9. The Ungodly Baptism of the Heretics.

1. His fifth epistle was written to Xystus, bishop of Rome. In this, after saying much against the heretics, he relates a certain occurrence of his time as follows: For truly, brother, I am in need of counsel, and I ask your judgment concerning a certain matter which has come to me, fearing that I may be in error.

2. For one of the brethren that assemble, who has long been considered a believer, and who, before my ordination, and I think before the appointment of the blessed Heraclas, was a member of the congregation, was present with those who were recently baptized. And when he heard the questions and answers, he came to me weeping, and bewailing himself; and falling at my feet he acknowledged and protested that the baptism with which he had been baptized among the heretics was not of this character, nor in any respect like this, because it was full of impiety and blasphemy.

3. And he said that his soul was now pierced with sorrow, and that he had not confidence to lift his eyes to God, because he had set out from those impious words and deeds. And on this account he besought that he might receive this most perfect purification, and reception and grace.

4. But I did not dare to do this; and said that his long communion was sufficient for this. For I should not dare to renew from the beginning one who had heard the giving of thanks and joined in repeating the Amen; who had stood by the table and had stretched forth his hands to receive the blessed food; and who had received it, and partaken for a long while of the body and blood of our Lord Jesus Christ. But I exhorted him to be of good courage, and to approach the partaking of the saints with firm faith and good hope.

5. But he does not cease lamenting, and he shudders to approach the table, and scarcely, though entreated, does he dare to be present at the prayers.

6. Besides these there is also extant another epistle of the same man on baptism, addressed by him and his parish to Xystus and the church at Rome. In this he considers the question then agitated with extended argument. And there is extant yet another after these, addressed to Dionysius of Rome, concerning Lucian. So much with reference to these.

Chapter 10. Valerian and the Persecution under him.

1. Gallus and the other rulers, having held the government less than two years, were overthrown, and Valerian, with his son Gallienus, received the empire. The circumstances which Dionysius relates of him we may learn from his epistle to Hermammon, in which he gives the following account:

2. And in like manner it is revealed to John; 'For there was given to him,' he says, 'a mouth speaking great things and blasphemy; and there was given unto him authority and forty and two months.' Revelation 13:5

3. It is wonderful that both of these things occurred under Valerian; and it is the more remarkable in this case when we consider his previous conduct, for he had been mild and friendly toward the men of God, for none of the emperors before him had treated them so kindly and favorably; and not even those who were said openly to be Christians received them with such manifest hospitality and friendliness as he did at the beginning of his reign. For his entire house was filled with pious persons and was a church of God.

4. But the teacher and ruler of the synagogue of the Magi from Egypt persuaded him to change his course, urging him to slay and persecute pure and holy men because they opposed and hindered the corrupt and abominable incantations. For there are and there were men who, being present and being seen, though they only breathed and spoke, were able to scatter the counsels of the sinful demons. And he induced him to practice initiations and abominable sorceries and to offer unacceptable sacrifices; to slay innumerable children and to sacrifice the offspring of unhappy fathers; to divide the bowels of new-born babes and to mutilate and cut to pieces the creatures of God, as if by such practices they could attain happiness.

5. He adds to this the following: Splendid indeed were the thank-offerings which Macrianus brought them for the empire which was the object of his hopes. He is said to have been formerly the emperor's general finance minister ; yet he did nothing praiseworthy or of general benefit, but fell under the prophetic saying,

6. 'Woe unto those who prophesy from their own heart and do not consider the general good.' Ezekiel 13:3 For he did not perceive the general Providence, nor did he look for the judgment of Him who is before all, and through all, and over all. Wherefore he became an enemy of his Catholic Church, and alienated and estranged himself from the compassion of God, and fled as far as possible from his salvation. In this he showed the truth of his own name.

7. And again, farther on he says: For Valerian, being instigated to such acts by this man, was given over to insults and reproaches, according to what was said by Isaiah: 'They have chosen their own ways and their abominations in which their soul delighted; I also will choose their delusions and will render unto them their sins.' Isaiah 66:3-4

8. But this man madly desired the kingdom though unworthy of it, and being unable to put the royal garment on his crippled body, set forward his two sons to bear their father's sins. For concerning them the declaration which God spoke was plain, 'Visiting the iniquities of the fathers upon the children unto the third and fourth generation of them that hate me.' Exodus 20:5

9. For heaping on the heads of his sons his own evil desires, in which he had met with success, he wiped off upon them his own wickedness and hatred toward God.

Dionysius relates these things concerning Valerian.

Chapter 11. The Events which happened at this Time to Dionysius and those in Egypt.

1. But as regards the persecution which prevailed so fiercely in his reign, and the sufferings which Dionysius with others endured on account of piety toward the God of the universe, his own words shall show, which he wrote in answer to Germanus, a contemporary bishop who was endeavoring to slander him. His statement is as follows:

2. Truly I am in danger of falling into great folly and stupidity through being forced to relate the wonderful providence of God toward us. But since it is said that 'it is good to keep close the secret of a king, but it is honorable to reveal the works of God,' Tobit 12:7 I will join issue with the violence of Germanus.

3. I went not alone to Æmilianus; but my fellow presbyter, Maximus, and the deacons Faustus, Eusebius, and Chæremon, and a brother who was present from Rome, went with me.

4. But Æmilianus did not at first say to me: 'Hold no assemblies;' for this was superfluous to him, and the last thing to one who was seeking to accomplish the first. For he was not concerned about our assembling, but that we ourselves should not be Christians. And he commanded me to give this up; supposing if I turned from it, the others also would follow me.

5. But I answered him, neither unsuitably nor in many words: 'We must obey God rather than men.' Acts 5:29 And I testified openly that I worshipped the one only God, and no other; and that I would not turn from this nor would I ever cease to be a Christian. Thereupon he commanded us to go to a village near the desert, called Cephro.

6. But listen to the very words which were spoken on both sides, as they were recorded: Dionysius, Faustus, Maximus, Marcellus, and Chæremon being arraigned, Æmilianus the prefect said:

7. 'I have reasoned verbally with you concerning the clemency which our rulers have shown to you; for they have given you the opportunity to save yourselves, if you will turn to that which is according to nature, and worship the gods that preserve their empire, and forget those that are contrary to nature. What then do you say to this? For I do not think that you will be ungrateful for their kindness, since they would turn you to a better course.'

8. Dionysius replied: 'Not all people worship all gods; but each one those whom he approves. We therefore reverence and worship the one God, the Maker of all; who has given the empire to the divinely favored and august Valerian and Gallienus; and we pray to him continually for their empire that it may remain unshaken.'

9. Æmilianus, the prefect, said to them: 'But who forbids you to worship him, if he is a god, together with those who are gods by nature. For you have been commanded to reverence the gods, and the gods whom all know.' Dionysius answered:

10. 'We worship no other.' Æmilianus, the prefect, said to them: 'I see that you are at once ungrateful, and insensible to the kindness of our sovereigns. Wherefore you shall not remain in this city. But you shall be sent into the regions of Libya, to a place called Cephro. For I have chosen this place at the command of our sovereigns, and it shall by no means be permitted you or any others, either to hold assemblies, or to enter into the so called cemeteries.

11. But if any one shall be seen without the place which I have commanded, or be found in any assembly, he will bring peril on himself. For suitable punishment shall not fail. Go, therefore where you have been ordered.'

And he hastened me away, though I was sick, not granting even a day's respite. What opportunity then did I have, either to hold assemblies, or not to hold them?

12. Farther on he says: But through the help of the Lord we did not give up the open assembly. But I called together the more diligently those who were in the city, as if I were with them; being, so to speak, 'absent in body but present in spirit.' 1 Corinthians 5:3 But in Cephro a large church gathered with us of the brethren that followed us from the city,

and those that joined us from Egypt; and there 'God opened unto us a door for the Word.' Colossians 4:3

13. At first we were persecuted and stoned; but afterwards not a few of the heathen forsook the idols and turned to God. For until this time they had not heard the Word, since it was then first sown by us.

14. And as if God had brought us to them for this purpose, when we had performed this ministry he transferred us to another place. For Æmilianus, as it appeared, desired to transport us to rougher and more Libyan-like places; so he commanded them to assemble from all quarters in Mareotis, and assigned to them different villages throughout the country. But he ordered us to be placed nearer the highway that we might be seized first. For evidently he arranged and prepared matters so that whenever he wished to seize us he could take all of us without difficulty.

15. When I was first ordered to go to Cephro I did not know where the place was, and had scarcely ever heard the name; yet I went readily and cheerfully. But when I was told that I was to remove to the district of Colluthion, those who were present know how I was affected.

16. For here I will accuse myself. At first I was grieved and greatly disturbed; for though these places were better known and more familiar to us, yet the country was said to be destitute of brethren and of men of character, and to be exposed to the annoyances of travelers and incursions of robbers.

17. But I was comforted when the brethren reminded me that it was nearer the city, and that while Cephro afforded us much intercourse with the brethren from Egypt, so that we were able to extend the Church more widely, as this place was nearer the city we should enjoy more frequently the sight of those who were truly beloved and most closely related and dearest to us. For they would come and remain, and special meetings could be held, as in the more remote suburbs. And thus it turned out. After other matters he writes again as follows of the things which happened to him:

18. Germanus indeed boasts of many confessions. He can speak forsooth of many adversities which he himself has endured. But is he able to reckon up as many as we can, of sentences, confiscations, proscriptions, plundering of goods, loss of dignities, contempt of worldly glory, disregard for the flatteries of governors and of councilors, and patient endurance of the threats of opponents, of outcries, of perils

and persecutions, and wandering and distress, and all kinds of tribulation, such as came upon me under Decius and Sabinus, and such as continue even now under Æmilianus? But where has Germanus been seen? And what account is there of him?

19. But I turn from this great folly into which I am falling on account of Germanus. And for the same reason I desist from giving to the brethren who know it an account of everything which took place.

20. The same writer also in the epistle to Domitius and Didymus mentions some particulars of the persecution as follows: As our people are many and unknown to you, it would be superfluous to give their names; but understand that men and women, young and old, maidens and matrons, soldiers and civilians, of every race and age, some by scourging and fire, others by the sword, have conquered in the strife and received their crowns.

21. But in the case of some a very long time was not sufficient to make them appear acceptable to the Lord; as, indeed, it seems also in my own case, that sufficient time has not yet elapsed. Wherefore he has retained me for the time which he knows to be fitting, saying, 'In an acceptable time have I heard you, and in a day of salvation have I helped you.' Isaiah 49:8

22. For as you have inquired of our affairs and desire us to tell you how we are situated, you have heard fully that when we— that is, myself and Gaius and Faustus and Peter and Paul — were led away as prisoners by a centurion and magistrates, with their soldiers and servants, certain persons from Mareotis came and dragged us away by force, as we were unwilling to follow them.

23. But now I and Gaius and Peter are alone, deprived of the other brethren, and shut up in a desert and dry place in Libya, three days' journey from Parætonium.

24. He says farther on: The presbyters, Maximus, Dioscorus, Demetrius, and Lucius concealed themselves in the city, and visited the brethren secretly; for Faustinus and Aquila, who are more prominent in the world, are wandering in Egypt. But the deacons, Faustus, Eusebius, and Chæremon, have survived those who died in the pestilence. Eusebius is one whom God has strengthened and endowed from the first to fulfill energetically the ministrations for the imprisoned confessors, and to attend to the dangerous task of preparing for burial the bodies of the perfected and blessed martyrs.

25. For as I have said before, unto the present time the governor continues to put to death in a cruel manner those who are brought to trial. And he destroys some with tortures, and wastes others away with imprisonment and bonds; and he suffers no one to go near them, and investigates whether any one does so. Nevertheless God gives relief to the afflicted through the zeal and persistence of the brethren.

26. Thus far Dionysius. But it should be known that Eusebius, whom he calls a deacon, shortly afterward became bishop of the church of Laodicea in Syria; and Maximus, of whom he speaks as being then a presbyter, succeeded Dionysius himself as bishop of Alexandria. But the Faustus who was with him, and who at that time was distinguished for his confession, was preserved until the persecution in our day, when being very old and full of days, he closed his life by martyrdom, being beheaded. But such are the things which happened at that time to Dionysius.

Chapter 12. The Martyrs in Cæsarea in Palestine.

During the above-mentioned persecution under Valerian, three men in Cæsarea in Palestine, being conspicuous in their confession of Christ, were adorned with divine martyrdom, becoming food for wild beasts. One of them was called Priscus, another Malchus, and the name of the third was Alexander. They say that these men, who lived in the country, acted at first in a cowardly manner, as if they were careless and thoughtless. For when the opportunity was given to those who longed for the prize with heavenly desire, they treated it lightly, lest they should seize the Crown of martyrdom prematurely. But having deliberated on the matter, they hastened to Cæsarea, and went before the judge and met the end we have mentioned. They relate that besides these, in the same persecution and the same city, a certain woman endured a similar conflict. But it is reported that she belonged to the sect of Marcion.

Chapter 13. The Peace under Gallienus.

1. Shortly after this Valerian was reduced to slavery by the barbarians, and his son having become sole ruler, conducted the government more prudently. He immediately restrained the persecution against us by public proclamations, and directed the bishops to perform in freedom their customary duties, in a rescript which ran as follows:

2. The Emperor Cæsar Publius Licinius Gallienus, Pius, Felix, Augustus, to Dionysius, Pinnas, Demetrius, and the other bishops. I have ordered the bounty of my gift to be declared through all the world, that they may depart from the places of religious worship. And for this purpose you may use this copy of my rescript, that no one may molest you. And this which you are now enabled lawfully to do, has already for a long time been conceded by me. Therefore Aurelius Cyrenius, who is the chief administrator of affairs, will observe this ordinance which I have given.

3. I have given this in a translation from the Latin, that it may be more readily understood. Another decree of his is extant addressed to other bishops, permitting them to take possession again of the so- called cemeteries.

Chapter 14. The Bishops that flourished at that Time.

At that time Xystus was still presiding over the church of Rome, and Demetrianus, successor of Fabius, over the church of Antioch, and Firmilianus over that of Cæsarea in Cappadocia; and besides these, Gregory and his brother Athenodorus, friends of Origen, were presiding over the churches in Pontus; and Theoctistus of Cæsarea in Palestine having died, Domnus received the episcopate there. He held it but a short time, and Theotecnus, our contemporary, succeeded him. He also was a member of Origen's school. But in Jerusalem, after the death of Mazabanes, Hymenæus, who has been celebrated among us for a great many years, succeeded to his seat.

Chapter 15. The Martyrdom of Marinus at Cæsarea.

1. At this time, when the peace of the churches had been everywhere restored, Marinus in Cæsarea in Palestine, who was honored for his military deeds, and illustrious by virtue of family and wealth, was beheaded for his testimony to Christ, on the following account.

2. The vine-branch is a certain mark of honor among the Romans, and those who obtain it become, they say, centurions. A place being vacated, the order of succession called Marinus to this position. But when he was about to receive the honor, another person came before the tribunal and claimed that it was not legal, according to the ancient laws, for him to receive the Roman dignity, as he was a Christian and did not sacrifice to the emperors; but that the office belonged rather to him.

3. Thereupon the judge, whose name was Achæus, being disturbed, first asked what opinion Marinus held. And when he perceived that he continually confessed himself a Christian, he gave him three hours for reflection.

4. When he came out from the tribunal, Theotecnus, the bishop there, took him aside and conversed with him, and taking his hand led him into the church. And standing with him within, in the sanctuary, he raised his cloak a little, and pointed to the sword that hung by his side; and at the same time he placed before him the Scripture of the divine Gospels, and told him to choose which of the two he wished. And without hesitation he reached forth his right hand, and took the divine Scripture. Hold fast then, says Theotecnus to him, hold fast to God, and strengthened by him may thou obtain what you have chosen, and go in peace.

5. Immediately on his return the herald cried out calling him to the tribunal, for the appointed time was already completed. And standing before the tribunal, and manifesting greater zeal for the faith, immediately, as he was, he was led away and finished his course by death.

Chapter 16. Story in Regard to Astyrius.

Astyrius also is commemorated on account of his pious boldness in connection with this affair. He was a Roman of senatorial rank, and in favor with the emperors, and well known to all on account of his noble birth and wealth. Being present at the martyr's death, he took his body away on his shoulder, and arraying him in a splendid and costly garment, prepared him for the grave in a magnificent manner, and gave him fitting burial. The friends of this man, that remain to our day, relate many other facts concerning him.

Chapter 17. The Signs at Paneas of the Great Might of our Saviour.

Among these is also the following wonder. At Cæsarea Philippi, which the Phœnicians call Paneas, springs are shown at the foot of the Mountain Panius, out of which the Jordan flows. They say that on a certain feast day, a victim was thrown in, and that through the power of the demon it marvelously disappeared and that which happened was a famous wonder to those who were present. Astyrius was once there when these things were done, and seeing the multitude astonished at the affair, he pitied their delusion; and looking up to heaven he supplicated the God over all through Christ, that he would rebuke the demon who deceived the people, and bring the men's delusion to an end. And they say that when he had prayed thus, immediately the sacrifice floated on the surface of the fountain. And thus the miracle departed; and no wonder was ever afterward performed at the place.

Chapter 18. The Statue which the Woman with an Issue of Blood erected.

1. Since I have mentioned this city I do not think it proper to omit an account which is worthy of record for posterity. For they say that the woman with an issue of blood, who, as we learn from the sacred Gospel, received from our Saviour deliverance from her affliction, came from this place, and that her house is shown in the city, and that remarkable memorials of the kindness of the Saviour to her remain there.

2. For there stands upon an elevated stone, by the gates of her house, a brazen image of a woman kneeling, with her hands stretched out, as if she were praying. Opposite this is another upright image of a man, made of the same material, clothed decently in a double cloak, and extending his hand toward the woman. At his feet, beside the statue itself, is a certain strange plant, which climbs up to the hem of the brazen cloak, and is a remedy for all kinds of diseases.

3. They say that this statue is an image of Jesus. It has remained to our day, so that we ourselves also saw it when we were staying in the city.

4. Nor is it strange that those of the Gentiles who, of old, were benefited by our Saviour, should have done such things, since we have learned also that the likenesses of his apostles Paul and Peter, and of Christ himself, are preserved in paintings, the ancients being accustomed, as it is likely, according to a habit of the Gentiles, to pay this kind of honor indiscriminately to those regarded by them as deliverers.

Chapter 19. The Episcopal Chair of James.

The chair of James, who first received the episcopate of the church at Jerusalem from the Saviour himself and the apostles, and who, as the divine records show, was called a brother of Christ, has been preserved until now, the brethren who have followed him in succession there exhibiting clearly to all the reverence which both those of old times and those of our own day maintained and do maintain for holy men on account of their piety. So much as to this matter.

Chapter 20. The Festal Epistles of Dionysius, in which he also gives a Paschal Canon.

Dionysius, besides his epistles already mentioned, wrote at that time also his extant Festal Epistles, in which he uses words of panegyric respecting the passover feast. He addressed one of these to Flavius, and another to Domitius and Didymus, in which he sets forth a canon of eight years, maintaining that it is not proper to observe the paschal feast until after the vernal equinox. Besides these he sent another epistle to his fellow presbyters in Alexandria, as well as various others to different persons while the persecution was still prevailing.

Chapter 21. The Occurrences at Alexandria.

1. Peace had but just been restored when he returned to Alexandria; but as sedition and war broke out again, rendering it impossible for him to oversee all the brethren, separated in different places by the insurrection, at the feast of the passover, as if he were still an exile from Alexandria, he addressed them again by letter.

2. And in another festal epistle written later to Hierax, a bishop in Egypt, he mentions the sedition then prevailing in Alexandria, as follows:

What wonder is it that it is difficult for me to communicate by letters with those who live far away, when it is beyond my power even to reason with myself, or to take counsel for my own life?

3. Truly I need to send letters to those who are as my own bowels, dwelling in one home, and brethren of one soul, and citizens of the same church; but how to send them I cannot tell. For it would be easier for one to go, not only beyond the limits of the province, but even from the East to the West, than from Alexandria to Alexandria itself.

4. For the very heart of the city is more intricate and impassable than that great and trackless desert which Israel traversed for two generations. And our smooth and waveless harbors have become like the sea, divided and walled up, through which Israel drove and in whose highway the Egyptians were overwhelmed. For often from the slaughters there committed they appear like the Red Sea.

5. And the river which flows by the city has sometimes seemed drier than the waterless desert, and more parched than that in which Israel, as they passed through it, so suffered for thirst, that they cried out against Moses, and the water flowed for them from the steep rock, through him who alone does wonders.

6. Again it has overflowed so greatly as to flood all the surrounding country, and the roads and the fields; threatening to bring back the deluge of water that occurred in the days of Noah. And it flows along, polluted always with blood and slaughter and drownings, as it became for Pharaoh through the agency of Moses, when he changed it into blood, and it stank.

7. And what other water could purify the water which purifies everything? How could the ocean, so great and impassable for men, if poured into it, cleanse this bitter sea? Or how could the great river which flowed out of Eden, if it poured the four heads into which it is divided into the one of Geon, wash away this pollution?

8. Or when can the air poisoned by these noxious exhalations become pure? For such vapors arise from the earth, and winds from the sea, and breezes from the river, and mists from the harbors, that the dews are, as it were, discharges from dead bodies putrefying in all the elements around us.

9. Yet men wonder and cannot understand whence these continuous pestilences; whence these severe sicknesses; whence these deadly diseases of all kinds; whence this various and vast human destruction; why this great city no longer contains as many inhabitants, from tender infants to those most advanced in life, as it formerly contained of those whom it called hearty old men. But the men from forty to seventy years of age were then so much more numerous that their number cannot now be filled out, even when those from fourteen to eighty years are enrolled and registered for the public allowance of food.

10. And the youngest in appearance have become, as it were, of equal age with those who formerly were the oldest. But though they see the race of men thus constantly diminishing and wasting away, and though their complete destruction is increasing and advancing, they do not tremble.

Chapter 22. The Pestilence which came upon them.

1. After these events a pestilential disease followed the war, and at the approach of the feast he wrote again to the brethren, describing the sufferings consequent upon this calamity.

2. To other men the present might not seem to be a suitable time for a festival. Nor indeed is this or any other time suitable for them; neither sorrowful times, nor even such as might be thought especially cheerful. Now, indeed, everything is tears and every one is mourning, and wailings resound daily through the city because of the multitude of the dead and dying.

3. For as it was written of the firstborn of the Egyptians, so now 'there has arisen a great cry, for there is not a house where there is not one dead.' Exodus 12:30 And would that this were all!

4. For many terrible things have happened already. First, they drove us out; and when alone, and persecuted, and put to death by all, even then we kept the feast. And every place of affliction was to us a place of festival: field, desert, ship, inn, prison; but the perfected martyrs kept the most joyous festival of all, feasting in heaven.

5. After these things war and famine followed, which we endured in common with the heathen. But we bore alone those things with which they afflicted us, and at the same time we experienced also the effects of what they inflicted upon and suffered from one another; and again, we rejoiced in the peace of Christ, which he gave to us alone.

6. But after both we and they had enjoyed a very brief season of rest this pestilence assailed us; to them more dreadful than any dread, and more intolerable than any other calamity; and, as one of their own writers has said, the only thing which prevails over all hope. But to us this was not so, but no less than the other things was it an exercise and probation. For it did not keep aloof even from us, but the heathen it assailed more severely.

7. Farther on he adds:

The most of our brethren were unsparing in their exceeding love and brotherly kindness. They held fast to each other and visited the sick fearlessly, and ministered to them continually, serving them in Christ. And they died with them most joyfully, taking the affliction of others, and drawing the sickness from their neighbors to themselves and willingly receiving their pains. And many who cared for the sick and gave strength to others died themselves having transferred to themselves their death. And the popular saying which always seems a mere expression of courtesy, they then made real in action, taking their departure as the others' 'offscouring.'

8. Truly the best of our brethren departed from life in this manner, including some presbyters and deacons and those of the people who had the highest reputation; so that this form of death, through the great piety and strong faith it exhibited, seemed to lack nothing of martyrdom.

9. And they took the bodies of the saints in their open hands and in their bosoms, and closed their eyes and their mouths; and they bore them away on their shoulders and laid them out; and they clung to them and embraced them; and they prepared them suitably with washings and garments. And after a little they received like treatment themselves, for the survivors were continually following those who had gone before them.

10. But with the heathen everything was quite otherwise. They deserted those who began to be sick, and fled from their dearest friends. And they cast them out into the streets when they were half dead, and left the dead like refuse, unburied. They shunned any participation or fellowship with death; which yet, with all their precautions, it was not easy for them to escape.

11. After this epistle, when peace had been restored to the city, he wrote another festal letter to the brethren in Egypt, and again several others besides this. And there is also a certain one extant On the Sabbath, and another On Exercise.

12. Moreover, he wrote again an epistle to Hermammon and the brethren in Egypt, describing at length the wickedness of Decius and his successors, and mentioning the peace under Gallienus.

Chapter 23. The Reign of Gallienus.

1. But there is nothing like hearing his own words, which are as follows:

Then he, having betrayed one of the emperors that preceded him, and made war on the other, perished with his whole family speedily and utterly. But Gallienus was proclaimed and universally acknowledged at once an old emperor and a new, being before them and continuing after them.

2. For according to the word spoken by the prophet Isaiah, 'Behold the things from the beginning have come to pass, and new things shall now arise.' Isaiah 42:9 For as a cloud passing over the sun's rays and

obscuring them for a little time hides it and appears in its place; but when the cloud has passed by or is dissipated, the sun which had risen before appears again; so Macrianus who put himself forward and approached the existing empire of Gallienus, is not, since he never was. But the other is just as he was.

3. And his kingdom, as if it had cast aside old age, and had been purified from the former wickedness, now blossoms out more vigorously, and is seen and heard farther, and extends in all directions.

4. He then indicates the time at which he wrote this in the following words: It occurs to me again to review the days of the imperial years. For I perceive that those most impious men, though they have been famous, yet in a short time have become nameless. But the holier and more godly prince, having passed the seventh year, is now completing the ninth, in which we shall keep the feast.

Chapter 24. Nepos and his Schism.

1. Besides all these the two books on the Promises were prepared by him. The occasion of these was Nepos, a bishop in Egypt, who taught that the promises to the holy men in the Divine Scriptures should be understood in a more Jewish manner, and that there would be a certain millennium of bodily luxury upon this earth.

2. As he thought that he could establish his private opinion by the Revelation of John, he wrote a book on this subject, entitled Refutation of Allegorists.

3. Dionysius opposes this in his books on the Promises. In the first he gives his own opinion of the dogma; and in the second he treats of the Revelation of John, and mentioning Nepos at the beginning, writes of him in this manner:

4. But since they bring forward a certain work of Nepos, on which they rely confidently, as if it proved beyond dispute that there will be a reign of Christ upon earth, I confess that in many other respects I approve and love Nepos, for his faith and industry and diligence in the Scriptures, and for his extensive psalmody, with which many of the brethren are still delighted; and I hold him in the more reverence because he has gone to rest before us. But the truth should be loved and honored most of all. And while we should praise and approve ungrudgingly what is said aright, we ought to examine and correct what does not seem to have been written soundly.

5. Were he present to state his opinion orally, mere unwritten discussion, persuading and reconciling those who are opposed by question and answer, would be sufficient. But as some think his work very plausible, and as certain teachers regard the law and prophets as of no consequence, and do not follow the Gospels, and treat lightly the apostolic epistles, while they make promises as to the teaching of this work as if it were some great hidden mystery, and do not permit our simpler brethren to have any sublime and lofty thoughts concerning the glorious and truly divine appearing of our Lord, and our resurrection from the dead, and our being gathered together unto him, and made like him, but on the contrary lead them to hope for small and mortal things in the kingdom of God, and for things such as exist now—since this is the case, it is necessary that we should dispute with our brother Nepos as if he were present. Farther on he says:

6. When I was in the district of Arsinoë;, where, as you know, this doctrine has prevailed for a long time, so that schisms and apostasies of entire churches have resulted, I called together the presbyters and teachers of the brethren in the villages—such brethren as wished being also present—and I exhorted them to make a public examination of this question.

7. Accordingly when they brought me this book, as if it were a weapon and fortress impregnable, sitting with them from morning till evening for three successive days, I endeavored to correct what was written in it.

8. And I rejoiced over the constancy, sincerity, docility, and intelligence of the brethren, as we considered in order and with moderation the questions and the difficulties and the points of agreement. And we abstained from defending in every manner and contentiously the opinions which we had once held, unless they appeared to be correct. Nor did we evade objections, but we endeavored as far as possible to hold to and confirm the things which lay before us, and if the reason given satisfied us, we were not ashamed to change our opinions and agree with others; but on the contrary, conscientiously and sincerely, and with hearts laid open before God, we accepted whatever was established by the proofs and teachings of the Holy Scriptures.

9. And finally the author and mover of this teaching, who was called Coracion, in the hearing of all the brethren that were present, acknowledged and testified to us that he would no longer hold this opinion, nor discuss it, nor mention nor teach it, as he was fully convinced by the arguments against it. And some of the other brethren

expressed their gratification at the conference, and at the spirit of conciliation and harmony which all had manifested.

Chapter 25. The Apocalypse of John.

1. Afterward he speaks in this manner of the Apocalypse of John.

Some before us have set aside and rejected the book altogether, criticising it chapter by chapter, and pronouncing it without sense or argument, and maintaining that the title is fraudulent.

2. For they say that it is not the work of John, nor is it a revelation, because it is covered thickly and densely by a veil of obscurity. And they affirm that none of the apostles, and none of the saints, nor any one in the Church is its author, but that Cerinthus, who founded the sect which was called after him the Cerinthian, desiring reputable authority for his fiction, prefixed the name.

3. For the doctrine which he taught was this: that the kingdom of Christ will be an earthly one. And as he was himself devoted to the pleasures of the body and altogether sensual in his nature, he dreamed that that kingdom would consist in those things which he desired, namely, in the delights of the belly and of sexual passion; that is to say, in eating and drinking and marrying, and in festivals and sacrifices and the slaying of victims, under the guise of which he thought he could indulge his appetites with a better grace.

4. But I could not venture to reject the book, as many brethren hold it in high esteem. But I suppose that it is beyond my comprehension, and that there is a certain concealed and more wonderful meaning in every part. For if I do not understand I suspect that a deeper sense lies beneath the words.

5. I do not measure and judge them by my own reason, but leaving the more to faith I regard them as too high for me to grasp. And I do not reject what I cannot comprehend, but rather wonder because I do not understand it.

6. After this he examines the entire Book of Revelation, and having proved that it is impossible to understand it according to the literal sense, proceeds as follows:

Having finished all the prophecy, so to speak, the prophet pronounces those blessed who shall observe it, and also himself. For he says, 'Blessed is he that keeps the words of the prophecy of this book, and I, John, who saw and heard these things.'

7. Therefore that he was called John, and that this book is the work of one John, I do not deny. And I agree also that it is the work of a holy and inspired man. But I cannot readily admit that he was the apostle, the son of Zebedee, the brother of James, by whom the Gospel of John and the Catholic Epistle were written.

8. For I judge from the character of both, and the forms of expression, and the entire execution of the book, that it is not his. For the evangelist nowhere gives his name, or proclaims himself, either in the Gospel or Epistle.

9. Farther on he adds:

But John never speaks as if referring to himself, or as if referring to another person. But the author of the Apocalypse introduces himself at the very beginning: 'The Revelation of Jesus Christ, which he gave him to show unto his servants quickly; and he sent and signified it by his angel unto his servant John, who bore witness of the word of God and of his testimony, even of all things that he saw.' Revelation 1:1-2

10. Then he writes also an epistle: 'John to the seven churches which are in Asia, grace be with you, and peace.' Revelation 1:4 But the evangelist did not prefix his name even to the Catholic Epistle; but without introduction he begins with the mystery of the divine revelation itself: 'That which was from the beginning, which we have heard, which we have seen with our eyes.' 1 John 1:1 For because of such a revelation the Lord also blessed Peter, saying, 'Blessed are you, Simon Bar-Jonah, for flesh and blood has not revealed it unto you, but my heavenly Father.' Matthew 16:17

11. But neither in the reputed second or third epistle of John, though they are very short, does the name John appear; but there is written the anonymous phrase, 'the elder.' But this author did not consider it sufficient to give his name once and to proceed with his work; but he takes it up again: 'I, John, who also am your brother and companion in tribulation, and in the kingdom and in the patience of Jesus Christ, was in the isle that is called Patmos for the Word of God and the testimony of Jesus.' Revelation 1:9 And toward the close he speaks thus: 'Blessed is he that keeps the words of the prophecy of this book, and I, John, who saw and heard these things.'

12. But that he who wrote these things was called John must be believed, as he says it; but who he was does not appear. For he did not say, as often in the Gospel, that he was the beloved disciple of the Lord, or the one who lay on his breast, or the brother of James, or the eyewitness and hearer of the Lord.

13. For he would have spoken of these things if he had wished to show himself plainly. But he says none of them; but speaks of himself as our brother and companion, and a witness of Jesus, and blessed because he had seen and heard the revelations.

14. But I am of the opinion that there were many with the same name as the apostle John, who, on account of their love for him, and because they admired and emulated him, and desired to be loved by the Lord as he was, took to themselves the same surname, as many of the children of the faithful are called Paul or Peter.

15. For example, there is also another John, surnamed Mark, mentioned in the Acts of the Apostles, whom Barnabas and Paul took with them; of whom also it is said, 'And they had also John as their attendant.' Acts 13:5 But that it is he who wrote this, I would not say. For it not written that he went with them into Asia, but, 'Now when Paul and his company set sail from Paphos, they came to Perga in Pamphylia and John departing from them returned to Jerusalem.' Acts 13:13

16. But I think that he was some other one of those in Asia; as they say that there are two monuments in Ephesus, each bearing the name of John.

17. And from the ideas, and from the words and their arrangement, it may be reasonably conjectured that this one is different from that one.

18. For the Gospel and Epistle agree with each other and begin in the same manner. The one says, 'In the beginning was the Word'; John 1:1 the other, 'That which was from the beginning.' 1 John 1:1 The one: 'And the Word was made flesh and dwelt among us, and we beheld his glory, the glory as of the only begotten of the Father'; John 1:14 the other says the same things slightly altered: 'Which we have heard, which we have seen with our eyes; which we have looked upon and our hands have handled of the Word of life—and the life was manifested.' 1 John 1:1-2

19. For he introduces these things at the beginning, maintaining them, as is evident from what follows, in opposition to those who said that the Lord had not come in the flesh. Wherefore also he carefully adds, 'And

we have seen and bear witness, and declare unto you the eternal life which was with the Father and was manifested unto us. That which we have seen and heard declare we unto you also.' 1 John 1:2-3

20. He holds to this and does not digress from his subject, but discusses everything under the same heads and names some of which we will briefly mention.

21. Any one who examines carefully will find the phrases, 'the life,' 'the light,' 'turning from darkness,' frequently occurring in both; also continually, 'truth,' 'grace,' 'joy,' 'the flesh and blood of the Lord,' 'the judgment,' 'the forgiveness of sins,' 'the love of God toward us,' the 'commandment that we love one another,' that we should 'keep all the commandments'; the 'conviction of the world, of the Devil, of Anti-Christ,' the 'promise of the Holy Spirit,' the 'adoption of God,' the 'faith continually required of us,' 'the Father and the Son,' occur everywhere. In fact, it is plainly to be seen that one and the same character marks the Gospel and the Epistle throughout.

22. But the Apocalypse is different from these writings and foreign to them; not touching, nor in the least bordering upon them; almost, so to speak, without even a syllable in common with them.

23. Nay more, the Epistle— for I pass by the Gospel— does not mention nor does it contain any intimation of the Apocalypse, nor does the Apocalypse of the Epistle. But Paul, in his epistles, gives some indication of his revelations, though he has not written them out by themselves.

24. Moreover, it can also be shown that the diction of the Gospel and Epistle differs from that of the Apocalypse.

25. For they were written not only without error as regards the Greek language, but also with elegance in their expression, in their reasonings, and in their entire structure. They are far indeed from betraying any barbarism or solecism, or any vulgarism whatever. For the writer had, as it seems, both the requisites of discourse—that is, the gift of knowledge and the gift of expression—as the Lord had bestowed them both upon him.

26. I do not deny that the other writer saw a revelation and received knowledge and prophecy. I perceive, however, that his dialect and language are not accurate Greek, but that he uses barbarous idioms, and, in some places, solecisms.

27. It is unnecessary to point these out here, for I would not have any one think that I have said these things in a spirit of ridicule, for I have said what I have only with the purpose of showing clearly the difference between the writings.

Chapter 26. The Epistles of Dionysius.

1. Besides these, many other epistles of Dionysius are extant, as those against Sabellius, addressed to Ammon, bishop of the church of Bernice, and one to Telesphorus, and one to Euphranor, and again another to Ammon and Euporus. He wrote also four other books on the same subject, which he addressed to his namesake Dionysius, in Rome.

2. Besides these many of his epistles are with us, and large books written in epistolary form, as those on Nature, addressed to the young man Timothy, and one on Temptations, which he also dedicated to Euphranor.

3. Moreover, in a letter to Basilides, bishop of the parishes in Pentapolis, he says that he had written an exposition of the beginning of Ecclesiastes. And he has left us also various letters addressed to this same person. Thus much Dionysius.

But our account of these matters being now completed, permit us to show to posterity the character of our own age.

Chapter 27.— Paul of Samosata, and the Heresy introduced by him at Antioch.

1. After Xystus had presided over the church of Rome for eleven years, Dionysius, namesake of him of Alexandria, succeeded him. About the same time Demetrianus died in Antioch, and Paul of Samosata received that episcopate.

2. As he held, contrary to the teaching of the Church, low and degraded views of Christ, namely, that in his nature he was a common man, Dionysius of Alexandria was entreated to come to the synod. But being unable to come on account of age and physical weakness, he gave his opinion on the subject under consideration by letter. But all the other pastors of the churches from all directions, made haste to assemble at Antioch, as against a despoiler of the flock of Christ.

Chapter 28. The Illustrious Bishops of that Time.

1. Of these, the most eminent were Firmilianus, bishop of Cæsarea in Cappadocia; the brothers Gregory and Athenodorus, pastors of the churches in Pontus; Helenus of the parish of Tarsus, and Nicomas of Iconium; moreover, Hymenæus, of the church of Jerusalem, and Theotecnus of the neighboring church of Cæsarea; and besides these Maximus, who presided in a distinguished manner over the brethren in Bostra. If any should count them up he could not fail to note a great many others, besides presbyters and deacons, who were at that time assembled for the same cause in the above- mentioned city. But these were the most illustrious.

2. When all of these assembled at different times and frequently to consider these matters, the arguments and questions were discussed at every meeting; the adherents of the Samosatian endeavoring to cover and conceal his heterodoxy, and the others striving zealously to lay bare and make manifest his heresy and blasphemy against Christ.

3. Meanwhile, Dionysius died in the twelfth year of the reign of Gallienus, having held the episcopate of Alexandria for seventeen years, and Maximus succeeded him.

4. Gallienus after a reign of fifteen years was succeeded by Claudius, who in two years delivered the government to Aurelian.

Chapter 29. Paul, having been refuted by Malchion, a Presbyter from the Sophists, was excommunicated.

1. During his reign a final synod composed of a great many bishops was held, and the leader of heresy in Antioch was detected, and his false doctrine clearly shown before all, and he was excommunicated from the Catholic Church under heaven.

2. Malchion especially drew him out of his hiding-place and refuted him. He was a man learned in other respects, and principal of the sophist school of Grecian learning in Antioch; yet on account of the superior nobility of his faith in Christ he had been made a presbyter of that parish. This man, having conducted a discussion with him, which was taken down by stenographers and which we know is still extant, was alone able to detect the man who dissembled and deceived the others.

Chapter 30. The Epistle of the Bishops against Paul.

1. The pastors who had assembled about this matter, prepared by common consent an epistle addressed to Dionysius, bishop of Rome, and Maximus of Alexandria, and sent it to all the provinces. In this they make manifest to all their own zeal and the perverse error of Paul, and the arguments and discussions which they had with him, and show the entire life and conduct of the man. It may be well to put on record at the present time the following extracts from their writing.

2. To Dionysius and Maximus, and to all our fellow-ministers throughout the world, bishops, presbyters, and deacons, and to the whole Catholic Church under heaven, Helenus, Hymenæus, Theophilus, Theotecnus, Maximus, Proclus, Nicomas, Ælianus, Paul, Bolanus, Protogenes, Hierax, Eutychius, Theodorus, Malchion, and Lucius, and all the others who dwell with us in the neighboring cities and nations, bishops, presbyters, and deacons, and the churches of God, greeting to the beloved brethren in the Lord.

3. A little farther on they proceed thus: We sent for and called many of the bishops from a distance to relieve us from this deadly doctrine; as Dionysius of Alexandria and Firmilianus of Cappadocia, those blessed men. The first of these not considering the author of this delusion worthy to be addressed, sent a letter to Antioch, not written to him, but to the entire parish, of which we give a copy below.

4. But Firmilianus came twice and condemned his innovations, as we who were present know and testify, and many others understand. But as he promised to change his opinions, he believed him and hoped that without any reproach to the Word what was necessary would be done. So he delayed the matter, being deceived by him who denied even his own God and Lord, and had not kept the faith which he formerly held.

5. And now Firmilianus was again on his way to Antioch, and had come as far as Tarsus because he had learned by experience his God- denying wickedness. But while we, having come together, were calling for him and awaiting his arrival, he died.

6. After other things they describe as follows the manner of life which he led:

7. Whereas he has departed from the rule of faith, and has turned aside after base and spurious teachings, it is not necessary,— since he is without—that we should pass judgment upon his practices: as for instance in that although formerly destitute and poor, and having received no wealth from his fathers, nor made anything by trade or

business, he now possesses abundant wealth through his iniquities and sacrilegious acts, and through those things which he extorts from the brethren, depriving the injured of their rights and promising to assist them for reward, yet deceiving them, and plundering those who in their trouble are ready to give that they may obtain reconciliation with their oppressors, 'supposing that gain is godliness'; 1 Timothy 6:5 —

8. or in that he is haughty, and is puffed up, and assumes worldly dignities, preferring to be called ducenarius rather than bishop; and struts in the market-places, reading letters and reciting them as he walks in public, attended by a bodyguard, with a multitude preceding and following him, so that the faith is envied and hated on account of his pride and haughtiness of heart—

9. or in that he practices chicanery in ecclesiastical assemblies, contrives to glorify himself, and deceive with appearances, and astonish the minds of the simple, preparing for himself a tribunal and lofty throne, — not like a disciple of Christ—and possessing a 'secretum,' — like the rulers of the world—and so calling it, and striking his thigh with his hand, and stamping on the tribunal with his feet—or in that he rebukes and insults those who do not applaud, and shake their handkerchiefs as in the theaters, and shout and leap about like the men and women that are stationed around him, and hear him in this unbecoming manner, but who listen reverently and orderly as in the house of God—or in that he violently and coarsely assails in public the expounders of the Word that have departed this life, and magnifies himself, not as a bishop, but as a sophist and juggler,

10. and stops the psalms to our Lord Jesus Christ, as being the modern productions of modern men, and trains women to sing psalms to himself in the midst of the church on the great day of the passover, which any one might shudder to hear, and persuades the bishops and presbyters of the neighboring districts and cities who fawn upon him, to advance the same ideas in their discourses to the people.

11. For to anticipate something of what we shall presently write, he is unwilling to acknowledge that the Son of God has come down from heaven. And this is not a mere assertion, but it is abundantly proved from the records which we have sent you; and not least where he says 'Jesus Christ is from below.' But those singing to him and extolling him among the people say that their impious teacher has come down an angel from heaven. And he does not forbid such things; but the arrogant man is even present when they are uttered.

12. And there are the women, the 'subintroductæ,' as the people of Antioch call them, belonging to him and to the presbyters and deacons that are with him. Although he knows and has convicted these men, yet he connives at this and their other incurable sins, in order that they may be bound to him, and through fear for themselves may not dare to accuse him for his wicked words and deeds. But he has also made them rich; on which account he is loved and admired by those who covet such things.

13. We know, beloved, that the bishop and all the clergy should be an example to the people of all good works. And we are not ignorant how many have fallen or incurred suspicion, through the women whom they have thus brought in. So that even if we should allow that he commits no sinful act, yet he ought to avoid the suspicion which arises from such a thing, lest he scandalize some one, or lead others to imitate him.

14. For how can he reprove or admonish another not to be too familiar with women—lest he fall, as it is written, — when he has himself sent one away already, and now has two with him, blooming and beautiful, and takes them with him wherever he goes, and at the same time lives in luxury and surfeiting?

15. Because of these things all mourn and lament by themselves; but they so fear his tyranny and power, that they dare not accuse him.

16. But as we have said, while one might call the man to account for this conduct, if he held the Catholic doctrine and was numbered with us, since he has scorned the mystery and struts about in the abominable heresy of Artemas (for why should we not mention his father?), we think it unnecessary to demand of him an explanation of these things.

17. Afterwards, at the close of the epistle, they add these words:

Therefore we have been compelled to excommunicate him, since he sets himself against God, and refuses to obey; and to appoint in his place another bishop for the Catholic Church. By divine direction, as we believe, we have appointed Domnus, who is adorned with all the qualities becoming in a bishop, and who is a son of the blessed Demetrianus, who formerly presided in a distinguished manner over the same parish. We have informed you of this that you may write to him, and may receive letters of communion from him. But let this man write to Artemas; and let those who think as Artemas does, communicate with him.

18. As Paul had fallen from the episcopate, as well as from the orthodox faith, Domnus, as has been said, became bishop of the church at Antioch.

19. But as Paul refused to surrender the church building, the Emperor Aurelian was petitioned; and he decided the matter most equitably, ordering the building to be given to those to whom the bishops of Italy and of the city of Rome should adjudge it. Thus this man was driven out of the church, with extreme disgrace, by the worldly power.

20. Such was Aurelian's treatment of us at that time; but in the course of his reign he changed his mind in regard to us, and was moved by certain advisers to institute a persecution against us. And there was great talk about this on every side.

21. But as he was about to do it, and was, so to speak, in the very act of signing the decrees against us, the divine judgment came upon him and restrained him at the very verge of his undertaking, showing in a manner that all could see clearly, that the rulers of this world can never find an opportunity against the churches of Christ, except the hand that defends them permits it, in divine and heavenly judgment, for the sake of discipline and correction, at such times as it sees best.

22. After a reign of six years, Aurelian was succeeded by Probus. He reigned for the same number of years, and Carus, with his sons, Carinus and Numerianus, succeeded him. After they had reigned less than three years the government devolved on Diocletian, and those associated with him. Under them took place the persecution of our time, and the destruction of the churches connected with it.

23. Shortly before this, Dionysius, bishop of Rome, after holding office for nine years, died, and was succeeded by Felix.

Chapter 31. The Perversive Heresy of the Manicheans which began at this Time.

1. At this time, the madman, named from his demoniacal heresy, armed himself in the perversion of his reason, as the devil, Satan, who himself fights against God, put him forward to the destruction of many. He was a barbarian in life, both in word and deed; and in his nature demoniacal and insane. In consequence of this he sought to pose as Christ, and being puffed up in his madness, he proclaimed himself the Paraclete and the very Holy Spirit; and afterwards, like Christ, he chose twelve disciples as partners of his new doctrine.

2. And he patched together false and godless doctrines collected from a multitude of long-extinct impieties, and swept them, like a deadly poison, from Persia to our part of the world. From him the impious name of the Manicheans is still prevalent among many. Such was the foundation of this knowledge falsely so-called, which sprang up in those times.

Chapter 32. The Distinguished Ecclesiastics of our Day, and which of them survived until the Destruction of the Churches.

1. At this time, Felix, having presided over the church of Rome for five years, was succeeded by Eutychianus, but he in less than ten months left the position to Caius, who lived in our day. He held it about fifteen years, and was in turn succeeded by Marcellinus, who was overtaken by the persecution.

2. About the same time Timæus received the episcopate of Antioch after Domnus, and Cyril, who lived in our day, succeeded him. In his time we became acquainted with Dorotheus, a man of learning among those of his day, who was honored with the office of presbyter in Antioch. He was a lover of the beautiful in divine things, and devoted himself to the Hebrew language, so that he read the Hebrew Scriptures with facility.

3. He belonged to those who were especially liberal, and was not unacquainted with Grecian propædeutics. Besides this he was a eunuch, having been so from his very birth. On this account, as if it were a miracle, the emperor took him into his family, and honored him by placing him over the purple dye-works at Tyre. We have heard him expound the Scriptures wisely in the Church.

4. After Cyril, Tyrannus received the episcopate of the parish of Antioch. In his time occurred the destruction of the churches.

5. Eusebius, who had come from the city of Alexandria, ruled the parishes of Laodicea after Socrates. The occasion of his removal there was the affair of Paul. He went on this account to Syria, and was restrained from returning home by those there who were zealous in divine things. Among our contemporaries he was a beautiful example of religion, as is readily seen from the words of Dionysius which we have quoted.

6. Anatolius was appointed his successor; one good man, as they say, following another. He also was an Alexandrian by birth. In learning and skill in Greek philosophy, such as arithmetic and geometry, astronomy,

and dialectics in general, as well as in the theory of physics, he stood first among the ablest men of our time, and he was also at the head in rhetorical science. It is reported that for this reason he was requested by the citizens of Alexandria to establish there a school of Aristotelian philosophy.

7. They relate of him many other eminent deeds during the siege of the Pyrucheium in Alexandria, on account of which he was especially honored by all those in high office; but I will give the following only as an example.

8. They say that bread had failed the besieged, so that it was more difficult to withstand the famine than the enemy outside; but he being present provided for them in this manner. As the other part of the city was allied with the Roman army, and therefore was not under siege, Anatolius sent for Eusebius,— for he was still there before his transfer to Syria, and was among those who were not besieged, and possessed, moreover, a great reputation and a renowned name which had reached even the Roman general—and he informed him of those who were perishing in the siege from famine.

9. When he learned this he requested the Roman commander as the greatest possible favor, to grant safety to deserters from the enemy. Having obtained his request, he communicated it to Anatolius. As soon as he received the message he convened the senate of Alexandria, and at first proposed that all should come to a reconciliation with the Romans. But when he perceived that they were angered by this advice, he said, But I do not think you will oppose me, if I counsel you to send the supernumeraries and those who are in nowise useful to us, as old women and children and old men, outside the gates, to go wherever they may please. For why should we retain for no purpose these who must at any rate soon die? And why should we destroy with hunger those who are crippled and maimed in body, when we ought to provide only for men and youth, and to distribute the necessary bread among those who are needed for the garrison of the city?

10. With such arguments he persuaded the assembly, and rising first he gave his vote that the entire multitude, whether of men or women, who were not needful for the army, should depart from the city, because if they remained and unnecessarily continued in the city, there would be for them no hope of safety, but they would perish with famine.

11. As all the others in the senate agreed to this, he saved almost all the besieged. He provided that first, those belonging to the church, and

afterwards, of the others in the city, those of every age should escape, not only the classes included in the decree, but, under cover of these, a multitude of others, secretly clothed in women's garments; and through his management they went out of the gates by night and escaped to the Roman camp. There Eusebius, like a father and physician, received all of them, wasted away through the long siege, and restored them by every kind of prudence and care.

12. The church of Laodicea was honored by two such pastors in succession, who, in the providence of God, came after the aforesaid war from Alexandria to that city.

13. Anatolius did not write very many works; but in such as have come down to us we can discern his eloquence and erudition. In these he states particularly his opinions on the passover. It seems important to give here the following extracts from them.

14. From the Paschal Canons of Anatolius. There is then in the first year the new moon of the first month, which is the beginning of every cycle of nineteen years, on the twenty-sixth day of the Egyptian Phamenoth; but according to the months of the Macedonians, the twenty-second day of Dystrus, or, as the Romans would say, the eleventh before the Kalends of April.

15. On the said twenty-sixth of Phamenoth, the sun is found not only entered on the first segment, but already passing through the fourth day in it. They are accustomed to call this segment the first dodecatomorion, and the equinox, and the beginning of months, and the head of the cycle, and the starting-point of the planetary circuit. But they call the one preceding this the last of months, and the twelfth segment, and the final dodecatomorion, and the end of the planetary circuit. Wherefore we maintain that those who place the first month in it, and determine by it the fourteenth of the passover, commit no slight or common blunder.

16. And this is not an opinion of our own; but it was known to the Jews of old, even before Christ, and was carefully observed by them. This may be learned from what is said by Philo, Josephus, and Musæus; and not only by them, but also by those yet more ancient, the two Agathobuli, surnamed 'Masters,' and the famous Aristobulus, who was chosen among the seventy interpreters of the sacred and divine Hebrew Scriptures by Ptolemy Philadelphus and his father, and who also dedicated his exegetical books on the law of Moses to the same kings.

17. These writers, explaining questions in regard to the Exodus, say that all alike should sacrifice the passover offerings after the vernal equinox, in the middle of the first month. But this occurs while the sun is passing through the first segment of the solar, or as some of them have styled it, the zodiacal circle. Aristobulus adds that it is necessary for the feast of the passover, that not only the sun should pass through the equinoctial segment, but the moon also.

18. For as there are two equinoctial segments, the vernal and the autumnal, directly opposite each other, and as the day of the passover was appointed on the fourteenth of the month, beginning with the evening, the moon will hold a position diametrically opposite the sun, as may be seen in full moons; and the sun will be in the segment of the vernal equinox, and of necessity the moon in that of the autumnal.

19. I know that many other things have been said by them, some of them probable, and some approaching absolute demonstration, by which they endeavor to prove that it is altogether necessary to keep the passover and the feast of unleavened bread after the equinox. But I refrain from demanding this sort of demonstration for matters from which the veil of the Mosaic law has been removed, so that now at length with uncovered face we continually behold as in a glass Christ and the teachings and sufferings of Christ. 2 Corinthians 3:18 But that with the Hebrews the first month was near the equinox, the teachings also of the Book of Enoch show.

20. The same writer has also left the Institutes of Arithmetic, in ten books, and other evidences of his experience and proficiency in divine things.

21. Theotecnus, bishop of Cæsarea in Palestine, first ordained him as bishop, designing to make him his successor in his own parish after his death. And for a short time both of them presided over the same church. But the synod which was held to consider Paul's case called him to Antioch, and as he passed through the city of Laodicea, Eusebius being dead, he was detained by the brethren there.

22. And after Anatolius had departed this life, the last bishop of that parish before the persecution was Stephen, who was admired by many for his knowledge of philosophy and other Greek learning. But he was not equally devoted to the divine faith, as the progress of the persecution manifested; for it showed that he was a cowardly and unmanly dissembler rather than a true philosopher.

23. But this did not seriously injure the church, for Theodotus restored their affairs, being straightway made bishop of that parish by God himself, the Saviour of all. He justified by his deeds both his lordly name and his office of bishop. For he excelled in the medical art for bodies, and in the healing art for souls. Nor did any other man equal him in kindness, sincerity, sympathy, and zeal in helping such as needed his aid. He was also greatly devoted to divine learning. Such an one was he.

24. In Cæsarea in Palestine, Agapius succeeded Theotecnus, who had most zealously performed the duties of his episcopate. Him too we know to have labored diligently, and to have manifested most genuine providence in his oversight of the people, particularly caring for all the poor with liberal hand.

25. In his time we became acquainted with Pamphilus, that most eloquent man, of truly philosophical life, who was esteemed worthy of the office of presbyter in that parish. It would be no small matter to show what sort of a man he was and whence he came. But we have described, in our special work concerning him, all the particulars of his life, and of the school which he established, and the trials which he endured in many confessions during the persecution, and the crown of martyrdom with which he was finally honored. But of all that were there he was indeed the most admirable.

26. Among those nearest our times, we have known Pierius, of the presbyters in Alexandria, and Meletius, bishop of the churches in Pontus—rarest of men.

27. The first was distinguished for his life of extreme poverty and his philosophic learning, and was exceedingly diligent in the contemplation and exposition of divine things, and in public discourses in the church. Meletius, whom the learned called the honey of Attica, was a man whom every one would describe as most accomplished in all kinds of learning; and it would be impossible to admire sufficiently his rhetorical skill. It might be said that he possessed this by nature; but who could surpass the excellence of his great experience and erudition in other respects?

28. For in all branches of knowledge had you undertaken to try him even once, you would have said that he was the most skillful and learned. Moreover, the virtues of his life were not less remarkable. We observed him well in the time of the persecution, when for seven full years he was escaping from its fury in the regions of Palestine.

29. Zambdas received the episcopate of the church of Jerusalem after the bishop Hymenæus, whom we mentioned a little above. He died in a short time, and Hermon, the last before the persecution in our day, succeeded to the apostolic chair, which has been preserved there until the present time.

30. In Alexandria, Maximus, who, after the death of Dionysius, had been bishop for eighteen years, was succeeded by Theonas. In his time Achillas, who had been appointed a presbyter in Alexandria at the same time with Pierius, became celebrated. He was placed over the school of the sacred faith, and exhibited fruits of philosophy most rare and inferior to none, and conduct genuinely evangelical.

31. After Theonas had held the office for nineteen years, Peter received the episcopate in Alexandria, and was very eminent among them for twelve entire years. Of these he governed the church less than three years before the persecution, and for the remainder of his life he subjected himself to a more rigid discipline and cared in no secret manner for the general interest of the churches. On this account he was beheaded in the ninth year of the persecution, and was adorned with the crown of martyrdom.

32. Having written out in these books the account of the successions from the birth of our Saviour to the destruction of the places of worship,— a period of three hundred and five years, — permit me to pass on to the contests of those who, in our day, have heroically fought for religion, and to leave in writing, for the information of posterity, the extent and the magnitude of those conflicts.

BOOK VIII

Introduction.

As we have described in seven books the events from the time of the apostles, we think it proper in this eighth book to record for the information of posterity a few of the most important occurrences of our own times, which are worthy of permanent record. Our account will begin at this point.

Chapter 1. The Events which preceded the Persecution in our Times.

1. It is beyond our ability to describe in a suitable manner the extent and nature of the glory and freedom with which the word of piety toward the God of the universe, proclaimed to the world through Christ, was honored among all men, both Greeks and barbarians, before the persecution in our day.

2. The favor shown our people by the rulers might be adduced as evidence; as they committed to them the government of provinces, and on account of the great friendship which they entertained toward their doctrine, released them from anxiety in regard to sacrificing.

3. Why need I speak of those in the royal palaces, and of the rulers over all, who allowed the members of their households, wives and children and servants, to speak openly before them for the Divine word and life, and suffered them almost to boast of the freedom of their faith?

4. Indeed they esteemed them highly, and preferred them to their fellow-servants. Such an one was that Dorotheus, the most devoted and faithful to them of all, and on this account especially honored by them among those who held the most honorable offices and governments. With him was the celebrated Gorgonius, and as many as had been esteemed worthy of the same distinction on account of the word of God.

5. And one could see the rulers in every church accorded the greatest favor by all officers and governors. But how can any one describe those vast assemblies, and the multitude that crowded together in every city, and the famous gatherings in the houses of prayer; on whose account not being satisfied with the ancient buildings they erected from the foundation large churches in all the cities?

6. No envy hindered the progress of these affairs which advanced gradually, and grew and increased day by day. Nor could any evil demon

slander them or hinder them through human counsels, so long as the divine and heavenly hand watched over and guarded his own people as worthy.

7. But when on account of the abundant freedom, we fell into laxity and sloth, and envied and reviled each other, and were almost, as it were, taking up arms against one another, rulers assailing rulers with words like spears, and people forming parties against people, and monstrous hypocrisy and dissimulation rising to the greatest height of wickedness, the divine judgment with forbearance, as is its pleasure, while the multitudes yet continued to assemble, gently and moderately harassed the episcopacy.

8. This persecution began with the brethren in the army. But as if without sensibility, we were not eager to make the Deity favorable and propitious; and some, like atheists, thought that our affairs were unheeded and ungoverned; and thus we added one wickedness to another. And those esteemed our shepherds, casting aside the bond of piety, were excited to conflicts with one another, and did nothing else than heap up strifes and threats and jealousy and enmity and hatred toward each other, like tyrants eagerly endeavoring to assert their power. Then, truly, according to the word of Jeremiah, The Lord in his wrath darkened the daughter of Zion, and cast down the glory of Israel from heaven to earth, and remembered not his foot- stool in the day of his anger. The Lord also overwhelmed all the beautiful things of Israel, and threw down all his strongholds. Lamentations 2:1-2

9. And according to what was foretold in the Psalms: He has made void the covenant of his servant, and profaned his sanctuary to the earth—in the destruction of the churches—and has thrown down all his strongholds, and has made his fortresses cowardice. All that pass by have plundered the multitude of the people; and he has become besides a reproach to his neighbors. For he has exalted the right hand of his enemies, and has turned back the help of his sword, and has not taken his part in the war. But he has deprived him of purification, and has cast his throne to the ground. He has shortened the days of his time, and besides all, has poured out shame upon him.

Chapter 2. The Destruction of the Churches.

1. All these things were fulfilled in us, when we saw with our own eyes the houses of prayer thrown down to the very foundations, and the

Divine and Sacred Scriptures committed to the flames in the midst of the market-places, and the shepherds of the churches basely hidden here and there, and some of them captured ignominiously, and mocked by their enemies. When also, according to another prophetic word, Contempt was poured out upon rulers, and he caused them to wander in an untrodden and pathless way.

2. But it is not our place to describe the sad misfortunes which finally came upon them, as we do not think it proper, moreover, to record their divisions and unnatural conduct to each other before the persecution. Wherefore we have decided to relate nothing concerning them except the things in which we can vindicate the Divine judgment.

3. Hence we shall not mention those who were shaken by the persecution, nor those who in everything pertaining to salvation were shipwrecked, and by their own will were sunk in the depths of the flood. But we shall introduce into this history in general only those events which may be usefull first to ourselves and afterwards to posterity. Let us therefore proceed to describe briefly the sacred conflicts of the witnesses of the Divine Word.

4. It was in the nineteenth year of the reign of Diocletian, in the month Dystrus, called March by the Romans, when the feast of the Saviour's passion was near at hand, that royal edicts were published everywhere, commanding that the churches be leveled to the ground and the Scriptures be destroyed by fire, and ordering that those who held places of honor be degraded, and that the household servants, if they persisted in the profession of Christianity, be deprived of freedom.

5. Such was the first edict against us. But not long after, other decrees were issued, commanding that all the rulers of the churches in every place be first thrown into prison, and afterwards by every artifice be compelled to sacrifice.

Chapter 3. The Nature of the Conflicts endured in the Persecution.

1. Then truly a great many rulers of the churches eagerly endured terrible sufferings, and furnished examples of noble conflicts. But a multitude of others, benumbed in spirit by fear, were easily weakened at the first onset. Of the rest each one endured different forms of torture. The body of one was scourged with rods. Another was punished with insupportable rackings and scrapings, in which some suffered a miserable death.

2. Others passed through different conflicts. Thus one, while those around pressed him on by force and dragged him to the abominable and impure sacrifices, was dismissed as if he had sacrificed, though he had not. Another, though he had not approached at all, nor touched any polluted thing, when others said that he had sacrificed, went away, bearing the accusation in silence.

3. Another being taken up half dead, was cast aside as if already dead, and again a certain one lying upon the ground was dragged a long distance by his feet and counted among those who had sacrificed. One cried out and with a loud voice testified his rejection of the sacrifice; another shouted that he was a Christian, being resplendent in the confession of the saving Name. Another protested that he had not sacrificed and never would.

4. But they were struck in the mouth and silenced by a large band of soldiers who were drawn up for this purpose; and they were smitten on the face and cheeks and driven away by force; so important did the enemies of piety regard it, by any means, to seem to have accomplished their purpose. But these things did not avail them against the holy martyrs; for an accurate description of whom, what word of ours could suffice?

Chapter 4. The Famous Martyrs of God, who filled Every Place with their Memory and won Various Crowns in behalf of Religion.

1. For we might tell of many who showed admirable zeal for the religion of the God of the universe, not only from the beginning of the general persecution, but long before that time, while yet peace prevailed.

2. For though he who had received power was seemingly aroused now as from a deep sleep, yet from the time after Decius and Valerian, he had been plotting secretly and without notice against the churches. He did not wage war against all of us at once, but made trial at first only of those in the army. For he supposed that the others could be taken easily if he should first attack and subdue these. Thereupon many of the soldiers were seen most cheerfully embracing private life, so that they might not deny their piety toward the Creator of the universe.

3. For when the commander, whoever he was, began to persecute the soldiers, separating into tribes and purging those who were enrolled in the army, giving them the choice either by obeying to receive the honor which belonged to them, or on the other hand to be deprived of it if they disobeyed the command, a great many soldiers of Christ's kingdom, without hesitation, instantly preferred the confession of him to the seeming glory and prosperity which they were enjoying.

4. And one and another of them occasionally received in exchange, for their pious constancy, not only the loss of position, but death. But as yet the instigator of this plot proceeded with moderation, and ventured so far as blood only in some instances; for the multitude of believers, as it is likely, made him afraid, and deterred him from waging war at once against all.

5. But when he made the attack more boldly, it is impossible to relate how many and what sort of martyrs of God could be seen, among the inhabitants of all the cities and countries.

Chapter 5. Those in Nicomedia.

1. Immediately on the publication of the decree against the churches in Nicomedia, a certain man, not obscure but very highly honored with distinguished temporal dignities, moved with zeal toward God, and incited with ardent faith, seized the edict as it was posted openly and publicly, and tore it to pieces as a profane and impious thing; and this was done while two of the sovereigns were in the same city—the oldest of all, and the one who held the fourth place in the government after him.

2. But this man, first in that place, after distinguishing himself in such a manner suffered those things which were likely to follow such daring, and kept his spirit cheerful and undisturbed till death.

Chapter 6. Those in the Palace.

1. This period produced divine and illustrious martyrs, above all whose praises have ever been sung and who have been celebrated for courage, whether among Greeks or barbarians, in the person of Dorotheus and the servants that were with him in the palace. Although they received the highest honors from their masters, and were treated by them as their own children, they esteemed reproaches and trials for religion, and the

many forms of death that were invented against them, as, in truth, greater riches than the glory and luxury of this life.

2. We will describe the manner in which one of them ended his life, and leave our readers to infer from his case the sufferings of the others. A certain man was brought forward in the above-mentioned city, before the rulers of whom we have spoken. He was then commanded to sacrifice, but as he refused, he was ordered to be stripped and raised on high and beaten with rods over his entire body, until, being conquered, he should, even against his will, do what was commanded.

3. But as he was unmoved by these sufferings, and his bones were already appearing, they mixed vinegar with salt and poured it upon the mangled parts of his body. As he scorned these agonies, a gridiron and fire were brought forward. And the remnants of his body, like flesh intended for eating, were placed on the fire, not at once, lest he should expire instantly, but a little at a time. And those who placed him on the pyre were not permitted to desist until, after such sufferings, he should assent to the things commanded.

4. But he held his purpose firmly, and victoriously gave up his life while the tortures were still going on. Such was the martyrdom of one of the servants of the palace, who was indeed well worthy of his name, for he was called Peter.

5. The martyrdoms of the rest, though they were not inferior to his, we will pass by for the sake of brevity, recording only that Dorotheus and Gorgonius, with many others of the royal household, after varied sufferings, ended their lives by strangling, and bore away the trophies of God-given victory.

6. At this time Anthimus, who then presided over the church in Nicomedia, was beheaded for his testimony to Christ. A great multitude of martyrs were added to him, a conflagration having broken out in those very days in the palace at Nicomedia, I know not how, which through a false suspicion was laid to our people. Entire families of the pious in that place were put to death in masses at the royal command, some by the sword, and others by fire. It is reported that with a certain divine and indescribable eagerness men and women rushed into the fire. And the executioners bound a large number of others and put them on boats and threw them into the depths of the sea.

7. And those who had been esteemed their masters considered it necessary to dig up the bodies of the imperial servants, who had been

committed to the earth with suitable burial and cast them into the sea, lest any, as they thought, regarding them as gods, might worship them lying in their sepulchers.

8. Such things occurred in Nicomedia at the beginning of the persecution. But not long after, as persons in the country called Melitene, and others throughout Syria, attempted to usurp the government, a royal edict directed that the rulers of the churches everywhere should be thrown into prison and bonds.

9. What was to be seen after this exceeds all description. A vast multitude were imprisoned in every place; and the prisons everywhere, which had long before been prepared for murderers and robbers of graves, were filled with bishops, presbyters and deacons, readers and exorcists, so that room was no longer left in them for those condemned for crimes.

10. And as other decrees followed the first, directing that those in prison if they would sacrifice should be permitted to depart in freedom, but that those who refused should be harassed with many tortures, how could any one, again, number the multitude of martyrs in every province, and especially of those in Africa, and Mauritania, and Thebais, and Egypt? From this last country many went into other cities and provinces, and became illustrious through martyrdom.

Chapter 7. The Egyptians in Phœnicia.

1. Those of them that were conspicuous in Palestine we know, as also those that were at Tyre in Phœnicia. Who that saw them was not astonished at the numberless stripes, and at the firmness which these truly wonderful athletes of religion exhibited under them? And at their contest, immediately after the scourging, with bloodthirsty wild beasts, as they were cast before leopards and different kinds of bears and wild boars and bulls goaded with fire and red-hot iron? And at the marvelous endurance of these noble men in the face of all sorts of wild beasts?

2. We were present ourselves when these things occurred, and have put on record the divine power of our martyred Saviour Jesus Christ, which was present and manifested itself mightily in the martyrs. For a long time the man-devouring beasts did not dare to touch or draw near the bodies of those dear to God, but rushed upon the others who from the outside irritated and urged them on. And they would not in the least touch the holy athletes, as they stood alone and naked and shook their hands at

them to draw them toward themselves— for they were commanded to do this. But whenever they rushed at them, they were restrained as if by some divine power and retreated again.

3. This continued for a long time, and occasioned no little wonder to the spectators. And as the first wild beast did nothing, a second and a third were let loose against one and the same martyr.

4. One could not but be astonished at the invincible firmness of these holy men, and the enduring and immovable constancy of those whose bodies were young. You could have seen a youth not twenty years of age standing unbound and stretching out his hands in the form of a cross, with unterrified and untrembling mind, engaged earnestly in prayer to God, and not in the least going back or retreating from the place where he stood, while bears and leopards, breathing rage and death, almost touched his flesh. And yet their mouths were restrained, I know not how, by a divine and incomprehensible power, and they ran back again to their place. Such an one was he.

5. Again you might have seen others, for they were five in all, cast before a wild bull, who tossed into the air with his horns those who approached from the outside, and mangled them, leaving them to be token up half dead; but when he rushed with rage and threatening upon the holy martyrs, who were standing alone, he was unable to come near them; but though he stamped with his feet, and pushed in all directions with his horns, and breathed rage and threatening on account of the irritation of the burning irons, he was, nevertheless, held back by the sacred Providence. And as he in nowise harmed them, they let loose other wild beasts upon them.

6. Finally, after these terrible and various attacks upon them, they were all slain with the sword; and instead of being buried in the earth they were committed to the waves of the sea.

Chapter 8. Those in Egypt.

1. Such was the conflict of those Egyptians who contended nobly for religion in Tyre. But we must admire those also who suffered martyrdom in their native land; where thousands of men, women, and children, despising the present life for the sake of the teaching of our Saviour, endured various deaths.

2. Some of them, after scrapings and rackings and severest scourgings, and numberless other kinds of tortures, terrible even to hear of, were

committed to the flames; some were drowned in the sea; some offered their heads bravely to those who cut them off; some died under their tortures, and others perished with hunger. And yet others were crucified; some according to the method commonly employed for malefactors; others yet more cruelly, being nailed to the cross with their heads downward, and being kept alive until they perished on the cross with hunger.

Chapter 9. Those in Thebais.

1. It would be impossible to describe the outrages and tortures which the martyrs in Thebais endured. They were scraped over the entire body with shells instead of hooks until they died. Women were bound by one foot and raised aloft in the air by machines, and with their bodies altogether bare and uncovered, presented to all beholders this most shameful, cruel, and inhuman spectacle.

2. Others being bound to the branches and trunks of trees perished. For they drew the stoutest branches together with machines, and bound the limbs of the martyrs to them; and then, allowing the branches to assume their natural position, they tore asunder instantly the limbs of those for whom they contrived this.

3. All these things were done, not for a few days or a short time, but for a long series of years. Sometimes more than ten, at other times above twenty were put to death. Again not less than thirty, then about sixty, and yet again a hundred men with young children and women, were slain in one day, being condemned to various and diverse torments.

4. We, also being on the spot ourselves, have observed large crowds in one day; some suffering decapitation, others torture by fire; so that the murderous sword was blunted, and becoming weak, was broken, and the very executioners grew weary and relieved each other.

5. And we beheld the most wonderful ardor, and the truly divine energy and zeal of those who believed in the Christ of God. For as soon as sentence was pronounced against the first, one after another rushed to the judgment seat, and confessed themselves Christians. And regarding with indifference the terrible things and the multiform tortures, they declared themselves boldly and undauntedly for the religion of the God of the universe. And they received the final sentence of death with joy and laughter and cheerfulness; so that they sang and offered up hymns and thanksgivings to the God of the universe till their very last breath.

6. These indeed were wonderful; but yet more wonderful were those who, being distinguished for wealth, noble birth, and honor, and for learning and philosophy, held everything secondary to the true religion and to faith in our Saviour and Lord Jesus Christ.

7. Such an one was Philoromus, who held a high office under the imperial government at Alexandria, and who administered justice every day, attended by a military guard corresponding to his rank and Roman dignity. Such also was Phileas, bishop of the church of Thmuis, a man eminent on account of his patriotism and the services rendered by him to his country, and also on account of his philosophical learning.

8. These persons, although a multitude of relatives and other friends besought them, and many in high position, and even the judge himself entreated them, that they would have compassion on themselves and show mercy to their children and wives, yet were not in the least induced by these things to choose the love of life, and to despise the ordinances of our Saviour concerning confession and denial. But with manly and philosophic minds, or rather with pious and God-loving souls, they persevered against all the threats and insults of the judge; and both of them were beheaded.

Chapter 10. The Writings of Phileas the Martyr describing the Occurrences at Alexandria.

1. Since we have mentioned Phileas as having a high reputation for secular learning, let him be his own witness in the following extract, in which he shows us who he was, and at the same time describes more accurately than we can the martyrdoms which occurred in his time at Alexandria:

2. Having before them all these examples and models and noble tokens which are given us in the Divine and Sacred Scriptures, the blessed martyrs who were with us did not hesitate, but directing the eye of the soul in sincerity toward the God over all, and having their mind set upon death for religion, they adhered firmly to their calling. For they understood that our Lord Jesus Christ had become man on our account, that he might cut off all sin and furnish us with the means of entrance into eternal life. For 'he counted it not a prize to be on an equality with God, but emptied himself taking the form of a servant; and being found in fashion as a man, he humbled himself unto death, even the death of the cross.' Philippians 2:6-8

3. Wherefore also being zealous for the greater gifts, the Christ- bearing martyrs endured all trials and all kinds of contrivances for torture; not once only, but some also a second time. And although the guards vied with each other in threatening them in all sorts of ways, not in words only, but in actions, they did not give up their resolution; because 'perfect love casts out fear.' 1 John 4:18

4. What words could describe their courage and manliness under every torture? For as liberty to abuse them was given to all that wished, some beat them with clubs, others with rods, others with scourges, yet others with thongs, and others with ropes.

5. And the spectacle of the outrages was varied and exhibited great malignity. For some, with their hands bound behind them, were suspended on the stocks, and every member stretched by certain machines. Then the torturers, as commanded, lacerated with instruments their entire bodies; not only their sides, as in the case of murderers, but also their stomachs and knees and cheeks. Others were raised aloft, suspended from the porch by one hand, and endured the most terrible suffering of all, through the distension of their joints and limbs. Others were bound face to face to pillars, not resting on their feet, but with the weight of their bodies bearing on their bonds and drawing them tightly.

6. And they endured this, not merely as long as the governor talked with them or was at leisure, but through almost the entire day. For when he passed on to others, he left officers under his authority to watch the first, and observe if any of them, overcome by the tortures, appeared to yield. And he commanded to cast them into chains without mercy, and afterwards when they were at the last gasp to throw them to the ground and drag them away.

7. For he said that they were not to have the least concern for us, but were to think and act as if we no longer existed, our enemies having invented this second mode of torture in addition to the stripes.

8. Some, also, after these outrages, were placed on the stocks, and had both their feet stretched over the four holes, so that they were compelled to lie on their backs on the stocks, being unable to keep themselves up on account of the fresh wounds with which their entire bodies were covered as a result of the scourging. Others were thrown on the ground and lay there under the accumulated infliction of tortures, exhibiting to the spectators a more terrible manifestation of severity, as they bore on

their bodies the marks of the various and diverse punishments which had been invented.

9. As this went on, some died under the tortures, shaming the adversary by their constancy. Others half dead were shut up in prison, and suffering with their agonies, they died in a few days; but the rest, recovering under the care which they received, gained confidence by time and their long detention in prison.

10. When therefore they were ordered to choose whether they would be released from molestation by touching the polluted sacrifice, and would receive from them the accursed freedom, or refusing to sacrifice, should be condemned to death, they did not hesitate, but went to death cheerfully. For they knew what had been declared before by the Sacred Scriptures. For it is said, 'He that sacrifices to other gods shall be utterly destroyed,' Exodus 22:20 and, 'You shall have no other gods before me.' Exodus 20:3

11. Such are the words of the truly philosophical and God-loving martyr, which, before the final sentence, while yet in prison, he addressed to the brethren in his parish, showing them his own circumstances, and at the same time exhorting them to hold fast, even after his approaching death, to the religion of Christ.

12. But why need we dwell upon these things, and continue to add fresh instances of the conflicts of the divine martyrs throughout the world, especially since they were dealt with no longer by common law, but attacked like enemies of war?

Chapter 11. Those in Phrygia.

1. A small town of Phrygia, inhabited solely by Christians, was completely surrounded by soldiers while the men were in it. Throwing fire into it, they consumed them with the women and children while they were calling upon Christ. This they did because all the inhabitants of the city, and the curator himself, and the governor, with all who held office, and the entire populace, confessed themselves Christians, and would not in the least obey those who commanded them to worship idols.

2. There was another man of Roman dignity named Adauctus, of a noble Italian family, who had advanced through every honor under the emperors, so that he had blamelessly filled even the general offices of magistrate, as they call it, and of finance minister. Besides all this he

excelled in deeds of piety and in the confession of the Christ of God, and was adorned with the diadem of martyrdom. He endured the conflict for religion while still holding the office of finance minister.

Chapter 12. Many Others, both Men and Women, who suffered in Various Ways.

1. Why need we mention the rest by name, or number the multitude of the men, or picture the various sufferings of the admirable martyrs of Christ? Some of them were slain with the axe, as in Arabia. The limbs of some were broken, as in Cappadocia. Some, raised on high by the feet, with their heads down, while a gentle fire burned beneath them, were suffocated by the smoke which arose from the burning wood, as was done in Mesopotamia. Others were mutilated by cutting off their noses and ears and hands, and cutting to pieces the other members and parts of their bodies, as in Alexandria.

2. Why need we revive the recollection of those in Antioch who were roasted on grates, not so as to kill them, but so as to subject them to a lingering punishment? Or of others who preferred to thrust their right hand into the fire rather than touch the impious sacrifice? Some, shrinking from the trial, rather than be taken and fall into the hands of their enemies, threw themselves from lofty houses, considering death preferable to the cruelty of the impious.

3. A certain holy person,— in soul admirable for virtue, in body a woman—who was illustrious beyond all in Antioch for wealth and family and reputation, had brought up in the principles of religion her two daughters, who were now in the freshness and bloom of life. Since great envy was excited on their account, every means was used to find them in their concealment; and when it was ascertained that they were away, they were summoned deceitfully to Antioch. Thus they were caught in the nets of the soldiers. When the woman saw herself and her daughters thus helpless, and knew the things terrible to speak of that men would do to them—and the most unbearable of all terrible things, the threatened violation of their chastity, — she exhorted herself and the maidens that they ought not to submit even to hear of this. For, she said, that to surrender their souls to the slavery of demons was worse than all deaths and destruction; and she set before them the only deliverance from all these things—escape to Christ.

4. They then listened to her advice. And after arranging their garments suitably, they went aside from the middle of the road, having requested of the guards a little time for retirement, and cast themselves into a river which was flowing by.

5. Thus they destroyed themselves. But there were two other virgins in the same city of Antioch who served God in all things, and were true sisters, illustrious in family and distinguished in life, young and blooming, serious in mind, pious in deportment, and admirable for zeal. As if the earth could not bear such excellence, the worshipers of demons commanded to cast them into the sea. And this was done to them.

6. In Pontus, others endured sufferings horrible to hear. Their fingers were pierced with sharp reeds under their nails. Melted lead, bubbling and boiling with the heat, was poured down the backs of others, and they were roasted in the most sensitive parts of the body.

7. Others endured on their bowels and privy members shameful and inhuman and unmentionable torments, which the noble and law-observing judges, to show their severity, devised, as more honorable manifestations of wisdom. And new tortures were continually invented, as if they were endeavoring, by surpassing one another, to gain prizes in a contest.

8. But at the close of these calamities, when finally they could contrive no greater cruelties, and were weary of putting to death, and were filled and satiated with the shedding of blood, they turned to what they considered merciful and humane treatment, so that they seemed to be no longer devising terrible things against us.

9. For they said that it was not fitting that the cities should be polluted with the blood of their own people, or that the government of their rulers, which was kind and mild toward all, should be defamed through excessive cruelty; but that rather the beneficence of the humane and royal authority should be extended to all, and we should no longer be put to death. For the infliction of this punishment upon us should be stopped in consequence of the humanity of the rulers.

10. Therefore it was commanded that our eyes should be put out, and that we should be maimed in one of our limbs. For such things were humane in their sight, and the lightest of punishments for us. So that now on account of this kindly treatment accorded us by the impious, it was impossible to tell the incalculable number of those whose right eyes had first been cut out with the sword, and then had been cauterized with

fire; or who had been disabled in the left foot by burning the joints, and afterward condemned to the provincial copper mines, not so much for service as for distress and hardship. Besides all these, others encountered other trials, which it is impossible to recount; for their manly endurance surpasses all description.

11. In these conflicts the noble martyrs of Christ shone illustrious over the entire world, and everywhere astonished those who beheld their manliness; and the evidences of the truly divine and unspeakable power of our Saviour were made manifest through them. To mention each by name would be a long task, if not indeed impossible.

Chapter 13. The Bishops of the Church that evinced by their Blood the Genuineness of the Religion which they preached.

1. As for the rulers of the Church that suffered martyrdom in the principal cities, the first martyr of the kingdom of Christ whom we shall mention among the monuments of the pious is Anthimus, bishop of the city of Nicomedia, who was beheaded.

2. Among the martyrs at Antioch was Lucian, a presbyter of that parish, whose entire life was most excellent. At Nicomedia, in the presence of the emperor, he proclaimed the heavenly kingdom of Christ, first in an oral defense, and afterwards by deeds as well.

3. Of the martyrs in Phœnicia the most distinguished were those devoted pastors of the spiritual flocks of Christ: Tyrannion, bishop of the church of Tyre; Zenobius, a presbyter of the church at Sidon; and Silvanus, bishop of the churches about Emesa.

4. The last of these, with others, was made food for wild beasts at Emesa, and was thus received into the ranks of martyrs. The other two glorified the word of God at Antioch through patience unto death. The bishop was thrown into the depths of the sea. But Zenobius, who was a very skillful physician, died through severe tortures which were applied to his sides.

5. Of the martyrs in Palestine, Silvanus, bishop of the churches about Gaza, was beheaded with thirty-nine others at the copper mines of Phæno. There also the Egyptian bishops, Peleus and Nilus, with others, suffered death by fire.

6. Among these we must mention Pamphilus, a presbyter, who was the great glory of the parish of Cæsarea, and among the men of our time most admirable.

7. The virtue of his manly deeds we have recorded in the proper place. Of those who suffered death illustriously at Alexandria and throughout Egypt and Thebais, Peter, bishop of Alexandria, one of the most excellent teachers of the religion of Christ, should first be mentioned; and of the presbyters with him Faustus, Dius and Ammonius, perfect martyrs of Christ; also Phileas, Hesychius, Pachymius and Theodorus, bishops of Egyptian churches, and besides them many other distinguished persons who are commemorated by the parishes of their country and region. It is not for us to describe the conflicts of those who suffered for the divine religion throughout the entire world, and to relate accurately what happened to each of them. This would be the proper work of those who were eye-witnesses of the events. I will describe for posterity in another work those which I myself witnessed.

8. But in the present book I will add to what I have given the revocation issued by our persecutors, and those events that occurred at the beginning of the persecution, which will be most profitable to such as shall read them.

9. What words could sufficiently describe the greatness and abundance of the prosperity of the Roman government before the war against us, while the rulers were friendly and peaceable toward us? Then those who were highest in the government, and had held the position ten or twenty years, passed their time in tranquil peace, in festivals and public games and most joyful pleasures and cheer.

10. While thus their authority was growing uninterruptedly, and increasing day by day, suddenly they changed their peaceful attitude toward us, and began an implacable war. But the second year of this movement was not yet past, when a revolution took place in the entire government and overturned all things.

11. For a severe sickness came upon the chief of those of whom we have spoken, by which his understanding was distracted; and with him who was honored with the second rank, he retired into private life. Scarcely had he done this when the entire empire was divided; a thing which is not recorded as having ever occurred before.

12. Not long after, the Emperor Constantius, who through his entire life was most kindly and favorably disposed toward his subjects, and most

friendly to the Divine Word, ended his life in the common course of nature, and left his own son, Constantine, as emperor and Augustus in his stead. He was the first that was ranked by them among the gods, and received after death every honor which one could pay to an emperor.

13. He was the kindest and mildest of emperors, and the only one of those of our day that passed all the time of his government in a manner worthy of his office. Moreover, he conducted himself toward all most favorably and beneficently. He took not the smallest part in the war against us, but preserved the pious that were under him unharmed and unabused. He neither threw down the church buildings, nor did he devise anything else against us. The end of his life was honorable and thrice blessed. He alone at death left his empire happily and gloriously to his own son as his successor,— one who was in all respects most prudent and pious.

14. His son Constantine entered on the government at once, being proclaimed supreme emperor and Augustus by the soldiers, and long before by God himself, the King of all. He showed himself an emulator of his father's piety toward our doctrine. Such an one was he.

But after this, Licinius was declared emperor and Augustus by a common vote of the rulers.

15. These things grieved Maximinus greatly, for until that time he had been entitled by all only Cæsar. He therefore, being exceedingly imperious, seized the dignity for himself, and became Augustus, being made such by himself. In the mean time he whom we have mentioned as having resumed his dignity after his abdication, being detected in conspiring against the life of Constantine, perished by a most shameful death. He was the first whose decrees and statues and public monuments were destroyed because of his wickedness and impiety.

Chapter 14. The Character of the Enemies of Religion.

1. Maxentius his son, who obtained the government at Rome, at first feigned our faith, in complaisance and flattery toward the Roman people. On this account he commanded his subjects to cease persecuting the Christians, pretending to religion that he might appear merciful and mild beyond his predecessors.

2. But he did not prove in his deeds to be such a person as was hoped, but ran into all wickedness and abstained from no impurity or licentiousness, committing adulteries and indulging in all kinds of

corruption. For having separated wives from their lawful consorts, he abused them and sent them back most dishonorably to their husbands. And he not only practiced this against the obscure and unknown, but he insulted especially the most prominent and distinguished members of the Roman senate.

3. All his subjects, people and rulers, honored and obscure, were worn out by grievous oppression. Neither, although they kept quiet, and bore the bitter servitude, was there any relief from the murderous cruelty of the tyrant. Once, on a small pretense, he gave the people to be slaughtered by his guards; and a great multitude of the Roman populace were slain in the midst of the city, with the spears and arms, not of Scythians and barbarians, but of their own fellow citizens.

4. It would be impossible to recount the number of senators who were put to death for the sake of their wealth; multitudes being slain on various pretenses.

5. To crown all his wickedness, the tyrant resorted to magic. And in his divinations he cut open pregnant women, and again inspected the bowels of newborn infants. He slaughtered lions, and performed various execrable acts to invoke demons and avert war. For his only hope was that, by these means, victory would be secured to him.

6. It is impossible to tell the ways in which this tyrant at Rome oppressed his subjects, so that they were reduced to such an extreme dearth of the necessities of life as has never been known, according to our contemporaries, either at Rome or elsewhere.

7. But Maximinus, the tyrant in the East, having secretly formed a friendly alliance with the Roman tyrant as with a brother in wickedness, sought to conceal it for a long time. But being at last detected, he suffered merited punishment.

8. It was wonderful how akin he was in wickedness to the tyrant at Rome, or rather how far he surpassed him in it. For the chief of sorcerers and magicians were honored by him with the highest rank. Becoming exceedingly timid and superstitious, he valued greatly the error of idols and demons. Indeed, without soothsayers and oracles he did not venture to move even a finger, so to speak.

9. Therefore he persecuted us more violently and incessantly than his predecessors. He ordered temples to be erected in every city, and the sacred groves which had been destroyed through lapse of time to be speedily restored. He appointed idol priests in every place and city; and

he set over them in every province, as high priest, some political official who had especially distinguished himself in every kind of service, giving him a band of soldiers and a bodyguard. And to all jugglers, as if they were pious and beloved of the gods, he granted governments and the greatest privileges.

10. From this time on he distressed and harassed, not one city or country, but all the provinces under his authority, by extreme exactions of gold and silver and goods, and most grievous prosecutions and various fines. He took away from the wealthy the property which they had inherited from their ancestors, and bestowed vast riches and large sums of money on the flatterers about him.

11. And he went to such an excess of folly and drunkenness that his mind was deranged and crazed in his carousals; and he gave commands when intoxicated of which he repented afterward when sober. He suffered no one to surpass him in debauchery and profligacy, but made himself an instructor in wickedness to those about him, both rulers and subjects. He urged on the army to live wantonly in every kind of revelry and intemperance, and encouraged the governors and generals to abuse their subjects with rapacity and covetousness, almost as if they were rulers with him.

12. Why need we relate the licentious, shameless deeds of the man, or enumerate the multitude with whom he committed adultery? For he could not pass through a city without continually corrupting women and ravishing virgins.

13. And in this he succeeded with all except the Christians. For as they despised death, they cared nothing for his power. For the men endured fire and sword and crucifixion and wild beasts and the depths of the sea, and cutting off of limbs, and burnings, and pricking and digging out of eyes, and mutilations of the entire body, and besides these, hunger and mines and bonds. In all they showed patience in behalf of religion rather than transfer to idols the reverence due to God.

14. And the women were not less manly than the men in behalf of the teaching of the Divine Word, as they endured conflicts with the men, and bore away equal prizes of virtue. And when they were dragged away for corrupt purposes, they surrendered their lives to death rather than their bodies to impurity.

15. One only of those who were seized for adulterous purposes by the tyrant, a most distinguished and illustrious Christian woman in

Alexandria, conquered the passionate and intemperate soul of Maximinus by most heroic firmness. Honorable on account of wealth and family and education, she esteemed all of these inferior to chastity. He urged her many times, but although she was ready to die, he could not put her to death, for his desire was stronger than his anger.

16. He therefore punished her with exile, and took away all her property. Many others, unable even to listen to the threats of violation from the heathen rulers, endured every form of tortures, and rackings, and deadly punishment.

These indeed should be admired. But far the most admirable was that woman at Rome, who was truly the most noble and modest of all, whom the tyrant Maxentius, fully resembling Maximinus in his actions, endeavored to abuse.

17. For when she learned that those who served the tyrant in such matters were at the house (she also was a Christian), and that her husband, although a prefect of Rome, would suffer them to take and lead her away, having requested a little time for adorning her body, she entered her chamber, and being alone, stabbed herself with a sword. Dying immediately, she left her corpse to those who had come for her. And by her deeds, more powerfully than by any words, she has shown to all men now and hereafter that the virtue which prevails among Christians is the only invincible and indestructible possession.

18. Such was the career of wickedness which was carried forward at one and the same time by the two tyrants who held the East and the West. Who is there that would hesitate, after careful examination, to pronounce the persecution against us the cause of such evils? Especially since this extreme confusion of affairs did not cease until the Christians had obtained liberty.

Chapter 15. The Events which happened to the Heathen.

1. During the entire ten years of the persecution, they were constantly plotting and warring against one another. For the sea could not be navigated, nor could men sail from any port without being exposed to all kinds of outrages; being stretched on the rack and lacerated in their sides, that it might be ascertained through various tortures, whether they came from the enemy; and finally being subjected to punishment by the cross or by fire.

2. And besides these things shields and breastplates were preparing, and darts and spears and other warlike accoutrements were making ready, and galleys and naval armor were collecting in every place. And no one expected anything else than to be attacked by enemies any day. In addition to this, famine and pestilence came upon them, in regard to which we shall relate what is necessary in the proper place.

Chapter 16. The Change of Affairs for the Better.

1. Such was the state of affairs during the entire persecution. But in the tenth year, through the grace of God, it ceased altogether, having begun to decrease after the eighth year. For when the divine and heavenly grace showed us favorable and propitious oversight, then truly our rulers, and the very persons by whom the war against us had been earnestly prosecuted, most remarkably changed their minds, and issued a revocation, and quenched the great fire of persecution which had been kindled, by merciful proclamations and ordinances concerning us.

2. But this was not due to any human agency; nor was it the result, as one might say, of the compassion or philanthropy of our rulers—far from it, for daily from the beginning until that time they were devising more and more severe measures against us, and continually inventing outrages by a greater variety of instruments—but it was manifestly due to the oversight of Divine Providence, on the one hand becoming reconciled to his people, and on the other, attacking him who instigated these evils, and showing anger toward him as the author of the cruelties of the entire persecution.

3. For though it was necessary that these things should take place, according to the divine judgment, yet the Word says, Woe to him through whom the offense comes. Matthew 18:7 Therefore punishment from God came upon him, beginning with his flesh, and proceeding to his soul.

4. For an abscess suddenly appeared in the midst of the secret parts of his body, and from it a deeply perforated sore, which spread irresistibly into his inmost bowels. An indescribable multitude of worms sprang from them, and a deathly odor arose, as the entire bulk of his body had, through his gluttony, been changed, before his sickness, into an excessive mass of soft fat, which became putrid, and thus presented an awful and intolerable sight to those who came near.

5. Some of the physicians, being wholly unable to endure the exceeding offensiveness of the odor, were slain; others, as the entire mass had swollen and passed beyond hope of restoration, and they were unable to render any help, were put to death without mercy.

Chapter 17. The Revocation of the Rulers.

1. Wrestling with so many evils, he thought of the cruelties which he had committed against the pious. Turning, therefore, his thoughts toward himself, he first openly confessed to the God of the universe, and then summoning his attendants, he commanded that without delay they should stop the persecution of the Christians, and should by law and royal decree, urge them forward to build their churches and to perform their customary worship, offering prayers in behalf of the emperor. Immediately the deed followed the word.

2. The imperial decrees were published in the cities, containing the revocation of the acts against us in the following form:

3. The Emperor Cæsar Galerius Valerius Maximinus, Invictus, Augustus, Pontifex Maximus, conqueror of the Germans, conqueror of the Egyptians, conqueror of the Thebans, five times conqueror of the Sarmatians, conqueror of the Persians, twice conqueror of the Carpathians, six times conqueror of the Armenians, conqueror of the Medes, conqueror of the Adiabeni, Tribune of the people the twentieth time, Emperor the nineteenth time, Consul the eighth time, Father of his country, Proconsul;

4. and the Emperor Cæsar Flavius Valerius Constantinus, Pius, Felix, Invictus, Augustus, Pontifex Maximus, Tribune of the people, Emperor the fifth time, Consul, Father of his country, Proconsul;

5. and the Emperor Cæsar Valerius Licinius, Pius, Felix, Invictus, Augustus, Pontifex Maximus, Tribune of the people the fourth time, Emperor the third time, Consul, Father of his country, Proconsul; to the people of their provinces, greeting:

6. Among the other things which we have ordained for the public advantage and profit, we formerly wished to restore everything to conformity with the ancient laws and public discipline of the Romans, and to provide that the Christians also, who have forsaken the religion of their ancestors, should return to a good disposition.

7. For in some way such arrogance had seized them and such stupidity had overtaken them, that they did not follow the ancient institutions which possibly their own ancestors had formerly established, but made for themselves laws according to their own purpose, as each one desired, and observed them, and thus assembled as separate congregations in various places.

8. When we had issued this decree that they should return to the institutions established by the ancients, a great many submitted under danger, but a great many being harassed endured all kinds of death.

9. And since many continue in the same folly, and we perceive that they neither offer to the heavenly gods the worship which is due, nor pay regard to the God of the Christians, in consideration of our philanthropy and our invariable custom, by which we are wont to extend pardon to all, we have determined that we ought most cheerfully to extend our indulgence in this matter also; that they may again be Christians, and may rebuild the conventicles in which they were accustomed to assemble, on condition that nothing be done by them contrary to discipline. In another letter we shall indicate to the magistrates what they have to observe.

10. Wherefore, on account of this indulgence of ours, they ought to supplicate their God for our safety, and that of the people, and their own, that the public welfare may be preserved in every place, and that they may live securely in their several homes.

11. Such is the tenor of this edict, translated, as well as possible, from the Roman tongue into the Greek. It is time to consider what took place after these events.

That which follows is found in Some Copies in the Eighth Book.

1. The author of the edict very shortly after this confession was released from his pains and died. He is reported to have been the original author of the misery of the persecution, having endeavored, long before the movement of the other emperors, to turn from the faith the Christians in the army, and first of all those in his own house, degrading some from the military rank, and abusing others most shamefully, and threatening still others with death, and finally inciting his partners in the empire to the general persecution. It is not proper to pass over the death of these emperors in silence.

2. As four of them held the supreme authority, those who were advanced in age and honor, after the persecution had continued not quite two years, abdicated the government, as we have already stated, and passed the remainder of their lives in a common and private station.

3. The end of their lives was as follows. He who was first in honor and age perished through a long and most grievous physical infirmity. He who held the second place ended his life by strangling, suffering thus according to a certain demoniacal prediction, on account of his many daring crimes.

4. Of those after them, the last, of whom we have spoken as the originator of the entire persecution, suffered such things as we have related. But he who preceded him, the most merciful and kindly emperor Constantius, passed all the time of his government in a manner worthy of his office. Moreover, he conducted himself towards all most favorably and beneficently. He took not the smallest part in the war against us, and preserved the pious that were under him unharmed and unabused. Neither did he throw down the church buildings, nor devise anything else against us. The end of his life was happy and thrice blessed. He alone at death left his empire happily and gloriously to his own son as his successor, one who was in all respects most prudent and pious. He entered on the government at once, being proclaimed supreme emperor and Augustus by the soldiers;

5. and he showed himself an emulator of his father's piety toward our doctrine. Such were the deaths of the four of whom we have written, which took place at different times.

6. Of these, moreover, only the one referred to a little above by us, with those who afterward shared in the government, finally published openly to all the above-mentioned confession, in the written edict which he issued.

BOOK IX

Chapter 1. The Pretended Relaxation.

1. The imperial edict of recantation, which has been quoted above, was posted in all parts of Asia and in the adjoining provinces. After this had been done, Maximinus, the tyrant in the East—a most impious man, if there ever was one, and most hostile to the religion of the God of the universe—being by no means satisfied with its contents, instead of sending the above-quoted decree to the governors under him, gave them verbal commands to relax the war against us.

2. For since he could not in any other way oppose the decision of his superiors, keeping the law which had been already issued secret, and taking care that it might not be made known in the district under him, he gave an unwritten order to his governors that they should relax the persecution against us. They communicated the command to each other in writing.

3. Sabinus, at least, who was honored with the highest official rank among them, communicated the will of the emperor to the provincial governors in a Latin epistle, the translation of which is as follows:

4. With continuous and most devoted earnestness their Majesties, our most divine masters, the emperors, formerly directed the minds of all men to follow the holy and correct course of life, that those also who seemed to live in a manner foreign to that of the Romans, should render the worship due to the immortal gods. But the obstinacy and most unconquerable determination of some went so far that they could neither be turned back from their purpose by the just reason of the command, nor be intimidated by the impending punishment.

5. Since therefore it has come to pass that by such conduct many have brought themselves into danger, their Majesties, our most powerful masters, the emperors, in the exalted nobility of piety, esteeming it foreign to their Majesties' purpose to bring men into so great danger for such a cause, have commanded their devoted servant, myself, to write to your wisdom, that if any Christian be found engaging in the worship of his own people, you should abstain from molesting and endangering him, and should not suppose it necessary to punish any one on this pretext. For it has been proved by the experience of so long a time that they can in no way be persuaded to abandon such obstinate conduct.

6. Therefore it should be your care to write to the curators and magistrates and district overseers of every city, that they may know that it is not necessary for them to give further attention to this matter.

7. Thereupon the rulers of the provinces, thinking that the purpose of the things which were written was truly made known to them, declared the imperial will to the curators and magistrates and prefects of the various districts in writing. But they did not limit themselves to writing, but sought more quickly to accomplish the supposed will of the emperor in deeds also. Those whom they had imprisoned on account of their confession of the Deity, they set at liberty, and they released those of them who had been sent to the mines for punishment; for they erroneously supposed that this was the true will of the emperor.

8. And when these things had thus been done, immediately, like a light shining forth in a dark night, one could see in every city congregations gathered and assemblies thronged, and meetings held according to their custom. And every one of the unbelieving heathen was not a little astonished at these things, wondering at so marvelous a transformation, and exclaiming that the God of the Christians was great and alone true.

9. And some of our people, who had faithfully and bravely sustained the conflict of persecution, again became frank and bold toward all; but as many as had been diseased in the faith and had been shaken in their souls by the tempest, strove eagerly for healing, beseeching and imploring the strong to stretch out to them a saving hand, and supplicating God to be merciful unto them.

10. Then also the noble athletes of religion who had been set free from their sufferings in the mines returned to their own homes. Happily and joyfully they passed through every city, full of unspeakable pleasure and of a boldness which cannot be expressed in words.

11. Great crowds of men pursued their journey along the highways and through the market-places, praising God with hymns and psalms. And you might have seen those who a little while before had been driven in bonds from their native countries under a most cruel sentence, returning with bright and joyful faces to their own firesides; so that even they who had formerly thirsted for our blood, when they saw the unexpected wonder, congratulated us on what had taken place.

Chapter 2. The Subsequent Reverse.

1. But the tyrant who, as we have said, ruled over the districts of the Orient, a thorough hater of the good and an enemy of every virtuous person, as he was, could no longer bear this; and indeed he did not permit matters to go on in this way quite six months. Devising all possible means of destroying the peace, he first attempted to restrain us, under a pretext, from meeting in the cemeteries.

2. Then through the agency of some wicked men he sent an embassy to himself against us, inciting the citizens of Antioch to ask from him as a very great favor that he would by no means permit any of the Christians to dwell in their country; and others were secretly induced to do the same thing. The author of all this in Antioch was Theotecnus, a violent and wicked man, who was an impostor, and whose character was foreign to his name. He appears to have been the curator of the city.

Chapter 3. The Newly Erected Statue at Antioch.

After this man had carried on all kinds of war against us and had caused our people to be diligently hunted up in their retreats, as if they were unholy thieves, and had devised every sort of slander and accusation against us, and become the cause of death to vast numbers, he finally erected a statue of Jupiter Philius with certain juggleries and magic rites. And after inventing unholy forms of initiation and ill-omened mysteries in connection with it, and abominable means of purification, he exhibited his jugglery, by oracles which he pretended to utter, even to the emperor; and through a flattery which was pleasing to the ruler he aroused the demon against the Christians and said that the god had given command to expel the Christians as his enemies beyond the confines of the city and the neighboring districts.

Chapter 4. The Memorials against us.

1. The fact that this man, who took the lead in this matter, had succeeded in his purpose was an incitement to all the other officials in the cities under the same government to prepare a similar memorial. And the governors of the provinces perceiving that this was agreeable to the emperor suggested to their subjects that they should do the same.

2. And as the tyrant by a rescript declared himself well pleased with their measures, persecution was kindled anew against us. Priests for the images were then appointed in the cities, and besides them high priests by Maximinus himself. The latter were taken from among those who

were most distinguished in public life and had gained celebrity in all the offices which they had filled; and who were imbued, moreover, with great zeal for the service of those whom they worshipped.

3. Indeed, the extraordinary superstition of the emperor, to speak in brief, led all his subjects, both rulers and private citizens, for the sake of gratifying him, to do everything against us, supposing that they could best show their gratitude to him for the benefits which they had received from him, by plotting murder against us and exhibiting toward us any new signs of malignity.

Chapter 5. The Forged Acts.

1. Having therefore forged Acts of Pilate and our Saviour full of every kind of blasphemy against Christ, they sent them with the emperor's approval to the whole of the empire subject to him, with written commands that they should be openly posted to the view of all in every place, both in country and city, and that the schoolmasters should give them to their scholars, instead of their customary lessons, to be studied and learned by heart.

2. While these things were taking place, another military commander, whom the Romans call Dux, seized some infamous women in the market-place at Damascus in Phœnicia, and by threatening to inflict tortures upon them compelled them to make a written declaration that they had once been Christians and that they were acquainted with their impious deeds—that in their very churches they committed licentious acts; and they uttered as many other slanders against our religion as he wished them to. Having taken down their words in writing, he communicated them to the emperor, who commanded that these documents also should be published in every place and city.

Chapter 6. Those who suffered Martyrdom at this Time.

1. Not long afterward, however, this military commander became his own murderer and paid the penalty for his wickedness. But we were obliged again to endure exile and severe persecutions, and the governors in every province were once more terribly stirred up against us; so that even some of those illustrious in the Divine Word were seized and had sentence of death pronounced upon them without mercy. Three of them in the city of Emesa in Phœnicia, having confessed that they were

Christians, were thrown as food to the wild beasts. Among them was a bishop Silvanus, a very old man, who had filled his office full forty years.

2. At about the same time Peter also, who presided most illustriously over the parishes in Alexandria, a divine example of a bishop on account of the excellence of his life and his study of the sacred Scriptures, being seized for no cause and quite unexpectedly, was, as if by command of Maximinus, immediately and without explanation, beheaded. With him also many other bishops of Egypt suffered the same fate.

3. And Lucian, a presbyter of the parish at Antioch, and a most excellent man in every respect, temperate in life and famed for his learning in sacred things, was brought to the city of Nicomedia, where at that time the emperor happened to be staying, and after delivering before the ruler an apology for the doctrine which he professed, was committed to prison and put to death.

4. Such trials were brought upon us in a brief time by Maximinus, the enemy of virtue, so that this persecution which was stirred up against us seemed far more cruel than the former.

Chapter 7. The Decree against us which was engraved on Pillars.

1. The memorials against us and copies of the imperial edicts issued in reply to them were engraved and set up on brazen pillars in the midst of the cities, — a course which had never been followed elsewhere. The children in the schools had daily in their mouths the names of Jesus and Pilate, and the Acts which had been forged in wanton insolence.

2. It appears to me necessary to insert here this document of Maximinus which was posted on pillars, in order that there may be made manifest at the same time the boastful and haughty arrogance of the God-hating man, and the sleepless evil-hating divine vengeance upon the impious, which followed close upon him, and under whose pressure he not long afterward took the opposite course in respect to us and confirmed it by written laws.

The rescript is in the following words:

Copy of a translation of the rescript of Maximinus in answer to the memorials against us, taken from the pillar in Tyre.

3. Now at length the feeble power of the human mind has become able to shake off and to scatter every dark mist of error, which before this besieged the senses of men, who were more miserable than impious,

and enveloped them in dark and destructive ignorance; and to perceive that it is governed and established by the beneficent providence of the immortal gods.

4. It passes belief how grateful, how pleasing and how agreeable it is to us, that you have given a most decided proof of your pious resolution; for even before this it was known to every one how much regard and reverence you were paying to the immortal gods, exhibiting not a faith of bare and empty words, but continued and wonderful examples of illustrious deeds.

5. Wherefore your city may justly be called a seat and dwelling of the immortal gods. At least, it appears by many signs that it flourishes because of the presence of the celestial gods.

6. Behold, therefore, your city, regardless of all private advantages, and omitting its former petitions in its own behalf, when it perceived that the adherents of that execrable vanity were again beginning to spread, and to start the greatest conflagration—like a neglected and extinguished funeral pile when its brands are rekindled,— immediately resorted to our piety as to a metropolis of all religiousness, asking some remedy and aid.

7. It is evident that the gods have given you this saving mind on account of your faith and piety.

Accordingly that supreme and mightiest Jove, who presides over your illustrious city, who preserves your ancestral gods, your wives and children, your hearths and homes from every destructive pest, has infused into your souls this wholesome resolve; showing and proving how excellent and glorious and salutary it is to observe with the becoming reverence the worship and sacred rites of the immortal gods.

8. For who can be found so ignorant or so devoid of all understanding as not to perceive that it is due to the kindly care of the gods that the earth does not refuse the seed sown in it, nor disappoint the hope of the husbandmen with vain expectation; that impious war is not inevitably fixed upon earth, and wasted bodies dragged down to death under the influence of a corrupted atmosphere; that the sea is not swollen and raised on high by blasts of intemperate winds; that unexpected hurricanes do not burst forth and stir up the destructive tempest; moreover, that the earth, the nourisher and mother of all, is not shaken from its lowest depths with a terrible tremor, and that the mountains upon it do not sink into the opening chasms. No one is ignorant that all

these, and evils still worse than these, have oftentimes happened hitherto.

9. And all these misfortunes have taken place on account of the destructive error of the empty vanity of those impious men, when it prevailed in their souls, and, we may almost say, weighed down the whole world with shame.

10. After other words he adds: Let them look at the standing crops already flourishing with waving heads in the broad fields, and at the meadows glittering with plants and flowers, in response to abundant rains and the restored mildness and softness of the atmosphere.

11. Finally, let all rejoice that the might of the most powerful and terrible Mars has been propitiated by our piety, our sacrifices, and our veneration; and let them on this account enjoy firm and tranquil peace and quiet; and let as many as have wholly abandoned that blind error and delusion and have returned to a right and sound mind rejoice the more, as those who have been rescued from an unexpected storm or severe disease and are to reap the fruits of pleasure for the rest of their life.

12. But if they still persist in their execrable vanity, let them, as you have desired, be driven far away from your city and territory, that thus, in accordance with your praiseworthy zeal in this matter, your city, being freed from every pollution and impiety, may, according to its native disposition, attend to the sacred rites of the immortal gods with becoming reverence.

13. But that you may know how acceptable to us your request respecting this matter has been, and how ready our mind is to confer benefits voluntarily, without memorials and petitions, we permit your devotion to ask whatever great gift ye may desire in return for this your pious disposition.

14. And now ask that this may be done and that you may receive it; for you shall obtain it without delay. This, being granted to your city, shall furnish for all time an evidence of reverent piety toward the immortal gods, and of the fact that you have obtained from our benevolence merited prizes for this choice of yours; and it shall be shown to your children and children's children.

15. This was published against us in all the provinces, depriving us of every hope of good, at least from men; so that, according to that divine

utterance, If it were possible, even the elect would have stumbled Matthew 24:24 at these things.

16. And now indeed, when the hope of most of us was almost extinct, suddenly while those who were to execute against us the above decree had in some places scarcely finished their journey, God, the defender of his own Church, exhibited his heavenly interposition in our behalf, nearly stopping the tyrant's boasting against us.

Chapter 8. The Misfortunes which happened in Connection with these Things, in Famine, Pestilence, and War.

1. The customary rains and showers of the winter season ceased to fall in their wonted abundance upon the earth and an unexpected famine made its appearance, and in addition to this a pestilence, and another severe disease consisting of an ulcer, which on account of its fiery appearance was appropriately called a carbuncle. This, spreading over the whole body, greatly endangered the lives of those who suffered from it; but as it chiefly attacked the eyes, it deprived multitudes of men, women, and children of their sight.

2. In addition to this the tyrant was compelled to go to war with the Armenians, who had been from ancient times friends and allies of the Romans. As they were also Christians and zealous in their piety toward the Deity, the enemy of God had attempted to compel them to sacrifice to idols and demons, and had thus made friends foes, and allies enemies.

3. All these things suddenly took place at one and the same time, and refuted the tyrant's empty boast against the Deity. For he had boasted that, because of his zeal for idols and his hostility against us, neither famine nor pestilence nor war had happened in his time. These things, therefore, coming upon him at once and together, furnished a prelude also of his own destruction.

4. He himself with his forces was defeated in the war with the Armenians, and the rest of the inhabitants of the cities under him were terribly afflicted with famine and pestilence, so that one measure of wheat was sold for twenty-five hundred Attic drachms.

5. Those who died in the cities were innumerable, and those who died in the country and villages were still more. So that the tax lists which formerly included a great rural population were almost entirely wiped out; nearly all being speedily destroyed by famine and pestilence.

6. Some, therefore, desired to dispose of their most precious things to those who were better supplied, in return for the smallest morsel of food, and others, selling their possessions little by little, fell into the last extremity of want. Some, chewing wisps of hay and recklessly eating noxious herbs, undermined and ruined their constitutions.

7. And some of the high-born women in the cities, driven by want to shameful extremities, went forth into the market-places to beg, giving evidence of their former liberal culture by the modesty of their appearance and the decency of their apparel.

8. Some, wasted away like ghosts and at the very point of death, stumbled and tottered here and there, and too weak to stand fell down in the middle of the streets; lying stretched out at full length they begged that a small morsel of food might be given them, and with their last gasp they cried out Hunger! Having strength only for this most painful cry.

9. But others, who seemed to be better supplied, astonished at the multitude of the beggars, after giving away large quantities, finally became hard and relentless, expecting that they themselves also would soon suffer the same calamities as those who begged. So that in the midst of the market-places and lanes, dead and naked bodies lay unburied for many days, presenting the most lamentable spectacle to those that beheld them.

10. Some also became food for dogs, on which account the survivors began to kill the dogs, lest they should become mad and should go to devouring men.

11. But still worse was the pestilence which consumed entire houses and families, and especially those whom the famine was not able to destroy because of their abundance of food. Thus men of wealth, rulers and governors and multitudes in office, as if left by the famine on purpose for the pestilence, suffered swift and speedy death. Every place therefore was full of lamentation; in every lane and market- place and street there was nothing else to be seen or heard than tears, with the customary instruments and the voices of the mourners.

12. In this way death, waging war with these two weapons, pestilence and famine, destroyed whole families in a short time, so that one could see two or three dead bodies carried out at once.

13. Such were the rewards of the boasting of Maximinus and of the measures of the cities against us.

Then did the evidences of the universal zeal and piety of the Christians become manifest to all the heathen.

14. For they alone in the midst of such ills showed their sympathy and humanity by their deeds. Every day some continued caring for and burying the dead, for there were multitudes who had no one to care for them; others collected in one place those who were afflicted by the famine, throughout the entire city, and gave bread to them all; so that the thing became noised abroad among all men, and they glorified the God of the Christians; and, convinced by the facts themselves, confessed that they alone were truly pious and religious.

15. After these things were thus done, God, the great and celestial defender of the Christians, having revealed in the events which have been described his anger and indignation at all men for the great evils which they had brought upon us, restored to us the bright and gracious sunlight of his providence in our behalf; so that in the deepest darkness a light of peace shone most wonderfully upon us from him, and made it manifest to all that God himself has always been the ruler of our affairs. From time to time indeed he chastens his people and corrects them by his visitations, but again after sufficient chastisement he shows mercy and favor to those who hope in him.

Chapter 9. The Victory of the God-Beloved Emperors.

1. Thus when Constantine, whom we have already mentioned as an emperor, born of an emperor, a pious son of a most pious and prudent father, and Licinius, second to him, — two God-beloved emperors, honored alike for their intelligence and their piety—being stirred up against the two most impious tyrants by God, the absolute Ruler and Saviour of all, engaged in formal war against them, with God as their ally, Maxentius was defeated at Rome by Constantine in a remarkable manner, and the tyrant of the East did not long survive him, but met a most shameful death at the hand of Licinius, who had not yet become insane.

2. Constantine, who was the superior both in dignity and imperial rank, first took compassion upon those who were oppressed at Rome, and having invoked in prayer the God of heaven, and his Word, and Jesus Christ himself, the Saviour of all, as his aid, advanced with his whole army, proposing to restore to the Romans their ancestral liberty.

3. But Maxentius, putting confidence rather in the arts of sorcery than in the devotion of his subjects, did not dare to go forth beyond the gates of the city, but fortified every place and district and town which was enslaved by him, in the neighborhood of Rome and in all Italy, with an immense multitude of troops and with innumerable bands of soldiers. But the emperor, relying upon the assistance of God, attacked the first, second, and third army of the tyrant, and conquered them all; and having advanced through the greater part of Italy, was already very near Rome.

4. Then, that he might not be compelled to wage war with the Romans for the sake of the tyrant, God himself drew the latter, as if bound in chains, some distance without the gates, and confirmed those threats against the impious which had been anciently inscribed in sacred books—disbelieved, indeed, by most as a myth, but believed by the faithful,— confirmed them, in a word, by the deed itself to all, both believers and unbelievers, that saw the wonder with their eyes.

5. Thus, as in the time of Moses himself and of the ancient God- beloved race of Hebrews, he cast Pharaoh's chariots and host into the sea, and overwhelmed his chosen charioteers in the Red Sea, and covered them with the flood, in the same way Maxentius also with his soldiers and body-guards went down into the depths like a stone, Exodus 15:5 when he fled before the power of God which was with Constantine, and passed through the river which lay in his way, over which he had formed a bridge with boats, and thus prepared the means of his own destruction.

6. In regard to him one might say, he dug a pit and opened it and fell into the hole which he had made; his labor shall turn upon his own head, and his unrighteousness shall fall upon his own crown.

7. Thus, then, the bridge over the river being broken, the passageway settled down, and immediately the boats with the men disappeared in the depths, and that most impious one himself first of all, then the shield-bearers who were with him, as the divine oracles foretold, sank like lead in the mighty waters; Exodus 15:10 so that those who obtained the victory from God, if not in words, at least in deeds, like Moses, the great servant of God, and those who were with him, fittingly sang as they had sung against the impious tyrant of old, saying, Let us sing unto the Lord, for he has gloriously glorified himself; horse and rider has he thrown into the sea; a helper and a protector has he become for my salvation; and Who is like you, O Lord; among the gods, who is like you glorious in holiness, marvelous in glory, doing wonders. Exodus 15:11

8. These and the like praises Constantine, by his very deeds, sang to God, the universal Ruler, and Author of his victory, as he entered Rome in triumph.

9. Immediately all the members of the senate and the other most celebrated men, with the whole Roman people, together with children and women, received him as their deliverer, their saviour, and their benefactor, with shining eyes and with their whole souls, with shouts of gladness and unbounded joy.

10. But he, as one possessed of inborn piety toward God, did not exult in the shouts, nor was he elated by the praises; but perceiving that his aid was from God, he immediately commanded that a trophy of the Saviour's passion be put in the hand of his own statue.

11. And when he had placed it, with the saving sign of the cross in its right hand, in the most public place in Rome, he commanded that the following inscription should be engraved upon it in the Roman tongue: By this salutary sign, the true proof of bravery, I have saved and freed your city from the yoke of the tyrant and moreover, having set at liberty both the senate and the people of Rome, I have restored them to their ancient distinction and splendor.

12. And after this both Constantine himself and with him the Emperor Licinius, who had not yet been seized by that madness into which he later fell, praising God as the author of all their blessings, with one will and mind drew up a full and most complete decree in behalf of the Christians, and sent an account of the wonderful things done for them by God, and of the victory over the tyrant, together with a copy of the decree itself, to Maximinus, who still ruled over the nations of the East and pretended friendship toward them.

13. But he, like a tyrant, was greatly pained by what he learned; but not wishing to seem to yield to others, nor, on the other hand, to suppress that which was commanded, for fear of those who enjoined it, as if on his own authority, he addressed, under compulsion, to the governors under him this first communication in behalf of the Christians, falsely inventing things against himself which had never been done by him.

Copy of a translation of the epistle of the tyrant Maximinus.

14. Jovius Maximinus Augustus to Sabinus. I am confident that it is manifest both to your firmness and to all men that our masters Diocletian and Maximianus, our fathers, when they saw almost all men

abandoning the worship of the gods and attaching themselves to the party of the Christians, rightly decreed that all who gave up the worship of those same immortal gods should be recalled by open chastisement and punishment to the worship of the gods.

15. But when I first came to the East under favorable auspices and learned that in some places a great many men who were able to render public service had been banished by the judges for the above-mentioned cause, I gave command to each of the judges that henceforth none of them should treat the provincials with severity, but that they should rather recall them to the worship of the gods by flattery and exhortations.

16. Then when, in accordance with my command, these orders were obeyed by the judges, it came to pass that none of those who lived in the districts of the East were banished or insulted, but that they were rather brought back to the worship of the gods by the fact that no severity was employed toward them.

17. But afterwards, when I went up last year under good auspices to Nicomedia and sojourned there, citizens of the same city came to me with the images of the gods, earnestly entreating that such a people should by no means be permitted to dwell in their country.

18. But when I learned that many men of the same religion dwelt in those regions, I replied that I gladly thanked them for their request, but that I perceived that it was not proffered by all, and that if, therefore, there were any that persevered in the same superstition, each one had the privilege of doing as he pleased, even if he wished to recognize the worship of the gods.

19. Nevertheless, I considered it necessary to give a friendly answer to the inhabitants of Nicomedia and to the other cities which had so earnestly presented to me the same petition, namely, that no Christians should dwell in their cities—both because this same course had been pursued by all the ancient emperors, and also because it was pleasing to the gods, through whom all men and the government of the state itself endure—and to confirm the request which they presented in behalf of the worship of their deity.

20. Therefore, although before this time, special letters have been sent to your devotedness, and commands have likewise been given that no harsh measures should be taken against those provincials who desire to follow such a course, but that they should be treated mildly and

moderately—nevertheless, in order that they may not suffer insults or extortions from the beneficiaries, or from any others, I have thought meet to remind your firmness in this epistle also that you should lead our provincials rather by flatteries and exhortations to recognize the care of the gods.

21. Hence, if any one of his own choice should decide to adopt the worship of the gods, it is fitting that he should be welcomed, but if any should wish to follow their own religion, do thou leave it in their power.

22. Wherefore it behooves your devotedness to observe that which is committed to you, and to see that power is given to no one to oppress our provincials with insults and extortions, since, as already written, it is fitting to recall our provincials to the worship of the gods rather by exhortations and flatteries. But, in order that this command of ours may come to the knowledge of all our provincials, it is incumbent upon you to proclaim that which has been enjoined, in an edict issued by yourself.

23. Since he was forced to do this by necessity and did not give the command by his own will, he was not regarded by any one as sincere or trustworthy, because he had already shown his unstable and deceitful disposition after his former similar concession.

24. None of our people, therefore, ventured to hold meetings or even to appear in public, because his communication did not cover this, but only commanded to guard against doing us any injury, and did not give orders that we should hold meetings or build churches or perform any of our customary acts.

25. And yet Constantine and Licinius, the advocates of peace and piety, had written him to permit this, and had granted it to all their subjects by edicts and ordinances. But this most impious man did not choose to yield in this matter until, being driven by the divine judgment, he was at last compelled to do it against his will.

Chapter 10. The Overthrow of the Tyrants and the Words which they uttered before their Death.

1. The circumstances which drove him to this course were the following. Being no longer able to sustain the magnitude of the government which had been undeservedly committed to him, in consequence of his want of prudence and imperial understanding, he managed affairs in a base manner, and with his mind unreasonably exalted in all things with boastful pride, even toward his colleagues in the empire who were in

every respect his superiors, in birth, in training, in education, in worth and intelligence, and, greatest of all, in temperance and piety toward the true God, he began to venture to act audaciously and to arrogate to himself the first rank.

2. Becoming mad in his folly, he broke the treaties which he had made with Licinius and undertook an implacable war. Then in a brief time he threw all things into confusion, and stirred up every city, and having collected his entire force, comprising an immense number of soldiers, he went forth to battle with him, elated by his hopes in demons, whom he supposed to be gods, and by the number of his soldiers.

3. And when he joined battle he was deprived of the oversight of God, and the victory was given to Licinius, who was then ruling, by the one and only God of all.

4. First, the army in which he trusted was destroyed, and as all his guards abandoned him and left him alone, and fled to the victor, he secretly divested himself as quickly as possible of the imperial garments, which did not fitly belong to him, and in a cowardly and ignoble and unmanly way mingled with the crowd, and then fled, concealing himself in fields and villages. But though he was so careful for his safety, he scarcely escaped the hands of his enemies, revealing by his deeds that the divine oracles are faithful and true, in which it is said, A king is not saved by a great force, and a giant shall not be saved by the greatness of his strength; a horse is a vain thing for safety, nor shall he be delivered by the greatness of his power.

5. Behold, the eyes of the Lord are upon them that fear him, upon them that hope in his mercy, to deliver their souls from death.

6. Thus the tyrant, covered with shame, went to his own country. And first, in frantic rage, he slew many priests and prophets of the gods whom he had formerly admired, and whose oracles had incited him to undertake the war, as sorcerers and impostors, and besides all as betrayers of his safety. Then having given glory to the God of the Christians and enacted a most full and complete ordinance in behalf of their liberty, he was immediately seized with a mortal disease, and no respite being granted him, departed this life. The law enacted by him was as follows:

Copy of the edict of the tyrant in behalf of the Christians, translated from the Roman tongue.

7. The Emperor Cæsar Caius Valerius Maximinus, Germanicus, Sarmaticus, Pius, Felix, Invictus, Augustus. We believe it manifest that no one is ignorant, but that every man who looks back over the past knows and is conscious that in every way we care continually for the good of our provincials, and wish to furnish them with those things which are of special advantage to all, and for the common benefit and profit, and whatever contributes to the public welfare and is agreeable to the views of each.

8. When, therefore, before this, it became clear to our mind that under pretext of the command of our parents, the most divine Diocletian and Maximianus, which enjoined that the meetings of the Christians should be abolished, many extortions and spoliations had been practiced by officials; and that those evils were continually increasing, to the detriment of our provincials toward whom we are especially anxious to exercise proper care, and that their possessions were in consequence perishing, letters were sent last year to the governors of each province, in which we decreed that, if any one wished to follow such a practice or to observe this same religion, he should be permitted without hindrance to pursue his purpose and should be impeded and prevented by no one, and that all should have liberty to do without any fear or suspicion that which each preferred.

9. But even now we cannot help perceiving that some of the judges have mistaken our commands, and have given our people reason to doubt the meaning of our ordinances, and have caused them to proceed too reluctantly to the observance of those religious rites which are pleasing to them.

10. In order, therefore, that in the future every suspicion of fearful doubt may be taken away, we have commanded that this decree be published, so that it may be clear to all that whoever wishes to embrace this sect and religion is permitted to do so by virtue of this grant of ours; and that each one, as he wishes or as is pleasing to him, is permitted to practice this religion which he has chosen to observe according to his custom. It is also granted them to build Lord's houses.

11. But that this grant of ours may be the greater, we have thought good to decree also that if any houses and lands before this time rightfully belonged to the Christians, and by the command of our parents fell into the treasury, or were confiscated by any city— whether they have been sold or presented to any one as a gift,— that all these should be restored

to their original possessors, the Christians, in order that in this also every one may have knowledge of our piety and care.

12. These are the words of the tyrant which were published not quite a year after the decrees against the Christians engraved by him on pillars. And by him to whom a little before we seemed impious wretches and atheists and destroyers of all life, so that we were not permitted to dwell in any city nor even in country or desert,— by him decrees and ordinances were issued in behalf of the Christians, and they who recently had been destroyed by fire and sword, by wild beasts and birds of prey, in the presence of the tyrant himself, and had suffered every species of torture and punishment, and most miserable deaths as atheists and impious wretches, were now acknowledged by him as possessors of religion and were permitted to build churches; and the tyrant himself bore witness and confessed that they had some rights.

13. And having made such confessions, as if he had received some benefit on account of them, he suffered perhaps less than he ought to have suffered, and being smitten by a sudden scourge of God, he perished in the second campaign of the war.

14. But his end was not like that of military chieftains who, while fighting bravely in battle for virtue and friends, often boldly encounter a glorious death; for like an impious enemy of God, while his army was still drawn up in the field, remaining at home and concealing himself, he suffered the punishment which he deserved. For he was smitten with a sudden scourge of God in his whole body, and harassed by terrible pains and torments, he fell prostrate on the ground, wasted by hunger, while all his flesh was dissolved by an invisible and God-sent fire, so that the whole appearance of his frame was changed, and there was left only a kind of image wasted away by length of time to a skeleton of dry bones; so that those who were present could think of his body as nothing else than the tomb of his soul, which was buried in a body already dead and completely melted away.

15. And as the heat still more violently consumed him in the depths of his marrow, his eyes burst forth, and falling from their sockets left him blind. Thereupon still breathing and making free confession to the Lord, he invoked death, and at last, after acknowledging that he justly suffered these things on account of his violence against Christ, he gave up the ghost.

Chapter 11. The Final Destruction of the Enemies of Religion.

1. Thus when Maximinus, who alone had remained of the enemies of religion and had appeared the worst of them all, was put out of the way, the renovation of the churches from their foundations was begun by the grace of God the Ruler of all, and the word of Christ, shining unto the glory of the God of the universe, obtained greater freedom than before, while the impious enemies of religion were covered with extremest shame and dishonor.

2. For Maximinus himself, being first pronounced by the emperors a common enemy, was declared by public proclamations to be a most impious, execrable, and God-hating tyrant. And of the portraits which had been set up in every city in honor of him or of his children, some were thrown down from their places to the ground, and torn in pieces; while the faces of others were obliterated by daubing them with black paint. And the statues which had been erected to his honor were likewise overthrown and broken, and lay exposed to the laughter and sport of those who wished to insult and abuse them.

3. Then also all the honors of the other enemies of religion were taken away, and all those who sided with Maximinus were slain, especially those who had been honored by him with high offices in reward for their flattery, and had behaved insolently toward our doctrine.

4. Such an one was Peucetius, the dearest of his companions, who had been honored and rewarded by him above all, who had been consul a second and third time, and had been appointed by him chief minister; and Culcianus, who had likewise advanced through every grade of office, and was also celebrated for his numberless executions of Christians in Egypt; and besides these not a few others, by whose agency especially the tyranny of Maximinus had been confirmed and extended.

5. And Theotecnus also was summoned by justice which by no means overlooked his deeds against the Christians. For when the statue had been set up by him at Antioch, he appeared to be in the happiest state, and was already made a governor by Maximinus.

6. But Licinius, coming down to the city of Antioch, made a search for impostors, and tortured the prophets and priests of the newly erected statue, asking them for what reason they practiced their deception. They, under the stress of torture, were unable longer to conceal the matter, and declared that the whole deceptive mystery had been devised by the art of Theotecnus. Therefore, after meting out to all of them just

judgment, he first put Theotecnus himself to death, and then his confederates in the imposture, with the severest possible tortures.

7. To all these were added also the children of Maximinus, whom he had already made sharers in the imperial dignity, by placing their names on tablets and statues. And the relatives of the tyrant, who before had been boastful and had in their pride oppressed all men, suffered the same punishments with those who have been already mentioned, as well as the extremest disgrace. For they had not received instruction, neither did they know and understand the exhortation given in the Holy Word:

8. Put not your trust in princes, nor in the sons of men, in whom there is no salvation; his spirit shall go forth and return to his earth; in that day all their thoughts perish.

9. The impious ones having been thus removed, the government was preserved firm and undisputed for Constantine and Licinius, to whom it fittingly belonged. They, having first of all cleansed the world of hostility to the Divine Being, conscious of the benefits which he had conferred upon them, showed their love of virtue and of God, and their piety and gratitude to the Deity, by their ordinance in behalf of the Christians.

BOOK X

Chapter 1. The Peace granted us by God.

1. Thanks for all things be given unto God the Omnipotent Ruler and King of the universe, and the greatest thanks to Jesus Christ the Saviour and Redeemer of our souls, through whom we pray that peace may be always preserved for us firm and undisturbed by external troubles and by troubles of the mind.

2. Since in accordance with your wishes, my most holy Paulinus, we have added the tenth book of the Church History to those which have preceded, we will inscribe it to you, proclaiming you as the seal of the whole work; and we will fitly add in a perfect number the perfect panegyric upon the restoration of the churches, obeying the Divine Spirit which exhorts us in the following words:

3. Sing unto the Lord a new song, for he has done marvelous things. His right hand and his holy arm has saved him. The Lord has made known his salvation, his righteousness has he revealed in the presence of the nations.

4. And in accordance with the utterance which commands us to sing the new song, let us proceed to show that, after those terrible and gloomy spectacles which we have described, we are now permitted to see and celebrate such things as many truly righteous men and martyrs of God before us desired to see upon earth and did not see, and to hear and did not hear. Matthew 13:17

5. But they, hastening on, obtained far better things, being carried to heaven and the paradise of divine pleasure. But, acknowledging that even these things are greater than we deserve, we have been astonished at the grace manifested by the author of the great gifts, and rightly do we admire him, worshiping him with the whole power of our souls, and testifying to the truth of those recorded utterances, in which it is said, Come and see the works of the Lord, the wonders which he has done upon the earth, he removes wars to the ends of the world, he shall break the bow and snap the spear in sunder, and shall burn the shields with fire.

6. Rejoicing in these things which have been clearly fulfilled in our day, let us proceed with our account.

7. The whole race of God's enemies was destroyed in the manner indicated, and was thus suddenly swept from the sight of men. So that

again a divine utterance had its fulfillment: I have seen the impious highly exalted and raising himself like the cedars of Lebanon and I have passed by, and behold, he was not and I have sought his place, and it could not be found.

8. And finally a bright and splendid day, overshadowed by no cloud, illuminated with beams of heavenly light the churches of Christ throughout the entire world. And not even those without our communion were prevented from sharing in the same blessings, or at least from coming under their influence and enjoying a part of the benefits bestowed upon us by God.

Chapter 2. The Restoration of the Churches.

1. All men, then, were freed from the oppression of the tyrants, and being released from the former ills, one in one way and another in another acknowledged the defender of the pious to be the only true God. And we especially who placed our hopes in the Christ of God had unspeakable gladness, and a certain inspired joy bloomed for all of us, when we saw every place which shortly before had been desolated by the impieties of the tyrants reviving as if from a long and death-fraught pestilence, and temples again rising from their foundations to an immense height, and receiving a splendor far greater than that of the old ones which had been destroyed.

2. But the supreme rulers also confirmed to us still more extensively the munificence of God by repeated ordinances in behalf of the Christians; and personal letters of the emperor were sent to the bishops, with honors and gifts of money. It may not be unfitting to insert these documents, translated from the Roman into the Greek tongue, at the proper place in this book, as in a sacred tablet, that they may remain as a memorial to all who shall come after us.

Chapter 3. The Dedications in Every Place.

1. After this was seen the sight which had been desired and prayed for by us all; feasts of dedication in the cities and consecrations of the newly built houses of prayer took place, bishops assembled, foreigners came together from abroad, mutual love was exhibited between people and people, the members of Christ's body were united in complete harmony.

2. Then was fulfilled the prophetic utterance which mystically foretold what was to take place: Bone to bone and joint to joint, Ezekiel 37:7 and whatever was truly announced in enigmatic expressions in the inspired passage.

3. And there was one energy of the Divine Spirit pervading all the members, and one soul in all, and the same eagerness of faith, and one hymn from all in praise of the Deity. Yea, and perfect services were conducted by the prelates, the sacred rites being solemnized, and the majestic institutions of the Church observed, here with the singing of psalms and with the reading of the words committed to us by God, and there with the performance of divine and mystic services; and the mysterious symbols of the Saviour's passion were dispensed.

4. At the same time people of every age, both male and female, with all the power of the mind gave honor unto God, the author of their benefits, in prayers and thanksgiving, with a joyful mind and soul. And every one of the bishops present, each to the best of his ability, delivered panegyric orations, adding luster to the assembly.

Chapter 4. Panegyric on the Splendor of Affairs.

1. A certain one of those of moderate talent, who had composed a discourse, stepped forward in the presence of many pastors who were assembled as if for a church gathering, and while they attended quietly and decently, he addressed himself as follows to one who was in all things a most excellent bishop and beloved of God, through whose zeal the temple in Tyre, which was the most splendid in Phœnicia, had been erected. Panegyric upon the building of the churches, addressed to Paulinus, Bishop of Tyre.

2. Friends and priests of God who are clothed in the sacred gown and adorned with the heavenly crown of glory, the inspired unction and the sacerdotal garment of the Holy Spirit; and thou, oh pride of God's new holy temple, endowed by him with the wisdom of age, and yet exhibiting costly works and deeds of youthful and flourishing virtue, to whom God himself, who embraces the entire world, has granted the distinguished honor of building and renewing this earthly house to Christ, his only begotten and first-born Word, and to his holy and divine bride; —

3. one might call you a new Beseleel, the architect of a divine tabernacle, or Solomon, king of a new and much better Jerusalem, or also a new

Zerubabel, who added a much greater glory than the former to the temple of God; —

4. and you also, oh nurslings of the sacred flock of Christ, habitation of good words, school of wisdom, and august and pious auditory of religion:

5. It was long ago permitted us to raise hymns and songs to God, when we learned from hearing the Divine Scriptures read the marvelous signs of God and the benefits conferred upon men by the Lord's wondrous deeds, being taught to say 'Oh God! We have heard with our ears, our fathers have told us the work which you did in their days, in days of old.'

6. But now as we no longer perceive the lofty arm and the celestial right hand of our all-gracious God and universal King by hearsay merely or report, but observe so to speak in very deed and with our own eyes that the declarations recorded long ago are faithful and true, it is permitted us to raise a second hymn of triumph and to sing with loud voice, and say, 'As we have heard, so have we seen; in the city of the Lord of hosts, in the city of our God.'

7. And in what city but in this newly built and God-constructed one, which is a 'church of the living God, a pillar and foundation of the truth,' 1 Timothy 3:15 concerning which also another divine oracle thus proclaims, 'Glorious things have been spoken of you, oh city of God.' Since the all-gracious God has brought us together to it, through the grace of his Only-Begotten, let every one of those who have been summoned sing with loud voice and say, 'I was glad when they said unto me, we shall go unto the house of the Lord,' and 'Lord, I have loved the beauty of your house and the place where your glory dwells.'

8. And let us not only one by one, but all together, with one spirit and one soul, honor him and cry aloud, saying, 'Great is the Lord and greatly to be praised in the city of our God, in his holy mountain.' For he is truly great, and great is his house, lofty and spacious and 'comely in beauty above the sons of men.' 'Great is the Lord who alone does wonderful things'; 'great is he who does great things and things past finding out, glorious and marvelous things which cannot be numbered'; Job 9:10 great is he 'who changes times and seasons, who exalts and debases kings'; Daniel 2:21 'who raises up the poor from the earth and lifts up the needy from the dunghill.' 'He has put down princes from their thrones and has exalted them of low degree from the earth. The hungry he has filled with good things and the arms of the proud he has broken.' Luke 1:52-53

9. Not only to the faithful, but also to unbelievers, has he confirmed the record of ancient events; he that works miracles, he that does great things, the Master of all, the Creator of the whole world, the omnipotent, the all-merciful, the one and only God. To him let us sing the new song, supplying in thought, 'To him who alone does great wonders: for his mercy endures forever'; 'To him which smote great kings, and slew famous kings: for his mercy endures forever'; 'For the Lord remembered us in our low estate and delivered us from our adversaries.'

10. And let us never cease to cry aloud in these words to the Father of the universe. And let us always honor him with our mouth who is the second cause of our benefits, the instructor in divine knowledge, the teacher of the true religion, the destroyer of the impious, the slayer of tyrants, the reformer of life, Jesus, the Saviour of us who were in despair.

11. For he alone, as the only all-gracious Son of an all-gracious Father, in accordance with the purpose of his Father's benevolence, has willingly put on the nature of us who lay prostrate in corruption, and like some excellent physician, who for the sake of saving them that are ill, examines their sufferings, handles their foul sores, and reaps pain for himself from the miseries of another, so us who were not only diseased and afflicted with terrible ulcers and wounds already mortified, but were even lying among the dead, he has saved for himself from the very jaws of death. For none other of those in heaven had such power as without harm to minister to the salvation of so many.

12. But he alone having reached our deep corruption, he alone having taken upon himself our labors, he alone having suffered the punishments due for our impieties, having recovered us who were not half dead merely, but were already in tombs and sepulchers, and altogether foul and offensive, saves us, both anciently and now, by his beneficent zeal, beyond the expectation of any one, even of ourselves, and imparts liberally of the Father's benefits—he who is the giver of life and light, our great Physician and King and Lord, the Christ of God.

13. For then when the whole human race lay buried in gloomy night and in depths of darkness through the deceitful arts of guilty demons and the power of God-hating spirits, by his simple appearing he loosed once for all the fast-bound cords of our impieties by the rays of his light, even as wax is melted.

14. But when malignant envy and the evil-loving demon nearly burst with anger at such grace and kindness, and turned against us all his

death-dealing forces, and when, at first, like a dog gone mad which gnashes his teeth at the stones thrown at him, and pours out his rage against his assailants upon the inanimate missiles, he leveled his ferocious madness at the stones of the sanctuaries and at the lifeless material of the houses, and desolated the churches,— at least as he supposed—and then emitted terrible hissings and snake-like sounds, now by the threats of impious tyrants, and again by the blasphemous edicts of profane rulers, vomiting forth death, moreover, and infecting with his deleterious and soul-destroying poisons the souls captured by him, and almost slaying them by his death-fraught sacrifices of dead idols, and causing every beast in the form of man and every kind of savage to assault us— then, indeed, the 'Angel of the great Council,' the great Captain of God after the mightiest soldiers of his kingdom had displayed sufficient exercise through patience and endurance in everything, suddenly appeared anew, and blotted out and annihilated his enemies and foes, so that they seemed never to have had even a name.

15. But his friends and relatives he raised to the highest glory, in the presence not only of all men, but also of celestial powers, of sun and moon and stars, and of the whole heaven and earth, so that now, as has never happened before, the supreme rulers, conscious of the honor which they have received from him, spit upon the faces of dead idols, trample upon the unhallowed rites of demons, make sport of the ancient delusion handed down from their fathers, and acknowledge only one God, the common benefactor of all, themselves included.

16. And they confess Christ, the Son of God, universal King of all, and proclaim him Saviour on monuments, imperishably recording in imperial letters, in the midst of the city which rules over the earth, his righteous deeds and his victories over the impious. Thus Jesus Christ our Saviour is the only one from all eternity who has been acknowledged, even by those highest in the earth, not as a common king among men, but as a trite son of the universal God, and who has been worshipped as very God, and that rightly.

17. For what king that ever lived attained such virtue as to fill the ears and tongues of all men upon earth with his own name? What king, after ordaining such pious and wise laws, has extended them from one end of the earth to the other, so that they are perpetually read in the hearing of all men?

18. Who has abrogated barbarous and savage customs of uncivilized nations by his gentle and most philanthropic laws? Who, being attacked

for entire ages by all, has shown such superhuman virtue as to flourish daily, and remain young throughout his life?

19. Who has founded a nation which of old was not even heard of, but which now is not concealed in some corner of the earth, but is spread abroad everywhere under the sun? Who has so fortified his soldiers with the arms of piety that their souls, being firmer than adamant, shine brilliantly in the contests with their opponents?

20. What king prevails to such an extent, and even after death leads on his soldiers, and sets up trophies over his enemies, and fills every place, country and city, Greek and barbarian, with his royal dwellings, even divine temples with their consecrated oblations, like this very temple with its superb adornments and votive offerings, which are themselves so truly great and majestic, worthy of wonder and admiration, and clear signs of the sovereignty of our Saviour? For now, too, 'he spoke, and they were made; he commanded, and they were created.' For what was there to resist the nod of the universal King and Governor and Word of God himself?

21. A special discourse would be needed accurately to survey and explain all this; and also to describe how great the zeal of the laborers is regarded by him who is celebrated as divine, who looks upon the living temple which we all constitute, and surveys the house, composed of living and moving stones, which is well and surely built upon the foundation of the apostles and prophets, the chief cornerstone being Jesus Christ himself, who has been rejected not only by the builders of that ancient building which no longer stands, but also by the builders— evil architects of evil works— of the structure, which is composed of the mass of men and still endures. But the Father has approved him both then and now, and has made him the head of the corner of this our common church.

22. Who that beholds this living temple of the living God formed of ourselves— this greatest and truly divine sanctuary, I say, whose inmost shrines are invisible to the multitude and are truly holy and a holy of holies— would venture to declare it? Who is able even to look within the sacred enclosure, except the great High Priest of all, to whom alone it is permitted to fathom the mysteries of every rational soul?

23. But perhaps it is granted to another, to one only, to be second after him in the same work, namely, to the commander of this army whom the first and great High Priest himself has honored with the second place in this sanctuary, the shepherd of your divine flock who has obtained

your people by the allotment and the judgment of the Father, as if he had appointed him his own servant and interpreter, a new Aaron or Melchizedec, made like the Son of God, remaining and continually preserved by him in accordance with the united prayers of all of you.

24. To him therefore alone let it be granted, if not in the first place, at least in the second after the first and greatest High Priest, to observe and supervise the inmost state of your souls—to him who by experience and length of time has accurately proved each one, and who by his zeal and care has disposed you all in pious conduct and doctrine, and is better able than any one else to give an account, adequate to the facts, of those things which he himself has accomplished with the Divine assistance.

25. As to our first and great High Priest, it is said, 'Whatsoever he sees the Father doing those things likewise the Son also does.' John 5:19 So also this one, looking up to him as to the first teacher, with pure eyes of the mind, using as archetypes whatsoever things he sees him doing, produces images of them, making them so far as is possible in the same likeness, in nothing inferior to that Beseleel, whom God himself 'filled with the spirit of wisdom and understanding' Exodus 35:31 and with other technical and scientific knowledge, and called to be the maker of the temple constructed after heavenly types given in symbols.

26. Thus this one also bearing in his own soul the image of the whole Christ, the Word, the Wisdom, the Light, has formed this magnificent temple of the highest God, corresponding to the pattern of the greater as a visible to an invisible, it is impossible to say with what greatness of soul, with what wealth and liberality of mind, and with what emulation on the part of all of you, shown in the magnanimity of the contributors who have ambitiously striven in no way to be left behind by him in the execution of the same purpose. And this place—for this deserves to be mentioned first of all—which had been covered with all sorts of rubbish by the artifices of our enemies he did not overlook, nor did he yield to the wickedness of those who had brought about that condition of things, although he might have chosen some other place, for many other sites were available in the city, where he would have had less labor, and been free from trouble.

27. But having first aroused himself to the work, and then strengthened the whole people with zeal, and formed them all into one great body, he fought the first contest. For he thought that this church, which had been especially besieged by the enemy, which had first suffered and endured the same persecutions with us and for us, like a mother bereft of her

children, should rejoice with us in the signal favor of the all-merciful God.

28. For when the Great Shepherd had driven away the wild animals and wolves and every cruel and savage beast, and, as the divine oracles say, 'had broken the jaws of the lions,' he thought good to collect again her children in the same place, and in the most righteous manner he set up the fold of her flock, 'to put to shame the enemy and avenger,' and to refute the impious daring of the enemies of God.

29. And now they are not—the haters of God—for they never were. After they had troubled and been troubled for a little time, they suffered the fitting punishment, and brought themselves and their friends and their relatives to total destruction, so that the declarations inscribed of old in sacred records have been proved true by facts. In these declarations the divine word truly says among other things the following concerning them:

30. 'The wicked have drawn out the sword, they have bent their bow, to slay the righteous in heart; let their sword enter into their own heart and their bows be broken.' And again: 'Their memorial is perished with a sound' and 'their name have you blotted out forever and ever'; for when they also were in trouble they 'cried out and there was none to save: unto the Lord, and he heard them not.' But 'their feet were bound together, and they fell, but we have arisen and stand upright.' And that which was announced beforehand in these words—'O Lord, in your city you shall set at naught their image,' — has been shown to be true to the eyes of all.

31. But having waged war like the giants against God, they died in this way. But she that was desolate and rejected by men received the consummation which we behold in consequence of her patience toward God, so that the prophecy of Isaiah was spoken of her:

32. 'Rejoice, thirsty desert, let the desert rejoice and blossom as the lily, and the desert places shall blossom and be glad.' Isaiah 35:1 'Be strengthened, you weak hands and feeble knees. Be of good courage, you feeble-hearted, in your minds; be strong, fear not. Behold our God recompenses judgment and will recompense, he will come and save us.' 'For,' he says, 'in the wilderness water has broken out, and a pool in thirsty ground, and the dry land shall be watered meadows, and in the thirsty ground there shall be springs of water.'

33. These things which were prophesied long ago have been recorded in sacred books; but no longer are they transmitted to us by hearsay merely, but in facts. This desert, this dry land, this widowed and deserted one, 'whose gates they cut down with axes like wood in a forest, whom they broke down with hatchet and hammer,' whose books also they destroyed, 'burning with fire the sanctuary of God, and profaning unto the ground the habitation of his name,' 'whom all that passed by upon the way plucked, and whose fences they broke down, whom the boar out of the wood ravaged, and on which the savage wild beast fed,' now by the wonderful power of Christ, when he wills it, has become like a lily. For at that time also she was chastened at his nod as by a careful father; 'for whom the Lord loves he chastens, and scourges every son whom he receives.'

34. Then after being chastened in a measure, according to the necessities of the case, she is commanded to rejoice anew; and she blossoms as a lily and exhales her divine odor among all men. 'For,' it is said, 'water has broken out in the wilderness,' Isaiah 35:6 the fountain of the saving bath of divine regeneration. And now she, who a little before was a desert, 'has become watered meadows, and springs of water have gushed forth in a thirsty land.' Isaiah 35:7 The hands which before were 'weak' have become 'truly strong'; and these works are great and convincing proofs of strong hands. The knees, also, which before were 'feeble and infirm,' recovering their wonted strength, are moving straight forward in the path of divine knowledge, and hastening to the kindred flock of the all-gracious Shepherd.

35. And if there are any whose souls have been stupefied by the threats of the tyrants, not even they are passed by as incurable by the saving Word; but he heals them also and urges them on to receive divine comfort, saying, 'Be comforted, you who are faint-hearted; be ye strengthened, fear not.' Isaiah 35:4

36. This our new and excellent Zerubabel, having heard the word which announced beforehand, that she who had been made a desert on account of God should enjoy these things, after the bitter captivity and the abomination of desolation, did not overlook the dead body; but first of all with prayers and supplications propitiated the Father with the common consent of all of you, and invoking the only one that gives life to the dead as his ally and fellow-worker, raised her that was fallen, after purifying and freeing her from her ills. And he clothed her not with the ancient garment, but with such an one as he had again learned from the

sacred oracles, which say clearly, 'And the latter glory of this house shall be greater than the former.' Haggai 2:9

37. Thus, enclosing a much larger space, he fortified the outer court with a wall surrounding the whole, which should serve as a most secure bulwark for the entire edifice.

38. And he raised and spread out a great and lofty vestibule toward the rays of the rising sun, and furnished those standing far without the sacred enclosure a full view of those within, almost turning the eyes of those who were strangers to the faith, to the entrances, so that no one could pass by without being impressed by the memory of the former desolation and of the present incredible transformation. His hope was that such an one being impressed by this might be attracted and be induced to enter by the very sight.

39. But when one comes within the gates he does not permit him to enter the sanctuary immediately, with impure and unwashed feet; but leaving as large a space as possible between the temple and the outer entrance, he has surrounded and adorned it with four transverse cloisters, making a quadrangular space with pillars rising on every side, which he has joined with lattice-work screens of wood, rising to a suitable height; and he has left an open space in the middle, so that the sky can be seen, and the free air bright in the rays of the sun.

40. Here he has placed symbols of sacred purifications, setting up fountains opposite the temple which furnish an abundance of water wherewith those who come within the sanctuary may purify themselves. This is the first halting-place of those who enter; and it furnishes at the same time a beautiful and splendid scene to every one, and to those who still need elementary instruction a fitting station.

41. But passing by this spectacle, he has made open entrances to the temple with many other vestibules within, placing three doors on one side, likewise facing the rays of the sun. The one in the middle, adorned with plates of bronze, iron bound, and beautifully embossed, he has made much higher and broader than the others, as if he were making them guards for it as for a queen.

42. In the same way, arranging the number of vestibules for the corridors on each side of the whole temple, he has made above them various openings into the building, for the purpose of admitting more light, adorning them with very fine wood-carving. But the royal house

he has furnished with more beautiful and splendid materials, using unstinted liberality in his disbursements.

43. It seems to me superfluous to describe here in detail the length and breadth of the building, its splendor and its majesty surpassing description, and the brilliant appearance of the work, its lofty pinnacles reaching to the heavens, and the costly cedars of Lebanon above them, which the divine oracle has not omitted to mention, saying, 'The trees of the Lord shall rejoice and the cedars of Lebanon which he has planted.'

44. Why need I now describe the skillful architectural arrangement and the surpassing beauty of each part, when the testimony of the eye renders instruction through the ear superfluous? For when he had thus completed the temple, he provided it with lofty thrones in honor of those who preside, and in addition with seats arranged in proper order throughout the whole building, and finally placed in the middle the holy of holies, the altar, and, that it might be inaccessible to the multitude, enclosed it with wooden lattice-work, accurately wrought with artistic carving, presenting a wonderful sight to the beholders.

45. And not even the pavement was neglected by him; for this too he adorned with beautiful marble of every variety. Then finally he passed on to the parts without the temple, providing spacious exedræ and buildings on each side, which were joined to the basilica, and communicated with the entrances to the interior of the structure. These were erected by our most peaceful Solomon, the maker of the temple of God, for those who still needed purification and sprinkling by water and the Holy Spirit, so that the prophecy quoted above is no longer a word merely, but a fact; for now it has also come to pass that in truth 'the latter glory of this house is greater than the former.' Haggai 2:9

46. For it was necessary and fitting that as her shepherd and Lord had once tasted death for her, and after his suffering had changed that vile body which he assumed in her behalf into a splendid and glorious body, leading the very flesh which had been delivered from corruption to incorruption, she too should enjoy the dispensations of the Saviour. For having received from him the promise of much greater things than these, she desires to share uninterruptedly throughout eternity with the choir of the angels of light, in the far greater glory of regeneration, Matthew 19:28 in the resurrection of an incorruptible body, in the palace of God beyond the heavens, with Christ Jesus himself, the universal Benefactor and Saviour.

47. But for the present, she that was formerly widowed and desolate is clothed by the grace of God with these flowers, and has become truly like a lily, as the prophecy says, and having received the bridal garment and the crown of beauty, she is taught by Isaiah to dance, and to present her thank-offerings unto God the King in reverent words.

48. Let us hear her saying, 'My soul shall rejoice in the Lord; for he has clothed me with a garment of salvation and with a robe of gladness; he has bedecked me like a bridegroom with a garland, and he has adorned me like a bride with jewels; and like the earth which brings forth her bud, and like a garden which causes the things that are sown in it to spring forth, thus the Lord God has caused righteousness and praise to spring forth before all the nations.' Isaiah 61:10-11

49. In these words she exults. And in similar words the heavenly bridegroom, the Word Jesus Christ himself, answers her. Hear the Lord saying, 'Fear not because you have been put to shame, neither be confounded because you have been rebuked; for you shall forget the former shame, and the reproach of your widowhood shall you remember no more.' 'Not as a woman deserted and faint-hearted has the Lord called you, nor as a woman hated from her youth, says your God. For a small moment have I forsaken you, but with great mercy will I have mercy upon you; in a little wrath I hid my face from you, but with everlasting mercy will I have mercy upon you, says the Lord that has redeemed you.' Isaiah 54:6-8

50. 'Awake, awake, you who have drunk at the hand of the Lord the cup of his fury; for you have drunk the cup of ruin, the vessel of my wrath, and have drained it. And there was none to console you of all your sons whom you brought forth, and there was none to take you by the hand.' 'Behold, I have taken out of your hand the cup of ruin, the vessel of my fury, and you shall no longer drink it. And I will put it into the hands of them that have treated you unjustly and have humbled you.'

51. 'Awake, awake, put on your strength, put on your glory. Shake off the dust and arise. Sit down, loose the bands of your neck.' 'Lift up your eyes round about and behold your children gathered together; behold they are gathered together and have come to you. As I live, says the Lord, you shall clothe yourself with them all as with an ornament, and gird yourself with them as with the ornaments of a bride. For your waste and corrupted and ruined places shall now be too narrow by reason of those that inhabit you, and they that swallow you up shall be far from you.

52. For your sons whom you have lost shall say in your ears, The place is too narrow for me, give me a place that I may dwell. Then shall you say in your heart, Who has begotten me these? I am childless and a widow, and who has brought up these for me? I was left alone, and these, where were they for me?'

53. These are the things which Isaiah foretold; and which were anciently recorded concerning us in sacred books and it was necessary that we should sometime learn their truthfulness by their fulfillment.

54. For when the bridegroom, the Word, addressed such language to his own bride, the sacred and holy Church, this bridesman, — when she was desolate and lying like a corpse, bereft of hope in the eyes of men— in accordance with the united prayers of all of you, as was proper, stretched out your hands and aroused and raised her up at the command of God, the universal King, and at the manifestation of the power of Jesus Christ; and having raised her he established her as he had learned from the description given in the sacred oracles.

55. This is indeed a very great wonder, passing all admiration, especially to those who attend only to the outward appearance; but more wonderful than wonders are the archetypes and their mental prototypes and divine models; I mean the reproductions of the inspired and rational building in our souls.

56. This the Divine Son himself created after his own image, imparting to it everywhere and in all respects the likeness of God, an incorruptible nature, incorporeal, rational, free from all earthly matter, a being endowed with its own intelligence; and when he had once called her forth from non-existence into existence, he made her a holy spouse, an all-sacred temple for himself and for the Father. This also he clearly declares and confesses in the following words: 'I will dwell in them and will walk in them; and I will be their God, and they shall be my people.' 2 Corinthians 6:16 Such is the perfect and purified soul, so made from the beginning as to bear the image of the celestial Word.

57. But when by the envy and zeal of the malignant demon she became, of her own voluntary choice, sensual and a lover of evil, the Deity left her; and as if bereft of a protector, she became an easy prey and readily accessible to those who had long envied her; and being assailed by the batteries and machines of her invisible enemies and spiritual foes, she suffered a terrible fall, so that not one stone of virtue remained upon another in her, but she lay completely dead upon the ground, entirely divested of her natural ideas of God.

58. But as she, who had been made in the image of God, thus lay prostrate, it was not that wild boar from the forest which we see that despoiled her, but a certain destroying demon and spiritual wild beasts who deceived her with their passions as with the fiery darts of their own wickedness, and burned the truly divine sanctuary of God with fire, and profaned to the ground the tabernacle of his name. Then burying the miserable one with heaps of earth, they destroyed every hope of deliverance.

59. But that divinely bright and saving Word, her protector, after she had suffered the merited punishment for her sins, again restored her, securing the favor of the all-merciful Father.

60. Having won over first the souls of the highest rulers, he purified, through the agency of those most divinely favored princes, the whole earth from all the impious destroyers, and from the terrible and God-hating tyrants themselves. Then bringing out into the light those who were his friends, who had long before been consecrated to him for life, but in the midst, as it were, of a storm of evils, had been concealed under his shelter, he honored them worthily with the great gifts of the Spirit. And again, by means of them, he cleared out and cleaned with spades and mattocks— the admonitory words of doctrine — the souls which a little while before had been covered with filth and burdened with every kind of matter and rubbish of impious ordinances.

61. And when he had made the ground of all your minds clean and clear, he finally committed it to this all-wise and God-beloved Ruler, who, being endowed with judgment and prudence, as well as with other gifts, and being able to examine and discriminate accurately the minds of those committed to his charge, from the first day, so to speak, down to the present, has not ceased to build.

62. Now he has supplied the brilliant gold, again the refined and unalloyed silver, and the precious and costly stones in all of you, so that again is fulfilled for you in facts a sacred and mystic prophecy, which says, 'Behold I make your stone a carbuncle, and your foundations of sapphire, and your battlements of jasper, and your gates of crystals, and your wall of chosen stones; and all your sons shall be taught of God, and your children shall enjoy complete peace; and in righteousness shall you be built.'

63. Building therefore in righteousness, he divided the whole people according to their strength. With some he fortified only the outer enclosure, walling it up with unfeigned faith; such were the great mass

of the people who were incapable of bearing a greater structure. Others he permitted to enter the building, commanding them to stand at the door and act as guides for those who should come in; these may be not unfitly compared to the vestibules of the temple. Others he supported by the first pillars which are placed without about the quadrangular hall, initiating them into the first elements of the letter of the four Gospels. Still others he joined together about the basilica on both sides; these are the catechumens who are still advancing and progressing, and are not far separated from the inmost view of divine things granted to the faithful.

64. Taking from among these the pure souls that have been cleansed like gold by divine washing, he then supports them by pillars, much better than those without, made from the inner and mystic teachings of the Scripture, and illumines them by windows.

65. Adorning the whole temple with a great vestibule of the glory of the one universal King and only God, and placing on either side of the authority of the Father Christ, and the Holy Spirit as second lights, he exhibits abundantly and gloriously throughout the entire building the clearness and splendor of the truth of the rest in all its details. And having selected from every quarter the living and moving and well-prepared stones of the souls, he constructs out of them all the great and royal house, splendid and full of light both within and without; for not only soul and understanding, but their body also is made glorious by the blooming ornament of purity and modesty.

66. And in this temple there are also thrones, and a great number of seats and benches, in all those souls in which sit the Holy Spirit's gifts, such as were anciently seen by the sacred apostles, and those who were with them, when there 'appeared unto them tongues parting asunder, like as of fire, and sat upon each one of them.' Acts 2:3

67. But in the leader of all it is reasonable to suppose that Christ himself dwells in his fullness, and in those that occupy the second rank after him, in proportion as each is able to contain the power of Christ and of the Holy Spirit. And the souls of some of those, namely, who are committed to each of them for instruction and care— may be seats for angels.

68. But the great and august and unique altar, what else could this be than the pure holy of holies of the soul of the common priest of all? Standing at the right of it, Jesus himself, the great High Priest of the universe, the Only Begotten of God, receives with bright eye and

extended hand the sweet incense from all, and the bloodless and immaterial sacrifices offered in their prayers, and bears them to the heavenly Father and God of the universe. And he himself first worships him, and alone gives to the Father the reverence which is his due, beseeching him also to continue always kind and propitious to us all.

69. Such is the great temple which the great Creator of the universe, the Word, has built throughout the entire world, making it an intellectual image upon earth of those things which lie above the vault of heaven, so that throughout the whole creation, including rational beings on earth, his Father might be honored and adored.

70. But the region above the heavens, with the models of earthly things which are there, and the so-called Jerusalem above, and the heavenly Mount of Zion, and the supramundane city of the living God, in which innumerable choirs of angels and the Church of the first born, whose names are written in heaven, Hebrews 12:22-23 praise their Maker and the Supreme Ruler of the universe with hymns of praise unutterable and incomprehensible to us—who that is mortal is able worthily to celebrate this? 'For eye has not seen nor ear heard, neither have entered into the heart of men those things which God has prepared for them that love him.' 1 Corinthians 2:9

71. Since we, men, children, and women, small and great, are already in part partakers of these things, let us not cease all together, with one spirit and one soul, to confess and praise the author of such great benefits to us, 'Who forgives all our iniquities, who heals all our diseases, who redeems our life from destruction, who crowns us with mercy and compassion, who satisfies our desires with good things.' 'For he has not dealt with us according to our sins, nor rewarded us according to our iniquities;' 'for as far as the east is from the west, so far has he removed our iniquities from us. Like as a father pities his own children, so the Lord pities them that fear him.'

72. Rekindling these thoughts in our memories, both now and during all time to come, and contemplating in our mind night and day, in every hour and with every breath, so to speak, the Author and Ruler of the present festival, and of this bright and most splendid day, let us love and adore him with every power of the soul. And now rising, let us beseech him with loud voice to shelter and preserve us to the end in his fold, granting his unbroken and unshaken peace forever, in Christ Jesus our Saviour; through whom be the glory unto him forever and ever. Amen.

Chapter 5. Copies of Imperial Laws.

1. Let us finally subjoin the translations from the Roman tongue of the imperial decrees of Constantine and Licinius.

Copy of imperial decrees translated from the Roman tongue.

2. Perceiving long ago that religious liberty ought not to be denied, but that it ought to be granted to the judgment and desire of each individual to perform his religious duties according to his own choice, we had given orders that every man, Christians as well as others, should preserve the faith of his own sect and religion.

3. But since in that rescript, in which such liberty was granted them, many and various conditions seemed clearly added, some of them, it may be, after a little retired from such observance.

4. When I, Constantine Augustus, and I, Licinius Augustus, came under favorable auspices to Milan and took under consideration everything which pertained to the common good and prosperity, we resolved among other things, or rather first of all, to make such decrees as seemed in many respects for the benefit of every one; namely, such as should preserve reverence and piety toward the deity. We resolved, that is, to grant both to the Christians and to all men freedom to follow the religion which they choose, that whatever heavenly divinity exists may be propitious to us and to all that live under our government.

5. We have, therefore, determined, with sound and upright purpose, that liberty is to be denied to no one, to choose and to follow the religious observances of the Christians, but that to each one freedom is to be given to devote his mind to that religion which he may think adapted to himself, in order that the Deity may exhibit to us in all things his accustomed care and favor.

6. It was fitting that we should write that this is our pleasure, that those conditions being entirely left out which were contained in our former letter concerning the Christians which was sent to your devotedness, everything that seemed very severe and foreign to our mildness may be annulled, and that now every one who has the same desire to observe the religion of the Christians may do so without molestation.

7. We have resolved to communicate this most fully to your care, in order that you may know that we have granted to these same Christians freedom and full liberty to observe their own religion.

8. Since this has been granted freely by us to them, your devotedness perceives that liberty is granted to others also who may wish to follow their own religious observances; it being clearly in accordance with the tranquillity of our times, that each one should have the liberty of choosing and worshiping whatever deity he pleases. This has been done by us in order that we might not seem in any way to discriminate against any rank or religion.

9. And we decree still further in regard to the Christians, that their places, in which they were formerly accustomed to assemble, and concerning which in the former letter sent to your devotedness a different command was given, if it appear that any have bought them either from our treasury or from any other person, shall be restored to the said Christians, without demanding money or any other equivalent, with no delay or hesitation.

10. If any happen to have received the said places as a gift, they shall restore them as quickly as possible to these same Christians: with the understanding that if those who have bought these places, or those who have received them as a gift, demand anything from our bounty, they may go to the judge of the district, that provision may be made for them by our clemency. All these things are to be granted to the society of Christians by your care immediately and without any delay.

11. And since the said Christians are known to have possessed not only those places in which they were accustomed to assemble, but also other places, belonging not to individuals among them, but to the society as a whole, that is, to the society of Christians, you will command that all these, in virtue of the law which we have above stated, be restored, without any hesitation, to these same Christians; that is, to their society and congregation: the above-mentioned provision being of course observed, that those who restore them without price, as we have before said, may expect indemnification from our bounty.

12. In all these things, for the benefit of the aforesaid society of Christians, you are to use the utmost diligence, to the end that our command may be speedily fulfilled, and that in this also, by our clemency, provision may be made for the common and public tranquillity.

13. For by this means, as we have said before, the divine favor toward us which we have already experienced in many matters will continue sure through all time.

14. And that the terms of this our gracious ordinance may be known to all, it is expected that this which we have written will be published everywhere by you and brought to the knowledge of all, in order that this gracious ordinance of ours may remain unknown to no one.

Copy of another imperial decree which they issued, indicating that the grant was made to the Catholic Church alone.

15. Greeting to you, our most esteemed Anulinus. It is the custom of our benevolence, most esteemed Anulinus, to will that those things which belong of right to another should not only be left unmolested, but should also be restored.

16. Wherefore it is our will that when you receive this letter, if any such things belonged to the Catholic Church of the Christians, in any city or other place, but are now held by citizens or by any others, you shall cause them to be restored immediately to the said churches. For we have already determined that those things which these same churches formerly possessed shall be restored to them.

17. Since therefore your devotedness perceives that this command of ours is most explicit, do thou make haste to restore to them, as quickly as possible, everything which formerly belonged to the said churches,— whether gardens or buildings or whatever they may be— that we may learn that you have obeyed this decree of ours most carefully. Farewell, our most esteemed and beloved Anulinus.

Copy of an epistle in which the Emperor commands that a synod of bishopsbe held at Rome in behalf of the unity and concord of the churches.

18. Constantine Augustus to Miltiades, bishop of Rome, and to Marcus. Since many such communications have been sent to me by Anulinus, the most illustrious proconsul of Africa, in which it is said that Cæcilianus, bishop of the city of Carthage, has been accused by some of his colleagues in Africa, in many matters; and since it seems to me a very serious thing that in those provinces which Divine Providence has freely entrusted to my devotedness, and in which there is a great population, the multitude are found following the baser course, and dividing, as it were, into two parties, and the bishops are at variance—

19. it has seemed good to me that Cæcilianus himself, with ten of the bishops that appear to accuse him, and with ten others whom he may consider necessary for his defense, should sail to Rome, that there, in the presence of yourselves and of Retecius and Maternus and Marinus, your colleagues, whom I have commanded to hasten to Rome for this purpose, he may be heard, as you may understand to be in accordance with the most holy law.

20. But in order that you may be enabled to have most perfect knowledge of all these things, I have subjoined to my letter copies of the documents sent to me by Anulinus, and have sent them to your above-mentioned colleagues. When your firmness has read these, you will consider in what way the above-mentioned case may be most accurately investigated and justly decided. For it does not escape your diligence that I have such reverence for the legitimate Catholic Church that I do not wish you to leave schism or division in any place. May the divinity of the great God preserve you, most honored sirs, for many years.

Copy of an epistle in which the emperor commands another synod to be held for the purpose of removing all dissensions among the bishops.

21. Constantine Augustus to Chrestus, bishop of Syracuse. When some began wickedly and perversely to disagree among themselves in regard to the holy worship and celestial power and Catholic doctrine, wishing to put an end to such disputes among them, I formerly gave command that certain bishops should be sent from Gaul, and that the opposing parties who were contending persistently and incessantly with each other, should be summoned from Africa; that in their presence, and in the presence of the bishop of Rome, the matter which appeared to be causing the disturbance might be examined and decided with all care.

22. But since, as it happens, some, forgetful both of their own salvation and of the reverence due to the most holy religion, do not even yet bring hostilities to an end, and are unwilling to conform to the judgment already passed, and assert that those who expressed their opinions and decisions were few, or that they had been too hasty and precipitate in giving judgment, before all the things which ought to have been accurately investigated had been examined—on account of all this it has happened that those very ones who ought to hold brotherly and harmonious relations toward each other, are shamefully, or rather abominably, divided among themselves, and give occasion for ridicule

to those men whose souls are aliens to this most holy religion. Wherefore it has seemed necessary to me to provide that this dissension, which ought to have ceased after the judgment had been already given by their own voluntary agreement, should now, if possible, be brought to an end by the presence of many.

23. Since, therefore, we have commanded a number of bishops from a great many different places to assemble in the city of Arles, before the kalends of August, we have thought proper to write to you also that you should secure from the most illustrious Latronianus, corrector of Sicily, a public vehicle, and that you should take with you two others of the second rank, whom you yourself shall choose, together with three servants who may serve you on the way, and betake yourself to the above-mentioned place before the appointed day; that by your firmness, and by the wise unanimity and harmony of the others present, this dispute, which has disgracefully continued until the present time, in consequence of certain shameful strifes, after all has been heard which those have to say who are now at variance with one another, and whom we have likewise commanded to be present, may be settled in accordance with the proper faith, and that brotherly harmony, though it be but gradually, may be restored.

24. May the Almighty God preserve you in health for many years.

Chapter 6. — Copy of an Imperial Epistle in which Money is granted to the Churches.

1. Constantine Augustus to Cæcilianus, bishop of Carthage. Since it is our pleasure that something should be granted in all the provinces of Africa and Numidia and Mauritania to certain ministers of the legitimate and most holy catholic religion, to defray their expenses, I have written to Ursus, the illustrious finance minister of Africa, and have directed him to make provision to pay to your firmness three thousand folles.

2. Do thou therefore, when you have received the above sum of money, command that it be distributed among all those mentioned above, according to the brief sent to you by Hosius.

3. But if you should find that anything is wanting for the fulfillment of this purpose of mine in regard to all of them, you shall demand without hesitation from Heracleides, our treasurer, whatever you find to be necessary. For I commanded him when he was present that if your

firmness should ask him for any money, he should see to it that it be paid without delay.

4. And since I have learned that some men of unsettled mind wish to turn the people from the most holy and catholic Church by a certain method of shameful corruption, do you know that I gave command to Anulinus, the proconsul, and also to Patricius, vicar of the prefects, when they were present, that they should give proper attention not only to other matters but also above all to this, and that they should not overlook such a thing when it happened. Wherefore if you should see any such men continuing in this madness, do thou without delay go to the above-mentioned judges and report the matter to them; that they may correct them as I commanded them when they were present. The divinity of the great God preserve you for many years.

Chapter 7. The Exemption of the Clergy.

Copy of an Epistle in which the emperor commands that the rulers of the churches be exempted from all political duties.

1. Greeting to you, our most esteemed Anulinus. Since it appears from many circumstances that when that religion is despised, in which is preserved the chief reverence for the most holy celestial Power, great dangers are brought upon public affairs; but that when legally adopted and observed it affords the most signal prosperity to the Roman name and remarkable felicity to all the affairs of men, through the divine beneficence—it has seemed good to me, most esteemed Anulinus, that those men who give their services with due sanctity and with constant observance of this law, to the worship of the divine religion, should receive recompense for their labors.

2. Wherefore it is my will that those within the province entrusted to you, in the catholic Church, over which Cæcilianus presides, who give their services to this holy religion, and who are commonly called clergymen, be entirely exempted from all public duties, that they may not by any error or sacrilegious negligence be drawn away from the service due to the Deity, but may devote themselves without any hindrance to their own law. For it seems that when they show greatest reverence to the Deity, the greatest benefits accrue to the state. Farewell, our most esteemed and beloved Anulinus.

Chapter 8. The Subsequent Wickedness of Licinius, and his Death.

1. Such blessings did divine and heavenly grace confer upon us through the appearance of our Saviour, and such was the abundance of benefits which prevailed among all men in consequence of the peace which we enjoyed. And thus were our affairs crowned with rejoicings and festivities.

2. But malignant envy, and the demon who loves that which is evil, were not able to bear the sight of these things; and moreover the events that befell the tyrants whom we have already mentioned were not sufficient to bring Licinius to sound reason.

3. For the latter, although his government was prosperous and he was honored with the second rank after the great Emperor Constantine, and was connected with him by the closest ties of marriage, abandoned the imitation of good deeds, and emulated the wickedness of the impious tyrants whose end he had seen with his own eyes, and chose rather to follow their principles than to continue in friendly relations with him who was better than they. Being envious of the common benefactor he waged an impious and most terrible war against him, paying regard neither to laws of nature, nor treaties, nor blood, and giving no thought to covenants.

4. For Constantine, like an all-gracious emperor, giving him evidences of true favor, did not refuse alliance with him, and did not refuse him the illustrious marriage with his sister, but honored him by making him a partaker of the ancestral nobility and the ancient imperial blood, and granted him the right of sharing in the dominion over all as a brother-in-law and co-regent, conferring upon him the government and administration of no less a portion of the Roman provinces than he himself possessed.

5. But Licinius, on the contrary, pursued a course directly opposite to this; forming daily all kinds of plots against his superior, and devising all sorts of mischief, that he might repay his benefactor with evils. At first he attempted to conceal his preparations, and pretended to be a friend, and practiced frequently fraud and deceit, in the hope that he might easily accomplish the desired end.

6. But God was the friend, protector, and guardian of Constantine, and bringing the plots which had been formed in secrecy and darkness to the light, he foiled them. So much virtue does the great armor of piety possess for the warding off of enemies and for the preservation of our

own safety. Protected by this, our most divinely favored emperor escaped the multitudinous plots of the abominable man.

7. But when Licinius perceived that his secret preparations by no means progressed according to his mind—for God revealed every plot and wickedness to the God-favored emperor—being no longer able to conceal himself, he undertook an open war.

8. And at the same time that he determined to wage war with Constantine, he also proceeded to join battle with the God of the universe, whom he knew that Constantine worshipped, and began, gently for a time and quietly, to attack his pious subjects, who had never done his government any harm. This he did under the compulsion of his innate wickedness which drove him into terrible blindness.

9. He did not therefore keep before his eyes the memory of those who had persecuted the Christians before him, nor of those whose destroyer and executioner he had been appointed, on account of the impieties which they had committed. But departing from sound reason, being seized, in a word, with insanity, he determined to war against God himself as the ally of Constantine, instead of against the one who was assisted by him.

10. And in the first place, he drove from his house every Christian, thus depriving himself, wretched man, of the prayers which they offered to God in his behalf, which they are accustomed, according to the teaching of their fathers, to offer for all men. Then he commanded that the soldiers in the cities should be cashiered and stripped of their rank unless they chose to sacrifice to the demons. And yet these were small matters when compared with the greater things that followed.

11. Why is it necessary to relate minutely and in detail all that was done by the hater of God, and to recount how this most lawless man invented unlawful laws? He passed an ordinance that no one should exercise humanity toward the sufferers in prison by giving them food, and that none should show mercy to those that were perishing of hunger in bonds; that no one should in any way be kind, or do any good act, even though moved by Nature herself to sympathize with one's neighbors. And this was indeed an openly shameful and most cruel law, calculated to expel all natural kindliness. And in addition to this it was also decreed, as a punishment, that those who showed compassion should suffer the same things with those whom they compassionated; and that those who kindly ministered to the suffering should be thrown into bonds and into

prison, and should endure the same punishment with the sufferers. Such were the decrees of Licinius.

12. Why should we recount his innovations in regard to marriage or in regard to the dying— innovations by which he ventured to annul the ancient laws of the Romans which had been well and wisely formed, and to introduce certain barbarous and cruel laws, which were truly unlawful and lawless? He invented, to the detriment of the provinces which were subject to him, innumerable prosecutions, and all sorts of methods of extorting gold and silver, new measurements of land and injurious exactions from men in the country, who were no longer living, but long since dead.

13. Why is it necessary to speak at length of the banishments which, in addition to these things, this enemy of mankind inflicted upon those who had done no wrong, the expatriations of men of noble birth and high reputation whose young wives he snatched from them and consigned to certain baser fellows of his own, to be shamefully abused by them, and the many married women and virgins upon whom he gratified his passions, although he was in advanced age — why, I say, is it necessary to speak at length of these things, when the excessive wickedness of his last deeds makes the first appear small and of no account?

14. For, finally, he reached such a pitch of madness that he attacked the bishops, supposing that they— as servants of the God over all— would be hostile to his measures. He did not yet proceed against them openly, on account of his fear of his superior, but as before, secretly and craftily, employing the treachery of the governors for the destruction of the most distinguished of them. And the manner of their murder was strange, and such as had never before been heard of.

15. The deeds which he performed at Amaseia and in the other cities of Pontus surpassed every excess of cruelty. Some of the churches of God were again razed to the ground, others were closed, so that none of those accustomed to frequent them could enter them and render the worship due to God.

16. For his evil conscience led him to suppose that prayers were not offered in his behalf; but he was persuaded that we did everything in the interest of the God-beloved emperor, and that we supplicated God for him. Therefore he hastened to turn his fury against us.

17. And then those among the governors who wished to flatter him, perceiving that in doing such things they pleased the impious tyrant, made some of the bishops suffer the penalties customarily inflicted upon criminals, and led away and without any pretext punished like murderers those who had done no wrong. Some now endured a new form of death: having their bodies cut into many pieces with the sword, and after this savage and most horrible spectacle, being thrown into the depths of the sea as food for fishes.

18. Thereupon the worshipers of God again fled, and fields and deserts, forests and mountains, again received the servants of Christ. And when the impious tyrant had thus met with success in these measures, he finally planned to renew the persecution against all.

19. And he would have succeeded in his design, and there would have been nothing to hinder him in the work, had not God, the defender of the lives of his own people, most quickly anticipated that which was about to happen, and caused a great light to shine forth as in the midst of a dark and gloomy night, and raised up a deliverer for all, leading into those regions with a lofty arm, his servant, Constantine.

Chapter 9. The Victory of Constantine, and the Blessings which under him accrued to the Subjects of the Roman Empire.

1. To him, therefore, God granted, from heaven above, the deserved fruit of piety, the trophies of victory over the impious, and he cast the guilty one with all his counselors and friends prostrate at the feet of Constantine.

2. For when Licinius carried his madness to the last extreme, the emperor, the friend of God, thinking that he ought no longer to be tolerated, acting upon the basis of sound judgment, and mingling the firm principles of justice with humanity, gladly determined to come to the protection of those who were oppressed by the tyrant, and undertook, by putting a few destroyers out of the way, to save the greater part of the human race.

3. For when he had formerly exercised humanity alone and had shown mercy to him who was not worthy of sympathy, nothing was accomplished; for Licinius did not renounce his wickedness, but rather increased his fury against the peoples that were subject to him, and there was left to the afflicted no hope of salvation, oppressed as they were by a savage beast.

4. Wherefore, the protector of the virtuous, mingling hatred for evil with love for good, went forth with his son Crispus, a most beneficent prince, and extended a saving right hand to all that were perishing. Both of them, father and son, under the protection, as it were, of God, the universal King, with the Son of God, the Saviour of all, as their leader and ally, drew up their forces on all sides against the enemies of the Deity and won an easy victory; God having prospered them in the battle in all respects according to their wish.

5. Thus, suddenly, and sooner than can be told, those who yesterday and the day before breathed death and threatening were no more, and not even their names were remembered, but their inscriptions and their honors suffered the merited disgrace. And the things which Licinius with his own eyes had seen come upon the former impious tyrants he himself likewise suffered, because he did not receive instruction nor learn wisdom from the chastisements of his neighbors, but followed the same path of impiety which they had trod, and was justly hurled over the same precipice. Thus he lay prostrate.

6. But Constantine, the mightiest victor, adorned with every virtue of piety, together with his son Crispus, a most God-beloved prince, and in all respects like his father, recovered the East which belonged to them; and they formed one united Roman empire as of old, bringing under their peaceful sway the whole world from the rising of the sun to the opposite quarter, both north and south, even to the extremities of the declining day.

7. All fear therefore of those who had formerly afflicted them was taken away from men, and they celebrated splendid and festive days. Everything was filled with light, and those who before were downcast beheld each other with smiling faces and beaming eyes. With dances and hymns, in city and country, they glorified first of all God the universal King, because they had been thus taught, and then the pious emperor with his God-beloved children.

8. There was oblivion of past evils and forgetfulness of every deed of impiety; there was enjoyment of present benefits and expectation of those yet to come. Edicts full of clemency and laws containing tokens of benevolence and true piety were issued in every place by the victorious emperor.

9. Thus after all tyranny had been purged away, the empire which belonged to them was preserved firm and without a rival for Constantine and his sons alone. And having obliterated the godlessness

ecognizing the benefits conferred upon them by their love of virtue and their love of God, and their to the Deity, by the deeds which they performed in en.

God's help, of the Tenth Book of the Church History of amphili.

[illegible] , with [illegible]